PRISM ME A LIE
TELL ME A TRUTH
TEHELKA AS METAPHOR

Our only possible hope

For the young people of India
Remember, if it wasn't for the battle
The couch would make you into a potato
Seize the magic of the struggle

—

Be the change that you want to see in the world.
                                        – Mahatma Gandhi

CONTENTS

GRATITUDE

I feel a profound sense of gratitude as I finish writing this book. I would like to thank Pramod Kapoor who understood the value of a book that was not banged off in three months with speedily researched, sensationalized material to become a cheap bestseller. He gave me the space and time to write what I believe is solid journalism and to make it feel that I am leaving something of value behind. (Is she going somewhere? Aren't we all? The boring oft-repeated pandit-at-chautha cliché – *Jo atha hai, voh jatha hai*!) I am grateful to Priya Kapoor for being so open to ideas and bringing her energy to the project.

After almost four decades in journalism, in print, television and the web, I was given this enormous opportunity to learn and grow when Roli Books commissioned me to write on Tehelka's Operation West End. It really is the best place for a journalist to be in: to have the time and space to research, study, analyse and write. I can say with confidence that I have learnt more in the last five years than I did in ten, chasing politicians to catch one bite.

I would like to thank all the computer doctors who helped me through my computer crashes and tearful crises: Bhupinder, Rakesh Sharma, Anubhav Chawla, Deepak Mishra, Jalaj and Gurvinder Singh. I am thankful to my editor Adil Tyabji, whose marvellous, eccentric persona brought some sense of punctuation and desperate formality to the book. A huge amount of gratitude to Nandita Bhardwaj, Roli Books editor, for her stubborn meticulousness and sigh-laced patience in the face of my over-intense reactions towards missed deadlines. More than that, she reminded me of what is now being seen as the second wave of feminism. In an interview, CNN's Soledad O'Brien questioned Michelle Obama about giving up her career for Barack and her children. O'Brien insisted, 'Sometimes your career helps to define who you are.' Michelle responded, 'It doesn't for me. What I do in my *life* defines me. A career is one of the many things I do in my life. I am a mother first. Where do I get my joy and my energy first and foremost? From my kids.' When I boasted about how nobody in my family was back from work before 10.00 p.m., Nandita in her quiet way said, 'That's not what it's about.' I have learnt and I agree. Thanks to Roli Books team particularly Neelam Narula and Supriya Saran. A big thanks to my transcriber Tara Kapur who was diligent and a joy to work with. To the young and bright lawyer Anjolie Singh for working so hard on my manuscript. A hug and gratitude to Mohit Gujral who put his mind in gear for me and Dilip Mehta for his bullying, my photograph and the title. To Feroze Gujral, she knows for what. To Dr Rajiv Bhasin for giving me the push to let go of the book finally. To Swapan Seth for his invaluable advice. To Dilip Cherian for his ideas, advice and wonderful supply of information about everybody and everything. To Rashna Imhasly for her contributions in the book as well as her unquantifiable personal help. To Atul Punj, Aimee and Ashok Bajaj, Reshma and Shashank Bhagat; Kavita and Hari Bhartia; Mohini Bhullar, Rtta (Gudsie) Kapur and Iftekar Chisti; Astad Deboo, Sona Jha, Pam and Raman Kapoor, Roshni, Rita and Naresh Khattar; Nila Mehta, Preeti and Rati Puri; Rajeev Sethi, Isabel Sahni, Rashme Uday Singh, Jyoti Suri, Bholi and Naveen Trehan, for always being there.

I would like to thank all the lawyers (who do not want to be mentioned), particularly, Fali Nariman, Chander Uday Singh, Diya Kapur and Shyel Trehan for their time and extremely valuable advice.

And the biggest surprise of all, my son-in-law Raoul Bajaj, who took the time to read this tome twice, mark passages and actually did a huge job of editing and critiquing the book. He also bullied my daughter Shonan to do time on the book. I want to thank Shonan for being a natural born Buddhist in her spirit and for always being there for me. I want to thank my older daughter Shyel for putting big lines through pages of my book, exclaiming, 'Boring! Boring! Boring!' Whether I listened to her or not, is another matter. Having called me her worst client often enough, I thank her for her patience. I want to thank my son-in-law Pankaj Sahni for putting out fires. And thank you to my husband Naresh for actually breaking his norms and reading something other than medical literature. I would like to thank my father, V.V. Purie, who blessed me with his spirit, his irreverent nature and dislike for hypocrisy.

I would like to thank all my friends and family who have tolerated my neglect of them; some with understanding, some with bemusement or irritation (how can a book take so long and why waste so much time writing a book? A book? Where's the money in a book?); some with incredulity (she is just ditching because she doesn't like to go out!).

Right! When you get an assignment like this, it is the best place to be.

INTRODUCTION

Akira Kurosawa wrote about the meaning of his film *Rashomon* (1951) in his book *Something Like an Autobiography* (1982):

> One day just before the shooting was to start, the three assistant directors Daiei had assigned me came to see me at the inn where I was staying. I wondered what the problem could be. It turned out that they found the script baffling and wanted me to explain it to them. "Please read it again more carefully," I told them. "If you read it diligently, you should be able to understand it because it was written with the intention of being comprehensible." But they wouldn't leave. "We believe we have read it carefully, and we still don't understand it at all; that's why we want you to explain it to us." For their persistence I gave them this simple explanation: "Human beings are unable to be honest with themselves about themselves. They cannot talk about themselves without embellishing. This script portrays such human beings – the kind who cannot survive without lies to make them feel they are better people than they really are. It even shows this sinful need for flattering falsehood going beyond the grave – even the character who dies cannot give up his lies when he speaks to the living through a medium. Egoism is a sin the human being carries with him from birth; it is the most difficult to redeem. This film is like a strange picture scroll that is unrolled and displayed by the ego. You say that you cannot understand this script at all, but that is because the human heart

itself is impossible to understand. If you focus on the impossibility of truly understanding human psychology and read the script one more time, I think you will grasp the point of it."

It was the right place. Sharing a New York taxi. Writer Gita Mehta pointed me in the direction of *Rashomon* when I tried to relate the story of Tehelka to her. Where else but in a city where egoism is not a sin but rather a badge of success?

What has *Rashomon* come to mean today? Simply expressed: different versions from all the participants of the same event and the impossibility of establishing One Truth. Kurosawa based his film on Japanese writer Ryunosuke Akutagawa's book *Rashomon* (1915). Akutagawa's work can appear deceptively simple. The stories are about a woman's rape and a man's murder. All the participants in the incidents tell the story of how the rape and murder took place but none of the stories are the same.

Akira Kurosawa's legendary film *Rashomon* was based on the book, but instead of following the book literally, he rather pushed Akutagawa's intent. If readers of the book or film viewers try to figure out the truth of what actually happened chronologically in the story, they are wasting their time. It isn't really about what happened but about the impossibility of determining the final, certain truth and, more crucially, how each version is important in itself. Each person's perspective distorts events and reality. Can there be an absolute truth about any event? The conclusion at the end of *Rashomon*: absolute, objective truth is impossible to establish, but then, here too there is a Rashomon. That's what the film and the book meant to me. Only to me.

To lay the blueprint of *Rashomon* on Tehelka is irreverent but downright irresistible. From September 2000 to January 2001, a couple of journalists from the website, Tehelka. com, worked out a sting operation, clandestinely videotaped army officers, the president of the party in government, the close colleague and president of the party of the defence minister, bureaucrats, defence ministry officials, while they accepted money from the sting operatives and sold information. The defence minister's party colleague is on tape discussing how the money offered would be used for her political party. They also supplied army officers with sex workers and filmed them in hotel rooms. In the case of all the characters on the videotapes, those mentioned in the tapes, as well as those in some way connected to the story, each incident has that many different versions. Not one person agrees that any particular event took place in the same way. Who is telling the truth? They all are, as they choose to believe it. Add to that strategically subversive lawyers' selective facts and you have a pile of conflicting stories. This is a chiaroscuro play of truth and memory. They all remember it the way they want to.

Milan Kundera has written: 'To take, with Cervantes, the world as ambiguity, to be obliged to face not a single absolute truth but a welter of contradictory truths (truths embodied in imaginary selves called characters), to have as one's only certainty the wisdom of uncertainty, requires no less courage' (*The Art of the Novel*, 1986). Kundera said, in a 1980 interview to Philip Roth, 'The novelist teaches the reader to comprehend the world as a question. There is wisdom and tolerance in that attitude. In a world built on sacrosanct certainties the novel is dead.' But this is not a novel. It is a journalist's Rashomon on the events around Tehelka's Operation West End sting: how they did it, their motivations, and how, in varying degrees, it destroyed everyone involved. There should be, at least, some certainties. One cannot apply the 'wisdom of uncertainty' to, say, Nicole Simpson's murder. Either you believe O.J. Simpson is guilty or not. And much the same way, people around the world formed judgements about Simpson's guilt that most often reflected and projected their own identity and background.

Without much doubt, it can be predicted that politicians, particularly, will read political leanings into the writer's opinions. It is possibly difficult for them to believe, there are neutral journalists. It was a coincidence that a particular party happened to be in power at that time. It could have been any other. The story would, in all likelihood, have been the same. Let it be clear, the author is not anti-BJP, not anti-Congress, not anti-Samata Party, not anti-Samajwadi Party, not anti-Communist or any other party. The levels of corruption may be up and down a few drops, but clearly it is rampant across the board. It happened to be BJP's kismet that it was in power when Tehelka decided on the sting operation.

Commissioned to write about Tehelka, what was expected to be a bang-off book in six months developed into six years of intense research, lengthy interviews and, not surprisingly, became a book that reached beyond Tehelka. It is about India. It is about what happens. And most important of all, it happens under such a 'nice' veneer that we do not notice the rot. It would be risky to not comprehend the book as your own story. It could be anybody's. It could very well be yours.

This book attempts to examine what happens to each player's thinking and psyche as the drama unfolds. Political policies create sociocultural phenomena and mindsets. Just as in the Stalin period of the Soviet Union, the culture of fear-psychosis so permeated every person's life that it was impossible to separate political policy from the interior life of any citizen. It was a tapeworm lodged in every citizen's brain: children reporting on parents, neighbours reporting on each other, fellow workers reporting on peers. It was contagiously pervasive. Indira Gandhi's Emergency rule in 1975 created a frighteningly similar paranoid culture in Delhi during those years. There was self-censorship in speaking freely even in social situations and caution crippled a substantial section of the mainstream press. It is difficult to believe how quickly people changed, from those who took their fundamental right of freedom of speech for granted, to being too afraid to express a political opinion even in a private home. What happened to the journalists and particularly to the investors of Tehelka is not commonly known. Frank Kafka wrote *The Trial* (1925) about a man accused of a crime he is not aware of and how that destroyed him. That would be one day in the life of Shankar Sharma and Devina Mehra, the couple who invested in Tehelka. The State's multi-dimensional attack on their lives is far worse than other stories, because it is invisible. No human rights organizations raised the flag for them. How do you substantiate with documentary evidence the before and after pictures of the interior consciousness that has undergone changes that will never recover? The Unbearable Changes of Being that occur when you find yourself in jail sweating next to killers and pimps. The most traumatic and indelible change is how you begin to view yourself. From an achiever and a winner, you become the hunted and a victim. You turn more and more inward within yourself and can relate to others only through the prism within which the State has enveloped you.

In the story of Operation West End, listening to each character's version you enter their variegated surround. The three principal players could not be more different from one another. Mathew Samuel, the man who initiated the sting operation and was largely responsible for it, was a villager with a dream of making it in Big City journalism. Samuel would rather use paper by rolling it into a point to clean his teeth than write one correct sentence in English on it. Aniruddha Bahal sold brassware, nurtured ambitions of becoming a novelist, but ended up as an investigative reporter. Tarun Tejpal, for his part, better known for his writing skills with no known desires to become an investigative reporter, shot into fame as one, though he did no investigating. Kumar Badal, a Tehelka reporter, was imprisoned for six months and two weeks on the basis of the police finding his phone number in the possession of arrested wildlife poachers. With the Tehelka team and their journalistic spirit, you are in an area where there is always adventurous electricity about stories, often in language that was repeatedly pointed out in the Commission of Inquiry as 'obscene'. Milan Kundera defines 'Obscenity: the root that attaches us most deeply to our homeland.'(*The Art of the Novel*, 1986). NRIs (non-resident Indians) will often soothe their homesick hearts on meeting up with Indian friends and curse away to replenish their connection to their motherland (yeah, right). As Natalie Angier wrote in an article, 'The History of Swearing', in *The New York Times* (20 September 2005), 'In some settings, the free flow of foul language may signal not hostility or social pathology, but harmony and tranquillity.' In 'polite' society, a presumptuous phrase anyway, such language is not used. But, the same lawyers in the Commission of Inquiry on Tehelka, who primly pointed out Mathew Samuel's 'foul' language and used it as a weapon to discredit him, could well be using the same language in private. A significant part of the Tehelka team's story is that the investigators are, to their perplexity, being investigated. They were supposed to be the good guys. What happened here?

Anil Malviya, alias Rajiv Sharma, got involved at the outset of the sting operation after a chance meeting with Mathew Samuel on a train. Malviya sold advertising space and had nothing to do with journalism. When the sting began heating up, he reportedly decided to opt out. Malviya reportedly died in Allahabad before the sting was made public. It seemed a little too convenient. The man who was involved at the start of the clandestine taping and allegedly organized the sex workers suddenly dies. Did he really die or just disappear? Did Mathew Samuel and Aniruddha Bahal pin the procuring of the women on a dead man who could no longer defend himself? I surprised his relatives to get an interview.

Shankar Sharma and Devina Mehra's lives remain the most damaged. During the dotcom boom they casually invested in Tehelka an amount that was to them small change. Their lives were transformed from being among the most successful brokers on the stock exchange, to being hounded by government agencies, which infected every part of their lives. This young, self-made couple was dragged down from their financial orbit into Delhi's swamp of politics and journalism. Their business in India closed down, their bank accounts were frozen, they were not permitted to trade on the Bombay Stock Exchange, which was their livelihood. For five years they found themselves consumed with fighting never-ending court cases. Sharma spent two-and-a-half months in jail for his connection with Tehelka and was accused of financial irregularities. Questions to be answered are: Were Sharma and Mehra part of a larger conspiracy to destabilize the government and make a killing on the stock market? The BJP government lawyers accused them of conspiring with arms dealers such as the Hindujas, notorious for their connection with Bofors. These questions are investigated.

Jaya Jaitly was president of the Samata Party when she met with Tehelka's reporter Mathew Samuel in Defence Minister George Fernandes's house, where Samuel presented a packet of money. Jaya Jaitly and George Fernandes occupy an old-world, *jholawala* space where materialism is still a bad word and social activism the motivator. But, as with so many *jholawalas*, there are juxtaposing inconsistencies. Jaya is a journalist's dream. She has been obsessed with her own defence since the exposé on 13 March 2001. Jaya is sultry, attractive, and virulently articulate, but again the facts are through Jaya's kaleidoscope. Jumbled colours at different angles, but clear to her. She is known for her work with crafts and artisans, and has spent her life working for the underprivileged. That George Fernandes and Jaya Jaitly share a rather special feeling for each other is obvious. Furious at the innuendoes, Jaya elaborates on her feelings for him.

An interview with George Fernandes displays his devastated psyche in his fury against the journalists for destroying Jaya's career. Yes, Tehelka also transformed George Fernandes's inner being. He is a man full of contradictions that makes him all the more intriguing.

Bangaru Laxman, then the president of the Bharatiya Janata Party, could not fathom what he did wrong when he took money 'for the party'. He was convinced that it was part of his job as president. Has he been more maligned than he deserves? Laxman could be a walk-on in any Bollywood movie for a corrupt politician. Yes, he does so look the part. His interview shows that there is no crisis of values here. Laxman's surprise at the fuss over taking money from a supposed arms dealer shows that the interior moral life of most politicians has been regulated to expediency, convenience, and survival.

The army officers, skulking around in a cloak of opprobrium, exist in a world of ingrained rules and regulations. Living in almost Victorian format, they were the 'naughty boys' who got caught. Their regulated lives on autopilot sequence with anticipated promotions now lie in smithereens around them, along with confused and depressed families: all for one mistake. But, it rarely takes hours or days to extirpate one's life. It is that split-second decision: jumping a red light, experimenting with a new recreational drug, stealing from a department store, hitting and running away, relishing a White House intern, buying a gun from Mumbai mafia that can U-turn your life forever. How you react to the army officers' predicament will in turn reflect your own values. Were my own reactions while watching the sex tapes justified? Many questions are raised. Should such men be forgiven? I attempt to answer the big question that puzzles many women and brings a curious, bemused smile to men: Why do men do what they do?

The Army Court of Inquiry is a realm by itself, apparently untouched by political considerations or vote-bank politics. The army announced their investigation two days after the Tehelka exposé, and it was completed in two-and-a-half months. The army is not an understanding wife who will look the other way nor is it a politician, ensuring that justice is not done but appears to have been done. The army court did not buy the argument that the tapes were 'doctored'. Although some of the officers attempted to 'fix' their trials through old boy contacts, the army showed how a commission of inquiry really should be conducted.

The Indian government ordered a commission of inquiry on Tehelka which was constituted on 24 March 2001. The frame of reference of the inquiry by the government had some rather dubious inclusions that set a damaging precedent for journalists. The messenger of bad news had better be prepared to pay the price of exchanging his normal work and personal life with one that involves only court appearances and his defence. One judge resigned in the midst of the inquiry when questions were raised about his integrity, another judge took over and the inquiry went into a slow trot in a completely different direction. What happened there?

What are the ramifications of the pinpointed, topic-related interest taken by Soli Sorabjee, the then attorney general of India (appointed by the BJP), and his self-interpreted role in the Commission? The impact his presence made was completely missed by a bored press who had moved on to the next story. Will his interventions set a precedent for future attorney generals?

When the Congress-led alliance won the general elections in May 2004, the lawyers representing the Union of India changed, as did the attorney general of India. The judge sitting on the Commission then had to adjust his breeches: suddenly the good guys were the bad guys. The lawyers of those caught on tape were confused for a bit when they found the government lawyers, instead of protecting them as had been the case in the past, were protecting the other side and often checked them from badgering witnesses. It has become clear that justice is not based on the principle of right or wrong but more on who hired or appointed you.

In the Commission, Justice K. Venkataswami repeatedly rejected the argument that the tapes were doctored. When Justice S.N. Phukan took over from Venkataswami, he accepted that the doctoring of tapes was a possibility. Immediately the lines were drawn. The Tehelka team perceived him as pro-government and anti-Tehelka; all the others were relieved that Phukan was on their side. The 'experts' performed a technological battle, armed with displays on how easy it is to alter what a person is saying. Tehelka had its own experts. Displays of the magic of video technology stirred up a buzz in the Commission. Which one of the 'experts' has a handle on the truth?

Then you have the Others. The second rung fixers, small-time wheeler-dealers, bureaucrats; who live in a planet where the biggest boast flies you to the moon. R.K. Jain, treasurer of the Samata Party said, 'If you are purchasing Qutab Minar, why don't you sell Taj Mahal to me?' in justification of all the lies bandied about. There are always numerous versions: the first, what they said in the Operation West End tapes; the second, what they said in the Army Court of Inquiry; and the third, what they said in the Commission of Inquiry. And I, presume, a fourth version for the wife at home. More often than not, none of them match. That brings up the question: Why do we, Indians, find it easier to lie than tell the truth?

An examination of values is churned up here. The values of the lawyers, who seem to be the only ones to have benefited from Operation West End and end up as collaborators in the diversion of justice. Most of the Tehelka lawyers, however, worked without a fee. Obviously, the lawyers' truth is chosen according to which facts will help to exonerate their client and destabilize the accuser's credibility. Does the cliché, constantly thrown by lawyers, that 'every individual is entitled to a defence', mean that lawyers need not adhere to any principles whatsoever?

The journalists' truth is what makes a good story. Journalists will sometimes don blinkers if a new fact kills their story. Although Tehelka created a new paradigm in Indian journalism, the presentation of the story raised questions of slanted editing. Where should journalists draw the line? Why is there no law for privacy in India? Where are the values of Indian journalism going? Editors of leading news organizations are interviewed for their perspective. Also to be considered: are the spin-doctors way ahead of the news-hungry journalists and taking them for a disingenuous ride?

As always various conspiracy theories were floated. Who are the active participants in promoting these? Unravelling those bring some intriguing answers.

After the exposé, and as the consequent developing events began to unfold, each person involved was deeply changed. It was not an easy time for those caught on tape and even worse for those who caught them. This book then explores the inner lives of these people. How events fracture, heal, splinter again and thereupon crush the interior of beings. How many of them are able to heal, recover, and reconstruct themselves? Each one applies a different form of balm.

When you listen to each player in the Operation West End network and their lawyers, you return to *Rashomon*. Whose truth is the Truth? The videotapes should be considered apodictic. But doubts about them have also been raised. When Jaya Jaitly makes a statement on the tapes, who is she addressing? Each person in that room has a different version and watching the tapes it is almost impossible to tell. Whose reality are we to accept?

In the making of *The Matrix* trilogy, Larry and Andy Wachowski, the writers and directors, decided that they would not declare the meaning or basis of the film to avoid what they feared would become a dogma. They wanted to leave an open space for reflective interpretation. Larry explained that the film was about introducing questions and does not provide answers. The film asks: What is reality? Larry discussed with integral thinker Ken Wilber his exploration of the philosophy of the Upanishads, the inquiry into what is Truth; how we arrive at rational conclusions, and how the film raised these eternal questions.

In *The Matrix*, Morpheus (Laurence Fishburn) tells Neo (Keanu Reeves), 'The Matrix is the world that has been pulled over your eyes to blind you from the truth'. At another moment, Morpheus tells Neo,

> **How would you know the difference between the dream world and the real world? What is real? How do you define real? If you're talking about what you can feel, what you can smell, what you can taste and see, then real is simply electrical signals interpreted by your brain. This is the world that you know.**

> The world as it was at the end of the twentieth century. It exists now only as part of a neural – interactive simulation that we call the Matrix. You've been living in a dream world, Neo. This is the world as it exists today. Welcome to the desert of the real.

The philosophical questions in *The Matrix* are those that are written about in the Upanishads' illumination of Maya (illusion). What is Maya? 'That which is truly not, but appears to be is Maya.' How do you know what is which? That's the point. You don't know. But the knowledge not the acceptance, of not knowing makes the difference. Maya is the purely physical and mental reality in which our everyday consciousness is entangled, which veils the true reality that one can only experience through meditation, psychological unravelling and perhaps terrific mushrooms that take you beyond your immediate experience. It is the realization that there is more than what we daily see, hear and feel; the realization of how much we do not know. The journey of Man (Neo) begins when he breaks through these daily illusions. That's what makes life worth living: finally learning that it isn't worth anything much at all. There is something much bigger out there and that's when you really enjoy the ride.

Yes, the Tehelka story is based on facts, but which of these are in double bold, which are in italics and which are in fine print? That perception lies in the eyes of the beholder and his own reality. The story is then heuristic. It is an interfusion of the projection of idealism, on the one hand, and the annihilating power of those who rule, on the other. Sounds simple; virtually a cliché of David and Goliath. The twist here is: Can David ever survive Goliath? In these times of global multinationals and One superpower, where is the story of the small company or any small country winning? David has been merged; taken over in an acquisition, or simply shocked and awed out of existence. It is a battle between those who are part of the system and those who want to change it because they see it as hurting the larger good. Tehelka's journalists are not part of the establishment although they would certainly like to turn it on its head. The commonality that both warring factions shared was that they both pushed the edges of the law. One side did it for financial profit, the other for journalistic gain. Tehelka's tale, if read with scrutiny and the necessary speculation, would then expectedly culminate in disparate opinions. The reader participates in the Rashomon and his/her reactions, then, become part of the story.

It is my belief that Indian mythological literature was written using protagonists and characters in an attempt to instigate dialogue about ethics and conduct. The worshipping of these characters, to me, is sacrilegious to the intent of the scriptures. The establishment of eternal dilemmas in the Mahabharata and Ramayana and their catalysing effect on daily life is the goal of the scriptures. They are written for people to react to. That there is disagreement in the interpretation signifies the success of the intent. For each individual must make them his own. For Mahatma Gandhi, the Mahabharata was a message of peace. When asked how he came to that conclusion when the epic is all about war, Gandhiji answered by putting his palm to his heart and said, 'From here.' Given that Hinduism does not have a single book of dogma, but rather a series of philosophical, lifestyle guidebooks, that are all open to interpretation and always hold the question mark in reverence, there is a historical and traditional freedom in personal perspective. In some way, it also explains why Indians find it so difficult to simply obey rules. In writing about Operation West End, Tehelka, and all that went with it, the attempt is to follow that tradition of interpretation. Yes, there are facts, but they are subject to my and your interpretations.

Above all, the book brings up the issue of ethics or the lack of them in our lives: in journalism, in the legal profession, in government. In our acceptance of corruption – we are like this only – consequently adjusting our lives and decisions by cooperating with it, are we damaging ourselves, our national character and the future of India?

I conducted over forty interviews, all of which were recorded on audiotapes with the subjects' permission. Four legal luminaries have vetted the manuscript to ensure that all information serves the purpose of public interest and is based on established facts.

Is there a clear conclusion in the book? Yes, there is, but it is only my conclusion. Readers must come to their own.

As loud and different as every singular story is, it knits into another, while forming a separate entity sometimes nudging the whole. The trick, then, lies in balancing it all. There is good and there is evil, yet both those colours are in all of us. To some, the comfort of knowledge only comes after certainty. Yet, there is great wisdom in looking at life in shades of grey. It is in the hazy hue of grey that you will find a crystal of truth.

CHARACTERS

Ahluwalia, Major General Manjit Singh: Additional Director-General of Ordnance Services, Army Headquarters. Introduced to Operation West End by Lieutenant Colonel V.P. Sayal. Was involved in general discussions about army procurement and equipment. Tehelka said they gave Rs 50,000 to Sayal to give to Ahluwalia, Sayal admitted to keeping the money for himself.

Badal, Kumar: Reporter in Tehelka who was arrested on the basis of arrested wildlife poachers found with Badal's phone number.

Bahal, Aniruddha: Head of the Investigation Cell of Tehelka. Took all the decisions about Operation West End, and Mathew Samuel reported to him daily.

Berry, Lieutenant Colonel V.K. (Retd): Formerly with Corps of Signals Service Department. Retired from DGQA as a senior quality assurance officer. Attempted to be a middleman and worked as a consultant for Mohinder Pal Sahni. Took West End to meet Major Sarabjeet J. Singh in a hotel.

Choudary, Major General P.S.K.: Additional Director-General, Weapons and Equipment (ADR, WE). Seen on tapes advising West End on the procurement procedures and current army requirements. Accepted a gold chain and Rs 1 lakh from West End.

Gupta, Deepak: Son of R.K. Gupta (an RSS trustee), reportedly working with his father in arms deals as a middleman. Introduced West End to Rakesh Nigam, reportedly a second-rung middleman.

Gupta, R.K.: Known to be an RSS trustee and dabbling in arms deals. Made extravagant boasts to West End about his proximity to the prime minister and Brajesh Mishra (security adviser in the Prime Minister's Office). Claimed he gave the BJP Rs 3 to 4 crore every month, made Rs 100 crore a year in commissions, and that he paid George Fernandes through Jaya Jaitly.

Jain, R.K.: Treasurer of the Samata Party. Spoke in detail and offered to show minutes of meetings with George Fernandes and commissions collected on behalf of the Samata Party on numerous defence deals.

Laxman, Bangaru: President of the party in government, the Bharatiya Janata Party. Seen on tapes accepting money from Mathew Samuel. Resigned on 14 March 2001.

Jaitly, Jaya: President of the Samata Party during the taping of Operation West End. Resigned from the party and has failed to renew her membership of it. Was seen in Operation West End tapes with Mathew Samuel in Defence Minister George Fernandes's house.

Malviya, Anil: Alias Rajiv Sharma in the Operation West End tapes. Small-time advertising space salesman who colluded with Mathew Samuel in the initial tapes. Reportedly died of a heart attack in Allahabad before the tapes were aired.

Mehra, Devina: Director of First Global Stockbroking Pvt. Ltd along with her husband invested Rs 3.5 crore in Tehelka.

Mehta, L.M.: Additional Defence Secretary. Was introduced to West End by Major General S. P. Murgai. Met West End and was accused of accepting a gold chain which he denied.

Murgai, Major General S.P. (Retd): Former Additional Director-General, Quality Assurance. Murgai introduced West End to Surendra Kumar Sureka, a businessman from Kanpur, who took them to Jaya Jaitly.

Nigam, Rakesh: Reportedly a second-rung arms dealer. West End offered him Rs 2 lakh to introduce them to Yogendra Narain, defence secretary.

Pant, H.C.: Staff Officer in the Ordnance Factories Cell. Was additional secretary to Hiren Pathak, minister of state for defence.

Phukan, Justice S.N.: Appointed by the Government of India to head the Commission of Inquiry into the Tehelka exposé on 4 January 2002 after Justice Venkataswami resigned.

Sahni, Mohinder Singh: Mistakenly referred to as Mohinder Pal Sahni in Tehelka transcripts. Allegedly an arms dealer middleman and then Consul General of Belize.

Samuel, Mathew: Maverick, aspiring journalist who started the clandestine videotaping of defence ministry officials and army officers.

Sasi, P.: An assistant (post between an upper division clerk and lower division clerk) in the Ordnance Services, Army Headquarters. Calls himself Sashi Menon rather than P. Sasi, his actual name in order to upgrade his caste. The first person who began selling documents to Operation West End and led them to Colonel Anil Sehgal.

Satya Murthy: Private Secretary to Bangaru Laxman. Was reportedly given Rs 10,000. Met with West End a second time to finalize a commission for a defence deal.

Sayal, Lieutenant Colonel V.P. (Retd): Last posting as Commandant of 24 FAD (Forward Ammunition Depot). Was attempting to become a middleman between the army and suppliers of arms and equipment. Introduced West End to Brigadier Iqbal Singh, Major General Murgai and Major General Manjit Singh Ahluwalia.

Sehgal, Colonel Anil: Director, Armaments in the Army Headquarters, in charge of procurement of spares for the army. Sehgal reportedly took money from West End in exchange for information on army requirements and starred in sex tapes with prostitute.

Seth, Suhel: Co-CEO of Equus, an advertising agency. Was part of the core group that formed Tehelka.com but dropped out before any work started.

Sharma, Lieutenant Colonel Bhav Bhuti: Assistant Director, Air Formation Signals, QMG Branch, Air Headquarters. Is seen on tapes drinking with West End poseurs and prostitutes in a hotel. Was not paid any money and was only interested in women.

Sharma, Shankar: Director of First Global Stockbroking Pvt. Ltd, along with his wife Devina Mehra, invested Rs 3.5 crore in Tehelka for a 14.5 per cent equity stake.

Singh, Brigadier Iqbal: Deputy Director-General, Procurement Progressing Organization in the MGO (Master General Ordnance) Branch, Army Headquarters. Singh was seen on tapes with Mathew Samuel and Lieutenant Colonel V.P. Sayal (Retd) in a hotel.

Singh, Narender: Assistant Financial Adviser, Ministry of Defence. Advised Tehelka on arms deals and details of army procurement procedures. He is accused of accepting Rs 10,000 from them.

Singh, Major Sarabjeet J. (Retd): Formerly in the Infantry Division in the army, now reportedly a middleman aspirant. Singh introduced West End to Major General Satnam Singh.

Singh, Major General Satnam: GOC 8 Mountain Division. Also Director-General of Operations in the Drass-Kargil sector. Got roped in inadvertently and provided West End with general information on army equipment and procurement.

Sureka, Surendra Kumar: Mistakenly called Sulekha in the Tehelka transcript. Businessman from Kanpur who supplied clothing to the army. Took West End to meet Jaya Jaitly. Accused of accepting Rs 1 lakh from them.

Tejpal, Minty: Tarun Tejpal's brother who worked with him in Tehelka.

Tejpal, Tarun: Editor-in-Chief of Tehelka.com. Played a key role in fielding the media after the exposé on 13 March 2001. He was the media face of Tehelka.

Raman, Vijay: Video editor who worked on the Operation West End tapes.

Venkataswami, Justice K.: Appointed by the Government of India on 24 March 2001 to head the Commission of Inquiry to probe the Tehelka exposé.

Venkatesh, Raju: Private secretary to Bangaru Laxman. Was reportedly given a gold chain to provide West End access to Bangaru Laxman.

OPERATION WEST END TEAM

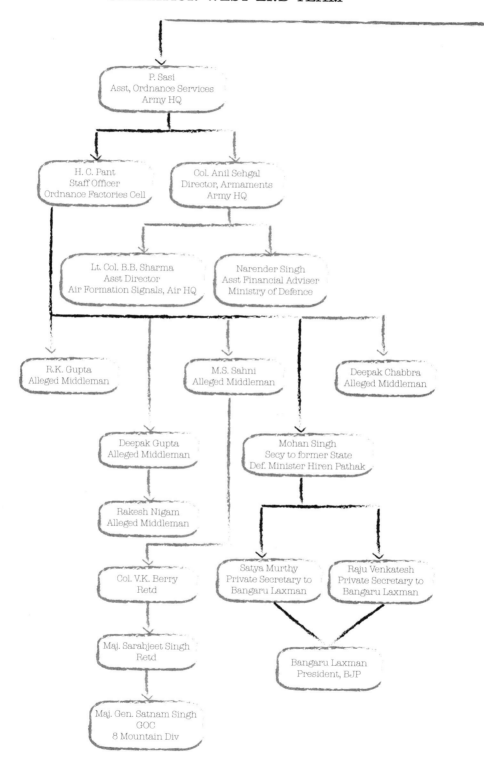

Mathew Samuel · Aniruddha Bahal

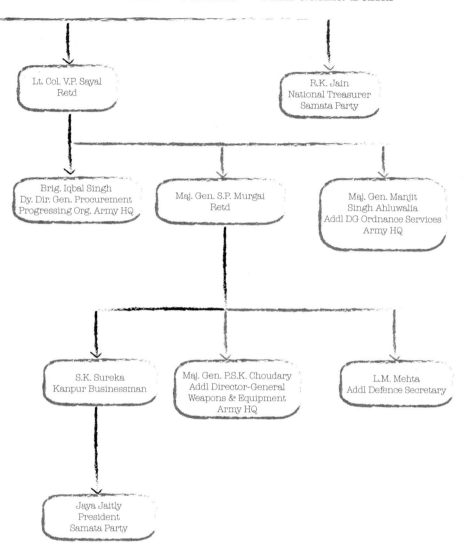

1   Grate Expectations
The Breaking Story

Imperial Hotel, New Delhi. 3.00 p.m., 13 March 2001. Website Tehelka.com showed four-and-a-half hours of videotapes in which Tehelka reporters posing as arms dealers bribed army officers, defence ministry officials as well as the BJP president Bangaru Laxman. In the defence minister George Fernandes's residence, Jaya Jaitly, president of the Samata Party met fictitious representatives of a company unknown to her who offered a financial donation to her political party. Jaitly directed where the money should be sent and explained how the money would be used for the Samata Party.

13 March 2001. What could be more ordinary than a date? Yet what makes a particular date unforgettable? Perhaps your life changing, irretrievably, for the worse? That morning, Tarun Tejpal had no inkling of this. He was wired with the 'centre of attention' charge. He had waited for this moment: the biggest journalistic coup in India's history. His website, Tehelka. com, was going to raze them all: the government, other news organizations, competitors, the lot. Wouldn't there be a slight tinge of gloating when his former bosses saw what he was worth? A lucky few get to experience this kind of euphoria. The sense of achievement and then just awaiting the accolades. Your interior being is in a pitch. A soft high that you can feel its colour inside. Your own faith in yourself is no longer shaky. You feel so right. Touched by an invisible hand that keeps the tension around you in a confident incandescence. As editor-in-chief of Tehelka, Tarun felt he had finally done what he had always wanted to do. Good journalism without some businessman with his eye on advertising revenue telling him what he couldn't do. Tehelka would be on the map of India forever. They would be heroes of all good citizens who believed in transparent governance. The value of the Tehelka website would soar. They would be rich. His wife's unfailing support would be rewarded. They would tell nostalgic stories of the bad old times when money was tight. Tarun's expectations were natural, given the outcome of journalistic exposés the world over.

The Tehelka team had used three cameras hidden in a briefcase, a handbag, and a tie, had bribed to obtain sensitive information, classified documents, and introductions to people involved in arms deals for the Indian Army. The reporters had filmed army officers with sex workers they had supplied. The journalistic sting was called Operation West End, after the fictitious company Tehelka created to uncover corruption in the government, army, and defence ministry. Sixteen individuals allegedly accepted money from the purported representatives of West End. The journalists portrayed themselves as arms dealers who wanted to supply non-existent hand-held thermal cameras. Tehelka taped them for four months, starting September 2000.

It was around 10.00 in the morning when Tarun put in a call to his investor in Mumbai, Shankar Sharma of First Global Stockbroking. Tarun told him that Tehelka was about to explode with a Big Breaking Story. He didn't give any details, only informed Shankar that they were going to show a political defence exposé. Shankar responded by telling him, 'Don't do it'. He pointed out to Tarun that they were in the midst of negotiations for funding with Subhash Chandra of Zee TV and it would be bad timing.

> **Shankar**: Look boss, doing anything controversial right now, anything that has political overtones is going to just blow your financing plans away.
> **Tarun**: I can't stop this because it's become very dangerous. There's a real risk we are running now. If they get hold of this, we're going to be in trouble. I can't stop it. It's way too big now.
> **Shankar**: If you can't stop it, then you can't stop it.

In Shankar's Rashomon, all business decisions should be based on whether they will make a profit. As he heard Tarun talk about the story he was about to break, Shankar did not share his enthusiasm. He only saw losing future funding. Shankar lived in a different surround. Mumbai's financial fundamentalism is a planet removed from Delhi's twisted politics and journalism. The twain shall never meet. Shankar too had no idea how his own life would be transformed.

The second phone call Tarun said he made was to film star Amitabh Bachchan, who was on the board of directors of Tehelka at that time. Tarun said he told Amitabh they were about to break a big story and as he was on the Tehelka board he wanted to inform him. Tarun said Amitabh asked him if he would like to tell him what the story was about. Tarun said he declined and Amitabh accepted that. Now this is where Rashomon begins and repeats itself through many incidents. When I contacted Amitabh Bachchan he professed ignorance. He said he didn't remember any phone call from Tarun. When reports of the phone call were printed in the newspapers at that time, there was no denial from Amitabh. Yet, in fairness to Amitabh, if he were to refute every incorrect story printed about his life that is all he would be doing. He did tell me that when he was asked to become a member of the Tehelka board he pointed out the potential conflict of interest as he was on the board of Sahara and his own AB Corp, both in the media business. Tarun had told Amitabh that he could step out of it if it ever became a conflict. When I repeated to Tarun that Amitabh could not recall his phone call, Tarun, with a bitter laugh, said how funny it was that people found it difficult to demonstrate support for him. Amitabh did subsequently remove himself from the Tehelka board through a letter to Tarun, which Tarun announced on 5 September 2001. No surprise there.

On that same capacious day, Tehelka's Mathew Samuel, the journalist–investigator and representative of the fictitious arms company, had no hint what a depressing night lay ahead. Mathew Samuel was the man who initiated the Operation West End investigation. He was flying back from Kerala, following instruction from Aniruddha Bahal, his boss and head of Tehelka's investigation cell. Samuel sat in the plane, quiet excitement gurgling inside him. All the gruelling work he had put in would now be shown to the world. Maybe his disgruntled wife, who couldn't deal with his weird working hours, would now understand. It was his dream to be recognized as a serious, investigative journalist.

None of the people shown on the Operation West End tapes, all of whose lives would be shattered by the afternoon, were aware of what lay in store. Ah, yes! There were a few. R.K. Jain (treasurer of the Samata Party) had become suspicious and traced Samuel's cellphone number to Tehelka. His nephew nosed Samuel down to the Tehelka office and Operation West End's cover was blown. Tehelka was forced to push out the story before it was actually ready. That nexus informed each other: the man they had met as Mathew Samuel, representative of West End, a multinational arms manufacturer, was actually a Tehelka journalist. They also knew now that he had videotaped them taking bribes and in sexual acts. Some of them contacted Samuel, frightened, angry, and hurt. *Why* had he done this? One of them begged Samuel not to expose the tapes because his daughter was about to be married. It would ruin all their lives, he said. Tehelka had no choice but to air the story as quickly as possible. In retrospect, the story was not journalistically ready. The transcriptions of the tapes had been hurriedly done. There could be errors, and as it turned out, there were plenty. There were still many loopholes and unchecked facts. There had been no crosschecking of damning allegations. Would that even have been possible given the nature of the story? The people clandestinely taped were a breed apart from the helpless, common masses. These were the sort who were used to fixing people who got in their way. Who could blame the Tehelka team for having nightmares? The story was ticking RDX that had to be flung out of the office.

On the morning of 13 March 2001, journalists all over Delhi began receiving calls from Tehelka, inviting them to come to a press conference at Imperial Hotel at 2.30 p.m. I received a call from Shoma Choudhary, Tehelka's Literary Editor. My response to her was: 'Okay, I'll send someone.' Shoma: 'No, Madhu. For this, I think, you better come yourself.' When I arrived at the Imperial ballroom, Tarun, with his brother Minty Tejpal, was standing at the top of the stairs. Minty first and then Tarun echoing his words, said, 'The government is going to fall. The government is going to fall.' They were tense, but it was a happy tension. How could he have guessed he was counting governments before they hatched?

As the tapes were screened, cellphones began ringing. As names were mentioned, journalists watching the tape, called people they knew and warned them they were on the tapes or had been mentioned. Jaya Jaitly was ordering her daughter's wedding invitation card when she received a phone call that stunned her. Jaya couldn't even remember this meeting with Mathew Samuel. In a state of alarm, she rushed back to the defence minister's home, 3 Krishna Menon Marg. Army officers on the tapes began getting phone calls. At Army Headquarters, senior brass huddled into one office to watch the Zee telecast of Operation West End. There they saw army officers drinking, shooting the breeze, pouring out classified information, handing over documents, and accepting bribes. Bangaru Laxman, the president of the ruling Bharatiya Janata Party (BJP), was on tape, accepting money from Mathew Samuel on 5 January 2001 without so much as glancing at him. The tapes also showed Jaya Jaitly, president of the Samata Party, on 28 December 2000, being offered a packet at the defence minister's house. She did not, at any point, refuse the money. Jaya gave instructions on where the money should be sent and explained how it would be used. She did not touch the packet.

While the ruling party was working out a damage-control exercise, the country was shocked. Okay, but not that shocked either. Everybody in India is aware of corruption, but who had ever proved it on camera? There was no sympathy for those caught on tape. If anything, there was glee and masala excitement. Yes, in the early days of the exposé, Tehelka did have its brief moments of Camelot. Tarun Tejpal, with whom most of the press was familiar because of his work with *India Today* and *Outlook* magazines, was a hero. Aniruddha Bahal was known to some journalists from a cricket match-fixing exposé he had done. Nobody knew who Mathew Samuel was. Where then was Samuel while all this was happening? Why wasn't he sharing the glory with Tarun and Aniruddha? Samuel's story often turns into a yesteryear Bollywood weepy.

When Samuel returned to Delhi from Kerala that evening, he discovered his Kashmiri landlord had decided to throw him out because of his Tehelka connection. His landlord was wary of any 'trouble'. Samuel was walking the streets with his wife and little child, desperately looking for a house. When Samuel called him in frustration and anguish, Tarun suggested he move into the Tehelka guesthouse. Samuel, the man responsible for it all was the first to feel the perniciousness of the aftermath.

By 3.00 p.m., when the Lok Sabha reconvened, Priya Ranjan Dasmunsi, the Congress chief whip, was pumping with excitement when he interrupted the discussion on the Farmers' Rights Bill. The Opposition already had copies of the transcripts of Operation West End and were baying for resignations. Many members of the Opposition had been invited to Imperial Hotel. They then turned out in full strength in Parliament. (The late) Madhavrao Scindia, senior member of the Congress, was forthright, 'The matter concerns national security; we want an explanation from the government on what seems to be irrefutable evidence. If the government cannot refute these allegations it has no moral right to continue.' Jaipal Reddy, the Congress spokesman, said, 'In the history of this country, we have never had such explosive evidence of corruption. It is equivalent to Pokhran III. It's not just money that changed hands. India's national security has been severely compromised.'

When Opposition members were screaming in Parliament, George Fernandes had no idea what was going on. He was embarrassed as they brayed for his resignation. He reportedly smiled in a daze and repeatedly asked them to calm down.

The Opposition gleefully and noisily demanded the immediate resignation of Prime Minister Atal Bihari Vajpayee. He comfortably retorted, 'Let them make a case for the resignation of the government. This is a political demand.' When asked about the rumours of a conspiracy behind Tehelka's exposé, Vajpayee said, '*Daal mein kuch kaala hai* [there is something fishy]'.

In the Rajya Sabha, the then leader of the Opposition, Dr Manmohan Singh, raised the issue soon after Finance Minister Yashwant Sinha had finished his reply to a call attention motion on the stock market crisis. Yashwant Sinha rejected the Opposition's demand for a Joint Parliamentary Committee to probe into the crash in share prices over the past few days. Sinha said, 'We are in complete control of the situation and therefore there will be no JPC probe'. Sucheta Dalal (*The Indian Express*) later wrote that Shankar Sharma had timed the Tehelka exposé to sabotage the stock market crash discussion in the Rajya Sabha, crediting Shankar with remarkably prescient qualities.

Opposition politicians had a bash up fest, zeroing in on the Prime Minister's Office. Brajesh Mishra, principal secretary to the prime minister, had been mentioned in the Operation West End tapes. Ranjan Bhattacharya, Vajpayee's foster son-in-law, had also had his name bandied about.

Although the Opposition was having a premature dance party on the BJP's grave, if a little thought had gone into it they might have realized it could well have been them. The Tehelka group clearly has no affiliation with any political party. Corruption in India had not developed overnight during the BJP regime. It was a twin, born along with Independence: real Midnight's Children. Jawaharlal Nehru himself was scrupulously honest, but he turned a blind eye to the corruption around him. The first reported virus eruption came as early as 1945, when T. Prakasam, a freedom fighter from what is today Andhra Pradesh, accepted money at political functions from poor peasants and then insisted on keeping it for his personal use as compensation for his sacrifices during the freedom struggle. Prakasam only forwarded the money to the Congress Party after a shakedown from Mahatma Gandhi himself. Allegedly, the first arms deal with a commission took place when Krishna Menon was high commissioner in London (1947-52), in the purchase of jeeps (Rs 80 lakh). Other contracts included Mitchell bombers, rifles and armoured cars. An outraged press wrote about it, there was havoc in Parliament but Nehru did nothing. The case was closed in 1955 and Menon was later, significantly, appointed defence minister. Subsequently, other cases of corruption were reported, involving Partap Singh Kairon, Bakshi Ghulam Mohammed, and T.T. Krishnamachari. No action was taken. The concept of India had begun, and in corruption we had only just begun.

During Indira Gandhi's premiership corruption flourished not only among politicians, but spread to epidemic proportions in the bureaucracy. Numerous books have been written about the abundance of corruption right through Indian history. It should be part of the curriculum in schools because corruption has catalysed historical events. Parliamentary history is replete with questions being raised about politicians: from Jagjivan Ram's ingenuous excuse for not paying taxes at all ('I forgot') to the fur coat allegedly given to Indira Gandhi by Dharam Teja, the first of all the operators. (Teja duped banks and financial institutions into funding his virtually non-existent Jayanti Shipping Company, and in 1965 fled to Costa Rica. The Indian government was in the process of extraditing him when he died with his sullied reputation in tact.) There is not a political party that has not been touched by some scandal or the other. In March 2001, the Opposition parties would have done well not to get too comfortable in an extraordinarily vulnerable glasshouse.

On Breaking Story Day, the Lok Sabha had to be adjourned as Opposition members shouted, *'Gali gali mein shor hai, yeh sarkar chor hai* [in every street the word is out, this government is a thief]'. It was almost as bad in the Rajya Sabha where members demanded the arrest of the people on the tapes. Arun Jaitley, law minister, was in the Lok Sabha. By the time he got back to his office at 5.00 p.m. his staff had downloaded the transcripts of Operation West End from the Tehelka website. A super rapid reader with an unfailing, photographic memory, Jaitley was fully prepared by 6.00 p.m. when Prime Minister Vajpayee called him to his office. Right after the meeting with senior party members, the government issued a statement read by (the late) Pramod Mahajan, then minister for information technology and communications: 'The attention of the government has been drawn to the Tehelka tapes. The government is ready and willing for a thorough debate in Parliament and an inquiry, if necessary. The government has nothing to hide. The guilty will not be spared. No innocent reputation will be allowed to be tarnished.' The prescient part of the statement was: *'No innocent reputation will be allowed to be tarnished.'* The words were carefully chosen. It had a portentous resonance. Tehelka should have put their ears to the ground. And listened. They would have heard a slow, slow drumroll.

In an interview two years later, Arun Jaitley recounted, 'I was called to the prime minister's house, along with Pramod Mahajan and [M.] Venkaiah Naidu. The prime minister had also called for Bangaru Laxman. I was sent in to grill Bangaru Laxman. I concluded, *"Yeh bilkul jhoot* account *nahin hai* [this is not an entirely false report]." It was decided that Bangaru must resign.' As simple as that. Not for Bangaru Laxman, who could not comprehend what he had done wrong. Wasn't he supposed to collect money for the party and doesn't everyone? When Laxman first heard of the tapes his initial reaction was, 'My conscience is clear.' He pointed out, 'You can't run a big party like the BJP without accepting cash donations'. His conscience may have been clear, but the prime minister's reaction was also clear: resign. Vajpayee had to save himself and his government. A puzzled and deflated Laxman reflected that because he belonged to the Dalit community there must have been a conspiracy to push him out.

That evening, Vajpayee's damage control team waited for George Fernandes to arrive. Fernandes delayed the meeting while he read the Operation West End transcripts. It was reported that Fernandes did strongly propose that the government should fight it out and he not resign, following Jaya Jaitly's advice to him. The following day a contrary buzz was generated by the government spin-doctors that Fernandes had offered to resign.

That same night, senior officers of the defence ministry and the armed forces were called for a meeting by Fernandes to decide on what action should be taken against army officers caught on the Tehelka tapes. Much later in the night, all the army officers in the Operation West End tapes were summoned to the defence ministry and interrogated. The following day, on 14 March, Fernandes suspended three officers in his ministry because of the revelations in the Tehelka tapes: H.C. Pant (staff officer in the Ordnance and Factory Board); Narender Singh (assistant financial adviser); and P. Sasi (assistant in the Ordnance Services, Army Headquarters). The army immediately suspended Major General P.S.K. Choudary (additional director-general, weapons and equipment) for his alleged role in the

Tehelka scandal. Choudary was the only officer who immediately admitted he had accepted bribes of Rs 1,00,000 and a gold chain. Choudary's timing of admission of guilt would have serious significance later. Other officers on the tapes, by now posted outside Delhi, were asked to report back but none of them admitted anything.

A day after the exposé, pandemonium again reigned in Parliament, with Opposition members shouting slogans against Fernandes. Prime Minister Vajpayee said his government was ready for an inquiry. Then the damage-control exercise finally got into gear. Rural Development Minister Venkaiah Naidu told reporters there seemed to be a big conspiracy behind the Tehelka revelations. There was suspicion on who funded the sting operation. Along with Naidu, Jana Krishnamurthy, acting president of the BJP, called the Tehelka tapes a conspiracy to defame the party and to destabilize the government. Krishnamurthy praised Bangaru Laxman for his resignation on moral grounds. When reporters asked Krishnamurthy whether journalists carrying briefcases would be banned from the BJP party offices, he responded with a broad smile, 'Let's see what happens'.

The government's team then slowly crunched into warfare mode. They followed the basic rules of combat propaganda.

First: the psychological operations to affect the enemy's reasoning. Three days after the exposé the BJP's media cell issued a press release accusing Tarun Tejpal of links with Congress leader Arjun Singh, who the BJP said was behind Tehelka's sting operation. Various departments in the government were informally asked to start digging for dirt on the Tehelka team. The government arrested six persons who were allegedly planning to kill Tarun Tejpal. Tarun was given Z-category security, which meant he was watched every second by security personnel who reported to the government. There is a Rashomon in this too. I was told that the 'would be killers' were prosecuted in Patiala House. Yet, Tarun said he had received no threatening calls.

Second: the warfare that denies accurate information to the enemy. This involved appointing the Commission of Inquiry, with Tehelka not being able to figure out what was happening to them in the Commission until too late in the game.

Third: physical destruction, which means any method to debilitate the enemy. This was effected through numerous raids on the First Global and Tehelka offices.

Fourth: security measures to keep the adversary from learning about capabilities and intentions. No one in First Global or Tehelka could put a finger on who the one man was or who were the men who issued all the orders and so cohesively coordinated the attacks against them.

Fifth: the information attack. Plant sufficient damaging information, counter-information, and disinformation to keep Tehelka busy defending itself instead of focusing on the corrupt caught on tapes. A series of stories were planted: Subhash Chandra of Zee TV did it to improve his ratings; the Hindujas were behind it to engineer the fall of government and get out of the Bofors scandal; investors conspired to make a killing on the stock market. One report said the ISI was behind it, another that the CIA was. The triumphant accusers were rapidly morphed into the bewildered accused.

How did the Sensex behave on 13 March 2001? Even that was to become a controversial issue, interpreted by government lawyers as crashing because of Tehelka, with the Tehelka investors' lawyers presenting a completely contrary view. On 13 March, Shankar Sharma said his office stopped trading the moment he had spoken to Tarun over the phone. First Global began trading after 4.00 p.m. when the Tehelka episode was aired on Zee News. Given the Indian tendency to always presume there is a conspiracy within a conspiracy, it was presumed that Shankar Sharma traded through other people. I questioned Tejpal about this:

> **Madhu**: The fact that you spoke to Shankar Sharma from your cellphone on the morning of your press conference showing the tapes at Imperial Hotel has led to the opinion that Sharma then started dumping stock expecting a crash. Did he discuss with you what he would be doing?
>
> **Tejpal**: If they are tapping phones, why don't they reveal the conversations? In fact, Shankar was advising me not to go ahead with the exposé. He said it would jeopardize my future and investments into Tehelka would be a problem. He was worried and did not want to get involved in anything like this and I tried to reassure him. Now First Global is being dragged into this for nothing. This was straight journalism and not anything personal against anyone or any government.

After all, how could anything possibly be as simple or as it appears to be? is the Tehelka story as straight as the Tehelka journalists claim? Or does it appear to be a conspiracy and unexpectedly, isn't?

The story of Tehelka has its application in our daily lives. At every step, will you bend? Lie down? Crawl? Break? Or sing: Get up, Stand up, Stand up for your rights? Or just turn your face away? Even more important, will you stand up for someone else when you have nothing to gain and perhaps something to lose? You cannot live in a country like India and ignore your choices. The Tehelka story can be dismissed as just another story. That would be hopelessly optimistic. The story is about you and me.

Joseph Campbell said, 'The journey is the goal.' In India, the journey forcefully becomes the goal, whether or not you want it that way. Don't forget, this is, after all, India. Not a soft state. Not a hard state. But a state of the eternal maze. And, just when you think you've found your way out of the maze, you find another one planted on top of you. As in the Upanishads and the film *The Matrix*, in Operation West End, go figure: What is the truth? What is reality? What is Maya? India is the state of the eternal Maya. One layered on another.

2 Kick-Ass Journalism is Born

Kevin Hollander [Alan Alda]: I'm who Americans trust for their news.
Max Brackett [Dustin Hoffman]: You really shouldn't let a marketing slogan go to your head.

– Costa-Gravas's film Mad City *(1997)*

Suhel Seth recalled, 'Like all good Indians they must have thought, why should they share the booty with a rank outsider?' It didn't take long to sour. Figure this: a bunch of dotcom cowboys decide to ride the cash horse by creating what Seth called 'an in-your-face, web-based news portal, which could be downloadable and printed out'. Tarun Tejpal contacted Aniruddha Bahal about his idea and was surprised when Bahal showed him his laptop with the same idea and a business plan. Bahal had already spent some months in search for funding. Besides Bahal, Tarun also had Shoma Choudhary on board and thought Suhel Seth, co-CEO of Equus would round off a good team.

What were this *Chak De* team's credentials? Tarun Tejpal had the widest experience in journalism. Writing was a hallowed art form for him. He had worshipped at the Authors' Altar since childhood. For Tejpal, the idea of Tehelka was not only that of seeing some cash action in the dotcom flush, he was more interested in Owning the journalism he produced. He wanted to publish what he believed in: not only in terms of content but also in style. It was the ownership of ideas and direction that catalyzed change in the system. His style was not Gonzo Journalism. It was not New Journalism. It was basically Kick-Ass Journalism. Tejpal wanted to own Kick-Ass Journalism. While working in news organizations, Tejpal had always nurtured a powerful undercurrent in his heart: that he was meant for bigger and better things (don't we all?). Tehelka was the path that would take him to where he most wanted to be.

All Aniruddha Bahal ever wanted to do was escape the narrowness of his background. No city slicker or Page 3 social climber, Bahal's interest in the Big City is not to be cool and make money, though of course money doesn't hurt. It is to fulfil his fantasies of adventure nurtured in his childhood by reading books, of which his favourite is *Catch-22* (Joseph Heller, 1961). His choice is portentous, in that the book's leitmotif is how destructive bureaucratic rules can be.

Bahal got his first job in journalism when Tarun Tejpal hired him for *India Today*. He had no qualifications for the job, but he was clear that journalism was where he wanted to be. Tarun moved to *Outlook* and Bahal followed him. Bahal resigned from *Outlook* in 1999, joined a sports magazine, *Cricket Talk*, and was having trouble with his boss when Tarun called him. Bahal became a recognizable name after his match-fixing exposés in *Outlook* magazine.

Tejpal and Bahal had much in common. Their vision for journalism was the same. Both were ambitious. Both had guts. Both loved literature. Both nursed dreams of becoming famous writers. Neither of them favoured any political party. Neither had any fear of playing a dangerous game. Both loved the high but, as it turned out, it was the commonalities that created the edginess between them. This was no yin and yang. It was yang and yang. Both lacked the yin to balance the relationship. So it had to crack to expose the misfit. Didn't Bollywood teach them anything? There is never room for more than one hero at the top. *Ek myaan mein doh talwaarenh nahin samaati* [one scabbard cannot accommodate two swords].

Suhel Seth, besides running his advertising agency, is also an actor on the Delhi stage and has dabbled in films. He has made his mark on the scene through myriad means. His column in *Business India* and *Financial Express*, which he calls 'Kick Ass', actually borders on the conventional and serenely mild. One can patronizingly add that it is improving. Seth sharply compensates for his lack of height with his wit, intense networking, and clean good-boy looks. He is rarely seen at parties without a *jhatki-pataki* draped over his arm. For all his frequently *chod*-peppered language in real life, he can skilfully switch to an ornamental, urbane patrician mode when he knows his conversation is being recorded.

Seth had earlier started a website called Brand Quiver and believed he had the experience of revenue models for such a venture. He recalled,

> We all got pretty excited, and from his house we resolved that we should first decide how this company should be constituted. In the flush of excitement, I rang Russi Mody in Kolkata and said, "Would you be interested in sitting on the board", to which he said "Yes". Somebody said, "I am going to get Amitabh Bachchan." Tarun said "I will get Naipaul." This was the way in which this whole flurry of activity began. What was decided was that Tarun, Minty, Aniruddha, and I would be the principle shareholders in the company.

They agreed they would make a presentation to Ashok Wadhwa of Ambit Finance in Mumbai and figure out how much the business was worth and whether anyone would invest in it. According to Seth, 'It was a tacit understanding between Tarun and myself that I would get about 30 per cent equity in the company and 70 per cent would be split into 50 and 20; 50 for the two Tejpal brothers and 20 for Aniruddha Bahal.' The portal had been registered by Bahal's relative in the US much earlier.

Seth made the presentation to Wadhwa in Mumbai, along with Minty, Bahal, and Tarun. Seth said,

> The pedigree came from Tarun's journalistic career. Aniruddha Bahal was touted as an investigative journalist, I came in from the perspective of an investor who would advise on how we should market the website. During the presentation Ashok Wadhwa didn't put down any numbers on paper but he put out numbers on the board which form part of my affidavit to the Venkataswami Commission. When that figure was put up everyone was pretty excited. As we were leaving the boardroom, I asked Tarun to join me for dinner that night. He said, "No, we are meeting an old school friend of Minty's called Shankar Sharma who runs a company called First Global. We hope to discuss valuation and those kinds of issues with him."

Aniruddha Bahal recalled:

> Everybody was talking in the air at that time: *Yeh hoga, voh hoga, yeh idher, arey* [laughs] *pachaas revenue stream bana diya usney* [this will happen, that will happen, he made 50 revenue streams]. Then Wadhwa just got up out of the blue and wrote a figure on the board. We didn't even know whether he was saying yes or no. He wrote this figure, $8 million. He had this fancy board out there, on which everything you wrote would be recorded [laughs]. It could also print out everything that was written on the board. The printer wasn't working so Suhel Seth was screaming madly [laughs] *ki* what are the figures he's written? When we walked out of Ashok Wadhwa's office it was all settled. He was a VC [venture capitalist] and he would take 5 per cent on par and then he would dilute. He fixed the evaluation at eight [million dollars], which is like Rs 36 crore, and then he would try to place, say, 10 per cent of it. His own brokerage [fee] would be 5 per cent. So basically he was getting free equity which he would pay at par and then offload 10 per cent over a period of time. There was no need to go to other VCs after that. Suhel cancelled all the appointments that were made. We were just too euphoric at that point of time. I remember walking out of the offices and then Suhel in his inimitable style and all these four letter words, *pata nahin kya ho gaya* [don't know what happened]. I asked Tarun, what it meant? He said boss, *ho gaya* [boss, it's done] and then immediately, Suhel took all of us to the President Hotel coffee shop. There on the tablemat is the original. Suhel wrote down the exact equity structure. The Xerox copy is in the affidavit, as approved by all in Suhel's handwriting.

After the pitch to Wadhwa, the dinner that night at Shankar Sharma's home was full of talk about the worth of their yet-to-be-launched website. Because Shankar and his wife Devina Mehra were experienced professionals on the Bombay Stock Exchange, Tarun was looking for some feedback about Ashok Wadhwa. Sharma told him that he was a 'bit of a dodgy guy'. Wadhwa had told them it would take him a couple of weeks to raise the money. Something must have clicked in Sharma's head because a week later he arrived in Delhi and spent a whole day with Tarun. On the way back to the airport, Sharma told Tarun he was open to funding Tehelka on the same terms as Wadhwa. Tarun told Sharma that he had given Wadhwa his word. The following week Tarun called Wadhwa a couple of times and found that he neither took the calls nor returned them. Then Tarun left a message, 'Either call me back or I am not going to call you again. I am going to move on.' Wadhwa returned his call. He told Tarun he was coming to Delhi and they would work something out. Tarun made it clear that he would not wait. Tarun said they had a higher comfort level with Sharma and had decided to switch to him. Sharma sent Tehelka Rs 27 lakh the following week.

When they returned to Delhi, the adventurous camaraderie turned. Minty and Tarun interrupted Suhel during his rehearsal for a play and took him to the car park. Suhel recalled that they told him, 'There is a huge issue. We can't afford 30 per cent'. When Suhel reminded them of their deal, they offered 10 per cent, to which Suhel responded, 'Then I am not interested. You guys carry on. I am not too keen on all these things and besides, I don't know Shankar Sharma. I don't know who the potential investors are going to be. I don't know their credibility.' Suhel recounted:

> Minty, strangely enough, was very aggressive in his tone and manner; very aggressive and very wild, not in the sense of wild as in angry, but he was a tangential kind of a guy. I had kept telling Tarun, even earlier, that Minty was a bit of a dicey kind of character because you never knew in which way he'd swerve and you can't take these risks with the corporate world. Minty kept saying [in his dude style]: "*Yaar*, but what will you bring to the party?" We will get money from Shankar Sharma, and okay, if you do the marketing then we can pay you a commission for that. I realized they obviously believed, after their conversation with Shankar Sharma, that they were on a winning wicket.

At that point Suhel realized they wanted him out. 'Which was fair. I took a very logical perspective of this. So I told Tarun and Minty, "Look, this is the way it is and I don't mind stepping aside."' To this Tarun responded, "Can we still use your office?" I said, "Of course" because I was not going to be undignified and say get the hell out of my office. The only other time I heard about Tehelka was on that 13 March.'

Tarun invited Suhel to the press conference on 13 March, saying, 'Something mega is about to happen. I can't tell you what but it is going to pull the government down.' Suhel said he laughed it off saying everyone thinks he can pull the government down. Suhel reported that Tarun said, 'It's the kick-ass stuff that's going to pull this government down and you must be at this press conference.'

> **Seth:** I obviously didn't go to the press conference. That was a busy day for me and that's where it ended.

Madhu: Thank you, Suhel.

Seth: So, how was it, my dear?

In all probability, a question Seth has asked of many a woman in different circumstances.

∽

What was Tarun's version of his interaction with Suhel?

Tarun: We discovered that Suhel is just a talker. He will not do. So initially when we had started out, I had the largest share in the company: 45 per cent, Suhel had 30, and these kids had the remaining whatever. Then we discovered *yeh kuch karta nahin* [he doesn't do anything], so we scaled him down. Minty had a very bad spat with him. Minty was one of the guys who actually told him so many hard truths to his face, *yaar*. It was in my house and it was pretty embarrassing. Minty said, "You just lie, boss, that's my problem with you. You may like your flamboyant style, but I don't like it. I hear you lying, using my brother's name also and my brother has great credibility because he has never done any funny thing in his life. So if you keep doing that, it's not good for me or my brother or any of us here, boss or Tehelka." Minty was like direct, boss. You know he's also a little mad, *yaar*, and Suhel just shrank. He didn't say a word. At that point his equity came down to 2 per cent. It had begun with 30 and now it had come down to 2. It was pretty embarrassing. But Suhel was cool. He said yeah, okay, whatever you guys think is okay; 2 per cent is fine. [Laughs]. It was so bizarre! By then we discovered that he also had his finger in ten pies. He had a 5, 10, 20 per cent stake in 10 different dotcoms that were coming up. Brand.com, HT.com, bloody some cricket.com which Raian [Karanjwala] had started. The guy was spread all over. We figured that this guy was just kind of just throwing his fishing net all over the place. It wasn't about creating something or doing something.

Minty freaked out because once, just the day before, we were sitting in Suhel's house, and Suhel was calling up somebody from *Business India*; what's her name? Farzana? And, then he gave all this hype about Tehelka and 90 per cent of it was lies. Then he called up a correspondent for a business paper and started giving the same thing. We've got 26 correspondents, in 26 cities of the world and we've got everything lined up. The three of us sat there listening to this bullshit, *yaar*; complete lies. Everybody has a different way of functioning. Maybe it works for Suhel to just speak through his hat, boss, but we don't do it. Two days later when Minty said, "Boss you're just bullshitting all the time and it's not good enough. At the end of the day there is work to be done." By that time the actual shareholding was constituted, he was out of the picture altogether. But to his, I must say, to his credit, *yaar*, he was always good to me.

The uncoupling happened because Suhel Seth's muse is not journalism. Advertising always embellishes. It seeks to glorify the utterly mundane. Journalism must intrinsically always be iconoclastic. It had the makings of a bad marriage. The journalists could not see the value of Seth's style. He was, after all, only doing his job.

⤙

Tarun euphorically resigned his job soon after the Mumbai trip but Bahal had initial reservations.

> **Bahal**: Just on the strength of that verbal thing, Tarun resigned from *Outlook*. But I was in a big [sighs] state of doubt, till the money came. Should I resign from *Cricket Talk* or not? You can understand. I am middle class, dependent on my monthly salary. If I don't get paid, I can't pay my rent. But even I took that gamble and resigned from *Cricket Talk*. That was one of the gutsiest decisions I've ever taken in my entire life, because this place needed all the energy, *na*? We were presuming on the basis of a verbal assurance that money would come.
>
> We had to hunt for offices, put together a core team, plan the site; what was going to be there. This whole energy; what to do now? We didn't even have a company and that's how this whole UD & MD nonsense came up. Because then Shanks said there is a company, a UD & MD, *isi ko ley lo* [take this], which is a normal thing to do. Hundreds of people do it all the time. That's what these companies are registered for: to start working immediately. Otherwise we go to Registrar of Companies, which takes months, *yaar*. So the first cheque that Shanks sent, maybe Rs 20 or 15 lakh went to Tarun's personal account because we didn't have a company. It was a big accounting thing to explain later to the Income Tax people: *bhai yeh company nahin thi toh issliyeh aisey kiya* [there was no company so that is why we did it like this]. He transferred that money when UD & MD came. Now they have made it into such a big sinister conspiracy which makes you want to sit and hold your head. [Laughs] What is this? Then UD & MD was the vehicle, so I transferred the name of Tehelka to UD & MD. That's how it all got started, that's all.

NOTE

UD & MD Agencies was a 'shell' company registered by Shankar Sharma and Devina Mehra's accountant, Neeraj Khanna. It was a company created for such a possibility of starting a new business whenever an opportunity arose. UD & MD stands for: Usha Divya & Madan Lal Daya Bhai.

3 The Catcher on the Fly

Tom Grunnick [William Hurt]: What do you do when your real life exceeds your dreams?
Aaron Altman [Albert Brooks]: Keep it to yourself.

— James Brooks's film Broadcast News *(1987)*

Roll on text on Operation West End tapes:

> We at Tehelka.com managed to sell the Lepage 90, the ALION and, the Kreuger 3000 to the Indian defence establishment – ostensibly fourth generation hand-held thermal cameras and, needless to add, non-existent.
> This is how we did it.

Yes, but did they actually sell all this high-faluting, dangerous sounding stuff? Did they hand over arms and thermal cameras, and take money for them? Is this the story then of how they didn't do it yet claimed they did? Aniruddha Bahal declared to the Commission of Inquiry on Tehelka that an evaluation letter for these products was issued by the Army Headquarters. The army officers denied any such letter was issued. Who was telling the truth? Did this letter actually exist?

What is a Lepage 90? Aniruddha borrowed the name Lepage from his favourite book *Catch-22*:

> Yossarian sidled up drunkenly to Colonel Korn at the officers' club one night to kid with him about the new Lepage gun that the Germans had moved in.
> "What Lepage gun?" Colonel Korn inquired with curiosity.
> "The new three-hundred-and-forty-millimeter Lepage gun," Yossarian answered. "It glued a whole formation of planes together in mid-air."

Right. Did Aniruddha make a portentous choice for his lead? Was everything then fiction? Was some of it fiction? Can't be, because there are the tapes for all to see. Or, were they 'doctored', as Jaya Jaitly vehemently declared? There was enough on the tapes to rile Jaya Jaitly, then president of the Samata Party and a close colleague of Defence Minister George Fernandes. The man responsible for recording virtually all the Operation West End tapes was Tehelka's Mathew Samuel.

The first recording was of P. Sasi, an assistant in the Ordnance Services, Army Headquarters. On the tapes, Sasi told Mathew Samuel: 'One battalion, 300 quantity. We have 360 battalions. One battalion: 36 quantity, 36 piece for one battalion. So we have 360 battalions. 360 into 3.' He also informed him about the ammunition that needed to be imported, '25 ammunition, 66 ammunition,135 ammunition, 150 for Bofors. They import all these, *na*?'

Sasi not only provided detailed information about the Indian Army's requirements, but also handed over confidential documents. How much then did Sasi sell his country for? In the Army Court of Inquiry (ACI), Sasi was asked:

ACI: As per the Tehelka script you have received the following amounts. Is it true?

Date	Place	Amount
(i) 6.09.2000	India Gate	Rs 2000
(ii) 25.09.2000	Hotel Orchid	Rs 20,000
(iii) 1.11.2000	Sasi's residence	Rs 10,000
(iv) 18.11.2000	Sasi's residence	Rs 20,000

Sasi: It is true. But I took that Rs 20,000 on September 25, as loan and gift worth Rs 10,000 on November 1 for distribution to friends.

So, India was for sale for Rs 52,000.

ACI: During this conversation you have discussed about a Russian company which supplied Noga Lights which illuminates inside the tank. You have also discussed about payments made to that firm. Quantity received so far. Did you make this statement?

Sasi: Yes, I did make the statement.

ACI: Is this item in the inventory and is this being dealt by you?

Sasi: It is there in the inventory and OS-16(b), where I am working, deals with it.

ACI: Why did you divulge the above information?

Sasi: I divulged it under the influence of liquor.

ACI: Are you aware that you are not supposed to divulge this information?

Sasi: Yes.

ACI: Have you signed the certificate in connection with Official Secrets Act?

Sasi: Yes. I have signed a certificate at the time of my entry into service. I do not remember whether I sign such certificate every year.

ACI: During this conversation you have also discussed about foreign firms KBP Russia, Rousvorqhvia, Dalpat (Holland) EI supplying items to the army. Is this true?

Sasi: Yes, I made the statements under the influence of liquor.

The court played the videotape showing Sasi's conversations with Mathew Samuel and Rajiv Sharma/Anil Malviya.

ACI: Did you hand over documents pertaining to II Tubes and Photomis to Mr Samuel Mathew and Mr Sharma?

Sasi: Yes. But these documents I have taken out from an old supply order.

ACI: Did you take anyone's permission in the office to hand them over to Mr Samuel Mathew?

Sasi: No.

ACI: During this conversation you were heard saying that the document is secret, signed by your boss and many higher-ups and hence it should not be shown to anybody? Is it true?

Sasi: Yes. Just to impress.

ACI: You were also seen showing the circuit diagram of the equipment from the supply order and asking not to show it to anyone. Is it true?

Sasi: Yes.

ACI: During the meeting at Hotel Orchid on September 25, 2000, you have discussed with Mr Samuel Mathew and Mr Sharma about procurement of LCD-Flake's multimeter and also showed a supply order signed by Colonel Anil Sehgal. Is this true?

Sasi: Yes. Just bluffed.

ACI: You have also discussed about DGPS Rovers, its supply order, IDE Thermal and its supply order signed by Colonel Anil Sehgal. Is this true?

Sasi: Yes.

How did a man like Mathew Samuel (wrongly called Samuel Mathew in ACI tapes) succeed in bribing his way into a network of army officers, politicians, bureaucrats, wheeler-dealers, and record it all on 105 tapes? It worked like this. Tarun Tejpal ran the Tehelka website: contracting famous writers, raising funds, hiring staff, and all the administrative stuff. Certainly not the kind of work Tejpal enjoyed. Aniruddha Bahal was in charge of the Investigative Cell; Mathew Samuel worked under Bahal.

Tarun repeatedly said in his cross-examination that he did not know the details of the sting operation, but everybody found that difficult to believe. Tarun became the public face of Tehelka after the story broke because he played the role of editor-in-chief, standing by his reporters in press conferences. He got all the media coverage, sometimes to Aniruddha's umbrage. But it was Mathew Samuel who was the core of the investigative journalistic siege carried out by Tehelka, along with Aniruddha. Or, as Samuel said, Aniruddha was 'guaaaiding' him. Samuel is responsible for permanently changing the paradigms of pursuit in journalism in India, yet no one has heard him speak publicly. His photograph has never been published. He doesn't give interviews. The few he gave in Kerala after the Tehelka story broke were to the Malayalam press, after which he was instructed by Aniruddha to zip it up and he did. Samuel agreed to an interview with me, explaining: 'Because of your work. You not scared of anybody.'

The first thing Samuel told me when I started interviewing him was, 'Maddumm, my English is not very well. My age is only thirty-three. Five years back I came here. I did not complete my degree. That is why I am not good in English.' When I assured him that I could understand him quite clearly, he carried on with confidence.

In the Commission of Inquiry, when Aniruddha Bahal was asked by lawyer Sidharth Luthra why he chose to hire Mathew Samuel, Bahal said, 'First of all, because he listens to me. Secondly, his remarkable store of leads to hot stories, and finally, because of Samuel's Kerala background, he had a natural ability to blend in with the clerk bureaucracy in the capital.' Samuel works on his skill to blend into the scenery. I asked him:

Madhu: What if a journalist takes your picture and blows your cover while you are investigating a story?

Samuel: One thing that Gawd given another one grace. Suppose you have vaatched me here, you can vaatch me after three-four days, in another one I can change my look very well. I can become a Asharaff coming from Bawmbay. That I did. Some story. I'm doing that. It's not like suddenly, if we can, many times we met, that kind of, I can change it very well.

Going with everyone, going there. Taking cycle rickshaw. Here, there. I'm not bothered about you are providing only car. So who bothered about me? Those who only having head weight, and claiming they are only coming out that way. I'm, as it is, uuuzsual. Thousand people walking, I'm one of them. How can you catch one idiot is going like that? It's possible? I don't think so. Hundred crores people are here.

As I began the first of numerous interviews with him, Aniruddha Bahal called Samuel on his cellphone and told him to stop the interview with me. Aniruddha shouted at him and sounded upset. Samuel got nervous, red in the face, and said, 'Awkay! Awkay! Awkay! Awkay!' He looked as if he was under pressure, but on the other hand, he seemed used to it. I expected him to bring the interview to a close; tell me he could not continue. But, totally in character, he said, 'Awkay!' to Aniruddha and looked at me silently for a few seconds: thinking. I was apprehensive. I asked him whether we could resume the interview. After internalizing his feelings, missing just one beat, taking a deep breath, he carried on unaffected.

Who is Mathew Samuel? Samuel is noticeably ordinary, yet unnoticeably extraordinary. He is not a college graduate, yet self-educated in conceptual thinking. He is around 5ft 10in tall. Heavy set, overweight, nondescript clothes. He doesn't breathe air, only smokes. A plebeian face. Determinedly average. Samuel's father was an upper division clerk in the

Electrical and Mechanical Engineers and his mother was a clerk in a cooperative bank. Samuel left his Kerala village, Pathirkal, (population 800, 'in booth', as he says) with the cliché in his heart of making it big in the city. By any means. With no one to pull strings for him, no godfather, no family background with a recognizable name in the right circles, he was at the bottom of the Malthusian mass. What made him different was the rumble in his belly. Samuel was hungry for adventure journalism.

Diane K. Obson, in her Introduction to *A Joseph Campbell Companion*, explains it:

> That step, the heroic first step of the journey, is out of, or over the edge of, your boundaries, and it often must be taken before you know that you will be supported. The hero's journey has been compared to a birth: it starts with being warm and snug in a safe place; then comes a signal, growing more insistent, that it is time to leave. To stay behind your time is to putrefy. Without the blood and tearing pain, there is no new life.

Guts, gumption and the excitement of wanting to be part of the action. Scratch the surface of any good journalist and these three elements will hit you: the driving urge to blow the lid off dishonest, powerful people and to make a positive difference to people's lives is a strong motivation amongst journalists. Sounds terribly old school. Unfortunately, it *is* old school. Today's journalism is increasingly leaning towards catching one juicy quote in a rush to make a story, and, sadly, there is also corruption. Media tycoons are more interested in the expansion of their tycoonism rather than the pursuit of good journalism. Yet old-school journalists continue to exist who believe in the nobility of the profession as a public service.

Is Samuel's ethos as simple as that? Not quite. There is an element in Samuel that has also figured out that supplying information to news organizations means money. Samuel's thrill in digging up scoops isn't purely altruistic. There are editors of dailies who have put down money for his information, but will never publicly acknowledge that. Samuel has figured out his weakness and strength, and is obviously capitalizing on his strength. He knows he cannot write a story in English. In his mind, those who matter don't read the Malayalam press. He wants to play with the big boys. So what does he do? He does investigative work; only half the work of a journalist but the crucial part.

When civilians who are not journalists, particularly lawyers, question Samuel about his motivations for doing Operation West End, it is impossible for them to comprehend the peculiarly simple reasons. Only a journalist who has experienced the excitement of landing a scoop will understand. If you interrogated Tehelka's lawyers on why they took on the Tehelka's cases without fee, given the zeitgeist, who would believe they were doing it for belief in principles? But that is the truth. Does Samuel look for glory in his own way? He clearly has no interest in celebrity of the Page 3 type. But he does want to be acknowledged by his peers as a good journalist.

The first time Samuel saw a television set was when it was brought to his village for the Asian Games in 1982. He said about 300 people watched that single television.

Samuel: That time TV came. So that all Dellli, in my mind. So after cawllij, Dellli was my dream. If suppose we will watch like local speeches, political leaders will speech, everyone started from Dellli. Then only he will come to Trivandrum. The mind set up is that, almost all the local speeches like political speeches and everyone, we will vaatch them. Vaat this idiot is saying.

The school in his village is only up to class IV. Samuel then went to St Stephen's in the slightly larger village of Pathanaparam. The hub of the village is a teashop run by a Muslim, Mammeni. 'Every morning we will assemble there and take 20 tea. We will discuss politics, international politics, including Iraq matter [ha! ha! ha!]. So all the tawpics are stupid. No one knows vaat eggzackly.' Evenings were spent playing volleyball and football in a rice paddy field after cultivation was over for the day. His home was the only one in the village that subscribed to the daily *Malayala Manorama*, which he studied every day.

Samuel: So Dellli kind of news I'm looking really this thing. After of course, your brother Aroon Purie and Arun Shourie. I was not that matured also, then some people told me who are elder to me, they are the legend of Indian journalism. Such kind of a tawpic started in the cawllij type debate. That is roooral cawllij. Remote village. Cawllij is in the hill. Only 1,300 students there. And we will discuss up to nuclear weapons to everything like that and we will take all the high profile people name, vaat they said, vaat they did. That is the composite culture in our village.

Samuel said he also edited the college magazine.

Samuel: We started a culub. In my rrooorral area. Companion, Atts and Sports Club.
Madhu: Atts?
Samuel: Oooof! [Banging his head in frustration] Atts! Atts! A-R-T-S. Atts! How we get that money, you know? You heard about Christmas carols singing in Kerlla? We 10 people will go night … with staaar and Santa Claus make up. We'll go and sing the song. Ha! ha! huh! So they will give five rupees, ten rupees, two rupees, one rupee. That is a bigger story. Ha! huh! Around three hundred rupees we collected and we bought carom board, chessboard, some books, and we started literacy campaign. Vaat happened? Ha! ha! huh! ha! One day, we're playing cricket. Cricket is like, our bat is coconut tree's big thing, *hai na*, that is our bat. Cricket is very esspensive game, *hai na*. I hitted the bawl and it went on the asbestos on another one. The bawl hitted asbestos roof, another one roof, another one guy. Then entire people come and burnt up our culub.
Madhu: Why did they burn down your club?
Samuel: Because asbestos is costing around hundred and fifty rupees. That day the culub stopped. Ha! ha! ha!

Madhu: So, how did you land up in Delhi?

Samuel: One thing you know, I know each and every nook and corner of Dellli road. Why? That's a story. After I came here, for vaat purrpus I came here, you know? Any idea?

Madhu: You came here … wait … uurrr … uummm … you wanted to see Delhi?

Samuel: Yes! And another purpose, you know. Fussst thing. Nobody know. The real reason I came here to visit Dellli. Before that, near to my home, my relative home, they got a telephone connection. My mother was very much jealousy. She given this number to her parents place in Palaghat. So two-three times they called up to her to connect my mother. After one or two times they also fed up. I was also in students' politics. She told me if I can go and collect a telephone connection from some politician. Then I went and met this Suresh. He was a member of Parliament. I was the cawllij general sekitry also. Then I told him I am planning to coming to Dellli to visit these places. He told me, vaatever you book this telephone, this paper, take it with you. So come with that paper. So if I am there, I will take the, I don't know vaat he said.

In 1995, Samuel told his mother he would go to Delhi and get her a telephone connection, keeping his real goals a secret. When Samuel arrived on a freezing winter day in Delhi in his lungi and no warm clothes, he called Suresh's number. There was no answer. An autorickshaw driver took him to Hotel Sher-e-Punjab in Paharganj. He went in to negotiate the rates, returned to find that the autorickshaw had vanished.

Samuel: He left with the briefcase. Becawz of that I stayed in Dellli.

Madhu: What was in the briefcase?

Samuel: My druss. Some money. Only thousand rupees. Otherwise tomorrow I have to go book the ticket for return. So I don't have the money to go and book the ticket return.

Right!

Madhu: This is a classic Hindi movie story. Village hick comes to town and gets taken for a ride.

Samuel: This really happened. Then, in my pawkit I have only 600-700 rupees. Suppose I am going to stay him, there is only two or three days programme here. I will give the paper to him, then he will take it and come back to Kerlla and return the paper. That way in my mind.

Samuel's adventures then began. He called his brother-in-law, ironically a police officer, who sent him a car the following day. Meanwhile he decided to go and watch a movie:

Samuel: Just I'm valking and vatching vaat bloody going on that is New Dellli. Coming in a mind, *hai nah*, that is villaige *sey aata hai* [come from a village]. Such a big rush where movie going on. People are pulllling like that. In our villaige no people pulllling like that get the ticket. So I decide, no, don't watch movie. I go back to hotul. Then I bought from roadside, short pant, I don't have anything, towel, brrrush, the whole thing *leh keh* I went to that place. I have only 400 rupees. Then he given that address, I went to that place. I just going to start my wurrrk to vaatch everything, Parliament House, India Gate, Qutab Minar, where is T.N. Seshan sitting. This are the targets. Vaat is Humayun Road, vaat is Akbar Road, vaat is 10 Janpath, it's appearing in newspapers, Race Course, but actually this. *Usney mujhey gaddi mey bhej diya, gaddi mey jao*, Central Secretariat *jayega* [he sent me in a car to go see the Central Secretariat]. Then I started walking on the path. I am vatching all the names. Lawts of names, member of Parliament, this name, that name. Two three times *hum usko ghoom liya* [I went around] Central Secretariat. I want to pass Talkatora Stadium, Jawaharlal Stadium also, Asiad happened there, *nah*.

While trekking through his pilgrimage, Samuel came across the house of Vayalar Ravi, who he had met a couple of times in Kerala. Samuel had also approached him to help in withdrawing a case filed against him for burning a bus during a students' agitation. Samuel walked into Ravi's house and was surprised that when he met Ravi, he insisted Samuel replace his absconding secretary.

Samuel: I told Ravi, I'm planning to go next year study then finish my degree. "Then why you are going back? You stay here. Kerlla!?! You stay here. My sekitry not here. You do my wurrk." Only one wait. I said I want to talk to my parents. Then he said, "I'll telephone your parents. Talk to your parents." Then I talked to same my neighbour with the phone. [Ha! ha! ha!]
Madhu: And your mother said, "Where's my phone?"
Samuel: Ha! Ha! Huh! No. I said I'm not coming. I got a small job here. She said, "Vaat job? You went for another wurrk!" I said, Mr Vayalar Ravi told me to stay here. I said I'm not feeling well. After one or two weeks I will come back. My mother doesn't even like me send me away. Vayalar Ravi instruct his cook to take me buy pants, shoes. Then I open his letters and pass to him. Phone call coming in Malayali, I answer. Rrrust, I pass to him. So he told me I am going for my wife's medical check up to US, so you have to look after. Vaaat I have to look after? I don't know anything. Rreally borrring job. Anything come when I am going to interact with someone in INS [Indian Newspaper Society]. I will take the newspaper every day Malayalam, all the Mallu those papers, they come to know bloody I am sekitry to this guy. One of the guys in INS, his name is Ismail, now he's wurrking with *Gulf Today*. He told me, "Why you are sitting

alone? Sometime you come and sit here." Cook and myself only there. He will prepare the food. He's like a friend. Only for me and really happy. We stay, morning wauk up, *itna thund mai* [in freezing cold]. He's a Tamilian. He also encouraging, otherwise second day third day I decided to go back because of the cold. He told me to stay, stay, stay, stay.

During the three months Samuel stayed with Valayar Ravi, he started hanging about his friend Ismail in the INS Building.

> **Samuel:** I am enjoying bloody INS Building. I very much proud. Bloody I am in INS Building. That kind of feeling. Lawts of journalists there. I respecting them. They not even notice me. Who the idiot he is. Then I saw some of them the TV. Some senior leaders are walking there. I am vaaatching them very keenly. Suppose you told me to vaaatch something, if you put me a wurrrk, I will give A to Z about that. Gawd given such kind of a talent. Then I started vaaatching, vaat these people are doing. Then I come to know vaat they're doing is a rubbish thing. Ha! ha! ha! So I thought I was a big fool. Just taking that *Mid Day* and *Evening News*, this kind of English newspapers, just translating into Malayalam, sending that. Then I rrreally felt baaaaad. I thought anyone can do that. There is no necessity go for higher studies London, Oxford like that. Just after one week I watch all the Malayali dailies, including *Deccan Herald*, this kind of this thing. Going, come back, writing, going. Like a routine process. Then I was vaaaatching vaaat they're writing, second day. The same idiomatic piece are coming. Nothing new. Then I started reading dailies. Patiently, *Hindustan Times*, *Times of India*, *Asian Age*, *Pioneer*, *Hinnndu*, *Indian Express*, then I would tell, "*Yaaar*, you missed this portion, *yaar*," to this Ismail. "This is good news. Oh, that I missed."

Ismail gave him some translations to do, which progressed into sending him for minor reporting assignments. Samuel's modus operandi developed at this point:

> **Samuel:** Some day, Ismail told me that some Malayali will die somewhere, like poison, suicide, he told me, you take the report and come back. I'm not chatting with high high profile, I'm chatting with low profile. Like, "Vaat happened?" Like that. Like Malayali connection wurrked out. Then Ismail told me, "*Yaar*, this profession is good for you." I thought this is very simpble. Then I started writing.

Samuel was never paid and didn't get any bylines. He said he familiarized himself with the roads of Delhi by walking to all the political party offices. Bored numb with his job with Valayar, he jumped at an opportunity to work on a current affairs programme on Doordarshan, which came up through Ismail's friend. With the Rs 1400 salary he was given he moved into a flat in Munirka Vihar with Ismail's friend Rajeevan, who was reportedly challenged or 'ekksentrik' as Samuel said.

> **Samuel:** I was very keen to lain [learn] each and everything. I will wawk up early morning 5 o'clock. That time the project was in trial pilot episode. Without money. I will walk from Munirka to INS. I very bold. Becawz of money matter. I'm vaaatching how they writing script. Then I started to give story line. Some of the seniors are sitting, they are not that happy. Why bloody idiot coming and suddenly giving this? Like ego wurrrked out. He did 20-25 stories. Around 16 stories I given. Those stories are very hit in Kerlla. Suppose who knows this idiot programme, for who will give interview? So I will go early morning to some other leader's home. Sometimes he outside to come back to visit all the visitors. I will go and tell, I need a interview. Not like a telephone I am making.

Samuel worked on television programmes for Telefocus and his mother was sufficiently proud 'to tell a hundred people' when his programme was being aired. Samuel believed that there was no clout in Malayali journalism, and despite his lack of fluency in English, he decided that the English press was where he wanted to be. His mother arrived in Delhi on her way to a cousin's wedding in Chandigarh. Samuel's boss in Telefocus lent a car for her to go sightseeing in Delhi. She loved it and told a somewhat shocked Samuel that she planned to stay. In establishing herself in Delhi, she not only started going to Sunday church, she managed to arrange a marriage for a horrified Samuel. 'I was very very resisssting marriage. I seen only once. I seen only one girl, I fixed up. This is normally, traditional way of Kerrla. We are very orthodox family. She is from near my village. Her family. But she born and brought up in Delllhi. Educated from Air Force School,' he said.

Telefocus wound up and Samuel found himself a job with Metro Heavy Engineering, a company that hosted a sports exhibition. Samuel helped with that, but when the show was over, he found himself cutting and pasting newspaper clippings about sports goods for his boss to read. 'Then he told me to wurrrk there as a PR executive. Bloody vaat I do with PR? After exhibition over, borrring job. Thuh! No wurrrk at all. So I'm verry restless person. That's my nature,' Samuel said. He got a job at *Competition Careers* magazine, where he said he didn't last because the kind of research he did was too 'hard' for the magazine. After six months Samuel joined the afternoon tabloid *Mid Day*, which also did not work out. 'In *Mid Day* also, the editor told me, I did an investigative story on the Sports Authority of India, bribing. The second day, the entire Sports Authority appeared in the Parliament also. They told me, they will finish this guy, the editor and everything. So they told me, we not able to afford you. John told to one Naqvi there, and he told me, it won't wurrrk out here,' Samuel recalled.

After his fiasco in *Mid Day*, Samuel heard that Tehelka was recruiting and showed up. Aniruddha asked him, 'What can you deliver?' He impressed Aniruddha with his explosive stockpile of story ideas. He was obviously not blind to Samuel's shortcomings but saw some potential in him and he was hired. Samuel had a contact in the Income Tax Department in Pune, and Aniruddha sent him there to dig deeper into the cricket match-fixing scandal.

It was Mathew Samuel's chance meeting on a train with an advertising space salesman, Anil Malviya, that set the sting operation rolling. Casual, boastful conversation exchanged in the small corridor of a train where all the smokers huddle. Samuel told Malviya that he was travelling back from Pune where he had been sent by Aniruddha Bahal to investigate rumoured income-tax raids on match-fixing cricketers. Malviya was aware of Tehelka's recent match-fixing exposés and was interested in selling Tehelka's advertising space. Sensing that Samuel was hungry for hot stories, Malviya boasted that he knew of many 'tehelkas' in the Indian Army. He gave Samuel details of corruption in procurement of consumer items in the Indian Army's canteen service department in Mumbai. Malviya told Samuel how private corporations bribed army officers to introduce their products in the army. Besides selling space in the MTNL directory, Malviya represented companies who wanted their products procured by the army and was part of the bribing process. Malviya asked Samuel if Tehelka would be interested in getting advertisements for their website, and Samuel told him that he was not authorized to discuss such matters and would have to speak to Bahal or Tejpal.

Samuel: Meanwhile he asked me he knows Tehelka.com and match-fixing and that kind of stuff. Then he told me I have much more tehelka. I said, "What kind of tehelka you have?" He told me that kind of stuff. The story was about the then current Railway Board chairman. Name is Ashok Kumar. I did a story because of that he got suspension. Story is, heh, heh, heh, heh, he was Railway Board chairman, that time he went to Germany for procorring some material from Germany.

Madhu: Ashok Kumar was the one who went to the sex workers?

Samuel: Yes. Malviya gave me the lead and then I followed it up. He gave me the source in the railways. Then I make the story like that like that. Then he told me another stuff on ... [off the record] procorrmunt. There is a ... procorrmunt for arrmy and navy and other armed forces. There is a contractors for their benefit they are ... [off the record] and this thing then I suddenly clicked. India is such a holy country and those who are soldiers they *never* forgive *that*. That they are getting this kind of a things they are fighting in the war. Again I am insisting that he tell me the rrust of the matter.

Madhu: What was Anil Malviya's motivation in giving you information and getting involved?

Samuel: Like me, like I'm doing, just fun. He also liked me. I also like him very very. He will give lawts of stuff, like a journalistic view. He's a gem. He's a minds of stories. Just we're chatting. That time he told me, vaat can I do here? After this, if the story is good then Tehelka will pay you something. Then he told me he knows one brigaydier here, he can give you some good inside story.

When they arrived in Delhi, Malviya invited Samuel for drinks at the YWCA Blue Triangle where he was staying. Essentially a run-down dump. In a drunken, machismo-driven state, they spoke about possible stories they could do to expose corruption in the army. Neither was clear where to begin. Samuel, for his part, was clear that this was exactly what he had wanted to do all his life. No, not get drunk and shoot the breeze. Samuel wanted to break the Big Story. He yearned for the Big Journalism Scoop.

In their fantasy laden drunken haze, they gabbled about possible stories they could do related to the army since Malviya had information. Samuel said he vaguely knew a fellow Malayali, Sashi Menon in the Army Headquarters. Samuel said they decided to make a fake visiting card with Malviya's alias Rajiv Sharma, created a new email address – rangoonsharma@yahoo.com. They showed up the next morning at Army Headquarters in South Block.

Samuel: Sunil Nair [who worked with Anil Malviya]. I told this Sunil to go find this and ask reception where is this Sashi Menon. He told me his name is Sashi Menon. [Samuel lowers his voice to a whisper.] Basically, he is a backward class. For twunty years, he is Sashi Menon. Maddumm, Menon is a forward class. We went two, three reception. Everywhere there is no such person here. We are rrreally … then we decided to go back. Meanwhile I had just take out ahver vehicle, that time Sasi's coming. With his cigrutt smoking. [Heh, heh.] That time Sasi doesn't even know my name clearly. He will call Thomas, some Thomas I am like. I said, Sasi, we are waiting for you. For vaat purrpus? I said, one of my friends is here. He needs some help. Sasi *bola* [Samuel strikes an arrogant pose with a cigarette in his hand, mimicking Sasi] "What help?" *Maineh Sasi ko kaan meh bola, thodda paisa milney ka hai* [I whispered in Sasi's ear, a little money has to be obtained]. If you vahnt to do, you can do. I intarduced this is Rajiv Sharma. He started talking. Hawffiss in Chile, you and there [here and there]; we supply to pin to tack [meaning: we can supply anything from pins to pin tacks]. Sasi said, "Awkay, awkay, awkay. Vaat information you need?" Rajiv saying, "I know all the information. You tell me vaat you need, then only I can supply to you." Sasi saying, "I can come and meet you. Where you are staying?" That time he was not staying in a single good room. He was staying in a dawmitry. [Heh! heh!] He said, "You just come in uh hostel. I'll be there."
Madhu: Didn't Sasi wonder why Malviya was staying in a hostel if you have an office in Chile and all the other stuff?
Samuel: No, we didn't say he is staying there. We just said, just you come. I went to the awffiss. Without talking to Aniruddha, I took the cams, tapes; I reached the hostel around 5 o'clock. *Pura check kar diya, battery hai, subh kuch theek hai* [I checked everything, the battery, everything was okay]. That fussst we have started. I am also big surprise. *Bloody kaisa hoga yeh* [bloody how will this happen]? [Ha! heh! heh!] Then I went to Grindlays Bak there, near Sardar Patel Marg. So I withdraw Rs 2000. Then I given to Rajiv Sharma, "You give him the money." So we decided to give Rs 2000. Fussst we decided to give 5000. Then Sunil Nair said, there is no need to give 5000. He not even deserving for that. He's only having 2000, 1000. Each and every, that is a very intrrussssting matter.

That is vaat is mystery absolutely. Such a junior guy, how he knows how the details. Becauze without these kind of people they the superior cannot even move anything. These people only know the entire data thurrruhly. Seniors, hawfissars will come, after three years they will go. In their tenure, only one procorrmunt will happen. Juniors are staying bloody twunty years there. They are handling all the things. So Sasi giving that each and every details superiors ask him. *Yeh kya karna hai, yeh kidhar post karna hai, yeh kaisey karna* [what to do, where to post, how to do this]. So he's the one giving the details. He's the man giving the percentage also. *Issey itna mileyga, ussey itna mileyga* [he'll get this much, the other one will get that much]. Rrrreally! That is the intrussting tawpic we got after Oprayshun Wust End. Superior they are depending these juniors, because they are getting only three years posting.

In the transcripts of the unedited tapes, the conversation that takes place during the first meeting with Sasi is baffling. The whole scene is straight from a B-grade Bollywood movie with three drunks acting B-grade drunks.

From the unedited Operation West End tapes:

Sasi: As far as he is concerned, he will get it done somehow.
Malviya: Then you have to get it done.
Sasi: If one person gets chilli chicken, why should he have rotten egg curry? He won't have egg curry.
Malviya: You listen to what I am saying.
Sasi: Isn't that so? The man who is getting chicken ... a full chicken ... why should he search for an egg?
Samuel: Sorry?
Sasi: For an egg.
Samuel: What he is telling is ... amount is ... now he is . . . no, no.
Sasi: A man who is getting full chicken ....
Samuel: Why should he cut a ....
Sasi: Why should ... he should go for an egg?
Samuel: Because sometimes the egg is golden ... you tell him this. Chicken may not be that good, but the egg may be a golden egg. I may be a golden egg. Maybe the size of a chicken ...
Sasi: Because the army . . . Civilian can be bended easily.
Samuel: I can assure you, Mr Sasi, that he will agree and he will happily tell me ...
Sasi: Okay, only after all this is done, give him money.
Malviya: Okay, we'll give it.
Samuel: Yeah, yeah, we will give it. We won't give it all in one go.

Picture this: A bunch of serious lawyers, intelligence officers, bureaucrats, ministers, pouring over this transcript trying to decipher what it means. Did Samuel really say: 'I may be a golden egg. Maybe the size of a chicken?'Yes, he did. That is Sasi's language and so of course, it becomes Samuel's too. One hundred hours of tape, a lot of it with dialogue that is pure drivel. Sometimes Samuel talks absolute gibberish to kill time, to goad the person on to talk more. He may as well be grunting and burping, because his words mean about as much.

Samuel's lack of fluency in the language that represents power, status and education, made him an easy target of the Lawyers of those Caught on Tape (LOCOT) in the Commission of Inquiry. R.P. Sharma, the lawyer of Colonel Anil Sehgal (on tape taking money and starring in sexual escapades), trashed Samuel in the cross-examination in the Commission of Inquiry:

Sharma: What are your qualifications?
Samuel: I have not completed my graduation.
Sharma: Have you had any formal education in journalism?
Samuel: No.
Sharma: Any experience in detective journalism?

What on earth is 'detective journalism'? You stop writing from handouts from the government?

Samuel: No.
Sharma: Why have you been changing jobs so frequently?
Samuel: Because I am esspecting something better will come.
Sharma: I put it to you that it was the result of your incompetence or because of the dubious means that you might be using in your profession.
Samuel: Denied.

Samuel does not fill the bill of the stereotype. His prospects of being employed by a mainstream standardized style manual editor of a daily newspaper would be extremely low, where often a spiffy school and Oxbridge background is enough to disguise a low I.Q. and lack of journalistic ability. Anyone who knows journalism is aware that regional and Hindi-belt reporters are the ones who get the stories. If you can get past their passion for creating in-house politics, they are the best reporters. Put yourself in Samuel's position. He is acutely aware of his lack of grammar and vocabulary. Men whose profession entails playing on words and using just that technique to trap you, are now questioning him. He was nervous about making a fool of himself. He could have demanded that the cross-examination be carried out in Malyalam. Then he would not only have been able to handle it, he would not have curbed his natural irreverence for those for whom he has no respect.

Here's an example of the intimidation of Samuel by R.K. Handoo, counsel for Rakesh Nigam (called a second-rung middleman for defence deals):

Handoo: Will I be right that you tried to lure Mr Nigam with money, with models, and all the lurings were spurned by Mr Nigam?

Samuel: It is not about Nigam I am mentioning this. I am just boasting this. It was just boasting. In my good memory, I never offered Mr Nigam any woman. That I can say.

Handoo: I did not say that you offered but you tried to lure him.

Samuel: I do not understand the meaning of looorrrre.

Handoo: You can boast, but you do not know the meaning of lure.

Samuel: I do not know the meaning.

Justice Venkataswami: Induce.

And the presiding judge imagined he was helping Samuel? As far as Samuel was concerned, 'induce' was even more baffling than 'lure'.

On the same day, C. Mohan Rao, counsel for Gopal Pacherwal (president of the Samata Party in Rajasthan and disputedly on tape with Jaya Jaitly), adopted the same tactic:

Mohan Rao: Mr Samuel, did you have any political leanings?

Samuel: I am not getting the meaning.

Justice Venkataswami: He does not understand the word "leaning".

The judge began to empathize with Samuel's predicament but the counsel was suspicious.

Mohan Rao: In his affidavit he has stated quite a few things. Now "leaning" is not a very difficult word.

Samuel: I have earlier said that I am verrry poooor in English.

Mohan Rao: Do you have any political affiliation?

Samuel: [Sigh of relief] No.

Again on the same day, N. Hariharan, counsel for P. Sasi capitalized on Samuel's weakness established by previous counsels:

Hariharan: Can you just tell me the meaning of the word *"raison d'être"* that you have mentioned? What is the meaning of *"raison d'être"*?

Samuel doesn't quite figure English, so to push him into French was diabolic.

Samuel: In my affidavit I have mentioned it?

Hariharan: I do not know. Do you know the meaning of that word, that is what I am asking.

Samuel: Really. I do not know the meaning. I do not know.

Hariharan: Could you give me the meaning of the word "slander"? What does slander mean? S-l-a-n-d-e-r? We are testing your memory.

Samuel: The meaning of slander I can tell in Malayalam.

Hariharan: In English.

Samuel: I can tell you the Malayalam meaning.

Hariharan: Simplify it in English. It doesn't matter.

Samuel: I am not getting the exact word for slander.

Hariharan: So you cannot?

Samuel: I can tell you the ordinary Malayalam meaning of slander; what it means.

Hariharan: That I can understand.

Samuel: The English meaning I am not able to give.

Hariharan: Could you give the meaning in English is the simple question I am asking you?

Samuel: I have answered it. I will not be able to give it.

Hariharan: Very well. You cannot.

Samuel: I cannot.

Then Hariharan completely changed the subject and got into details of Samuel's affidavit. The intimidation was embarrassing. Imagine how Samuel felt, or as he would say, 'Just imaaaagine'. He would go home to his wife and see in her eyes what he felt like in the Commission. Less of a man. Less of an educated man. Samuel can be likened to a man of his generation and ilk: Matt Drudge, known for breaking the Clinton-Lewinsky story on his website The Drudge Report. Drudge, too, did not go to any snotty schools or colleges. The closest he came to journalism was working as a clerk in CBS, where he did everything from folding T-shirts in the gift shop to delivering messages. Much like Samuel, he kind of fell into 'journalism'. Drudge's father, panic-stricken over his son's non-achiever status, gifted him a computer. Fooling around on the Internet, Drudge found how easy it was to create a website and post information. On 17 January 1998, at 21:32:02 (PST), Drudge posted his ticket to fame: '*Newsweek* kills story on White House intern'.

This was the clear differential between old journalism and cyber journalism. *Newsweek* sat on it because they wanted to confirm with Monica Lewinsky that it was her voice on the tapes. According to the tenets of journalism, they would want to get the other side of the story, but could *Newsweek* reporter Michael Issikoff actually call the White House and expect 'their side of the story'?

Six months after his scoop (2 June 1998), Drudge was the guest speaker at the prestigious National Press Club in Washington. Doug Harbrecht, journalist with *Business Week* and the president of the club made it clear in his introduction that he did not support Drudge's form of reporting. Chief guest Drudge was told there were many in the room who did not even consider him a journalist. He was barraged with questions about cross-checking facts and getting 'the other side'. One of his answers: 'What I do is a formula where I follow my conscience – and this is upsetting to some people – but I maintain that conscience is going to be the only thing between us and the communication in the future, now. And I'm very happy with my conscience.' That is Samuel saying, as he did in his cross-examination: 'I know what is right and what is wrong'. Drudge pointed out: 'I can print something without an editor. This is where we are now.' Cyber journalism has turned the old rule book on its head.

The question arises: Is Mathew Samuel a professional journalist? Samuel represents an optimistic spark illustrating, in a conceptual sense, that the least likely could have the potential to succeed in India. Samuel knew he had to get out of his village to become more than what he was born to be.

Not all the editors in India of the major dailies and weekly magazines are qualified journalists. Shekhar Gupta, Vinod Mehta, M.J. Akbar did not go to schools of journalism but can compete with the best in the world. On the other hand, there are many functioning journalists who are ignorant of even the basic fundamentals of journalism. Unlike the legal and medical profession where entry is restricted through study and qualifying degrees, anyone can become a journalist, even without a college degree.

Today bimbo socialites, boring retired civil servants, aspiring social hitchhikers, cobweb ridden geriatric journalists, and full-blown losers are given acres of column space in leading newspapers.

Degree and diploma courses for journalism have only recently been introduced in India. In this context, is Mathew Samuel less respectable than the rest in the marketplace?

Exposing corruption in government, and now even in the corporate sector, has always been a goal for journalists. In America, nothing is sacrosanct. Not private lives, not national security, not foreign affairs. Until 2005, Indian journalists had stayed away from the sexual escapades rampant amongst those in power. A charming term 'foster', coined by an unknown, in a sense covers everything and we really find it distasteful to go any deeper. From Sitaram Kesri, Mayawati, Narasimha Rao, Uma Bharti to Chandra Shekhar gossip flourished, but more in amusement and nobody really cared what they did in the privacy of their bedrooms. Even Samuel, when questioned on whether he had investigated Jaya Jaitly and George Fernandes's relationship, said he had no interest in their private lives. Samuel did have a goal in exposing corruption and said he did see it as a public service.

Then there is the questioning fine line of, did he do it for fame and money or was there an altruistic motivation? Is it ever possible to demarcate the motivation so clearly? Did Mahatma Gandhi lead the freedom movement for the independence of his country or to gain mass followers and fame? Could he indeed have even been successful without the mass support? Did Kiran Bedi revamp Tihar Jail only for the betterment of the inmates or to personally excel in her career? It, of course, all comes together. It is rare that one can find a singular motivation in action. So when a human being is involved in work that is philanthropic and results in celebrity, what are his motives? Are they so clear-cut that positive action for public good cuts out the consequent fame that follows? It would be a rare human being who does not want acknowledgement of his work. How then does one analyse Samuel's motives? The role of journalists as watchdogs of government and power is a tradition. To dig up the truth is also a tradition. To antagonize those who do not benefit from the exposure of uncomfortable truths is again journalism's tradition. To completely remove Samuel from such motives would be unfair. Was he using altruistic motives as a cover for a murkier ambition? He was not involved in the financial side of Tehelka. Not even the LOCOT accused him of that. He was not playing the stock market. At worse, we could say he did it to further his career. Not a crime. No matter how much the LOCOT tried to denigrate him, Samuel, the man who was really responsible for the clandestine taping, collecting documents, bribing, and providing sex workers, never believed at any point that he had done anything wrong.

Does one completely trust what Samuel says? There are sufficient stories doing the rounds about Samuel's chicanery. He dismisses them all with a confident sweep as 'jealousy'. A former friend of Samuel's from Kerala, Madhu Shekhar, filed an affidavit on 28 May 2001 in the Commission of Inquiry. Madhu Shekhar has been an assistant editor with the Publications Division, in the Ministry of Information and Broadcasting, since 1991. There were rumblings in the Commission that it was one of Jaya Jaitly's lawyers who had arranged for this man to come forward, and he was Jaya's witness. Jaya did ask me if I was aware of Madhu Shekhar's testimony. For everything that Madhu Shekhar has spoken about, Mathew Samuel's Rashomon played out with his own version. Madhu Shekhar's version of the story, in his affidavit, was that as no respectable journalist would go around with a spy cam, Tarun Tejpal hired Samuel because he was a known con man. According to Madhu Shekhar, Samuel was a student-activist of the Congress Party in Kerala and was involved in petty criminal cases, and had been charged with burning buses. He had failed his pre-degree examinations twice and never graduated. Shekhar said that Samuel came to Delhi as an errand boy of Vayalar Ravi, member of Parliament of the Congress Party. There, he misused gas and telephone coupons and quotas and was removed from Ravi's house. In Madhu Shekhar's story, Samuel met a certain Mr George who was producing a current affairs programme for Doordarshan called *Notam* in Malayalam, working as a production assistant. Madhu Shekhar gave evidence to the Commission about Samuel's name-dropping, conning various people including his wife's parents. Samuel allegedly conned people into believing that he could get the General Sales Agency for Air India in the Gulf and pocketed money from them without delivering anything. Shekhar said that Samuel took Rs 75,000 from Shivaram Kandoth of Manorama Vision for the film *Roses* to be shown at Mahadev Auditorium, New Delhi, which never transpired. Shekhar recounted how Samuel took Rs 12,000 from a Mr Raiseen from Guwahati with the promise that he would introduce him to Jaya Jaitly and George Fernandes. Samuel even called Shekhar up one night saying he had run out of money while entertaining Jaya Jaitly and needed Rs 6000 to pay the hotel bill. Shekhar said that Raiseen paid him that amount the following morning. At an appointed time when Samuel was supposed to take Raiseen to meet Jaya Jaitly, he did not show up. Shekhar stated that he frequently helped Samuel write stories for his various jobs as he was unable to write.

On 6 September 2001, Samuel filed his own Rashomon of the story in response to Madhu Shekhar's allegations. He stated that Madhu Shekhar's affidavit was 'only an effort to discredit me and to carry out a slander campaign; to try and malign me so as to deflect the attention of this Commission from the real issue'. He denied all Madhu Shekhar's allegations.

Who is telling the truth? I do not believe that Madhu Shekhar stories could be entirely untrue, yet they had once been friends and had fallen out. There was an undercurrent of revenge and bitterness. The fact that Madhu Shekhar happened to be Jaya Jaitly's witness and was brought to the Commission by her lawyers also made it a bit unsavoury. Whatever the truth is, even if Madhu Shekhar is given the benefit of doubt, there is no doubt that Samuel did record 105 videotapes. Had Samuel done all the bribing that he did, and he did it without a camera, given Samuel's credibility factor, who would have believed him?

S.A. Arsalan from Guwahati, also a Jaya Jaitly witness, arrived at the Commission with the goal to do damage to Mathew Samuel. Arsalan, a businessman, supplied the government with roofs, tube-oil, and overhead raisings. He wanted to get into supplying the army. Arsalan said he gave Mathew Samuel Rs 12,000, who had told him he would introduce him to George Fernandes and Jaya Jaitly. According to Arsalan, Samuel then disappeared and he never got to meet any of the people to whom introductions had been promised. Kavin Gulati, counsel for Tehelka, grilled Arsalan and got on record that if Samuel had allegedly cheated him in 1998, why had he made no effort to file any case and only decided to come forward when Madhu Shekhar approached him and brought him to Jaya Jaitly's house a week before he appeared before the Commission.

Mathew Samuel is clear in his moral concepts. In the world according to Samuel, he has decided what is right and what is wrong. He is passionately against corruption. His motivations are mixed with a zeal to push the borders of conventional journalism, his awe of consorting with 'big' people and marvelling how an 'idiot' like him is able to do all that he does. His concept of a lie is truly, let's face it, Indian. A little bit of exaggeration, a little bit of boasting, a little bit of Monica by his side, and Samuel is ready to mambo number 5. Any discrepancies in his statements cannot always be seen as blatant lies. You could call them a 'shift from the truth'. For example, Samuel tells me in detail how, when he first arrived in Delhi, an autorickshaw driver took off with his briefcase. He went to a cinema hall but didn't see a movie because the ticket booth was too crowded. In the Commission, speaking of the same evening, he says he went to see a movie and his pocket was picked. In his mind, that's not really a lie. He has just shortened the story. The end result is the same. He was left with no money because it was stolen from him.

When asked who Mr X was, in one interview with me he said he was Deepak Gupta's friend. On another day, when I asked the same question, he said Mr X was Deepak Gupta's son because he remembered him ordering ice cream. No earth-shattering difference, but in an investigation where a minor point could lead to the resolution of a major dispute in evidence, it could become crucial. So, when Samuel insists vehemently that Gopal Pacherwal was in Jaya Jaitly's room and both Gopal Pacherwal and Jaya deny it, whom do you believe?

Samuel was forced to face the issue of lies when Major General P.S.K. Choudary (on tape taking money), suspended additional director-general, weapons and equipment, questioned him in his cross-examination before the Commission:

Choudary: Mr Samuel, did Major General P.S.K. Choudary ever tell you that he will take you out for dinner?
Samuel: No.

Choudary: Did you tell someone that Major General Choudary had offered to take you out to dinner?

Samuel: That I do not recollect.

Choudary: May I draw your attention to the transcript: "Murgai: That also can't that be done? No, no you are saying that today Choudary will take you to dinner. Samuel: That is cancelled." Did you say this?

Samuel: Yes. I stated it.

Choudary: So it is obviously a lie stated by you?

Samuel: Not like that.

Choudary: What is it if it is not a lie?

Samuel: Just like that I said.

Choudary: I suggest to you that you have told Major General Murgai a lie that Major General Choudary will take you out for dinner.

Samuel: Denied.

Choudary: Is this also a sort of boasting and lying?

Justice Venkataswami: This is for arguments. If you are saying like this for every question, there will be no end to it.

Choudary: Without understanding the meaning of boasting, basically he has been saying that he has been boasting all along. I want to explain the dictionary meaning of boasting and lying to tell him that it is not a boast, it is a lie. Do you understand the meaning of boasting?

Samuel: Yes.

Choudary: What is it? Can you tell me?

Samuel: It is like telling something.

What did Choudary expect? For Samuel, it is like telling something and anything.

Choudary: Telling something can be anything. Do you understand the meaning of the word lie?

Samuel: A lie is a lie.

What Samuel was saying is: What's the problem?

Choudary: I suggest to you that the derogatory form of boasting is a lie.

Samuel: Thaaaat I do not know.

Choudary: I also put it to you that with reference to the false statements made by you earlier, when queried, you have stated that you are boasting, whereas you were lying, since you did not know the difference between lying and boasting.

Samuel: Denied.

Here we have an educated Major General advancing to Samuel a literal argument about the value judgement of two words; to Mathew Samuel of all people. 'So it is a lie stated by

34

you?' Choudary asked. Of course it was a lie. I cannot fathom why Samuel got into the rut of denying whatever was asked of him. Everything Samuel did on the tapes was a lie. He misrepresented himself, deceived people by not telling them he was a journalist working for Tehelka, and led them to believe all kinds of lies in order to bring them into the net of the sting operation. Under these circumstances, if Samuel had claimed a dinner invitation that hadn't really been received, how much did it matter?

Jaya Jaitly also brought up the subject of Samuel's lies when she appeared before the Commission of Inquiry. Jaya pointed out:

> Your Lordship, there are two or three different types of lies which are contained in this entire document. That is why from the very first day, even to the press, I have said it is a bundle of lies. One is a lie about the actual conversation, how it took place, what I said where. The other lie was what they have propagated, as spoken by various people, who are either under the influence of alcohol, or gossiping, or trying to promote how great they are and show something. All those people have either denied what they have said, or they have said they were fooling, all that is hearsay.
>
> However, the worst lies were uttered, where nobody informed Tehelka of any such thing. In Tape 40, if I remember correctly, there is a very interesting episode, which has come out in the government transcript, where Mr Samuel is talking to Mr Pant. Suddenly, there is a whole chunk. But Mr Samuel interjects in the middle of the conversation: "Jaya Jaitly's daughter's wedding tomorrow", which is utterly meaningless in the context. This tape is supposedly dated 22 November, but my daughter was married on March 30th, after the Tehelka tapes were released. So if he is saying, "tomorrow", which date is he talking about? This was a lie that they propagated to others to show some familiarity or whatever for their purpose.
>
> The second was even worse. Mr Samuel is talking to Rakesh Nigam. He says to Rakesh Nigam, "You know that Jaya Jaitly's daughter, she has now become the CSF Thompson Vice President and she has an office in Meridien Hotel." My daughter is a Bharata Natyam dancer. She does not know anything about any company. I have never heard of CSF Thompson till these tapes came out. Why the gentleman is telling anybody, whom he calls a middleman, that my daughter is working for a French company, which is supposedly in arms manufacturing? And Rakesh Nigam is not saying anything. He says, I do not know. He says, no, no. But is it not a bad thing she should be working like that, waiting for him to say that "Yes these politicians are very bad?" Why concoct a lie?
>
> Then, after the meeting with me he goes to meet Murgai and Sureka. He tells Sureka, yes, she told me in Malayalam I can go and meet her any time. Why tell that lie? They were all there. What he said in Malayalam is known to everybody. Every Malayalee here would know it.

The fourth lie is he is supposed to have met me, I have no confirmation of the date, they are supposed to have met me on 28th December. But on the transcript of 21st December, Samuel is telling Major General P.S.K. Choudary "I have paid money to Jaya Jaitly." How can he be saying something when he has not even met me? So, this is a self-manufactured lie, is a whole new facet of this story, which I have discovered while going through these documents.

The final one is, after he had supposedly met me, he has gone to meet Major General Choudary. He tells Major General Choudary, "I have met Jaya Jaitly. Jaya Jaitly is so happy with me that she has already invited me for dinner to her home." Why tell lies like this? And Major General Choudary says, "I do not know. You can take care of the politicians. I am not bothered." So, "you can take care of the politicians" is taken out and then put in the transcript, which is shown to the whole world.

This major set of lies, combined with the tampering, it is so clear, Sir, that I have been trying to say from the very beginning, because it will be my description of the events and my view of the events. I believe that it is just like asking for an x-ray. Two or three doctors may see my arm. But I feel my arm is broken, surely an x-ray will tell the truth.

Jaya felt her arm was broken. But what was really broken? Much, much more than that. A part of her soul had, kind of, fractured. The sense of being with which she had lived her life had disappeared. Suddenly her passion for her work became passion for the defence of her name. Her compassion for the under privileged had morphed into compassion for herself. Would that not create a perpetual discomfort in her soul?

What Jaya said does raise the question: Why does mendacity come so easily to Indians? To what can we attribute this collective programming of mind and habit? Of course, there are many collective experiences that create particularities in a national character. One of the most important collective experiences has been that of being colonized by the White Man. In that, a technique of survival evolved where you held back what you really thought, said what the White Man wanted to hear and kept your inner Indian self to yourself. This personality trait possibly triggered the phrase 'inscrutable Indians'. We had to be. If we were not, how could millions of Indians have worked for the British and retained their jobs? Dishonesty, euphemistically called tact, was a survival tactic. Then, the collective perception evolved of what according to us is really dishonest. Paying lip service to your listener, glossing over uncomfortable facts, tactical diversionary answers became the norm. So, whatever was collectively done became right. Our democracy has developed, is continuing to evolve but our value system is slower in changing from the entrenched positions.

Consequently, it is tough to change a subterranean, collective, pervasive consciousness where deceit has become the norm. To my knowledge, it has not been taken up nationally as an issue that needs to be discussed or changed. With the White Man no longer ruling us, why then have we not changed? It is because we have transferred the same colonized collective consciousness to the authority figures in our lives. Whether it is a strict parent, a stern boss, or disapproving husband/wife, there is a greater tendency to lie in an attempt for peace and accord. Telling the truth only creates trouble one is forced to deal with. Honesty within relationships is not a highly regarded value. Harmony and tranquillity are considered far more important. When Samuel's honesty comes up as an issue before the Commission, it is clear that Samuel is honest according to Samuel. (WATS – World According to Samuel.) That is the norm. Each person individually draws the line on how far he allows himself to be dishonest. Stopping at a red light in India is optional. Which rules you obey and break in India is an extremely individualistic decision taken without any consistency, even by the same person. We are not on automatic that all rules have to be obeyed. Every Indian is a practicing royal eccentric and decides as according to whim. *Sabh hero baney huey hain* [everyone has made himself a hero]. Samuel is only a direct product of his environment.

Journalists and lawyers live a Rashomon on a daily basis. Truth as journalists see it is a debatable issue; truth as lawyers see it, is even more so. Journalists see the truth that gives them a good story. Lawyers see the truth that defends their client. Although the Commission of Inquiry for Tehelka was set up to ostensibly get to the truth, whose choice of truth was it going to get at? The lawyers' or the journalists'?

Towards the end of Franz Kafka's book *The Trial*, when a befuddled K. is wondering why he is being falsely accused, he is told, 'One does not have to believe everything is true, one only has to believe it is necessary.' K. responds, 'Depressing thought. It makes the lie fundamental to world order.'

When R.P. Sharma, lawyer of Colonel Anil Sehgal questioned Samuel in the Commission, he asked him:

Sharma: Forget about a journalist, even as a citizen, do you know that the prevention and detection of crime is the exclusive prerogative and responsibility of the civil police?
Samuel: I know vun thing like this is rrright and that is wrrrrong. I do not know about the prevention and detection and all that.

Doesn't that just say everything about Mathew Samuel? He followed his conscience in the manner he knows right from wrong. He was following one of the principles of journalism as set out in Project for Excellence in Journalism on the website www.journalism.org in their Statement of Shared Purpose: 'Its practitioners must be allowed to exercise their personal conscience. Every journalist must have a personal sense of ethics and responsibility – a moral compass.' Viktor E. Frankl writes in *Man's Search for Ultimate Meaning* (2000), 'In fact, conscience reaches down into unconscious depths and stems from an unconscious ground; it is precisely those momentous, authentic – existentially authentic – decisions that take place completely without reflection and thus unconsciously.' Samuel is answering his questions from his moral unconscious conscience. Frankl goes on to say: 'Moral self-scrutiny is also only possible afterward. The judgments of conscience, in the final analysis, are inscrutable.' In the 'scurrilous' tapes, when Samuel was with a sex worker, he asked her to trust him, urged her to go with the army officer and promised to take care of her;

incredibly, Samuel began kissing her. If Samuel were to look at the tape today, he would probably bang his head in disbelief at his actions. Frankl points out that just as animals are misled by vital instincts, so can man go astray unless one is living one's conscience on a highly personalized level, aware of the full implications of each situation. In these particular tapes, Samuel floated away with the 'reality' of the drama he had created, forgot he was only a fictitious representative of a fictitious company and that consequently it was a fake situation. He became one of the players, forgetting his conscience.

Back to the Commission. Sharma then seriously warmed up, cut swiftly into Samuel: 'As a citizen, aren't you aware that detection of crime and bringing the offenders to justice is the sole prerogative and responsibility of the police?'

Samuel answered from (WATS) the Gospel according to Mathew Samuel: 'Yes. It is of the police. I want to add here. Sometimes they fail, because of which some journalist is coming and detecting these matters.'

In this, Samuel was quoting the tenets of journalism, in his own language.

Sharma then was on a terrific roll, loving it all and going for the kill. Oddly, the kill of a flummoxed soldier who believed he had done his duty, thought he would win medals, and cannot figure out why he is the one being interrogated.

Sharma thundered: 'Are you aware that as a citizen in terms of Section 39 of the Criminal Procedure Code … if a person comes to know about the commission of a crime or the intent to commit a crime, it is the duty and responsibility of the citizen to immediately report the matter to the police?'

Samuel has by now created what can safely be called Samuelisms: 'I really respect the Indian Penal Code and everything. But I do not know the ABCD of the Indian Penal Code and Section 39. Nothhhhhing!'

Samuel was cross-examined 31 times by 16 lawyers before the Commission of Inquiry. Samuel's goal was to expose corruption and he didn't quite see the necessity of checking whether what he did fell within the purview of existing laws. His intention was clean, so what was there to question?

Then is Mathew Samuel a hero? A hot air artist? Good or bad? Obviously, he is not all 'good' and not all 'bad'. It is a disservice to offer easy answers. I expect the reader to feel for a complicated Samuel, understand his motivations, and see what picture of Samuel emerges when the jigsaw puzzle fits into place. He is very simple, but not easy.

P. Sasi had known Mathew Samuel since 1998. Sasi said of Mathew Samuel before the Commission:

> He is my friend. He is my thick friend at that time. He is a good friend. I have given a certificate to Rajiv Sharma also, because once he asked me what type of a person Samuel was. I asked him, "Why are you asking all this to me, when you know him better than me?" He says, "No, I am going to set up an office here and he will be the chief liaison officer." So I said, he is a good man.

Sasi is a short, stocky man given to wearing shiny, half-sleeved shirts. His glasses don't seem to belong on his nose and there is the affectation of a white *tikka* from puja, or perhaps it is a petition prayer to God. In Vigyan Bhavan Annexe, where the Commission hearings were held, Sasi sat arrogantly. Strutted around. Really quite bouncy.

P. Sasi didn't seem in the least bit affected that he was the 'opening door' to Operation West End; not in the least bit embarrassed or sheepish as were the army officers. He seemed to enjoy the fact that here he was on the same platform as Jaya Jaitly and his bosses, defending himself, just like them. He truly appeared to relish sharing their boat.

Sasi's manner showed contempt for everybody, especially his own boss. In the 'scurrilous tapes', Sasi makes lewd jokes, holds his whiskey glass like a trophy, and makes an issue about smoking as if it was an act of sophistication and brashly prances about. Sasi was suspended but still collected 60 per cent of his salary. His wife runs a crèche in their home for children to supplement their income. He joined the government in the chief administrative office as a lower division clerk in 1981 and was promoted to the position of an upper division clerk in 1986. He met Mathew Samuel in 1998 when he was the personal assistant to the minister of state for human resource development. After a series of jobs, he landed up in the Master of General Ordnance (MOG), as assistant in the Ordnance Service Directorate, with Colonel Anil Sehgal as his boss.

Sasi recounted to the Commission that he gave Colonel Sehgal's residence telephone number because the West End representatives had told him that all these officers were guiding them in supplying CSD (Canteen Stores Department) items: 'CSD item means in the form of light cloth, clothing items, mosquito nets all those things. They are registered vendors of the DGS&D (Director-General Supplies and Disposal). The DGS&D registered vendors can compete with the Ministry of Defence for any tender and purchase.'

It became obvious that these products were P. Sasi's focus of interest. His office was directly involved in issuing supply orders for HHTIs (hand-held thermal Imagers). Sidharth Luthra (counsel for Tehelka) played the tapes where documents and money are exchanged between Mathew Samuel and P. Sasi.

Luthra: Can you identify the person, who says, "*Udhar notes bhi hai uska ...?*"
Sasi: I think all sequences were changed. These were manipulated because the sequences and other things were changed. Because in this lawn they used to come to my office in the lunchtime. They know that I used to go to India Gate lawn for a rest. On so many occasion, so many things have happened. So, this has been edited or unedited wherever it suits Tehelka only. But in reality what has happened is not there. So, these scenes and the situations are exactly changed. I have to explain all those things. Later I will explain.
Luthra: My question was simple. Whose voice is this?
Sasi: There is no lip movement and there is no head. How can I say that?
Luthra: Can you identify the voice of the person speaking about the battalions?
Sasi: The voices are coming from the backside. So, without knowing the exact

lip movements and other things I cannot be sure about the voice. But it seems to be my voice in the resemblance only. I cannot say very surely.

Luthra: Who is saying, "by 3 o'clock I am getting all the document. I have told him for the full money". Can you identify who said this?

Sasi: I cannot.

Luthra: It says, "Valuation *ke kaam mein… Sahib se baat…*" Can you identify the voice there?

Sasi: Actually I am not present there. I am getting the voice. The voice seems to be mine. But I am not there.

Funny stuff here. Sasi can identify everybody else on the tape but he can never identify himself. When Luthra asked him who was working in Colonel Sehgal's office with him: 'No. For the last two years, from 2001 onwards, for the last one-and-half years I am not going to office. So, everything is off. Tehelka has made me an off.'

Sasi made himself an 'off' and he described himself better than anyone else could. When asked to identify people on the tapes demonstrated in the Commission, his answers bordered on contempt. Sasi stated: 'So far in these tapes, the edited tapes, there was no such portion, which we have seen in the Commission and from the downloaded portion, there was no such thing so far. It is a surprise tape, which he is showing me and asking me to identify.'

When confronted by Dayan Krishnan (counsel for the Commission) about divulging confidential information and documents, P. Sasi was quite airy and insouciant about it:

Krishnan: Let me ask the question again. The various dialogues I have drawn your attention to contain certain information. Can this information, to which I have drawn your attention, be divulged to a person who is not authorized to receive?

Sasi: This information is already available. It is not in that form, but the actual information is available there.

Krishnan: Therefore, is it your contention that this information can be divulged?

Sasi: If somebody knows that directory …

Krishnan: Therefore, you say you can divulge it?

Sasi: Yes.

Tehelka's lawyer, Sidharth Luthra did mention that P. Sasi was one of the toughest nuts to crack, since he had one of the best lawyers, Hariharan, who had prepared Sasi for any kind of questions. Sasi did not seem to care at all about how he would be perceived. Sasi is a direct result of his surround. Stories about corruption in every field, every section of society, every industry, even in schools and colleges, in the practice of medicine, in the judiciary as well as the lawyers, in the police; there is no area where corruption has not been exposed. The tired argument that it always existed but was only being exposed now is not acceptable. A psychological change has taken place.

Globalization has not only meant the opening up of markets and the freedom to make money without restrictions but has lifted the mental reservations of the post-independence era, where the 'larger good' of the poverty-stricken masses was considered a high priority. All the reams written on how misled Pandit Jawaharlal Nehru and Indira Gandhi were in their socialist dreams do not take away from the fact that a vision for the poor is as essential to a global economy for India as ever before. The acknowledgement of that failure has hurtled us into the noisy, self-oriented capitalistic world. The lower income groups can no longer be called 'the have-nots', having joined the upper-class club of: we will get what we want no matter what. Gracefully called 'aspirations', the new lower middle class want everything and they want it yesterday. In government too, the mindset has moved away from promising the poor an economic future to making each individual shine. To make your buck any way whatsoever and enjoy the fruits of the consumer religion is evangelized day in and day out in television and print advertising. The words 'ethics', 'morality', 'honesty' have a sanctimonious, preachy tone to them: an immediate turn-off. You may as well be talking about a thesis on the archaeological history of the 113 BC Heliodorus Vedic column in Beshnagar. Who cares?

Economic liberalization has created a new class structure that cuts across almost all income levels. This class, the GABAMs (Get-Ahead-By-Any-Means) exists in government, the bureaucracy, the judiciary, the police, the army, private industry, students, all the professions, even NGOs; the list is endless. In other words, they are everywhere. The second class is much smaller, the HAAOs (Honesty-Against-All-Odds). As has happened historically in India many times, two opposite poles develop with comparable strengths. More and more people are becoming socially aware and are moving into areas of charitable community work, whether full or part-time. But, it is a daily struggle to stay honest in India. HAAOs are treated badly as goody-goodies are treated in school. They are spitting at the sky. In fact, when a bureaucrat or police officer stands up for honesty, it makes news. As our leaders ride the nation to the new world of consumer fundamentalism, transformational leadership has been reduced to providing a better economy. Will a booming economy alone make India a global player? A sincere transformational leadership must drive a wide psychological and sociological change within the nation. This was something Mahatma Gandhi understood intuitively and worked towards without the need for image creators, event managers, or spin doctors to spread his message. Individualism has infected India, and the disease is killing off exactly that which pulls a nation together: commonality of ethics. At this point, india has a pseudo-transformational leadership (PTL) that is destructive. PTL is not confined to the party in power; it is rampant in all the opposition parties. When Mayawati was criticized for having a lavish birthday-bash at state expense and wearing an astronomical diamond necklace, she retorted that higher castes do as they like, when a Dalit's daughter does it, they scream. Mayawati was saying that I can compete in corruption with the best of them. In 2007, Mayawati declared Rs 52 crore with no visible connection to a revenue stream other than 'donations from supporters'. The reaction was: 'Well, that is what she declared! How much has she not declared?' [Please do check out http://www.ibnlive.com/news/left-lost-trust-vote-won-hearts-of-indians/70360-3.html Karan Thapar's riveting interview with

CPI General Secretary A.B. Bardhan, where Thapar nails Bardhan about their strange alliance with Mayawati.]

Authentic transformational leadership must provide along with provisions for basic needs, inspirational motivation, the necessity for discipline, caring for others, and the glamorization of these ideals. It must make you look and feel like a superior person, if you are last in line but you wait in the queue. At a films award show in Dubai, an altercation was reported when Amar Singh found himself and his friend/brother, Amitabh Bachchan, in eleventh row seats and not the first. He counted them? A truly great man brings his dignity to the chair he sits on and doesn't need a throne to exalt and prop him up. Are then people in the eleventh row lesser human beings? Bachchan's stature is such that nobody would respect him any less, probably more, if he sat on a stool.

Why is national honesty necessary at all for India to become a global player? Figure this: you get out of bed sweating because there has been no electricity all night because it has been stolen on the streets around your house. You try to take a shower and there is no water; your neighbour has stolen water from your tank. You give your child a glass of milk that has been mixed with water and blotting paper. You drive your children to school in a car where the petrol has been adulterated or your driver has made a deal at the petrol pump. You are paying for more petrol than is in your car. Or, you drop your child to the school bus and pray, because you know the driver has no regard for speed limits or red traffic lights. Your child goes to the school where you have had to pay a bribe called a donation to get admission. You go to work and you watch as co-workers do whatever they can to dishonestly squeeze the employers for every penny, be it fake meal bills, travel accounts, or theft of stationery, microphones, and the like. You visit the Zee TV offices in Mumbai and the staff is frisked by their own security to catch pilferers. You go shopping to Modern Bazaar in Delhi and if their staff is helping you carry your bags out, they are body-searched before they are allowed to leave. If you are a journalist, you have the choice of which business house or political party to take money from to write a story. When you eat lunch, you know that all the spices and lentils have been mixed with spurious additives. The bottled water you drink has been officially declared contaminated. If you have a friend or relative in a hospital, you have to ensure that the glucose bottles he is being fed intravenously are not contaminated. Used infected syringes picked up from hospital garbage are repackaged in a way that even a doctor can't tell for certain whether they are new. Life-saving medicines with the same packaging as the genuine ones have nothing but powder in the capsules. Fake versions of popular American and European face creams are flooding the market. A neighbour offers to send a man to your house who will fix the electricity meter to minimize your bill. if you are building a house, you have to stand there all day to ensure that the contractor is not mixing sand in the cement. If you want to open a shop, you will have to pay off the real estate mafia and the police. Even when you move into a new home, you will be forced to pay exorbitant dues to the colony's residents' association. Journalists have proven that you can buy a driver's licence, marriage certificate, and even had arrest warrants issued for the president of India and the chief justice of India for a price. You can buy your way into college and pay to have your result fixed. Your parents will help you buy leaked examination papers. Someone can even get a death certificate in your name and kill you off on paper to take over your property. If you own property and do not build on it immediately, someone else will sell off your land and build multi-story apartments on it. Your cellphone ID can be used by someone else if you call a certain number and you will end up paying all the thief's bills. Snazzy looking highways are soon reduced to rubble with iron rods sticking out as the road wears off. The road is supposed to be eight inches thick. The money for one inch goes to the guy who awarded the contract to the contractor. The money for the second inch goes to the chief engineer. The money for the third inch goes to the supervisor on site. The money for the fourth inch goes to the contractor himself. So, a road that is supposed to be eight inches thick, is reduced to four inches. Yet, as always in India, there is the opposite. E. Sreedharan built the world-class Delhi Metro, where there is no visible corruption and he met the deadline.

Indians have the expertise to invent a scam seconds after a product is introduced. The ingenuity, time and effort put into making money dishonestly can only be guessed at. All this cannot happen in an insular fashion. Everybody is in on the game. It is not only socially acceptable but also admirable to be a scamster. So how does it affect India's attempt to become a global player? The answer is simple: it hurts. If you can't trust a partner not to slice the cream for himself in a business, why should you invest? If you can't trust a manufacturer to supply the same goods that he showed you as samples, why should you buy from him? If you can't take the word of your supplier to meet a deadline, why should you take the risk? China's scandals in adulterated drugs, milk and eggs, displays exactly where this takes a country.

Today we see hypocrisy and sophistry as basic ingredients for success. The pseudo-transformational leadership is setting an example that is being followed diligently: political expediency, political corruption, political profit, and self-promotion. A senior minister Z in the Bharatiya Janata Party told me about a fellow minister Y who came to him and complained about all the scams being reported in the newspapers. Y asked him to control the press as he had contacts with the media. Z's answer was: 'Why don't you stop doing all the scams and the reporting will stop.' To this Y replied: 'Listen, everybody does it. When our turn comes, how can you stop it?' Every time there is an exposé, a band-aid is placed to fix it but the core root of corruption, which is the national psychological mindset, is not addressed. Colonial shackles are thrown away, wars have been won, nations have been transformed when the citizens have had transformational leadership. India is in a state of the materialist dogma shooting around us like greased lightning. It possibly sounds reactionary, but yes, we are losing our values to a brash audacity that has no room for humanitarianism. An opportunity is being missed because Indians do have a mindset that if humanitarianism was promoted, we would grab it.

Yes, all humans are multi-dimensional: not all evil, not all good. P. Sasi seems to break that axiom. Philosopher Jean-Jacques Rousseau (1712-88) wrote at length about the root cause of evil: 'Man, seek the author of evil no longer. It is yourself.' Why do so many of us then end up doing what is wrong? According to Rousseau, it is because of all the other influences of society that make us forget it. That is certainly applicable in P. Sasi's case. It was socially acceptable to be dishonest and he saw no wrong in it. In 1961, when philosopher Hannah Arendt (1906-75) covered SS Lieutenant Colonel Adolf Eichmann's trial in Jerusalem for *The New Yorker* magazine, she wrote about 'the banality of evil'. The culture of the Nazis made it easy for Eichmann to send Jews to gas chambers. There was no moral dilemma. Arendt wrote, 'The sad truth is that most evil is done by people who never make up their minds to be good or evil'. What P. Sasi did was so ordinary and commonplace in his mind that the question of making a choice between right and wrong never arose. Those who function honestly are heretics. Corruption is a cottage industry as well as a national commercial megacorporation. Expecting honesty is considered quaint and anxiously pious. If it isn't done to protect oneself from being transferred to a 'punishment posting', it is a retirement plan for the future.

P. Sasi was found guilty of corruption and misconduct by the defence ministry's Chief Vigilance Officer R.P. Bagai on 26 May 2001. But it was only on 13 February 2008 that Sasi was arrested by the CBI for handing over sensitive information including documents of supply orders and contracts related to procurement of weapons and the Indian Army's requirements.

P. Sasi was not extraordinary in his air of ascendance in taking bribes, selling documents, and divulging confidential information. As India exists today, he was just being 'normal'. P. Sasi is a living symbol of our system. A statue of P. Sasi should be erected in South Block. Until the corruption network is sabotaged, his statue should stay right there. All defence ministers should take a good, hard look at him.

H.C. PANT

Sasi got into what must have been routine for him. He introduced Samuel to H.C. Pant, a staff officer in the Ordnance Factories Cell since 1993, not deputy director, as reported in Operation West End. Pant had worked as officer on special duty to Minister of State for Defence Hiren Pathak from October 1999 to November 2000. P.Sasi had been his lunch buddy for the past fifteen years. Pant proved to be a multiplying force for the Tehelka journalists when he went on to introduce them to five key people, a circle which in turn networked further. In the Operation West End tapes, Pant reassured Samuel: 'Don't worry about these things. Once the job is done, everything takes care of itself. Why do you worry about these things?' Pant elaborated on the route of the channels:

> You have to go through the DG Infantry. DG Infantry will recommend it to DGOS (Director-General Ordnance Services) or MGO. DGOS will then give it to General Choudary. DG (Director-General) Infantry General Shankar Prasad has to recommend it first of all. I will get you an appointment with General Shankar Prasad. Then I will speak to … have already spoken to General Choudary. But he said, the recommending authority is we people. Then it will go to DGOs. Then you meet Colonel Pandey there. One of my friends is there.

Pant expressed his admiration for Major General P.S.K. Choudary, who he considered a 'smart chap'. He mentioned that Choudary had tied up with a friend of his for a house in Vasant

Vihar which cost Rs 1.86 crores. Pant said, 'That is why I know his ins and out. I have told him, 'Brother, how do you get so much money?' He says, 'No, no'. I said (joking), 'Saala, I will have you locked up'. Pant advised Samuel that Choudary's wife and daughter acted as his middle(wo)men and that he should move through them. Pant then allegedly accepted Rs 20,000 from West End. He discussed the kind of gifts that would be appropriate for Choudary. That was not enough so Pant boasted about his connection to RSS trustee R.K. Gupta and his son. Their property in Jhandelwalan was donated to the RSS. Pant mentioned that at one point of time Atal Bihari Vajpayee used to live there.

On 4 April 2001, in the Army Court of Inquiry, Pant said that he did not speak to Major General P.S.K. Choudary but did raise the subject with Deepak Chabbra, reputed to be an arms dealer, who said in the Commission that he was only a construction engineer.

The army court asked Pant to elaborate on what he knew about Choudary's flat in Vasant Vihar.

> **Pant:** The plot belonged to Deepak Chabbra. He sold it to one Dr Choudary, who in turn built three separate floors, one flat each and a basement on that plot. The total cost of the building was approximately 1.86 crore. I am not aware of the cost of each floor, but was told that Major General Choudary had purchased one floor.

Pant said that he had obtained all this information from Deepak Chabbra.

The ACI asked Pant:

> **ACI:** During your discussion with Mathew Samuel at various times, you have been mentioning that if he had to get his product through then he would have to give gratification at various stages. Is this true?
>
> **Pant:** As far as civilian setup particularly with public-dealing departments, paying gratification for getting anything done is a normal practice. But I am not sure about the army. However, giving gifts during Diwali is normal practice.

In the Commission of Inquiry, on 28 January 2002, Pant was questioned by Tehelka lawyer, Sidharth Luthra:

> **Luthra:** According to the Operation West End transcripts, you said: "Pant: We will get it shortlist [sic]. We will then meet General Choudary for this. Before that we want to meet these people. I have told my man to tell his daughter. She will be coming to him today."
>
> **Pant:** I do not recollect the conversation. I have told Deepak Chabbra that Samuel wanted to meet you in this regard.

Luthra asked Pant about the sum of Rs 20,000 he received from Tehelka. He played the tape.

Pant: I have not accepted anything. I would request you, My Lord, to let him refer to my affidavit in this regard.

Luthra: You are in the Ministry of Defence. As you have just told us, Mathew Samuel has told you about thermal imagers working at minus 40° centigrade and you have taken him to Mr Gupta. Was it not your duty, as a public servant working in the Ministry of Defence, to report this matter to the defence authorities that this is what this person is doing?

Pant: That is why I am here in the witness box. This is what I have told you also. There is a departmental inquiry going on under Rule 14 against me.

Pant insisted through all the questions that he had only been discussing a holiday resort project with Mathew Samuel and had nothing to do with defence procurement. He was, noticeably invited by Mohinder Singh Sahni, an alleged arms dealer, to a party.

Major General P.S.K. Choudary then questioned Pant on all the talk about his wife that Pant had bandied around in the West End tapes:

Choudary: In your conversations with Mathew Samuel, you have referred that my wife and my daughter were my agents and the way to me was through them.

Pant: I have not referred that. Chabbra told me that General Choudary does not meet anyone. All these negotiations he has been doing only through his wife and daughter.

Choudary: What negotiations are you talking about?

Pant: Regarding that flat at Vasant Vihar.

Choudary: So you are talking about the flat purchased by my daughter in Vasant Vihar and it has nothing to do with any official transactions.

Pant: Yes.

Siddharth Aggarwal, counsel for the Commission, took his turn with Pant and got him to admit that he fixed up meetings with contractors to exploit political connections which was necessary if a product was to be successfully sold. Aggarwal confronted Pant with the West End transcripts where he discussed Bharat Electronics' programme for the next five years. Using the transcripts of the tapes, he accused Pant of handing over futuristic requirements that were to be handed over to the government. Aggarwal read details from the transcript:

"Pant: If you have to do business, you see this. What I will give you, the futuristic developments.

Tehelka: Haan.

Pant: What the government's thinking about the …"

And then, five lines below that, Pant said:

"Pant: No, entrance. I will make you the entry. Entry point is no problem for me. See these futuristics, you see if you can supply any of these things. This is a committee report I am going to give to the government."

Pant vehemently denied all that he reportedly said. He claimed he did not know what a hand-held imager is and said, 'My Lord, I am purely an administrative officer. I have nothing to deal with any of the technicalities or the technical equipment at all.' Pant also said he could not recollect anything that Aggarwal read out to him from the transcripts related to defence procurement.

Aggarwal finally said.

I put it to you that your action as depicted here may lead to a conclusion that you have acted against the interest of national security.
Pant: Not at all. No, I have not received any money from them. The video clippings have been doctored and it is a camera trick.

Well, the CBI saw no camera tricks. Pant was suspended from service on 26 May 2001, the defence ministry's Chief Vigilance Officer R.P. Bagai found Pant guilty of corruption and misconduct in the Tehelka exposé on corruption in defence deals. But it was only on 31 August 2006 that the CBI charged Pant for demanding and accepting bribes amounting to Rs 70,000 in order to facilitate procurement of orders for the supply of hand-held thermal imagers to the Indian Army. According to Tehelka's report, they had paid Pant Rs 60,000. The CBI reported that within a short span of about two weeks, between 22 November 2000 and 9 December 2000, Pant held seven meetings with Tehelka journalists. The CBI's proceedings continue. Whether he actually ends up in jail depends on which party is in power, what kind of strings Pant can pull and who he knows.

Sasi had just begun. He led Mathew Samuel to his boss, Colonel Anil Sehgal. That woke up Aniruddha. This could prove to be a big story. What information and documents did Sehgal sell to Tehelka and for how much? It turned out that Sehgal was interested not only in money. When money comes, can sex be far behind?

4 The Death of a Salesman
The Birth of a Journalist

Reluctant interviewee: Fuck, fuck, fuck, fuck, fuck. Can you use that?
Aaron Altman [Albert Brooks]: Depends on how slow a news day it is.

– James Brooks's film Broadcast News *(1987)*

As written on the Tehelka website: Starting his career with India Today *in 1992, Aniruddha Bahal moved to the science and environment magazine* Down to Earth, *followed by* The Financial Express. *He was part of the original team that launched* Outlook *magazine in 1995 and has reported on a range of subjects from environment to travel, sports and defence. He is best known, though, for his groundbreaking investigation on match-fixing which rocked international cricket. Rumoured to seduce his sources with his hyena laugh.*

Samuel: *Subeh* Aniruddha *ah gaya* [Aniruddha came in the morning]. I said to Aniruddha, Sasi is asking three lakhs then his bawss Brigaydeer will talk. Aniruddha said, "*Phhaah! Chutiya! Hum kehan deh sakta hai* [Phhah! (Hindi expletive as in fucker!) How can we give that much]?"

Then I said, "Aniruddha, we can give 20,000?" He said, "*Kyon? Ismey kya chaleyga?* [Why? What will work in this?]" I remumber that. I said, "Suppose we get one meaty Birgaydeer, he's selling me Brigaydeer, he's dealing with almost all those action items."

Aniruddha began to sniff a good story. He told Samuel to start with Rs 20,000 for Sehgal. Samuel crafted out a plan to throw off Sasi.

Samuel: Daylibrutly, vaat I did, Sasi bloody know I'm vurrrking with Tehelka. Unfortnately, I told him that, fussst meeting. Then I told Sasi that vaatever money you get, you have to give me 10 per cent commission, because I vant to prove my credibility, that I am doing it for the money and not for a story. That money we can spare for Malviya's stay. Esspenses you have to meet, *nah*, so bloody I'm saying here stay.

Samuel then moved to fix up the meeting:

Samuel: Sasi said Kernel Sehgal will come dyerrrect to there. Myself and Malviya will go, to Kernel Sehgal … opposite Dhaula Kuan. So Malviya said we should buy some frrruts, *mithai, kithai, humarey haath mey subh kutch hona hai* [sweets, we should have everything in our hands]. So *itna samaan pakadh kar hum uppar gayey* [so carrying all this stuff in our hands we went up]. He also surprised. *Kya leykar aah raheh hai. Usmey phhool bhi hai. Phhool rakhney ki jaganh nahin, aisa rakh kar gayey* [What have you brought? There are also flowers. There was no room for the flowers, we were carrying so much]. Ha, ha, [Samuel laughs his belly holding laugh]. "*Pappa aiyey, badda pappa aiyey* [father has come, big father has come]. He's very fun man. *Theek hai* [okay]. So Sasi was intarduced both of us. Sasi said don't tell my bawss that you are a journalist. You tell with Malviya you are doing vurrk. Otherwise he'll scared. He will not tell you anything. After that, we given Rs 20,000 [the money was given in stages at every meeting]. Everything Sasi pre-arranged. We got all this on camera.

Then he started talks. The percentage basis. How Sehgal can help us. How he can gayde us. How he can reach into materialize our supply. Bloody we don't know vaat kind of product we have to. Sehgal is asking hundred times, "Vaat kind of product you have? Vaat product you have?" Vaat we know vaat product we have? Ha, ha, heh. [Really enjoying himself.] Then he given lawt of stuff. Then he instructed to Sasi. He gave the drinks also. I also had one. Sasi *nahin piya* [Sasi didn't drink]. In front of his bawss how can he take? He instructed to Sasi, "*Ja keh almara khol keh, dawkumunts padda hai, usko deh doh* [go and open the cabinet, there are documents there, give those to them]."

Madhu: What documents were these?

Samuel: Rrelated to arrrmy procorrrmunt. Second day, Sasi dawkuments *deh diya; Sasi ko bhi paisa deh diya, batth khathum* [second day, Sasi gave the documents; Sasi was given the money, the matter was over]. That's also recorded. One is HHTI. I don't know even that time how to pronounce this [Samuel slowly and painfully enunciates] hand-held thermal binoculars. And II Tube. Intensive imager. So fitted for the tank. *Maineh tho, yeh kya, tube kya hai* [I asked, vaat is this tube]? *Uska sab* [all the] details, these are the things we need. Then after one day Aniruddha look at some tapes. That time he said, "Okay, now we can go." Meanwhile Sasi this guaide inform us you have to meet some other people also. I am not like this a big chain. Minister and ministry also takes a percentage and everything. Then Aniruddha fussst drafted a letter, like

Verghese George wrote a letter to Rajiv Sharma, Indian, that such and such vaatewer you given the information, we can follow the procedure that, I need more information on this. Computer *mey draft kar key*, Pranav Dutta *ko deh diya* [they drafted it on the computer and gave it to Pranav Dutta, graphic designer in Tehelka]. He decided the letter pad and Wust End, Aniruddha put the name.

Then again meeting Sasi and we again giving money. Happened every time we meeting Rs 2,000 he collecting. After that again we want to meet Kernal Sehgal to give money again to get some information. Meanwhile Sasi giving dawkumunts with procorrmunt information for arrrmy posts and capacity started. He given the instruction from Kernel Sehgal.

Madhu: That kind of information could fall into the wrong hands.

Samuel: Yeeesily! That is vaat I am saying. All the dawkumunts that is written, "Confidential" "Most Confidential". All that I got.

Madhu: But that has not come out in the Commission.

Samuel: No. That also Sasi's lawyer, Union of India lawyer, rrrust of the lawyer, we want to supposed to deposit [the documents] with the Commission. They are saying requesting Commission do not allow them to submit to the Commission. Just imaaaaagine!

How can Union of India lawyers? That, you know, if we are submitting, again *voh hangama ho jayeyga* [chaos will be created], how this leaked. We have submitted. The dawkumunts are in the Commission. I submitted. Arrrmy Court of Inquiry asked me to submit the dawkumunts. They say for them it is the "Most Confidential" matter. And here also, tapes *mey records hain*. That is a *Crrross almarah* [Cross cabinet] there. You operate, inside three locker there, then you have to take dawkumunts. When you open the *almarah* [cabinet] there is one key there, *uskey neechey dusra key hai, woh khole key* [below that is another key, that will open it]. Sasi how? Sasi manage *hai na*. He will tell, go and take photostat and return it back. Just imaaaaagine! These people are talking vaat rubbish vaat we did and I am very much concerned about this matter, Maddumm. This is very serious.

Madhu: What kind of information was he dumping?

Samuel: He was asking vaat kind of supply you want to do to army, so he can give all the details, vaat are the other suppliers are doing, how they are achieving the supply order, through whom, percentage basis, how these people are dumbping these products in army depots that is not using because of the date, expired dates, that kind of information. Each and every tawpic he knows very well. I really surprised. Malviya also surprised. Every day Sasi is leaving at 4 o'clock and I am recording. This camera we had got for match fixing story. In a briefcase. After three, four meetings with Sasi, I told Aniruddha this was happening.

This was a dream coming true for Aniruddha Bahal. It was not by mere accident that he was in charge of the investigative cell in Tehelka. How did an individual selling brassware and office equipment from Moradabad end up as an incendiary investigative reporter? Aniruddha Bahal's background scarcely destined him for the most sensational journalist sting operation in India. Aside from running away from home at fourteen to find his fortune in Mumbai and, at the age of twenty-four, writing a book, (A Crack in the Mirror) nothing would suggest the kind of focused zeal he demonstrated in Operation West End. Bahal's father worked for the National Airports Authority of India. His somewhat mundane background after his birth in Meerut, included school in Calcutta until class IV and then high school in Ahmedabad. He followed the predictable trajectory and got a BA degree from Allahabad University.

As mentioned earlier, on a visit to Delhi in 1991, he simply turned up at the India Today office and harassed Tarun Tejpal into giving him a job as a sub-editor. Bahal had a germ in his head that he had to get out of where he was. Moradabad was too small to contain his goals. Bahal took the first step in what the American scholar Joseph Campbell has brilliantly set forth in his treatise, The Hero of a Thousand Faces (1949) where the archetype of a hero at various stages is examined through the prism of mythology. 'The hero, therefore, is the man or woman who has been able to battle past his personal and local historical limitations to the generally valid human forms.' The 'hero' here is not necessarily Superman or a perfect human being who solely performs good deeds, but any man who reaches a threshold point he must cross in order to embark on an adventure that brings new meaning to his life. Of course, this prototype has been used in books and films all over the world.

Strolling around Connaught Place, Aniruddha saw India Today's board and walked in. Tarun Tejpal saw his CV, told him he would get back to him, and presumed that was the end of it. Aniruddha had other ideas. He sat in the India Today reception from early morning until Tarun left at night, for a week, waiting. 'I couldn't go out or come in, without this guy being there,' Tarun recalled. 'The moment I would cross he would stand up, waiting for an answer. One week it went on. I went bananas. I couldn't get in and out of the bloody office, yaar. I finally hired him as a trainee just to get him out of the reception.'

Aniruddha joined India Today in December 1991 and surprised everyone when he quit India Today in January 1994 for the Centre for Science and Environment's magazine Down to Earth. He was there for just seven months, but the stint gave him the opportunity to travel to all corners of India that turned out to be a great learning experience. When Tarun joined Financial Express, he called Aniruddha to join him there. When Tarun quit Financial Express to join Outlook magazine, Aniruddha followed him there too. Tarun said,

> The great thing about Ani is he is a do-er. He's not a nuance guy. He's not a finesse guy. What he wants to do, what he has to do, he'll get the job done. He won't do more than that, because he always had a big play for himself and he always had big ambition. If he was told, send him somewhere "Yeh rahee ek story, laana hai [here's the story, so get it]" he'd get it for you, whichever way he did it. He is a single child and I don't think he has an articulate relationship

51

with too many people in the world. I won't be surprised if I am the only person he has a relationship like that in the whole world. I don't think he has it even with his wife or parents.

This is clearly Tarun's Rashomon, and I can just hear Aniruddha groaning and laughing his hyena laugh!

He is in that sense a fairly lonely kind of guy and lot of him is lived in his head. In class IX he had devised this whole plot on how one can assassinate the American president without being caught. He was full of these fantastical potboiler imaginings. Somewhere with me he has a connection that goes way beyond the professional. There is a bond and the bond I think has to do with the fact that I'm probably the one person in the world he can talk to, and with whom he feels okay. Because he is socially gauche, he's the kind of guy who'll say or do the wrong thing. But there is also the kind of hammer to go ahead and break down the wall and do what he has to do.

Socially gauche? Yes, Aniruddha definitely doesn't seek to fit in the social whirl. There is this story that did the rounds. It was Holi (in 2001 Holi was on March 9, four days before Operation West End was to be shown at Imperial Hotel) and Tehelka had decided they would close their offices for the morning on the holiday but open up at 4.00 p.m. When Aniruddha, totally focused on working on Operation West End showed up at the office, he found it locked. He was tense about completing the story. He arrived at Tarun's house to pick up the key at around 5.00 p.m. and found about a hundred people there still in a Holi mood. As he waited for Tarun to give him the key, one of Tarun's friends decided to rub colour all over Aniruddha, despite Aniruddha explaining to him that Holi was over and he was on his way to work. Tarun's friend ignored his protests and continued to apply colour on Aniruddha, who of course lost it and proceeded to give the fellow a solid thrashing.

Vinod Mehta, editor-in-chief of *Outlook*, said, 'Aniruddha always believed we were wasting our time in journalism by ringing up people and asking for on the record interviews and doing journalism in the conventional way.' Whenever he went on an assignment abroad he bugged Mehta to give him money to buy hidden cameras. Mehta gave the money once and Aniruddha did buy two hidden cameras. Mehta said he allowed him to buy the cameras to keep him happy but kept asking him how he was going to use them, 'given the business we are in'. Aniruddha gave *Outlook* two good stories using those cameras. He smuggled himself into the West Indies cricket team's dressing room and recorded a famous cricket star making racist comments about the white Zimbabwe team. The cricketer called up Vinod and told him, he would never had made those statements had he known he was being recorded. Vinod said, 'There was a big stink.' He also sat with a Pakistani cricketer in a car in London and recorded him talking about other cricketers who were suspected of match-fixing. *Outlook* did not use that tape but Mehta said: 'The Pakistani cricketer got so scared he gave him a lot of other information on the record.'

Mehta marvelled at Tarun and Aniruddha's way of getting apparently impossible things done. Mehta recalled,

> When Mark Mascarenhas invited Sachin Tendulkar to his home in America, Aniruddha wangled an invitation for himself and the *Outlook* photographer. I was delighted that we would have pictures of Tendulkar in the Jacuzzi. But then three weeks later I got very upset. They did a huge profile of Mark Mascarenhas in the magazine, which was a puff job. They did it behind my back. Then I realized it was payment, as it were. So none of us were surprised that to get that story they had used that kind of method and prostitutes. We know these chaps quite well.

Mehta added,

> Aniruddha is actually a very simple guy. He's got this kind of mind which sees things like that but basically he's a simple sort of person. I think as far as Tehelka was concerned, he just wanted to make a big bang. He just wanted the biggest story and the biggest story was to trap politicians taking money. I don't think that he had any other motives.

Was Aniruddha getting frustrated at *Outlook*? Mehta thought so,

> Because we'd never allowed him a free run of play on many of the ideas that he had. Many of the ideas that he had were very interesting, but we said get them but in the proper way and we didn't have any gadgets. Actually this whole conceptualization of the sting; it was a brilliant conceptualization. You must concede that. But I think 99.99 per cent was Aniruddha's idea.

Bahal worked with *Outlook* from 1995 until 1999, when he was offered a huge jump in salary (Rs 16,000 to Rs 1 lakh) to join Mark Mascarenhas in *World Tel* for a cricket magazine. Bahal was not entirely comfortable at *Cricket Talk*. There were problems, and Bahal had donned his fantasy hat. Meanwhile, he had already put together plans for a news website when Tarun, having quit *Outlook* in February 2000, called him with a similar idea.

Bahal's essentiality of always pushing his own edge and reaching outside his existing environment began to rumble. Tehelka was born to take Tejpal and Bahal into an entirely different orbit from that which neither of them had experienced earlier. They gave Tehelka their best in terms of time, energy, effort, and doggedness. It was a solid website.

In May 2000, Bahal put Tehelka.com on the map with an undercover investigative story on match-fixing in Indian cricket. He did this with the cooperation of former cricketer Manoj Prabhakar, using the same hidden camera he later used for Operation West End.

In his cross-examination before the Commission of Inquiry on Tehelka, Bahal said:

> We took the decision that the empty cassettes would be with me. During that period, I was on call 24 hours a day. I do not think I have ever taken even a Sunday off for the last two or three years, except may be two or three Sundays. If I have been travelling, it's on Tehelka's work or if I am in Delhi, on most holidays I am in office.

Bahal wholly focused on his mission and everything else fell by the wayside. Both Bahal and Tejpal have another thing in common: absolutely loyal, supportive wives. As Bahal said, 'I wouldn't have been able to do it otherwise'. In keeping with his background, Bahal had an arranged marriage and has two daughters. His wife, Reema, knew nothing about Operation West End. The first time Reema learnt of it was when she turned on the television set on the afternoon of 13 March. Bahal laughed and said,

> They knew with the excitement, *kuch honeh wala hai, kuch kar rahein hain* [something is about to happen, they are doing something]. But that is all. I've been blessed with a family who just leaves me alone. And they just support me. What support? They just keep praying [laughs]. If I hadn't had this kind of family, I couldn't have done West End. If I had a wife who asked me, "Why are you returning at 12 o'clock?" I couldn't have ever told her and that would have led to serious family complications. That's the grace of God, that I don't have that kind of family.

In the end, it was Bahal who not only shed light on why and how Operation West End took place, but was also able to argue on principles of journalism with the LOCOT, who tried to portray him as an unscrupulous opportunist. Samuel's concepts and language are in a world exclusive to himself (World According To Samuel – WATS), and Tarun Tejpal said he did not know enough about the operation. Bahal said that the idea of Operation West End was triggered by the Bharatpur ammunition depot that caught fire, the Kandahar hijack, and Kargil, all related to national security issues. He said that national security was considered a holy cow and there were no answers given when related questions were asked, even in Parliament. Even Defence Minister George Fernandes had spoken about middlemen in arms deals and he felt a story was begging to be done.

Samuel's relationship with Aniruddha was complex. Neither one of them could have accomplished Operation West End without the other. Samuel's coarse thinking was balanced and nurtured by Aniruddha's eye on the larger story. Aniruddha gave Samuel money to bribe people and trusted him. Samuel did say, 'More than Tarun, I liked Aniruddha', but there was underlying tension:

Madhu: Did you have a good relationship with Aniruddha? Did you have any fights?
Samuel: Yes, Aniruddha I had a good relationship. Yes, three, four times I forward my resignation.

Madhu: Why?

Samuel: Becawz sometimes he will uncontrol his talks. Like shouting. But I was doing the same job before, but he forgot that. I did or not did. Sometimes, I rreally, how can, I did the wurrk, the result got. It's not like suddenly pushing and everything. Unnecessarily he will shout. Oh, you're not doing this. After only he come to know, he already did. I felt very angry that time. Three, four times I resigned.

Madhu: What did he say when you resigned?

Samuel: After I resigned, he will come to my home. Then he will tell, I am carrying lawts of pressure in my head. You know, financial position there. I went for collecting money to give your salary. How you feel? Like that. I rrreally like him. Then I will say, I am sorry and I back. Suppose I will switch off my mobile due to some other operation, then he's not feeling well. Why I switched off my mobile? If I switch off becawz of the recording matter, we want to record properly, disturbance will come, the tawpic can also change, that also he don't like. He think I am doing something else. That is vaat, he's not responding. He have very short temper. Without knowing he will shout. But finally he will come to know. And he will tell, "Yah! Really!" That also I saw, those who are close to him, then only he will shout.

Madhu: Did he ever say he was sorry?

Samuel: Many times.

Aniruddha's symbiotic relationship with Samuel functioned through many layers. Samuel turned to him even in his personal life.

Madhu: How was your family life affected by your work?

Samuel: I will not chat with anything with my wife. But I'll tell you one thing. I have a very important assignment with Kernel Saiyal tape-recording meeting going on. That night I promised my wife I be there for cake cutting for my kid's birthday.

Madhu: Usual story!

Samuel: Yeah, uzzzual story. Then I forgot that to go there. Then that day, she left the home. She talked to Aniruddha, said, "I'm taking my kid, I'm going." So that day I reached my home around 3 o'clock. Every morning I have to give the tape, charge it, then have to confirm it has charged it or not. Most of time I reached 2.30.

Madhu: Then what happened? Did she come back?

Samuel: No. Then Aniruddha came in the night. Talked to her. He was here 4 o'clock in the morning. He talked to Annie.

Madhu: Then she … understood?

Samuel: Understood. No! Not understood! She told me I'm not bothered about your fame or anything. She saying I want a small, happy family. She born and brought up in Delllhi. We have one boy and one gell. After she got to know I took this bloody risk, she having this problem. Why you are taking this kind of risk? Now she is staying with her parents.

Madhu: Is she going to come back to you?

Samuel: Yes, told me she will come back.

Madhu: So this messed up your personal life completely?

Samuel: Yes. My horoscope also saying. My personal life like that. He told me I will again do three, five stories like that. They told me, but your life is like that. When I'm doing any story I could not able to sleep. I am not a person to go on six-seven hours. I am not a person to come and chat with you. I'm not bothered with mileage matter. I have to engage it every time. Something other something or I'll not feel well.

Madhu: Does Annie understand this?

Samuel: She not understand. Every time she like 10 o'clock going, 5 o'clock back. After, kids playing.

Madhu: She may come around later.

Samuel: She always neeeedle me like that. If we are talking, call will come. She's not bothered some big people are calling. She told me many times. I need only very caaalm life. You have to away from all that. She is a biggg nuwwweeesance. Every time she asking me, "If something happened to you, vaaat will happen to me?" Fusst she asking only some time. Now she asking every day, every day, so many time. Soooo many time. Tooooo many time. "If something happen to you, vaaat will happen to me?" Again and again. Really a big nuwweeesance.

Madhu: So what did you tell her?

Samuel: I tell her, "How I know vaat happen to you? I gone." Now she is vurrrking. I told her to start vurrrk. Most of the time she is sitting in the home, then only feelings will come.

When Samuel brought Anil Malviya to meet Aniruddha, he figured that Malviya wanted to get into the advertisement side of Tehelka and found the best way to get in was to give hot leads to stories. That suited Aniruddha fine. Samuel was still too raw to go out on his own. Aniruddha said the most difficult part of Operation West End was to find an entry point in the arms procurement business. Once they got that, the next step that befuddled them was the kind of product they could pretend to sell? Aniruddha said, 'Malviya was confidence personified. He was one of those blustering, aggressive salesmen who just get in. He would tell you that a water purifier is a bloody air-conditioner also. That's the kind of guy he was.' When they first started the story, none of them had any idea it would grow to the level it did. Aniruddha said,

Maybe people think that in October, November, it was valuable. No, it wasn't. It grew incrementally. How can you know where you are going? Suddenly then, oh boy, what are we sitting on? We could have gotten flat in a week. Nobody knows what we're going to get. In a way it was just madness; just going through like that. Who has ever even thought …? For six, eight months maybe, I slept two hours a day. There was so much paranoia at that time. The only thing I was meticulous about is keeping the tapes in custody.

When Samuel brought in Colonel Sehgal's tapes, Aniruddha had reason to get excited. Sehgal had readily shared inside information about the current situation in army procurements. Sehgal told Samuel:

You have to break this thing of BE-Delft, a PSU. As of late, there is a policy that nothing is to be imported. There are many people interested in that. So you have to get the nexus broken up at the top. BE is Bharat Electrical. Delft is Holland. Holland has branched out from itself after the US sanctions. What you have to do is get a little open, because they have been talking big. They have been taking us for a ride. And somehow bureaucracy also. And things have been manipulated in the ministry that delay things deliberately to suit them.

When Sehgal and his friend Lieutenant Colonel Bhav Bhuti Sharma (assistant director, Air Formation Signals) were entertained by West End with drinks and women in a Delhi hotel, there was the following exchange:

West End: Sir, I want to ask … another one thing. One Mr B.S. Yadav sitting in the Air Headquarters. It's a foreign cell. Sales he is dealing, I think in that.
Sharma: They have got their own procurement. They are basically dealing with Russians directly, and …
Sehgal: *Nahin*, everything, everyone has got work. Unlike … unlike us.
Sharma: Because those kind of PNCs [price negotiation committees] and negotiations are done at the ministry level. We don't involve ministry in our work. We do it directly.
Sehgal: *Yeh behanchod, inhoney bahut sahi kaam kara. Saara kuch apney haath mein rakha* [these sister-fuckers have done it right. They have kept everything in their own hands].
Sharma: *Ma chudaaye* [mother-fucker], no CDA, nobody. We issue the tender, call the bloody parties, do the PNC, give the supply order.
West End: *Is baat par mein sahab ek baar phir haath milaunga ki mainey aapney sahab sey mila* [on this question, sir, I will again shake hands that I met my sir] this is what he has said, *Yeh mujhey kaha gaya tha* [that is what I was told].
Sharma: *Hum toh … raag me phanstey hi nahin na* [we don't get stuck in all this].
West End: *Usmey toh mai …* [in that …]
Sehgal: So many bloody water-tight compartments.

West End: *Billkul* [exactly].

Sehgal: The left ball don't know what the right …

⤸

According to Tehelka, Colonel Sehgal then demanded Rs 2 lakh to give further documents relating to the procurement of hand-held thermal cameras and other equipment. When Samuel gave him Rs 20,000, Sehgal was clearly insulted at the small sum. He demanded, 'What will I do with this? Let me tell you something. You keep this. Give it all tomorrow.' When Samuel explained that they were going slowly and he would eventually receive the total amount, Sehgal told him, 'There are some principles in life', meaning that taking a small bribe was beneath his principles. Sehgal then instructed Samuel what to write in letters about the transfer of technology to vice-chiefs and various other senior officers and to keep the rates a bit low. Sehgal said,

> See, the guy will think twice before signing … *Behanchod* [sister-fucker], see I have a counter offer and all these fuckers know about it. Either I give money *behanchod* to all of them. Include all. This *mader chod* [mother-fucker] is the way here. Not everyone gets the money. Whoever does the contract, gets it.

Sehgal warmed up to the subject and informed Samuel that money has to be paid all the way up, right up to senior lieutenant generals. Sehgal said, '*Yaar*, that goes on the powers of Brigadier Singh. May have to go to RM [*raksha mantri* (defence minister)] also.'

Tehelka: Who is RM?

Sehgal: *Raksha Mantri*. It will go to Fernandes sahib also.

Sasi: He also …

Sehgal: That *behanchod* is so moneyhungry that one can just go on about it. [Sehgal rose up to make himself another drink.]

Sehgal (continued): All these politicians are *chutiyas* [fuckers]. They are all different behind your backs.

Tehelka: So we'll have to pay there also. If we meet five, we have to pay them all. We have no idea whether they will or won't do the job. It will be singled down to one person.

Sehgal: And, thereafter, I will tell you who the bastard is. I don't want to teach all the tricks because it has reached such a stage. Send a letter to the *raksha mantri* also. Address it to the *raksha mantri* and give a CC to everybody, *behanchod*.

Tehelka: RM first? Sir, then how he will collect the money?

Sehgal: *Behanchod*, there are numerous channels for him.

Tehelka: Those people themselves will contact us.

Sehgal: They will come on their own; they will contact on their own. All that you have to ensure, that it can function upto minus 40 degrees.

Besides handing over classified documents and supplying secret information to West End, Sehgal was entertained with sex workers by the Tehelka operatives. This exposure of how the officers made themselves so utterly vulnerable did not set off appropriate alarm bells. Instead there was outrage from all directions, including the press, that the Tehelka journalists had taken their quest that far. It was constantly brought up in the Commission of Inquiry by lawyers to browbeat Tehelka journalists and to make them appear sleazy and unscrupulous. This was not, however, supposed to be a trial of the character of Tehelka journalists. However unethical it may have been deemed to be, it still exposed the threat to India's security.

The Army Court of Inquiry (ACI) showed no sympathy for the officers on trial. The ACI was not interested and not prepared to listen to any lame excuses. On 14 April 2001, Colonel Anil Sehgal, 471 Engineer Brigade (as the 15th witness) handed over a written application to the ACI, which stated that he did not want to make any statement, citing Article 20(3) of the Constitution of India: 'No person accused of any offence can be compelled to be a witness against himself.' Obviously done on the advice of his lawyer, Sehgal did not endear himself to the ACI with his first step. The army court informed Sehgal that as this was only an inquiry, undertaken to arrive at the truth and any information he divulged would not incriminate him, he therefore had no protection under Article 20. Under Army Rule 179(4), the ACI was empowered to put questions to elicit the truth. Sehgal was entitled to decline to answer but he could not prevent the ACI from asking questions.

Most of the lawyers for the accused army officers were former army officers or para-military officials, chosen for their intimate knowledge of the mechanics of the armed forces.

Sehgal answered some basic questions about his area of work and relationship with P. Sasi. He informed the court that as director, Armaments in Army Headquarters (January 1998 to January 2001) his duties included provisioning for all Users 'A' equipment of the armament side and also of their fire control instruments. He did deal in thermal cameras and II Tubes. When he was asked:

ACI: How many times have you met the representatives of M/s West End?
Sehgal: On legal advice I decline to answer that question.

The army court then proceeded to grill Sehgal – did he take Rs 40,000 from Tehelka and give them documents and information related to army equipment, was he entertained by West End representatives in Park Hotel, were Lieutenant Colonel B.B. Sharma, Mathew Samuel and P. Sasi present, did West End operatives visit him at his home in Arjun Vihar, did he talk to them about the procedures for procurement and the bribing of various people to clinch the deal, did he ask P. Sasi to get 'parachutes' implying condoms?

Sehgal's response to all questions was, of course, 'On legal advice, I decline to answer this question'.

At this stage, the court played the unedited videotape showing Sehgal's meeting with Sasi, Mathew Samuel, and Rajiv Sharma (Anil Malviya).

ACI: Do you recognize your self and your voice in the videotape?

Sehgal: On legal advice I decline to answer the question.

ACI: Did this meeting take place at your residence on 21 September 2000?

Sehgal: On legal advice I decline to answer the question.

ACI: It is seen from the tape that when a sum of Rs 20,000 was given to you by Mr Sharma of M/s West End as gratification at your residence you were heard saying "*Issey kya hoga*" or words to that effect and you wanted the total amount as agreed to be given on the next day. Is this statement true?

Sehgal: On legal advice I decline to answer the question.

At this point Colonel Anil Sehgal submitted that he did not wish to see the tape any further. Who can blame him? He undertook not to raise any objection at any stage that he had not been afforded the opportunity to inspect/view the unedited tapes produced before the court.

ACI: It is seen from the transcript that you have indulged in unnatural sex with a call girl provided by M/s West End on 18 September 2000 at Hotel Park. Is this true?

Sehgal: On legal advice I decline to answer the question.

ACI: It is also seen from the transcript that while you were in the company of that girl you rang up Lieutenant Colonel B.B. Sharma in the other room at the same hotel, where he was in the company of another call girl and asked him to come down to your room. Is this true?

Sehgal: On legal advice I decline to answer the question.

Colonel Anil Sehgal was the only witness who refused to answer questions. Rather a creatively capricious stand for an army officer to take in an Army Court of Inquiry but obviously it was done on the advice of his lawyer. But then, any accurate description of Sehgal's lawyer, R.P. Sharma, is putting it euphemistically. The first option was to give full cooperation to the court, pour out all the information, admit guilt with contrition, and fall into a tumble at the mercy of the court, Bollywood a la Shakespearean shtyle. Perhaps R.P. Sharma figured that the quality of mercy is strained in the Army Court of Inquiry. Sharma and Sehgal could, however, have considered that this was not an investigation unravelling a mystery. There were tapes that clearly showed what had happened. The court was simply going through the academic exercise of verifying the actions with the players. Any information Sehgal confirmed or denied about his behaviour would still be weighed against what was visible on the tapes. At this point his refusal only became a statement with the connotation: do whatever you have to do; I am not going to assist you to do it. To many it would imply a complete contempt of the court and its proceedings. R.P. Sharma was using a ploy, too clever by half, but would it really help his client? My suspicion is that Sehgal was too overwhelmed by the enormity of the impact of the exposé on his life and his family, to think straight. Was there any hope in going out with dignity? Would anyone ever look at him and not think of the West End tapes? Would he ever look into his own eyes in the mirror and not see his disgrace? As it came to pass, refusing to answer questions did not help Sehgal much but it did save him the agony of re-living what he had done.

On 21 January 2002, Sehgal appeared in the Commission of Inquiry and his answer to the first relevant question was:

> I would like to submit that reference be made to my affidavit where I am an 8B noticee. But I am sorry, I cannot answer any of these questions in the light of the facts contained in the affidavit and I seek protection. I have been informally charge-sheeted and any disclosure on my part will prejudice my defence there in the prosecution by the army.

All subsequent questions were answered with, 'I am sorry. I cannot answer the question.'

The wives of Colonel Anil Sehgal and Brigadier Iqbal Singh resorted to loyalty by filing charges against Tehelka for blackmailing their husbands with the sex tapes. Kiran Sehgal wrote:

> This blackmailing was in the form of seeking the setting up of meetings with the officials concerned. My husband has been living with a constant threat of exposure since Rajiv Sharma and Samuel Mathew first told him about the filming of certain scenes that he had with the prostitutes …. Caught on the horns of a dilemma he finally caved in to the demand for fixing a meeting. To get rid of the pressure of Sharma and Mathew and also without affecting the interests of the organization [army], he referred them to Narender Singh – a junior level officer in the Ministry of Defence – who was not concerned with the equipments which their company was apparently selling.

Tehelka responded by scoffing at the charges while denying them. Aniruddha Bahal said:

> First the army officers claimed that the tapes were doctored, now all of a sudden they claim they were being blackmailed by us? Does this mean that now they are admitting that it is they who are in the tapes? This is a very welcome change. So far, they had not even admitted that they were on the tapes with the sex workers.

I met Colonel Anil Sehgal and his wife Kiran, along with his lawyer R.P. Sharma. Kiran's steadfast loyalty to her husband made me uneasy for her. Sehgal said that the meetings that took place did not occur as they were projected.

> **Sehgal:** After they entrapped me, they started phoning me up to get them more people. They came to my house, and when there was an argument my wife came out and saw them. Just to wash my hands off them I sent them to meet people. They had come for a different purpose. They knew I used to get

drunk around 8.30. By 9.00 I was drunk and then went to bed. That was my ritual. When they came and I asked them to open their briefcase, then they said *bhago, bhago* [run, run]. Sasi brought them as friends. After the hotel scene, they told me, "We have you on camera. We are going to expose you unless you introduce us to people in the Ministry of Defence." I lived in constant fear and they were constantly threatening me.

Kiran said, 'He has been slogging day and night for the army and this is what he gets for it.' I asked Sehgal to walk me to my car and then asked him: 'I've seen the tapes with you in the hotel. You told your wife nothing happened. I did not want to say anything in front of her. But I know what I saw.' Despite repeated coaxing from me that he tell the truth, Sehgal stuck to his story: nothing happened between him and the sex worker. Perhaps he may have confided the truth, had I had been a male journalist and up to boozin' with the boys.

The Tehelka episode metamorphosed Sehgal into giving up liquor and becoming a vegetarian. He spent a large part of his time praying in his puja room, moving as far as he could from his past behaviour. How do you put the past behind you? Sehgal speaks of his destiny and bad luck, but who is this Destiny? It would be nice to meet Destiny, who takes the blame for the antics of mortals. No matter how ferociously Sehgal wants to put the past behind him, how can he prevent it being thrust upon him wherever he goes? Like a sex worker who goes straight and marries into society, the fear of meeting a former client must cling like an unwanted odour. However desperately she wants to put the past behind her, a surprise encounter can fling her back into her past life, no matter how hard she tries to pull away. William Shakespeare wrote in *The Tempest*, 'Whereof what's past is prologue'; the past is only the beginning of what will come next.

How do you define the past that is always present? Many scientists and philosophers have studied and evolved theories of Time. How do you define the present if the past never leaves? In 1907, Henri Bergson, in his controversial third book, *L'Evolution Creatice* (Creative Evolution) elaborated on his theory of Time. He defined two types of Time: basically man-made time in terms of physics, measured with a clock as opposed to Real time, which is the Time of inner experience. Real time is not measurable because the way a person feels time depends on the experience. As Albert Einstein said, 'Put your hand on a hot stove for a minute and it seems like an hour. Sit with a pretty girl for an hour and it seems like a minute. *That's* relativity.'

In Time in terms of physics, the past disappears as the next moment appears. However, in Real time, each moment takes its texture from the past. In Real time, the present cannot exist without the past. Colonel Anil Sehgal has to live in Real time. Not matter what he does, the past will always bump into him and stare him down. Even if he disguised himself and nobody recognized him, simple words like 'tapes', 'call girls', 'investigative journalists' would create yet another crack in his interior being. The past creates an invisible aura that encloses the person completely. How do you fight your way out of a coffin if the lid is not visible? But everybody wants to be happy, as is evidenced by the burgeoning industry of New Age, Middle Age, and Old Age gurus. Not one of them will advise you to live in the past. All will tell you to live in the moment. This existing and passing second. Is there an easier way to live with the past than to simply believe it didn't exist and doesn't matter any more? It is reduced to a survival technique. Then doesn't forgiveness also fall into the same category? Not to forgive is to hang on to the unpleasant past, so you forgive to free yourself of the ugly past and presto you are happy. Or, are you? Ask someone who was molested as a child. Poor Colonel Anil Sehgal. He couldn't be more trapped had they jailed him for life. Isn't the most favoured sentence dished out after an unconscionable act: 'It's all in the past. Let's look ahead'? A favoured sentence, yes, but the saddest portent clouded in an impossible hope. The past is the out-breath of the present in-breath. You cannot breathe in again until you have breathed out. The past is in the present. The past is here to stay. It is only the present that goes away.

On 12 January 2005, Colonel Anil Sehgal was sentenced to four years' rigorous imprisonment and cashiered from the army by a five-member General Court Martial headed by Brigadier Kuldip Singh. Sehgal was convicted for illegal gratification of Rs 20,000, for accepting hospitality of liquor and sex workers, and for meeting arms dealers without the permission of the Directorate of Military Intelligence.

NARENDER SINGH

Warmed up with a touch of money, Colonel Anil Sehgal helped out the Tehelka journalists by confidently directing them to Narender Singh, who displayed the historically established nexus with the ease with which he accepted the bribe. 'I will give a parallel line in the finance division. They will come into picture only where there is a procurement proposal. Before that they have nothing to do,' said Narender Singh, assistant financial adviser in the Ministry of Defence, as he pocketed Rs 10,000 as an advance from West End (4 November 2000). The Tehelka team had learnt that it was not sufficient to grease defence ministry officials and army officers; finance division officials were an important link in getting a deal approved.

Narender Singh gave Samuel a fairly clear picture on how the system worked:

I will tell you there are number of persons to be contacted. Contacting one person in the defence ministry will not help. There are a number of persons. One person will be holding the project; another will be sitting in the PNC. So there will be four-five at working levels. So I am more concerned with people who are at the working level. So, then it is your job; if there are any problems I will tell you, you will have to handle this person or that person.

Narender Singh then gave Samuel details about the numbers involved:

So you will think of giving the best price in the first quote. So, even if you are by one dollar, you are higher than them. You have no chance. Whatever you have done it goes in the drain. So, nowadays, that 21 per cent is out of the question. But now for the last one-and-a-half years, the latest instructions have come that contract is to be based on the L-1, that is the lowest offer received. All higher offers are to be summarily rejected. No talking to them. It's only two-three per cent and you see 100 crore. I will not try to misguide you because our association will be very long also. Right now, Ordnance has nothing to do with it. They will not come into picture, neither PPO will come. It is only WE and Infantry and Mechanization and Artillery.

Narender Singh was one of the few who admitted he had made a mistake in not reporting West End to the police, although he did deny taking any money. He did not once say that the tapes were doctored or fictitious.

On 19 April 2002, Narender Singh tried to explain his actions before the Commission of Inquiry:

N. Singh: Actually, what I was feeling was, what happened in the first meeting was, he suddenly started showering me with offers: we can give you a percentage of cut. He said, we can give you visa to USA, we can give you visa to UK for two years or three years, you can go and enjoy. Then he also mentioned that he can give some money, gifts, something like that. Then as per Tehelka's own commentary, if you have a look at the Tehelka prepared Transcript No. 28 at the end, it says, "Narender Singh looks peeved and troubled and thereafter Tehelka leaves." In the wake of such offers, it is mentioned there. So my intention was, this man has got a job, he should know what exactly is the procedure. His intention was somehow or other to influence my mind, corrupt me by one method or the other.

Sidharth Luthra (Tehelka counsel): Despite these inducements, these offers to corrupt you, giving you a visa to send you abroad, you did not report this meeting to any superior officer, did you? You did not file a complaint in any of the police stations against this man?

N. Singh: I think this is a fault on my part. I should have done that. But what happened to me, I took pity on him. I thought people were misguiding him and somehow or other I should put him on the right track. That was my approach. Had I known that he is such a type of person, who has come with some ulterior motives, I should have reported. That is my fault. I agree.

Narender Singh pointed out passages that had been edited out of the broadcast tape, where Mathew Samuel asks him for further introductions. From the unedited transcripts:

Samuel: No, I told you, *na*, what Mr Narender Singh, we want to do now is creating a network. Without creating a network, it won't work out sir. The army officers also told me. Is somebody there?

N. Singh: No.

Samuel: *Yah*, you even told me; you told me in that case also you will introduce some people.

N. Singh: No, I never told you.

Samuel: No, whom we will meet Issar?

N. Singh: If you ask me, it is not possible.

Samuel: *Nahi*, do you have any channel? Do you know any channel?

N. Singh: No, no channel. I told you last time.

Narender Singh had reason to be peeved that anything that pointed to his honesty had been removed with an editorial slant. However, his honesty did not stretch to acknowledging that he took the money.

Luthra: I put it to you that Mr Mathew Samuel has offered to you and you have accepted the sum of Rs 10,000.

N. Singh: I never accepted anything.

Dayan Krishnan (counsel for the Commission) questioned Narender Singh on this statement in the Operation West End tapes where he said, 'So then it is your job. If there are any problems, I will tell you. You will have to handle this person or that person.' Again, N. Singh elaborated that his completed sentence, which had been edited out, included, 'How you tackle has to be your problem. Even I can't tell you how to tackle. So, frankly speaking, I do not have that kind of connection with Mr Issar or anybody. And, even if he wants, our system, you have seen, it is not one body decision.'

Krishnan then asked N. Singh that in the procurement of HHTIs, whether he would discuss these details with a middleman or defence dealer. N. Singh said indeed he would. He pointed out that he had been dealing with imports for the last 5–6 years and the first thing he would do is issue a RFP (Request for Proposal) containing the detailed terms and conditions. He would ask for two samples for trial, the amount for a bank guarantee and ask for the L-1 price. N. Singh insisted this was not a secret document and was sent to all the embassies as well as to all the military attachés posted abroad with the request that it may be circulated to all the known vendors. He said it would be a crime if they knew of a vendor and did not let him compete. They wanted more competition and that was the reason he was giving away all the detailed information. Krishnan adamantly pointed out that Singh should not have given away information about army requirements. According to Singh, 'There are two types of information when we are dealing with procurement cases. One is pre-contact information. When something is going on, the meetings are being held; then if we leak out something, it is criminal. But after everything has been done, if army wants new vendors, then it is our duty to give that procedural information.'

Even if you give Narender Singh the benefit of confusion and tune into the daily ethos of middlemen, there is the niggling matter of Rs 10,000.

Narender Singh was suspended from service one day after the exposé (14 March 2001). The chief vigilance officer in the defence ministry, R.P. Bagai declared Narender Singh guilty of corruption and misconduct on 26 May 2001. It was only on 30 November 2006 that the new government (UPA) had the CBI file a charge-sheet against him.

He is charged for commission of offences punishable under the Prevention of Corruption Act 1988.

〜

The LOCOT used innumerable methods to distract the Commission from getting to the truth. Thousands of questions were asked about the call girls simply to create an ambience that Tehelka journalists were just a dirty, sleazy bunch. N. Hariharan, counsel for P. Sasi (Samuel's first contact lead) asked hundreds of questions related to purchase of tapes, cameras, and the process of editing. Hariharan spent half an hour on lockers that were taken by Aniruddha and Tarun in Standard Chartered Bank to store the tapes. After detailed questions about the cost of the lockers, how the payment was made, who operated them, the size of the lockers, Hariharan came up with his great exposé:

> **Hariharan**: I put it to you that the biggest locker that exists in Standard Chartered Bank is measuring 400 mm in height, 524 mm in width and 470 mm in depth.

Well, so what? When Hariharan, got to this point he abruptly changed the subject.

〜

A subject that never elicited any clear answers from Bahal was: Who was the friend who gifted these hidden cameras to him in London? Immediate suspicion pointed to the Hindujas. They stood to gain by discrediting George Fernandes. For over 12 years they had allegedly successfully stalled the Bofors investigation, but with George Fernandes and Arun Jaitley, they had reached a stone wall. When the counsel for Bangaru Laxman (then president of the BJP), Sunil Kumar questioned Aniruddha, the truth finally emerged:

> **Kumar**: So, you go to London with the idea of spy camera and briefcase and you get a gift of the spy camera and briefcase?
> **Bahal**: No. I went to London so that I could check out some equipment. I have lots of friends in the area. They are familiar with me, because I have done some stings in London, some of which came through and some did not. I am a sufficiently well-known name in cricket reporting and they respect me. So, I have friends and they thought of helping me out.
> **Kumar**: That is all right. We appreciate that. But before going to London you had the idea and you got these gifts in London. Do you think that the spy cameras or briefcase cameras, sophisticated equipment, these are all gift items?
> **Bahal**: It depends on who is giving them to you.
> **Kumar**: In the normal course of events?
> **Bahal**: I would not see these as normal gifts.
> **Kumar**: No?
> **Bahal**: No. They would be given to you by someone who knows about them and who knows what you need. This particular friend of mine, who himself

gave it to me, his name is Shekhar Bhatia. You can take it down. He is a mainstream journalist. He worked for *Daily Express*. Now he is a freelancer. He is a UK citizen. He has been a journalist for 20-25 years in London.

It was obvious that Aniruddha Bahal was apprehensive of giving Bhatia's name; wary of getting a friend involved in Tehelka's imbroglio. However, given the curiosity about the hidden cameras, it is worth getting into the details.

In answer to Sunil Kumar's questions, Bahal said:

Bahal: If you assemble a brand new, maybe both units combined may cost Rs 50,000. Believe me, it is cheap in London. If you go to the manufacturer, not the people in the shops but the people who are making it, you can get these concealed cameras for £50. You could get second-hand analogue devices. Analogue devices which we used are no longer in vogue. Sony has outdated them. So, these analogue devices, they were just going for second-hand prices.

Kumar: Will you kindly look at Page 8 of you affidavit dated 18 April 2000? It says:

"The pinhole is a wide-angle Plano convex lens (3.6mm to 4mm) covering 80 degrees or thereabouts. The scanning is of 400 television lines. The sensing device is 1/3 inches coloured CCD. Auto electronics IRIS (aperture) auto white balance (grey level). It has a sensitivity of 1 Lux D/N operating. Voltage of +12 volts. The make is possibly Kocum (South Korean)."

From where did you get these details?

Bahal: We called an audio-video specialist to our office, who had helped us previously with the equipment.

Kumar: But, did he not say that the details of the make, etc. could not be given without removing the camera by disturbing the briefcase and taking out the pinhole, etc. and so he has not touched that.

Bahal: No, he has not. I think he has opened it from outside. What he did was from the inside; he opened the small black box and he saw the circuits. He cannot unpeel it from the side. The problem in unpeeling from the side is that the alignment between the pinhole and the lens would go. And that is the crucial bit. Otherwise the camera hits a dark spot. So, if you unalign it from the pinhole then the whole purpose of the unit goes. The model number and make is maybe at the side to the wall.

The three cameras, in a briefcase, in a woman's handbag and in a tiepin, are mind-boggling to see. The briefcase and handbag look like any bags. The pinhole is so tiny that it is virtually undetectable to the naked eye. With the tiepin camera, one has to be excruciatingly careful to hide the cable connecting the controls through a hole in one's pocket. While it is on, it vibrates slightly.

Analysing Aniruddha's motives one has to accept that literary fiction influenced him immensely. In May 2003, Bahal published his own novel, *Bunker 13* (Faber and Faber). On 3 December 2003, Bahal won the Literary Review Bad Sex Award and was funnily enough quite happy about it. He said he got a free trip to London, connected with all his friends, met Sting who handed him the award, and it focused attention on his book. The guilty passage that got him there:

> She is topping up your engine oil for the cross-country coming up. Your RPM is hitting a new high. To wait any longer would be to lose prime time . . . She picks up a Bugatti's momentum. You want her more at a Volkswagen's steady trot. Squeeze the maximum mileage out of your gallon of gas. But she's eating up the road with all cylinders blazing.

You've got to laugh!

Did Tehelka have a political agenda against the BJP government? No. The sting would have been done no matter which party was in power at the time. Aniruddha pointed out, 'Whoever was in the tapes, it was their misfortune that it happened now. If dotcom money had been available and this easy venture of capital had been there early 1990, then maybe this would have happened to the Congress as well.'

Aniruddha also pointed out that the impact was deeper than it would have been in the 1990s because of the plethora of television channels. The BJP was not geared for instant reactions to microphones thrust in front of them. For the first 48 hours there was silence from the government. Aniruddha said,

> It took them 48 hours to think of some spin and then Arun Jaitley came out and Pramod Mahajan came out and a few others. By that time, Bangaru had resigned, so they had something to say and then they started spinning, *ki nahin Jain toh* he's a loudmouth, he's a braggart. Then their next spin was, one braggart was conning another braggart.

But there was the needling issue of the girls who were supplied to the army officers. I asked Samuel:

Madhu: Did Aniruddha ever bring up the moral issue, about what is right and what is wrong?
Samuel: No, he never told me. Suppose the story is running, this they needed. Then I informed to Aniruddha, these people are telling they need this much. The moment I got that, they are going on that way. I never want to deviate from that way, to some other way.
Madhu: Were you aware you were committing a crime? Why was the moral aspect of it not discussed at all?

Samuel: Uh, uh, suppose if you ask me this question, no. I'm really the hangover of the story. I'm rrreally keeeen on the story. I'm not even bothered about vaat security matter concerned, vaat are other moral things in between. I'm only focused on story. Twunty-four hours. My wife also shouted at me many times. I could not able to sleep every night. I would talk in the story sleeping. I was too keeeen and focused on story. I never even got a chance is vaatever we did is wrong or right.

Madhu: Let's talk about the girls. Did they ask for the girls?

Samuel: Yes. Sasi asked for the gells.

Madhu: For himself or for Sehgal?

Samuel: For Sehgal. How I know? I doesn't even know anything related to Dilli culture, really. I am coming from a very roooral background of Kerala. In my knowledge, the gells coming from Bawmbay. Malviya arranged. That is also verrry inntrussting. After "Singn-is-King" left, "Mister Style" [names changed] want to screw that woman. He started touching like that and she telling, I am feeling lots of cold, sne suddenly opened the door, and told me that he is just like my father's age, I don't allow. I said you can go. Then he complained also. Then I say, next time I will arrange a good babe. They will not say like that.

Madhu: Malviya was organizing these women … right?

Samuel: No, Malviya, yes, of course.

Madhu: Who organized the women?

Samuel: Malviya.

Madhu: No, who really did?

Samuel: Malviya.

Madhu: No, who organized them?

Samuel: Malviya. Malviya.

Madhu: He organized them?

Samuel: Yes, maddumm. Malviya organized them. Sasi fixed up a meeting with Kernel Sehgal Park Hotel. Before the meeting going Sasi is tell is Brigaydeer is very much intrussted female. Before fixing that meeting Sasi said you are not giving the money? We said we are not giving. We don't have the money. Definitely he will come. In further discussion, uh uh, you have to fix a female. Ana, so he will come. He will take drinks, take your hospitality, and then you will go. Then he said if you can take Mr Sehgal in your pocket it can help our company every time. So then it started going on little smooth way. But the female matter suddenly stuck up. This I told Malviya, *kaisey karey* [how do we do this]? Malviya said just give some time. I went outside to procorr likkker. Hotul *sey likkker zyada paisa* [the hotel liquor is expensive].

At another point in the interview, Samuel said that it was P. Sasi who got the liquor.

Madhu: Where were the girls from?

Samuel: They are from Bawmbay based. So his Bawmbay kannnekshun vurrrked out. He arranged. One officer only needed unnatural sex. But she won't take, no. That some conversation happened in between. Malviya fixed the problem. A big fight happened.

Madhu: Is the fight on tape?

Samuel: This is not on tape. This is off from camera. Vaat his demand? The female has to … She said I will not. Big fight happening, between gell and awfficer. And one of our awffiss's staff, Aniruddha's staff, sekitry acted like a call gell. She carried another one camera. She acted like, she will say I don't have, like headik, then she can move. She said I'm not well. I'll come back another day. Malviya arranged this gell. Malviya is a very terrific man. Sharma choose one girl. This guy had a problem with that gell. The unnatural sex matter. Malviya sorted out. He said you do it; these are the big people here. He'll give Rs 500, like that something happened. He convinced her. So after that everything we recorded. Aniruddha was downstairs. So there is lawt of jawks happening between these gells and everyone. (Heh, heh!) Sometimes they want to listen to music. How can I listen to music? Then nothing will recorded. Music will mix everything. They want to on the TV. So I said, "No TV."

Madhu: The reason?

Samuel: Reason is TV is on both sound will micksed.

Madhu: No, I mean, what reason did you tell them?

Samuel: TV and this kind of thing is not good for this space. Only this and consummate here, that's all.

⌒

In the Commission of Inquiry, Mathew Samuel was targeted on this issue. Notwithstanding all the intimidation tactics employed by the lawyers in full force in the Commission, Samuel did give as good as he got when he believed he was on firm ground.

For instance, R.P. Sharma, counsel for Colonel Anil Sehgal, in his cross-examination of Samuel:

Sharma: Would you please explain to the Honourable Commission that on your own admission, the girls, which you have provided . . . if no prostitutes were provided, I am asking you, what were the credentials of those girls then, if you say they were not prostitutes or, as is usually said, call girls? Who were they?

Samuel: They were women.

Sharma: For what purpose you provided them?

Samuel: That is better known to your client.

A heated discussion took place as the lawyer complained that Samuel had ruined the lives of the officers' families.

Samuel: May I answer the question? Denied.

Sharma: What have you denied?

Samuel: You have said that I have ruined the officers' families; the wives and daughters of the officers.

Sharma: That is the first question. This question is not that. This is the consequence of your misdeeds. As a journalist – you were a journalist – were you not aware that procuring a call girl for someone else is a serious crime punishable under Section 5 of the Suppression of Immoral Traffic in Women Act?

The moment a lawyer started quoting Acts and the law, Samuel was in quicksand.

Samuel: I do not know.

Sharma: Did Colonel Sehgal ask you to provide a call girl for him?

Samuel: Kernel Sehgal never asked me directly give me money; give me prostitutes. The demand comes through Sasi. If you allow me, I can show you the details.

The Commission of Inquiry on Tehelka did not permit Samuel to go into the details, but the Army Court of Inquiry not only showed the tapes in their court but also grilled the officers. The ninth witness in the ACI was Lieutenant Colonel Bhav Bhuti Sharma who was conspicuous in the Operation West End tapes for not wanting any money. His needs began and ended in a dark world of the erotic. He was ardently graphic in the unedited West End tapes:

3.75 centimetres ko millimetres meh convert karo to 375 hai. Bade-bade rajah, maharajah ... ek seh ek maharajah, Akbar-Bakbar voh ... rag meh Taj Mahal banava gaya uss chakkar mey, yeh dekhiye 1.5 inch keh chakkar meh banava gaya bechara. Aur kya hai? Ab martey dum bhi aadmi ki aankhey khuli rahti hai ki ek baar aur dikha do ki kaisi hai. Log pakad kar bundh kar detey hain ... bahut ho gaya bundh karo, ho gaya [convert 3.75 centimetres to millimetres to 375. Big kings ... each and every king, Akbar-Bakbar ... made the Taj Mahal for this entanglement ... look at this ... he built it for the 1.5 inch entanglement poor fellow. What else is there? Even when a man dies his eyes remain open that show to me once more what she is like. People then close them ... it is too much ... now close them.)

Sharma proved to be the unusual man who liked the lights switched off when he was with the girl.

5 Who is Tarun Tejpal? 'I'm a Mad Punjabi'

Aaron Altman [Albert Brooks]: Let's never forget, we're the real story, not them.
— James Brooks' film, Broadcast News *(1987)*

Army Court of Inquiry: Were you entertained by any call girls at Hotel Park on 18 September 2000?
Lieutenant Colonel B.B. Sharma: No. There were two girls who were present with us in the room. They were talking and they organized the drinks and snacks. They also used to go out and enter the room in between once in a while.
ACI: Were you alone with any girl in any room during your stay in the hotel?
Sharma: No.
ACI: Are you aware as to whether Colonel Anil Sehgal was with any girl alone in any room during your stay at the hotel?
Sharma: I am not aware nor did Colonel Anil Sehgal mention this to me.

The Army Court of Inquiry played a videotape.

ACI: Do you recognize yourself and Colonel Anil Sehgal in the video clippings that you had just seen?
Sharma: Yes, I can recognize myself and Colonel Anil Sehgal, as well as our voices in the tape.
ACI: It is shown on the videotape which you had just seen, that you and Colonel Anil Sehgal, during your discussion at the hotel, asked for two "parachute"/ "plastic *ka moja*" or words to that effect (implying condoms) from a nearby shop. Is this statement true, and if so, what for you asked them?

Sharma: I did make the statement, but I do not recollect in what context I made the said statement.

ACI: It is seen from the unedited videotape that when there was a conversation at the hotel regarding the call girls, you had asked where the girls had been kept. You were also seen and heard saying that two girls were to be brought but now there was one and what would happen to her or words to that effect. Did you make this statement? If so, in what context did you make the said statement?

Sharma: The statement made by me is factually correct. But I do not recollect in what context I said so since the statement was made under the influence of liquor.

ACI: It is seen/heard in the unedited videotape that when the man who was sent to get the condoms returned without them, you and Colonel Anil Sehgal claimed that it would be a risky affair to go ahead without them (implying condoms) since these days one has to be very cautious or words to that effect. Did you say so? If so, what were you referring to?

Sharma: I said so, but the conversation was regarding procuring spare parts for the aircrafts.

The court cautioned the witness that he was under oath and his answers should be truthful. 'Spare Parts?' Was Sharma's next line that he was late because of traffic? Or that he had missed school because his neighbour's grandmother died?

Sharma's 'ishtyle' of talking is unique. In a conversation with Colonel Sehgal and the Tehelka sting soldiers:

Sehgal: *Ek ghante baad hoga na? . . . tu, tum kya uper ek ghanta lagaoge. Tum jao, abhi jao* [after an hour it will happen, isn't it?... Are you going to take one hour upstairs? Go now].

Sharma: *Nahin, nahin, voh dikkat nahin hai. Kam to... do* minute *ka* 1.5 inch *ka khel hai sara* [no, no, there's no problem. It is a game of one minute of 1.5 inch].

Lieutenant Colonel Bhav Bhuti Sharma, was assistant director, Air Formation Signals at Air Headquarters when he participated in the shenanigans with his friend Colonel Anil Sehgal. His job included processing landline communication projects for sanction by the competent financial authority and provision of telephone exchanges. This also covered underground cables and fibre optic cables. He maintained liaison with BSNL, public-sector units and other suppliers of electronic equipment and supplies. He stated he was in no way involved in the procurement of any equipment for the army. Mathew Samuel had mentioned that Sharma was never interested in money.

In his statement, Sharma pointed out, as he was unaware that his conversations were being recorded, he was not under oath so there was no need for him to be careful about statements made in a casual atmosphere. You have to hand it to him for ingenuity. But, Sharma did discuss equipment procurement with Mathew Samuel. There are only a few noticeable points about Sharma on the Operation West End tapes. He is known for his store of jokes. Since he switched off the lights during his sexual encounter, the visual details are sparse but the audio is explicit. Most significant is how he boasts that in his department they do not have to go through any channels: can order the products themselves, without any interference from anyone.

On the West End tapes, Sehgal and Sharma were in the hotel room drinking and sharing stale, memorized jokes. The Tehelka sting operatives brought the conversation back to their own focus.

> **West End**: *Toh yeh toh sahab, yeh jo aapney kaha hai,* this, we can … *issmey aap jo cheez kahengey, hum sabh kara saktey hain* [so sir, the thing that you mentioned, we can get it done].
> **Sharma**: No, but I told you. We're basically … we are dealing with proprietary items. You have to tie up with those people.
> **West End**: *Hum* tie up *karva lengey. Aap jis sey boliyey, hum* tie knot *subh bandhva lengey* [we will tie it up in a knot. You tell us who; we will tie it up].
> **Sharma**: *Theek hai* [okay].
> **West End**: *Aap bataa dijeyey, aap hi ko bataana hai kissey tie bandhvana hai aur kissey knot bandhavana hai, kissko naada baandhana hai. Sub hum kar dengey. Aur aap pin se lekar jo bhi cheez aap kahengey hum pahunch a …* [you tell us who we can tie up, who to tie a knot with, who we tie with a tape. We will do it all. You tell us what to supply, from a pin onwards, we can supply that].
> **Sharma**: Thursday, Thursday *tak … Thursday ko 221 number kamrey mein aajao, Vayu Bhavan mein* [come to meet me in room number 221 at the Vayu Bhavan].
> **West End**: *Theek hai* [okay].
> **Sharma**: Then I'll explain to you. This is not the right time to explain to you. Because you will also not … you can grasp something, but I will not be able to put it across correctly. Then I'll show you what all is actually happening.

Sharma then explained to the West End team:

> **Sharma**: *Chaar* option *aatey hain na Crorepati mein? Toh hum aapko dus option dey dengey. Baaki ghumate turn kartey rehna* [they give you four options on Crorepati (the 'Kaun Banega Crorepati' programme on TV) we will give you ten options. Then you can keep spinning it].

The Army Court of Inquiry, of course, questioned Sharma about his meeting with Mathew Samuel in his office:

> **ACI**: What did you discuss with Mr Mathew Samuel?
> **Sharma**: On his enquiry, I told him that we undertake provisioning of some

electronic equipment and that the contract is awarded to the vendor selected by a board of officers as per existing procedure and tendering norms. On his asking me about payment and kickbacks, i told him that there is no system of kickbacks and everything is transparent in Air Force.

ACI: Did Mr Mathew Samuel inform you about the company which he claimed that he was representing?

Sharma: No. He did not tell me. In fact I came to know about M/s West End only when the present inquiry started. He did not give me any visiting card either.

ACI: If you did not know about the company of Mr Mathew Samuel or his antecedents as claimed by you, firstly, how did you clear him to visit your office and secondly, without knowing his job, was it right for you to part with the information which you provided to him especially when you are dealing with procurement of sensitive equipment?

Sharma: During our meeting at Hotel Park, Mr Mathew Samuel had expressed his desire to venture into communication sector. i presumed that he would have brought his company's profile for examination when he came to my office. Therefore, I allowed him to come to my office. The information which was given to Mr Mathew Samuel is commonly known to various vendors whom we deal with. I, in any case, was not involved with procurement of any equipment of sensitive nature. Therefore, in my opinion, there was nothing wrong in parting with the information I provided him.

The army court then asked Sharma why he spoke to Samuel at all in his office as he had not brought his company's profile. Sharma's answer again illustrates how good we are at answering questions without answering questions: 'Since they were venturing into communication sector, I generally gave him a rough idea about the procedure.'

However, all of West End operative's questions to Sharma were about army equipment procurement and not about any communications sector. The army court then proceeded to ask Sharma whether he took permission from any higher authorities to meet Samuel in his office, whether he informed any higher authority about the meeting, and whether he received any brochures of West End. Sharma answered in the negative to all of these questions.

It became apparent that Mathew Samuel did try to leave a bag of cash with Sharma at the Staff Officers Club, which he refused to take without asking what it contained.

How would you describe an air force officer whose only property is a 270 sq. yard plot in Lucknow, his wife is a teacher in the army school in Delhi Cantonment, is not interested in money but is willing to risk the little that he has for a few hours with a hired woman? Not evil. Just sad.

Lieutenant Colonel B.B. Sharma did not face a court martial. He was simply dismissed from the army through administrative action.

Bringing sex workers into Operation West End generated the greatest controversy around Tehelka. After Anjali Mody broke the story in *The Indian Express*, editors and journalists found a reason for not supporting Tehelka. It became officially sleazy. Traditionally, feminists have objected to prostitution as exploitation of women. This would certainly apply to minor girls being kidnapped or bought and then sold. However, many divergent and controversial views have emerged, which include perspectives from adult working sex workers who see it as a powerful method of economic empowerment. Tarun found himself in an excruciatingly uncomfortable position and said repeatedly he did not know Tehelka journalists were bringing sex workers into the story. Nobody believed he could not have known. But there was no reason for him to apologize for them. If Indian army officers are shown to be so vulnerable, it puts security on a pretty shaky footing. Yet Tarun has continued to be embarrassed and defensive on this issue. Pressure from the female journalist force in the Tehelka office was a factor.

N.K. Khetarpal, counsel for Major General P.S.K. Choudary, put Tarun on the spot:

Khetarpal: You had knowledge at that particular time that money was given to particular persons?

Tejpal: I did know that.

Khetarpal: Meaning thereby that you have authorized them to give money to different persons for the purpose of projecting your story?

Tejpal: As I said earlier, I have given Aniruddha Bahal a free hand to progress with the story as deemed fit.

Khetarpal: This free hand includes the employment of women for that purpose?

Tejpal: No. That is a separate issue. We have already clarified that. That is something we came to know later. Aniruddha will answer that himself, because it is not for us to answer that.

Khetarpal: I am asking you whether you authorized them?

Tejpal: I did not authorize.

Khetarpal: Meaning thereby that the use of women by Aniruddha Bahal and Mathew Samuel was without the authorization of Tehelka.com?

Tejpal: Yes. There was no authorization as such.

Khetarpal: But you own the correctness of such methods?

Tejpal: Given the circumstances of the case and what it revealed, I think the decision they took, which was in the heat of the story, I think in the long run the decision was not to be faulted so easily.

The day Tarun denied that he was not aware of the sex workers being used in the story, that was when the cracks in the relationship between Tarun and Aniruddha began to surface. C. Mohan Rao, counsel for Narender Singh, also targeted Tarun Tejpal on this issue:

Rao: You said you were not aware. But when you came to know about the use of prostitutes, did you approve of it?

Tejpal: I did not approve of it. But we tried to conduct ourselves as honourably as we could. Now that the footage had been obtained, we were honourable about the footage.

Rao: Did you ask them what necessitated the use of prostitutes?

Tejpal: Yes, I did.

Rao: What was the answer?

Tejpal: They said they needed to do it to stop the story from getting derailed.

Rao: How is it possible? If they did not provide prostitutes, how is it possible that the entire operation will get derailed?

Tejpal: You have to remember that Aniruddha Bahal and Mathew Samuel were not working as reporters of Tehelka.com. They were working as arms dealers. And clearly …

Rao: I am putting a simple question to you. You said that the explanation given by your reporters to you is that they have to utilize this method to prevent the operation from getting derailed.

Tejpal: I was trying to answer before you interrupted me. I was trying to say they were posing as arms dealers. These kinds of demands were made of arms dealers and they were trying to fulfil these demands so that the story would go on from wherever they were. They did not want to be exposed as not being arms dealers.

Rao: Your explanation is that they did not want to get derailed, in which case the operation cannot go forward. Is it the reason or they wanted to put pressure on the people?

Tejpal: I do not think that is the case. As I said, I cannot speak for these matters, because I was not present and I am not handling them.

Rao: I am putting one suggestion. It is directly by blackmailing that you are preventing it.

Tejpal: Certainly not.

Rao: What was the necessity, I am again putting it to you, to film this act? One is the question of demand and providing it.

Tejpal: It is a question that Aniruddha Bahal and Mathew Samuel will answer when it comes to them.

Rao: I am asking you as editor-in-chief. Just answer in general terms. You do not seem to have thought of what would have been in the mind of Bahal at that time. I am asking you what was the necessity of filming the act?

Tejpal: I would imagine, you have to see that there are 105 hours or more hours of tape. But the only relevant material is five or six hours. The point is that the camera is not controlled all the time in a sting operation. You switch it on because you do not know when you will catch the crime or catch the actual evidence. So, it is possible that the camera was switched on, because you did not know what you will get.

Rao: But your reporter knew at that time what is going to happen.

Tejpal: You would have to ask the reporter.

Rao: I am putting it to you as the editor-in-chief. What was the necessity of filming that?

Tejpal: You have to ask the reporter, as I said.

Rao: Can you find any reason for filming it?

Tejpal: I just gave you the reason. I said, you do not know at what point evidence will present itself. You have no control over these cameras. Because, once they are set up, they just keep moving. Then you cannot say, all right something is happening, I am going to start this. It is a sting operation.

Rao: Do you know that there are two different rooms and the person went into another room only for this and there was no scope of any further evidence except the filming of the very act itself?

Tejpal: No. I do not know whether there were two rooms or anything else of that kind.

Rao: Is it not clear that your reporters were filming the army officers having intercourse? Is it not clear to you?

Tejpal: Is it not clear? What is there on the tapes is there on the tapes. If they are on the tapes, nobody can deny what is on the tapes. It is clear to both of us.

Rao: Do you know that the wives of both army officers, Colonel Sehgal and Brigadier Iqbal Singh, have complained that their husbands were blackmailed by Tehelka after filming them in a compromising position?

Tejpal: I deny that completely.

〜

If you look at the sting operation as a whole, for Bahal and Samuel, testing the officers' honesty was done through money, gifts such as gold chains, pastries, and then women just became part of the package. For them, it was to prove that army officers can be compromised through many methods, women being one of them. It does raise Tarun's question: 'Suppose we had been the ISI?' Supposing the women had been part of the ISI network? But, Bahal and Samuel could have considered that there was an important problem about using women, in that it raises the issue about *their* rights as only one of them knew she was being filmed.

Tarun earlier said in one of his cross-examinations that no Tehelka staffer was involved in the sex tapes. Later, he corrected that version. Kirit Rawal, additional solicitor general for the Union of India (unfortunately, Kirit Rawal died on 26 April 2005 after a brave fight against cancer), raised this issue:

Rawal: Were you at this point of time aware as to who were the girls who were working for this?

Tejpal: No. I was not.

Rawal: Is it true, because it is one of the facts which has come in the affidavit that even a person who was working in your organization was requested to perform those services?

Tejpal: That is not true at all.

Rawal: Was any of your female staffers part of the sting operation?

Tejpal: Not part of any sexual activity.

Rawal: I am talking of the sting operation.

Tejpal: Not to my knowledge. You will get a more accurate response from Aniruddha Bahal.

Rawal: Are you aware that *The Indian Express* of 24 August 2001, carried a story: "Tehelka today said that some staffers posed as prostitutes during the sting operations under the guise of multinational arms dealer. The head of the investigation team of Tehelka, Aniruddha Bahal, said this while dismissing fears about women used by the team being exposed."

Tejpal: The story was denied the day it appeared.

Rawal: You have denied that. Tehelka.com denied it … and this is what I am quoting to you, In a statement here today, Tehelka editor-in-chief, Tarun Tejpal said: "… the information was given to me by Aniruddha Bahal." In response to question on the safety of the prostitutes, he said that there was no intention of ever releasing the tapes involving the prostitutes and there was no question of their coming to any harm. Bahal went on to say that, in fact in one session one of our staffers went posing as a prostitute. "It was a pre-planned thing. Our staffer feigned an asthma attack to make her escape. It was all planned."

Tejpal: Bahal will have to answer that question.

⌣

The lawyers of those caught on tape often raked up the issue of sex on the Tehelka.com website as a means of discrediting the entire operation. Sunil Kumar, counsel for Bangaru Laxman, set sail on a red herring boat with Tarun:

Kumar: Would you please tell this Commission whether the "S Spot" was on your website?

Tejpal: What is the "S Spot"?

Kumar: If there was any.

Tejpal: I do not think so. Nothing comes to mind when you say "S Spot" I have heard of "G Spot" but not "S Spot".

Kumar: "S Spot" is an advisory on sex, which was on the site of Tehelka. I have downloaded it and I will get it marked and exhibited also before the Commission. Was there an "Erotic Reader" on your website?

Tejpal: There was.

Kumar: This "S Spot" was not part of the "Erotic Reader"?

Tejpal: If you are asking me, was there or is there a sexual advisory on the site, there was and continues to be a sexual advisory on the site, where a very eminent sexologist from Chennai gives advice to a lot of confused souls about sexual issues. It is still there. It was there and it is still there now.

Kumar: Does it have the title "S Spot" now?

Tejpal: "S Spot" does not strike me. But if it is about a sexual advisory on the site, it is there even now. It was not just then.

Kumar: How many items of sex you keep on the site?

Tejpal: I will not be able to tell you accurately, but I think the advisory is updated every two weeks. It depends on when the readers write in. There are questions of all kinds. When the questions are asked, they are sent to the sexologist, who is in Chennai. He answers those questions. They are put on the site, where the readers can access them.

Kumar: I am not on the questions. I am on sex items on your site; the items of sex on your site.

Tejpal: Define items of sex? What items on sex? Is it that there are stories about the sexual mores of Indians? That could be a sex item. Are you asking, do we put up any pornography? We do not put up any pornography. I have never put up any pornography.

Kumar: When you are on a website, if you go for a search on sex, it says you have so many items. That is what I meant when I asked you whether your website has items of sex.

Tejpal: It does not as a rule.

Kumar: I would like to confront the witness with some results from the website. Please look at page 5 of the compilation. "Search Results" from Tehelka.com found 437 items on the subject of sex. I am showing 1 to 10. Do you admit that this is a correct representation?

Tejpal: It may well be correct.

Kumar: Will you please answer yes or no and then give your explanation?

Tejpal: I cannot answer yes or no if it deviates from the truth. I said it may well be, because as my own counsel also said, there is no way I can be standing here and tell you that these are 437 items – as everybody knows, Net allows manipulations. But I am willing to give you the benefit of doubt. It may well be correct. You can carry it from there.

Kumar: … These are the articles or items, which are available, just like "Erotic" found 108 items, now showing 41 to 50.

Tejpal: I would like to make one minor clarification. If somebody keys in a word, for example, "erotic" into the search engine, then wherever the word "erotic" appears, you could be saying "I find eating apples extremely erotic" – it could show as one entry. That is one thing you have to keep in mind that whenever the word appears, no matter how many times it appears it will show that …

Kumar: Kindly look at those items, what is given. It is not that a word erotic has been found.

〜

Justice Venkataswami lost his patience with this lawyer:

Venkataswami: What is your question on this?

Kumar: You are reported to have made this statement: "A core editorial ambition of Tehelka.com was to create a media platform that reflects and process life in all its range, from highbrow to lowbrow, from high culture to low culture, from cerebral to sexual; more than politics, art, and sports, sex is intrinsic to our life."

Tejpal: I stand by that statement entirely. Even today I stand by that.

Kumar: My suggestion to you at this moment is that Tehelka.com was no journalistic endeavour of yours. It was a purely money-making device by sensationalizing these things significantly by featuring sex on your website.

Tejpal: I deny that entirely.

Well, Sunil Kumar certainly took his time getting there. Does the fact that Tehelka might have been using the subject of sex to increase traffic to the site in any way discredit what was found on the tapes?

Kajal Basu, features editor with Tehelka, who was in the thick of it when Operation West End was being constructed, spoke about the women used in the sting.

Madhu: Tarun said in the Commission that he didn't give his approval to use girls in the sting.

Basu: That's crap. There's no way. There is absolutely no way, because he was in touch with them on day-to-day basis. They were sitting upstairs all the time, having these marathon meetings and discussions. But what is appalling is that even after obviously having planned it for so long, they did not reach the conclusion that you shouldn't be taping anything at all. Stop the camera at the door.

Madhu: But the camera is in there by itself. Nobody could walk in and switch it off.

Basu: That's true. But, again in terms of story itself, I don't think the story would have been possible in any other country. Certainly not anywhere in the West, because America has the law of entrapment.

I asked Tarun about how the erotica channel on the Tehelka website was constantly brought up in the Commission of Inquiry:

Tejpal: Yes, it was brought up in the Commission, I said, "Yes, of course, we did", because my conviction was that sexuality is not just intrinsic, but it is an incredibly intrinsic part of all our lives, boss. Probably more than fucking politics and cinema. How do we just completely slice off all kinds of representations we do in mass media or in art? Even in writing and art, all this precious stuff, this inability to engage directly with something that is so fundamental to us. It just leaves me cold. The obsession was to create a platform – that's why

Tehelka had a phenomenal literary channel. At the other end we had this hardcore investigative streak, where it was about giving freedom to the people to pursue stories.

Tarun has always been a huge fan of Naipaul, to the point of hero worship. Naipaul, being one of the first of his genre of writers, did not have an easy beginning. The rejections and struggle to make it are then only seen as part of the process. With Naipaul's precedent in mind, there is a romance in the struggle. Yet it is only romantic if it culminates in success. Tarun was dogged about making it. But not, funnily enough, as a famous investigative journalist. Hardly anyone believed him, when he was cross-examined in the Commission of Inquiry on Tehelka, when he said he did not know the details of what Aniruddha Bahal and Mathew Samuel were doing. He said he would get a general report every fortnight or so, without any real specifics. Curiously, he was doing what he was least equipped to do. In fact, Tarun was living the Peter Principle. He was not writing. When Tehelka broke the story, Tarun was in the forefront. All over the press, giving interviews on television. He had to stand by his reporters and by his company. Tarun said, 'I didn't do the story. My dignity lay in standing by my fucking reporters; fighting to the last and seeing it through. My original gift lay in creating the space for them to do it. I'm trying to the best of my ability and I will see it through till the end.'

Tarun Tejpal has repeatedly brought up 'Kafkaesque' in his interviews in the aftermath of the Tehelka exposé, and it is in character for him to relate a situation to literature. It speaks loudly about his interior life, how he sees himself, and how he sees others around him: through literature, a prism through which he seems to have lived all his life.

The son of an army officer, Tarun went to school all over the country: Bangalore, Mumbai, Bareilly, Jhansi, and finally went to DAV College in Chandigarh, majoring in economics. Although he passed his exams with a first division, he never bothered to collect his degree. It became a joke in *India Today* magazine, with the personnel department, which could not understand why a man who had only passed high school was rising in the magazine and getting huge jumps in salary. Reading played a central role in his growing years and Tarun always knew he wanted to be a writer. His army officer father had a huge influence on Tarun, including him in conversations about the United Nations, history, and literature. Even so, his identity through his college career was shaped by sports and, according to Tarun, he was a 'jock and a college star'. He said he didn't attend a single class; only played basketball for Punjab University and enjoyed stipends for food and shoes. With a decided antipathy towards formal education, Tarun also mentioned he was a debating star and president of the Speakers' Association of the college as well as the Quizzers' Association. He got a first division in his college degree by studying for three days, which he eloquently explained: 'That's the *hokum* of the fucking system, boss. *Tum do din pad lo, na, dus saval pad lo, yeah, dus mein se teen aa gaye, to first aah gaye. Ek aya tho pass ho gaya. Teen aah gaye, panch aah gaya toh* you're a star, *yaar* [you study for two days, study ten questions, out of ten if three questions come, you get a first division. If one comes, then you pass. If three come or five come, you are a star]'.

His first job was with the late Marcus Mirch, a stage actor who produced a magazine called *India 2000*. When the office closed in the evenings, Tarun would go for a walk around Chandni Chowk, the ancient bazaar in Old Delhi, drink lassi at the railway station, and return to sleep in the office as he had no money to rent even a garret. *India 2000* closed down, and Tarun returned to Chandigarh where he did nothing but read for ten months. In 1985, insanely in love with Geetan, now his wife, Tarun was determined to write but had to find a job before marrying her in the face of the disapproval of her parents. Both Geetan and Tarun walked into editor Rahul Singh's office in *The Indian Express*. He hired Tarun at Rs 2100 a month and Geetan as a trainee. Armed with his job, Tarun invited Geetan's parents to his parents' home and basically told them,

> I give a fuck for your middle-class moralities, your middle-class ambitions; what you want your daughter to do, what you want me to do. I'm really not interested in you. I'm going to do what I'm going to do. Apart from which I'm going to get married to your daughter next month. If you guys want to come, you can come. If you guys don't want to come, it's fine by me.

They got married but Tarun recalls the ceremony was a dismal affair, with only a handful of people from Geetan's family. Within six months, Tarun quit *The Indian Express* and joined *The Telegraph*. When Tarun applied to M.J. Akbar, the editor, for leave he was told: 'Punjab is too important now. You can't go on leave.' Tarun gave in his resignation.

Four months out of work, with the arrival of a baby and no money, Tarun took up Shekhar Gupta's offer to come for an interview at *India Today*, Delhi. Tarun was the rare person who did not want to become a correspondent and opted for the copy desk. Prabhu Chawla negotiated his salary down to Rs 4500 on a trial basis, upon which Tarun promptly asked for a loan of Rs 2000 to get his belongings from Chandigarh. Tarun said he enjoyed his run with *India Today* and found a great equation with the editor-in-chief, Aroon Purie. He ran the books section and then, encouraged by Aroon, started writing essays for the magazine. After five years he was bored. 'The curious part about *India Today* is you learn a lot,' Tarun recalls,

> But one of the great failings of *India Today* is that it doesn't have the innate flexibility to accommodate eccentricity, excessive talent, and some amount of maverick behaviour. It is a mistake to imagine that you can put everybody into the same kind of mould. Because the best people will never fit your mould, boss, and you have to have room for your best people. It was so difficult to leave *India Today*. The one great gift Aroon has is that he has the ability to create the illusion that "This is the world". When you work in *India Today* or *Aaj Tak*, everybody who works there thinks "This is the world". I was one guy who used to keep knocking it, saying, please remember *India Today* is only a drop in the world. The world is a very big place, boss. But the people who were working there thought, "This is it".

Prabhu Chawla, who had by then joined *The Financial Express*, hired Tarun as consulting editor to revamp the paper. Tarun was out of there in six months, and met Deepak Shourie, who had left *India Today* to start a weekly magazine called *Outlook*. Tarun joined Vinod Mehta, the editor-in-chief of *Outlook*, who said about him, 'He was my number two here but he became absentee number two'. Mehta said he would come for half an hour in the morning and disappear for three-hour lunches. Tarun was busy with a publishing company he had started, Indialnk, and parties. Mehta recalled that he gave Tarun an introduction to V.S. Naipaul, who was Mehta's friend, and found that pretty soon Tarun had ensconced himself as Naipaul's friend. Mehta said, 'Most of the time he was spending cultivating his own sort of relationships, which had nothing to do with work'. The bust up came on a really bad day when Mehta was trying to close the issue for the week. As he paced up and down, he realized he was missing a deputy editor. Mehta could not take it any longer. He peremptorily told Tarun 'I don't think you are in this. If you don't want to work here, you leave'. Mehta said that since he had shouted at Tarun in front of the other staff, Tarun decided to leave. Mehta didn't stop him. He said, 'Tarun did not even serve out his notice period and in three days he was gone'.

Mehta believed that Aniruddha had already put Tehelka in place when Tarun joined him. He didn't have too many options. He had burnt his bridges with Prabhu Chawla (now back at *India Today*) and not much was happening in the publishing business. Mehta said that when Tarun was with *Outlook*,

> He was fretting about a lot because he wanted to become famous. He wanted to become big. He wanted to be editor-in-chief. He wasn't sure whether he wanted to be a journalist or not, maybe some hot-shot publisher. It didn't matter which area. He wanted to be famous. So he started Indialnk and had one big book but could not stay the course. The publishing ended in court with his partner. In journalism, also, he wasn't sure. It was just taking too long for him. He was number two, or number three here. In *India Today*, he was not even that. But he was seen as a bright spark. If he had stayed the course maybe another five, seven, eight years, maybe he would have risen to the top in *India Today*. But I think, that waiting period was hurting him too much.

Mehta reckoned that Tarun saw Tehelka as his big opportunity:

> Once the Tehelka sting was done, Tarun moved in a big way. In the projection of Tehelka I think he played a major role, which Aniruddha may not have been able to play. I think there was some resentment on the part of Aniruddha that most of the kudos of Tehelka are going to Tarun, when actually Aniruddha had done all the hard work. And Tarun had just done the presentation.

Although Tarun said that Vinod Mehta was a great person to work with, he realized that there could be only one editor and he itched to hold the reins in his own hands to create his own vision. Kajal Basu, features editor in Tehelka, spoke about Tarun:

> Writing is his strength. We always thought that he should be writing. But I think somewhere along the line, Tarun actually made a fairly radical decision that his strengths lay in organizing rather than writing himself. Which is why he started IndiaInk along with Sanjeev Saith. He wrote some wonderful poetry while he was in *The Express* in Chandigarh. He never carried that forward. It was the decision that he took somewhere that, at the end of the day, he wasn't going to be the creative person but would opt to foster creativity. He was frustrated with that. He used to keep complaining all the time that he is meeting about 10-20 people a day. Trying to get funds, whatever. I don't know how much of that was a romanticized sense of his own place in the scheme of things. I do think he imagined himself as a fairly big magnate. But you've got to know if you are capable of building or holding on to an empire. I think Tarun has been ambitious for a long time.

While interviewing the Tehelka team, I found numerous characteristics common to all of them. The most important was a pinpointed focus that they wanted to do more than the ordinary that makes everything else trivia; fall by the wayside. Everything boiled down to that one focus.

Tarun, Aniruddha Bahal, and even Mathew Samuel, for all the differences in their personalities, have common characteristics. Known for his theories on humanist psychology, American psychologist Abraham Maslow's term 'self actualization' closely mirrored these Tehelka characters. Tarun's path, as Abraham Maslow said, involved the continuous desire to fulfil potentials, to 'be all that you can be'. It is a matter of becoming the most complete, the fullest, 'you'.

Carl Rogers developed it further and described it as a single 'force of life' he calls 'the actualizing tendency'. We're not just talking about survival: Rogers believed that all creatures strive to make the very best of their existence. If they fail to do so, it is not for a lack of desire, but because their basic needs are not met. As Maslow explains it, there are capacities that clamour to be used and cease their clamour only when they are well used. The unused capacity can become a disease centre or else atrophy and disappear, thus diminishing a person. Every moment then is an urge to meet that fulfilment. This is far more than just the ambition to be rich. The person then evolves to becoming complete, developing to the fullest extent in his Self, which makes the term 'self actualization' self-explanatory.

Maslow gives examples of people who were self-actualized: Eleanor Roosevelt, Mahatma Gandhi, and Albert Einstein. To that I would add, Mother Teresa, Vinoba Bhave, Kiran Bedi, Medha Patkar, Baba Amte, Aruna Roy. This does not mean that the person has to accomplish worldwide fame, although it would not unexpectedly happen. It simply means being so narrowed to your goals that nothing else matters. Maslow lists many characteristics, but one that is most applicable is a difficult word, but still worth looking at:

Gemeinschaft. This means the qualities of social interest, compassion, and humanity. This archetype resists acculturation, that is, they are not susceptible to social pressure – they are indeed nonconformists but not necessarily rebels. There is an unwillingness to conform just for the sake of it.

Okay, Tarun is no Gandhi, but his life is a clear process of realizing the actualized man that can be simplified by some to a mere voracious ambition. One person he worked for raised doubts about Tarun's integrity. 'I'm not so sure about Tarun and what he did,' he said, with narrowed eyes. He could have been expedient in the effort to realize his ultimate goals, but he does epitomize the actualized man, in that, he strongly believes in a *method* of journalism: to write with freedom, without the shackles of some editor ordering you to temper your views so as not to offend powerful authorities or commercial interests. Tarun got restless when he found his life in a state of homeostasis, however successful it was in other people's eyes. The *jholawala* in him will never quite go away. Clearly, he does not identify himself with the powerful or owners of companies, although he owns Tehelka. There is thus a dichotomy there: now in a position of deciding the future of people who work for him, he still sees himself as the underdog, just doing a job.

> **Madhu:** Tehelka was part of the dotcom fever and money was big, so it had to be part of your goal to make big bucks.
>
> **Tejpal:** No, the most important thing was to get a chance to do journalism the way you would like to do it. To actually not just be a journalist, but be an owner of the kind of journalism you do. Because I had great frustration, both through *India Today* and *Outlook*, because in *India Today*, we were made into masons. People like me wanted to be architects. If somebody had given me funding to start a magazine, or television channel, paper, I would have done that more readily. But money at that stage in time was miraculously available for dotcoms, so I took that route. I have always talked about my idea of both great art and great media, which is that they should marry ideally both high culture and low culture. I'm not just a guy who reads Franz Kafka. I'm also a guy who can look at pornography and get turned on. I'm not just a guy who likes to listen to a bit of one sonata, I'm also a guy who likes to fucking kiss my wife's ass. What I'm saying, high and low culture is part of all our lives. And there is actually no disjunction there. It's the frailty of being human. In my opinion, a great media platform should reflect our lives in entirety, not just one aspect of it. That's why we had an erotica channel.

The Commission of Inquiry, before which Tarun had presumed he would see the corrupt punished, turned out differently. Very differently. It was intriguing that in the millions of questions thrown at the Tehelka team, there was a screaming absence of questions from the government lawyers to those Caught on Tape (COT). A point that Tarun made in his cross-examination by (the late) Kirit Rawal:

Rawal: With regard to the various allegations and the transactions in question, what would you think of the Honourable Commission of Inquiry?

Tejpal: I have, as I said, full faith in the Commission of Inquiry, but I have also seen the government stance, which you represent in the Commission of Inquiry. I know for a fact that the government has not bothered, and you the Counsel did not even bother to cross-examine any of the other witnesses. I know that the government has not bothered even to file a single line in any of the affidavits that have been filed in the Commission against any of the other witnesses, or any of the other accused. I know for a fact that the government has filed reams and reams of totally dishonest affidavits against us and I know today I am standing here, being cross-examined by the additional solicitor general of India, for one full day. I suppose that pretty well establishes the prejudice of the government.

On whether Tarun believed the government was taking appropriate action, namely the Army Court of Inquiry, Rawal asked again:

Rawal: My question is, is this action or inaction?

Tejpal: I doubted it because we were at the end of one and a half months of being charged with all kinds of completely baseless charges from conspiracy theory to ISI, Dawood Ibrahim and there was nothing that had not been thrown at us.

On further questioning, Tarun pointed out the unfairness of the treatment meted out to Tehelka:

Tejpal: What we are saying is that while there is constant action against Tehelka which, in an ideal situation, should have been lauded for the public interest work it did. Instead of that, while Tehelka is being acted against, there is no discernable sign of any action against those found guilty, including by the government counsel at the Commission. I will say that. No government counsel at the Commission has bothered to file an affidavit against those found guilty of corruption or even to cross-examine them.

Rawal: As far as the government counsel are concerned, or even your counsel are concerned, they act as per instructions of the clients. They are not independent. I am trying to explain it. Do not take it as personal.

Tejpal: Clearly, from what the honourable additional solicitor general says, it shows that the government, who is your client, is interested in probing us and not those found guilty of corruption.

Rawal: If I do not cross-examine those army officers who have been extensively cross-examined by others and I have no facts to elicit from them. Here "I" mean the government cross-examining them, because these are army officials who have come forward and they have to say what they have to say. Government has no view, because it wants to be informed as to what the Commission may conclude. Is it something, which is favourable or unfavourable to the government? What is cross-examination?

Tejpal: I think what is important is that government has not resolved in trying to nail the only people who have been found guilty of corruption. I think the government has only resolved to nail those who have done the hard work of exposing corruption.

Milan Kundera writes about Kafka:

> He does not ask what internal motivations determine man's behaviour. He asks a question that is radically different: what possibilities remain for man in a world where the external determinants have become too overpowering that internal impulses no longer carry weight?

Anyone who has faced the Indian legal system will recognize the experience. Before your case comes to court, the planning, the choice of lawyer to face which particular judge and what plea you will take that will give the judge the opportunity to rule in your favour, are decisions that will establish your fate. Tarun and the entire Tehelka team found themselves embroiled in the machinations of the Commission. They had no other life.

What Tarun experienced was borderline humiliation: being politely, officially, interrogated as if he was a financial scamster, a traitor, and, yes, even a sexual pervert. One lawyer questioned Tarun on being a pimp and his wife as 'available'. This was a world away from the vision Tarun had of himself as a writer and his work. The most curious aspect was that Tarun for his own part had done nothing. Yet stood accused. He took responsibility for 'almost' everything about Operation West End.

In his deposition with his own lawyer Kavin Gulati, Tarun explained his involvement in Operation West End:

> **Tejpal:** I would like to reiterate here that Tehelka does not just do investigation. It does 20 stories a day. The best of writers and columnists in the world write for Tehelka. At that time when we broke the story, we had 40 journalists working in the office. There was a lot of journalistic work going on that had nothing to do with the investigation. There are seven editors in Tehelka. I was responsible for looking after them. Aniruddha Bahal runs his investigative cell separately, largely because it was very, very necessary in the investigation department to keep a high degree of secrecy, because the kind of stories that they were doing could get jeopardized very easily if there was loose talk happening. In fact, the investigation cell within the office is separate from the rest of the editorial.

Gulati: Questions are being raised about ethics of such a sting operation. Do you think that such an operation was ethical?

Tejpal: Absolutely. I have no doubt at all about the ethics of the sting. Apart from the fact that such stings are carried out all over the world and they are ways of exposing corruption. I am absolutely clear that in a country like ours – where corruption has become so rampant and it has become impossible to shame our public figures – the journalists need more and more resourceful and aggressive means to unearth what is wrong with people who are in public office. Here I would like to draw a very clear line, and it is a line that Tehelka has followed, that we are not interested, Tehelka is not interested, in the private lives of anybody. The only thing that Tehelka looks at is people who abuse public money, public power and public office. If you look at the Tehelka tapes, or any other investigations that Tehelka has done, they are always not focused on the private life of individuals; they are rightly focused on the abuse of public office.

When R.P. Sharma, counsel for Colonel Anil Sehgal cross-examined Tarun, he asked him about the ethics of a sting operation:

Sharma: Are you aware that in the United States, except the FBI, no other agency can undertake a sting operation?

Tejpal: Are you aware that in England every journalist undertakes this?

Sharma: I am asking you a question about USA. You cannot put a counter question to me.

Tejpal: I am not totally aware of USA. But I have been told that there it is a grey area.

Sharma: It is not a grey area. I will give you material. It is a fact. It is only in India all these things are allowed.

Tejpal: In England?

Sharma: You say, "I don't know about America." I do not know about England.

Tejpal: Let me tell you, in England it is par for the course all the time.

Sharma then changed the subject.

During the Tehelka team's cross-examinations, it emerged that none of them had ever read the Code of Conduct laid down by the Press Council. If you are undertaking a sting operation, it wouldn't have hurt to check out just how far one can go. But had they strictly followed the code, they would not have been able to undertake it at all. Come to think of it, most journalists would not have read it until summoned by the Press Council.

N.K. Khetarpal, counsel for Major General P.S.K. Choudary, too zeroed in on Tarun on the subject of ethics:

Khetarpal: Are you aware that there is a code of conduct laid down for journalists?

Tejpal: I am not aware of any code of conduct.

Khetarpal: Do you call Aniruddha Bahal and Mathew Samuel as journalists?

Tejpal: I think they will go down in Indian journalistic history as the finest investigative reporters.

Khetarpal: I put it to you that the Press Council of India in the year 1996 has laid down the details of the code of conduct to be followed by journalists.

Tejpal: I am afraid I have not read them.

Khetarpal: I am reading out to you from the norms of journalistic conduct laid down by the Press Council under the chairmanship of Mr P.B. Sawant. I will read those which are important and relevant here.

Tejpal: I would like to say here that Mr P.B. Sawant, whom he is quoting, has been on record a dozen times to applaud Tehelka's West End investigation. The guidelines that have been read out are all extremely honourable. But almost all of them have a distinct qualifier – you can go through them one by one – and the qualifier is, "unless it is in the public interest". Our investigation was nothing except in public interest.

⌣

Vibha Datta Makhija, counsel for Sudhir Choudhrie, questioned Tarun on the ethics of not cross-checking names for verification of statements. When Makhija said, 'You are not ruling out there would be some inconsistencies, some untruth and some vacuum might be there in your stories. Tarun responded, 'I said that. Nobody says we are foolproof. We work with limited resources. No matter what our intentions are, it is difficult business. We may have made some glitches, we may have made mistakes. But there is nothing motivated or with intention'. Makhija asked whether he could vouch for whatever was said on the tape was true. Tarun replied, 'A lot of allegations or comments that were made would require further investigation for which we never had the resources'.

Makhija got what she wanted on record for her client.

⌣

Kavin Gulati, counsel for Tehelka, gave an opportunity to Tarun to explain why Tehelka broadcast the story nationally, without going to the government:

Gulati: If you were doing this story in national interest, why did you not show these tapes to a responsible state functionary, such as the president or the prime minister? Why did you straight away show this on national TV?

Tejpal: I think the journalist's understanding of national interest is the people of India, and in our case it is the people of India. I think the national interest is reflected through the people. The journalists are responsible not to the systems of authority but to the people. If anything, they are meant to be the watchdogs of the various pillars of authorities. As far as we were concerned, we were very clear that the story belonged with the public in the public domain and I have to say this, that for two or three months we lived in immense fear, immense tension that if a word of the story got out, somebody would raid us, somebody would seize the tapes or somebody would attack us. We knew that there are many vested interests involved in a story like this, who would be upset by the fact of our exposure. We were very afraid; very, very tense. The moment we managed to start screening the story on March 13 at the Hotel Imperial, it was at that time that we first began to feel a sense of relief, because we felt now the story is in the public domain, now everybody is responsible for the story, not just us. It is true it may not have turned out that way, but that is the way we felt when we broke the story, and I still think the story actually belongs to the public. Our own interaction with the establishment has been very, very disappointing. We have no reason at all to trust the establishment on any issue. I do not think we could have gone to the establishment with the story.

The Hinduja name created another problem. In the dotcom boom, one of the keys of survival was to supply content to other websites. In normal circumstances, it would mean nothing. However, for journalists who had just undertaken a sting operation to unearth corruption in arms deals, to approach the Hindujas for a business deal was bound to raise questions. With the Hinduja name associated with the Bofors scandal since 1987, it was a curious coupling. When Tehelka had taken such a high moral ground on corruption in arms deals, the decision to go to the Hindujas, even for something as harmless as selling content, was injudicious and hypocritical.

Kirit Rawal, additional solicitor general for the Union of India, took issue with Tarun on this:

Rawal: Mr Tarun, you mentioned in one of the answers a few days back that you had gone for a meeting with the Hindujas but actually did not meet them.
Tejpal: I said, I had gone to the building where their office is situated. We have a correspondent in London called Charulata Joshi. She does business development and writes for us for the website. She is a journalist. At that point, we were trying very hard to get some revenue arrangement with various other portals. The only thing we have to sell is content. Among the people she had spoken to, it seems that Hindujas also had a website. So, when I was in London, she said, "I am going to meet them. Would you like to come along?" She told me that they were also keen to meet me. I actually went to their office with her. But I did not go in, because I was aware, and I am glad that I did not go in, that anything I do at this moment could be misconstrued or painted in the wrong light, particularly by the government. So, I actually never went in. Till date I have never met or spoken to any of the Hinduja brothers.
Rawal: This awareness: when did it come?
Tejpal: I said, actually I was at the building. Then I did not go in. It then struck

me that it would be misconstrued, no matter what our intentions were, they would be misconstrued. By then there has been a well-established history of everything that we did being misconstrued.

Rawal: How long did you wait when she carried on that meeting?

Tejpal: Around half an hour, up or down 5 or 10 minutes. I actually did not stay there. I went down the road, sat in McDonald's and ate a burger or something.

Rawal: You felt that your going would be a problem. But your authorized representative going is not a problem.

Tejpal: That is correct.

Rawal: You had mentioned on that day – correct me if I am wrong, because I was not present – when you deposed, you mentioned that they were also involved in arms deal and that is one of the reasons why you actually did not go into their office.

Tejpal: That is right.

Rawal: This awareness of Hindujas being arms dealers came to your mind only after you entered their office?

Tejpal: I think there is no Indian who is not aware of that. We are all aware of it. But the fact that it can be misconstrued; that all kinds of sinister motives could be read into it, that particular awareness came right there and I took the decision there is no way I am going in there. I did not want to meet any of them.

Rawal: I put it to you that this whole story of having gone and not met them is wrong.

Tejpal: That is totally wrong. It is absolutely true.

⌣

Then Rawal changed the subject. It is intriguing, that lawyers ask why did you think this at this time, why not at that time? Does anyone know why a certain thought occurs at a particular time and not at another? Just by raising the oddity of the time of thought, it makes the thought appear false and insincere. I was also told by Kirit Rawal that there was a close connection between Tarun Tejpal and the Hindujas. He pointed out that Ram Jethmalani was the Hindujas' lawyer. Jethmalani is also Tehelka's lawyer. Charulata Joshi is very close to Jethmalani. Her wedding took place at Jethmalani's house. Ipso facto, the Hindujas must have bought Tehelka the spy cameras in London, put the money in Shankar Sharma's Mauritius shell company, in which there are two NRI partners, and hit George Fernandes who was going after them in the Bofors case. Sounds interesting as conspiracy theories go, but it has too many holes and is largely based on conjecture.

Shankar Sharma's lawyer Mahesh Jethmalani elaborated on this:

Madhu: Kirat Rawal, the Union of India lawyer, said that there was a connection between Tarun Tejpal and Hindujas.

Jethmalani: These are irrelevant coincidences, really. Frankly, you can't say that because two people were in a particular place, they conspired to commit murder. These are harmless coincidences, whereas it's got to be much deeper than that. If you infer conspiracy from such innocuous circumstances then everybody is a conspirator in this country. The fact of the matter was that they were caught in the wrong. They were caught with their pants down. Supposing it was the Hindujas? Let me put it differently: so what? It doesn't make your wrongdoing any less condemnable, just because the ultimate source was somebody who himself was tainted. You've got to judge what happened on that tape on its own merit, irrespective of who exposed it.

Madhu: But your father Ram Jethmalani is the Hindujas' lawyer as well as Tehelka's.

Jethmalani: In fact, the Hindujas kept telling Ram, please don't take this case. They kept telling Ram at that stage, because of you being a Tehelka lawyer we're going to get screwed in court. You know how businessmen are. They would actually tell Ram that, look at this case, you're getting high profile and we're suffering in the Bofors case.

In Operation West End, the journalists pushed ethics and the law to achieve their goal. But it was evident that the one element they had greater faith in than anything else and relied on for their sting's success was the Weakness of Man.

If anyone knew the truth about how much Tarun actually knew, it would be Mathew Samuel:

Samuel: My very well knowledge, Tarun doesn't know exackly vaat was in the tapes. After they edited, after going through me, then only he knows. I am 101 per cent, Tarun is not part of this. That is the irrrony. Somebody else did it. Everybody thinks Tarun did it. He knows nothing. I am not blaming. Suppose I am vurrking with you, you will get the credit. It is absolutely normal. It is stupid. This is absolute nonsense. How can it be? Nobody knows I am just starting with Malviya.

Madhu: Did you ever discuss with Tarun that you did the story and the media focus is on him?

Samuel: I naaaiverrr chat with him. I never blame to Tarun also: why you are taking credit? After CBI raid there was a letter found from Aniruddha to Tarun saying that me, Samuel and myself did the story, why you are taking the credit? CBI got it. It was published in many of the newspapers. Then two days later, I asked Aniruddha, "Who is actually doing all the stories?" But no matter. I am doing these stories, just like a fun. Enjoying. Not like getting celaibraity and all that. I hate this like kind of people. Who knows me like he is the idiot who did. I never go and bloody tell anyone I am a journalist. Now also. That is all stupidity. Leave it.

Madhu: Were there any other motives other than journalistic?

Samuel: Not possible. Aniruddha is a nice man. He is <u>core</u> journalist. Tarun knows nothing vaat we have, ven we have. Even Aniruddha doesn't even know vaat is in the tape. This stock market thing is all rrrrubbish. How they do it if I don't tell them anyting? Just I will give, these are the tapes. Some idea but I was busy. I was recording.

Madhu: You didn't actually …

Samuel: Spelt out vaat is in tape? No. I don't have time. He'll not insist, tell me, tell me, vaat's in tape. Not like that. That kind of a nature we have got.

Madhu: What do you think of Tarun now?

Samuel: Tarun having a big celaibraity now. Ha! Huh! I'm really proud of that. Team work. I was also part of that. Really I was part of that. Sometime, he will call, "Tiger, Tiger, Tiger." He knows also I am leeeeeeest intrrrusssted in essposure. I away from this kind of stuff.

Madhu: What do you think of Tarun's deposition? When he was asked whether he trusted Aniruddha, he said "Yes". When he was asked whether he trusted Mathew Samuel, he said, "I don't know".

Samuel: Hmmm.

Madhu: He was asked this question in different ways many times, but he never confirmed that he trusted you.

Samuel: Hmmmm.

Madhu: Did you feel that Tarun did not trust you?

Samuel: Hmmmmm. I never reported Tarun anything. Till today. He never asked me also. Most of the time Tarun also feel little guilty this thing also. Suppose he also think that he's a chief of this thing. I have to report him. I have to come and talk his second floor. I merely visited one or two times. That related to official matters. I never went and report him.

Madhu: What about other people in the office? Did they ever ask you what you were up to?

Samuel: I nevvvver interact with these people. One time this Kajol Basu agitated against me: why you vant car?

Madhu: The car was a big issue?

Samuel: Car was a big issue. They are editor, I am only reporter. Ha, ha, ha. After story broke they felt that …

Madhu: Then you were a hero?

Samuel: In awfiss, they said you, bloody, did this! I don't have any personal ambitions or anything. Suppose you are vurrrking with me then you will come to know. I'm only bothered I have to deliver you a story, then you only will give the money. Simbple thing. Maddum, you know, the truth, Brajesh Mishra was waiting for me in India International Centre. You believe that?

Madhu: No, actually, I don't. It is hard to believe. It's just that those kinds of people don't function like that.

Samuel: He was waiting for me more than one owwher. What happened there is awfiss politics there. Tarun's mama's name is called Kapil something. He denied to give the car to me. How I will go auto rickshaw? Appointment arranged by R.K. Gupta. You believe? He's waiting for an arms dealer. So I have to give some money to him. Maybe he's a big lucky man.

Madhu: Did you get back to him after that?

Samuel: How can I back to him? He was waiting for me one owwher. Real loss. That time I was using the car. That time big problem. Why Samuel is using this Esteem car? Just a new joined. He is only a special correspondent and they are not getting the car. Editors they are not getting the car. Kapil mama he was in charge of accounts. And he thought I am a big man here, how he can use every time my car? Lot of awfiss politics there.

Madhu: Did you bring this up with Tarun?

Samuel: I never chat with Tarun this matter. This I told Aniruddha many times. He said, "Fuck off these bastards. Why I was not informed?" I was trying to arrange taxi. That day even taxi was not even coming. Suppose I am going to arrange this meeting it is not a simpble thing. Just imaaagine to get Brajesh Mishra. I managed that. Then after the second meeting Aniruddha saw the cash on the tapes then he come to know the real face of the story. Then he told me the story is little good. Meanwhile I told him our budget is this much: that time the budget was 6 lakhs. So he want to go with this story little bit up. Then I got some appreciation from him also. Then I also become energized. Almost every time I will vurrk out, vaat to talk, how to talk; I was keeeenly vaatching vaat Malviya was talking. Everything I grasped very fastly. Action, female matters and everything, interaction hotel and everything. Aniruddha also told me I think so we can run the story. I say we can build up the story. Aniruddha says we can publish the story right now. I said, "Bawss, give me two-three days. I will do something. Please."

LIEUTENANT COLONEL V.P. SAYAL

Mathew Samuel decided to push the sting operation laterally when he and Malviya had a near miss with Colonel Sehgal.

Samuel: We went to Sehgal home and there we gave 20,000. Then he said, you have to give rrust of the money. Don't do this kind of *hera pheri* [hanky panky] like a fish market. Then he say to opun the briefcase.

Madhu: Sehgal got suspicious?

Samuel: Yes. In the therd meeting he told me, opun the briefcase. That is only very intrussting matter. Malviya maintained the situation well. He said, I will not opun. There is something special there. I will not opun. Then he said, "If you are not willing, we are going." Finally we said we are going. We left and landed up in Tehelka awfiss.

Madhu: What did Sehgal say?

Samuel: Saying, just opun, pleeeease opun. Pleading.

Madhu: Pleading? Not ordering?

Samuel: Pleeeeading. Please opun, bawss. Anyway we want to away from there. Suddenly Malviya really scared. Aniruddha said if it is any problem we can break the story tomorrow. I told Aniruddha, give me two-three days. Then I went to Sasi. I told him that, "Sasi, lissun. So why could not we able to opun briefcase? Because we kept some magazines." You know that stuff.

Madhu: That doesn't seem like a good excuse. Army guys are used to all that.

Samuel: Sasi believed me. Sasi said he thought you are tape-recording something.

Soon after their encounter with a suspicious Sehgal, Malviya dropped out of the operation citing it as being too risky. After a couple of days, while waiting for P. Sasi outside his office, he noticed a forty-year-old civilian sitting near the Army Headquarters gates giving documents to suppliers. Samuel approached him, got his name, Suresh, address and phone number and the same evening went to meet him to ask for help.

Madhu: To whom was he giving documents on the road?

Samuel: Suppliers, vendors, agents, *ayega, na* [come, no]? Ficksed appointments. He knew those people, he ficksed appointments and give the dawkumunts. I said I want to meet some senior awfissars. He said I have one friend. His name is Lefftnunt General Saiyal. Retired awffissar. After about second day he arranged a meeting with him. Ashok Hotul. *Phut gaya, phut gaya* [ass busted, ass busted]. He dealing only with mosquito net. I talking like Patton tank. In between the meeting, I lernt vaat Malviya is talking. Meanwhile, we have that borshurr [brochure] and everything ready. I gave this card and borshurr to Saiyal. Saiyal said, "*Ismey kuch nahin hai* [there is nothing in this]. I want to know, who are you? You are CBI agent? Pakistan ISI?" He vant to know my credibility. *Udhar sey Saiyal key saath shuru ho gaiya* Jaya Jaitly [there I started with Sayal to get to Jaya Jaitly]. After that Saiyal started his vurrk. Saiyal supposed to ask make availability I will give 5,000. Then he vants to know where I'm staying. He vant to visit my home. Many time he asked me. Then I saw one mad, pathetic man staying in Janakpuri near to my home; he won't allow any outsiders, visitors in his home.

Madhu: How do you know him?

Samuel: From one chai wallah. He won't allow anyone. He's a very mad man, like that. *Uskey ghar mey bees key uppar kutta bhi hai* [there are more than 20 dogs in his house]. I given to Saiyal his address. Saiyal came, *bees kutta ah gaya* [20 dogs showed up]. So he asked me, "How many dawgs you have, *yaar*?" Ha! Ha! Ha! "How can you feed?"

Lieutenant Colonel V.P. Sayal was the second link in the chain of Operation West End. Sayal, with his army contacts from his past, led Mathew Samuel to Brigadier Iqbal Singh, Major General

Ahluwalia, and Major General Murgai. It was Murgai who introduced Samuel to Surendra Sureka who led him to Jaya Jaitly. Lieutenant Colonel Sayal (Retd) was responsible for trapping many of the army officers. Sayal had the iniquitous distinction of also fooling Mathew Samuel.

Sayal started as a radio operator in the Indian Air Force until 1967 and took premature retirement in 1991. His last post was as Commandant of 24 FAD [Forward Ammunition Depot]. His first job after retirement was with Swetang International as their deputy general manager, exporting groceries and general items to Russia. Any mention of Russia is sufficient to set off alarm bells for anyone looking to unearth arms deals. Sayal left that company in 1994 and started supplying clothing items to the army.

He was doing liaison work for a number of companies who were on the look out for orders from various ministries, including the Ministry of Defence. Samuel and Sayal first met in the reception of Army Headquarters. They met again at Hotel Ashok for drinks and dinner, and then followed it up with about fifteen more meetings.

Sayal was suspicious of Samuel right from the outset. He questioned him many times about his background and his company. Despite his suspicions, why did Sayal get involved with Samuel? In his deposition before the Commission, Sayal explained how it happened:

He lured me with lots of things. In fact, because of my age factor plus my ill health, I was in search of a job. He lured me by saying that if we get a breakthrough in this, we are going to have an office here in which you will have a suitable place.

Sayal invited his old colleague, Brigadier Iqbal Singh, prospective procurement officer to a Delhi five-star hotel, for drinks and dinner. When Singh arrived there he discovered the entertainment included a woman. Sayal told Singh that Samuel's London-based firm was interested in supplying night vision devices to the army. Singh enquired what spadework had been done so far. Sayal answered that they knew that the army did need them, and although CSF Thomson had bagged the contract, their product did not meet the requisite standards. They were having problems in the inspection stage. The aim was to get West End shortlisted. Singh then instructed Samuel to write a letter giving details of the product along with a brochure and an assurance that West End was willing to give trials on no-cost no-commitment basis. Singh said that then their equipment should be evaluated.

Singh told Samuel he should cultivate Major General P.S.K. Choudary of the Weapons & Equipment Division. Samuel responded by telling him that as he did not know Choudary, he would need his help. Singh informed Samuel that he would try but that Choudary didn't fall in his chain of command. At this point, the Operation West End transcript reported that Samuel handed over Rs 50,000 to Brigadier Iqbal Singh, which he accepted. If you watch the tapes, that is not exactly how it happened. Samuel told Singh he had brought a small gift for him and pulled out a wad of money. Singh shook his head, pushed the money away and said, 'What for, *yaar*?' Sayal coaxed Singh, 'Please, please'. Singh said, 'First let your job be done'. On further persuasion from Sayal, Singh looked confused and said, 'For whom?' Sayal interjected, 'If you have a problem taking it with you, I will deliver it at your place'.

Singh responded, 'You do like this, let your job be done first'. When Samuel persisted, Singh said, 'Let us say I am not able to help you, then?' Sayal said, 'No problem'. Singh then took the money from Samuel and handed it to Sayal, who quickly put it in his hungry briefcase. Then, inexplicably, Singh talked as if he had accepted the money and told him that he would talk to Lieutenant General Dhillon, Master General Ordnance. Singh said, 'My job is to look after … up to MGO, but Choudary is not my department'. When Samuel questioned him further about Lieutenant General Dhillon, Singh told him that organizing a meeting with Dhillon was within his power, if not at home then in his office. Samuel informed him that the office would be dangerous and Singh replied then he would organize it at Dhillon's house.

Sayal took the money to give to Singh later, but Singh said he never received it. When Nilay Dutta, counsel for Jaya Jaitly, cross-examined Sayal, he brazenly admitted to pocketing the money:

> **Dutta:** The Brigadier left and you are back at home.
> **Sayal:** That is what I am telling. While going itself he said, "Sayal, do not ever… because this is the first time and last time I am meeting you. I do not need money." In fact, I pocketed that money myself and whatever expenditures I have incurred, I have utilized that.
> **Dutta:** That Rs 50,000 remained with you and did you explain this to Mr Samuel Mathew later on that I have kept it with me?
> **Sayal:** Later on, I told him I have given it to brigadier.
> **Dutta:** You said that you have given it to brigadier and you kept it with you?
> **Sayal:** I kept it with me, because he did not accept it. So, I kept that money with me.
> **Dutta:** Would it be a fair assessment to say that if Mathew Samuel believed that you had handed it over to Brigadier Iqbal Singh, you are misleading Mathew Samuel?
> **Sayal:** Yes, because he had started misleading me. I also started misleading, because I wanted money. He posed himself, that it is a multinational company, whatever it is. I felt, if that be so, my main aim was to get money from them.
> **Dutta:** Do you think that you did something wrong that day?
> **Sayal:** Well, whatever the assessment, I took that money. Since he did not take it, I pocketed it myself. It is in my statement.
> **Dutta:** Don't you realize that Rs 50,000, which you kept yourself, has now become subject matter of this Honourable Commission and that is why Brigadier Iqbal Singh is lying as a heart patient in the hospital? Don't you think it is very wrong?
> **Sayal:** The fact is I kept the money myself.

Sayal was quite unmoved by Dutta's outrage. It appeared shockingly heartless in the Commission, but, Major General P.S.K. Choudary, in his interview with me, hinted that Sayal was covering up for other officers who he had trapped along with Samuel.

However, Brigadier Iqbal Singh did explain to Samuel the procedures he should follow, to write to the WE Directorate, provided details of the product, say that they were willing to give trials at a 'no-cost no-commitment' basis and that their equipment would be evaluated. Why was he giving all this information to a stranger? To be fair to Brigadier Iqbal Singh, he had no idea he was going to meet Samuel. He accepted a dinner invitation expecting only Sayal. When he was leaving the hotel he admonished Sayal: 'I am in no way in this sort of game, the way you treated me here.' But, there was the rather pathetic interaction with the woman, which can only be described as all pain, no gain.

With Samuel's promise of a job, Sayal went around trying to impress him by introducing him to as many people as he could. Yet, Sayal himself was not terribly impressed with Samuel:

> **Sayal:** To tell you frankly, I found so many things when he started coming closer to me and opening up. I found him a chain smoker, a very heavy boozer. Also, wherever we used to have critical words to be spoken, he used to keep something in the mouth, some sort of iron ball sort of thing, he used to crack it. That is how I have seen in many places the words are not spoken by a person attributed to him; though these words are spoken by Samuel himself. Twice I have noted it. Thirdly, he had the knack of telling I have 2 per cent share in the company, West End International: I have got this, I have got that, I can provide whatever you want, that type of boasting. Accordingly, one has to boast also.

Sayal said that Samuel had promised to pay him Rs 3 lakh and give him an air-conditioned car.

> **Sayal:** That man touched my feet saying, if you are not going to take me to Brigadier Iqbal Singh and Major General Ahluwalia, I will lose my job. That sort of drama he played. I must have been paid a maximum of Rs 35,000 to Rs 40,000, whereas I spent a lot more for running about, finding a place for their accommodation, for meeting people.

Sayal insisted that a lot of the sentences on the tapes were not his. Sayal told the Army Court of Inquiry that the tapes were doctored: 'In the Operation West End tapes and transcripts, it is stated: "Our next meeting with General Ahluwalia takes place 10 days later. Here he accepts a token bribe of Rs 50,000, which is never delivered to him."' According to Sayal, the money was never given to him, never delivered to Ahluwalia, that it was not asked for and not accepted. Samuel insisted that the money was handed over later, off camera. Major General Ahluwalia cross-examined his friend of twenty years, Lieutenant Colonel Sayal, who agreed that Ahluwalia had refused to take any money, had tried to discourage Samuel, and did not want to get involved. Ahluwalia also got Sayal to admit that his visit was purely social, stemming from an old friendship, and Ahluwalia had no idea that Samuel would be present. Ahluwalia had informed him that he had no role to play in the procurement of HHTI and had never handed over any manual relating to the procurement procedure for HHTI. Sayal agreed that Ahluwalia had tried to discourage them because this kind of venture was beyond them.

Sayal was engaged in what he called liaison work, and it was part of the deal to use all his army contacts. After all, he was a retired ordnance officer and was in the loop about what needed to be done to get contracts for his clients. Gifts of money, entertainment that included booze and women, were all part of that arrangement. For him, nothing that Samuel did was that extraordinary, but having been in the field, he continued to be suspicious of Samuel as he certainly did not measure up. Did Sayal sell his country down the drain? He connected people, collected money for that, and was basically doing what he perceived was his job. Sayal's lack of any introspection that he was doing anything wrong seems intrinsically part of this ethos.

Sayal appeared in the Army Court of Inquiry on 28 March 2001 as the fifth witness. Major General P.S.K. Choudary interrogated Sayal and established that the latter had never met or spoken to him except in court. To all of Choudary's questions, which were related to Sayal's discussions about Choudary in the Operation West End transcripts, Sayal's answers were, 'I do not remember'.

When the Army Court of Inquiry questioned him, it transpired that when Sayal was supplying clothing to the army, the DQA(S) at the time was Major General S.P. Murgai. The court was obviously cognizant of this murky connection, and asked Sayal to confirm the figures supplied by Tehelka about the amount of money paid to him, totalling Rs 80,000. Sayal insisted that the numbers were fabricated. He also maintained that he had no knowledge of Samuel's plan to give Brigadier Iqbal Singh Rs 50,000. The Army Court of Inquiry dug out some intriguing facts about Sayal's dealings with other army officers. He supplied Rs 2 crore worth of blankets from Mahavir Woollens to the army and did meet Brigadier Nijahwan in the tender opening process. The ACI questioned Sayal about his association with Brigadier Nijahwan, the officer in charge of processing the tenders for these supplies:

ACI: It is mentioned in the Tehelka transcript that during your conversation with Mr Sukhdev Singh and the Tehelka team, you said that Brigadier Nijahwan was one person who for everything straight away says, "*Mujhe kya doge, bolta hai* [what will you give me, he says]" or words to that effect? Did you make this statement and if so, when and on what occasion did Brigadier Nijahwan tell this to you?

Sayal: Yes, I said so, but it is factually not correct. Brigadier Nijahwan never said any such thing to me. I was trying to impress the representatives of Tehelka by making tall talks.

ACI: It is mentioned in the transcript that during the said meeting you told the representatives of Tehelka that money has to be paid to Brigadier Nijahwan, Brigadier Iqbal Singh, Lieutenant General J.S. Dhillon and that the amount should not be in mere thousands. You told them to keep Rs 2 lakhs ready. Did you make this statement? And if so, why and what for you claimed that money has to be paid to the army officers named by you?

Sayal: I did make the statement. But I was repeatedly being prompted by the representatives of West End to take the names of army officers. I also in the bargain indulged in making tall claims and loose talk. Factually, no army officer had ever asked for any money from me.

ACI: It is seen on the tape that you also told that money will have to be paid to all these people. Did you mean that for getting things done you had to bribe people in the system?

Sayal: I decline to answer.

Sayal understood in an instant that he would be opening the proverbial can. It became clear that Sayal was just one of many army officers who take early retirement and then use their contacts made while working for the army to set up related businesses.

SURESH NANDA

Legend has it that it all began with Admiral Sardari Mathradas (S.M.) Nanda who was appointed Chief of Naval Staff on 1 March 1970. In December 2003, Admiral 'Charles' Nanda published his memoirs entitled *The Man Who Bombed Karachi* (who was of course himself). He was awarded the Param Vishisht Seva Medal in 1966. In the 1971 Indo-Pak war, Nanda was reportedly instrumental in turning around India's defensive position into a proactive one. As the British and the US had shown apprehension in contributing to India's naval strength, Indira Gandhi turned to the Soviet Union. The Indian Navy acquired eight Osa class missile boats, each carrying Styx missiles, in mid-1971 from the Soviet Union. This formed the 25th Missile Vessel Squadron comprising *Vijeta, Vidyut, Vinash, Veer, Nashak, Nipat, Nirghat,* and *Nirbhik*. The Soviets cautioned that these boats had limited range and should only be deployed defensively close to home base. Nanda ignored all the Soviet warnings and, in Operation Trident, ordered frigates to tow the Osa missile boats in the dark of night close to Karachi harbour. In the early hours of 4 December 1971, the Indian Navy successfully bombed Karachi and sank two Pakistani warships. In Operation Python, on the night of 8 December 1971, in a second attack, two more ships were sunk and the Keamari oil refinery was destroyed. It turned the war in India's favour. Nanda was a hero. Was.

After he pseudo-retired on 28 February 1973, Nanda took over as chairman and managing director of the public sector company, Shipping Corporation of India, Ltd. A short while later, Nanda became the inventor of a new profession: retired armed service officers dabbling in the supply of defence equipment. Equipped with the technical requirements of the armed services, a knowledge of the defence products available, and already drinking buddies with the companies producing them, there was no way he could lose. Nanda's company, Crown Corporation hired ex-servicemen who could obtain classified specifications about equipment from the armed forces. Nanda claimed he was helping retired servicemen, but was he helping India? When defence decisions are based on personal profit and not what is beneficial to the country, it is unnerving and dangerous. His son, Lieutenant Commander Suresh Nanda took premature pseudo-retirement from the navy and ran their office in London.

On 22 February 1999, the issue of middlemen subverting India's security was brought into the public domain by sacked Chief of Naval Staff, Admiral Vishnu Bhagwat. In a dispute over the appointment of Vice Admiral Harinder Singh, who Bhagwat refused to accept, Defence Minister George Fernandes exerted his authority and dumped Bhagwat on 30 December 1998, two days after his appointment. At a press conference two months later, Bhagwat said he had informed George Fernandes on 4 and 8 May 1998 about the nexus between Crown Corporation and naval officers. He pointed a finger at Fernandes of his long friendship with Admiral S.M. Nanda since the 1960s when Nanda was chairman of Mumbai's Mazagon Docks and Fernandes a trade union leader. Bhagwat charged that even after he informed Fernandes of corrupt naval officers, the defence minister met Nanda before and after the day he was sacked. Bhagwat agitated,

> Admiral Nanda and his son, Suresh Nanda are the agents for the MTU engines for the Army tanks Vijayanta and Arjuna, and the HDW submarine. Globe-Tek, Crown Corporation, the names keep changing and so do directorships and their partnerships and front companies, but it is the same people who are middlemen for foreign interests peddling arms to India.

The Nandas continued to deny their company had links with any defence deals yet their names keep popping up in connection with T-90 tanks, advanced jet trainers, and the Admiral Gorshkov ship. In the late 1980s, the CBI and Income Tax Department raided the Nandas' homes and offices, in an investigation into HDW deals. The distraught, ex-hero admiral wrote a letter to Indira Gandhi complaining about this treatment. Mrs Gandhi was not in the least bit receptive. They now have the reputation of being the largest arms dealers in India, apparently dislodging the earlier king, M.K. Jajodia, group chairman of Monnet International Ltd.

R.K. Jain, treasurer of the Samata Party, whose ranting gossip on the West End tapes threw Jaya Jaitly into a wild fury, had elaborated on how Suresh Nanda of Crown Corporation offered him Rs 1 crore for a deal involving armoured recovery vehicles for which Nanda was the agent. This you have to read verbatim from the Operation West End tapes.

R.K. Jain: Armoured recovery vehicle was my first case which I did it for Slovakia.
Tehelka: Okay.
R.K. Jain: When George was defence minister for the first time [gestures]. After one year, then he became another defence minister.
Tehelka: Yeah, yeah.
R.K. Jain: This is I am talking about the first time when he became the defence minister. As soon as he became the defence minister, after six or seven months ...?
Tehelka: Okay.

R.K. Jain: Suresh Nanda approached me for armoured recovery vehicle. He was the agent for the Slovakian company.

Tehelka: What was the product?

R.K. Jain: Armoured recovery vehicle.

Tehelka: Oh! Yeah, yeah.

R.K. Jain: There were 250 vehicles were there. The tender was worth say 250 crores.

Tehelka: Okay.

R.K. Jain: There were two ... three, competitions – Slovakia, Czechoslovakia and there was a company from Poland.

Tehelka: Okay.

R.K. Jain: Boomer?

Tehelka: Yeah, yeah, that jet plane and everything.

R.K. Jain: Nanda approached me. Czechoslovakia's price was the lowest, second Slovakian, third was the Poland.

Tehelka: *Haan, Haan.*

R.K. Jain: He said, "I will give you one crore rupees in advance ..."

Tehelka: Okay.

R.K. JAIN: "You get disapproved the last one ... Czechoslovakia because they are so lower that we cannot match their price."

Tehelka: Okay.

R.K. JAIN: "If you can push him out. Delegation is going on to the ... delegation has been ordered to go to Czechoslovakia. Stop this delegation, and technically reject this company. Here are the documents."

Tehelka: Hmm.

R.K. JAIN: "By which it's proved that this company is closed for the last two years. They will start only after getting this order."

Tehelka: Yeah, yeah.

R.K. JAIN: "I will give one crore rupees. And I will give you ... if they are technically disapproved, then you are my agent."

Tehelka: Yeah.

R.K. JAIN: "For this particular ... perks ... and I will give you so much of commission."

Tehelka: Okay.

R.K. Jain: I said, "Fine." He gave me the correspondence. I took the correspondence to George.

Tehelka: Hmm.

R.K. Jain: And he said, "All right, I'll reject it." He is a very intelligent man. Next day he called Rajiv Goba.

Tehelka: Hmm.

R.K. Jain: He said, "Ring up to this Indian Embassy in Czechoslovakia and find out whether this company is closed for the last two years or not."

Tehelka: Hmm.

R.K. Jain: And he rang up. It was closed.

Tehelka: Hmm.

R.K. Jain: He told me, "…said the company is closed for the last two years. There is no point of a delegation to go. And therefore this company is technically disqualified." [*Jain's phone is ringing.*]

Tehelka: Okay, it is manipulated.

R.K. Jain: He wrote straight away on the file himself. He never goes and orders to a joint secretary. He wrote it himself, and sent the file back. Nanda gave me one crore rupees. He called me, "Yes, Mr Jain, the file has come down. Like you know George … "

Tehelka: Yeah, yeah.

R.K. Jain: "The file is down, my work has been done, I am very happy. You take your one crore rupees." I said, "Fine, give it to me."

Tehelka: Yeah, this kind of work.

R.K. Jain: After that …?

Tehelka: Yeah.

R.K. Jain: After that, the bugger could not get lowest into the PNC. Poland become the lowest.

Tehelka: Okay.

R.K. Jain: Then he started running around. "Mr Jain …" I was very angry, "You bastard." And on the instruction of George Fernandes, Rajiv Goba attended that PNC to see that what is happening in the case.

Tehelka: Hmm.

R.K. Jain: Party was wanting money. We just came into the power. We had no money.

There was no confirmation that the company was actually closed except an alleged phone call. At the Commission, Jain said he was just gossiping and talking tall. But facts seem to match what he later claimed was gossip.

Central Vigilance Commission chief, N. Vittal said in March 2001, that his inquiry on 'defence purchases had reached its final stages and action against officers and bureaucrats against whom prima facie evidence was found would be recommended. The exposé of Tehelka.com only confirmed and vindicates our initial findings.' He mentioned Suresh Nanda in the 250 Armoured Recovery Vehicles deal from a Slovak company when he pushed out the lowest bidder PSP Bohemia. Other bidders, including Nanda, had protested that PSP Bohemia was not an original manufacturer and would supply old ARVs.

When all these accusations were flying around, George Fernandes attempted to clarify this and stated, 'When a report was received that the Czech company was planning to procure surplus stocks, break them down, improve them and sell them off, the defence ministry decided against procuring the ARVs from any foreign company and ordered 87 vehicles from BHEL and BEML.' Fernandes said that the defence attaché in Prague had shot down since Czech Bohemia was not an original manufacturer.

Yes, but the CBI reported in October 2006, that the defence ministry purchased VT-72 B ARVs from Unimpex, an agent of ZTS Martin, a Czechoslovakian company since 1993 through the public sector company BHEL. Oh ho! And who is the agent of Unimpex but none other than Suresh Nanda. The CBI reported that officers of Ministry of Defence allegedly 'abused their official positions and wilfully ignored the lowest technically suitable offer of PSP Bohemia for supply of 8 ARVs.' The CBI reported in October 2006, that Nanda paid R.K. Jain, treasurer of the Samata Party, Rs 1 crore to get George Fernandes, then defence minister, to reject the proposal to send a technical team to check on PSP Bohemia. The CBI charged that Suresh Nanda of Unimpex, who they discovered was also not an original manufacturer, got part of the ARVs order and the government suffered a loss of Rs 51.83 crore. By dealing with Unimpex, the ministry violated the Defence Purchase Procedure 1992. CBI reported that Nanda laundered the money from Unimpex through acquisition of assets in the names of family members and companies. There is, of course, a more detailed report but that is beyond the scope of this book to include.

The tragedy here is that many reading this will say, 'What a smart guy!' It was reported that Suresh Nanda was also involved in the Rs 60 crore Barak Missile deal for INS Virat.

Although the Government of India offers the facility for middlemen to register as agents for foreign arms dealers, it is virtually unheard of. It would mean that they would be – horror of horrors – subject to Indian income tax laws and would have to actually pay income tax. Additionally, they would not be able to collect their money in countries outside of India, as most of them do. The USA has the FCPA (Foreign Corrupt Practices Act) and the Sarbanes-Oxley Act, which prevent middlemen from bribing companies to appoint them as their representatives. This keeps the middlemen out. So Russia and Israel are easier targets.

Suresh Nanda has reportedly been a non-resident Indian since 1984. He is one of the directors of Crown Corporation, which he first said exported engineering goods. He owns another company, Dynatron Services, which he said, provides maintenance and after-sales service for equipment which is sold in India. He was cross-examined in the Commission of Inquiry on 25 June 2002 by Dayan Krishnan, counsel for the Commission:

Krishnan: What kind of equipment does Dynatron service?
Nanda: We started with servicing of diesel engines which were sold, which were supplied to the navy from a German company called MTU. Those companies saw in us a competent company to be able to keep the products they have sold already in the country in a state of constant availability; in a high state of readiness so that the machinery was available at all times.
Krishnan: Apart from the German companies you have mentioned, are any of your clients having their equipments put on any defence-related projects or with defence?
Nanda: I told you about the Propeller Company VA Tech. It has propellers installed in coastguards offshore patrol vessels.
Krishnan: I was asking you a while earlier as to whether you or your family concerns were dealing with the Ministry of Defence in your business activities in India. Have you or they dealt with the Ministry of Defence?

Nanda: As I have said, the company Dynatron Services had dealings with the defence ministry undertakings. It is an authorized service organization for MTU engines. If you see the international catalogue of MTU, it will say that Dynatron Services is the organization in India for repair of MTU engines, which are fitted on ships and generating sets. Even for merchant ships generally coming here, if it is MTU guard ships, the servicing is done by Dynatron and for that we have to contact the defence organization.

Krishnan wanted to end the cross-examination but Nanda had not had his full say. He went on to add:

Nanda: One more thing I would like to say because you have asked about defence. I have one more company which has dealings with defence, and this is a company called Crown Corporation. The Crown Corporation is a Government of India recognized export house. We export defence equipment from India to foreign countries. As per the government policy, the Crown Corporation have been exporting things like parachutes, submarine batteries, aircraft ground hauling equipment and trucks for use by foreign armies. Tata trucks we have exported. For this, we have been given awards by the Government of India on three consecutive years. We have Shri Pranab Mukherjee giving us awards. I have got photographs with me. We have shown exceptional results. Several crores worth of goods we have been exporting every year. So, in that respect, Crown Corporation only exports defence equipment from India and perhaps the only or the largest private sector company in the country. The Crown Corporation has never imported anything on defence into the country. So, I think that is something which has a connotation of defence dealing but there should be a difference between imports and exports.

Krishnan: How many employees does Crown Corporation have?

Nanda: It is about 10 or so.

Krishnan: Similarly with Dynatron?

Nanda: In Dynatron we have about 60, because servicing is done in various parts of the country.

Krishnan: Of these people who are working in Crown Corporation as well as those who work with Dynatron, are there any retired defence service personnel?

Nanda: Yes.

Krishnan: What is their proportion? How many would they be?

Nanda: They are primarily retired people. More than 50 per cent are retired defence personnel.

So much for that!

Krishnan: Am I correct that the Israel Aircraft Industry (IAI) is not one of the companies for whom you are an authorized after-sales support organization?

Nanda: Yes, we are not.

Krishnan: Do you in your individual capacity or Dynatron or any other companies for whom you are associated with deal with Israel Aircraft Industry in India?

Nanda: No, we do not.

Krishnan: Do you deal with them anywhere in the world?

Nanda: No, we do not.

Krishnan: Would I therefore be correct that you would not have an occasion to make phone calls to them if you do not deal with them.

Nanda: Not necessarily.

Krishnan: I am presently showing you two telephone numbers out of the summoned documents which have been given to you earlier, it is one telephone number occurring at two places. Would you be able to identify that number which has been made out of your cellular phone? The number I referred to is 98100....

Nanda: Outgoing from which phone?

Krishnan: Outgoing from the cellular phone 98100... Is that your number, Mr Nanda?

Nanda: Yes, the number is mine.

Krishnan: Would you be able to identify the number please?

Nanda: I am not able to identify.

Krishnan: I put it to you that this number 98100... is the number belonging to the Israel Aircraft Industry and is used by its office in Delhi. Would you be able to clarify to this honourable Commission as to why you were making telephone calls to them?

Nanda: This is June 2000, both on the 14th. I cannot remember why but I have no business dealings with that company. Could be for a social purpose.

Social? Sky dancing with Top Gun planes?

After a break and discussion with his own lawyer, Harvansh Chawla, Suresh Nanda is re-examined by his own counsel:

Chawla: Were you ever contacted by Israeli people for security reasons because we understand you are neighbouring the Israeli Embassy?

Nanda: Yes. Actually Israeli Embassy and my house share a common wall and they were contacting me for making an opening in the wall in case they need to escape from their house through a back door. That is true; they approached me number of times for this purpose.

The calls Krishnan was questioning Nanda about were outgoing calls from his phone.

A paper from income tax intelligence found its way to me in the summer of 2003. In that, it was clear that raids were planned on Admiral S.M. Nanda, Suresh Nanda, their associates mentioned included R.K. Jain and two retired naval officers, Avneesh Tandon and K.K. Batta. The list included two houses on Prithviraj Road, two farmhouses, office space in Nehru Place, three houses in Defence Colony, Claridges Hotel, eight flats in Delhi, Chennai, Kolkata, and Goa, and houses in Moscow, Ukraine, London, and Slovakia. This note stated the investigation would include: Auto Mellara gun system and its ammunition for the navy, MTU engines for all the naval ships and their spare parts, naval spare parts from Russia and Ukraine on a regular basis, Unimpex of Slovakia, Thompson CSF of France, MTU of Germany, HDW of Germany, Westland of United Kingdom, for helicopters and a number of Russian Ukrainian companies for SKS submarines and spare parts for it. Neither the raid nor the investigation took place while the BJP government was in power.

So what is wrong with making money as a middleman for arms? Not much, since the government has made it possible for anyone to register as a middleman. But who will, when the kind of fees middlemen charge would then be taxed and would the government then allow such high commissions? Additionally, should decisions for the best security for the nation be influenced by some middleman's connection and his profit motive rather than the best product?

On 27 February 2006, the press reported that the CBI had arrested R.K. Jain on charges of corruption, for demanding and accepting money from West End International and promising to get them an arms supply contract. On 10 October 2006, the CBI (now under the UPA government) did finally carry out the postponed raids on 27 Nanda properties in Delhi, eight others in Gurgaon, Chandigarh, and Mumbai. Besides a crore and a half in cash, the CBI reported that they had found incriminating documents and links with five other middlemen (four are in the Operation West End tapes) as well as R.K. Jain, former Samata Party treasurer. The investigation in progress is like all soap operas; there is always a new development with no ending in sight. On March 8 2008, Suresh Nanda, his son Sanjeev, his accountant Bipin Shah were arrested in a hotel in Mumbai, allegedly in the act of bribing deputy director of income tax Ashutosh Verma so he would fudge a probe on their tax evasion. After being denied bail on 5 April 2008, Suresh and his son Sanjeev, by a Delhi court, they were let out after 53 days on 29 April 2008. Saga continues. Don't even bother to watch this space. You could write it yourself.

↩

BRIGADIER IQBAL SINGH

When Lieutenant Colonel Sayal (Retd) brought his friend Brigadier Iqbal Singh into Operation West End's net, he was Deputy Director-General Procurement Progressing Organization in the MGO's Branch, Army Headquarters. Iqbal Singh completed his deposition in the army court on 14 April 2001 as the fourteenth witness. Singh's job involved processing offers received from foreign vendors against the indents floated for import of spare parts. He told the court that he knew Lieutenant Colonel Sayal as they had served together in 1986-88. He had met him at army social events, but when they met in September 2000 it was after a long gap. Sayal brought Mathew Samuel to his house uninvited. Samuel had offered his help when Singh told him that his daughter's visa to the United States had been rejected. Singh reported, 'I wish to apprise the Honourable Court that at no stage I sought Mathew Samuel's help for this purpose, as I had not liked his behaviour at the first sight itself and the mannerism in which he bragged to show himself big'. He repeatedly declined Sayal's invitations due to personal commitments but eventually gave in and reluctantly agreed to dine with him at a hotel.

Brigadier Iqbal Singh generated many different Rashomon's in me. I saw the 'scurrilous' tapes and was angered and saddened. I met his lawyer and that angered me even more. However, when I witnessed Iqbal Singh's cross-examination in the Commission and subsequently read the transcripts, I felt uncontrollable pity. This Singh was different from the other army officers. He was meticulous in his own defence and there was enough on the tapes to show that he was not happy with his encounter with Mathew Samuel which his old friend Sayal had set up for him. Although Samuel was told by Sayal that he had delivered the money to Singh, there is doubt that it ever happened. No matter how much Iqbal Singh protested subsequently, Singh's relatives, friends, acquaintances, and fellow army officers remembered only what they saw broadcast on 13 March 2001. Singh's lament became just part of the cacophony of other protesting officers who were guilty. In the unedited tapes which were not broadcast, Iqbal Singh furiously abused Sayal in the hotel lobby as he left. Singh said, 'I am not involved in such things'.

Then there was the problem with the woman in the room. When Singh first saw her, he was confused. He thought it was a social evening and she might be Samuel's wife. When it became clear that she was there for his entertainment, he protested and asked her to be sent away. Singh said, 'Get this female out of there. She is locked up in the bathroom. *Aiy, behanchod, kithey ley aya* [hey, sister fucker, where have you brought me]? After some time, she can leave. *Acha nahin lagta. Hammey bhi accha nahin lageyga* [it doesn't look nice. I don't like this]'. What is dichotomous is that during dinner, Singh said that he felt bad about sending off the woman and that she should be called back to share their meal. She returned to eat with them and after dinner Sayal went off ostensibly to call for Singh's car. Samuel told Singh he was standing outside for a smoke (wink, wink) and the hapless, sitting officer (duck) was left with the woman to – aw, just rhyme it – and the third entity in the room, his conscience.

6 God of Small Flings

Edward Lewis [Richard Gere]: I will pay you to be at my beck and call.
Vivian Ward [Julia Roberts]: Look, I'd love to be your beck and call girl, but um, you're a rich, good-looking guy. You could get a million girls free.
Edward: I want a professional. I don't need any romantic hassles this week.

– Gary Marshall's film Pretty Woman *(1990)*

The woman, on the happy-plump side, is seen earlier on the tapes going to the bathroom and fitting the camera in the handbag. Neither a sex worker nor an employee of Tehelka, she had voluntarily agreed to be taped. When she was in the room, she sat on the bed, very quietly. A kind of lower-middle-class quietness, where sitting and doing nothing is a normal way of life. She looked comfortable just sitting, listening and watching. There was no social, neurotic need to 'make conversation'. She also gave the impression of being a sport; that attractive quality found in many sex workers when it is a voluntarily chosen profession. That game-for-anything trait so vividly portrayed in Sanjay Leela Bhansali's film *Devdas*, when the courtesan Chandramukhi, played by Madhuri Dixit, dances and has boarding school *hulla-gulla* type of fun with inebriated men to the song *Shishe se shisha takraaye*. Sorry, can't see that song being played out with a wife.

What does a sex worker offer? More than the obvious, she offers freedom. A woman who doesn't have to be taken care of. A woman who doesn't have to be thought about. A woman who asks no questions. A woman who does not seek commitment. A woman who is always happy to see him. A woman who has no complaints. A woman who does not discuss the children's problems. A woman who does not bring up household problems. In short, a woman who has no needs and makes no demands except to be paid.

And then, there are men like *Zorba the Greek* in Mihalis Kakogiannis's 1964 film, who 'open their belts and look for trouble'. Anthony Quinn gave Zorba's character his passion when he said; 'God has a very big heart but there is one sin he will not forgive: if a woman calls a man to her bed and he will not go. I know because a very wise old Turk told me.' Zorba characterizes the man who is hungry for life with commitment in its entire catastrophe, with the pain, questions, demands, problems that come packaged with love. What then happens to men when faced with a momentary escapist temptation for a dip in the hassle-free woman?

Brigadier Iqbal Singh's lawyer C.M. Khanna had demanded of me, 'Tell me, which man would not? Tell me one man who would walk away! Give me one name!' Oooh, the pressure of identifying a name! 'Give me one name!' he bellowed. How about Rama?

Tehelka's official position on the acquisition of the prostitutes is that the late Anil Malviya, alias Rajiv Sharma, organized them. The truth is, the woman with Brigadier Iqbal Singh was not a sex worker or an employee of Tehelka. She was divorced, alone, and elected to form part of the operation. She was aware she was being taped and had been instructed by Tehelka on the use of the camera in the handbag. She had been reassured that she would not have to go all the way. One can only speculate about her motivation. There was no sexual act between this woman and Brigadier Iqbal Singh.

With Sayal and Samuel gone, Singh had this soporific, boring conversation with the woman. Where does she live? There was some dull exchange about Noida. Her 'job', which she said, is 'Very much distance. Lots of work. We have to work twelve hours at a stretch. Holidays *toh hota hai* [we do get], *sir*. I am in marketing, so I have to go …' Then Singh gestured to the woman and she … .

I forgot. Which man would not? They were stopped by room service. They resumed but Singh then interrupted himself. He got up, straightened himself, and sat on the chair facing the bed. He asked the woman to give him her number so he could call her directly and not through Samuel. She refused and asked for his number instead. So Singh never got her number. Never got laid. But got royally screwed all the same. When Samuel returned he sensed there had been no action. He offered Singh a much better girl and boasted he could procure models for him. Singh told him it wasn't that, it was just that he was not mentally prepared for this. Samuel then offered to wait in the lobby if he wanted to have a go. Singh refused.

Names were thrown around. Singh advised Samuel on who was crucial and who was not. He repeatedly stressed to Samuel the need to cultivate Choudary. On speaking about cornering the MGO, Samuel offered to arrange women for any officers. At that point, Singh said, 'Give him one plus cuts also'.

'One plus cuts'? Kavin Gulati, counsel for Tehelka, grazed Singh over the coals on this issue in the Commission. Gulati asked him three times and never really got a satisfactory answer. Here is the third round.

Gulati: You said this conversation was doctored. You never said these words?
Singh: No, no, what I mentioned in my examination-in-chief: I had just touched upon the issues which according to me they were doctored. And the next sentence which he is now saying, I said on so and so date; he is referring to this, "Give him one plus cuts also". He is referring to this sentence now.
Gulati: We were talking of commission.
Singh: When you say "one plus cut" it is not a commission. It is a token amount

as per his language and Samuel has said so in the statement that Iqbal Singh said that you give a token amount to the MGO when you meet him for the first time and when the court asked him, how it was to be given? Iqbal was to take it and give it to MGO or you were to give it to the MGO, he says, "I was to give it directly to the MGO." Now where is that conversation?

Singh pointed out in a painfully detailed way, how a 'one plus cut' was Samuel type of language which Samuel had used elsewhere. Singh said that language of that kind was not in his vocabulary so the tapes had been doctored.

Justice Venkataswami who had patiently heard all of Singh's arguments somewhat sympathetically earlier, then asked him:

Venkataswami: One thing I want to say. You are under no obligation to oblige or please this Tehelka man, Mathew Samuel. Why did you not cut him short, "Don't talk nonsense, all this commission business. Don't talk to me?" Why did you not say that?
Singh: My Lord, this is the only sentence here.

The Indian style of using words to say nothing.

Venkataswami: He is talking about commission. Why did you not cut him saying, "No, don't talk this nonsense?"
Singh: My Lord, I was myself a guest of somebody there and that guest of somebody was a guest of somebody again, as the situation was. Behaving in a rude manner, telling somebody … .
Venkataswami: In a polite manner also you could have said all these things.
Singh: I have said so. God is kind to me. I am not looking for these things. I have no commitments in life. I have said it. But the unfortunate part is that he does not understand decent language.
Venkataswami: All right.

Throughout his evening with Samuel and Sayal, Iqbal Singh was a man who was going through the stereotypical struggle between doing the right thing and giving in to temptation. You can see he was uncomfortable. He politely dodged accepting the money, but was really put to the test when he was left alone with the woman. He said that he had paid his respects for 30 seconds at the gurudwara before arriving at Park Hotel and that God saved him from succumbing. One of the tenets of the Sikh code of conduct: 'He who regards another man's daughter as his own daughter, regards another man's wife as his mother, has coition with his own wife alone, he alone is a truly disciplined Sikh of the Guru. A Sikh woman shall likewise keep within the confines of conjugal rectitude.'

In a situation such as this, the religious teachings in one's upbringing become entwined subconsciously with one's being. What Iqbal Singh is referring to is the invisible and intangible quality of conscience. By unconsciously feeling what he 'ought' to do, he ends up putting a break on himself. The other army officers who were offered women, seemed to have no issues with their conscience; their machismo enculturation annihilated any qualms, though none whatsoever were visible. Others who have seen the tapes, disagreed. In their Rashomon, 'Singh did not decide it was the wrong thing to do. He was interrupted by a knock on the door and at no point did his face show any remorse or embarrassment or understanding that it was wrong.'

For some unfathomable reason, Singh was more than forthcoming to Samuel with information about the army's procedures and requirements for equipment. There is a sense that Singh is a 'pleaser'. He unconsciously lives up to what is expected of him in a social situation even though it goes against his grain. Singh advised Samuel; told him that MGO was his department, promised to cultivate Dhillon, and spoke of pay-offs. Yet, he was a man at odds with himself. He spoke as if he was going along with them, observed the handing over of money, but didn't take it himself. He allowed himself a beginning with the woman, but then he cut himself short of sleeping with her. When Singh was leaving, he abused Sayal and told him this was the first and last time he was coming to the hotel. Singh told Sayal that he should have known he did not get entangled in these kinds of things.

Major General Ahluwalia mentioned that there is a certain decorum of hospitality observed between officers in the army. He too, like Iqbal Singh, found it difficult to be impolite and simply throw them out. In India there is a strong culture where the word 'No' is an ugly one. Most people find it hard to say 'no', and curiously people find it even more difficult to accept a 'no'. If some business tycoon ignorant of a journalist's natural negative bias, calls and asks you to do a public relations story on his new car being launched or whatever, if you react with an outright 'no' there is hell to pay. If you say 'yes' and don't do it at all, that is all right. To respond with an outright 'no' is taken as an insult but a 'yes' saves their face/honour. Either you understand the honour culture or you don't. In fact, the word 'honour' barely ever surfaces in daily life in Western cultures today, except in the Hispanic/Latino world. The same is true of the Yes/No culture: either you get it or you don't. In India, you never turn down an invitation; always say you will try. Singh explained this rather common condition in the Commission:

> **Singh:** The situation was such. When I say, I did not like him. I did not hate him. You don't want to develop friendship with everybody you come across. His impression towards me was something different which I did not appreciate. And the environment at that point was this that either I should say, Thank you very much, I am going back, or I go ahead with him. I mean I could not say "yes", or I could not say "no". Sometimes you want to withdraw but the situation is such that you cannot withdraw from a situation, I will put it that way. And let me tell you one more trait of me. I simply cannot say "no" to anybody, even to my enemy. It is very difficult for me to say "no" to anybody. You can say weakness, shortcoming, or whatever; to tell somebody that I am not doing it for you or tell somebody that I will do it for you ... I mean harsh words to that effect, I will put it that way, I won't use generally against anybody.

It is not only the difficulty of saying 'no', but also a panic to avoid confrontations at all costs. Valerie Victoria, expressed it rather charmingly in 'Indians Can't Say No' on a website, www. stylusinc.com, that guides Western businessmen through Indian culture:

> Nonverbal communication is important in every society. Problems arise when two cultures meet, and the physical nonverbal signal means one thing in one culture and has quite another meaning in the other culture. In India, shaking the head from side to side is a visual way to communicate to the speaker that you understand what they are saying and in many cases that you agree with them. On the other hand, in the American culture this is how disagreement and a definite "no" is conveyed. I have finally come to the conclusion that the Indian culture does not have a nonverbal way to express "no" because they are so kind that they have no verbal way of saying "no".

This inability to not say 'no' is not, however, as weak and silly as it would be considered in the West. In India, it is part of being a good human being who is generous to a fault. In the West, the term 'can't say no' is used in a derogatory sense about promiscuous women. In India, it is used flatteringly, to show how large-hearted a person is or to denote a weakness of excessive love: a sign of unconditional love or even deep friendship. As part of that culture, Singh was a polite, conflicted mess. Torn between what he knew was wrong, trying to be polite to an old friend, sorely tempted by a sweet-natured, plump girl, he ended up spouting a lot of meaningless rubbish. Had he meant all his advice to Samuel and his plans to help him further, he would have followed it up with action; would have asked Sayal for the money or would have informed Samuel that he had not received it. That did not happen.

There are, however, contradictions in what Singh said. Compare what he said in the Army Court of Inquiry to what he said in the Commission.

Army Court of Inquiry:

> **ACI**: You were also heard saying to the lady, "Sorry to keep you waiting. We were discussing something." What have you to say?
> **Singh**: I do not recognize my voice but it appears to be my voice.
> **ACI**: Did you tell the lady that your daughter also studied in Jesus & Mary's College as shown in this frame?
> **Singh**: Yes. I did mention this to her but it was when I met her initially.
> **ACI**: On the video clipping just shown you are seen with the lady sitting on the area of the chair and you are fondling the woman's breasts. Do you recognize yourself?
> **Singh**: It is not me.

It talks like Singh, it walks like Singh, it fondles like Singh, it asks for phone numbers like Singh, and then of course, as usual, it must be another duck.

At the Commission, Iqbal Singh was noted for his aggressive and rough manner with lawyers. But, it is reported that after he saw the tapes in the commissioner's chambers, he was decidedly shaken. In the Commission:

> **Singh:** Now in this tape, page No.1, I am supposed to have said [reads from transcript] "Lady: Jesus and Mary. Singh: Jesus and Mary? My elder daughter has studied in this." Now either I have to lose my balance of mind by taking excessive drinks or drugs, what they served me, or something wrong has to be with me because my daughter has never gone to this college.
>
> **Venkataswami:** But you have said this.
>
> **Singh:** I have never said this. Now, how these tapes have been manipulated, I gave you an example the other day when I showed one voiceover of Mr Aniruddha Bahal which I had got it made in my presence. I have only shown you part one of that, part two I will be showing you after I finish this; that how words can be picked up from wherever you desire and incorporated in this to look like as if you are talking those, because neither the lips movement can be seen nor the face can be seen where you can actually say that, yes, this man is saying so and so because his lip movement are showing so and so.

Whose lip movements were saying, 'I did mention this to her but it was when I met her initially' in the Army Court of Inquiry? Was Singh now going to claim that he was manipulated in the ACI with 'excessive drinking or drugs'? The ACI was in no mood for fantasies.

Army Court of Inquiry:

> **ACI:** You have stated before the court that Lieutenant Colonel Sayal came with Mathew Samuel to your residence unannounced. What would have been your reaction if Lieutenant Colonel Sayal had told you that Mr Mathew Samuel would be accompanying him for the meeting?
>
> **Singh:** I would have politely declined to meet him after verifying his antecedents.
>
> **ACI:** If that be so, why did you then discuss about the procedure for procurement of night-vision devices in detail with Mr Mathew Samuel?
>
> **Singh:** I did not discuss anything in great detail. I categorically told that I do not deal with night-vision devices which is a WE subject. I only told them to write an official letter regarding user trials.
>
> **ACI:** You have told the court that Lieutenant Colonel Sayal, while extending the invitation for dinner at a hotel, did not inform you that Mr Mathew Samuel would also be there. If that be so, what was the necessity for you to have discussed again with Mr Mathew Samuel about the procedure for procurement, organizing a meeting with MGO, cultivating Major General P.S.K. Choudary, etc?
>
> **Singh:** The dinner was exclusively organized by Lieutenant Colonel Sayal as told to me. On reaching the hotel I was surprised to find Mr Mathew Samuel there. To avoid an embarrassing situation to Lieutenant Colonel Sayal I was forced by circumstances to stay there till the dinner was over.

In the ACI, numerous questions began with 'If that be so why did you … '. The army brass was not giving any of the officers the benefit of doubt. It was patently clear that the army did not believe them. The ACI then barbecued Singh on why he had not reported the meeting to the Deputy MGO as required, why he said he would organize a meeting with the MGO, why he had pointed out to Samuel all the people to be cultivated, why he had said he was the man who paid all the money for all equipment imported, why he had implied he could influence Lieutenant General Dhillon, why he spoke to the lady about naval exercises in which he had been involved, the reasons for accepting or rejecting grenades not meeting specifications, percentage of commission paid. Most of Singh's answers were Nixonesque non-answers with a lot of words. The ACI was not buying his act.

ACI: Were you entertained by any lady at Hotel Park on 5 November 2000?
Singh: No I was not entertained.

He must have been bored; perhaps the ACI should have defined 'entertained'.

ACI: Are you sure you did not indulge in any sexual activity at the hotel?
Singh: Yes. I am very sure. I did not indulge in sexual act.

Here he graduated from Nixon to Clinton talk. He did not indulge in the 'sexual act' but did he engage in 'sexual activities'? Anyway, the ACI played the unedited videotape showing Singh and the lady. When questioned, Singh said he did not recognize the lady, did not remember what she was wearing, said she seemed similar but her hairstyle was different, denied any conversation about his rank and other ranks in the army, denied discussing the Sukhoi deal and the upgradation of MIG-29 in front of her, and denied asking for her phone number. After viewing the tape and seeing himself in embarrassing activities, Singh said, 'The involvement shown is not mine.'

The Army Court of Inquiry recommended a General Court Martial against Brigadier Iqbal Singh. The General Officer Commanding (GOC-in-C), Western Command, seconded the recommendation. A screaming question: If the army could act promptly and take action against the officers, why was the Tehelka Commission taking years? When you add up the number of all the people on the tape, add the Tehelka team, add the lawyers of the people even mentioned in the tape, all of their witnesses and all the lawyers trying to trip whose versions did not suit them, you can imagine what happened in the Commission. Venkataswami created a relaxed ambience, was extremely patient, attentive, often asked pointed questions to flaky defendants, but with that many numbers to deal with, it was like presiding over a barely controlled fish market. It was a lawyer's dream.

L.K. Upadhyay, (incidentally, ex-army officer) counsel for Lieutenant Colonel Sayal, asked Brigadier Iqbal Singh the same question repeatedly six times, getting similar answers each time. Justice Venkataswami finally got fed up and asked him:

Venkataswami: I don't know whether you are doing a criminal trial or…
Upadhyay: No, My Lord. I am not doing criminal trial at all. My Lord will permit

me because they are very relevant. I don't want to pre-warn anybody about it. I am happy that nobody is understanding where I am leading to. I am happy about it, rather.

Very sharp and very useless. Julia Roberts and Richard Gere in *Pretty Woman*:

Vivian (Julia Roberts): You must be a lawyer.
Edward (Richard Gere): How did you guess?
Vivian: You have that sharp and useless look about you that all lawyers have.

Upadhyay was feeling really sharp that nobody in the Commission, specially the presiding judge, could figure out where he was going with his barrage of questions. Upadhyay is also ex-armed forces. After six questions, it was clear he was going to a place that brought no explanation for the questions. At the end of it all, what did he get out of Brigadier Iqbal Singh? That his client, Lieutenant Colonel Sayal was an upright officer, which had no relevance to the matters before the Commission. He has Singh quoting Sayal in the tapes, saying, 'I want to serve with respect. I want to serve with honour, as I have served in the army.' Could words cost any less?

What was the story Singh told the Commission? He had won four awards. 'In the long history of the Army Ordnance Corps of 225 years, I am the only officer, who has received four decorations up to the rank of full Colonel,' Singh stated. He painstakingly made points for his defence in a 33-page affidavit:

1. I was still in uniform at 6 o'clock in the evening. I made them sit for about five minutes till I changed, but when I see the tape here, I am already in civilian dress. That indicates they have taken the shot somewhere and tried to superimpose it on that.
2. The participation of Aniruddha Bahal is a major participation. He got his pre-conceived plans, executed through Mathew Samuel as well as the girl, who was brought by him.
3. When the girl is brought to the room a second time, she is teaching Samuel how to operate the camera. She was better trained than Samuel was and it is not Samuel that was providing the training.
4. After they see me off the first question Bahal is asking Samuel – pardon me for using straightforward language – he is asking Samuel, did he use so and so and perform that?
5. I made it a point to tell him that I did not leave the room while this woman went out, because briefcases were lying here and suddenly the camera goes off. The latter part of the conversation that you would have doubted me had your money been lost, to which he said, sorry, sorry, that is not there in the tape. But the first part of the conversation, "I did not leave the room…" is there. The full conversation should have been there. In conclusion, the tapes are doctored.

6. Samuel offered the same girl to Lieutenant Colonel Sayal later. This means Samuel was aware from where she had come. Arun Malviya, who Samuel claimed had arranged the girl, was out of town.

7. There was more than one girl. Firstly they all dress alike, like air hostesses.

8. When Samuel offered the money, I refused it and Samuel tried to persuade me. While these arguments were on Lieutenant Colonel V.P. Sayal also tried to persuade me by saying, please, please … Sir. Making gesture with my right hand I told Sayal to please take care of his friend who was drunk and unnecessarily arguing. Taking advantage of gesture of my hand pointing towards Mr Samuel, he thrusted some money on to my hand, which I passed it on to Lieutenant Colonel V.P. Sayal in the same motion to sort out directly with him. Sayal then put the money and in the briefcase and later apologized to me.

In his affidavit, Iqbal Singh pointed out the portion on the tapes where he said to Samuel, 'No, no, she is not required. If she wants to leave, she can go. She was not required.' He had also said, 'Get this female out of here. Why is she locked up in the bathroom?' Singh stated in his affidavit, 'Tehelka attempted to supply sex workers to me, demand for which was never, I repeat, never made by me. On the contrary Mathew Samuel made several attempts to induce me subsequent to this event also but met with failures as I rejected his inducement with contempt.'

Iqbal Singh reminded the court that Mathew Samuel had stated in the Army Court of Inquiry that Iqbal Singh had not introduced him to any other officers or lobbied for West End.

Iqbal Singh, in great detail, in his affidavit said that his dinner was spiked with some kind of drugs that made him 'uncomfortable and excited'. He mentioned all the available 'party drugs' and added, 'above mentioned drugs create sensual images and promote proximity, putting the process in a fast forward mode. The arousal is fantasy oriented. The abuser may not remember anything after the intoxication wears off.'

The problem here is a bit of a catch-22. If Iqbal Singh was 'drugged' by Samuel, then why did he not go all the way with the girl? Why did he ask Samuel to send her away? In the tapes, Singh looked like he was in control of his senses. If he was drugged and did not know what he was doing, he would have taken the money, taken the girl, enjoyed his dinner and thanked everybody and gone home a happy man. But he didn't. He verbally rejected the money, asked for the girl to be sent away and roundly abused Lieutenant Colonel Sayal later. He should not be able to recall what actually happened. Yet, he was able to correct what he calls mistakes in the tapes.

In conclusion of his affidavit, Singh stated:

Tarun Tejpal and his team are the most appropriate examples of traitors and enemies operating within the country and must be punished as per

law of the land for causing character assassination of Armed Forces officers and demoralizing the Army and playing with the National Security besides committing crime against the nation.

The 'demoralization of the army' is a bogey that is pulled out when any negative news about the army is published. It does not stand. Is it not presumptuous to believe that if a couple of officers who are involved in questionable activities with dubious arms dealers and are punished for it, the whole Indian Army will snowball into mass demoralization?

On 14 October 2005, the General Court Martial sentenced Brigadier Iqbal Singh to two years' rigorous imprisonment and was dismissed from service. Singh was found guilty of acceptance of a bribe and violation of the Army Code of Conduct, which included enjoying the hospitality of a sex worker. The GCM observed in the order that Brigadier Singh had wilfully accepted Rs 50,000 from the Tehelka sting operative. It said that Singh was fully aware that he will be offered Rs 50,000 in a hotel and even after accepting the money he continued to enjoy liquor and the girl. The GCM pointed out that Brigadier Singh repeatedly asked the sex worker for her telephone number, which proved he was aware and in his senses.

Was the order and sentencing a bit of an over kill and unfair? Brigadier Iqbal Singh did not get the money, he did not get the girl and yet his professional career is over. Singh's manner of defence played a powerful role in how the GCM reacted. He was known to be rude and rough with the lawyers. Worst of all, Singh and the recording officer Brigadier S.S. Gill were caught in trying to change and forge Aniruddha Bahal's summary of evidence in the court martial. On 15 June 2005, when Aniruddha Bahal was being questioned in the GCM, Brigadier Iqbal Singh got up and insisted on interrogating Lieutenant Colonel V.P. Sayal who had turned into a hostile witness. Judge Colonel Tripathi told Brigadier Iqbal Singh that he would be permitted to do that if he had new points to raise. When Brigadier Iqbal Singh, generally freaked out, the presiding officer Major General P. Khanna ordered him to maintain the dignity of the court. Far from taking that advice, Brigadier Iqbal Singh then screamed, yelled and stormed out of the court, upon which he was arrested. Singh said his counsel had advised him to disassociate himself from the proceedings of the GCM. How could he possibly have imagined he could do that?

Lieutenant Colonel Sayal seemed the most professional in his career of corruption. Sayal's next victim was Major General Manjit Singh Ahluwalia. They had worked together when Sayal was a captain and Ahluwalia was a major. When Sayal arrived with Samuel at Ahluwalia's house, Ahluwalia was surprised to see Samuel when he expected Sayal's wife. Ahluwalia then casually made a mistake that cost him his career in the army.

Think about it. These are all army officers one could meet in an ordinary social setting. At the Gymkhana Club, which has its share of members from the armed services or at a party in a friend's home. It makes you wonder: How many of the people you meet, who are so correct and polite, have a dark side and lead a double life? Is there anyone who doesn't hide a dark side? All these men had no qualms about tasting these women. J.M. Coetzee (Nobel

Prize for Literature, 2003), in his brilliant but depressing novel, *Disgrace* (2000), explores the dark side of a professor who has a sexual relationship with a student. He has no regrets and justifies his sexual activities with an intellectual monologue about the essentiality to follow all one's desires for a meaningful life. He has sex with numerous partners but is forced to re-examine his hedonistic, promiscuous position after his daughter is raped. Were the rapists then also justified in satisfying whatever urges propelled them? There are many allusions to dogs and sexual promiscuity. He finds himself in a job where he assists putting dogs to sleep and there is a dog on the book jacket.

Ram Gopal Verma's film *Nishabd* (2007), delves into the web of dark obsession where Vijay (Amitabh Bachchan), an old man falls for his daughter's eighteen-year-old friend Jia (Jiah Khan). The film was a box office flop. It had to be. No wife would take her husband to see this kind of a story. No point giving the old geezer ideas. No young people want to see the potential of their father's misbehaviour. No man could admit to his family he wanted to see it. Sad, because it is an important film. It is a deep, serious work of art where (WARNING: SPOILER AHEAD! STOP READING IF YOU DON'T WANT TO KNOW!) in the riveting last scene, Vijay explains to his wife's brother, Shridhar (Nassar) what stops him from killing himself, even though he has lost everything. Every day, he drives to a cliff and stands at the edge and contemplates jumping to his death. In a heart-breaking performance, Vijay (Amitabh) says:

> *Aisa nahi hai ké mai marné sé darrta hun. Parr socha ké uské yaadon ké saath kuch din aur jee lu* [it is not as if I am afraid of dying. But then I think, just to be with her memories, I could live for a few more days].

When the camera pans to his brother-in-law's face, there is no judgement or reproach in his eyes. Instead, there is a look of recognition between two men of the dark state of being. Two raw nerves touching delicately, in an almost shared anguish but too awkward for one man to comfort the other.

Can we then, understand why the army officers did what they did?

7 Why do Men do What They do?

A close friend of mine told me, "Look, once it hits a man, a man doesn't care which woman it is. He becomes an animal and he's got to do it. Nothing matters. All his commitments, his true love, everything rushes out of his head. All he wants to do is to just do it. And after it's over, he doesn't want to see the woman for one second more. He'll push her out. He will be filled with remorse and regret, hit his forehead and wonder what got into him. He hates the fact that he did it. But when he's on fire, nothing can stop him. He will hate himself afterwards. That's how men are."

I won't pretend to understand this condition of men. In a conversation with a group of women, we went around the table asking each woman if she would tolerate her husband having a one nightstand. All the women said they would not understand it. Could they be just out of touch with reality and the labyrinth men are caught in? When I checked back with my friend, he said, 'Okay, don't understand it. Just forgive it.'

What is in the sex tapes? Is it even relevant to go into the details? Is it part of the unravelling of Tehelka? Am I looking for reasons to exclude it from the book because of my own personal squeamishness about the incidents? Will the focus of the book turn on this chapter given our own sexual repressions and, therefore, greater excitement and prurient interest in sexual revelations? That would be disheartening. Is it possible to hope that this chapter will be treated the same way as any other? If every aspect of the events in Operation West End is being analysed, then should any particular area be excluded? These tapes may be sexual, but they are not erotic. There are women engaged in a professional job and there are men who, without any emotional connection, are performing a sexual act. The incidents raise two important issues in Tehelka's sting operation: firstly, it exposes the vulnerability of army officers and, secondly, should the journalists have gone as far as they did? How could these army officers have allowed themselves to be so accessible in this area? Was it unfair of the Tehelka journalists to have offered the officers what men reportedly find impossible to turn down? Why do men find it so difficult to say 'no' to casual sex? Can you blame them? When a woman is offering herself, paid for or even otherwise, is it comprehensible that a regular guy, not enlightened or idealistic or highly principled, will just give in? Is it simply a part of a man's being? There can be no definitive answers to these questions. As this entire field is subjective and personal, there can be only Rashomon answers. But, there are answers. What exactly did the army officers do?

There are two prostitutes in a hotel room making small talk with the woman from Tehelka, who is posing as a prostitute. They talk about jobs as 'extras' in Bollywood. One of them asks for contacts in the film industry and says she has been in group dances in films. She points out, 'Vehaan give and take ka hisaab hai [there it is a matter of give and take]'. She says, 'Abhi toh mera figure itna naheen hai. Uss time mera figure bahut hee acha tha [I don't have such a good figure now. At that time I had a great figure]'. She explains that she lost her figure after she had an abortion.

These are the girls of the feel-good generation. The itch to make it out of their lower middle-class milieu into money: a life which means that when the electricity disappears, you switch on the generator, no water means you turn the water pump on, not arriving for work stinking of sweat in the bus, umpteen visits to the beauty parlour, a constantly evolving wardrobe, replacing steel drinking glasses with real glass glasses to be changed when chipped, and most important of all, living with hope that life can improve. Hope is an élitist commodity; a luxury item. Frustrated acceptance of circumstances is a national state of mind and mood. The opportunity to break out of that is a luxury item, and the feel-good factor has been offered for the first time since India's independence. The transition of the feel-good generation into aspirational citizens is cracking established norms. Young people are moving away from poverty-stricken families to strike out on their own in whichever way they can. Can you blame them? Of this phenomenon there is no analysis on a governmental or national level on how it will affect Indian society. The second step, after a sociological analysis, would be how to prevent this change from being socially destructive. At this point we are dashing through a Mistaken Modernity (Dipanker Gupta, 2000), much like a vegetarian, teetotaller, virgin villager, who goes wild in the city with all the goodies to which he never had access to earlier.

In 1943, Hermann Hesse wrote in The Glass Bead Game:

Another possible immunization against the general mood of doom was cynicism. People went dancing and dismissed all anxiety about the future as old-fashioned folly; people composed heady articles about the approaching end of art, science and language.

He could be writing about what is happening in India today.

The fact was that a breakdown of outmoded forms, and a degree of reshuffling both of the world and its morality by means of politics and war, had to take place before the culture itself became capable of real self-analysis and a new organization.

We already have had enough of politics and war but it has not led us to 'self-analysis and a new organization'. Instead, the leap into consumerism has numbed the brain. We have stopped introspection and subsequent philosophical evolution that could enable us to evaluate the direction we are going in, which part of our culture we should restore and maintain, and which discard. Although there have been some terrific books by Dipanker Gupta (*Mistaken Modernity*) and Pavan Varma (*Being Indian*, 2004) that analyse Indian sociological trends, nothing has been undertaken at a national level that addresses this serious issue. Where are we going? What is happening to our youth? It is easy to dismiss the tripe on Page 3 and television programmes with eight year olds in heavy makeup and seductive outfits doing bumps and grinds, but should it only be dismissed and ignored? The Censor Board is more obsessed with cutting out kisses and sex than with what has become the Indian Idol. Censorship is just not the solution. The answer lies in raising questions and awareness. Television channels and the print media have played a violent role in subverting values to the lowest denominator. What leads the media is their perception of what their target audience is hungry for; give it to them. Consequently, interest existing within a margin of society snowballs into interest within the majority. They feed into each other, with the media then sufficiently encouraged to believe it is on the right track then to dish up even more. The Mumbai film industry has, in fact, been more responsible in creating films that highlight the dilemmas and dichotomies in Indian society. At this point, Page 3 journalism has taken the place of the mindless, pandering Bombay films of the 1970s and 1980s. It is not until one begins to really see oneself and be made aware, can any thinking process of the choices of right and wrong begin. The girls in the Operation West End tapes are a direct product of a society out of control, blazing towards what is erroneously perceived to be 'modern'.

⤻

Back to the hot tapes. The Tehelka poseur had earlier placed the handbag with the camera on the cabinet. One of the prostitutes asks the poseur whether she can look at the handbag. When the poseur responds in panic, *Kyun* [why]?', she responds, '*Mujheh purse rakhney ka bahut shawk hai* [I love purses].' The poseur answers, '*Abhi naheen, baad mein dikhaungi* [not now, I'll show you later].' The men arrive. Anil Malviya and Mathew Samuel are entertaining two army officers and P. Sasi in a hotel room. Alcohol is flowing but they are drinking in the cheap thrill manner of schoolboys sneaking cigarettes. The atmosphere is heavy with testosterone-laden guffawing. The girls are trying to entertain the men with rather lame memorized jokes. One of the army officers asks the girls to tell some 'non-veg.' jokes. It is a stag night state of mind. They want the works. The girls are young, plain, and lower middle-class. In my interview with Samuel, he was fumbling in attempting to describe the girls to me. He looked me up and down and mumbled. I had a strong feeling he was stopping himself from saying, 'Well, they dressed like you'. Well, I am safely middle-aged. He did say they didn't look like prostitutes. He said, 'More like the kind of girls you see hanging around Priya Cinema.' They do not look like street prostitutes or the corny caricature Kareena portrayed in the Bollywood film *Chameli*. They could be college kids, they could be secretaries in a mid-level office, they could be girls who have arranged marriages. The ubiquitous question: Why are they doing this? Are we looking at this aspect of the expanse of consumerism at all? Shining the streets of India like Pat Pong? Does the feel-good factor mean a girl can now buy handbags? The Tehelka poseur 'gets' a coughing fit and blames the pollution. Anil Malviya says that she has a cold and asks the Tehelka poseur to leave, which she does, leaving the handbag with the camera in position in the hotel room.

The drinking and jostling continue. The army officers laugh at P. Sasi, suggesting that he is not going to get any that night. Sasi brashly boasts about what he did in Mumbai in a Zen car behind the Taj Hotel. It is a little too easy to be judgemental and prudish about this, but it raises many questions. What is it that makes emotionless sex outside of marriage so exciting? It has to be forbidden for it to become exciting, and danger adds to the eroticism. It is not only acceptable but a man who does it, is admired by other men. Their masculinity is reassured by each other. Little girls used to play 'House House'. Now these army officers are playing 'Men Men'. A Napoleon complex played out to prove masculinity. Today's man seems to be trapped in living up to a macho hype. He has either a brainwashed duty to respond to his libido or he has to live up to what is hyped as masculinity. How much of it is real libido or is he being railroaded by an environment in which any other behavioural trait would make him less of a man? A perceived wimp.

A woman's copious use of her sexual urges makes her rapidly into a 'whore' or a 'nymphomaniac'; never, ever more 'womanly'. The male equivalent to nymphomania is 'satyriasis', a word so rarely used it is virtually unknown. The accepted concept of *mardana*, first of all, in essence, means physical strength and power. Then, the natural expectation is for the strong and powerful to help and nurture the weak. We expect that from stronger nations, we expect that from strong leaders, we could expect that from strong men. Does the very act that makes some of them feel they have validated their masculinity, so carelessly and without emotion is it done, that it in some form actually reduces them?

In the Ramayana, Lord Rama epitomizes the perfect man. He is strong but always faithful to his wife Sita. So much so, that when Ravana's sister, Surpanakha offers herself to him, he cuts off her nose in disgust. Ravana, though a renowned scholar and intellectual, is depicted as an evil man because he lusted after another king's wife. Women are constantly reminded of Sita's devotion to Rama, as a norm to follow, yet men are never reminded of the strength of Rama's fidelity to Sita. Why is this ideal man not in the Indian male's psyche at all? Why is there no focus on the reason why Ravana is portrayed as an evil man? There is so much propaganda about Sita's devotion to her husband and how she followed him wherever he went to serve as a reminder to all Indian women, but the powerful message about how men should behave, as outlined in the Ramayana, is ignored. One of Mahatma Gandhi's favourite hymns, *Vaishnav Janate*, outlines the correct conduct of man. It includes; '*Par stree jeneh maate reh* [consider someone else's wife/daughter as your mother].' Why has pseudo-*mardana* overtaken what is ingrained in our scriptures?

Is today's man noble and honourable; words hardly used in today's parlance? This self-centred insecurity of his own masculinity guides his need to unflinchingly land in any geographical area, without any discrimination. And all this is done to the thundering applause of his buddies. I wonder how many men would think twice about doing it if their locker-room buddies looked at such acts with derision and contempt. There is a great deal of egging each other on. A man who turns down an offer from a woman is not admired and respected for his strength of character, but is mocked for being tied to his wife's dupatta and viewed as a coward. Ironically, he is made to feel less of a man. In an interview, Ricardo Montalban, the Latino actor who exuded machismo to the hilt, was asked, 'How would you describe a great lover?' Montalban replied, 'A great lover is not a man who continually goes from woman to woman, for any dog in the street can do that. No, a great lover is a man who can captivate and nurture the love of one woman her entire life.' To be fair, there are insecure women who will do the same thing. Notably, this is not done to validate their femininity but in order to validate their allure and ability to attract. It is so easy to see in women the cause as insecurity, yet so difficult to see the same in men. Indian women have fought vociferously to have obvious wrongs righted: battered wives, dowry deaths, sati, child marriage…It is near impossible to fight a subterranean, ingrained concept handed down from generation to generation, insidiously and silently implemented. Yet, it has the effect of powerfully warping the minds of young boys who grow up with a twisted view of manhood and teaches young girls that it is the norm to accept it. There are young fathers who plant the seeds by encouraging their sons with dirty talk, leering at women, with the belief they are being open and leading them into a healthy attitude towards sex. When this young boy grows up and gets married, he continues the learned machismo, and a disconnect develops when the wife demands fidelity. He is only doing what he has been trained to do and cannot but feel that fidelity undermines his manhood. Will these boys ever then comprehend the value of sex to be experienced with a consensual passion of love with a maintained commitment? Will they ever really understand the value of fidelity? In the Commission of Inquiry there was a Victorian air of embarrassment and superior piety when the 'scurrilous' tapes were mentioned. Are we expected to believe that no one in that room had ever been to a sex worker or had sex outside marriage? One sensed a huge hypocrisy in matters of sex.

In the 'scurrilous tapes' the first thing one of the army officers does is to ask a girl for her phone number: 'How do I get in touch with you?' He tells her, 'I would like to do it the other way'. When she does not agree, he says you are 'already disappointing'. Defensively, she says, 'First let me know you well. Let's see if you are a gentleman.' Why is the word 'gentleman' used so often by sex workers? Perhaps because they encounter so many who are not? The army officers were doing what their environment has taught them. To paraphrase Milan Kundera, he says that the only stupidity in the modern world is to accept past norms as the only way of seeing things. The army officers were following the mental format that is deeply engraved in the collective consciousness. As you watch the tape, you rage at the officers' stupidity and despair for the young girls. In some way it is difficult to blame either group. They are products of the current that engulfs us.

One of the officers whispers to a girl and she responds, '*Nahin, nahin, aisa nahin hoga* [no, no, it won't happen like that]' *Kaun Banega Crorepati* is playing on the television and Amitabh Bachchan's familiar, sonorous voice can be heard offering options. If only Bachchan knew who was watching him and that his television image would figure on the Operation West End tapes. The officer whispers to that girl again and she emphatically gestures, 'No, No', with her index finger. One of the army officers wriggles closer to the girl; she squirms away. A discussion in Punjabi follows. Two girls are whispering to each other. 'Preeti' has some 'technical limitations' as the army officer refers to it. Mathew Samuel takes her aside and says, 'I can talk to her some personal talks'. He sits very close to her, puts his arm around her, and repeatedly asks her quietly whether she trusts him or not. He tells her he will take care of everything. He tells her to go with the army officer and everything will be all right. Mathew Samuel, tells her: 'It is my responsibility. You go with him. I will take care of everything.' (Here, of course, you wonder, what will Samuel do? How will he 'take care of everything'? Charge into the bedroom at the opportune moment and drag the army officer away from the girl?) Preeti: 'Okay, *agar kuch hoowa* [if something happens]?' Mathew Samuel: 'I am here, *nah*.' Isshh, it's the '*main hoon nah*' syndrome, a clear signal that *woh kahin nahin hoga* [he will not be there]. Incredibly, in the process of trying to convince her, Samuel has a little cuddle with her and kisses her. Has Samuel stopped thinking? Has he lost track of the purpose for which he is there? He has apparently forgotten the camera is rolling. Meanwhile, the army officer announces in rather crude terms what he is planning to do. Eventually Samuel is able to persuade the girl to go with the officer.

The girl and the officer are now in the bedroom. There is a mirror behind the headboard and the officer sprawls across the moss-green bedspread with one hand in his pocket, the other behind his head. He is wearing a cream shirt and beige trousers. They walk about the room, which the officer says was used for a meeting the day before. She sneezes and says a quiet, 'sorry'. She points to the briefcase lying on the cabinet and asks, 'What's this?' The officer answers, '*Samaan pada hai* [some luggage lying around]'. She says, 'Very strange', which should also have occurred to the officer. He tells her, 'Samuel meeting *key leeyey laya hoga* [Samuel must have brought it for the meeting]'. Why did he not open it and check it out, if only out of curiosity? As Aniruddha Bahal pointed out to me in an interview, 'That fellow Jain's guy went to Airtel, got the address and then landed up at Tehelka's office, which is what all of them should have done from the beginning. But they were dumb enough. These brigadiers and generals, if they had done just a little bit of checking. You're meeting this, PPO, the procurement officer, he's in such a sensitive post, Brigadier Iqbal Singh, MGO's office, all these retired generals and so on. Choudary and all of them. That stupid visiting card of Samuel. That was a print out from office'.

The officer and the girl begin their proceedings.

At this point, Preeti asks, 'Can we do one thing? Can we switch off the lights?' The officer says, '*Nahee* [no]'. Will anyone ever answer the question why men always want the lights on and women want them off? Preeti suggests, '*Hum peheley bath ley leyn* [first let's take a bath]'. The officer drags, '*Bath ka time naheen hai* [there is no time for a bath]'. Preeti persuades him, '*Kyon naheen*? Two minutes it will take. *Chalo, chalo*. [why not? Let's go, let's go]'. The officer groans, '*Baap re baap* [slang: father oh father]'. 'Let's go, we'll take bath,' she coaxes. She ties up her hair and pulls him to the bathroom. There are sounds of a shower running. The officer comes out, pulls off the bedspread, lies down, and lights a cigarette. The girl returns with a towel wrapped around her and says brightly, 'Fresh, fresh *lag raha hai nah* [aren't you feeling fresh, fresh]?' The officer says in a resigned voice, 'Sweetheart, whatever you want'.

There is a knock on the door. Room service. The officer says twice, 'Please come after some time'.

It is boring. He gives her instructions. He asks her how long she has been doing this and she tells him she has been at it for six months. He asks whether she has a boyfriend, and she tells him that he is a carpenter in a furniture shop. She says she is doing her best as this is her first time doing this. The officer responds that there is a first time for everything. The engagement ends and she charges to the bathroom. Sounds of the shower running while he gets dressed. She comes out in a towel and dresses. She has a clean, young body. 'Sorry, sir,' she says to him. 'Well done,' he replies without much enthusiasm. 'It's my first time, that's why,' she tells him, which is somehow hard to believe. She brushes her hair; he then borrows her brush and tidies his hair. The officer then reprimands her for lying to him about it being her first time. He asks her about where she is staying and for how long. She gives vague answers about staying with a friend. She asks if she can help herself to some chocolate from the mini-bar. She coaxes him to share it, '*Aik* bite, one bite; after this, sweet *khana chaheeyey* [have one bite; after this it is good to have sweets]'. He takes a small bite, saying, '*Therey karan kha raha hoon naheen tho kadwa aadmi kabhi meetha naheen khatha* [I am eating it for your sake because a bitter man never eats sweets]'. He picks up the phone, calls someone, tells them he is done, and they should come up.

In the other 'scurrilous' tape, the officer insists that the lights are switched off. Nothing much can be seen. The woman does the job according to the officer's instructions and there is barely any verbal communication.

'Why do men do what they do?' is a question that has intrigued me ever since I watched the 'scurrilous tapes'. Why do they risk so much, their careers, sometimes even a presidency, losing their families, for what seems so small and fleeting? In the brilliant film, *The Man from Elysian Fields* (written by Philip Jayson Lasker and directed by George Hickelooper), Dena Tiller, played by Juliana Margulies, trying to understand her husband's actions, asks the gigolo she has hired from the same escort service she has discovered her husband works for: 'What makes a man do what you do?' The gigolo, Nigel Halsey, played by Michael Des Barres, responds breezily: 'I think of it as our mission of giving joy to others, my darling.' Dena again asks in a soft, serious tone: 'Actually, I really need to know the truth.' Nigel picks up her tone and replies in a quiet, sombre voice: 'Fucking is the last resort for a man who feels impotent.'

It is no coincidence then, that when men start experiencing viropause, the confusion they experience for lack of information is frightening and they often end up catapulting themselves through a mid-life crisis by either serially changing partners to a younger brand or start a wild carnival of extra-curricular romps. Today, of course, women do the same thing. Couples who have been married for many long years are known to develop a blind eye for each other. They do not see each other, even when they are looking. There is a revealing opening scene in Stanley Kubrick's, *Eyes Wide Shut* (1999), a complex film about the vagaries of marriage. The husband and wife were played by Tom Cruise and Nicole Kidman while they were still married to each other.

Bill and Alice Harford [Cruise and Kidman], an attractive couple in their thirties, are in evening clothes preparing to leave for a party.

Alice: [looking in mirror] How do I look?

Bill: You look great.

Alice: My hair okay?

Bill: Perfect.

Alice: You're not even looking at it. [Bill kisses her neck.]

Bill: It's absolutely beautiful. You always look beautiful.

Alice: Oh, shut up . . . OK, let's go.

When Bill tells Alice that she looks 'great', at that point of time, Alice is looking anything but 'great' and he answers without looking at her. She has glasses perched awkwardly on the tip of her nose and her hair is a mess. He responds to her without actually seeing her. The blind eyes glaze over wide shut.

In *The Man from Elysian Fields* (2001), Byron Tiller, a gigolo played by Andy Garcia, informs his middle-aged, not very attractive client:

Byron: I've made reservations for us at the Huntington.

Lady (the client): My husband eats there.

Byron: We can go somewhere else.

Lady: It won't matter. He looks right through me.

Byron: That's impossible.

Lady: Thank you

Byron: He's probably very busy at work.

Lady: So he tells me.

Byron: You know when a man is concerned in taking care of his family sometimes his priorities can get all scrambled. It has nothing to do with love.

Lady: For what I am paying you, I expect you to be on my side in everything.

Byron: Excuse me.

The most common excuse dished out by men who are caught in an extra-marital affair is that it was 'just sex'. Women, when caught, have been known to say it was because they felt neglected. Men will insist there was no emotion. That may be true, but either way, it doesn't seem to fly with the women. The magic of that one special relationship, emotional, physical, shared experiences of family, is lost. Even so, there are many women who say, 'It is inevitable. That is what all men do. May as well accept it.' Rather like saying that a man will suck his thumb forever.

On 4 May 2005, Hollywood star Goldie Hawn dropped this pearl when she appeared on America's ABC morning television programme *The View*:

Men spread their seed. That's what they do. I've done a lot of thinking about this because I've had a lot of men cheat on me in my life. All women have. So the question is: What are you going to do about it? Is it in our nature to be true to one person? A marriage paper doesn't do anything but sometimes close a

door psychologically. I've always said, if I'm in a cage and you leave the door open, I'm going to fly in and fly out, but I'll always come home.

Or, not. Methinks, Deepak Chopra has gone to her head. Hawn's wisdom outraged women who had a different perspective from this kind of gender bending. Sex expert Sue Johanson, who had been invited by *The View* to discuss sex education for children, was then asked to address the point Hawn had made. Hawn also said that she understood why men cheated: because it was 'biologically correct in the species'. She said, 'It's just the way I try and keep myself feeling happy because otherwise we're going to be feeling miserable all the time'. According to Johanson's Rashomon, she ticked off Hawn and said, 'I don't agree with you. I do think we are adults, we can make rational decisions and we can look at the consequences and say, "Hey, woah, if I do this, if I go out spreading my seed, what's going to be the long-term result?"'

Did the army officers do what any man would do given the opportunity? Haven't there been enough revelations over the years of high-profile men who have risked their careers, family and destroyed their lives, for something that is so fleeting and transitory? The urge must be a profoundly powerful force for them to do that. I turned to my trusted friend, Rashna Imhasly (renowned psychotherapist and author of the book *The Psychology of Love*) to answer this question. I will put it in layman's language, as I understood it. After what Rashna explained to me, and working with her concepts, I came to the conclusion that there are three categories of men that represent the different levels of the spectrum of conscious evolution: the Serial Sexualizer, the Collared Man, and the Hero of the Heart. Today, you can replace 'man' for 'woman' in any of these categories, because women have shown that they are no slouches in sexual profligacy. The first type represents the primordial level, comprises those who are still totally governed by their instincts. They are the kind of men who are like wild geese; things just happen to them without conscious awareness. They are still very much at the level of the *muladhara chakra*. They are the type of men who have sex outside marriage any chance they get. The Serial Sexualizer is the type of man who will never be satisfied; he is like a bottomless pit; a void that can never be filled with every subsequent sexual act. His instincts are operating, he is not connected to his rational function, and it is as good as masturbating. It is over in seconds; the memory is a nuisance, nagging the conscience, and would rather be forgotten. It is a continual cycle of looking for the next fix. There is the excitement of the hunt, the capture, a quick fix, and it is over until the next demand arises. It is the force of Eros in its raw and blinded form, still acting out of the primordial first *chakra*, the seat of *kundalini* energy. It is the animal in him and, of course, natural. When a person plays with sex outside marriage, it is fulfilling the need for a confirmation that he is wanted and needed. He is still caught in the mother complex, where he was treated like a god and where all his narcissistic needs were automatically met. The woman, for her part, is caught in the princess complex, when she was treated as extra special. He continues to demand what he thinks is his birthright; caught up in this primal erotic euphoria he thinks this is the be all and end all of existence. He is blinded by this need and is unaware of the fact that it is the drive that has him, instead of him having the drive.

The only time he feels a 'real man' is when he can get a sex fix outside the home. He begins to believe the secret is his true freedom.

> Little does he realize that he is living what in psychological language is called the "split psyche" – the instinctual and rational self are polarized. Such men live in two different worlds: the mundane life at home with the socially acceptable mask that is required and the other is the high-risk, secret life where his drives have to be met. [*The Psychology of Love*, 1997]

When Kama's arrow, the sex drive, hits a man, he is forced to make a choice. If he chooses sex for the sake of sex, he is stuck in this labyrinth in a never-ending cycle.

> The labyrinth is symbolic of the path to Self. It at the same time permits and prohibits; only those qualified and equipped with the necessary knowledge can find the centre; those entering without knowledge are lost. Each one has to journey through his/her own labyrinth of right and wrong paths to reach one's centre and gradually work one's way out; the path is about attaining the realizations of the trials and tests all initiations and rites of passage from one level of consciousness to the next. [Op. cit.]

However, if a man is stuck in the labyrinth then he continues to need the constant reaffirmation of his virility and seeks it at every step. He regresses to me, myself, and I. 'I will do what I want, to please Me.' (Op. cit.) As a layperson's observation, I have seen that the more successful and powerful the man is in his professional life, the more selfish is his attitude. He works hard, so the world *owes* him. Yes, it is exciting to be with a new woman, but is it excitement or just projection? Is it because the woman is actually exciting or because the man is projecting his own excitement at doing something forbidden on to her, thereby believing it is the woman who is exciting? Would he spend his life with her? Most often, not, but she is great on the side. It is, however, only because she is on the side that makes her hot. This excitement is then projected from the man himself on to her: that she is exciting. It is only the emptiness in his soul that begs for excitement that convinces him that she is exciting. It is actually because she is not the always available one at home, whose newness has certainly worn off. Subsequently, when this babe on the side has been around too long and the sameness begins to wear and tear, she is dumped.

Why is there the constant need for affirmation of who one is and why is he addicted to this level of existence? Is it because he wants to escape the mundane life with its daily problems with his wife and escape into a fantasy world that keeps him on a constant high? (a high that is fake and fleeting because it is not grounded in reality).

Machismo cultures encourage this wandering in the labyrinth, as the more women a man has conquered, the higher is the esteem extended to him in the locker room. Historically, the Indian culture fully accepted man's visits to the *kotha* (courtesan's house), and this was considered a highly cultured expression of lifestyle. When the courtesans degenerated from ladies who were accomplished poets and singers to impoverished girls *jhatkoing* to Bollywood songs, wealthy men stopped the tradition of *kotha* visits. However, having a mistress on the side was considered what *rajwadey key log* [royalty, landowners, and wealthy men] must do. The women's attitude was ingrained with: *Theek hai. Mard hai. Shawk toh rakhtey hain. Ek doh rakhail toh hogi.* (it's fine. He is a man. He is a connoisseur. He must have one or two mistresses). A friend tells the story of how his grandmother would admire his grandfather when he dressed to go to the *kotha* in his perfumed, finely embroidered kurta; proud that she was married to a man who embodied taste and masculinity. Rashna told me that she has also found this more among Latino men, and where the collective ideal in a society about what a man is expected to be remains at an infantile pre-conscious stage. She has witnessed that more and more men in India seem to have no conscience about their extra-marital affairs and refer to it as the Clinton Factor: if Bill Clinton did it, it is all right for everybody else to do it too. This, however, is where the conflict begins. More and more Indian women no longer carry the burden of submission and acceptance as their mothers did. Unafraid to assert themselves, horns are then locked and confusion prevails because it is difficult to identify, what is traditional and what is modern. Today's Indian woman will more likely take revenge by doing her own share of lap-dancing. What then do we have here? A lot of men who are looking for it and a lot of women ready to give/take it. When collective consensus believes that infidelity is part of their tradition as well as being 'cool', there is very little hope for individual consciousness to develop as an individual's moral code takes refuge in the collective consensus. In India this 'morality' has been blurred to begin with.

The double game of the constant of telling lies, the inevitable boredom of one sex act after another, finally reaches a saturation point. Many men/women feel this keeps them 'young' as the anxiety of being older means you are no longer sexual. It is as desperate, as sad, and as obvious as a facelift. It doesn't make anyone any younger. It only makes it obvious that there is great discomfort in the process of aging. It only makes them look like what they really are: sexually desperate, middle-aged men trying to be what they think is young, who have not arrived within themselves. Would it surprise them to learn that as soon as such men walk away from a woman after a sexually innuendo-laden conversation feeling macho and cool, that the woman is contemptuous and laughs at him as being a pathetic creature? Alternatively, when a woman does the same thing, he turns and mocks her with his friends.

The second category is what I have called the Collared Man. He is either held by his wife on a tight leash or by his own unquestioning obedience of what is deemed by him to be the 'oppressive' rules of society. He would love to have wild, kinky sex but at most he can fantasize about it. He is not able to participate and swim in the current of life because he is too weak and does nothing. He is bored with his wife and his only thrills are pornographic films and magazines. His erotic desires (*muladhara chakra*) are as active as any man's, but too afraid to follow through with its strong urges. He remains a sexually aroused stymied celibate outside his marriage. A highly frustrated man whose sexual urges are expressed by leering at women, talking dirty but never really acting on his impulses. Alternatively, if unable to do that, he can become the irritable and angry man who feels he is the victim of the world at large. Nevertheless, he remains a man who never attempts to try to civilize his primal instincts and his inner growth towards conscious awareness is stunted. He too, like the first category of men, is caught in the double game of the split personality. He follows the norms of society yet his urges continue to be played out in his inner world. His instincts remain repressed not transformed. Tightly held by his wife's leash, he is not truly faithful to her because he chooses to be so but only because he feels controlled by her.

According to Rashna, the force of Eros is part of humanity and arouses our impulse to enter the game of life in order to become involved. In everyday language, it is normal to screw around, but you will be stuck and degenerate in the morass until you become aware of yourself. Individual conscience can only mature when it is forced into the labyrinth. Love when it is experienced, with its passion and its pain, leads us closer to discover more of who we are. A single route of right and wrong choices that must be made, leading us to the centre of our being. It makes us dare the forbidden, pulling us at the same time into love's shadows. Each person needs to experience being in the current of life and experience it to its fullest in order to civilize his drives. The Collared Man remains suppressed, his drives are never tested, and they do not die a natural death. They eat away inside of him; he is not a balanced man. He continues to exist, and remain frustrated and angry at never having lived his life to its full potential. The experience of the labyrinth is necessary for the man to evolve and reach his own decision of staying true to his meaningful relationship.

As Rashna relates and connects Greek mythology to human psyche and relationships, she points out that this is where Hera, the Goddess of Boundaries steps in. Hera is the Greek goddess who represents the force that protects the values of the home, family and marriage. Hera's virtue is about finding fulfilment within partnerships. She is said to be continually jealous. Jealousy, if correctly used, is an energy that creates essential boundaries in social life. If every being lusted after whoever they chose, there would be chaos in the world social order. Jealousy acts as a reminder and creates boundaries without which unchecked passion can lead one astray. Hera acts as the force of union and attachments, mutual interdependency and protects relationships. She is the force that represents consistency and companionships.

When a person gives in to his temptations and he can feel within him the destruction that follows, the pain he will cause his family and decides on his own that this is not his path any longer, he then moves on to higher levels of consciousness. It is a journey that he must undertake on his own. It is only after he has tested out his drives and he can get in touch with his feeling function and then chooses to retrain his drives, is he a truly transformed person. This, as you will see, happened to the army officers involved in the 'scurrilous tapes'. No degree of nagging from a wife and rules from society can kill the sexual urge. He has to experience it himself to then apply his own restraints. It is only by conscious effort that this primal force can be re-channeled.

The third group of men belongs to what I call the 'Hero of the Heart' category. It is about civilizing the animal within, which is the next step. Rashna pointed out that if the force of civilization did not step in and create the 'Thou shalt not's' of society, there would be complete mayhem. The creation of the family system goes along with progressive civilization, where partners take care of each other and their offspring. Those who walk this path of having had the experience of sex outside the bounds of marriage and have been lucky enough to get caught, and then discover for themselves through the process the devastation they have caused, are often transformed. Through the experience of the affair, they have learnt to respect the boundaries and the safe harbour that a stable relationship offers and have at the same time gained the wisdom of the right choice through the process of living through it.

As Rashna explains in *The Psychology of Love*, the process that an individual faces when he encounters the war within himself, leads to a crisis. The Chinese pictograph for 'crisis' is made up of two characters: danger and opportunity. When the man happens to be caught or exposed, he is then forced to make a choice. Now here is the crucial turning point. If the man comes back to his wife after having lived through his affair, it is a decision he has taken after having walked through the fire. It is the transformation of energy: a psychic process where he has resolved the conflict between blind instinct and freedom of choice. The process brings him closer to his inner self which has been touched and transformed through the experience. By going through the dark recesses of the right and wrong paths of the labyrinth, he has learnt for himself what brings him lasting happiness and satisfaction. His soul has understood what it really needs: an emotional steadiness along with the excitement of sex and the security of a future. It becomes his responsibility to make sex with his wife exciting. He rises to the category of the Hero of the Heart. It goes without saying that in this case, his wife too, must understand the journey he must take in order to be truly there with her/him, not just physically, but with his heart, mind and soul. If the wife understands the process, despite the hurt and pain, they can both evolve and rebuild their relationship on a higher plane. Yes, it is a frightening risk the wife must take in accepting that everybody needs the space to widen sexual experiences and emotionally mature to a more humane level. Although there is a perceived high level of risk involved in this acceptance, there is no less risk in the false sense of security if she is married to the first two categories of men discussed earlier. His presence may be with her ostensibly, but his heart and libido will be somewhere else. A phoney fidelity to appease a wife is not a true, deep relationship and teeters within realm of fragility. It is a contrived drama being played out where neither can be truly happy.

I suspect that many men are caught between the two categories: being the Collared Man in the wife's presence and playing the naughty Sexual Serializer who continues to play the double game. If a man continues to be periodically unfaithful to his wife and is sufficiently careful never to be caught, he remains at the pre-conscious level all his life; his instincts will rule him; he will never be master over them. It takes an accident of synchronicity for a man to evolve into becoming a Hero of the Heart.

This is not an indictment of men, but rather empathizes with them for the gender role that entraps them. For centuries, art and literature have glorified the philandering man, from Don Juan to Casanova. Albert Camus wrote about Don Juanism in *The Myth of Sisyphus*: 'It is because he [Don Juan] loves them with the same passion and each time with his whole self that he must repeat his gift and his profound quest.' Reflectively justifying his own love life, which encompassed multiple contiguous affairs, Camus wrote, 'Why should it be essential to love rarely in order to love much?' We can intellectualize, analyse, theorize, but in the end it can be something as simple as lawyer Raian Karanjwala commented, 'I'll tell you why men do it: because it is fun'. So is eating five bowls of ice cream and throwing up on someone else.

In *Outlook* magazine (12 December 2004), a sex survey conducted by Dr D. Narayana Reddy, reported that in 15 years, extra-marital sex has risen 3.3 times for men and 14.6 for women. The report stated that 30 per cent of those surveyed admitted to extra-marital sex, 36 per cent men and 18 per cent women. It does bring a smile when you read that 23 per cent of the women did it 'to get even'. Infidelity is so ubiquitous that it seems odd that there are laws, social and legal, against it. As we are reminded, it saves us from utter chaos where families ensure that everyone is cared for. Even so, society seems to be moving towards the inevitability of it, as reflected in three major films released in 2004. *Closer*, directed by Mike Nicols and adapted by Patrick Marber from his play, looks at the essential dichotomy of love. In Caryn James' article, *Partners Who Cheat But Tell the Truth* (8 December 2004) in *The New York Times*, the zeitgeist is clear:

> And when Anna leaves Larry for Dan, Larry quizzes her about the sexual details of her affair. She flings hurtful truths at him, using honesty as a dagger. At times Patrick Marber's screenplay too flatly articulates the theme of dangerous truth, but *Closer* remains shrewd about today's emotional climate. The characters may be over-the-top selfish, but they stand as symbols of a world in which doing anything for love and self-fulfillment is valued, and also has consequences.
>
> *Closer* never hints at going back to the bad old pre-Kinsey days of sexual ignorance or of restricting sexual freedom. Instead, it analyses the emotional fallout of the inevitable betrayals. What makes *Closer* so contemporary, what may make viewers squirm most of all, is the film's own honesty, its cool acceptance of infidelity as one more fact of life.

James starts the article with:

> "We said we'd always tell each other the truth," she reminds Dan, who responds with bitterness and a burst of common sense: "What's so great about the truth? Try lying for a change – it's the currency of the world." They are hardly the first couple to deal with love and betrayal, but with their agonized honesty they may be the most up to date.

James then wrote about *Kinsey*, a biographical film about the sex researcher who produced *The Kinsey Report*:

Kinsey, the hauntingly eloquent film about the pioneer of sexual research, may be the season's most astute films; and in both, the most wrenching scenes involve revelations of infidelity. When Kinsey (Liam Neeson) tells his wife, Mac (Laura Linney), that he has slept with one of his research assistants, she momentarily falls apart. She is not upset that the assistant is a man, but she is devastated by the betrayal.

She has been attracted to other men, she says, but has stayed faithful to their marriage vows, which her husband refers to as "social restraints".

"Did you ever think that those restraints keep people from hurting each other?" she asks.

But for Kinsey, truthfulness is more important than fidelity. Having carried so many other people's sexual secrets, he says, he can't bear to keep anything from his wife. His painful honesty doesn't resemble selfishness because Mr Neeson so profoundly captures the character's complexity: his earnestness, the depth of his intellectual passion and the remnants of childhood repression.

Writing about *Alfie*, starring Jude Law, James wrote:

> When Alfie betrays his best friend by sleeping with his girlfriend, he tells the audience in one of his asides to the camera, "Even lying to myself comes easily." Throughout the film, it's the lying, not the womanizing, that makes him a cad.

With the currency of today, honesty has become a weapon and a refuge. Many might pray for the days when lying was easier to say as well as to hear.

Again, in the film, *The Man from Elysian Fields*, Byron writes a book about how his marriage failed, and at his book launch reads the final chapter:

> In a moment when she would turn, he would never see her again. There were things that he knew he should have said, that he wanted to say, but when he looked into his wife's face, all he could remember was what the old man had said, "Be careful of women who are content to love you just as you are. It's a sure sign they settle too easily." His wife loved him too much to be willing to settle. But he no longer had the conscience to change. He had convinced himself that everything he was doing, he was doing for her. He had mastered the fatal technique of believing his own lies. And one day his wife and child were gone. He had everything a man could ever need except the reason to wake up every morning. That single split second after you open your eyes and there is that someone to turn to, who loves you, who loves you even more and holds you even tighter through your defeats and through your victories. He poured himself another Scotch, knowing then he would spend the rest of his life trying to gain that split second back.

The army officers must now spend all the years after Operation West End's exposé trying to regain that split second back. That split second contained love and respect for them. Yet it remains; there are some things in life that cannot be pieced together again. The cracks always show, and sometimes even shatter, to replay the past.

The Man from Elysian Fields ends with a narration by Luther Fox, (played exquisitely by Mick Jagger) who runs the gigolo stable.

Luther Fox says,

> I'd spent years trying to pleasure women. I've come to the conclusion that what's important is knowing how to please only one. Now there's something to write about.

There has to be a postscript to all these generalizations about man/woman relationships. All though sociologists as well as journalists record trends in societies, it must be added here, that today's young adults show a definite change away from the old 'need for infidelity' syndrome. Experiencing other relationships before making a commitment and partners ready to perform as much if not more than sex workers, the 'excitement' is now viewed with squeamishness as just plain seedy and pathetic for those who simply can't get it on in real relationships. The feedback I get from young people is that infidelity and talking dirty is just plain 'middle aged'.

The jury is clearly divided on whether sex workers should have been used in Operation West End. The first violation was that, apart from the Tehelka poseur and one woman who set up the camera bag, the others were unaware they were being filmed. As the Tehelka journalists were basically filming for a sting, the only value of which was depicting it to the general public at large, it was a gross violation of the women. Kajal Basu, features editor in Tehelka at that time spoke on this subject.

> **Madhu:** I have got two three different versions of this. I was told that women in the office got to know that women were being used in the sting, they were up in arms and went to Aniruddha and told him it was unacceptable.
> **Basu:** What had happened is that Ani again is like a bulldozer. He made some statement to the press and it came out in print that women in the office had also participated in the story itself, and I think that was somewhere very close to the revelation that sex workers have been used. All the women in the office went up in flames.
> **Madhu:** Because of that statement?
> **Basu:** Because of the statement. I remember all of us marched down to Ani's cabin and he was *gheraoed* [surrounded] there for one hour and a half. Finally we got an apology out of him. Initially he said nothing wrong and you guys are not supposed be here telling me what to do; that I shouldn't have done this and so forth. Finally, they managed to sit on his head and get an apology out of him. There is no reason to have taped any of that nonsense. That's where I

think everything just started falling apart because there is no business to it. Nothing justifies something like this.

Madhu: Besides *gheraoing* Aniruddha, was there an uproar in the office that he had said that a woman from the office was involved?

Basu: Not an uproar. You couldn't be happy about something like this. But it's so much like what Tarun would do. So much like what Minty would do, so much like what Ani would do. I don't think they had any qualms. The qualms and the conscience came in hindsight. I don't think the qualms were there when it actually got done.

Madhu: But maybe as journalists they saw it as okay; we are giving them money now we are giving them girls. It was just one more item.

Basu: Exactly, exactly. And that's ridiculous really because at the end of the day the story is a human story. To ignore something as fundamental as this or to break a rule as fundamental as this. It's not done.

Madhu: It's kind of surprising because both Tarun and Aniruddha are sensitive in terms of gender issues and women.

Basu: No, they are not.

Madhu: They are not?

Basu: They are not. They might talk about it but I don't think it really goes very deep. It doesn't go very deep. Nor with Minty.

Madhu: No, Minty is this macho guy but with Tarun and Aniruddha, as I know them, are politically correct.

Basu: They are politically correct, but when it comes to the crunch, it doesn't work. The question was: what's wrong with being a sex worker and you can find fault with that. The question itself. Then comes the question of what's wrong? If there is nothing wrong in being a sex worker then why couldn't we use the sex worker for a story? I think there's something fundamentally wrong in both asking the question itself and in using commercial sex workers for a story like this. But I don't think that it struck him that way. Certainly it wasn't impromptu. The decision wasn't because someone tailgated them. It certainly took place over a space of weeks, because I do know that they went looking for a girl in Bombay. It took time to locate a girl in Bombay who would be willing to come down to Delhi.

Mathew Samuel spoke about the Tehelka staffer who helped in the sting operation:

Madhu: You said in your cross-examination that one or two tapes were the work of a woman from Tehelka. Who was she?

Samuel: That was ... she is also from Kerala. She resigned because no money is getting.

Madhu: Which tapes did she do?

Samuel: She did Ketan Mehta, private sekitry to minister for state, defence ministry.

Madhu: Did she give him money?

Samuel: No, she just taped. We used two tapes. We are just talking.

Madhu: What other tapes did she do?

Samuel: That one with Kernel Sehgal and the call gells. She acted like call gell, set the camera, then she said she sick and left.

Madhu: Did she volunteer to do it or did someone ask her to?

Samuel: I don't know. See, she knows something is going on but she doesn't know vaat. I only know after coming to hotul, Aniruddha told me she is also coming.

⌒

Aniruddha Bahal explained his reasons for including the women in the sting operation.

Madhu: Aniruddha, the media was supporting Tehelka throughout, then when the prostitute story broke, there was a divide.

Bahal: There was no divide. It was just *The Indian Express*. So if you can consider *The Express* on one side, the others were, like, *theek hai*, you shouldn't have done it.

Madhu: Why did you bring in the girls? You were telling me at one time, when we met casually that you wished you had taped their demand for girls.

Bahal: Yeah.

Madhu: Did they make the demands over the phone?

Bahal: Lots of phones. There were lots of meetings, which weren't recorded also. Every time you are meeting, you're not going with a briefcase and recording those meetings. And, which I kept saying, there were hundreds of hours on the phone, which went unrecorded. How can you record conversations on a mobile? You need a clamp. It's a kind of suction device, which you put on the thing and you don't have those. You're travelling *idher udher mobile mein bath karna hai khatum bath* [here, there, everywhere you talk on the mobile and the talk is over]. So all those conversations are unrecorded. The one landline number from which Samuel made calls, or received calls, was a stand-alone number, because we couldn't give the PBX number in any case. So anybody who picked it up, knew what to say; it was just usually Samuel or me. We couldn't give any other number because, if somebody has a caller ID and he calls back. We couldn't call from the PBX line also, because caller ID would come. Even landlines have caller ID and they would call back and somebody would answer, "Tehelka"; that would expose us immediately.

Madhu: Tehelka was seriously criticized by the press for using sex workers and the way the story broke it looked as if Tehelka was hiding that fact.

Bahal: How do you say that we've held that information? We didn't. If we had, I can understand it being a big problem of ethical transgression. If we had not given these so-called sex tapes to the army court or the Venkataswami Commission and somebody had broken the story, then it would be a problem.

We had already given it to the authorities; both tapes as well as transcripts. In fact I remember, because Justice Venkataswami before he resigned, all the tapes were viewed in the Commission. All the tapes were played over six weeks. Everybody could come and see the tapes: the original tapes, playing in Hi8. He called me to his office and he said, please point out the scurrilous tapes to me. So I gave them these numbers. I said you can play anything you want. But they didn't want to do it. So then I said okay then, these, these, these tapes, and he saw those portions before me. In fact, there are portions in some tapes where there is only conversation, not the visuals. Venkataswami said, that is fine, that I'm not stopping, that will be played. K.K. Paul, the police commissioner was sitting there when he's watching those tapes. What do you mean we were hiding it? In hindsight, there were two things that I would have done. I would have maybe included it comprehensively in the voiceover and said for reasons of these graphic images that we have not included it in the four and a half. That would have solved everybody's problems, *yeh tape hai, deh diya hain* [here are the tapes, we have given them]. So that, if there was a charge *ke press ko kyu nahin bataya* [why didn't you tell the press]?

Madhu: But why did you use sex workers? You wanted to show that they were vulnerable from all sides?

Bahal: One is that, look at the extent of the vulnerability. It means you can make them do anything. If you're an intelligence agency or something then the sky's the limit; on the way that they have been compromised.

Madhu: Colonel Anil Sehgal's wife accused Tehelka of blackmailing her husband with those tapes.

Bahal: All that came up after the exposure in *The Indian Express*. Why didn't she bring it up earlier? It began two, three days after that because they had to give an explanation for that. Iqbal Singh doesn't mention it in his affidavit about these things. No blackmail, nothing. Sehgal doesn't mention it in the Army Court of Inquiry or in the Venkataswami Commission. Nobody says anything about it, till the day that it comes out. Then they write to the army, I don't know whatever explanation they started coming out in the media.

Madhu: Colonel Sehgal said that West End spiked his drink.

Bahal: *Haan.* Sehgal goes and says that he doesn't meet Samuel again. Whereas in fact, there is a small five minute meeting subsequently.

Madhu: Colonel Sehgal said I met him because he was blackmailing me, that's why, although I caught him with the cameras . . .

Bahal: Oh hoh!

Madhu: . . . and he forced me to introduce him to Narender Singh.

Bahal: All bunkum! Why Narender came through? There was a different collegiums of ways that Sehgal and Sasi also were responsible.

Madhu: He said, "I only introduced them afterwards because they were blackmailing me."

Bahal: Why would we be so interested in meeting a man with that process? It is totally false. Nothing like that happened. In fact, we were so scared after that, when Samuel goes and meets Sehgal again, in that last bit, with the device in his satchel. We knew that he suspected the briefcase, but satchel he wouldn't suspect. All these are explanations after the fact. If there was an iota of truth, they should have come up before *The Indian Express* broke the story. Why didn't they come up with this in the Army Court of Inquiry? Why are they coming up with all this after the exposé in *The Indian Express*?

Madhu: Going back to the girls: that has been an area where you have been criticized. Why did you do it? Why did you need the girls there?

Bahal: The demand came from them and please, please don't forget that we were defence middlemen. We were acting in that whole mode. We were even talking in that mode. So now they're saying, why did you say that on tape? Samuel *ney itni baar toh usse aisi bath karra tha* [Samuel spoke like that so many times], you're talking loosely. You're not bloody stiff-legged journalists, for God's sake, you're just middlemen. Sehgal, PPO was a very, very important post. Actually, then it started off in my mind, that this is an additional ground on which to be a part of the story. It was later on that you could say that we had second thoughts whether to put it or not; that it would derail the story, but initially we said we would put it in. Even at the screening I remember telling at least two, three journalists that this had happened. For God's sake, we had given all the tapes, including the sex tapes, to the army, way back in March. We had given all the tapes in May 2001 to the Commission. Then *The Indian Express* comes out with this story in August, as if we have been trying to hide it? How the hell have we been trying to hide it? The Army Court of Inquiry has happened on this girls business.

Madhu: So who got the girls?

Bahal: [Silence. Off the record.]

Cut in Tape, and then:

Bahal: But obviously there, no rules were flouted, nothing. It was the public interest thing. It wasn't for personal. But these people who are holding positions of such sensitivity; for them to be compromised in this manner. What if we had been someone else? These tapes wouldn't even have come to your knowledge.

Madhu: I was told by someone working in Tehelka that the women in Tehelka were up in arms and they threatened to resign.

Bahal: All bullshit. Nothing like that happened. My secretary went, because somebody had to. This is all part of records, so I have no problems. She went and she faked an asthma attack and left when things started getting shirty.

Because we needed someone to handle the camera there. So the Commission knows about this. There's nothing. The name is there.

Madhu: Any of the other girls?

Bahal: No. None of the other girls. Nobody else, because we didn't need. After that, it was just those two episodes.

Madhu: Did other people in the office know?

Bahal: Nobody knew. How can you talk about this story in office, *yaar*? The very nature of the story is such. There would be so many times that Samuel in the Esteem coming in with a briefcase and going out. People were naturally curious; *bhai kidher ja raha hai, kya kar raha hai* [hey, where is he going, what is he doing]? [Laughs]. *Esteem mein ata hai, idher jata hai, mein jata hoon, udher jata hai, idher jata hai* ... [he comes in an Esteem, goes here, I go here, go there...].

In the Commission of Inquiry, R.P. Sharma, counsel for Colonel Anil Sehgal, zeroed in on Aniruddha Bahal:

Sharma: The first one is the blatant violation of the law of the land by the so-called investigative agencies composed of only graduates. Under what provision of law did you undertake Operation West End while knowing, as an enlightened citizen that it was the role of the police or the CBI?

Bahal: I think the media is a watchdog in any democracy. I am not aware of any provisions of law that prohibit me from doing what I did.

Sharma: Were you aware that in terms of Section 39 of the Criminal Procedure Code, you as a citizen of this country were supposed to pass on the information or intelligence that you have gathered through your staff to the police or the CBI, if you do not have the confidence of the local police? Why did you perform that role? This you will have to explain yourself. I will read out Section 39. "Every person aware of the position or of the intention of any other person to commit any offence punishable under any of the following sections of the Indian Penal Code, which includes sections 161 to 165, which relates to corruptions shall (so it is mandatory for the citizen) in the absence of any reasonable cause (which he did not have), the burden of proving his innocence shall lie upon the persons who aware for giving this information to the nearest magistrate or police officer of such commission or intention." I want a simple answer.

Bahal: The primary function of the media is to the people, which that particular media has to address to. In this case ...

Sharma: My question is simple. Did you comply with the provisions of the law of the land as mandated in Section 39 of the Criminal Procedure Code?

Bahal: I think if you read the clause, which you [just] read me, there would be reasonable cause there.

Sharma: Reasonable cause for what? For not reporting? What is the reasonable cause, you explain? I understand your explanation. What is the reason for not reporting to the law enforcement agencies, which the Constitution has set up. Why did you not do it? What is the reasonable excuse for not doing it as a law-abiding citizen, if you are?

Bahal: Which particular clause are you reading?

Sharma: Section 39 itself is clear. Have you got it? " . . . shall, in the absence of any reasonable excuse, the burden of proving it . . . shall lie upon the persons who are there". Now you have to give an answer.

Bahal: Yes, I am giving an answer. As I said, the beholden duty of any media anywhere in the world lies not with the authority of that particular state, but the media is basically to report facts as they see it to the people. In case of a newspaper, it would be the daily readers; in the case of television, it would be the viewers. In the case of Internet, it is whoever is reading them on the Net. So, there is no obligation on the part of the media, as I understand it and as many of my colleagues in the media would understand it, to report to the authority on what stories they are doing or what they are not doing, or what they would like to do.

Sharma: In other words, according to you, the members of the media are above the law of the land.

Bahal: No, that is not what I said.

Now this is a tricky one. If every journalist were to report every story that he was covering and which concerned illegal activity, a lot of stories would die before we got them out. While producing the video magazine *Newstrack* (TV Today) we did sometimes break the law to get stories. Journalist Nutan Manmohan climbed through a window of a sealed hooch factory to get the story after numerous deaths of people who had consumed the illegally made alcohol produced there. How could she have called the authorities from a remote village, informing them she was about to break the law to get a story? When *Newstrack* got Shiv Sena activists on camera admitting to the conspiracy to bring down the Babri Masjid, the CBI got after *Newstrack* to provide them with details. Sometimes journalists are just better investigators.

However, Arun Shourie, the pioneer of activist journalism and ex-minister in the BJP coalition, gives us something to consider in his code of ethics for journalists:

Professionalism – specially good professionalism – puffs up the professional. He begins to insist that as he is such a good professional he is entitled to more than the ordinary citizen, and that he is entitled to special privileges merely because he is such a good professional – privileged access for one, the right to be taciturn about his assertions, for another – and he is entitled to them even though he is neglecting the duties that are his as an ordinary citizen.

Arun Shourie's third paragraph in the code would give Aniruddha something to think about:

> I affirm that I shall be a citizen first and last and not a mere professional; in particular I shall not claim for myself any more than I would urge for the ordinary citizen; but simultaneously being a citizen, I shall wholeheartedly and relentlessly devote myself to the public benefit.

These are personal dilemmas every journalist must face, which arise in every day situations but even more when covering a war. Are you a journalist first or are you a patriotic citizen, which may mean you cover up negative stories about the army? Almost all the journalists covering the Kargil war faced this dilemma.

Sharma then shifted to the second law Tehelka violated:

> **Sharma:** For your information, in terms of Sections 131 of the Indian Penal Code, "any person who attempts to seduce a member of the army, navy or air force from his duty or from his allegiance shall be liable to be sentenced to imprisonment for life". Such is the grave offence which your team has committed.
>
> **Bahal:** What is the question?
>
> **Sharma:** The question is, have you or have you not committed an offence in terms of Section 131 of the IPC?
>
> **Bahal:** No, I have not.
>
> **Sharma:** Now I come to the question under the heading "Call Girls". You call them call girls; I would call them as white collared prostitutes, because they come from decent families, highly educated, this and that. They have used the term "call girl". Was doing business in flesh trade also part of your activity in Tehelka.com?

This is a new one! White collared prostitutes! The dictionary defines 'white collar' as 'belonging or pertaining to the ranks of office and professional workers whose jobs generally do not involve manual labour or the wearing of a uniform or work clothes.' Sorry, honourable counsel, this does not work. Sex workers' work does involve manual labour and they do wear work clothes, which are usually very different when they are off duty.

> **Bahal:** No, not at all.
>
> **Sharma:** Would you please disclose the source of procurement of the call girls for use in your operation?
>
> **Bahal:** I plead Article 20.

According to the Constitution of India, under Fundamental Rights and Right to Freedom, Article 20 is about Protection in respect of conviction for offences. Article 20(3) states: 'No person accused of any offence shall be compelled to be a witness against himself'.

Sharma was thrown completely off guard; seemed surprised and then went ballistic:

Sharma: How Article 20(3) comes in? [Objection] You have admitted all these questions and answers for the consumption of whom? My Lord, these should be taken into consideration by My Lord at the time of finalization of the findings of the Commission. I am asking you a simple question. I would not ask the names; that is not proper; that was also disallowed by My Lord. What is the source from where you procured the call girls?
Bahal: I said I have already answered your question.
Sharma: What?
Bahal: Article 20.

Sharma gave up:

Sharma: I put it to you that you are trying to evade an answer, which has a direct nexus with the truth or otherwise of the story that you are taking.

What does Bahal's modus operandi to recruit the call girls have to do with the fact that Sharma's client, an army officer, is on the tapes with a sex worker? Then Bahal got fresh:

Bahal: I do not know, as a matter of law, can a suggestion follow a pleading of Article 20?

Justice Venkataswami played referee and got them out of this jam.

Venkataswami: He is saying you are deliberately avoiding an answer to the suggestion which he has given. You may accept or deny it.
Bahal: No.
Sharma: As an enlightened citizen concerned primarily with the public interest, as your MD has been claiming and you also claimed that, were you not aware of the law of the land? Yesterday I quoted to Mr Tarun Tejpal and now I quote it to you. Section 5 of the Suppression of Immoral Traffic in Women Act, 1956, which says the procurement of prostitutes and supply to any person is punishable with three years of imprisonment. Are you aware of the law or not?
Bahal: Well, since then I have been aware of this, many lawyers that we have basically consulted with, do not think that we have violated any provision of law.

⌒

Tehelka's lawyer and Aniruddha's friend, Kavin Gulati talked about the prostitutes they brought in:

144

Madhu: What advice did you give to the journalists about the prostitutes?

Gulati: They could have been prosecuted for that. In fact, I've been dying to answer that in a public forum, but I chose not to because I did not project myself at all. What is this story, Madhu? This story is about corruption. How do you corrupt a person? Only with money? It is women, it is liquor. It's not only these army officers. It is there in our system. Prostitution is not something which does not happen. It's very rampant. You walk the roads of Bombay. There are all these people who are doing it on an every day basis. See much of it was: Did I supply these women? Did they ask for it? How does that matter tell me? For example, if you are a colonel in the army, supposing I push a woman inside your hotel room, where you are there on a foreign jaunt, going with a technical team to evaluate a new system in Russia and you have these beautiful ladies being shoved into your room. Does it behove an army officer to entertain such people, when you're on official duty? So I'm saying forget this business of who forced whom, the fact that you've agreed to be with them and do whatever you did, is good enough. That is part of the story according to me. Aniruddha and all, in their cross-examination, they were trying to be defensive, by saying all this, that "they were the ones who demanded it and we did not offer", and things like that. But according to me, they chickened out there. Because the fact is that this is the story. This is what happened, whether they demanded it or not. How is that relevant at all? But, I think by that time when they faced cross-examination they were scared and they knew of the consequences.

Madhu: This fellow, Anil Malviya; he was the guy who was supposed to have procured the girls?

Gulati: Yeah, that's what the cross-examination says, yeah.

Madhu: But it seems to be like a convenient sort of thing because Malviya as far as we have been told, is dead.

Gulati: [sighs.]

Madhu: It seems to have been palmed off on to Malviya.

Gulati: That looks like, but the fact of the matter is that if you see those tapes, where he is there, that is just the beginning of the story. Samuel, of course, started developing in confidence much later. But at that point of time he was a very glib talker and very smooth generally. [Pauses] And, he was the one who was actually interacting with Sehgal [pauses] so I really don't know. I've asked these people and I've spoken to Samuel also at length. When this issue came up, I would have personally liked that they would have taken a stand, and said, "All right, Tehelka – whether it be Malviya, or whether it be Samuel, or whether it be anybody – Tehelka has done this and we stand by it whatever be the consequences. You send us to jail? Fine." But they said "No, we have to say who was the source. They are asking us the source. We are telling you the source." And then of course the judge stopped it at a point, saying that, whether names should be brought in. There was a long, drawn argument where the attorney general had appeared and I had appeared for Tehelka. The judge passed an order where I had shown them instances, where the judge had right from the beginning said that, why drag names? Because on one hand the government was saying, we want to protect these ladies. I said, "If you're wanting to protect these ladies, why tarnish their reputations? There are so many people doing it in the country, why get these people out in the front? What do you achieve by doing that?" That is when the judge stopped it. He said, "Nothing doing". Because to a stage, they do accept that these girls were procured. From where they were procured, who procured them, what were their names; the judge was of the view that the fact that you've admitted to this much, is good enough for me. Because if I have to say that you were unethically doing this, I can still say that, because you do admit to this extent, that as a part of the team, some Malviya did it – so what? It was a Tehelka story which was emerging. So why get into names and things like that and who procured them?

Madhu: So you feel that it was the right thing for them to do. In terms of using one more thing to corrupt. To show that they can be corrupted.

Gulati: We are all adults, and if one is susceptible to such corruption then they must be exposed. Because the other side was saying that, "We want to bring these girls who have been misused back into the mainstream." Who is going to believe that? It is happening all over.

Before we judge the army officers too harshly, there has to be some understanding that they were just doing what their immediate culture, society's ethos, and their unenlightened libidos led them to do. When the armty officers engaged with sex workers, did it in any way make the Indian Army vulnerable? The answer has to be a resounding: Yes! Female spies in war and peace have been and are commonly active. From Mata Hari (real name, Margaretha Geertruida Zelle McLeod) during the First World War, to numerous famous women during the Second World War and the Cold War. Today, there are thousands of women reportedly working secretly for the newly evolved cyber information spy links, such as the US intelligence community's worldwide, super-secure intranet Intelink. Evidently, the power women have to entice and extract information has traditionally been used as a political weapon. According to Camille Paglia (*Vamps and Tramps*, 1994), 'The prostitute is not, as feminists claim, the victim of men but rather their conqueror, an outlaw who controls the sexual channel between nature and culture.' Paglia has said that she viewed 'the prostitute as one of the few women who is totally in control of her fate, totally in control of the realm of sex.' In her perception there is a 'misunderstanding what prostitution is. Prostitution is Woman's command of men!' Awareness of this female power and the accessibility of the army officers, clearly answers the question. Tehelka proved beyond doubt that documents and information were handed over to the Tehelka sting operatives in exchange for money and women. What could be more vulnerable than that?

Should such men be forgiven? Their wives could forgive them. The nation should not.

8 The Errors of Comedy

Treason is like diamonds; there is nothing to be made by the small trader.
– Douglas William Jerrold (1803-57), British Humourist, Playwright

Samuel: I don't know vaat is bloody HHTI. Huh, I'm going to sell this product. Who talk taught me vaat is HHTI, you know? Major General Manjit Singh Ahluwalia. I'm going to sell my, I say I have my product, lawtz of products; one product I have is HHTI. I don't know really full name. Then he told me vaat is HHTI is hand-held thermal imager. Basically this people vants to know vaat is our capacity.

Ahluwalia asked me, "Tell me vaat is the specification, magnification?" Vaat I know? Then Ahluwalia started, "I know you are very recently joined this way. I am going to tell you eggzakly vaat this is." Then he essplained me vaat it is. Ahluwalia was showing me vaat he knows. Then I come to know, this is the matter.

Major General Manjit Singh Ahluwalia was additional director-general, Ordnance Services, Army Headquarters. When he appeared in the Army Court of Inquiry on 10 April 2001, he clarified that in his current assignment he had limited interaction with civil firms and 99 per cent of his processing was through public sector units. Operation West End tapes reported that Lieutenant Colonel V.P. Sayal (Retd) took Samuel to meet Major General Ahluwalia, and identified him as the DGQA. That was the first mistake. Ahluwalia was not DGQA. Lieutenant General Amarjit Singh was DGQA.

Lieutenant Colonel V.P. Sayal had worked with Ahluwalia when Sayal was a captain and Ahluwalia a major. Sayal took advantage of that connection and took Samuel to Ahluwalia's home. Ahluwalia offered them drinks and snacks, and the discussion veered towards army procurement. In this, Ahluwalia sensed Samuel's actual poverty and repeatedly told them that this game was too big for the likes of them. He told them that offers of a couple of thousand, a low brand whiskey, and driving a Maruti car would not get them very far. This can be construed to mean, don't offer me peanuts. If you want to get in the game, play big. There is no record of Ahluwalia taking money. Samuel said he gave it to Sayal to pass on to Ahluwalia. Sayal said Samuel never did. The fact that Sayal kept the money meant for Brigadier Iqbal Singh seems ominous. Anyway, Ahluwalia never got it.

But Ahluwalia gave Samuel an inside on how big and deep the corruption ocean is. Ahluwalia said to them,

> If you are talking about a deal which is 20 crore here, 60 crore there, make a profit of 5 crore, *saala*; if you come to my house to meet me on Diwali, you can't talk without bringing Blue Label. If you are talking of bloody making a couple of crore of rupees, you can't give me bloody Black Label also.

He went on to explain that it would easily cost Rs 25-30,000 to find out where a file is. Ahluwalia was on a roll,

> I've been here two years. I must have met at least 35-40 people. Every other fucker knows bloody Putin. Everybody knows George Fernandes. Everybody knows Saddam. They all say, "Get this done for me".
>
> It's a massive bloody system. There is no place for friends. There is no place for singleton. It requires very deep pockets. Nobody talks small. And I also ended up with bottles of Black Label, Blue Label in this bloody business. Because it is easier to come and bloody talk. As I said, if you're going to talk about a couple of crores, even to say "good evening". You have to present that bloody "good evening" properly.

Ahluwalia expounded on how, at every stage of an arms deal, as the file that went up to the next step, all the persons who could stop or move it make money. If a deal is worth Rs 60 crore, the question then is how much money the officer who will move the file sees upfront on that day. Only one line has to be written on that file and, according to Ahluwalia, nobody will forward a Rs 60 crore deal for a mere dinner at Maurya Sheraton hotel.

At the end of the meeting, when Samuel and Sayal rose to leave, Sayal tried to hand Ahluwalia a packet of money. Ahluwalia said, 'Don't be stupid', and refused it. Sayal responded, 'Okay, later then'. According to Tehelka, Sayal gave the money to Ahluwalia later, off camera. Ahluwalia has maintained he never received any money.

In the Army Court of Inquiry, Ahluwalia, in his sworn statement, vented his anger at Sayal, whom he had known for twenty years:

> At this stage I would like to also place on record the personality of Lieutenant Colonel Sayal. He is dim witted, thick skinned; one who does not take no for

an answer easily and is persistent like a leech. I was irritated to see him bring without my knowledge someone I did not know.

Ahluwalia pointed out that although he had known Major General P.S.K. Choudary since they were classmates, he refused to take Sayal and Samuel to him. He said that all his comments were sarcastic and frivolous in nature, and the army court should observe the tone of his conversation, which was basically to discourage them. He turned down a dinner invitation from Sayal at Maurya Sheraton.

In his statement, Ahluwalia was unforgiving to his now former friend Sayal:

> An elaborate trap has been laid to set me up, including using a retired colleague who at that stage I called a friend. This talk took place in the privacy of my home in my personal capacity in a most informal setting and was aimed at an old army colleague. Mr Samuel could never have had access to my residence but for the connivance of my former colleague who grossly betrayed my trust.

The Army Court of Inquiry questioned Ahluwalia about why he did not report the meeting with Sayal and Samuel to the higher authorities as required, why he spoke about thermal imagers to them, why he did not check Mathew Samuel's antecedents as required, and why did he not report the second meeting? Ahluwalia responded by saying that he thought he had dissuaded them enough to believe they had given up and did not then find it necessary either to report the encounter or check Samuel's antecedents. He said he did not report the second meeting because he had no proof that money had been offered, claiming too that he was provoked by Sayal into talking about the thermal imagers.

> **ACI:** In your conversation recorded in the videotapes/transcript, you had repeatedly said that the entire system is corrupt and that you have to pay bribes to get your work done. But in your statement to the court, you have said that you dissuaded them from entering in to the field. Is not your statement self-contradictory?
>
> **Ahluwalia:** My intention was to dissuade them. In fact, the method that I used was to tell them since they wanted to use dubious means I exaggerated the extent of dubious means so to imply that it was beyond their reach. I thought that this was the best way rather than sing the virtues of the system and get into a never-ending conversation.

Okay, how's this as an alternate for discouraging a never-ending conversation: 'The army does not allow agents or commissions. It is a watertight system. If anyone is caught they will be arrested. So I suggest you do not dabble in this game?' The conversation does confirm that corruption is rampant in the army and no one in India is surprised.

The Army Court of Inquiry questioned Ahluwalia about why he did not inform

Lieutenant Colonel Sayal and Mathew Samuel of the correct procedure for introducing an item. Ahluwalia's answers can only be described in the most politically incorrect way as 'an Indian state of mind'. He said, 'The frame of mind that I perceived about Lieutenant Colonel Sayal and Mr Samuel precluded my telling about the correct procedure to them.' About Ahluwalia's boasts about 'ending up with bottles of Black Label, Blue Label, in this bloody business', he explained that they were all frivolous statements. The army court pointed out that Ahluwalia had detailed the entire procurement procedure to Mathew Samuel but in contradiction had stated in court that he had only told them what was already in the public domain. Ahluwalia claimed it was not contradictory since, 'I only talked about "first trial evaluation and then procurement", and that WE deals with imported equipment while we deal with indigenous equipment, which is common knowledge.' What about the statements made by Ahluwalia that if West End did not have enough money to pay people off at every level there was no point in proceeding further? The court asked, 'Was it normal practice that without gratification no item can be procured into services?' Obviously, every serving officer knows the truth on this issue, but this was a clear attempt to place the situation on record. Ahluwalia was back in the 'India state of mind'. He answered, 'I am aware that procurement of defence equipment has adequate checks and balances to ensure that no corruption takes place. Mr Samuel and Lieutenant Colonel Sayal had indicated right in the beginning that they wanted to use dubious means. I therefore became wary of introducing such a firm into the system. Hence I exaggerated the dubious means to such an extent so that they were dissuaded from entering into the fray.'

The army court played the videotape with Samuel offering Ahluwalia money, which he refused to take, saying, 'This is, Sayal please, don't be stupid … *theek hai badh mein* [… okay later]'. But, he did not take the money. Ahluwalia had two choices in the Army Court of Inquiry: he could say what he did, which is, 'army procurement procedures are clean and there are enough checks and balances to prevent any corruption'. Alternatively, he could have said, 'I did not take any money from Samuel but the procurement system is corrupt and it is common practice to take money from vendors who represent major arms manufacturers.'

That would have opened a can of names and a necessity for evidence. Following that course, Ahluwalia would also have made himself a punching bag for all the arms wheeler-dealers and their network of corrupters and corrupted. Was Ahluwalia's conversation with Sayal and Samuel motivated by an intention to dissuade them or did they simply not interest him enough? He was not impressed by them at all. He knew Sayal was new to the game and had no idea how the big dudes played. The likelihood of Samuel measuring up to the well known, slick, suave arms dealers in the city was indeed laughable. After watching all the videotapes and reading the transcripts, could the army court believe that there was no corruption in equipment procurement? Or was this another conspiracy of collusion and just plain Omertá. Scratch the surface, stick to the fictitious element created in the West End tapes, do not go deep enough to actually dig out the real corruption involved in arms deals. Have the heads of all the army officers in the West End tapes and let all the other money-grabbing dogs lie low peacefully.

Ahluwalia is a truculent yet defeated man. He believes that Tehelka exploited the naiveté of the army officers and the base nature of human beings: 'You walk into a place with your wallet open, what do you expect?'

Ahluwalia told them in army language that this business was way out of their league, that arms dealers drive Mercedes cars, don't invite you to a club but to Maurya Hotel. This was interpreted as instructions. Ahluwalia has repeatedly said that if you read the transcripts in totality, he was discouraging Samuel. He has said he was quoted out of context when he told them they had to invest big money. He felt he had been quite rude to them.

Lieutenant Colonel Sayal then invited Ahluwalia to a party which he declined. Ahluwalia feels that he has been treated unfairly:

> I was found guilty on 13 March by the media. One fact is forgotten: I did not take any money. Tehelka people are blasé about what they have done to people's lives. A small mistake has ruined my life. For the last two-and-a-half years we have been miserable. My wife has been sick because of all this. My daughter is in college and she is a brave girl. My son is an investment banker in London. My family has been very supportive. But I have lost my rank and it will make a difference post-retirement. I am bitter because the organization has distanced itself. They ask me, "Why did you let him come into your house?" How did I know who they were? Sayal called up as an old friend and I did not want to be rude. I felt I had done no wrong. I knew I would come out of it. It's taking so much time. I should have been a three-star general by now. The last three years have been spent to redeem my honour. I have been sinned against more than I have sinned. This was like over speeding. I did meet them but I did not take any money. Samuel said he gave the money to Sayal who said he gave it to Ahluwalia. But the story has to be linked to a defence deal. Where was the defence deal? What has Bangaru Laxman got to do with defence deals?

As far as Ahluwalia is concerned, he got implicated because he allowed Sayal to bring Samuel to visit him. He said,

> It was a preconceived story. They catch hold of a clerk like P. Sasi who can be bought for Rs 1000. Two colonels like their whiskey and women. That is a crime against their families. Claiming it can lead to blackmail for state secrets is too far fetched. If they had caught Suresh Nanda or Choudhrie it was a different matter. Here people were just bragging about whom they knew. So? That happens all the time. It was not honest journalism. They had preconceived ideas and then tried to fix the jigsaw puzzle in places. Army officers by training are slightly different. I have been branded as a dishonest man. All I did was entertain these people and serve them drinks. I told them this was not the way to do things. It was too big for them and they should stay away. All that

was interpreted as advice on how to go about it. The mistake I made was that I did not report them.

On 27 August 2001, Ahluwalia filed a defamation case against Tehelka and Zee TV, asking for Rs 2 crore in damages and a front-page apology in all the prominent national newspapers.

Ahluwalia filed an additional statement before the Tehelka Commission, in which he stated:

> I am the only person in the entire episode who drove away the fake dealer and spurned the inducement offered. Despite being aware of this, Tehelka has crucified me through their media blitz being fully aware that as a serving service officer I am not permitted to go public and give vent to my version of the incident. The entire event has been directed by a person who, as a son of a retired army officer, was aware of the "soft belly" available in that it is the custom of service to show civil hospitality when a retired officer goes and meets a serving officer of his regiment. Also, the rules and regulations governing the service officers prevent them from speaking to the press or in any way making public their version of an incident. My family, I and my organization have paid a heavy price for this normal brotherly contact which has been totally distorted with the full knowledge that no forum is available to me to refute this allegation.

Ahluwalia stated that most of the top brass of the army do believe that he is innocent but are wary of dropping charges and reinstating him because of the anticipated uproar it would generate in the media.

After the Army Court of Inquiry concluded, Major General Manjit Singh Ahluwalia's services in the army were terminated in an administrative action instituted by Army Headquarters.

Lieutenant Colonel Sayal had only just begun with Ahluwalia. His next stooge was Major General S.P. Murgai, who for Samuel proved to be two steps closer to Jaya Jaitly.

9 Of Greedy Bondage

Money is the great power today. Men sell their souls for it. Women sell their bodies for it. Others worship it. The money power has grown so great that the issue of all issues is whether the corporation shall rule this country or the country shall again rule the corporations.
– Joseph Pulitzer, December 1878, St Louis Dispatch

Samuel: Murgy like a headmaster. Ha! Huh! Like a headmaster teach you students. He'll tell one matter hundred times. "The point is this," almost all the times he starting like that. His essplanation is very nice. So he will essplain, this I have to do, this I have not do. To go this money there, don't go this money there. He is very pungtual. If you do the vurrk, he will take the money on the spot. Ha! Ha! Huh! That's also.

Madhu: How did you create this rapport with him that you felt like his younger brother?

Samuel: Suppose this Saiyal is intarduced me, then I went there, then meanwhile vaat was my basic strategy I focused on. If suppose I was intarduced to General Murgy, I make a difference between Saiyal and Murgy. I said, "Sur, Saiyal told me you are like that, like that." Murgy said, "*Sala aisa bola* [bastard said that]? Samuel don't talk to him. What help he can do for you?" Why I did, suppose Saiyal come to know my past, my things from Tehelka, he won't believe that suddenly.

Major General S.P. Murgai (Retd) was the latchkey that opened the door to Major General P.S.K. Choudary, L.M. Mehta (additional defence secretary), and Surendra Sureka (Kanpur businessman) who claimed he knew Jaya Jaitly. Murgai was formerly additional director-general, quality assurance, and appeared in the Army Court of Inquiry (seventh witness) on 3 April 2001. The most striking sentence in his affidavit at the Commission was that Mathew Samuel 'thrusted' money on him. Murgai met Samuel at the DSOI [Defence Service Officers'

Institute] Club on 18 October 2000. Sayal was there with Samuel, and as they passed Murgai they were introduced to each other. Interestingly, Murgai had first met Lieutenant Colonel Sayal when Murgai was in the army working as director, quality assurance.

Murgai said he was promised a fabulous job by West End operatives at a dollar salary. In the Operation West End tapes Murgai spelt out each step of the movement of a file in the defence ministry and the army. He explained at which point money was necessary to nudge the file along. He also mentioned it would be a good idea to meet the MGO (master general ordnance) Lieutenant General Dhillon before Diwali since he was going off to the US after that, because he was waiting for Diwali gifts. Murgai said, 'Only a fool goes before that'.

> **Samuel**: Everyone intrrussted in their pocket. Verrry intrrusssting matter, if Saiyal and Murgy are sitting and three people, both Saiyal and Murgy talking in Punjabi against me. They don't know it's being recorded. *Woh mujhey abuse deh rahey* [they were abusing me]. Rrreally. Ha! Ha! Ha! Murgy saying, "Whatever that money, you take it." Saiyal saying, "I'm taking that money". I'm enjoying. Before I'm moving also, he saying, "Keep it to you Mat. Don't talk to him." So vaat is happening with General Murgy, went to up to this much level and doesn't even know vaat happened. Otherwise, Saiyal also will be in the picture.
>
> **Madhu**: This rapport you created with General Murgai? Did you discuss personal things with him?
>
> **Samuel**: No. If suppose we are starting talking talks, so suppose General Murgy needed car to go visit his daughter in South Ex. I'm always willing to give the car. "Sure, you take the car". Sometimes Murgy offered me, see suppose you need any drinks, he tells me, I will get from the canteen. I said I don't vant. And [great excitement in his voice] in Christmas he gave me two bottles of Peter Scott whiskey. Rrreally I forgot that. *Driver key saath bhej diya* [he sent it with the driver].

When interrogated by the army court, Murgai insisted that he had never promised West End any trial evaluation. The Army Court of Inquiry then played the tapes that showed Murgai telling Surendra Sureka and Mathew Samuel that he would get a trial evaluation letter issued and Samuel would receive a copy of the letter. The Court then repeated the question about the trial evaluation letter. Murgai's silence communicated more than any words. After a few long minutes, he picked up some bravado and said, 'The tapes have been doctored'. The army court asked him:

> **ACI**: Did Lieutenant Colonel V.P. Sayal meet you in connection with contracts for supply of uniforms by Rohit Exports, blankets supplied by Mahavir Woollen Mills, supply of combat boots by Tulsi Rubber products and SDE by Jammu Plywood?
>
> **Murgai**: I was not DQAS in 1994-95 and for the other contracts, I do not remember.

ACI: Is it correct that the inspection of the items in respect of the above contracts were carried out under the aegis of DQAS and its controllates?

Murgai: Inspection was carried out by controllates. He is the inspecting authority. Inspection is carried out by the QAEs controllates who were under my control.

That of course makes you wonder how deep and far the corruption extended? Everyone under Murgai had to play along.

The Army Court of Inquiry questioned Murgai about how he organized a meeting for West End with MGO Lieutenant General Dhillon. Murgai admitted that he was able to get an appointment for West End through Dhillon's staff officer, explaining that it was a UK-based firm dealing with electronic equipment who wanted to present their products. Murgai told the court that although he told Samuel that Dhillon had no role to play at the moment, they insisted on it and paid him Rs 20,000. Murgai said, 'They wanted to pay the money for the professional advice I had rendered, which I reluctantly took at their insistence.'

The court then grilled Murgai about his connections with Surendra Sureka, the businessman who supplied the army with uniforms. Murgai insisted that Sureka was one of the contractors he had met a couple of times and had no deal with him. He also maintained that he was unaware that Samuel was planning to give Major General P.S.K. Choudary anything.

ACI: It is mentioned in the transcript that after Major General P.S.K. Choudary had left your residence, you stated, "So, you are happy with the...?" To which Mathew Samuel said, "Okay". It is also mentioned that thereafter Mathew Samuel said, "Then he opened ... he accepted my gift also", to which you said, "Yeah, very good", and then Mathew Samuel gave you Rs 25,000 which you took saying "Okay, that is good". Are the above statements true?

Murgai: The above statements are not true because this is a doctored conversation which Tehelka has used to their advantage. My statement, "yeah very good" is a neutral and casual remark. As regards money paid by Mathew Samuel, West End was making ad hoc payments to me. I had never asked for any money nor I knew that some payment will be made to me on that date. It was a deliberate ploy by West End to pay me immediately after Major General Choudary had left. However, since the money was given by Mathew Samuel on his own, I accepted it as ad hoc payment towards my consultancy relating to aspects on trial evaluation and procedure for vendor registration.

In answer to a question, Murgai described Mathew Samuel and his meeting with L.M. Mehta, who was presented with pastries and a packet. It is in dispute whether Mehta accepted the packet. Murgai admitted to having accepted Rs 90,000 from West End.

The Indian Army bars employment for two years after retirement. How did Murgai get around that? Murgai said: 'I received ad hoc payments for counselling that I had rendered.

I kept an account of it, whatever ad hoc payments I received which I reflected in my tax return.'

Major General Murgai did not snivel around, did not say he was drunk, did not say he was hypnotized like many of the others did. He admitted to receiving Rs 90,000. What indeed does this 'counselling' mean other than just one more way of getting around the law? How difficult can it be to work for someone and not get on the official payroll, and they can consult your butt off. Shouldn't there be some Intelligence follow-up on all these retired army officers who get into the arms supply business? Murgai can be heard saying on the tapes, 'No one has a price. It is negotiable. If that negotiation is there, it is because the system is corrupt. The man is not corrupt, the system is corrupt.' This is marvellous logic. Who mans the system? He later goes on to say:

> You are selling defence products. Defence products have got certain significance. They are going to be used in the field. The life of jawan is involved; the security of the country is involved. The people in uniform are not corrupt. The politicians who are there are not corrupt. The media is hyping them that they are corrupt.

All this said by a man neck deep in money taken to pull strings in the army to get people to meet Samuel, a virtual stranger to him.

Murgai met Samuel at a club and the following week he had him shaking hands with Lieutenant General Dhillon, MGO at Army Headquarters. Murgai then took him to meet Ketan Shukla, at that time private secretary to Hiren Pathak, then minister of state for defence production. Throughout all this, Murgai continued to advise Samuel in great detail about the procedure he should follow to get the evaluation letter for his product.

Further, Murgai claimed that he was not supposed to be at the meeting with Jaya Jaitly. It was purely accidental. How could it have been accidental when in a discussion with Samuel he outlined to Surendra Sureka, 'We will give two to Jaya Jaitly in that initially and one for you and one for me?' He is talking about lakhs of rupees.

Sidharth Luthra, counsel for Tehelka, took Murgai on every incriminating sentence he had uttered in the tapes, but the lawyer didn't get very far. Murgai suffered instant amnesia. Luthra read out conversations from the transcripts where Murgai is discussing how to bribe Major General P.S.K. Choudary. Murgai's response? 'I do not recollect'.

Although Murgai obviously thinks lowly of Samuel now, Samuel felt he had a great equation with Murgai. He said he explained every detail and nuance to him on how to function as an arms dealer. According to Samuel, he gave Murgai Rs 50,000 to give to L.M. Mehta to obtain the evaluation letter. Murgai denied ever receiving this money. Tehelka insisted that a gold chain was given to L.M. Mehta. Both Murgai and Mehta denied this.

Siddharth Aggarwal, counsel for the Commission, interrogated Murgai on the confidentiality of procedures to supply arms. Again, the answers he got from Murgai were on the lines of: the procedure is something arms vendors need to know and that he had not divulged any secret information. Murgai also fudged around by asking, 'Which document are you referring to?' Although the procedures were promulgated in 1992 and Murgai had been in the army for 38 years, he said he was unaware of the prescribed rules of procedure.

Aggarwal pinpointed, through his questions, how Murgai had picked up all the information on procurement procedure during the course of his duties. He repeatedly harangued him on this until Murgai finally admitted to this:

Murgai: The information gathered regarding the procurement procedure were as I understood during my service.
Aggarwal: Now, I put it to you that you have parted with information, which is marked secret within the Army and the Ministry of Defence, to West End International, which is a civilian concern.
Murgai: No, I have not.

In reality he had. How many of these retired bogey-fogies are doing this? Can this issue be taken so lightly and completely ignored by the Ministry of Defence? Counsel for the Commission, Aggarwal, got on Murgai's case on this.

Aggarwal: Are you in a position to tell us generally whether people from defence services are taking employment or consultancy with various arms manufacturers? Does this normally happen?
Murgai: I cannot say.
Aggarwal: [Reading from the transcript of the tapes.] You are saying, "Here in India, there are already companies existing, companies headed by people like me, who have been in the department, after retiring, they found their companies where they have found their employment. Couple of generals, couple of brigadiers, major generals ... It is a full fledged company who spread their wings. They are tackling at different levels, different projects. That is what is networking."
Murgai: Maybe.

This is the most important thing Tehelka exposed. Not Jaya Jaitly, not Bangaru Laxman. They exposed how laws are being flouted by some retired army officers who tip their whiskey glasses to the army with a golden handshake they give themselves. They are the *dalals* who sell classified information in the market to the highest bidder.

On 6 December 2004, the CBI registered a case of corruption against Murgai.

10 A Greased Passage to India

There is always free cheese in a mousetrap.

– Navjot Singh Sidhu, Cricket Commentator,
Politician and Former Cricketer

Remember H.C. Pant? Staff officer in the Ordnance Factories Cell who burped on a satisfying Rs 60,000? Well, the grease motivated him enough to take Samuel to meet a slew of 'dealers', the first among whom was Deepak Chabbra, deputy general director of Russian Technology Centre since May 2000. Chabbra is noticeable in the unedited Operation West End tapes only for all the people he named and implicated. He said he was a construction engineer but it turned out that he did a little more than that.

Deepak Chabbra was cross-examined at the Commission of Inquiry on 2 January 2002. The directors of his company are all Russian. According to a document read out by Kavin Gulati, counsel for Tehelka, Chabbra's job entailed: take a deep breath!

Overseeing the existing business interests of Russian Enterprise Developers and manufacturers of product of military assigning and representing them in various matters in India with the ultimate object to render services in the sphere of technical maintenance, modernization of Russian-made A&ME already in use in India to direct technical cooperation with the Indian undertakings. Additionally, to examine the prospects of collaborative development and marketing of Russian technologies, spare parts, components and other products covering Army, Air Force, Navy and all defence-related operations as and when and then eventual production in India. The third is to undertake export and import trading activities to produce a long-term assurance for comprehensive products support over the expected life of Russian made A&ME

in India as well as to translate into reality the potential for enhanced military technical cooperation between India and Russia with the intention of using market opportunities to create profitable business, leading to meet futuristic mandatory requirement of the Indian Army in modern military equipment.

Chabbra must certainly be one busy man. Besides all the above, he also said he was engaged in construction undertakings and international trading, in buying tungsten scrap from defence plants and exporting it to the US. But wait, it's not over yet. He also exports semi-precious jewellery. This profile matches that of a defence middleman but, of course, we have been told they do not exist. All of them have agreements for representation of foreign countries in some form, mostly with Russia. They also conduct other import/export business as a cover for the real thing. The finishing touch is that they often become the consul general of a country so small that it is often tinier than their own 'farm houses'.

> **Gulati:** What in your view is the role of a defence middleman?
> **Chabbra:** Middleman means some agency work. If somebody is working for a certain company, so he gets agency for that job done.
> **Gulati:** You have seen the profile. You are aware of the objects of the company. You are also aware of the company is [has to] to serve its defence part and also engage in the business of supplying spare parts. Would it be correct to say that this company or its agents were defence middlemen?
> **Chabbra:** There were no such middlemen involved at any time.

At the Commission, Gulati repeatedly pinned him down on his conflicting testimony. Chabbra denied meeting Mathew Samuel more than once, and never speaking to him over the phone. Gulati pulled out telephone records showing that Chabbra had made calls to Mathew Samuel. Chabbra just shrugged, 'I didn't remember'.

When Chabbra appeared at the Army Court of Inquiry on 10 April 2001, they were most interested in his connection and activities with Major General P.S.K. Choudary, as well as Mrs Choudary and their daughter. Chabbra made a series of conflicting statements about the Choudarys.

Chabbra said his brother had acquired a 250 sq. yd plot in Vasant Vihar on the basis of an agreement with Dr Pankaj Choudary to develop it. In this deal, Chabbra's brother got the basement and the builder the first and second floor of the building, with the builder responsible for the entire cost of construction.

> **Chabbra:** Some time after June 2000, the builder along with some prospective buyers for the first and second floors came to meet my brother. I was also present. At this stage, I was introduced to one Mrs Choudary and her daughter. They checked the documents pertaining to the plot and left thereafter. I have never met nor spoken to Major General P.S.K. Choudary. Mrs Choudary spoke to us and our wives on a couple of occasions, seeking our help with regard

to teething problems in the building. Subsequently, a broker approached us for hiring on rent the whole premises for a Middle East company. We met Mrs Choudary once again. The negotiation, however, did not materialize. Thereafter I have never met her.

ACI: Do you know which is the portion owned by Mrs Choudary in that building?

Chabbra: Mrs Choudary owns the second floor in that building which is approximately 1500 sq. ft.

In the original tapes, Chabbra clearly told West End that he would organize a meeting with Choudary. Also, as mentioned earlier, Chabbra had shot his mouth off about Major General P.S.K. Choudary's wife and daughter being deeply involved in collecting money and real estate deals but backed off when questioned by Choudary at the Army Court of Inquiry.

In the ACI, Major General Choudary asked Chabbra:

Choudary: It is alleged in Tehelka tapes that my wife and my daughter had been accepting money on my behalf, which accusation is attributed to you. Is it true?

Chabbra: It is not true.

Weird! Answers vary according to who the questioner is.

One year later (15 May 2002), at the Commission of Inquiry, when Kavin Gulati questioned Chabbra about his relations with Choudary, he changed his mind about all that he had said in the Army Court of Inquiry. This was after the 'doctoring demon' had been raised. Gulati asked Chabbra pointedly whether he was now denying he knew Major General P.S.K. Choudary. Chabbra's answers then bounced around between the Vasant Vihar property actually belonging to his brother, he had never really met Major General Choudary, professing ignorance about who had then bought the Vasant Vihar flat, and he forgot how much was paid. But he could not avoid admitting that he was finally aware that Major General Choudary's wife had in fact purchased the property. Gulati concluded by stating that Chabbra knew a lot more about all this in the Army Court of Inquiry and was now deposing falsely, which, of course, Chabbra denied.

In the unedited Operation West End tapes H.C. Pant and Chabbra can be heard discussing their forty-year-old friendship, as they grew up in the same neighbourhood, Gole Market, New Delhi. When questioned in the Army Court of Inquiry, Chabbra replied that he was only a casual acquaintance and had met him three or four years ago at Co-ordination Cell of DGOF (Ministry of Defence) when he dealt with a contract for export of Tungsten scrap. He denied it twice when questioned at the Commission of Inquiry, when Tehelka's lawyer Kavin Gulati accused him of deposing falsely.

Then Chabbra introduced yet another twist. In his cross-examination on 2 January 2002, Gopal Subramaniam, the senior counsel for the Commission, questioned Chabbra on the veracity of the tapes:

Subramaniam: You have gone through what is put against your name at various places? By and large, it is accurate?

Chabbra: Generally, yes. I believe so because it is being produced as a tape recorded statement. I must have said. Generally, I was there, I could have said so many things. I have not gone through exactly what I have said.

Subramaniam: And the same applies to Tape 43 also?

Chabbra: It must be all right. I do not deny all that. I was there. I would have said all that.

Subramaniam: Do you stand by what is stated in all these tapes?

Chabbra: Generally, yes.

Five months later, on 15 May 2002, Deepak Chabbra was re-summoned to the Commission. He was cross-examined by Medhanshu Tripathi, counsel for Tehelka, who read out Chabbra's earlier testimony:

Tripathi: So, you do not deny the tapes as such?

Chabbra: No, I deny it fully.

Tripathi: When?

Chabbra: Now. I am denying it. Because as you were reading these papers to me, I did not apply my mind. Now I retreat my statements and I now say that all these tapes are doctored and manufactured to suit your purpose.

Tripathi: You were on oath, I think, when you deposed before this Commission.

Chabbra: That is right.

Tripathi: Which part is doctored? Can you specifically pinpoint which part is doctored?

Chabbra: It is totally doctored. I have to see the tapes. Then, if you want, I can pinpoint.

Tripathi: Without seeing the tapes, you are saying that the whole part is doctored?

Chabbra: Even the transcripts, they are not pertaining to me. These things were never talked there.

Tripathi: And you made certain statements. On what basis you have made this statement?

Chabbra: It is incorrect.

Tripathi: So, you made a statement on oath incorrectly?

Chabbra: Because it was incorrect.

Tripathi: At this moment, I am putting it to you that you are making a false statement on oath.

Chabbra: I am making a correct statement.

Tripathi: Why should the Commission believe you? On what basis?

Chabbra: I am making a correct statement now. I have made a correct statement earlier.

Tripathi: But earlier you were on oath and right now you are denying your earlier statement.

Chabbra: It was just read to me. I never accepted this.

Tripathi: Why did you say "Yes"?

Chabbra: It was just written there. I said, it is written there. That is all.

Tripathi: Are you connected with the RTC project?

Chabbra: I was connected with the RTC at that time. But it is a company which never took off. It has already died. It is already an aborted child.

Tripathi: Who is Alexander Popov?

Chabbra: He is with the company.

Tripathi: Which company?

Chabbra: The RTC company.

Tripathi: Please turn to page 9 of your earlier deposition. Please see Question No. 55. May I read it for you? "You have discussed this RTC project with Mathew Samuel?" Your answer is, "Right". Now you are saying you do not remember. So, your memory is quite short.

Chabbra: It is incorrect.

Tripathi: What is incorrect?

Chabbra: Whatever is said here – Question No. 55.

Tripathi: Why did you say "Right"?

Chabbra: I did not apply my mind at that time.

Tripathi: So, you are applying at this time?

Chabbra: Correct.

Tripathi: Is it under legal advice?

Chabbra: I am saying the truth, whatever is the truth, what I can remember today.

Now figure this conversation:

Tripathi: Did you discuss the RTC project with Mr Pant?

Chabbra: No.

Tripathi: Please come to Question Nos. 146 and 147 at page 23. "How many times roughly have you spoken to Mr Pant after that?" Your answer was: "I don't remember exactly. Couple of times, maybe." Then the question: "In what connection?" The answer is: "Of course in my RTC connection. That was my main aim to talk to him."

Chabbra: Now, I am telling you, RTC is a paper company. It has not taken off. It has already died before it's taking off. It is an aborted child. Nothing to talk on RTC.

Tripathi: Why did you make this statement?

Chabbra: It was the situation then.

Tripathi: What situation was there?

Chabbra: RTC was there.
Tripathi: Therefore, you spoke to Mr Pant?
Chabbra: No. I did not speak to him.
Tripathi: Why have you said so in Question No. 147, "Of course in my RTC connection. That was my main aim to talk to him"?
Chabbra: It is incorrect.
Tripathi: That statement is incorrect?
Chabbra: Incorrect.

There is such an ease and social acceptance of lies being told, Chabbra does not flinch. It is surprising such persons were not charged with contempt.

When Siddharth Aggarwal, counsel for the Commission, questioned Chabbra about his conflicting statements at the Army Court of Inquiry, Chabbra reiterated: 'It is incorrect. Mr Pant had nothing to do with it. It is based on my memory. I think my memory has failed me here.'

More than that, all sense of honesty has failed him here.

Aggarwal confronted Chabbra with transcripts of the West End tapes where Chabbra is promising Samuel a meeting with Major General Choudary. Aggarwal read out bits where Chabbra discussed when money has to be paid. Pant said, '*Indent vindent…voh deyga* [indent, he will give it].' Chabbra replied, '*Kitne ke hai? Sara jugad hai* [how much is it? It is all arranged].' At this point, Chabbra said he could not remember anything since it had all happened two years ago. Irritated, Aggarwal said, 'That would be your answer for any question that I ask about this specific transcript.' Chabbra defiantly responded, 'I do not think you can question all these things, whatever you want to.'

Yes, but hours drag by with answers given that amount to nothing. Additionally, all those COT collaborated with one another to nix all that was recorded on tape. For each other. N.K. Khetarpal, counsel for Major General P.S.K. Choudary, questions Chabbra, in a way that not only helps his own client but also Chabbra. Read this:

Khetarpal: It is attributed to you in the statement of Mr H.C. Pant that you told him that General Choudary does not meet anyone and he is entering into all negotiations through his wife and daughter. Did you state so to Mr H.C. Pant?
Chabbra: That is all incorrect. I did not say anything to anybody.

'Anything to anybody?' This is Rashomon in action. This kind of collaboration between the clients through their lawyers to subvert facts, and thereby subvert what was on tape for all to see, continued throughout the proceedings of the Commission. There could not be a longer, twisted and diverted path from the truth.

Khetarpal: Have you ever met or ever spoken to Major General P.S.K. Choudary?

Chabbra: Never.

Khetarpal: Did you ever tell Mr Deepak Gupta that you had been dealing officially with Major General P.S.K. Choudary?

Chabbra: Never.

Khetarpal: Did you tell Mr Deepak Gupta that you knew Major General P.S.K. Choudary?

Chabbra: Never.

Khetarpal: Did you ever approach Major General P.S.K. Choudary for any favours?

Chabbra: Never.

Khetarpal: I put it to you that all statements made in different transcripts concerning Major General P.S.K. Choudary to you are all false?

Chabbra: Definitely. I have said that these Tapes 42 and 43 concerning me are false.

My question to Chabbra is: 'Did you ever tell the truth in the proceedings in the Commission?' Chabbra's honest answer would be: 'Never.' My next question: 'Which is the true representation of facts? First, what we saw and heard on the Operation West End tapes; or, second, what you said in the Army Court of Inquiry; or, third, what you said in the Commission of Inquiry. Which one is true?'

Why did it take Chabbra a year to realize that the tapes were 'false'? And why is the nature of the Commission such that any person can ramble on, not give answers, or give untruthful answers, and all that is done is to record the proceedings? Why can the commissioner not question the person being cross-examined about the veracity of the statements? A historical format is followed where the commissioner watches the proceedings as if watching a play; a bad one at that. He accepts the conflicting testimony, for after all, what does he have to do but simply file a report which will never see the light of the public's eye. It might as well be a drama critic's review.

Next on H.C. Pant's circuit was Deepak Gupta, son of the RSS trustee R.K. Gupta. Here they entered the world of a B-grade version of a Bollywood stereotype. So easily dismissible in films as an exaggeration, but how do you disbelieve a man who describes arms procedure incidents minutely, recounts details of mega-deals and buying off politicians and bureaucrats with a sleight of a hand? After convincing the Tehelka operatives to believe them, the wheeler-dealers then attempt to convince the Commission of Inquiry and the Army Court of Inquiry that all that were boasts and lies; now they are telling the truth. Gupta elaborated the procedures to Samuel:

MGO normally has three suppliers. You have to be one of them. If you become one of the three, then it is my job to pick you up. What happens is, that whole report is sent to the Ministry of Defence. Then they will have the tendering process. After which they have their PNC. That's where we can help you. Where we can tell you what to fill; what are the other rates that are likely to come. Political help comes only in areas where either you are L-1 or you are a single vendor. Now, if you look at the entire Russian business, it is all single vendor. If defence secretary is told, can defence secretary ask WE to go in for trial? That I will do. General Choudary is the man. Only he takes too much money. If he is ready to give the money, I can talk to even General Choudary.

Gupta proceeded to give his own job profile, which he said included power, defence, telecommunication and highways. In all these areas, he said, whatever money had to go to the government went through him. This gave him the access to get any instructions implemented.

Gupta spelt out how his operation worked. He stated that he operated from the Prime Minister's Office (PMO). He said,

Brajesh Mishra gives in suggestions, do this, this needs to be done, this file needs to stop, this file needs to begin. So we are in an area of big fish. We catch big fish. If you want to catch the big fish, it is 35 per cent business. But while the net is put for the big fish, there are people who hold the net. There is defence secretary, there are some joint secretaries, so I come to know.

Gupta gave details on how the network had to be pumped:

Now, at the user level, when it comes to army, air force, I have people operating in small areas. Small-time agents. They can be worked upon for clearance, clear our money, clear our order. Because main payments goes to bureaucracy and politicians. If you want political interference, politicians take four-five per cent, bureaucracy takes two per cent, user takes only one per cent. Eight per cent. Maybe one or two per cent expenses. Ten per cent is your expense. Commission in this business is fifteen per cent. Then you make five per cent.

Deepak Gupta appeared before the Commission of Inquiry on 30 January 2002, where he stated that his business interests included real estate, tourism, medical supplies, everything other than anything to do with defence. He is the director of United Group. Kavin Gulati (counsel for Tehelka) asked Gupta about his job profile which he had outlined for Mathew Samuel. This included defence and that he operated through the PMO.

When Kavin Gulati questioned him about his pontificating on kickbacks and commissions in defence deals, Gupta claimed he had picked up all the information hanging about Gymkhana Club where he said all this was commonly discussed. Although Gupta said he knew H.C. Pant only on a social level and never discussed defence procurement with him, Gulati pointed out that their discussions on Operation West End tapes were all related to arms deals, when the items go to WE for trials and various procedures. Gupta refused to accept that.

Siddharth Aggarwal (counsel for the Commission) then asked whether Gupta's father had donated any building to the RSS. Deepak Gupta replied that he had no idea. He insisted that he only discussed genuine business ideas with Mathew Samuel.

Aggarwal: Were illegal or unusual means to do genuine work discussed with Mathew Samuel?

Gupta: I do not remember.

To all of Aggarwal's questions about the discussions he had with Mathew Samuel and the means used to get work done in the arms procurement area, Gupta's answers were, 'I do not remember' or 'I was just puffing'. The contempt with which some of the questions were answered displayed the attitude of all these players. They had nothing to gain by telling the truth and nothing to lose by telling lies.

Aggarwal asked Gupta whether he knew that Mathew Samuel was engaged in the manufacture of arms. He quoted from the transcript:

Gupta: What is your company doing?

Samuel: No, we are basically manufacturers of arms equipment.

This is where Gupta started toying with the Commission:

Gupta: Arms, there are powers equipment. Arms could be anything. Arms do not specify anything. An air gun is an arm. You have sporting arms. Let us carry on, I did not understand what it matters.

Aggarwal: This is the line I am pointing out to you. I am asking you whether you are aware of it.

Gupta: One, I do not recollect, but I decided to discuss this matter because I had been through it.

Aggarwal: Well, we are obliged that you are discussing it with us.

As Aggarwal continued his interrogation, Gupta's answers became increasingly contemptuous, claiming that hand-held thermal imagers could also be used for hunting, as shown on Discovery Channel.

Aggarwal questioned Gupta on why any vendor would need political help to pull through a project. Gupta answered that it only meant discussing it with the bureaucrat concerned and nothing else. Aggarwal asked how he knew that only one vendor handled the entire Russian business in the defence sector, as stated in the Operation West End tapes. Gupta, of course, denied it. When Aggarwal asked Gupta about Deepak Chabbra's dealings with Major General P.S.K. Choudary, Gupta declared he presumed they may have a relationship but was only 'puffing' when he talked about his own proximity to Choudary.

Oh beauteous slide from truth! Let me count the ways I shift thee!

↝

H.C. Pant followed this established grid by taking Samuel to R.K. Gupta. If Deepak Gupta was from a B-grade film, his father *toh uska bhi baap hai*. Raj Kumar Gupta is seventy years old and is the chairman of MPPL Ltd. He is an engineer, and in his younger days worked in canals and irrigation with the government and then in construction. He began doing business in real estate in 1982 and then went into supplying medical equipment. In the Operation West End tapes, he boasted how Prime Minister Vajpayee ordered Bangaru Laxman, 'Whatever Gupta says, do it'. Gupta said, 'Bangaru Laxman is a useless fool. We should tell Bangaru that Brajesh Mishra should order from defence ministry.' H.C. Pant, who was present, added, 'Brajesh Mishra, principal adviser to PM; he will order the [sic] George Fernandes, defence minister or recommend some of this.' Gupta told Samuel, 12 per cent was given for an arms deals from Russia. He said,

> But they take back 50 per cent themselves. Out of that, users, they take one per cent. And the defence secretary will take one and a half per cent. He'll settle with one. Plus there are bureaucrats, joint secretaries, and there are others, from where we have to start?

Gupta also boasted: 'I killed Ranjan Bhattacharya [PM Vajpayee's son-in-law] and Brajesh Mishra both. I got through directly. PM blasted him.'

On the other hand, Gupta contradicted himself:

> If Brajesh Mishra tells the defence secretary, "it has to be done", the defence secretary is the last word. This Yogesh Narain, I went to. I will get it spoken by PM. Not PM himself, but Brajesh Mishra is PM. After that I will talk to Yogesh myself. I know him very well. He will want that somebody should tell him. Then I will tell Bangaru Laxman.

Gupta gloated that when he cut Ranjan Bhattacharya into pieces, the prime minister could not say, 'No, my son-in-law is getting 100 crore. Leave it.' Pointing to himself, Gupta said, 'We are his father's father'. He claimed Ranjan had not been able to figure who had cut him out. According to Gupta, Ranjan calls him 'uncle', adding:

> He doesn't know uncle has cut him to pieces. Who is the man who has taken half the order and he is left high and dry? He is still trying to find out who is the man behind it. He can't find out. If he finds out then I am not a good operator.

Yes, but all Indians know, children today walk into a store, and call the shopkeeper 'uncle'. Anybody is everyone's 'uncle'. Gupta made it clear that the picture he presented to Vajpayee was that he was collecting money for the BJP, so Vajpayee had no choice but to lend him the support he required. According to Gupta's claims, he was the backbone of the party while Ranjan was only the son-in-law. Gupta said, 'Once Ranjan comes to know his uncle was operating behind the scene, he'll come running here saying "Uncle, why you are doing this?" You are not talking to your bloody uncle, no man. You are the PM's son-in-law. Uncle has given his life for this party.' In Ranjan's Rashomon: I seriously do not think so.

Gupta told Samuel that he had spent over Rs 50 lakh to build the RSS headquarters in 1967. He said that during Indira Gandhi's Emergency he gave them Rs 1 crore and $500,000, 'When nobody was even prepared to listen to telephone calls'. Gupta said that he would take Samuel to the BJP office and show him how they respected him. He explained,

> You have to have this big heart if you want to work. This much I can guarantee you, your money will never go waste. I only take personal responsibility, because I can force them. I can also slap on the face if they don't do the work. If it's not paid back, I will have to pay the money. I will pay, don't worry.

Gupta confidently informed Samuel that he would start West End's work, but for that he would need money:

> You know, "Sir, this is five lakh rupees." When I do the work, I put Rs 20-25 lakhs in my pocket. I will just go and give to these, like defence secretary, five lakhs, the Ved Prakash Goyal, five lakhs for the party, then I go to Bangaru Laxman. You just give for no work. Brajesh's price is one crore. I don't want to go with him with money. We will handle. You don't worry. You keep Rs 20-25 lakhs ready. Then blast your work.

At a subsequent meeting, Gupta informed Samuel that he gave the BJP almost three-four crore every month. He said, 'Unless your file is prepared from below nothing can be done. I have arrangements up to joint secretary and under secretary. You will see the result in three-four months.' Gupta said that he had been told by the prime minister to only deal with the treasurer and president of the BJP and they would get the work done. Gupta gave details about how the deal is prepared from below and then the secretary of defence would tell him how much he would charge: 'One per cent, one and a half per cent. Rest you manage below.' He claimed that when the defence secretary wanted money, 'I'll give with my own hand. "Sir, this is a cheque worth two crore." So tell your principal to deposit in his account.'

When Samuel mentioned that Defence Minister George Fernandes would not take money, Gupta said, 'We have already tied with Jaya Jaitly. One or two per cent. We'll settle with Jaya. It's her job to give him or not give him. Our file is signed. She takes the money.'

Gupta claimed that he got the Russian Sukhoi deal through. He pointed out that he told the Russians that the user would 'tell you there are a hundred defects in your product, bureaucracy will put a spoke in the wheel, politicians will say it is no good.' He said he told all of them that they could not eat up people's money and they must do as they had promised. 'So,' he said, 'They came back to their senses'. Then he explained to Samuel the method the Russians use:

> How much commission do we pay to each person? The complete bill is 12 to 15 per cent. But 50 per cent they take back. With Russians that is the practice.

They have Swiss accounts or other accounts. They import something from here to their country at a little higher price. They channelize it all.

R.K. Gupta appeared before the Commission the day after his son's deposition. R.K. Gupta had the swagger of what is called a self-made man. From a rather low income background, he had made money through his wit and street-smarts. He aggrandized his exemplary, honest character. He seemed so accomplished in sliding the truth to where it suited him, he was in the worst place a man can be: where he begins to believe his own distortions. He preened about his bullet injuries:

> **R.K. Gupta:** On 6 March 1947 there were riots in Amritsar. I was a young man at that time. Fifteen years old. I was an ordinary worker of the RSS. We were called upon to defend the city of Amritsar because at that time incidentally lot of the Sikh brothers had gone outside for Hola Mohalla. Therefore, the Muslims attacked all at once. That is how I got those injuries by the double-barrelled guns. I have those injury marks still. If you want to see I can show you.
> **Kavin Gulati:** [Counsel for Tehelka, not particularly interested in the injuries]: Therefore, you are connected with the RSS since 1947.
> **R.K. Gupta:** That is my soul from childhood since 1939. But I am an ordinary worker. I have never been an office bearer.

1939? When he was eight years old he was politically connected with his soul?

> **Gulati:** You have said that you have been in the business of real estate. Have you also built a property in Jhandewalan?
> **R.K. Gupta:** Yes. I was ordinary *swayam sevak*. I was doing construction work for the army. I built cabin catering building at the airport in New Delhi. I also strengthened the existing airport. They called upon me. I did it gladly.
> **Gulati:** For the RSS?
> **R.K. Gupta:** Yes, but they paid for it.
> **Gulati:** When Mr Pant introduced you to Mathew Samuel, what exactly did he tell you about Samuel and this company?
> **R.K. Gupta:** How can I remember that? I told you I am an old man of seventy years. I do not remember.
> **Gulati:** You mentioned you were interested in watching Mr Pant's interest?
> **R.K. Gupta:** This is nothing. This is all bogus. Mr Pant had left. This is all fabricated.
> **Gulati:** Can I ask you where in your affidavit you have said that this is fabricated?
> **R.K. Gupta:** Kindly see page 4, last paragraph. [Reads from affidavit]: "That the deponent submits that the edited tapes commonly known as the Tehelka Tapes pertaining to the deponent are highly doctored and the digital imagery

technique has been used to superimpose words on the visual movements. Further, the editing has been done to join sequences in a different manner than the original." That means, doctored, fabricated, nonsense and rubbish.

Gulati: Mr Gupta, I would like to remind you that I am referring to the unedited tapes.

R.K. Gupta: When a film is prepared, there are lot of tapes which are prepared, which are edited and unedited and what they have omitted, what they have recorded and what they have not recorded. I say that it is fiction that they have created. It is a cinema like story which could sell, which they have created for mercenary matters. Their main and only one purpose was to earn money and to create a sensational story to get undue enrichment. That is what they have done. They would go to any length for that. They have gone to prostitutes. What else they could do? What can you expect from such people?

Such high moral ground? It gets even richer:

Gulati: I am suggesting to you at this stage that you have made this statement even without verifying from the unedited tapes and the transcripts what is the truth of the matter. Therefore, my suggestion to you is that you have to this extent falsely deposed in your affidavit in pararaph 8.

R.K. Gupta: I have not falsely deposed. I have correctly deposed to the best of my knowledge and very truthfully. I can die for truth. That has been my character.

That is clear from the Operation West End tapes. Gulati questions R.K. Gupta about his considerable knowledge of the mechanics of kickbacks in defence deals, to which he responds by saying that he is an educated man, reads nine newspapers a day, and all the information is from there. Then there is a priceless comment that explains away his detailed knowledge of Jaya Jaitly:

Gulati: During the course of cross-examination of Mr Pant, he had told us that you know Mr Bangaru Laxman and Mrs Jaya Jaitly very well. Is it correct?

R.K. Gupta: I am reminded of something. We friends were sitting and somebody asked, "Which actress do you like?" and I told, "I like Juhi Chawla. I love her." Then he asked, "Does she know you?" I said, "It is 50 per cent." I might have told him that I know Bangaru Laxman and Bangaru Laxman does not know me.

R.K. Gupta stated that all that we saw on the tapes were all fabricated, doctored, and superimposed. Or, he was 'puffing'? He acknowledged the veracity of statements that he chose. He admitted he was the trustee of Friends of India Society International, he does own properties in Khajuraho and opposite All India Radio in New Delhi.

R.K. Gupta spoke volubly about his scrupulous principles and impeccable character. Some could even have believed him, if it hadn't been for those damn tapes.

✆

Deepak Gupta patched Samuel to Rakesh Nigam, another wheeler, can't exactly say dealer. Nigam presented himself at the Commission of Inquiry as a marketing consultant. He was furious that the Tehelka journalists had presented him in the West End tapes as a 'second rung fixer'. It was the 'second-rung' that rankled him. He said he offered expertise in concepts and product selling. Nigam reluctantly mentioned the name of the company who had hired his consultancy, Iterate Pvt. Ltd. He added that he had been marketing a waterproofing compound for Kryton Built-mat Pvt. Ltd. He recounted that he had met his friend Deepak Gupta who had told him about West End, a company looking to supply night vision devices. He audaciously asked the Tehelka lawyer to stick to his affidavit where there was no mention of supplying to the army or anything to do with defence.

In the Operation West End tapes, Rakesh Nigam asked Samuel how much he would pay for an introduction to defence secretary Yogesh Narain. Samuel suggested two lakh as a token amount immediately and then adding more the following year. Nigam scoffed at him contemptuously, 'Mr Mathew, I will give you Rs 25 lakhs. You arrange for my meeting with one of my contacts, with defence secretary. People here talk in crores, you are talking two lakhs and five lakhs.' When Samuel meekly protested that nothing had actually happened, Nigam responded:

Getting an access there is itself an opening. Yeah, we are going to be looked after. Let's talk in terms where we can really make a breakthrough with the business. Two lakhs, five lakhs, ten lakhs people just throw for entertaining. Recently Deepak [Gupta] and I just incurred an expenditure of about a lakh of rupees, a week back.

Nigam mentioned the then minister of state for defence Hiren Pathak, 'Hiren Pathak is a very bold person. One or two jobs he did for me and we exchanged bags. And things moved very smoothly.' Nigam also boasted that he was able to outsmart other arms dealers when a deal was stuck and by handing over one crore he got things moving (MTR engines from Germany), Nigam said, for the Daimler Chrysler group, 'The bloody Indian agent was screwing these people. This went on for seven years.' He mentioned Dr Fisher and Heinz of Daimler Chrysler and said he gave them results in twenty days. He said he knew of the defence secretary's appointment a month-and-a-half earlier and that now people were astonished at the rapport he had established in such a short while.

It is interesting that Rakesh Nigam played his role before the Tehelka journalists as a man who had done major deals but was not well known because he chose that it be so. Nigam stated in his affidavit that all his talk in the Operation West End tapes about Chrysler, ALH, Fisher and Heinz, etc. was picked up from casual conversations with journalists. When Tehelka's counsel, Kavin Gulati, questioned him about this, Nigam said he had been at the bar in the Press Club when he got into an argument with a German journalist who was discussing Advanced Light Helicopters by HAL in Bangalore. He said the German journalist mentioned that Fisher and Heinz had been coming to India for seven or eight years but got no response from the Indian government. Nigam felt that this German and his friends were being anti-Indian so he got into an argument along with his Indian journalist friend. And who was this Indian journalist? Nigam replied that it was Chand Joshi.

Kavin Gulati, not being a journalist, was perhaps unaware that Chand Joshi, a legendary, veteran journalist had died on 25 January 2000. Joshi had been seriously ill during the last few years of his life, so the likelihood of his frequenting the Press Club was thin. At that point, Gulati was obviously informed by a journalist that Chand Joshi was dead. After two unrelated questions, Gulati went back to Chand Joshi:

> **Gulati**: You have said about the journalist friend of yours, Chand Joshi. Which newspaper did he belong to?
> **Nigam**: *Hindustan Times.*

Chand Joshi had been the bane of *The Hindustan Times* organization, often creating and leading strikes against the owners.

> **Gulati**: I am sorry to ask this question. Is he alive?
> **Nigam**: No. With a very heavy heart, I can tell you that he died sometime in 1999.
> **Gulati**: Therefore, Mr Nigam, when did this conversation take place?
> **Nigam**: It was some time in 1996-97.
> **Gulati**: And you remembered the names Heinz and Fisher?
> **Nigam**: Exactly, sir, because there was such a heated argument, as I have clarified.

But Nigam could not recall conversations he had with Mathew Samuel at the end of the year 2000, about Ukraine and Sukhoi. Gulati then took up the unedited tapes at the point where Rakesh Nigam is negotiating the price for introducing Mathew Samuel to the defence secretary.

> **Gulati**: My question to you is, why does organizing a meeting, especially when it is going to be official, require money?
> **Nigam**: I am sure you are representing Tehelka. You are not doing any job on charity. You are charging a fee. They have been able to convince themselves that Mr Learned Counsel is the right person to do their job. So, obviously, I am trying to bind this man by getting the maximum advance from him.

Funnily enough, Kavin Gulati, while representing Tehelka, was indeed 'doing charity'. But that is a distant world far removed from Rakesh Nigam's psyche, who would presume there would be an ulterior motive if money was not involved.

Gulati: Now 25 lakhs, you say, you are ready to give for arranging a meeting with the defence secretary. If it is an official meeting, my question to you is …
Nigam: I will come back to you. This is basically hypothetical conversation. I am sorry. Excuse me. I am giving this example to you. Hon. Justice sahab, please do not feel offended. Here is a person who comes to you and says, I can supply you Madhuri Dixit for Rs 2 lakhs. I know the value of Madhuri Dixit is about 50 lakhs or Rs 1 crore. So, it is just a question of countering. That two lakhs, no. I will give you Rs 20 lakhs. It was just a thought which had come up there. Why? Because I just wanted to get this official representation. That was my sole aim. I did not want him as you have been observing. People come here, do window shopping and go away.

Nigam's apology should have been directed to Madhuri Dixit and not to the sitting judge. A film star's public persona so easily becomes Rakesh Nigam's property to be bandied about. Could he replace the name of Madhuri Dixit with that of his wife or daughter or mother? Would he say: 'If I come to you and say I can supply you my wife for Rs 2 lakhs. I know the value of my wife is 50 lakhs or Rs 1 crore. I will give you Rs 20 lakhs?' His own anonymity to Madhuri Dixit makes the vulgarity possible. If he actually knew her, would he have used her name? Preity Zinta, the gutsy Bollywood actress who stood up to the Indian mafia in court, was correct when she objected to journalists treating film stars as sluts. Nigam's mother, if not Madhuri Dixit's mother, should wash his mouth out with soap.

Gulati questioned Nigam on his advice to Samuel in the Operation West End tapes about how to make a breakthrough, where he said, 'Two lakhs, 5 lakhs, 10 lakhs, people just throw away for entertaining.'

Nigam answered that he would take out a potential customer for a sandwich and coffee, if he wanted to sell his product. But, Gulati asked, would it cost Rs 10 lakhs? Nigam responded, 'Again, it is a hypothetical thing which you are mentioning. Either you frame your questions in a way that I am able to understand or I am not being able to put my views across to you.'

Gulati: I will reframe the question. My question to you is this: You said that Rs 2 lakhs, 5 lakhs, 10 lakhs expenditure for "entertaining". My question to you is what kind of entertainment requires this kind of expenditure?
Nigam: It was just a discussion which was taking place. I wanted to get the maximum amount of money from the agenda. If you recollect, which they have not very cleverly mentioned, in the same edited tape: 'Tehelka: Token amount if you can arrange a meeting with this man, defence secretary. It is just a half kind of promise from his level. It won't be worked out in 2000. It may be in 2001. Now, on the spot, I can give Rs 2 lakhs." And four bundles of 500-rupee notes were shown to me. He is not mentioning that. They have not even shown it on one of the videotapes. What has suited them, they have shown it. I will tell to you in this examination the way, the manner in which they have just

interpolated and mentioned things, which have no significance whatsoever. Whatever suited them, that has been brought by them. The learned counsel is mentioning of entertaining with Rs 2 lakhs, 5 lakhs, 10 lakhs, but he has not mentioned that Tehelka gave me Rs 2 lakhs which I have not accepted. It was just a hypothetical situation.

Gulati: Please also see the last two lines on the same page. "Recently, Deepak and I just incurred an expenditure of about one lakh of rupees a week back." Now, what was the purpose of this expenditure?

Nigam: It was not an expenditure. It was just my presence of mind. I was just blowing things out of proportion. *Mene usko dyia ki mene abhi kaam karaya hai aur Deepak aur mene ek lakh rupye kharch kar diye hai* [I got some work done and Deepak and I spent one lakh] because Deepak and I wanted to do a joint venture.

In answer to all the other questions, Rakesh Nigam's position was that either he did not recall the matter or that he was just blowing things out of proportion and boasting in order to get the job with West End. But Siddharth Aggarwal caught Rakesh Nigam in all his lies. Aggarwal asked him if he knew Dr Ketan Shukla (private secretary to Hiren Pathak), Hiren Pathak (minister of state for defence), Bangaru Laxman (president of the BJP party), Ranjit Issar (joint secretary in the defence ministry), Suresh Nanda, Sudhir Choudhrie, Karnail Singh (joint secretary in HAL), Om Prakash (joint secretary in the defence ministry), Brigadier Krishan Kiren, Lieutenant Colonel I.I. Singh, Commissioner P.V. Venugopal, Brigadier H.L. Bhandari. Nigam denied knowing any of these people. Then Siddharth Aggarwal pulled out Rakesh Nigam's Airtel cellular phone bill that proved that he had made calls to all these people whom he claimed not to know.

According to Nigam, he did not know 80 per cent of the numbers on the list. Aggarwal ended with: 'I put it to you that you have withheld material information from this Commission. Do you agree or deny?' Nigam's response was: 'To the best of my knowledge, I have not withheld any information. Since I am under oath, I am bound to give you the true and factual position.'

What indeed could this oath possibly mean if it is so evident that what we are getting is not the truth?

⤷

When H.C. Pant took West End to meet Mohinder Singh Sahni, he told them that Sahni had made Rs 26 crore out of the Rs 924 crore deal with the Czechoslovakian firm Skoda. Pant pointed out, 'That's how he got the money for his farmhouses and all this everything'. In the discussions, Sahni talked generally about deals, how they should be manipulated, when pressure should be applied, and on whom. Sahni advised Tehelka that they had to be technically competitive and to do that, he said, 'If we have to beat our enemy, we should know what we are doing'. Sahni told them all, 'If PCO is broken then we will have very big business'. Sahni was ready for action and told Tehelka that he would prepare a draft letter for them with all the specifications of the product and the reasons that would convince them to opt for West End's product. Sahni said rather grandly, 'I have to prepare a note. On the paper, I should be Napoleon.' At this point Sahni knew nothing about West End and little beyond cursory mention about the product he planned to promote.

Mohinder Singh Sahni, mistakenly identified as Mohinder Pal Sahni in the Operation West End tapes, presented himself before the Commission of Inquiry as a businessman involved in 'trading'. He was also the consul general of Belize, a 22,966 sq. km. country with a Caribbean coastline and a population of 272,945. Some businessmen acquire an appointment of consul general which gives them the privilege of putting a flag on their car (that may intimidate security personnel), a plaque outside their house and invitations from other embassies and other consul generals. Some consul generals represent countries so obscure that they are excruciatingly difficult to trace on a map and are tinier than the properties they own. And thus, we come to Mohinder Singh Sahni, who has since resigned from his position of honorary consul general.

When Kavin Gulati (counsel for Tehelka) questioned him about his status as consul general, Sahni's response was well rehearsed:

> I was in the States in Houston. It so happened I met one [of] their ministers. At that time, they did not have any Consulate here. So, they offered me to represent them in India. It is an honourable job. So, I accepted this. Then the minister interviewed me in Belize and after that, they recommended me to the Government of India and then it was cleared through the various agencies here. After that, it was gazetted and I was appointed the Honorary Consul General of Belize.

Sahni claimed that he had no dealings in defence, which completely belies what was seen and heard on the Operation West End tapes.

Kavin Gulati pointed to conversations in the unedited tapes, in which Sahni told Mathew Samuel: 'Don't spell it. Do not worry … I have people in the sense *ki* we have a team of hundred-twenty consultants … full team of our own. It is a very big power establishment. We have six groups, dealing in different areas like power, mining.' He also adds, 'Defence, petroleum … *Mere ko Berry se baat karao* [get me to speak to Berry]. Have you given the presentation to the Indian Army?'

> **Gulati:** You have said you do not deal in defence but here we find that you are saying that you also deal with defence.
> **Sahni:** As I already mentioned to you that I was trying to impress that I am capable of doing business.

He said he was putting together a project for security systems. Strangely, he denied that Lieutenant Colonel V.K. Berry and Major Sarabjeet Singh were employed by him. Sahni said both of them had come to him looking for jobs. Why then did he meet Lieutenant Colonel Berry? The consul general of Belize grandiloquently answered:

If somebody comes to you and requests you for a job, naturally, if he comes and sees me, that kind of responsibility I am carrying as the consul general, that also needs to have exposure with people who come to visit my consulate. It is courtesy to meet anybody who comes to meet me.

Sahni spoke about his connections with Major General P.S.K. Choudary, Bangaru Laxman, Mr Natarajan (deputy director of the DRDO) and Ranjit Issar (defence ministry) to the Operation West End poseurs. When asked at the Commission whether he knew them, Sahni denied any acquaintance whatsoever:

I was talking all these names just to impress Tehelka, who have made all this story against me and in no point of time I have accepted their any offer for any kind of giving money to anybody or taking money myself and it is by the grace of God that it happened.

Sahni detailed his connection with Bangaru Laxman on the tape but in the Commission it is put down to bragging. Sounds reasonable since the bragging culture is as much an institution as going to work, getting married, having children, then grandchildren, and eventually dying. It is the warp and weft of the fabric of business life. He saw nothing wrong with it or in pointing out that that's all it was. He sounded reasonable to himself. It is intriguing that the greatest braggarts are also the most gullible about other people's stories. The evening is spent listening to each other and going home marvelling at the other's prowess, subsequently worrying whether one's own boasts flew in the right direction. When questioned by Gulati about his stating that he was drunk at the meetings, Sahni clarified:

Sahni: You can see in my cassette how quickly I drink. Was I not drunk? I was least interested at that time. But, you know, being social and having status, I did not want to displease anybody. So, I was attending them. Nothing else.
Gulati: That should be all right. In paragraph 6 you have said that you have never acted as defence middleman. My question to you is, all these deals which you have discussed in the tape, where did you get all this information about these deals?
Sahni: These people were sitting there. The Tehelka people brought some people with them. If you go through the whole tape, at many places they are repeating a few words and then they are putting in the mouth on other side and some other people are sitting there. They are asking them and questioning them. If you go through this, I do not know the product at all. Many times I am asking them questions straight. Well, I have no knowledge of this product. But I was given a presentation. As a businessman I know many subjects and that is how I was impressing them.
Gulati: My suggestion to you, Mr Sahni, is that you have filed a false affidavit and that you have deliberately withheld information about the defence deals.
Sahni: It is not correct.

Siddharth Aggarwal's (counsel for the Commission) scepticism about Sahni's answers was obvious. Sahni told him he had never heard of Krasnopol. He did not know Major Sarabjeet Singh but vaguely remembered Sarabjeet had come to him for a job.

> **Aggarwal:** I am asking you, what do you understand by the phrase "suitcase person"? Because you say, "I'm not a suitcase person". What is a suitcase person?
>
> **Sahni:** They have shown in the cassette to everybody that there is corruption. They made a story out of it. They made me one of the tools in this.

Sahni sounded hurt.

Around the same time the Commission was in session, a memo found its way to me that showed that income tax intelligence was planning a raid on Mohinder Singh Sahni and his brother Maninder Singh Sahni's properties. The memo mentioned the Mokul group and various Russian and Czech defence production companies, one of which was Skoda Export Ltd. The raid never took place. If you need to ask: why not? Then you have not understood the Indian cultural heritage since Independence.

↩

Lieutenant Colonel V.K. Berry's dream was to be appointed country manager by a multinational firm. Then all his problems would be over and he had more than his share. Instead, Berry got entangled in the West End web and his already complicated, difficult life spiralled relentlessly, with no hope of recovery. Goaded by Tehelka, Berry said that he had begun this kind of work with reputed arms dealer Vipin Khanna for three years and had been in the field for nine. He said he was at an advantage because he had extensive technical knowledge of electronic warfare. He spoke about being involved in deals with Tadiran, Elistra, Symtech, and several others. When pressed, Berry admitted that it was all illegal. Berry said, 'What they used to do is they get into three-four companies. You give to one politician and get three-four companies signed with you directly. So you are loyal to nobody.' Lieutenant Colonel Berry introduced Samuel to Major Sarabjeet Singh, who was reportedly working for reputed arms dealer Mohinder Singh Sahni.

Lieutenant Colonel Berry, who appeared before the Army Court of Inquiry on 10 April 2001, was completely hoodwinked by the Tehelka operatives. With a mentally challenged child at home and having retired in 1990, Berry was particularly susceptible to West End's offer as their country manager with a dollar salary. Berry said in his deposition in the Commission:

> I had a mentally retarded child. That is why I had taken retirement. That is why I wanted to explain to you otherwise I would have remained in the Army all through and through. To bring up a mentally handicapped child is a Herculean task. That is why I was trying to find my feet as to what to do in my life as such. It took me good about two years to decide. It is better to do a job than anything else.

In a telephone conversation, a request for an interview was answered with the utmost anger, pain, and anguish. Lieutenant Colonel Berry shouted, 'You journalists have destroyed my life. You have no principles. All I was trying to do was get a job and take care of my family.' His wife's plea was even more wrenching, 'I am a simple housewife and I don't know much about these things. But, how can journalists do something that completely ruins us? Are there no rules? Is there no such thing as decency?' Berry's mentally challenged child died, Berry himself suffered a paralytic stroke and has little means of livelihood. For the journalists, it was a story. That's it. Today's newspaper is tomorrow's garbage. Tehelka paid a huge price for the story, financially, professionally, and personally. Some of those who they covered paid, sometimes, more than was due.

When P.N. Lekhi, counsel for Mohinder Singh Sahni, asked Berry, 'Did you not, at that time, realize that Tehelka was a conspiracy against the defence forces?' Berry replied, 'The thing is that the carrot hanging in front of me as a country manager and that was my dream. It is my dream even today that I want to become a country manager. They had utilized my sentiments and my emotions to meet their purpose.'

There was a sad bitterness when Berry said,

> I was trying to find my feet. I tried to get into an industry because I had a mentally retarded child. You must know how he is brought up. He needs 24 hours attention. I will put it that was that, it is the journalist who has some obligation towards these types of children and tries to project to the people as to what the difficulty these people are facing? I took my retirement as lieutenant colonel, not just like that. I was Gold medallist. I was an assistant professor in the army. I had so much of technical background that the project that I did 25 years ago, that is coming now on the production line.

Berry had served in the Corps of Signals and was an expert in telecommunications and electronics. He was in DGQA as a senior quality assurance officer. He said he had sent West End a fax asking for a confirmation of his appointment on 9 January 2001 but had received no reply.

The Army Court of Inquiry questioned Berry about the statements he had made on the Operation West End tapes related to procurement of Krasnopol ammunition for Rs 150 crore, Cornet-E (ATG Missiles) for Rs 250 crore, Gustav for Rs 85 crore, Tadiran deals, High Frequency Direction Finders for a Hungarian company for about 10 million dollars and Radio Set R-173. Berry admitted that he had spoken about these items only to impress West End to get a job but had not dealt in them. He informed the army court that he had served as DGQA from 1987 to 1990 and had worked for Vipin Khanna for three years.

ACI: Are you aware that Mr Vipin Khanna is one of the biggest arms dealers in Delhi?

Berry: I have no personal knowledge. But as per newspaper reports he is one of the many dealers.

ACI: When you were working with Mr Vipin Khanna, did you know what he was dealing with?

Berry: From whatever I knew about him, he was dealing with procurement of defence equipment/stores as also number of equipments/stores used in civilian life.

ACI: In the video clippings you were seen discussing about Tadiran Communications Equipment. How were you involved in this deal?

Berry: This equipment was procured for Cabinet Secretariat through Mr Vipin Khanna. I am not sure whether the same equipment was supplied by him to the defence services.

ACI: You have talked about 12 per cent commission having been paid in Tadiran deal out of which some commission was paid to late Rajesh Pilot. Is it true?

Berry: I did say so, but factually it was not true. I made these tall claims with a view to impress West End.

ACI: In the video clippings you were heard saying that for procurement of HFDF was 10 million dollars from a Hungarian company, for use of Signal Directorate of Army, a commission of 12 per cent was paid to user headed by General Bhalla. Is that statement true?

Berry: I do not know in what context I made that statement. But, it was factually incorrect. In fact, I was not at all involved in any manner with any deal either with procurement people or payment of money in that.

ACI: If it be so, then why did you take the name of General Bhalla and not others?

Berry: I took the name just like that. There is no truth in it.

The army court questioned Berry about statements he had made on tape about Major General Satnam Singh and Major Sarabjeet Singh (Retd) and user trials for thermal cameras. He was also asked about money being paid to Ram Mohan, DG, BSF in connection with a border-fencing contract. Berry had mentioned in the tapes that money was paid to the air chief for the Sukhoi deal. Berry repeated that all that he had said on the tape was factually incorrect.

I once again reiterate that I have never indulged myself in any defence project. I have never visited or dealt with any official connected with MOD in uniform or otherwise.

It was shocking to see myself on the video making irrelevant, unauthentic and rubbish statements about anything and everything, about anyone and everyone. These statements should be discarded as bazaar gossip. They are neither factual nor real. I never meant to harm or malign anyone. They are far from reality. I tender my apology for the same.

I was just gossiping and making very tall claims with the so-called president of West End International, my prospective employer who had been clandestinely video graphing me and I never knew that any meaningless gossip will be photographed and then used by them for exploitation and character assassination.

There was something about Lieutenant Colonel Berry that prevented you from clubbing him with the rest of the unscrupulous bunch. He believed he had been duped when all he was doing was trying to get a job. Tall claims are *rajma-chawal* to Indians; comfort food. Gossip, wholly concocted, becomes solid truth, with people swearing on their children. It is difficult to believe that the reason why Priyanka Gandhi doesn't want anything to do with politics right now is because she wants to spend time bringing up her children. That is far too boring and reasonable. The 'real' story is that she does not get along with her brother. Alternatively, even better, her macho husband doesn't want her to. Creating fictionalized stories are grist to the gossip mill.

Unfortunately, Berry's answers to the army court only raised more questions. On 31 January 2002, after telling the army court that he had nothing to do with the Tadiran deal, he contradicted himself in his deposition before the Commission when questioned by the relentless Tehelka lawyer, Sidharth Luthra:

Luthra: You said that you were providing consultancy services. Tell me what was your income in the year ending March 2001?
Berry: I filed an income tax return of about Rs 8 lakhs or something.
Luthra: That was all from consultancy?
Berry: Obviously from consultancy.
Luthra: Who were you providing this consultancy to?
Berry: To a foreign company.
Luthra: Which company?
Berry: Tadiron Electronic Systems of Israel.

This electronic surveillance system was supplied to the Ministry of Communications. Berry's association with Vipin Khanna did no service in his effort to establish his innocence. Berry had also gone to another alleged arms dealer, Mohinder Singh Sahni, for a job in his Surveillance Security Systems. Berry did state that Major Sarabjeet Singh was heading Surveillance Security Systems for Sahni but later contradicted himself:

Luthra: Let us turn to page 73 for a minute. Start with the line at the bottom.
"Berry: I will tell you … Sarabjeet Singh is sub agent of Sahni…"
Berry: I just said it is a presumption.

More discrepancies were exposed by Luthra which leads to the question: who is protecting whom? Why are there so many cloak and dagger answers? Luthra pointed out that Vipin Khanna denied on oath that Berry was ever employed by him. Berry reiterated that he did work for Khanna for about three years, but he insisted the work had nothing to do with procurement of arms or defence deals. He confirmed that he had asked Major Sarabjeet Singh to help him get the job with West End. Berry further said that he left Vipin Khanna because his ethics were not 'proper'.

> **Luthra:** [Reading from the transcript] "The guy who had accompanied me from Vipin's side. And there, the things went for a six. Because, even the guy whom you are paying, he does not know that whether you are going to pay him or otherwise or not." What do you mean by this?
> **Berry:** It means nothing. It is out of sense.

When P.N. Lekhi, lawyer for Mohinder Singh Sahni, asked Berry: 'So, every gossip that went on from both sides was a gossip most ill informed, misinformed in relation to how defence equipments are purchased; correct?' Berry enthusiastically agreed, 'True, totally ill informed and ill conceived ideas.' So would I if I had an alleged arms dealer's breath on my back.

N. Dutta, lawyer for Jaya Jaitly, extracted from Berry that when he spoke about bribing the air chief, it was only incorrect gossip. Now, there's another toughie's breath on Berry's back. In concluding his deposition, according to Berry, 'When I am saying generally gossip, you must understand a statistical analysis of any conversation, in a gossip, it is 90 per cent. But 10 per cent will have to be something.'

Luthra then asked him, 'What was the 10 per cent?' Berry quipped, 'I do not recollect. I was not having a recording device with me.' What indeed was the 10 per cent that was true?

⌒

Major Sarabjeet Singh (S.J.) introduced himself to Operation West End operatives as a 'fixer'. Although he comes across as a swashbuckler in the Operation West End tapes, when interviewed in the wake of the Tehelka exposé, he was dejected, lonely, and still trying to piece his life together. On the evening of 13 March 2001, a friend called him up and said, 'Sarabjeet, you are a big man now'. A puzzled Sarabjeet asked, 'How am I a big man?' His friend told him, 'Some stupid has put out stuff. Be careful.' Sarabjeet read the exposé the following morning and was appalled:

> I do not know how they have set their imagination to call me as the biggest arms dealer in Delhi. I was shocked. That is the height of lies journalists tell. It is so irresponsible that you malign an individual's name without any verification, without finding the truth. Without finding the facts, just on hearsay or on gossip you pass your judgement.

Sarabjeet Singh said he was only trying to help his friend Lieutenant Colonel Berry get a job with West End and took no money for it. There may have been an effort to make an extra buck, but that was not established. Most importantly, Sarabjeet had knowledge of subterranean deals that run parallel to the designated official procedures for arms.

Sarabjeet had retired in 1981, he said, because he was suffering from bullet and splinter injuries he sustained during the wars against Pakistan in 1965 and 1971. He worked for a

181

company that manufactured particle boards and then started his own business exporting rice, food grains, and agricultural equipment to Somalia. Sarabjeet traded in the jaggery plant and was introduced to Somalia's President Said Barre by the then Foreign Secretary Romesh Bhandari. When Barre asked him to produce a Somali film and promised, 'He would open the gates of Somalia to me if it was good', Sarabjeet did so without any expertise in film production. From then on, Sarabjeet did great business in Somalia, because 'there was nothing that Somalia did not need. We exported everything.' The scenario changed in 1987, when President Barre faced pressure from the World Bank and violence broke out amongst the unhappy and disgruntled Somalis.

Sarabjeet then tried to set up a factory of wood components, but he said that things did not work out because of an unstable political situation. Singh met his friend Wing Commander Randhawa and talked about setting up a local facility to erect electronic fencing. They got in touch with Mohinder Singh Sahni, who was in the business, to finance the project. Sahni sent both of them to Israel to study their systems. The idea was to take their technology and manufacture it indigenously for defence requirements. Lieutenant Colonel Berry also joined the company after Wing Commander Randhawa died. It was Lieutenant Colonel Berry who, at his own initiative, introduced Sarabjeet Singh to West End, to impress them. Sarabjeet reported that he avoided the invitation a couple of times but Berry asked him to do him a favour and help him out. Sarabjeet Singh said Berry told him that they were looking for a country head and he would be paid $3000 a month. He was told by Berry that he should try to impress West End. Sarabjeet told Samuel, 'Basically, you can call me a fixer. I will use a crude word but that is what it is.' Sarabjeet elaborated that he had friends at different levels, in the ministry, in the bureaucracy, in politics, and in the defence services. He also said he knew people at the junior level who were useful in providing information. Sarabjeet boasted that he organized the Rs 150 crore Krasnopol deal. He explained that the Russian missile (22 km range 152 mm laser designated artillery) was not cleared because it had failed five out of six tests. Despite that, Sarabjeet said he was able to push it through.

A jawan on duty in a border area gets to know that he is defending his country with a bomb that has failed a test five times out of six? I would like to see what these jawans would do to their senior officers who bought substandard equipment and exposed them to risk their lives, not for the nation but for their own profit motives. Sarabjeet gave details of the Krasnopol deal worth, ammunitions from the Kornet-E deal, and a Polish company called PCO for the supply of thermal image cameras and II tubes for tanks worth Rs 265 crore. He boasted about how he worked the Price Negotiating Committee for army procurements. He also stressed the absolute need for trust amongst the dealers, as nobody could be taken to court. After negotiating for his three-and-a-half per cent cut, the supplier then gives a bank guarantee. Sarabjeet said that he would only get half per cent himself and the three per cent would go to all the people he would have to pay off. This, he said, would include the chairman and the financial controller of the PNC. He said he was happy with his half per cent. Sarabjeet elaborated that the most important step is the trial report of the product. If the item is deemed unfit by the user, he said, it would never go through. Therefore the technical specifications have to meet the requirement and only when that is cleared can the item be short-listed. As Singh pointed out, 'To start with, associate them right from the beginning: the word "go". The metre, as I say, is down from the word "go". The 'metre', as in every movement of the file, means money has to be paid.

Sarabjeet Singh clarified the events that led to the meeting with Major General Satnam Singh. He said he was sitting alone in the coffee shop in Oberoi Hotel, when he called up Satnam's wife. He asked her what they were doing, and when she replied that they were free, Sarabjeet Singh invited them over for tea. Sarabjeet Singh said, as Major General Satnam Singh and his wife walked in, 'these jokers were out there and they came forward'. While they all sat together, Samuel and Aniruddha tried to ferret out information about procurement procedure.

Compare all that to Sarabjeet Singh's responses at the Army Court of Inquiry (ACI) on 16 April 2001:

ACI: During that [with Mathew Samuel] meeting, you have talked extensively about Krasnopol ammunition with particular reference to fixing that deal. Were you in any manner involved in that deal?

Sarabjeet Singh: No.

ACI: If that be so, on what basis you said that out of six tests only one was successful when it was trial evaluated?

Sarabjeet Singh: All I had said was based on news reports published from time to time after the Kargil War.

ACI: During the said meeting you also had said that in spite of pressure from some angles "we were able to push this deal through". What did you mean by that statement?

Sarabjeet Singh: Actually speaking, I knew nothing about Krasnopol. The statement was made by me as a tall claim only with a view to impress Mr Samuel Mathew.

ACI: What was the need to impress Mr Samuel Mathew if you had no intention of entering into defence deal?

Sarabjeet Singh: I tried to impress him only so that Lieutenant Colonel V.K. Berry can get a job with West End. In fact, my impression about Mr Samuel Mathew after the meeting was that he appeared to be a fraud.

ACI: You have talked extensively with Mr Samuel Mathew about a South African firm trying to clinch a deal for Krasnopol ammunition and you were trying to push out that firm. Is that true?

Sarabjeet Singh: All these information appeared in *Asian Age* from which I came to know about these details.

In answer to all the questions directed to him, Sarabjeet Singh's explanations were based on the fact that he was only trying to impress Mathew Samuel and none of it was true.

ACI: What was the necessity for you to call Major General Satnam Singh for a cup of coffee at the Oberoi's?

Sarabjeet Singh: It was only a coincidence that Major General Satnam Singh came and met the representative of West End. In fact Mr Aniruddha Bahal wanted to meet some serving General Officer for which I rebuked him.

ACI: Did you speak to Major General Satnam Singh yourself and invited him for a cup of coffee?

Sarabjeet Singh: Yes, I spoke to him and requested him to join me.

ACI: Did you invite the representatives of West End to join the meeting with Major General Satnam Singh?

Sarabjeet Singh: No.

ACI: If that be so, how come the representatives of West End joined you all for coffee and discussed about thermal cameras without being invited?

Sarabjeet Singh: I do not know.

Then, some schoolmarm should have shouted: If you don't know, then *who* will know?

In his deposition before the Commission, on 2 February 2002, he got the Sidharth Luthra (Tehelka's lawyer) treatment. Luthra grilled him on where he got all the information about Kornet-E, the company and the bomb. Sarabjeet Singh took the position that everything he said to the West End representatives was exaggeration and boasting. He wasn't a fixer. He was not involved in any arms deals. He met Aniruddha Bahal and Mathew Samuel on 5 January 2001, at Oberoi Hotel. An hour later he had invited Major General Satnam Singh and his wife for coffee at the same hotel. Aniruddha and Samuel just 'happened' to pass by and join them. Sarabjeet Singh said he did not invite them in order to introduce them.

Luthra: Colonel Berry thought you are a respectable person and you could have helped him getting a job. Yet, being respectable and responsible person you insisted on making these tall claims without any reference to Berry.

Sarabjeet Singh: When you start something imaginary, then the flight of imagination has no bounds. It carries on till it comes to the landing point. That is exactly what has happened in this case.

Sarabjeet did have serious regrets.

Luthra: In your affidavit in response, I find no mention of any meeting with General Satnam Singh. You have not disclosed anything deliberately. Have you?

Sarabjeet Singh: No, I will say that now. Now I am speaking. Whatever I am speaking here, I am speaking under oath. Therefore, I wish to disclose further that General Satnam Singh was totally innocent and I feel so guilty of having dragged such a reputed and a good officer of high integrity into this sort of situation. It is my doing. I did not realize it that I was dealing with such cronies. Otherwise, I would have made sure that I do not call him here. I would have never taken this risk of involving such a civilized, such a good officer into this situation. I am again deeply regretful of my action that I have landed the general for no rhyme or reason who was totally innocent and who was totally ignorant of this fact that I was inviting him for what.

Dayan Krishnan, counsel for the Commission, read sections from the Operation West End transcripts where Sarabjeet Singh is bragging away about all the fixing he has done in defence deals and the important people he knows. Krishnan then asked Singh:

Krishnan: Now, tell me how would all this have helped Berry get a job?
Sarabjeet Singh: I started that I know everyone whether it is in defence, whether it is in Army or it is in the Air Force or it is in Navy. I am a man who knows everyone. It was a continuation of the same build up that I was continuing with the same conversation. Whatever the information was in the back of my mind; I kept on rattling them out.

Sarabjeet Singh denied that he knew anyone in Mokul International and Skoda. Krishnan produced phone records that showed Sarabjeet Singh had made repeated calls to the chairmen of both those companies.

When you are involved in arms deals, even if it is on the periphery, you are playing with high stakes. When you lose out, you lose big. Sarabjeet Singh's life spun into a downward spiral. He lost all means of livelihood and his wife left him. Utterly disheartened, he said,

Can you believe, Madhu, that I went to the golf course; I play five days a week. I found a sea change in the attitude of people? Suddenly I found that I have become untouchable. People were trying to shy away from me. Trying to run away as if I have done something sinister. This is how it has affected my life. People started throwing expressions and passing comments. They, in no way, had the courage to say it on my face, because they know who I am. I can really give them back in a big way. I take no nonsense. I give no nonsense.

Sarabjeet Singh said that a number of his friends, his course-mates, stood by him: 'They are very understanding and they said that we know that you have done nothing wrong.'

Sarabjeet Singh said he lost two years of his life because of Tehelka, and this seriously damaged his social and working reputation. He said that as people avoided him, he did not want to embarrass them with his presence. He said that now he was starting his work again slowly and picking up the pieces. 'Two, three years I had to undergo this mental torture and misery all by myself. And who is to be blamed? This so-called journalism. So, this is what it is.'

Clearly there were some simple facts: Sarabjeet Singh had not accepted any money from West End and he had not intended to get his old friend Major General Satnam Singh involved in anything murky. Dispiritedly, he said,

I feel absolutely disgusting because he was an officer who was spotlessly clean. An officer who had such a good future. There was no stopping him becoming Lieutenant General. But unfortunately for a remark passed by the army against him that he was indiscreet. Where was he indiscreet, I really fail to understand? If you want to knock down someone, you can always find some excuse to knock him down. That is the army system. Unfortunately, it is very sad. I wish I had not invited him for a cup of tea. Poor chap, the very next day he went back to Kargil where he was posted. He had no business to be in Oberoi. He had not even the faintest idea about whom he is going to meet.

Sarabjeet Singh said that he had not subsequently met Satnam Singh. He said tearfully,

It had embittered him and rightly so because he feels slighted. Though I am very clear in my conscience that this was not my desire. Whatever happened was an accident. But, unfortunately, he had to suffer very badly. So he is right in thinking that if he had not come over for a cup of tea, he would not have undergone this torture. It is a torture.

Sarabjeet Singh despaired that Major General Satnam Singh had been his subaltern in Sikkim in 1966 and treated him like an elder brother. Today he cannot bear to look him in the eyes.

◡

Major General Satnam Singh appeared disturbed and upset when he appeared before the Army Court of Inquiry on 30 March 2001. He had reason to be. Singh got caught in the web wholly inadvertently. Major General Satnam Singh was posted as infantry chief in the Kargil sector and had come to Delhi on a short period of leave. He did not accept any gratification from the Operation West End operatives.

Major General Satnam Singh told the court that his conversation about HHTI, in reply to Aniruddha Bahal's questions, was casual and did not give away any information. Bahal had testified that Satnam Singh did explain the specifications of HHTI, including the quality of image, portability of the equipment, low weight, and the rejections of the equipment supplied by Thomson and Elop. Bahal did confirm that the meeting was not a pre-arranged one. An examination of the tapes shows that the conversation really did not get into any specifics and was far too general to be of any consequence.

In Oberoi Hotel, Bahal asked Satnam Singh how long the evaluation trials take, say for example, for Thomson and El-Op. Satnam Singh replied, 'We can't be very specific about it. It is based on the type of equipment we have. You are dealing with these Image Intensifiers; they take a much shorter time than probably a weapon system will take.' Bahal continued asking rather basic questions, to which Satnam Singh said, 'You carry on trials, see your performances that have been identified by the company. See what we need. We either say "yes", or we say "no". Or, if the company can give us what we need, because some people have the capability to modify the equipment and things.' When Bahal questioned him further, Satnam Singh said, 'It's the quality of image that counts. Also, the other criteria is the portability. If it is going to be a Hand-held Image Intensifier, it should be something that doesn't add too much of weight.' Bahal asked Satnam Singh whether he was happy with the evaluation of Thomson and El-Op. Satnam Singh replied, 'It's not been fully accepted as such. It still has to come to my area for trials.' The trials were still being carried out in the plains and the equipment had not been tested in high altitude areas. The manner in which Aniruddha Bahal hyped up this encounter in the script of Operation West End created the impression that Major General Satnam Singh had exposed military secrets. Not quite. All that they discussed was common knowledge to anyone who reads newspapers.

On 11 April 2002, Major General Satnam Singh was questioned by Sidharth Luthra, counsel for Tehelka, at the Commission of Inquiry. Clearly, Satnam Singh was being grilled for a conversation that bore little importance in the larger scheme of West End. Luthra did his best to spin a web of intrigue and accused Satnam Singh of giving away army secrets but there really was little to go on. Of course, the Reader's Rashomon must come in here and judge how guilty Major General Satnam Singh was.

> **Luthra:** Are you aware that the army authorities have said that these procedure documents are secret documents and they have claimed privilege in law?
> **Satnam Singh:** To the best of my knowledge, it is not a secret document.
> **Luthra:** When they offered you this catalogue in relation to HHTIs, did it not dawn upon you that they are dealers or they are offering to sell this to the Army?
> **Satnam Singh:** Well, I did get a feeling and after that my conversation is very generic. I have not spoken of any specifics on any equipment.

The case against Major General Satnam Singh was flimsy at best. Satnam Singh and his wife accepted an invitation for tea with an old friend. The discussion with West End representatives was vague and general. His friend, Major Sarabjeet Singh, is consumed with regret and anguish. Guilty by tea association.

The Udhampur based Northern Command issued a 'strong censure' against Major General Satnam Singh for conduct unbecoming of an officer. In this case, as in some others, the journalists also bordered on unbecoming behaviour. There has to be at least some hint of presumed misconduct before you tape and catch any person who is passing by or drops in to have tea with a friend. Major General Satnam Singh's army career stands destroyed.

11 Lock, Stock and Two Smoking Secretaries

An honest politician is one who, when he is bought, will stay bought.
– Simon Cameron, American Politician (1799-1889)

Bangaru Laxman, then president of the party in power, the Bharatiya Janata Party, accepted Rs 1 lakh in cash from Mathew Samuel without so much as glancing up and quickly tossed it in his drawer. When Laxman flew in from Hyderabad on the morning of 13 March, 2001, he had no idea what Delhi had in store for him. A reporter from *Telegu Daily* called him in the afternoon and informed him that Tehelka was airing these tapes. He watched it play out on the Zee News.

Laxman said,

> It was shocking because I never thought that this particular thing was filmed. They meant to show it to the whole world. I felt it very, very bad. You could have given an objective thing. After all, they wanted to put a story, they could have verified with me and then taken my side also.

What then was his 'side'? Laxman was upset that Tehelka reported that he was 'anxiously' gazing at the briefcase, to be opened awaiting the hundreds of dollars he would receive. He pointed out, 'Whoever watched the film cassette saw I was most reluctantly and absent-mindedly attending them.' Absent-minded? True. It was just another day's work.

The day after he put the money in his desk, did he think about it? Unlikely. For Tehelka, it was *The Day*. Aniruddha and Samuel attempted to get access to Bangaru Laxman because they had heard he was making money from business houses. R.K. Gupta asked for Rs 25 lakh for an introduction to Laxman, according to West End. Mohinder Singh Sahni allegedly sought Rs 10 lakh. Eventually, H.C. Pant sent Mohan Singh (private secretary to the former minister of state for defence, Hiren Pathak) to introduce West End to Raju Venkatesh, Laxman's private secretary.

The first sentence Mathew Samuel uttered when he was introduced to Laxman was, 'So I am chief representative. It's written in my liasoning this thing'. Without any waste of time in small talk, he immediately told Laxman that they were interested in investing around Rs 5000 crore in India and had moved a proposal to the prime minister. He told him that they wanted to introduce hand-held thermal cameras and needed help because they were competing with CSF-Thomson and El-Op. Samuel said, 'Now, I need your favour ... uh ... to defence secretary.' According to Tehelka, Laxman answered, 'I know him, but now at what stage the proposal is?' Samuel, clearly nervous, replied, 'The proposal is ... if defence secretary will send the ... proposal ... already the file is with the defence secretary. Already users ... that means they will decide which item they will use or not. So they'll send the file to defence secretary.' Laxman did not look up but continued to mutter 'Hmmm ... hmmm'. Samuel said, 'So what should we do, thinking on these lines. So if defence secretary will agree, so our company will be shortlisted. We will get around Rs 60 crore order.' Laxman pointedly asked, 'Who are the people who will help this? There must be some committee which must have gone in.' Samuel, as vague as ever and totally out of his depth, said,

No, that is they've approved. That PNC will open in January first week. Before we have ... Sir, there is one reason, I'll tell you very frankly, openly. So in the bureaucratic and in the political level, they will not allow in the third company into the fray. Reason, two companies are already supplying.

Samuel worked out a second meeting with Laxman by giving a gold chain to his secretary Satya Murthy and Rs 10,000 to his other secretary Raju Venkatesh. In his affidavit, Satya Murthy said that every time he took a cigarette from Mathew Samuel, he would feel numb. At the Commission, Tehelka's lawyer Sidharth Luthra made chutney of that excuse.

Luthra: Is it not correct that the first time he came to Mr Laxman's office, he offered you a cigarette?
Satya Murthy: Yes.
Luthra: And you say you felt numb?
Satya Murthy: Yes.
Luthra: And despite that, on each occasion Mr Samuel would offer you cigarettes and you would accept them, knowing fully well that you would feel numb?
Satya Murthy: I was not knowing. Whenever I smoke the cigarette, I used to feel something different. But I did not know that. Every time he is offering and it is happening.
Luthra: Did you consult a doctor?
Satya Murthy: No.
Luthra: Did you ever complain to anyone that the cigarette had an adverse effect on you?

Satya Murthy: No.

Luthra: Isn't it possible that you are not a smoker and, therefore, by smoking a different brand of cigarette you felt different?

Satya Murthy: It is not smoking a different brand, because I do not have a particular brand. I am not a regular smoker.

Luthra: You said you felt numb. Why were you continuing to meet Mr Samuel again and again, although you felt numb with the cigarettes he offered?

Satya Murthy: After meeting so many times .....

Luthra: I am talking about the first meeting. You meet on the first meeting. He gives you something. You say it does not suit you. Why did you continue to meet him and why did you continue to accept his gifts, his entertainment, his lunch, his job, his gold chain?

Satya Murthy: Yes. We have become very friendly after so many meetings.

Luthra: I am talking of the first meeting. After the first meeting, when you felt numb .....

Satya Murthy: He used to meet me very often. I have like that feeling.

Luthra: Did you inform Mr Laxman about the cigarettes and this feeling?

Satya Murthy: No.

Two days after West End gave Bangaru Laxman the money, Mathew Samuel said he started receiving calls from Laxman asking him when they were visiting him next. Satya Murthy took the initiative of showing up at Oberoi Hotel where Aniruddha Bahal had taken a suite, to ask for more money. Satya Murthy promised them that he would introduce them to Ved Prakash Goyal, the BJP treasurer. Satya Murthy also told them that Goyal had asked him to 'screw' Gupta. With West End operatives goading him along, Satya Murthy said it was true that Gupta was involved in the Sukhoi deal. He said, 'They were here about a month back. Sukhoi. Because myself and Mr Laxman, we operated. We operated, very ... nobody, nobody can smell.' He boasted, 'It's like a very small needle behind that kind of congested place and we're very cautious.' He did add, 'Even the money, what you giving, we give it to the party. We won't take it.' When West End representatives said that Laxman spoke about an overseas account, Satya Murthy said, 'I'm doing it in London now'.

Satya Murthy mentioned that R.K. Gupta, Mohinder Singh Sahni and Sudhir Choudhrie were involved in the Sukhoi deal. He did admit that he made money from it and was quite happy. He said that only south Indians could do these kinds of deals because, although they sought a higher percentage, they were the most trusted. West End then offered to give Laxman $31,500, and Satya Murthy promised to set up the meeting for 6.00 p.m. the following day. When asked how many foreign accounts Laxman had, Satya Murthy said, 'He must be having five or six'. He added that he was supposed to have gone to Thailand for this kind of work.

Somehow, this conversation has just too much of feeding of names and gas to be credible. West End leads Satya Murthy into it and he just runs with what is being suggested. It is difficult to believe that a man in Satya Murthy's position would be making money out of a deal as big as Sukhoi, but then there are many known examples of business people who want work done by bureaucrats, who tip everyone in that office from the peon upwards.

At the Commission, Luthra went after Satya Murthy, in his way. Hey, Sidharth, pick on someone your own size. Here was this guy from a village in Andhra Pradesh being lunched and cigaretted by the likes of Mathew Samuel, and promised a job in London, with an undreamt of salary. It would be surprising to find a person in that position who would not succumb to giving an entry to a boss, who in any case happens to be available. The transcript does show Mathew Samuel leading him to names like Brajesh Mishra and Mohinder Singh Sahni. Satya Murthy did not exactly volunteer them but acquiesced to all of Samuel's suggestions. Satya Murthy mentioned he was going to Thailand for a wire transfer of money. Thailand? Why did he not just say, 'Phoren'?

At the second meeting, Samuel introduced Aniruddha Bahal to Laxman, saying rather incongruously, 'Sir, my boss is here. In in … a … in Oberoi executive … executive suite'. Samuel then said, 'For the party fund, I have Rs 5 lakhs. I will give you Rs 1 lakh for just the beginning. A New Year's gift.' Samuel asked Laxman about R.K. Gupta. Laxman replied that Gupta had asked him if he would entertain work from West End. At this point, Samuel handed over Rs 1 lakh to Laxman and said, 'Sir, this is a small gift … small gift'. Laxman responded, 'Oh, no, no … '. Samuel persisted, 'It's a small gift for the New Year party. Right?' Laxman opened his drawer and without looking up, took the wad of currency from Samuel and tossed it into his desk. Samuel tried to set up another meeting with Laxman and was told to come at 5.00 p.m. the following day. Samuel asked, 'Rupee or dollar?' Laxman sealed his fate by saying, 'Dollars. You can give dollars'. Samuel also confirmed that they could come directly to Laxman after fixing an appointment with his secretary.

When I asked Laxman about this conversation, he said that conversation was doctored. He pointed out,

If you look to the preceding conversation, I was referring to them that my treasurer knows whether dollars are accepted, whether there is any other account, all these things I said, you meet my treasurer. But, they had a definite script. They had certain things which they want to put into my mouth.

The next time Samuel showed up with Aniruddha Bahal, they asked Laxman if he could help in getting the item they were selling, shortlisted. Laxman responded, 'On Brajesh Mishra? How?' Bahal elaborated that R.K. Gupta had asked for Rs 20 lakh to introduce them. He also said that West End would give 4 to 5 per cent commission but were confused on what to do with the treasurer. Bahal asked, 'Do we wire or transfer the money?' Laxman said, 'Yeah, yeah. I will tell you …' When Bahal grilled Laxman about the procedure to follow, Laxman said, 'Yeah, yeah. I will tell you'. Then Laxman contradicted himself and said, 'Look, no. Probably you know may be knowing the procedure better than me.' Bahal said, 'Yeah, yeah. That's why I was here. But things don't move in India without some political …' Laxman said, 'Yes, that is true, provided … We shall try to do that. So far we have been taking the help of Brajesh Mishra to organize this because Brajesh Mishra is there on a number of committees apart from principal secretary to prime minister.' Laxman added that they turned to Brajesh Mishra because he had access to defence, foreign, and other related ministries. According to Laxman, Mishra was the liaison between the prime minister and the bureaucracy. Laxman admitted that Mishra was the lynchpin in all the dealings and promised to obtain all the requisite information. Laxman also told them that the prime minister's foster son-in-law, Ranjan Bhattacharya, was not involved in defence deals but dabbled in other things. Laxman promised to meet them the following day and explain the system of procurement to West End. Inexplicably, Tehelka excluded the following conversation in the unedited tapes from the broadcast tapes and edited transcript:

Tehelka: So we should meet tomorrow? Possible?
Laxman: Yes. You will bring cash?

Laxman recalled,

I found my lips were there, but there is no sound. Nothing is coming out. When I was not speaking, something was coming out. There was no sync. At one point of time, they were explaining something. Then I said there must be some committee, some system through which these things might be going. "Sir, system is there, but we are only afraid that the bureaucrats, bureaucratic setup, will not allow any new competitors to come into the field." I said that shouldn't take place. So, they told me that, "Sir, these things are decided by the defence secretary." I told them I don't know defence secretary. Now they have interfered with that particular scene and sentence, and then removed that "don't". While removing the "don't", the "t" remained. So there it appears as though, *ke bhai* I told them I know, they wanted to show that I know defence secretary and I can get this. That "t", fortunately remained. So I demonstrated before the Commission. And ultimately Prashant Bhushan [Tehelka's lawyer] had to say that the benefit of doubt in this particular thing can be given to Bangaru Laxman. They had a definite scheme and script, so the names, which they wanted, they should come into the audio, video.

So, after some time I realized these things are irrelevant. Why they are asking? So I had to answer in some way. If you watch my whole tape, I think it runs into thirty to forty minutes or so, *meine jo usme kaha hai, voh paanch minute se zyada nahin hai* [what I said there, could not have been more than five minutes]. Rest of the time they were talking. And they got some certain terminology and that they wanted to put into my mouth and get a nod from me. *Ke iss tereh se unho ne kiya hai* [this is how they did it].

Laxman broke through the entrenched caste system when, in spite of being the son of a Dalit pump operator in Metro Waterworks, Hyderabad, he rose to become the president of the BJP. He joined the RSS when he was twelve years old, studied up to the 10th class in a government school in Nampally, Hyderabad, and then dropped out to work to help support his family. Laxman went to Evening College, Osmania University, for a Bachelor of Arts degree and then a law degree from Law College in the same university. He was enrolled as a lawyer but never got to practice. He became involved in fighting against the Emergency called by Indira Gandhi and went to jail for fifteen months. He held low level government jobs in the electricity department, railways, and the auditor general's office. Laxman was preparing for the IAS examination in 1969 when Jan Sangh President Deendayal Upadhyaya was murdered. Laxman had great regard for Upadhyaya and reacted by resigning his job to become an active political worker. He said he never aspired for political power, but inspired by Upadhaya, he said was interested in public service. He was appointed president of the Andhra Pradesh BJP unit and served as president of All India Scheduled Castes Morcha for over seven years. He held various positions in the BJP until he was appointed president of the party in 2000.

Can you blame the Tehelka journalists for their exuberance after catching the president of the party in government accepting money on camera? Bangaru Laxman was utterly bewildered about the fuss. Wasn't he, as president of the BJP, supposed to take money? Wasn't that his job? How else could a party run? When asked about how his wife and his four children reacted, he answered,

> They knew it pretty well this money was taken for the party and given to the party. Therefore they were not seeking my explanation *ke bhai*, why did you take money? After all, it was part of the job. But they did feel: why did they choose you? And, naturally they were hurt.

On the evening of 13 March 2001, Venkaiah Naidu, the (late) Pramod Mahajan, Anant Kumar, and Arun Jaitley arrived at Laxman's house. They wanted to know Bangaru Laxman's side of the story. Laxman said that someone called him from the BJP and told him that the leaders had met and discussed his resignation. Laxman said he immediately sent in his resignation because, 'I don't want to cause any embarrassment to the party, on account of this'. He recalled that there was a history in the BJP of leaders resigning in the event of any serious allegations. He pointed out that L.K. Advani, Yashwant Sinha, and Madan Lal Khurana all handed in their papers when allegations were levelled against them.

When asked if it was common for him to accept donations in his normal working day as president of the BJP, Laxman said, 'It happens. Wherever I went, some people come with currency garlands. Even those have been accounted for. I did not know what I did wrong.' Well, no receipt was issued. When asked by the Tehelka lawyer in the Commission whether Laxman was aware of the rule that he could not accept more than Rs 20,000 in the year 2000, Laxman fallaciously replied: 'It is for the contributor to ensure this is followed.' When questioned further, Laxman clarified, 'As far as we are concerned, we ensure that whether it is accounted in our books or not'. When it was pointed out that Ved Prakash Goyal (treasurer of the BJP) stated in his affidavit to the Commission that no receipt had been issued, Laxman looked puzzled and said, 'I don't think he has said so. He has not. No, no, he was not even asked about this.'

Laxman denied what he said about going to Brajesh Mishra for defence deals in the Operation West End tapes. He said, 'No, absolutely not. I was only saying that Brajesh Mishra being a member in the National Executive earlier, he was taken as secretary by the prime minister.'

Laxman stated that he was not aware that his personal secretary Satya Murthy took money to arrange meetings with him. Before he asked Satya Murthy to leave, he did ask him about it. Laxman said that Satya Murthy had explained to him that as his job with him was not permanent, West End induced him with many promises and he got sucked in by them.

It is noticeable that Bangaru Laxman is not living in financial discomfort. He has rented a large enough house and seems to have enough people still working for him. But he is despondent because, from leading an active political life, he is reduced to going to general programmes of the party or meetings of the Scheduled Caste Morcha of the BJP. He pointed out that from 1969 to the time he resigned, he invariably held some responsible position in the BJP. With a bitter laugh and sadness, he said, 'You can imagine the change'. He said there were certain people whose behaviour with him had changed, but most people were good to him. He pointed out that he was no socialite and always kept a low profile. He never projected that he was a fixer or doled out favours as an extension of his power. He said he was never spoken about as a man who could get things done. Laxman believed this was not the end of his political career; only an interruption. He said, 'Once the Commission's report is out and the truth is out, I will be free to pursue my political career'.

Did Laxman feel that he had been treated unfairly? 'Yes,' he said, 'I do feel but maybe it is a part of the whole plan laid by the Almighty'. Did this embitter him?' Laxman replied, 'No, I am not because surely I feel that I must have committed a mistake, therefore, I am being punished. If not now, maybe in the previous lives. You cannot escape.'

Laxman said,

> Certainly they have targeted me for two reasons. One is my humble background. A man coming from that background and going to such high, highest of position. Media was very kind to me during my tenure as president. Even international media was kind to me. So maybe that created a kind of jealousness for some people. Secondly, I was easily accessible. *Mere gate bandh nahin rehte teh* [my doors were never closed].

On 6 December 2004, the CBI registered a case of corruption against Laxman. Despite everything, Laxman still hangs on to his belief that he was targeted because he belonged to the Dalit caste. This despair brings him right into Insectpur, the land of the helpless, with karma as the only explanation for his misfortune. Perhaps, then, he wouldn't be shocked that a senior BJP politician, on hearing about Laxman taking money from Tehelka, said privately, '*Bhangi toh bhangi hee raheyga* [a *bhangi*, (low caste individual) will always remain a *bhangi*].' Don't test your naïveté by being shocked.

12 Thus Spake R.K. Jain
[Oh, heck, everything below is 'alleged', of course.]

The best ammunition against lies is the truth. There is no ammunition against gossip. It is like a fog and the clear wind blows it away and the sun burns it off.

– *Ernest Hemingway (1898-1961), Novelist*
in a letter to Adriana Ivancic

Madhu: What about when R.K. Jain called you to his office?

Samuel: That is also very inrrusssting part. I also sometimes very I enjoyed the story. Very very intrrussting. So then R.K. Jain said, "If your bawss is coming I can arrange to give a Mercedes Benz." I said there is no need. I know that our car have to use. It is our matter. Operating and everything, cams and everything. Then he said, "Vaat else?" I said, "Nothing else." He said, "He want to go to Agra?" I said, "I don't know his toor plan and everything." He said, "I can arrange a chawpper." Ha! Ha! Ha! Then he said, "He's intrrussted good babes?" Treasurer of Samata Party is arranging babes? The socialist party. George Fernandes heading the party. Treasurer of Samata Party is organizing babes, for whom? This I want to prove. So I said, "This I don't know. I can talk to him. I can tell you tomorrow." Then second day he called six, seven babes.

Madhu: Where did he show you the girls?

Samuel: [Shouting in amazement!] Inside his hawffiss, in Barakhamba Road! All the babes arrived there. They don't look like prostitutes kind of things. Like very hi-fi type. Vaat I supposed to say? Like suppose you go to PVR, Vasant Vihar; mostly I saw this kind of places. Vasant Vihar cinema, this type of female will come, *hai nah*? That kind of stuff came. Ha! Ha! Huh! Huh! Rrreally! If you go through the tape, *nah*, I rreally stuck. I don't know vaat to ask, vaat to do. I never thought he will call, he will do like that. Then he's asking, "You can ask. Which one you like?" In front of them. How can I say which one I like in front of some females? Others how they feel? Like my roooral background, vaat they will feel? I literally scared. Then this guy, Menon, he starting esskplanation of everything. The one who the pimp who accompany with them. He esskplaining to me and Jain. That she's hairless, she will do like that like that, very much enjoy. I am also literally you know in front of them. That is my fussst experience, *hai nah*. He saying they will do everything, natural, unnatural. One babe, her special her tongue. She will handle everything with that. So rreally after I heard that, I walked away from there. So one babe came to the Hotul Oberoi. This guy selected. Who selected? R.K. Jain. She came to the hotul. Aniruddha told me to send her back. She came to Oberoi. Aniruddha was staying. *Woh hamare room mey aah gayi thi* [she had come into our room]. Aniruddha told me to send her back. I told her, "That's enough. We are not intrrussted today. We have lawt of other business." Aniruddha said something, "We don't have mind right now to do anything. So we will call you." Bloody R.K. Jain was standing there. So no one asked this question in Commission. This gell went and talked to this Menon [pimp] and said that she enjoyed very well here. He's very happy. How can she say nothing happened? We already paid Rs 50,000 to R.K. Jain.

Perhaps the juiciest and potentially damning tapes, if you believe the guy, are those with R.K. Jain, who was the Samata Party treasurer since 1998. The Tehelka operatives did not need anyone to introduce them to R.K. Jain. Hearing a lot of rattling about Jain as the acting briefcase man for George Fernandes, the Tehelka journalists went directly to a highly accessible Jain. He was no slouch in the gossip department. Jain is seen and heard on the Operation West End tapes:

R.K. Jain: Jaya Jaitly is the second wife. But [George Fernandes] not officially married to Jaya Jaitly. She's president of the party also. So there are two defence ministers. One is George Fernandes, another is Jaya Jaitly.
West End: That's cute. Very cute.
R.K. Jain: I am basically the front of Jaya Jaitly and George Fernandes. If you want, I can show you the minutes of the meetings. It is cyclostyled in our different conferences. National conferences, that whenever the party needs money, Mr Jain will have to arrange that money and give it to the party. That is the job of the treasurer.

When West End asked Jain how much money he had generated for the Samata Party, he replied, 'Till now, I think I am worth … [then, correcting himself] I have given more than Rs 50 crore.'

Jain trained as a mechanical engineer in Ranchi, Bihar, and worked in export for numerous companies – Honda generators, oil, paper, steel, and beer. He then set up his own industry for acrylic fibre and then Pasupati Haryana Woollens Ltd. He worked in the Labour Cell of the Congress Party in Ghaziabad for five years, before being appointed treasurer of the Samata Party.

R.K. Jain's remarks in the Operation West End tapes are ostensibly facts but largely gossip. But, how then does he even know such details of the deals if it is all invented? Jain is upfront about his role in collecting money: 'Please consider that it is not hidden from the treasurer that the party is getting money. Money is withdrawn when I pass a cheque; when I sign it. And why should I lie? I would take money only in lieu of work done for you?'

Jain recounted how he was appointed treasurer of the Samata Party. He said, one day Fernandes called him and asked him for Rs 2.5 lakhs. Jain said, 'What is Rs 2.5 lakhs? You are such a big man. You should have asked for Rs 20 lakhs, 25 lakhs.' Jain arranged for the money and the following day, according to Jain, Fernandes called him up and asked him to become treasurer.

Jain said his first project was advanced jet trainers with three competing companies: the British Hawk, the French Alpha Jet, and the Russian MAPO-MiG. All of the below is alleged and according to Jain on the Operation West End tapes. Jain recalled that he went to Fernandes and told him that it was a big job worth Rs 3,600 crore. He said: 'If you bless me, then I'll take the agency from them and do it.' Fernandes reportedly replied that he would check it out and get back to him. The defence minister called Jain back and told him that the Russians have the lowest price and there was a good prospect of the order going to them. Jain alleged that Fernandes gave the go-ahead for the tie up. When Jain told the Russians that the ball was rolling, they insisted that they wanted to meet Fernandes first. Jain informed Fernandes who, according to Jain, said: 'But they should trust you. You are the treasurer. What is the point of exposing me? Why do you want to expose me?' Jain said he explained to Fernandes that he was not exposing him because it was an official appointment. The Russians agreed and Jain got into negotiating mode with them. He asked for 10 per cent commission for the deal. The Russians said they could not give more than 7 per cent. Jain said he explained to them that the Samata Party would expect 3 per cent, the Prime Minister's Office would expect at least 3 per cent, and then there were bureaucrats, ministers, and then, of course, himself. The Russians went off to meet Fernandes, and Jain reported that the next day Fernandes laughed and told him: 'The bugger was sweating. The chairman of MiG was sweating.' After that meeting, Jain was asked by the Russians to fly to Moscow to sign the agreement. Jain told Samuel that he was not allowed to fly without Jaya's permission. He said he went to Jaya Jaitly and told her that the Russians had called him to Moscow. Jain said that Jaya told him: 'No, no, Mr Jain, it is not safe. You don't fly because you are our treasurer. People are keeping an eye on you.' Jain recalled that he told Jaya that uness he flew there and signed the agreement, he could not do their job for them and there would be no commission for the party. Jain said that then Jaya gave him the go-ahead. Jain said when he arrived at the Moscow meeting, in a room full of MiG managers, he was told that they were not ready to sign for the air jet trainers but could work out some smaller deals. Jain said, 'My mood got spoilt because I took permission from the boss to fly to Moscow and they're not wanting to sign the agreement at that time. They were not confident of providing all the papers and licences, which are needed to approve them technically.' All of this, of course, according to Jain, at that time.

On 19 March 2001, George Fernandes clarified that the advanced jet trainer (AJT) contract was yet to be signed. Fernandes pointed out,

> It is noteworthy that the MIC MAPO [from press release of Fernandes's statement from the defence ministry] company whom I have alleged to have favoured was not even issued the request for proposal. The request for proposal was issued to only to the two companies which our air force had shortlisted namely the British Hawk and the French Alpha Jet. It is true that the Russians had been constantly requesting the government of India to consider their aircraft. However, I decided to go by the choice of the air force.

Jain related the story how a major arms dealer had positioned himself to represent both British Hawk and MiG. Jain said he met him for the first time in the presence of Pushkin, the chairman of MiG. Jain was amazed that the arms dealer had himself met all of the expenses required to bring all the MiGs to Bangalore from Moscow for demonstration because the Russians had no money. Jain said that the Indian arms dealer invited him to talk. At the arms dealer's home, he was asked to join forces with British Hawk, along with the dealer. It was explained to him that there was no point in them competing with each other. Jain said that he didn't want to run around with two companies while the arms dealer was hedging all his bets by covering both bases, but he agreed to help him on any other projects. The arms dealer proposed the upgrade of guns from 130mm to 155mm by Soltam of Israel. According to Jain, Abdul Kalam, then scientific adviser to the PM, had written that we should use indigenous items. Jain said that the file had been pending since Narasimha Rao's government, but Fernandes took the decision and did it.

According to George Fernandes, any implication that the contracts were manipulated was 'a complete lie'. He insisted,

> The procurement process was carried out strictly in accordance with defence procurement norms and the project was approved by the Cabinet Committee on Security after examination by the finance ministry. I had taken a decision in January 2000 that all procurements above Rs 75 crore should by examined by CVC, the files pertaining to this contract were sent to the CVC. The CVC did not find any evidence of malpractice in this case.

Jain said he also got an order from the French company Sagem.

Jain recounted the Barak deal, a system meant for air-to-air and surface-to-surface missiles on ships. Abdul Kalam had written on the file that it was no use importing this system; instead DRDO's Trishul and Prithvi missiles should be used. According to Jain, Suresh Nanda was representing the Israeli company, Barak, and had handed over Rs 1 crore to him. Jain said he went to Jaya Jaitly and asked her whether they could help Nanda get the order or he would have to return the sum of Rs 1 crore. According to Jain, Jaya kept the money and asked him for two days. When she called Jain, Jaya told him, 'I've spoken to the boss. Don't worry. He said he'll make everything fine.' According to Jain, when the file was called, Fernandes told Jain that he was overruling Kalam's comments but that he should not buy all seven at one go. The idea was to get one approved and then state that all ships were important, and on that basis buy the rest of the six. Jaya Jaitly, however, later stated emphatically: 'There was no question of him [Fernandes] overruling Kalam as Jain is supposed to have been saying.' Jain said he was told to push Nanda to work the system from below. After six months, Nanda had done his work and the file reappeared on Fernandes's desk. At the point of their discussion, the deal was being considered in the Price Negotiating Committee. In the Operation West End tapes Jain admitted to getting 3 per cent for the Samata Party and some for himself.

According to a clarification issued by George Fernandes on 16 March 2001, the defence ministry had approved a proposal by the Indian Navy for six Barak systems in 1996 and he had not gone against Dr Abdul Kalam, before he took over as defence minister on 19 March 1998. The decision was taken to meet the navy's requirement with the Barak anti-missile defence systems for immediate deployment and when the DRDO developed the indigenous system, it would be used. Fernandes pointed out that the urgency was triggered by Pakistan's purchase of P3C Orion aircraft fitted with air-to-surface missiles and the submarine-launched Exocet missiles.

On the Operation West End tapes, Jain elaborated that the modus operandi used was that one man would give a verbal guarantee of the amount in the presence of one or two friends. As soon as the money was transferred, Jain would show the slip and he would receive the money. Sometimes it was credited to Jain's brother's account abroad. Jain boasted that he got half per cent in the 600 crore Sultam deal. Jain claimed that he had to pay half per cent to the man who took him to the arms dealer and Jaya Jaitly allegedly insisted on nothing less than 3 per cent.

George Fernandes, furious at the allegations, said,

> I will not take any more time in dealing with the other insinuations against me. All that I want to say is that the accusations made against me are completely false. My public life extends over a period of 52 years. I have spent these years fighting for probity in public life and for upholding our democratic values and in fighting against all forms of injustice everywhere.

At the Commission of Inquiry, Jaya stated:

> They [Tehelka] are talking of R.K. Jain, listening to some nonsense from him and on the basis of that, without cross-checking they say that he [Fernandes] is indicted beyond redemption. In the other parts of the transcript, which I would not like to repeat here, there is Mr Jain talking, probably in a fit of drunkenness, where I am called the second defence minister; if you reach me, you have reached George Fernandes. This is extremely sad and insulting and can be only part of an unholy operation which cannot be called investigative journalism.

Dayan Krishnan, counsel for the Commission of Inquiry, questioned Jaya Jaitly on Jain's statements:

Krishnan: You have already told us about R.K. Jain and your association with him and so on. I just want to show you one or two things stated by R.K. Jain in your context in the transcript and seek some clarification. Please see the middle of page 76 of the transcript:
"R.K. Jain: And then I said, 'no I can't do it for less than 10 per cent.'"
Please see the whole paragraph.
Then he says, "In India you can't negotiate with ministers. Which means … normally, they try and keep 3 per cent and up to 2 per cent depending on the size." Then he went on to George Fernandes and so on. Lastly, he said, "Though I am not allowed to fly without the permission of Jayaji."
Let me show you all the things attributed to you and then put my question. At the bottom of page 76 as well, there is a statement attributed to you: "But I went to Jaya Jaitly. I said, 'Madam, they are calling me to Moscow.'" Then please see page 81, "At least what my party is going to get, what I am going to get … it has all been decided … That 3 per cent to the party." See page 80: "I told Jaya Jaitly, 'Look, so much of money he has already given to me now. If you accept that means we have to do something for the party.'"
Tell me, after the Tehelka tapes went public, what action did you take against R.K. Jain for making these statements against a reputed national party and its functionaries?
Jaitly: Sir, soon after the tapes were shown everywhere, I resigned my position. And therefore, for me to take action against anybody becomes irrelevant.
Krishnan: Were you aware of what action your party took?
Jaitly: As far as I know, I have been informed, later on he had resigned from the position and he has not showed his face since. As far as the party is concerned, he is non-existent.
Krishnan: Mr Jain in his deposition before this Commission has stated on oath that he is presently the president of your Delhi unit.
Jaitly: That is absolutely incorrect. I do not know how he could have said such a thing. The president of the Delhi unit was appointed by the current president in the middle of April or May some time and there is an appointment letter and an announcement in the press accordingly.
Krishnan: I put it to you that as national president of the Samata Party at the given time, functioning out of the residence of the defence minister, you have portrayed you have access to the Ministry of Defence.
Jaitly: I deny that completely.
Krishnan: I further put it to you that your action, as depicted in the transcripts and the tapes, as the president of a national political party, shows gross impropriety.
Jaitly: No, sir, I deny it.

Even if you decide that Jain was a blustering gossip, one cannot but wonder how, if he was not involved, he could have known such minute details of the various arms sales? He spoke of numerous deals and all the steps they went through but gets the name of a major arms dealer wrong, so could it be gossip? Surely, if he went to the arms dearler's house he would have known his correct name.

When R.K. Jain appeared before the Commission of Inquiry on 22 April 2002, Kavin Gulati, counsel for Tehelka, immediately asked him:

> **Gulati:** You respect Mr George Fernandes and Ms Jaya Jaitly, as appears from your affidavit. Is it not?
>
> **Jain:** I have a lot of respect for Mr George Fernandes. From my college time, I have been respecting Mr George Fernandes, because he is basically a leader of the labourers and I do not know why, but I always used to feel that he is one who really wants to do something for the poor people, for the labourers and he is a real socialist and that is the reason why I have always respect for him.
>
> **Gulati:** Would you then say anything which is detrimental to their interest?
>
> **Jain:** No, if you respect somebody then why will you speak against him without any reason. But if you have any reason therefore, you may not continue to respect him only because you have been respecting him earlier.
>
> **Gulati:** You are a member of a political party, that is, Samata Party. What would happen if you speak against Mr Fernandes and Ms Jaya Jaitly?
>
> **Jain:** Naturally they will throw me out of the party.

There is a glaring absence of any mention of respect for Jaya Jaitly. When asked about favours given to people who contributed to the Samata Party, Jain said:

> It is not necessary that everybody wants things in return. For example, I want to help somebody and I have given him money. It does not mean that I want something from him. It is not necessary all the time. There are so many people like that. It depends on the ideology of the party also. In my party, Mr George Fernandes has a very high reputation. I am feeling so bad that because of this Tehelka episode such a nice and such a dignified man is being dragged out to such kind of situation. They should all feel ashamed for this because finally there is nothing in this where Mr George Fernandes is involved. They will realize this later. This kind of exercise has really ruined the country.
>
> **Gulati:** Why did you introduce this firm DHK and its proprietor Lav Chadha to Mathew Samuel?
>
> **Jain:** Samuel wanted my help in the Ministry of Defence. When he realized I cannot do it, I cannot help him, he said, he could get defence related work done. He wanted that I should introduce him to some people, who want their work to be done. This raised doubts in my mind about the man who initially approaches me for getting help in defence matters and then states

that he can get the work done in defence matters. After I met the president [Aniruddha Bahal of West End], I realized that they are up to some mischief, because when I saw the president alighting from an old car I decided that I should find out. I wanted to keep him engaged. To keep him engaged, to find out the reality, I knew one person by the name of Lav Chadha. I thought I will use him to find out about their motive. To understand them and keep them engaged, I took them for a few other meetings. I wanted to catch them, and in fact I caught them in their office after a few meetings. I took 3-4 days before I could really know that these people are from Buffalo Network. Otherwise I would have caught them.

Gulati: In the same paragraph you have stated that you started boasting and taking names. What were you boasting about and what names were you taking?

Jain: I can get done any kind of work you want.

Gulati: Please specify.

Jain: I cannot remember what I really boasted, because it is all gossiping. The gossip is not remembered. I said whatever I could and he was pleased all the time. I was telling him, "Look, if you want to buy Qutab Minar, I am willing to sell Qutab Minar." He said, "All right, I will purchase Qutab Minar." Then I said, "If you are purchasing Qutab Minar, why don't you sell Taj Mahal to me?"

Gulati: Where have you said so in your affidavit that he was wanting to purchase Qutab Minar and he wanted to sell you Taj Mahal?

Jain: What I was trying to say is that he was talking of wrong things. He was talking of fake things. Whatever I was talking, I was also talking of fake things. When I say he is accepting my offer, he is accepting whatever I am saying to him. So, you keep on telling whatever you want so that he is impressed.

Jain's position on why he entertained Mathew Samuel at all when he became suspicious was that he was a businessman and was interested in setting up a hospital. This was motivated by the death of his first wife, due to medical neglect. Gulati, for his part, was suspicious of this ploy and asked a series of questions that demanded that Jain prove the hospital was not just a dream but actual work had gone into it.

Gulati asked Jain about the Rs 50 lakh he was expecting from Mathew Samuel. He read from Jain's affidavit:

Shri Samuel then suggested that I should render services for his company for consideration. To begin with, Shri Samuel asked me to arrange a couple of meetings for his President with various ministries, as well as businessmen, who were interested in investments. I suggested to him that since he had no concrete proposal for investment, it would be better for his boss to meet a few private businessmen/industrialists who had concrete proposals for investments in different area. Shri Samuel agreed and requested that there should be at least four to six meetings, as he wanted to impress his boss.

Gulati: Then you say, he asked me how much money I was expecting and after negotiations Rs 50 lakhs was settled. To make him meet various people in various ministries, you were demanding money, which was quantified into Rs 50 lakhs.

Jain: Not ministries. I said various possible buyers, possibly companies which are interested in having investment. In that private companies are also there, government companies are also there. If he is interested in investing into oil sector or communication sector, if I can identify them, the communication ministry is interested in having the funding for any kind of project that is used. Why not?

Gulati: You said already that for investment in these projects you will charge a certain sum of money. Do you know that charging such a sum of money is illegal?

Jain: I do not think it is illegal.

Gulati: Did you specify that you will charge this sum?

Jain: In case this is selected, if the investment is taken by this ministry, well, yes. Since I am your representative, for identifying this area for you, definitely some commission has to be paid.

Gulati brought up the discussion Jain had with Mathew Samuel about money that would be paid abroad.

Jain: The big money which he is offering me to take it to Ms Jaya Jaitly or George Fernandes. He asked, how do you get this money? Everybody knows what is havala. So, I just boasted myself, because I was not taking him to George Fernandes or Jaya Jaitly. There was no question of any havala transaction of money coming into the picture.

Gulati then turned to large sections that were edited out of the broadcast tape and read from the transcript:

"**Jain:** George is not like Yashwant Sinha. Takes money openly. Yashwant Sinha takes money. George does not take money. His image is that with very socialist background. It is not easy to give money to George. I told you that day also. You told me the same. He does limited work. Yashwant Sinha takes money. Digvijay Singh takes money. Sharad Yadav takes money. Paswan takes money. You have done any big work. I have got a loan. Just by chance I told you that. I have got loan from Yashwant Sinha for one of my brothers. Rs 30 crore, just I have to be open now, within four to five days, okay. Yashwant Sinha has very good terms and conditions with one of my colleagues, M.P. He is a BJP M.P. What is his name? Rudy. Okay. What state? Bihar."

Gulati: According to you, what you are saying is that Mr George Fernandes does not take money, but Mr Yashwant Sinha, Mr Digvijay Singh, Mr Sharad Yadav and Mr Paswan will take money. Is that what you are saying?

Jain: Yes. It is written there.

Gulati: Why did you say such a thing?

Jain: It is because, in the sense, he was talking in terms of investment, he want to make investment into this country. So, to show him as a big man, as a big man of contacts, to show him as a big man, I was just gossiping.

Gulati: So, would the Commission be entitled to assume correctly that you are also gossiping about Mr George Fernandes when you said he is an honest man?

Jain: Just to show that I was saying this, nothing else. Gossiping. When you say something, when you boast about something, everything is not false. Part of it is true even. As far as George Fernandes is concerned, what I said is true. When you talk about investment, to show you can get work done, to show that you have to boast and get things done. I fail to understand. There cannot be any illegal thing in this. What illegal things can be there? I am just surprised. If the project is false, perhaps one can think in those terms. But no illegality is involved when the project is genuine.

Gulati: Are you suggesting to the Commission that there is nothing wrong in paying the ministers?

Jain: I have not said that you will have to pay money to the ministers. You are already making an investment either to the private people or the government people. You are already investing. You should be happy that a big amount is coming to the country.

Gulati then reads from the unedited transcript:

"**Jain:** Listen to me. George is an honest man. You cannot go to him. People cannot go to him. When people cannot go to him through the main door, what do you do? Some other channel. Otherwise, why are they queuing up in front of the BJP gate? Why not the gate of Samata Party? And the Samata Party also nobody will be able to enter. This is what George Fernandes. But it is a matter of chance. As far as money is concerned, I am one of the most trusted men in the party. Okay, party knows because I am a businessman. I am not a politician. Okay. He knows that I am not interested in fighting an election. If I am given a seat for Rajya Sabha, I will be fine."

Gulati turned the page and read:

"**Jain:** Maybe you are not in the gang but you are not a bloody robber. But, at least to survive. Naturally, otherwise where the money? Without money, party will not be able to survive.

George does very few cases, which are good, very good cases. Then, where he feels that the party is interested party, is genuine party, money is saved and he tries to help. So unless and until I am secure from all these angles.

Jaya Jaitly is the president of your party. She is very close to George Fernandes. She will take money for the boss, like that some officer told me. He does not meet directly. You cannot. He is the man for PM's candidate. He cannot take risk of a small amount of Rs 50 lakhs. He meets you and you take advantage of that meeting, start talking about everywhere. So, he is finished. That is true. Sometimes, all right, if I meet someone officially does not matter. I am not going to tell you anything wrong of him. So there is safeguard. The safeguard is that the first is Jaya Jaitly. Jaya Jaitly also does not, because she also wants protection. Because, if anything goes wrong to Jaya Jaitly, it affects George Fernandes straightaway.

If Jaya Jaitly meets anybody who want to meet George Fernandes, everybody knows he is nothing. If you meet Jaya Jaitly and Jaya meets you, it more than means that you have met George Fernandes. I will try to fix up a meeting with George or Jaya, one of them. And there is a third person in command, who does all the work. That is S.K. Rajiv Goba, this is his PS. The three triangle, which works, because the boss tell Madam or he tells Goba that whatever Madam tells you. Do people come to Madam? It does not work for everybody. I go to her. She calls immediately Goba. The three will have a meeting. Goba will understand. Then he will give his views in two or three days, whether we should put our head into this or not. Then he is the man responsible for looking after the job. He is the man who goes to George Fernandes. "Please write like this"; he would give instruction to do the job by Jaya Jaitly. And I have my direct relationship with Goba.

All these Cabinet Ministers, they want to clearly keep safe. Nowadays, you know, within a minute everything comes into the papers like this what the minister has done. I know. I get it, money very carefully. If they take money, they take it carefully from those people to whom they are close. Okay, for example, like Mr George Fernandes. He is an honest man. He is very popular in India. You know, to run a party, you need funds, donations anyway. You cannot do without that. So, somebody or the other, companies will have to make some money. He has done it very, very quietly, with very limited people."

Gulati stopped reading and asked:

Gulati: I have read out certain portions to you. My question to you is this. Do you still maintain that you were trying to say that Mr George Fernandes is completely honest? Is it the definition of honesty?'

Jain: I am a businessman. They came to me as an investor, a company manufacturing binoculars. My interest was towards the investment. I should look after their investment. My interest was limited to that. They were technically rejected. Samuel spoke about defence again and again. He said his boss feels defence procurement is a big area for his company to invest. Somebody strong in defence area is required to be appointed by the company. Not to displease him, I agreed that I may help him out. He may have gone somewhere else, to somebody else otherwise. Time and again, to make him satisfied, I indulged in loose talk, so that the investment part is looked after by me only. I could have taken him to Jaya Jaitly but I never did that. I said, I knew Colonel Choudary, Dhillon, etc. But, in fact, I do not know any one of them. He agreed to do what I told him and I got encouraged to speak further. I was able to convince him, to let me handle the investment part. During the Bhagwat episode, I gathered some information and to impress him, whatever I could recollect, I told him to show that I am strong in the defence area. I indulged in gossip. The triangle of Jaya Jaitly, Goba and George Fernandes was to exploit the situation so that I can impress him and get work in the investment area. Anybody having common sense would know that by dropping the names of a few top people of a particular ministry, or people associated with them, the work can get done. Despite all these attempts, I did not take him to Jaya Jaitly. I even suggested absurd sum of Rs 3 crore for the company to give so that I can arrange the meeting. I estimated the binocular project would be worth about Rs 40 to 50 crore. I wanted to convince him that I cannot take him to meet Jaya Jaitly.

But the fact remains the fact, in the sense that I did not act if you see the 100 hour cassettes very carefully. Everybody, whoever sits in this Commission they will realize that at no point of time I indulged myself in doing so or in supporting Mr Mathew Samuel for doing the work in defence. The only thing, yes, I made some gossip. I made certain loose talk in that sense that he should not feel that a man who is the national treasurer of the party is not strong even in the party. If he senses like that, then my business will go away. But as far as action is concerned, I even did not try to phone Ms Jaya Jaitly. I never tried to go to the defence ministry or anywhere nearby there. The talk of General Choudary and all that is nonsense. I do not even know them.

Gulati: Why did you introduce Mathew Samuel to Mr Ram Vilas Paswan and Mr Santosh Gangwar, the ministers?

Jain: As I told you, he was interested in making investment in this country. I felt, because may be our communication ministry, our oil ministry, they may need some investment for their projects and that is why I thought, I told him also, that at this stage there is no concrete proposal. But still if you are interested in meeting them, there is no harm in making a courtesy call to him. Well, then you will be able to say, look, I will be able to get the man who is in a position, who can be able to identify the areas where your investment can be made. It was just a courtesy call meeting with no proposal; nothing of that kind.

Gulati: What amount was paid to you for arranging this meeting?

Jain: I was paid nothing.

Gulati: Did you demand something?

Jain: Yes.

Gulati: How much?

Jain: Not for the meeting. I said for the total consultancy, like my hospital, like private meetings, I said that I will try and locate certain areas for you, where your company can make an investment. If I do that, you will have to pay me a sum of Rs 50 lakhs for these services.

Gulati: So, as you are saying, Mr Jain, you demanded Rs 3 crores to arrange the meeting with Ms Jaya Jaitly and Mr George Fernandes and Rs 50 lakhs for the other services.

Jain: That is what I have been saying. You are saying the same thing, which I have been telling. Let me finish first. Let me say very clearly, in spite of the Rs 3 crores he offered to me, I did not take him to Jaya Jaitly. He is talking about only Rs 50 lakhs. We settled it at Rs 50 lakhs. I am trying to organize a number of meetings with him because I was supposed to locate certain areas for him, where this company could make investment. You very rightly said the same thing, which I want to tell the Commission.

Rakesh Jain had repeatedly said that he was suspicious of Mathew Samuel. Why then did he take Samuel to meet people? Jain said his suspicions arose when he met Samuel's boss (Bahal) who was supposed to be the head of a multinational company but arrived in a run-down Maruti car, simple clothes and wearing a baseball cap backwards. So he decided to string him along, continue the meetings and began nosing around about him.

When questioned about how he knew such intricate details about the various arms deals he has mentioned, Jain said that he picked up the information from the newspapers during the Admiral Vishnu Bhagwat episode relating to defence deals. Admiral Bhagwat was dismissed for his refusal to accept the appointment of Vice Admiral Harinder Singh as deputy chief of the naval staff (December 1998). Bhagwat's explanation for his refusal was that Vice Admiral Harinder Singh 'employed a communal appeal to divide the armed forces of the Union'. Bhagwat did talk to the press about underhand arms deals with ex-naval officers and reported arms dealer Suresh Nanda. However, the kind of details that R.K. Jain spoke of were never reported. Had that happened there would have been as much of an uproar as that created by the Tehelka exposé. Some of the information Jain said he picked up during conversations with Mathew Samuel. Jain said he mentioned names of arms dealers who he only knew socially.

Gulati asked Jain how he knew details about the Barak deal and Abdul Kalam, then scientific adviser and subsequently president of India. Jain tried to pass it off as general gossip he had picked up and said he didn't even know if it was true. Jain however had inside information. Abdul Kalam had not only made the noting Jain mentioned but George Fernandes himself confirmed this in his own affidavit.

Jain said he got suspicious when, after taking the West End representatives to meet the ministers, he had a couple of drinks with them at Oberoi Hotel and he was ill the next day. He was sure they had spiked his alcohol. Jain continued to deny that he accepted Rs 50,000 from West End.

In his answers to his lawyers, Jain was nonplussed about the fuss. He is a businessman, as he repeatedly reminded everyone, and was living by the Indian businessman's unwritten rules. Legalities are a mere formality where the businessman's creativity is inspired into how to get around them. For him it is only a challenging crossword puzzle that needs to be solved. Jain's indignation with Gulati for raising questions about issues which were his way of life are understandable. We are often reminded that Hinduism is a way of life, and equally is business and *hera pheri* a way of life.

There is a telling little tale in this. Jaya Jaitly said that R.K. Jain had disappeared after the exposé. Well, he hadn't disappeared at all. He continued to live in a tony area of Delhi and work in his Barakhamba Road office. When I called up R.K. Jain for an interview, this is how it went:

> **Madhu**: Mr Jain, I am writing a book on Tehelka. I would like to meet you and get your side of the story.
> **Jain**: Are you Mrs Trehan, wife of Dr Trehan?
> **Madhu**: Yes.
> **Jain**: Dr Trehan the dentist?
> **Madhu**: No, he is a cardiac surgeon.
> **Jain**: Oh, oh, oh. He operated on my father. Of course I will meet you. But, we respect your husband so much, why should you come? I will come to your house.
> **Madhu**: No, no, I think it is better if I come to your place.
> **Jain**: No, no, that would be impudent of me. Why should you take the trouble to come to my place? I will come to you.
> **Madhu**: No, Mr Jain, it is no trouble at all. I would like to come to your place.
> **Jain**: Okay, 11.00 a.m. tomorrow.

The following morning, I received a call from his office informing me that he could not meet me as he was busy in a meeting. At that point I suddenly remembered that our wonderful, businessman R.K. Jain had filed a case against me for defamation for printing in the *Wahindia* magazine what he had said in the Operation West End tapes. He had forgotten about this as well when we spoke the first time. Someone must have reminded him.

On 27 February 2006, the CBI on a list of charges arrested Jain: for corruption, for demanding and receiving money from West End and promising them a contract from the defence ministry. The CBI also raided three of Jain's properties.

Jaya Jaitly's fury directed towards R.K. Jain is highly understandable: he was after all someone who she naturally felt was beholden to her and Fernandes for his position in the Samata Party. The treasurer of her own party spraying names, describing deals with such sequential chronology, and making Jaya into a greedy, money-grabbing manipulator with cringe-generating innuendoes. Jain, who was suspicious of Mathew Samuel, succeeded in tracing his cellphone number to Tehelka.

> **Madhu:** Who blew the whistle on you first?
>
> **Samuel:** R.K. Jain's this guy, nephew.
>
> **Madhu:** What happened when R.K. Jain's nephew arrived at Tehelka's office?
>
> **Samuel:** He saw me there. I just jummmbed into Tarun's floor. He talked to the receptionist that he knows that I am here. He told, "So we know how to meet him." That day rrrreally Tarun scared. Ha! Huh! Ha! Ha!
>
> **Madhu:** They got suspicious and decided to trace your cellphone number?
>
> **Samuel:** Yes, yes. Then after that, I decided to, the same day I switch off my mobile, same number.

In one of the numerous interviews with Jaya Jaitly, she said to me, ' Jain found out, but Jain is an idiot. He didn't do anything about it. He didn't tell us even. If he had found out something so great, wouldn't he have come and said? '*Oh ho, logo ne hamseh baat kiyah aur aap keh paas ana chahteh thé, ya defence deal keh baat kar rahey* [oh ho, people have talked to us and they want to come to you; they were talking about this defence deal]. Something he would have said.' Which begs the question, was Jain supposed to talk to Jaya Jaitly about discussions relating to defence deals?

There was no way in which Jain could have figured the extent of the footage and who they had taped. How could Jain have known that Tehelka had Jaya Jaitly on tape in the defence minister's official residence?

13 The Sureka also Rises

I either want less corruption or more chance to participate in it.
– Ashleigh Brilliant, Writer, Columnist and Cartoonist

Operation West End tapes:

> **Murgai:** This … as far as Jaya is concerned … what he wants is a proper meeting and explain his case..
> **Samuel:** Not like hanky-panky. Everything I want to essplain.
> **Murgai:** We'll give two [lakh] to Jaya in that. Initially. And one for you, one for me. All right? [Sureka nodded.]

Major General Murgai introduced Mathew Samuel to a Surendra Sureka, a businessman from Kanpur. The Operation West End transcripts related to Surendra Sureka are most intriguing, in that they expose the planning of the meeting with Jaya Jaitly, how to give her the money, and the execution of the plan.

Samuel explained to Major General Murgai and Surendra Sureka that West End was competing with three other companies in selling their product, and that the defence ministry would take the final decision. Samuel said, 'That means George, I mean, George Fernandes. So that time, is the channel to George Fernandes is Mrs Jaya Jaitly. She will … she is the briefcase woman.' For this, Samuel said, he was willing to pay the usual commission of 3 or 4 per cent. Major General Murgai assured Samuel that Sureka could obtain an evaluation letter for West End. Sureka asked, 'But what will be my interest?' He elaborated that he would introduce West End to Jaya Jaitly, they could talk to her directly and tell her what percentage they would pay her. Sureka said he did not want to be paid for the introduction but was seeking something more permanent with West End. Major General Murgai explained the deal. Jaya Jaitly would be given Rs 2 lakh, Rs 1 lakh would go to Sureka, and Rs 1 lakh would go to Murgai. Samuel, fearful of being searched, suggested that Sureka should arrange the meeting with Jaya Jaitly at a hotel. Sureka told Samuel that it would either be at George Fernandes's or his own house. Sureka said, 'She will meet you just alone only. Nobody else will be there. You can talk as much as you want.' A worried Samuel stammered, 'You … you'll be there?' Sureka assured him that he would.

Tehelka mistakenly identified Surendra Kumar Sureka in the Operation West End tapes as Surendra Singh Sulekha. Mathew Samuel was not one for details. Sureka seemed to have some vague acquaintance with Jaya Jaitly. In Jaya's defence, she says she meets everyone and George Fernandes's house does have an open door ambiance. When questioned by Sidharth Luthra, Sureka admitted he had met her only twice before. Once at an exhibition at Pragati Maidan and then when he presented her with flowers when the Samata Party joined the NDA government. Thousands of courtiers show up with flowers when someone hits the power button. Obviously for Jaya, Sureka was a face in the crowd. Sureka has a textile-processing unit in Kanpur. He had been a major supplier to ordnance factories, which fall under the purview of the Ministry of Defence. He had met Major General Murgai when he was director (quality assurance) in the army. If the norm he played out on the tapes was anything to go by, the practice of money changing hands may have begun then. They all seemed so comfortable with it. He had kept in touch with Major General Murgai and mentioned to him that he was looking for business as he did not have much work. Major General Murgai then told him about West End and set up a meeting.

When Samuel, Murgai, and Sureka arrived at George Fernandes's house, they met a grey-haired man in a kurta who was addressed by all as Gopalji. Samuel had two hidden cameras, one concealed in his tie and the other in a briefcase. The tie camera was wired to a battery that was connected through a hole in Samuel's trouser pocket. While they engaged Gopalji in small talk, Samuel took out a wad of money and Sureka admonished him not to give it in that way. He suggested that it should be covered properly. Though of course, Samuel preferred it to be given in a way that would be visible to the camera hidden in his tie.

Major General Murgai and Mathew Samuel were made to wait for a few moments in one of the rooms in the defence minister's house. Surendra Sureka joined them and immediately asked for the money he had been promised earlier. Samuel paid Sureka the Rs 1 lakh he expected for the introduction and postponed paying Murgai.

Operation West End tapes:

[Samuel took out the money and gave it to Sureka.]
Samuel: Sir, this is one lakh. Count it, that.
Sureka: No, it's okay. You will go …
Samuel: I'm sorry that I couldn't able to … train that … he said he'll come at 6 o'clock. So, I waited there. You know that Krishna Saini? We are there? I couldn't able to wire transfer the money. I don't know that how to … you had asked me to bring it in an envelope, so why didn't they allow me to bring the briefcase inside?

Sureka: Because of the security reasons … they have cameras and everything …

Samuel: There is no camera inside this.

Sureka: We have to be very, very alert. Otherwise, you get questioned immediately. [Pause.]

Murgai: You organize your things a bit.

Sureka: You should always keep a packet in a packet. Don't give like this. This will impress him. [Samuel put the money in a plastic bag.]

Samuel: You are not given … that ….

Sureka: When you give somebody sweet, no … why do you pack it?

Samuel: Yeah, yeah.

Murgai: Now the question is what are they wanting?

Samuel: I will, you know … you know you are telling that. I will leave the …

Murgai: That is all right. But the point is, you still not understood. Who's got to give the clearance? I feel Choudary is well within his capability to take up the evaluation.

Samuel: And he … I told you no, so he need the … some reference for … if …

Murgai: Reference from where?

Samuel: If RM [*raksha mantri*] is … RM will …

Sureka: You give letter of copy of RM. You will get …

Samuel: I will give you a copy.

Sureka: That is my job, I will get it. I will get it done.

Murgai: We will get it done.

Samuel: If that RM will sign that "Go for evaluation", he will do.

Sureka: Yes, I will get it done.

Samuel: And he will short-list the company also, he told me.

Sureka: No, that is his … that is his …

Murgai: That is his.

Sureka: I can only talk about this evaluation.

Murgai: My dear sir …

Sureka: I can only talk.

Samuel: One thing I will ask. If I will give letter to General Murgai tomorrow, when you can do?

Sureka: Within 10 days.

🔁

Jaya's deposition before the Commission of Inquiry, in the presence of her own counsel, Nilay Dutta, showed that she had done considerable homework and was fully prepared with her arguments. The first point she made was that there was a discrepancy between the recordings of the two cameras deployed at her meeting, and this indicated that they had been switched on or off at different times and did not correlate. Alternatively, cuts had been made in the two recordings.

According to Jaya, if the two cameras, one in Samuel's tie in her room and the other in a briefcase facing a sofa in the waiting room, were recording simultaneously the sounds of both should match. That is, in the event of a sound of a door banging, the sound should come at exactly the same time in both the cameras. She pointed out that five times the bang is recorded at different times, with the time gap increasing between the two by about eleven seconds. An explanation for that is that Samuel kept switching his tie camera on and off, while the camera in the waiting room continued to roll.

Jaitly: After he finishes the talk with me and goes out and rejoins his briefcase after the conversation at that time in the room. The tape that was ahead is now back and the tape that was behind has now gone ahead. Your Lordship, this cannot happen unless the tapes have been tampered with.

The sounds – no matter where the cameras are, five cameras maybe in this room but my words will be picked up at exactly the same moment. The time difference shows that there has been a complete non-synchronization of the sounds on both the tapes. Why? Because they cut out various sections; the distance is short, the conversations are short and there is, therefore, no synchronization. The non-synchronization explains and is the key to open the door. Why should there be non-synchronization? Because tampering had been done.

Why was the tampering done? I have earlier said also when the expert witness was here originally he had shown that there were two specific words that were super-imposed which means that either those words were not said at all, or perhaps some other word was there, which needed to be covered up, or it had to be interpolated, but it was not interpolated with a cut.

One specific word was "West End". I had at the very beginning pointed out Tehelka had said in the transcript "West End". Even now, I believe to this date, the transcript, which is on the website, says "West End" … After our expert witness here showed your Lordship that it was not "West End", it was a very strange, synthetic, separate sort of a voice saying "CD West End". Mr Sureka is saying, "Here is Mr Samuel, they are a premier electronic company. I will be joining" so on. Suddenly, interpolated or re-recorded or superimposed on this is "CD West End", as if he is saying something at the bus stop and announcing a stop or something. It is not a part of the normal conversation, where he is sitting inside the room and telling about himself.

From the very first day that I saw the tape on March 13, I knew that I had never ever given an appointment or met anybody from any company, let alone West End. I had never heard of it.

Jaya said all this without a gap. I am not putting it all together. Defending herself was her pain reliever. She continued:

Jaitly: The second place where they needed to superimpose was at the portion where they are saying, "let's go", because I have very clearly told them that there is nothing in which I will intervene. They are all confused. They are saying, have you written the letter, no let us write the letter, then if there is no reply – all I have, in any case, assured them is that, if you do not get a reply – if we may write twenty representations to the government, we will assume that all right, let the fellows get a reply at least, even if the reply is "No, we are not interested in you," but courtesy demands a reply. Other than that, there is no question of any intervention. However, having said all that, Murgai is satisfied and he is saying, "Let us go; thank you very much". I am nodding and saying, "Thank you very much". Because it is "How do you do, how do you do" like that. So I said, "Thank you very much"; just before 'thank you' there is an interpolation which you can hear very clearly with the sound. There are five rhythmic beats like, dum, dum, dum, dum, dum. It goes like that. Why that sound came in? There is no music or any beat or anything in the room. That sound does not appear anywhere else. But if you listen carefully, you can hear those beats and then you hear "that two lakhs … *doh*" cut like that. That sound is so completely unusual and not part of the same level, not of the same pitch, nothing to do with that "thank you, bye bye" that is going on. I knew, therefore, that that two lakhs, since it had never been paid to me, nobody has subsequently got any two lakhs, therefore I knew that "two lakhs" had been interpolated by them, because they have to show the public in their presentation that I knew the company and that this amount was specified at some point wherever.

Now, apart from that, there is another very significant word which is just after "West End", where he is saying, "They are a premier electronics company; I will be joining them in this" is what he says. The transcript from the beginning till now, including the government's transcript, says, "defence"; "I'll be joining them in defence". I would request your Lordship to play the tape here. You can clearly hear and let everybody here listen; it is saying, "I'll be joining them in this".

I recollect very, very faintly, this man, who is in textiles, comes and says, "I would now be expanding into electronics". So, where is the question of defence? Why did they need to change that word "them in this"; mislead people into saying that they said "defence". Why? Because they wanted to show subsequently that West End Company I knew and the whole thing was all about defence, to put me in a bad light. However, I would request that in this 100-hour tape which I would request to be played here, the cut that my counsel had referred to is so blatant and there cannot be a cut in an unedited tape.

↜

Jaya continued uninterrupted about her conversation with Samuel:

Jaitly: At the very end, Mr Samuel speaks to me in Malayalam. He says, "Can

I come and see you, if there is any problem", in Malayalam. I found it very interesting that in the very first transcription given to the public by Tehelka they say four sentences, "Yes, you can come any time. Just give me the details" was not there. Actually, there should have been more sentences rather than less in the 100-hour tape.

Finally, when it comes to the actual thing, I am not saying, "You can come here any time," which in Malayalam would be 'Eppo venongil vannolu.' That is not what I am saying. He is asking, "Can I come to you any time?" and I am saying, "No, you can tell me on the telephone, if there is no response." Whenever you do not want to see anybody again, you say, "No, no, phone, do not come". In fact, this is a decent way of saying I do not want to see you again.

If you listen to all of these things, you will notice that cut, which is the most crucial thing, because the entire conversation, which formed the bulk of the meeting – of that meeting that they had, which was not a fixed meeting, actually took place at a completely different time. This becomes extremely significant, Your Lordship. That is why I have been saying from the very beginning that unless we check whether there is a cut in the original, whether what is lying here is the original, whether these cuts are there, were portions are shifted from here to there? Now I am saying it from my understanding. But I can never be a forensic analyst.

Then, after the meeting with me – I explained the Malayalam conversation – after that he goes to meet Murgai and Sureka. He tells Sureka, "Yes, she told me in Malayalam I can go and meet her any time". Why tell that lie? They were all there. What he said in Malayalam is known to everybody. Every Malayalee here would know it.

Jaya also protested about Tape No.22, where Mathew Samuel is seen getting into a Maruti van to go to Vasant Vihar. He is seen during the journey on tape but gets out of a Maruti Esteem. Jaya said, 'Unless there is a break and two separate tapes are put together, a person cannot get into a Maruti van and get out of a Maruti Esteem, if that journey has not been broken at any place.'

Obviously, Tehelka made the mistake of treating the story like any other news story package, taking cutaways, in non-synchronized time. (Cutaways = footage taken to supplement the story, such as the gate of the house.) In a sting story it is imperative that only the footage of the operation should be used without adding cutaways later. Anything else raises the flag of doctoring. Jaya then, in the Commission, showed tapes where she said there were discrepancies. She ran Tape 74, where she said there were three cuts, and if it was an unedited tape, there should have been no cuts. She displayed various tapes that had jump cuts. She pointed out that the tape goes from the Tehelka office, there is a cut and then Samuel is seen walking and not travelling in the car. Then it jump cuts to Fernandes's office. Of course, if the camera was switched off and started again, there would be jump cuts. No journalist is going to keep the camera running while sitting in a car travelling to

Fernandes's office. Jaya spent a lot of time pointing out all the 'cuts' as if that automatically meant that the tapes had been doctored. People in the Commission were surprisingly lacking in basic knowledge of television editing techniques.

Jaya insisted that 'CD West End' was what she called the 'superimposed sentence'. She said Tehelka's website had changed the transcript from 'CD West End' to 'Sir, you have explained'.

> **Justice Venkataswami:** What is the government translation?
>
> **Jaitly:** Government has said, "Sir you explained." I am also saying the government transcripts are wrong in many places. You may please hear it. I am still challenging it that it is "CD West End" that is being said. It is not a tone of voice that is fitting in with the rest of the explanation. It is not sounding like a self-introduction or part of what Mr Sureka is saying they are an electronics company.
>
> The next sentence is also very important, where I have challenged both Tehelka and the government. Because, he is saying "I will be joining them in this". He does not say "they will be starting them in the defence". It is "this", it is not "defence" and it is an important change, "starting something with them in this".

Jaya then pointed out in the difference in pitch when Samuel says 'Two lakhs *doh*' and the 'dum dum dum' sound where the two tapes do not synchronize. She said that in the footage the Tehelka team arrived in darkness but on the Zee TV tapes they entered the house in broad sunlight.

If you are banging your head, so was everyone else.

> **Jaitly:** At the end of this, after he has got into the car and is driving away. In this earlier Tape No. 73, he said, "*jaldi speed leh lo.*" Here the entire conversation to the driver is different, as I said then, different; it is very foul language and he is driving and it suddenly ends. So there is a lot of switching on and switching off of tapes or editing which means that the true scene was not filmed. They do not tally and there are cuts in both.

Yes, that is all very well but it is odd that the only areas that Jaya pointed out are 'doctored' are the points of accusation. They said she knew they were dealing in defence procurement and she accepted Rs 2 lakh.

When the counsel for Tehelka, Kavin Gulati took his turn to question Jaya, her manner changed. Clever enough to anticipate his questions, Jaya was ready and lay in wait. A cheetah looking at a snake, aware that he is there to sting. Gulati was clearly in awe of her. He knew he had to get rough with her on his client's behalf, but his sensibility of facing power, that too, in the shape of a woman, tamed him a bit.

Gulati: You do admit the meeting you had with Mr Mathew Samuel on 28 December 2000?

Jaitly: I would not call it a meeting, unless you define meeting.

Oops!

Gulati: A conversation?

Jaitly: Some event had taken place.

Gulati: But he was physically present in the room with you on that day?

Jaitly: I cannot vouch for it hundred per cent, because his face is never shown on the tape. I do not recollect his face. In fact, when I came to the Commission, and only when my lawyer pointed out to me that there is Mathew Samuel that I actually saw his face and even at that time I did not feel that I had seen that face before.

Gulati: You have just told the Commission of certain incidents. You said that "CD West End" was put in the transcript, "*doh lakh doh*" was never said, and "Thank you" was being said as a matter of courtesy. That is what you said yesterday. Now who are you having all this conversation with, if not Samuel?

Jaitly: I am not saying that it was not Samuel. I am only saying, if you ask me specifically, "Were you having a conversation with Samuel", because you have offered me this transcript and these tapes, I have to take your word for it, just as I have to take so far, your word for these transcripts also.

In the Tehelka Commission, there was an undercurrent of Jaya's status with George Fernandes. It was never actually spelt out but it was a looming shadow impossible to ignore. Given Jaya's fractious attitude, Kavin Gulati, counsel for Tehelka, stepped cautiously.

Gulati: You have stated in your affidavit that they wanted to make some contribution. You have stated at page 12 "they wanted to make some contribution" in paragraph 3. Who are "they" you are referring to?

Jaitly: They were the gentlemen who had come along.

Gulati: Please name them for the benefit of the record.

Jaitly: At that point of time, I knew the name Sureka. According to the transcript, I see that there was Samuel there. The third person, I did not know his name, because he was never introduced to me.

Gulati: You have stated in the paragraph 3 on page 12, that "I was also told that they wanted to make some kind of contribution". Who told you this?

Jaitly: Sureka. I would not talk to unknown people. Sureka being slightly known, having come and said *samarthak namaskar* and all that, if he says he would like to make a donation to the party, I would say "How nice".

Gulati: How much was the contribution to be made?

Jaitly: They never specified any amount. Neither did I ask.

Gulati: Has Sureka ever brought anybody else to you before this incident for giving contributions?

Jaitly: Never. He has never met me for any work at any time.

Gulati: So, were you not surprised when he came to you for this purpose?

Jaitly: No. I was not surprised because there is always a well wisher who comes.

Gulati: Did you enquire about the credentials of the person seeking to make this contribution?

Jaitly: No. I do not need to.

Gulati: Would you accept money from anybody who comes to you, including defence middlemen and criminals? You have not verified the credentials of a person so anybody can come.

Jaitly: He was not anybody. Our work in public life is not based on suspicion of people. It is based on trust and good will. If a person, who may have done *namaskar* a couple of times, expresses good will, and if he brings somebody from electronics, why on earth should I think of them as crooks, criminals or anything?

Gulati: In this meeting of the 28th, did you enquire from Sureka or Samuel why they wanted to make this contribution to you?

Jaitly: I did not. I took it in my mind that it was a contribution from Sureka, because he was collaborating with them.

Gulati: In your affidavit you say: "Since the visitors said they were from the electronics field, the mention of cameras and binoculars by them seemed most innocuous to me. I have never entertained arms dealers and did not in any way connect cameras and binoculars to arms." My question to you is, was there any discussion relating to the Ministry of Defence or any defence equipment?

Jaitly: There was no discussion other than what I follow on these tapes and I have only to deduce all the discussion was from there. They are not supplying, they are saying we have got these cameras and they are not replying to us. It seems to me even more of a preliminary to preliminary. They are wanting somebody to talk to them. They are not getting a reply. But even that is not clear, if you follow the subsequent conversation. I could take you to the transcript. Should we go through the transcript?

'They are not replying to us.' The 'They' here is the defence ministry. Jaya threw a distracting bone to Gulati with 'Should we go through the transcript', and he fell for it and answered her question rather than eliciting one from her.

Gulati: You can answer the question any way you want.

Once again, Gulati gifted Jaya a platform to yank the discussion into a tangent.

Jaitly: They are very confused amongst themselves. One is saying, "wait for a reply". One is saying, "first write a letter". One is saying, "they are not calling us". So I am not bothered with all this. I say I do not know how they function. We would not interfere. Only if there is any injustice and if an injustice is not getting a reply, a courteous reply saying, "you are rejected", even then, other than getting a reply to them, is no question of any intention and I have clearly expressed the opposite.

Gulati: So, do I take it then that there was a discussion with regard to defence equipment and the Ministry of Defence?

Jaitly: If saying "I do not know anything about the ministry, I would not interfere" is a discussion about the defence ministry, yes.

Gulati: And that you were willing to help them if they were treated unfairly?

Jaitly: It is the duty of every politician.

Gulati: My question to you is this. Did you as a matter of fact discuss anything about the Ministry of Defence or defence products and that you would be willing to help them if, as you say, they were being treated unfairly?

Jaitly: You have put three questions. I did not discuss any product. They have mentioned cameras and binoculars and I have passed it off completely. I have said, I do not know anything. I have discussed the defence ministry, as I said, by saying I do not know anything about the defence ministry and we do not interfere. In a general term, whichever may be the ministry, from the prime minister to the local municipality, if any public office is not dealing with the citizens as citizens expect them to do, in fairness and according to procedure, then it is the citizen's right to come to anybody, and in that context, I have responded to them.

〜

Jaya began dancing a salsa around Gulati, leaving him hearing only his own music.

Gulati: You have talked about testing of the product, whenever there is a new entry in that field, they have to test these things.

Now, observe Jaya's dips and dives with which she makes Gulati a passive spectator.

Jaitly: I will give my own personal experience about that. I am talking in very general terms. As everybody here knows, I am more interested in handicrafts than anything else. My purpose in our politics is to promote the idea of *Swadeshi* and cottage and village industries. To that end, I have definitely approached all the ministers in our party, who are in the ministries, to say that can they not have products from the rural and cottage sector. So the ministers followed up and in response, the Central Cottage Industries Emporium, the Handicraft Handloom Export Corporation and the KVIC held exhibitions and discussions with both these ministries to see that jams, pickles and stuff like that which is supplied, is used. At that point of time, I know they were told that we have to test everything, the price has to be right and the quality has to be right. I presume that is the rule for everything.

⟿

Jam and pickles?! Compare that to what Jaya said on the tapes which was all about testing and evaluation by the defence ministry? Jaya's jamming. Gulati gave up, and look at his response:

> **Gulati**: We will come back to this? [Why? Why not now?] Please see paragraph 5 on page 14 for a minute: "Subsequently, the visitors made a complaint about being unable to have their product tested". Subsequently to what?
> **Jaitly**: Subsequent to a long and irrelevant conversation.

Here's another great swish answer from Jaya:

> **Gulati**: Do you normally ensure that people get a fair deal in defence matters?
> **Jaitly**: I have ensured that women who have been thrown out of their homes, because some Major or Captain has come and said that he's thrown me out and married some other woman illegally, that is an unfair deal and a person is in defence, I have written to the ministry about such things. I have never written to the ministry, or taken up or spoken informally, or even entertained any issue and taken up, where there is any commercial interest involved.
> **Gulati**: Then in what capacity were you willing to ensure that West End would get a fair deal, as you have stated in paragraph 5 on page 14, the last line?
> **Jaitly**: A fair deal in this case means only a reply.
> **Gulati**: But in what capacity were you doing it? You are not connected with the Ministry of Defence.
> **Jaitly**: As a public worker. Whether the person is connected with the Ministry of Defence or not, every member of Parliament, every president of any political party, could be in the entire NDA or in the opposition, anybody can write to any ministry. If somebody comes to them saying we are not getting a fair deal, somebody can write them and say, give them a reply; please consider. Most of the time, they get a thing saying "Your matter is being examined" and it ends there.

⟿

Ah, 'anybody' can write, but who will listen to 'anybody'? The next question from Gulati should have been: can you give us an example or instance where you have written to someone and asked for a fair deal and they have answered, 'Your matter is being considered?' This is rather like a journalist who asks prepared questions but forgets to listen to the answers to follow through the thread and elicit a real answer.

> **Gulati**: Did you not think at any point during that conversation that a matter

relating to the Ministry of Defence being as sensitive as it is, it was best left to the ministry to deal with its own issue and that you should not in any manner intercede on anybody's behalf?

Jaitly: I do not think the defence ministry is so sacrosanct that if there are any real problems, a person who is well aware of his duties as a citizen in public life should refuse to touch it. Tomorrow those very same people may go out and tell the whole world that Jaya Jaitly refused to intercede because she was paid off by the other company who actually got the order. There are many who believe that the Ministry of Defence is sacrosanct and should not be polluted with unusual requests or favours. George Fernandes being one of them.

Gulati: Has it ever occurred to you that if you or the minister of defence asked the Ministry of Defence or an official to consider a particular company fairly, would not that officer get an impression, or would not the ministry be obliged to consider the company's case favourably?

Jaitly: There is no question of asking anybody to consider anybody favourably. At most, what anyone would say is, these people are shouting that nobody is writing a letter to them. That is all. There is no question of asking anybody to consider, neither do I approach any officer of any ministry.

This time Gulati did not let go.

Gulati: My question is slightly different. My question is, if an important person like you, or the minister of defence, tells a particular official in the Ministry of Defence, please consider the case, will it not ring bells in that person's mind? Will he not be obliged to consider this case?

Jaitly: No, sir. The question does not arise. Neither do I do it and I do not know how Mr Fernandes works in his ministry.

'The question does not arise'? In this *ji huzoor* culture where your next posting and promotion depends not on how well you performed your job but how well you pleased your boss? The question that does not arise is not doing what is suggested..

Gulati: At this stage I would like to confront the witness with the edited tape: the four and half hour tape; the portion where, according to us, a packet is being exchanged. I would like to put it to the witness.

The video film was shown.

Gulati: My question to you is two-fold. (1) what is inside this packet, and (2) who was this packet being handed over to?

Jaitly: I would have no idea what is in the packet and I have no idea who he is handing it to.

Gulati: Then why did you say "Gopalji, *aap rakh leejiye*"?

Jaitly: I have not said that.

Gulati: Did you know that there was money inside the packet?

Jaitly: No, not really. Nobody thinks at that time is it *mithai* [sweets] or is it something. If he is wanting to give something and since they have said "brought something for the party", my mind uppermost is on the National Council and Mr Srinivas Prasad was organizing it. So, I asked Samuel to send it to Srinivas Prasad. Beyond that, I am not concerned.

Gulati: Would you please take page 13 of your affidavit for a minute; the top four lines: "I said, please send this to Srinivas Prasad, our minister." This means, obviously, there is something there.

Jaitly: Must be. Something is something. I don't know what it is.

Gulati: If there is *mithai*, as you say, would you direct it to be sent to Srinivas Prasad?

Jaitly: No, I said, I corrected myself; I said that packet if there is no context, one may think anything. But they have said they have brought something for the party and there is a National Council. So I clarified already that I presumed that there was some donation in it.

Gulati: You presumed that there was some donation in it?

Jaitly: Yes. I have never said that I do not accept donations and I have said, I accepted their offer by asking them to send it to Srinivas Prasad.

Gulati: At this stage, I put a suggestion to you that the packet contained Rs 2 lakhs, which was offered to you in your office and you directed the same to be kept by Mr Gopal Pacherwal.

Jaitly: That is not true

Gulati now warmed to his prey, forgot his awe of Jaya, and dug in his teeth:

Gulati: Please see page 13 of your affidavit, paragraph 4: "I did not see any packet allegedly containing money being delivered to anyone in the room." Just now you told us that you had presumed that there was a donation in that. But this averment of yours in paragraph 4, is clearly to the effect that you did not see any packet allegedly containing money being delivered to anyone in the room.

Jaitly: No. If you read the sentence, what I am saying is, that the packet allegedly containing money was not seen being delivered to anybody in the room.

Gulati: How are you so sure of this fact?

Jaitly: I know what I saw or what I did not see.

Gulati: You have told us half an hour back that you do not remember anything about the meeting and your only memory is based on the tapes and the transcripts.

Jaitly: It is obvious. What I always do; I know that I never take money from anybody, other than in the party office, where there is an accountant who will receive it and deposit and give a receipt. Otherwise, if anybody gives a donation, I always ask that if somebody is wanting to print posters, please send it to that person. I do not handle money myself.

On 26 June 2002, Jaya continued with her deposition. This time she came prepared with tapes, a VCR, and a TV monitor. She pointed out that the same conversation takes place on two separate tapes, numbers 17 and 19. One tape is dated 20 October 2000, venue Park Hotel. The other is also dated 20 October 2000, place Park Hotel, and also states, Dr Ketan Shukla, Colonel Sayal, and General Murgai. Jaya said the beginning has exactly the same verbatim conversation.

> **Jaitly**: How can that happen in two separate tapes? One conversation has been placed inside tape No.19 and the same conversation placed inside tape No.17? Until there is some reorganization of the tapes, this cannot happen.

The other example:

> **Jaya**: I do not have the tapes here to show, but in Tape No.1 and Tape No.Y, not the transcripts, but the visuals are exactly the same, although they are supposed to be two different occasions.

Yes, but they were using two different hidden cameras.

⌣

Gulati then further questioned Jaya at length on her statement that she barely remembered the meeting on 28 December, and yet vividly recalled that no money was given.

> **Gulati**: If no money was paid to you, as you have said, why did you thank Mr Samuel?
>
> **Jaitly**: When somebody leaves, they either say "Good bye" or they say "Thank you very much". So, automatically one repeats, like, "How do you do". You never say, "How do I do"; you say "How do you do" back. It is a common conversational habit. They have added a nod in the transcript, I nod, in the transcript. But there is actually no nodding even over there. Somebody says "Thank you" and you'll say "Thank you", and toss your head a bit, which I have a habit of doing. That is all.
>
> **Gulati**: You remember even the nod?
>
> **Jaitly**: No. I am saying this is the characteristic of a person. To call a nod – if I am nodding, you cannot even see it. I am only pointing out errors in the transcript.

⌣

I don't know. To someone saying, 'how do you do', surely the response would be, 'fine, thank you'. But, I don't see how 'thank you' can elicit a 'thank you very much' unless you are really thanking someone for something.

Mathew Samuel was petrified during the meeting and was in a rush to leave once the packet was handed over. He knew only too well what could happen to him if he was caught with the hidden camera. He repeatedly suggested that it was time to go. They were about to leave when Jaya reminded them that she had ordered tea for them. Sense Samuel's panic to get out of there and the enforced courtesy of a cup of tea. They sat down again and more conversation took place. According to Jaya, conversations were switched around. A new conversation begins after she asked them to wait for tea. Gulati pointed out that she had not challenged that aspect until that moment. Jaya insisted that the conversation changed abruptly and there was a cut that showed that that was not the actual portion.

It makes perfect sense for the conversation to be renewed in a different manner; the natural corollary of trying to kill time while waiting for the tea to arrive. Samuel could very well have switched the camera off, thinking he was leaving and then switched it on again when he realized there was going to be more talk. This accounts for the cut in the tape.

Gulati then focused his attention on the Gopal Pacherwal issue:

Gulati: Was Gopal Pacherwal there or not? Do you see him in the tape or not?
Jaitly: I do not recognize anybody as Gopal Pacherwal.

Now this is rather odd. Sureka, the businessman who had brought Samuel to meet Jaya, repeatedly addressed the man in the kurta pyjama as Gopal. Samuel also asked him where he was based and he replied that he looked after the Samata Party in Rajasthan. Pacherwal is in fact president of the Samata Party in Rajasthan and only speaks in Hindi. Gulati read this conversation to Jaya.

Gulati: Now who is this person? Have you been able to identify this person exactly?
Jaitly: No. I have not. It is said that it is Gopal everywhere. But it is not identified as Gopal. You are saying it is Gopal. But I do not identify and I cannot say.
Gulati: You dispute that?
Jaitly: I cannot say whether it is Gopal or not. You will have to ask Gopal.

Gulati then asked Jaya if she had shown the tapes to Gopal, and her response was Jaya mambo:

Jaitly: Gopal Pacherwal is a very decent, humble and simple person, whom I have known since 1982; since I joined the trade union in which he was there. We have worked together for very long, on struggles for grassroots issues, important campaign issues, drug trafficking in Manipur-Burma border, salt agitation in Kandla, agitations to help the depressed classes and downtrodden people. He is an utterly simple person. If I speak to him in a manner that I have to interrogate him, when I know and he knows we have never had any financial dealing, it would be an insult to a person of his background.

A cleverly woven fabric interspersing Jaya's own work in her answer. There is no reason why she should not be lauded for it, but is it a relevant answer to the question? What did Samuel have to say about Pacherwal?

> **Madhu**: Have you identified Gopal Pacherwal for the Commission?
> **Samuel**: They haven't asked.
> **Madhu**: Because he has denied being there.
> **Samuel**: He's on the tape. He was there with me. I asked Jaya Jaitly, I have to give you, she told me give it to, "*Gopalji, rakh lijiyey* [Gopalji, keep this]."
> **Madhu**: Jaya Jaitly has given me two tapes, one unedited and one edited. She says in the unedited tape, there is no sentence, "Two lakh, *do*". She says that has been put in later in the edited tape.
> **Samuel**: *Unke diya huya tape mey nahin hoga, master may hai nah* [it may not be in the tape given to her, it is in the master]. Maddumm, nothing happened to the tape.
> **Madhu**: Were there two cameras or one camera in Jaya Jaitly's room?
> **Samuel**: Only one camera, tie camera, recorded her conversation.
> **Madhu**: What if she shows you a tape that does not have those words?
> **Samuel**: Tell Aniruddha to show you the master tape. He has master. Ask him to show you. Definitely it is there. Commission is not like idiot in some such matter. They know. They know entirely.

Sidharth Luthra said,

> **Luthra**: Kavin was the lead counsel for Tehelka from start to finish. For months on end he fought the battle alone and sacrificed the most as he was then starting off his individual practice. He brought me in at the evidence stage. He is a quiet and extremely competent person. A tenacious litigator but with a quiet manner, he gets the job done and most effectively. In fact, with our differing styles we kept the COT guessing as in Jaya Jaitly's case, who (I was later told) prepared for my cross examination, then made mistakes when Kavin cross examined her. She was not able to figure out his strategy or the effect of his questions. Despite his lineage in the profession being quite amazing, he is down to earth. Both his grandfather and father were highly respected judges at Allahabad and leading tax lawyers.'

With Jaya, Gulati went from strength to strength. He lost his earlier inhibitions and executed elegant pirouettes around Jaya's contortions. He thrice demanded to know how she could remember some details with such clarity and yet was totally vague about others?

> **Jaitly**: My Lord, since yesterday I have shown, I have pointed out many instances. I can only go by my own understanding, which I see very carefully by viewing

the tapes for hours on end. The cuts are there. The sentences are mixed up. There are so many things that have been hidden from the beginning from me. The type of conversation, everything that is today in the transcript that I have personally made, even after the government one, shows that it is completely different from my recollection. So, my recollection is not perfect. However, I recollect because I know that I never take money from people in this manner. If I am sitting in the party office and somebody comes to give a donation, "I'll see if the accountant is there", I say, "please give the receipt". Or if something is going on somewhere, I will say, "You pay the printer or do something". And when that person receives the money, I cannot presume that they will actually give it. Some people have sometimes given us a cheque and when you go to cash it, it has bounced. They just pretend that they are giving you a cheque. I know what I always do, because I am careful and I will not handle money like that, because somebody may say that I have walked off with it.

Where then does that leave us? With no real answer, and even Gulati cannot be blamed, because he did not fail for lack of effort. Jaya had reached a point in her deposition that all her answers were tailored to create doubts about the authenticity of the tapes and push for a forensic analysis. When Gulati explained to her that two tapes in different cameras at the same meeting could have differing timings because one was being switched on and off, Jaya grabbed the opportunity to say, 'Whether it was switched off or whether it was cut is something that only a proper analysis will say. We cannot be guessing between what you say and what I say'. She said that she believed so strongly that Tehelka had done an unfair job that she would still call the switching on and off as editing. She grumbled, 'I may have said many things to those people which are beneficial to me and harmful to them and he could have easily switched it off at that time, because he did not want that recorded. How do we know, that is the point.' When Gulati pointed out that the day before she had said that they could have switched it on and off and now she contradicted herself, Jaya jumped in again and said, 'If at all there is switching off and switching on, it can be found through forensic analysis; can also be a motivated exercise'.

I asked Samuel about the story of the camera vibrating in his underwear.

Samuel: Yes, supposing the camera is on, the switches vibrate. That is the interesting tawpic happened. It fell into my underwear. Then I decide to go because of this tension this I switched it off. Then again conversation started, again I switched on. That is the jummmb there.

Madhu: The jump in the tape?

Samuel: Uhuh, the jummmb in the tape. Then I switched off. Okay, I'm going. Then there is a tawpic there. Then I switched on. Then I decided to go. Then I switched off. Then again conversation starting. Then I switched on. That is waat.

Madhu: Didn't the remote vibrate when it was on? Jaya could have noticed it.

Samuel: How can notice? Switch is here. I am sitting.

Madhu: How many minutes is the tape with Jaya Jaitly?

Samuel: That I do not know. I never count any tape.

Madhu: Couldn't you just leave it on for the whole meeting?

Samuel: Leave it on means the battery matter is important. The battery will go around one hower somethinggk. After that I want to record Murgai's home giving money to Sureka. That also I want to record with that. Meanwhile, I told Murgai and Sureka, just I want to go to Connaught Place to give you. Please you go there, I will come back. Meanwhile I go to office. I given the camera everything. The briefcase camera I again took. Then I recorded briefcase camera.

Madhu: The tie camera you only used for Jaya Jaitly?

Samuel: No, for Bangaru Laxman we also used. That same camera we can make into bag also. That we used.

⌒

Yes, but how could Samuel know when to switch it off unless he could predict what Jaya was going to say? Why would he switch it off when anything Jaya said could incriminate her? I attempted to elicit more details from Jaya.

Madhu: In your deposition, in answer to the question, you said in your cross-examination that you presumed that the packet contained some donation. Your reply was, "Yes, I have never said that I do not accept donations and I've said I accepted their offer by asking them to send it to Srinivas Prasad." Then on page 13 of your affidavit, para 4, the second sub-paragraph, you contradict yourself and say, "I did not see any packet allegedly containing money being delivered to anyone in the room." So which is it?

Jaitly: It's both. Here I'm saying, I'm presuming there's money in it. I have not seen any money. Secondly, I did not see any packet being given to anybody else. I know I have not taken it. So, I have not even seen it being given to anybody else, which is what I've said right from the start.

Madhu: No, but when he says, "Madam, I'm offering this …"

Jaitly: Then I say, please send it to Srinivas Prasad.

Madhu: To whom were you saying it ? To the man sitting at your side?

Jaitly: I'm saying it to Mathew Samuel or whatever his name was. I'm not saying it to anybody else. We'll come to that. Supposing it had been Srinivas Prasad sitting next to me. I may have talked to him in English, but anyway, it's not Srinivas Prasad. The person whom they claim it is, is a person called Gopal Pacherwal, who only speaks Hindi. I have known him for twenty-five years. I would never dream of speaking one sentence to him in English.

Madhu: Who was the gentleman with the grey hair in the kurta?

Jaitly: The one whom they claim is Gopal Pacherwal? He is the president of our Rajasthan Party.

Madhu: So it is Gopal Pacherwal on the tapes?

Jaitly: I don't know. They are saying it's him. He's also saying he comes and goes from Rajasthan to Delhi.

Madhu: No, but who do you identify as the person in the tapes?

Jaitly: Very difficult to say. If you sit here for any length of time, you'll find umpteen people like that. Rather stout and kurta pyjama. Everybody looks the same.

Madhu: But it is somebody with grey hair and a kurta. It has to have been somebody from your office?

Jaitly: There could have been any number of people in that room.

Madhu: But why wouldn't that person come up and identify himself? Unless, of course, he has kept the money.

Jaitly: No, because we haven't a clue who it was.

Madhu: But when this guy gets up for the tea, you can see him quite clearly.

Jaitly: You can't see anybody on the tape. That is unedited, months and months later.

Madhu: But when you see it now, can you identify who that is?

Jaitly: I can't identify clearly, because it's not clear for me. Gopal Pacherwal has been asked. He says that he's come here often enough. He could have easily been in here at that time. He could have been in and out of the room. But no, he was never part of any discussion, in which anybody was giving me any money. Secondly, he would have no locus standi to even take any money. He's the president of the Rajasthan party. He has nothing to do with the Karnataka Sammelan.

Madhu: So your position is that when Samuel said, "Can I give it to madam?" you said, "Please send it Srinivas Prasad". Did you say that to the grey haired man in a kurta?

Jaitly: Yes, to him. Not to Gopal Pacherwal, because Gopal is not my clerk.

Madhu: So Gopal Pacherwal was there then?

Jaitly: No, no. I said it to Samuel. I said, he's organizing our conference in Mysore and I go on talking to them. The funny thing is that, if Gopal Pacherwal had been there, as part of the conversation, I would have said meet so-and-so. *Inkeh paas deh deejiyeh*, give it to him. I would do it differently. You can't keep a senior colleague of yours sitting there, not uttering a word. I have not mentioned Gopal Pacherwal or brought him into the conversation throughout.

Madhu: But there is somebody sitting there.

Jaitly: There could have been umpteen people sitting there.

Madhu: But why didn't you ask people in the Samata Party who was sitting there?

Jaitly: No, how? Which party people? From all over the country? They can come in here and sit any time. You've seen the other room the way it is arranged.

People who may be doing their own work, people may be getting something typed, waiting for it to be over, people may be getting some photocopying done. People may be waiting to meet me after they go. They may be all just sitting around. I never say *yeh log hai toh aap bahar jao* [there are people here so please leave].

Madhu: But in your battle to fix Tehelka, wouldn't it help you and your position to find the person and say, this is the guy who was sitting there?

Jaitly: Who will I find? I will have to ask hundreds and hundreds and hundreds of party people. Because people come from Faridabad, they come from Ghaziabad, they come from Rajasthan, they come from south India. They come from anywhere, at any point of time. There are days where every part of these rooms is full of party people. How can I say, *aap thé, aap thé, aap thé* [was it you, was it you, was it you]?

Madhu: But it leaves an unanswered question that doesn't help you.

Jaya said that Gopal had nothing in common with her regarding financial affairs, other than her organizing funds for his Rajasthan party. Understandably, Jaya shrugged that nobody notes down ordinary daily meetings in calendars. She is certain Gopal would not be part of any discussion on defence or money. Then Jaya gives her Rashomon of the incident, which successfully confuses the issue enough:

Jaya: So they could have got him on film if it is Gopal. Outside, there's somebody who goes in and they say *haan namaskar, namaskar Gopalji* [yes, hello, hello Gopalji], something like that they talk. And then that person sits down and he suddenly gets up and goes out. Then there is a cut. That's one of the famous cuts. Now, did they talk to him longer in there? There is a whole conversation between Murgai and this person Gopal. Now that conversation between Murgai and Gopal is going on in this room, when Murgai at the same time is talking to me. Can't be possible. Have they taken that section and put the audio here, to show that Gopal was the one in the room? Because these tapes were given much after.

When Jaya announced on *We the People* (NDTV) that Srinivas Prasad was not in the room with her, Samuel said Aniruddha called him back urgently from Kerala. It took Tehelka a month to figure out the man in the white kurta was Gopal Pacherwal. Kumar Badal had located him in Rajasthan and Jaya said in dismay, 'Kumar Badal had gone to him, who was later on in jail. He went off and he impersonated. He went to Gopal Pacherwal's house and then he wrote of Gopal Pacherwal as a multi-crore man, who's in hiding, being hidden by the party. Poor Gopal Pacherwal. He's really an ordinary Dalit fellow, who lives in a house with four of his brothers. It's not even a complete house. They don't have a car of their own. They don't have a vehicle, other than some motorcycle his younger brother has. He is a very poor and simple Lohia type who till today will come to Delhi in a bus'.

On 10 September 2001, V. Srinivas Prasad filed a criminal complaint against Tehelka on charges of defamation for making allegations of corruption in defence deals.

Madhu: But that point where, this guy who's sitting next to you takes the package from Samuel …

Jaitly: No, but does he? One, we don't know who the person is.

Madhu: Where did the package go?

Jaitly: I believe Samuel took it back.

Madhu: But Samuel does not have a packet when he leaves or in the car.

Jaitly: That is why this whole funny business of why Tape 73 ends in the office, with him lying to Aniruddha and why Tape 74 shuts off? Why does the tape that goes back to the office shut off in between? Why does he shut off both tapes and put on one again when he's going to the office? Then it's not in his *chuddie* [underwear]. And then he's asking Samuel, "*Achha* did you meet her inside, did you?" and he says, "Oh, *hoo haan*, no, she didn't allow me to take the briefcase, she said …" "Oh so she was also in the room?" "No, but *hmm haa*," all that whole transcript if you read of Tape 73, when he's talking to Aniruddha when he's got back, doesn't match with what happened here, as you can see it happened. Why is he lying to Aniruddha? Why didn't he just say – There was a man sitting next to Jaya Jaitly to whom I handed over the money – which is their claim one month later. At that point of time, when he actually supposedly had just done it, why didn't he go there and say so? He's instead telling him, "She didn't let me take the briefcase in." Untrue; I never stopped it. I didn't even know who he was or bringing the briefcase. Two: I switched off this camera and switched on the other camera: not true – the camera was on all the time. He doesn't say, "I've given her the money." Why not? I think he decided that why not pinch it and shove this two lakh, because he claims that Aniruddha told him wherever you give people money, you record it. If it's not shown, at least it'll be there on tape. That's a ridiculous position to take. That it doesn't matter if it's not shown, just record it in with your voice. How does that make it credible evidence at all, in the first place? But secondly he's shoved it in there, why didn't he put it where he's talking to me or supposedly handed it over?

Madhu: Then maybe he didn't doctor it in because if he were doctoring it he would have put it when he handed the packet over.

Jaitly: But he should have said it then. That there's two lakhs in this packet; he could have said then. But just when we're saying bye bye, thank you, thank you, he suddenly says, that's the two lakh, *doh*. Very quietly; is he whispering into my ear? No, he's nowhere near me.

Madhu: So according to you, the guy next to you didn't take the money and Samuel took it back?

Jaitly: Yes, because the guy next to me, Gopal Pacherwal, is somebody whom never in ten life times I would mistrust. He would not be sitting next to me and swallowing money.

Madhu: So then you admit it was Gopal Pacherwal next to you?

Jaitly: No, I'm saying, if it had been him, he would not be doing it. If it's anybody else, or him, or anyone, nobody would do such a thing. Gopal Pacherwal as I'm saying, how can somebody hand you something now, and you'll just go off with it. Wouldn't I tell you? Where's that money or do something with it, or anything?

Madhu: But you told him to send it to Srinivas Prasad?

Jaitly: No, I don't talk to Gopal in English, that's what I'm saying. I'm talking to Samuel. He said, "Can I give it to madam?" So I'm saying, "Send it to Srinivas Prasad, he's our minister, this–that, this–that." Otherwise I would have talked in Hindi, if I was telling anybody, whom I speak to in Hindi. Gopal Pacherwal, or otherwise. He probably realized that since I'd given him all these instructions, now he was left with this packet and therefore now he had to either go back and say mission failed or he would have had to take the whole trouble of sending it to Srinivas Prasad, which was not part of their story. It would have been a bore. So he decided to do this. That's one explanation I can perhaps give. Otherwise, as I'm saying, if I accept the offer, why should I say I didn't get it? In both, if I'm accepting, I'm accepting. But if, so where's the thing about the two lakhs? Nobody's saying that I've swallowed it. So? I'm not cheating [laughs] my party or cheating anybody. If I've said send it there, I washed my hands off the whole thing.

Madhu: So either the gentleman sitting next to you or Samuel kept the Rs. 2 lakh.

Jaitly: I can't see the gentleman, unless he was some stranger sitting there who realized that in all this *hadbad* [confusion] he could hook off with the money, because I had not noticed. Because I have not seen anybody; if I had, I'm not so dumb that if somebody's handed some money, I'm just not going to bother to register that.

Madhu: But in the unedited tapes, you can see the guy who gets up when the tea is served; you can see who it is. You should be able to identify him.

Jaitly: See, I have asked myself and I've asked umpteen people. The trouble is that honestly, U.P, Rajasthan, Haryana – you look at any party fellows – they all look the same. Gopal has said to me, "*Keh mujhh toh yeh sab cheez yaad hee nahin hai. Mein toh kahin wahaan aya hoga, nahin hoga, mujheh khayaal nahin* [I don't remember any of these things. I may have come there or I may have not, I cannot remember]." He knows and I know, that he would never be sitting in and participating in a meeting which is supposedly related to defence matters. If various people are in the room and various people hear various conversations, that's another matter. It could have happened. But he has no recollection of this at all. Being a person who only speaks Hindi, he doesn't understand fluent English. So, he may have been here in the last ten years or fifteen years, sitting in on umpteen conversations with all of us, but wherever it's in English he'd tune out. How would he know what's going on? He's not a *naukar* [servant] that he'll just take a package and hold it. He's senior to me in politics. [Gopal Pacherwal in his deposition in the Commission stated that Jaya Jaitly is senior to him in politics, as she is older than he is.] He was an MP earlier. He's not just an office clerk. So, in absence of any knowledge about all this, I can only guess as to what was possible or what was not possible.

Madhu: Are there any other Gopals in your office?

Jaitly: No. There may be millions of Gopals in a party somewhere, but not offhand.

Madhu: But what's the harm in Gopal saying, "Yes, it's me?"

Jaitly: He's also saying, in his deposition, what he's asked. The trouble again [is that] he is asked in Hindi; translate, all this business – but he has said *ke*, "*Mein toh udher ateh jata rehta hoon, mein toh, ho sakta hai ki mein tha. Lekin mein koi uss meeting mein kabhi nahin tha* [I keep coming and going from here, it is possible it was me. But I was never in that meeting]." Because if you're in a meeting, consciously knowing about it, you would know the subject matter, then he would remember. But this subject matter is of no connection with him.

Madhu: So he was sure that he wasn't there or not sure?

Jaitly: He says that if anybody talked about any packet and offered, he has never been involved in any packet-related work in my office. I think that's what he's saying. I don't know whether in the deposition it'll come out like that.

Madhu: He says he doesn't remember. He says that as far as he can recall he could have been there, might not have been there; that's what he says.

Jaitly: People like him, he's a Lohiawala. He's been with George Sahab since he was in his early twenties. Rajasthan is very close, he comes quite often; he may sit in any room, he can walk in here into this room very freely, any time he feels like, so how is he to say? Especially when conversations are going on in a language he doesn't understand. Where a person is being specifically spoken to, which is sounding as if it's Gopal, I believe that that was elsewhere. Maybe at another time or outside, patched in and the audio patched in.

Madhu: But it's the same guy who gets up for the tea.

Jaitly: That's much later, na? That's what I'm saying. That's where that big, fat cut is. He might have come in later for the tea. But that doesn't hang him and being a taker of money. How do we know, that that same tea serving person is the person who is supposedly … ; how do we know how everyone was sitting? There is no shot of everybody together in the room.

Madhu: But when he gets up for the tea, there is a very good shot of him.

Jaitly: But was he sitting there …

Madhu: And it is the same guy in the living room, where somebody says "Jairam Gopalji."

Jaitly: Could be. So he's saying that; he doesn't deny that as far as I gather. But it's that portion where that packet business went on; it's not, nowhere near the tea time.

Madhu: Are you saying that the chronology was switched?

Jaitly: The packet part chronologically came first. But I believe that the discussion about the defence probably came later. What would be the reason for them to cut at that point?

Madhu: The defence part does come later in any case.

Jaitly: Not after the tea; before the tea it comes. According to the edited [tape], it's this thing, then defence discussion, and out. As if there's no other conversation. But as you can see there's a hell of a lot more. Why that hell of a lot more was just bundled out? When there's a whole lot of other crappy conversation that goes on in many other tapes? Because, again, you wanted to tighten this one so much [so as] to make it look as if Jaya Jaitly was just there to make money. Anybody can be in the room, taking the money on her behalf. This whole hotchpotch with Srinivas Prasad now. What, if I'm saying send it, how can the man have been there from the beginning? How could they have made such a mistake of that nature? How could you think it's Srinivas Prasad? I'm saying they didn't even analyse what they were doing.

Madhu: I think it was done in a panic because R.K. Jain had discovered Samuel's identity.

Jaitly: But where's the panic? In February they come here and do cutaways. I don't believe that panic.

⤿

Jaya may not believe that panic but consider Samuel's *halat* [condition]. If he were caught with the cameras, he wouldn't have time to even kiss himself goodbye. No question about that. In the unedited tapes, as they stepped out of Jaya's office, Samuel continued his conversation with Murgai, who said: 'She will do everything. There is a proper way to talk to politicians.' Samuel replied 'She has taken the money'. Samuel had trouble locating his driver who was blissfully sleeping in the car with the radio music blaring and did not see Samuel come out or hear him call. Samuel got into the car, did not immediately switch off the cameras, and started screaming at the driver. '*Peecheh dekhna ko peecheh toh nahin aah reha? Gaana bhi nahin sunnah aisa jageh mai. George Fernandes koh gaand phadna hai. Behenchod, tum soh reha. Voh mera shooting kereh ga. Tum koh kyun bulaya? Doosra ko kyun nahin? Hamareh peecheh gaadi toh nahin hai?*' The driver replied: '*Nahin.*' Samuel: '*Peecheh gaadi toh nahin hai?*' Driver: '*Nahin.*' Samuel: '*Jaldi office pahunchna hai. Uddher seh ghar jana hai.*' (Look behind; is anyone following us? You cannot listen to music in a place like this. We are going to bust George Fernandes's ass. Sister-fucker, you were sleeping. They are going to shoot me. Why did they call you? Why didn't the other one come? Is there a car following us? Driver: 'No.' Samuel: 'Is there a car behind us?' Driver: 'No.' Samuel: 'We have to reach the office quickly. From there I go home.'

It can be safely confirmed that Mathew Samuel was in a state of total fright.

Jaitly: I believe the panic had something to do with Shankar Sharma and the stock market and something like that. Shankar Sharma knew he was already under inquiry. The inquiry which they claim is harassment is actually initiated one week before this exposé. Because SEBI said, check all these people who we think are doing hawala operations and he was one. It started one week before and that's why the court cases and all have been thrown out against Shankar Sharma, because the government has shown the court files which initiated the inquiry well before the exposé. They're using this cover blown as an excuse. One: there was no letter, so where is that cover blown, this, that and the other? Sure, Jain found out, but Jain is an idiot; he didn't do anything about it.

Samuel is in a panic to get out of the defence minister's home because of something happening to Shankar Sharma? This is not connecting the dots. It is invention.

The mystery of Gopal Pacherwal's presence is an important one to solve, because the real issue here is, who got the Rs 2 lakh? According to Jaya's Rashomon, Samuel kept it for himself. According to Samuel's Rashomon, he gave it to Gopal, who was instructed by Jaya to send it to Srinivas Prasad. In the tape, you do hear Jaya giving instructions in English to send the money to Srinivas Prasad. Jaya, on her part, said she would never speak to Gopal in English. In the West End tapes of the waiting room, it is true that Gopal only converses in Hindi. As the money was taken for Samata Party activities, whoever took it would have to account for it. At this moment, it remains a case of the missing two lakh.

The facts: Samuel was in Jaya's room. A packet of money was offered. Jaya did not refuse it. It did happen in the defence minister's home. Jaya did not check Samuel's credentials. Jaya did spend some time explaining how the money would be used. Jaya did give a long lecture on how decisions are only taken in the nation's interest, adding that the price and quality have to be right. Jaya was correct in saying that she did not handle the money at all. The money was clearly for the Party. She said that if somebody was not given even a fair chance, she could send word down to the ministry. That's it. To me she did not seem as guilty as she herself made it seem in her defence.

Dayan Krishnan, the counsel for the Commission, showed he was not in the least intimidated by Jaya. Krishnan started off by asking Jaya about her conversation relating to helping West End being considered by the defence ministry.

Krishnan: Let me just pause here for a moment. If the Ministry of Defence says "we cannot". What would you have done?
Jaitly: I do not care at all. I would not have asked the ministry whether they can or they cannot. All I have indicated in all this is that, if there is no response at all and in case that means that they are purposely …
Krishnan: Because I will go back where you said:
"Major General Murgai, … But initially they have not shortlist.
Jaya Jaitly: Hmmm … if there is any way, if they are refusing to test it, that is …
then we can step into the picture."

Jaitly: In between, in the 100-hour transcript, there is a whole section which was cut out. When I first saw the transcript and I came to this line, I said, I could not have possibly sounded so enthusiastic and proactive because I would never do such a thing and it was only when I got the 100-hour transcript that I realized that they have cut out a whole long thing, where they were trying to tell me that some two companies have been asked, they are not at all being paid attention to. The implication, as I understood it, was that they were being treated unfairly and that there was some hanky-panky. That is why I say, if there is any unfair practice. As I had mentioned earlier, if there is a complaint, which I presume to be genuine, and I do not pay attention to it, then there may be those other companies are paying off somebody. So, all I want to do is to send this so that the ministry can then deal with them. It is for the ministry.

Krishnan: This means you will only forward it to them.

Jaitly: Only forward, and that too I clarified, I would only send it to Sahab's office which is in the front portion of the house.

Krishnan: Then you say: "If they say, Yes, certainly we will consider your thing and get back to you by such and such a time." Then, over the page, "after a reasonable time, you can chat with them … send them a reminder …. and also you know that I will not have any direct … I will only request Sahab's office that somebody is not being considered even. So, please send a word down that if anybody is fairly offering a good quality thing and at a good price they should also be fairly considered." Please then look at next two sentences uttered by you, "Now when that happens, you do not want to feel that anybody has an extra interest…." Then you say a line later, "In the interest of the nation. So that … we will ensure that they do not neglect you…"

Jaitly: There is one line left out. I said here, "we do not want anyone to feel that he is … because we do not have any extra interest in anybody." That means we have extra interest in good quality and good price. I am making it very clear to them that I do not care about them as individuals or as a company or anything. I would only care about my country.

Krishnan: Now I take you back to your affidavit, where you say, "Our role is limited to forwarding any complaint or representation, which is on paper to any ministry with the presumption that these would be duly examined." Have you not clearly portrayed that you will do much more than merely forwarding a representation to the ministry?

Jaitly: No. I think in fact I have done quite the opposite; that I have clearly told them that I do not interfere, that I do not know and that I would only pass on this request. At the end, when he asked me in Malayalam, can he come if there is a problem, I said, no, you can give me the details on phone if there is no response. That is, all they will get is a response. If in any way I had been wanting to help them, most people would have said, "all right, give me the papers. I will see that your work is done" and not wasted so much time making small talk just for the sake of courtesy.

Krishnan: What troubles us, and so what I need you to clarify first is, then why do you say that you will ensure that they do not neglect them? And why did you also say that you will put in a word to sahib's office and ensure that the word goes down? I put it to you that you portrayed that you can do more than merely forwarding the representation.

Jaitly: No, sir. That is absolutely incorrect. It is the opposite.

On 4 April 2002, Sidharth Luthra, (counsel for Tehelka) in the Commission, questioned Surendra Sureka:

Luthra: Are you in the habit of introducing people to politicians?

Sureka: *Agar* [if] I was in the habit. If I have done something wrong, that's why I am standing here.

Luthra: You said, "What percentage you will give her, what will you give? Everything you talk her." By mentioning her, are you referring to Jaya Jaitly?

Sureka: Yes. Because he was telling sometimes, I will give 3 per cent, I will give 5 per cent. I went there for a business tie-up. Then I said, you will talk directly. I am not concerned with all these things and I will not charge anything I do not want any money for this introduction. My turnover is around five, six crore rupees. My total sale per year is five, six crore rupees. Then he was talking of 5000 crore rupees. I was getting some excitement. Oh, some big work is going to come to me. I get one crore rupees per showroom he was going to give me, finance me, to open the showroom. He was impressing me high. I was also trying to impress him – yes, *billkul* [absolutely] I can do anything. I can produce the sky over here.

Luthra: The next conversation, Shot No. 216. You are talking about a packet. Have you mentioned about this packet in your affidavit?

Sureka: No, it is not that packet. That packet I referred was for me. There are two packets concerned with me in this case.

Luthra: Do you recall the amount?

Sureka: I do not recall the amount. He said, some amount.

Luthra: Please see the next page 106. You were there during the entire conversation, weren't you?

Sureka: No, one or two times, I went out also. I was there when I introduced [Samuel] to Ms Jaya Jaitly.

Luthra: But you have not stated so in your affidavit, have you?

Sureka: I have not given in my reply completely because it was said that I was involved in some defence deal. I was not involved in any defence deal. According to me, I am doing this business for the last 30 years, since 1972. Defence deal starts from where? When some tender is there, when tender is opened. There are two types of tenders: limited tenders and advertised tenders. Advertised tenders are published in newspapers. Limited tenders are issued by the department to registered suppliers. When a tender is issued, when we participate, then the defence deal starts. So, that is why we have not given reply. I have mentioned in my reply that I am not at all involved in any defence deal and the talk was only for evaluation. Evaluation, I have stated in my affidavit, that it is the right of every citizen.

Luthra: Meeting at Major General Murgai's house on 28 December. Please go to page 117:

"Major General Murgai: You organize your things a bit.

Sureka: You should always keep a packet in a packet. Don't give like this. This will impress him."

Luthra: Is it your conversation?

Sureka: Yes.

Luthra: Please come to the bottom of the page.

"Major General Murgai: That is his.

Sureka: I can only talk about this evaluation."

Luthra: What evaluation are you talking about, Sir?

Sureka: Evaluation of that product.

Luthra: Which product?

Sureka: The product which he was going to offer.

Luthra: Please turn to the next page:

"Sureka: Within 10 days."

What do you mean by this?

Sureka: Within 10 days means, if you give me the letter of application for evaluation, I said, "Yes" it can be done within 10 days. It can be done within 24 hours.

Luthra: What would get done?

Sureka: Letter. It is a question of 5000 crore.

Luthra: I am asking you what do you mean "within 10 days"?

Sureka: My meaning is very simple. He was impressing me with 5000 crore rupees. I was impressing him with anything I can do.

The crucial point here: how did Sureka have a sufficient connection with Jaya Jaitly to have the confidence to take a stranger to her for a defence deal and give money for the party? At the Commission, Sidharth Luthra confirmed that Sureka had discussed introducing Samuel to Jaya Jaitly for the purpose of a defence product related to the defence ministry. Sureka agreed that he did it because he had been promised 5000 crore business.

Luthra: I put it to you that you received money from West End representatives.

Sureka: No, Sir, not at all. You just start the cassette. I want to prove myself now. This is the biggest question for me. I am a very religious person. Sir, let me explain. I could not sleep for nights together for this one lakh rupees. Even the newspaper of Kanpur had written against me lot of things. Then even they have written that Surender Sureka cannot take one lakh rupees and my God is here. I take this thing, Sir, that I have not taken one lakh rupees. I have not taken. I have not taken. Start the cassette. I will prove to you I have not taken. This is the only thing for which I am coming here to prove this thing. Otherwise there is no allegation against me. This one lakh rupees, I will not take. I will not take. I will not take and I have not taken.

Luthra: Evaluation procedures: you were supposed to get an evaluation letter done within 10 days. What is the normal time frame for that?

Sureka: I do not know. I have never done any evaluation. I do not know what is this. I am in the textile business. For 5000 crore business, I engaged myself with him. Not a single notice has been served on me till date. Only for this, I have to come for Delhi for more than 10 times, and apart from that, the fee of advocate is also there.

Surendra Sureka was a simple man. An ordinary businessman. He was living the 'business way of life'. Slipping money here, pulling strings there; how else can you get work done? Wasn't he supposed to grab at every opportunity to make money? He was God-fearing, but was the fear of God used as a warranty against the vagaries of life? Living with the fear that all the wealth might disappear with a flick of God's blink, some insurance is deemed necessary. Sureka's bewilderment at being portrayed as a dishonest man rankled him, like the grating on his neck from a label on a T-shirt. He came to the Commission to reclaim the image he projected of himself. He wanted to be seen in the way he wanted to be seen. Sureka left a frustrated man.

Sureka and Murgai had reassured Samuel that the letter for evaluation would be issued. Tehelka journalists believed it was. Did such a letter indeed exist?

14 The Feminine Mstake

If we do not believe in freedom of speech for those we despise we don't believe in it at all.
— *Noam Chomsky, American Philosopher, Author, Professor*

A senior minister in the BJP government described Jaya Jaitly:

> Jaya has the art of winning enemies. She has a sharp tongue, thinks she is the
> cat's whiskers and doesn't listen to anyone's advice. She gets totally obsessed
> with whatever she does, as is the case here with Tehelka. She is totally straight.
> She is very courageous and even when totally isolated, won't yield. There were
> very few persons who believed her completely, but she carried on.

But, hell, isn't she just the cat's whiskers? And who is the cat? Jaya is no ordinary, average
woman. A huge distance from it.

Jayalakshmi Chettur was an only child and thirteen years old when her father, K.K.
Chettur, died of a heart attack when he was India's first ambassador to Belgium in 1956.
Jaya and her mother were transported from living in a huge mansion to one room in the
barracks at Kota House, Delhi. Jaya's family owns a palace in Kerala but she pointed out that
they all slept on *chattais* (mats), because that was their culture. As a widow, Jaya's mother
went to work for the first time in her life as social secretary to the American ambassador.
Until she died, three years ago, she filled her life with social work, reading to students of the
Blind School, teaching municipal school students, and working in a clinic in South Enclave.
She did not own a house or car. Jaya said she imbibed her mother's values; of one who was
a raja's wife and then an ambassador's widow but always thought of what she could do for
others. In Jaya's life, she has introduced the rules she chooses to live by. Jaya explained,

So living on my terms means not doing anything I want, but doing what I believe in. This may not be what is understandable in the Delhi political scene. I know that it's certainly not understandable in the backward class kind of politics of Bihar. Therefore, I can understand why the men in the party don't have any empathy with me or my work. It's just part of a different way of life, perhaps.

Jaya returned to India after her father died and went to Convent of Jesus and Mary in Delhi, and then on to Miranda House, the hottest college in Delhi University at the time. She got a scholarship to Smith College in Massachusetts (USA) and graduated with a degree in English Literature in 1963. Before returning to India, she lived in London working for Air India, she said, to experience what it was like to live alone and earn her ticket back. Jaya married IAS officer Ashok Jaitly and started working with craftsmen and handicrafts. In 1977, Jaya met George Fernandes when her husband was posted as personal secretary to Fernandes, minister for industries, under the Janata Party government. Jaya's work ethos was influenced by the post-colonial zeitgeist of her family and was ingrained in her at an early age. Jaya recalled,

It's not that I've been financially comfortable at all. We've lived a rough lifestyle, in Jammu & Kashmir when we first got married. Our salary was Rs 500 a month. If I bought a kilo of cherries, we couldn't afford to have our guests eat it in one evening, because then there wouldn't be cherries for the rest of the week. We used to travel by *tonga* and money's never been an important consideration. But we have our self respect. We come from a very aristocratic, as I do, from my family. That's all reflected in one's thinking and in one's attitudes to life, not in show of money.

In Miranda House she was well known for the various activities she was into, but also, yes, for her hot, sultry looks. A man I met socially remembered his young, flirty days when he cycled with a teenage, capri-clad Jaya (then known as June Chettur) to swim with her at Gymkhana Club in Delhi. As he spoke, his eyes nostalgically misted over at the bewitching memory.

Sagarika Ghose, journalist, and now senior editor at CNN-IBN, was exposed to Jaya's personality when she was fourteen years old. Sagarika was a friend of Jaya's niece, Nandika, and lived next door to Ashok and Jaya Jaitly. To Nandika and all her friends, Jaya was known as Cheri, short for Cheriamma, meaning 'aunt' in Malyalam. Jaya is described as absolutely dazzling with her hip-length sinuous black hair in khadi kurtas and jeans, while most IAS officers' wives stuck to the safety of sarees. The young couple was the cynosure of all eyes when they broke into a jive at Nandika's birthday parties. While other officers' homes had the colonial chintz sofas and bland curtains, Jaya's home was filled with crafts from all over India. Mirror-work bedspreads, hand-crafted puppets. durries instead of carpets, an antique telephone attached to the wall instead of the boring, government-issue black. Ethnic chic way ahead of its time. She had begun working in Gurjari (a government-run shop that brought Gujarati rural crafts to Delhi) and had brought its culture home. More than anything else, she left an impression of a hurricane of energy and fun. She would bundle up a bunch of kids in the car and take them swimming. At Holi, rather than just playing with a few close friends as was commonly done, she dragged everybody out on the street to play with the entire neighbourhood. When some village women passed by singing, Jaya surprised everyone by knowing their lyrics and singing along with them. At one of Nandika's birthday parties, disaster struck when the birthday cake went crashing to the floor. Jaya jumped into her car with her dogs and miraculously returned with two cakes from some dinky shop she knew. Details like naming her dog Ghazi, rather than one of the usual post-colonial names like Tommy or Rover, expressed her personal style. Her car number was JK something, so the car was christened Jacob. Jaya was indelibly different from all the other mothers. As these moments were recalled, on serious reflection, Sagarika said, 'I simply cannot square the Tehelka allegation with the Jaya I know. She has always struck me as personally incorruptible, idealistic, and full of integrity. I can't imagine her as anything else.'

Then began Jaya's involvement with handicrafts, socialist politics, and George Fernandes. It's easy to see how it happened. The humdrum life of a government officer's wife compared to the excitement of being an activist of social change, all inspired by a charismatic, handsome man. Who wouldn't?

◡

To understand Jaya you also have to visualize the *mahaul* (atmosphere) of the times. Capitalism and making money were dirty words. It was a time when there was no Page 3, nor any recognized socialites. A socialite, then, was a boring dowager. 'Designer' in those days meant something you had designed, painted, or made yourself. Clothes were bought from Jama Masjid markets, Cottage Industries, Khadi Bhandar, and jewellery from Hanuman Mandir. The hippie culture infected the élite youth of India. Were we real real hippies? No, not really; of course not. But politically, we were consensually questioning established mores, so the accoutrements and uniform were an announcement of mission. Chiffon and pearls were symbols of derision and handmade street stuff made the required statement. In morphic resonance around the world, parents looked at their sons with shoulder-length hair and were embarrassed, as we showed up at social gatherings in crumpled khadi. How did a hick in Mid-West America know that a parent in Delhi mocked with the same question: 'Is it a boy or a girl?' Young people worked in villages with bewildered villagers wondering what they were doing there. Anyone and everyone was roped in to act in street theatre that shouted social and political messages. Culturally, socially, and politically, there were two battle camps: young people who continued to think like their parents and those who absolutely refused to. The influence of the hippie culture was high, in both terms of the word, and India became international hippies' Mecca for drugs and spirituality. The Beatles arrived in Rishikesh in kurtas and beads to sit at the feet of Maharishi Mahesh Yogi. Mia Farrow followed in hot spiritual pursuit. There were strange pangs when 'white' hippies connected with their Indian counterparts. Writing of the hippie invasion of India, nobody has ever said it better than Gita Mehta in her jewel of a book *Karma Cola* (1979):

Still others say the action began when that long red line of loonies came straggling in by way of Afghanistan, the Northwest Frontier, and the Punjab plains. What an entrance. Thousands and thousands of them, clashing cymbals, ringing bells, playing flutes, wearing bright colours and weird clothes, singing and dancing and speaking in tongues.

We looked at them; we wanted to be them. They looked at us and wondered why we couldn't stay as we were.

Mehta then summed it up:

The seduction lay in the chaos. They thought they were simple. We thought they were neon. They thought we were profound. We knew we were provincial. Everybody thought everybody else was ridiculously exotic and everybody got it wrong. Then the real action began.

Goa became the hippie capital of the world while the baffled Goans couldn't figure out this new breed of 'white man' who, more often than not, had no money. Pammi and Kamal Singh opened the first discotheque The Cellar, designed by Rajeev Sethi, at the corner of Regal building in Delhi. He hung an old car from the ceiling and painted the walls himself. For the first time, young people had their own place to hang around, smoke, dance and make out, and not have to tag along with their parents to Gymkhana Club. Unlike the parents, young people were dancing without touching for the first time, deemed sexier than ever. Sethi designed the interiors for another disco which had toilet seats as chairs for the customers. For the walls, Sethi did Pierrot make-up on himself, had me photograph him, and I developed the three-foot print in my bathtub. When a young group of actors took their play to Srinagar, one of the actresses brought her boyfriend along and they made a zeitgeist statement by taking a room for themselves. We, even as spectators, vicariously gloried in their assertion. Handsome young artist, Vivan Sunderam, lived with stunning singer Asha Puthli on top of a garage in Baroda where he painted. The social hub was the National School of Drama, in Delhi, where people like Naseeruddin Shah, Om Puri, M.K. Raina, Anupam Kher, Mala Thapar (now Singh), Kusum Haider, Rtta Kapur, Madhu Chopra enrolled, attracted by the charismatic, revered, despot Ebrahim Alkazi. I was nineteen years old when I got Alkazi suitably disconcerted when I irreverently accused him of being archaic for watching old film reels of Brecht and copying his style. (Giving an interview twenty years later, he had the amused courtesy of recalling the moment.) Heated political and social debates carried on for hours. Should Alkazi slap actors when he directed them, as he did? One actress felt it brought out the best in her but Madhu Chopra warned him, in loud, emphatic, terms, with her finger pointing in his face, never to touch her again.

The anti-Vietnam war movement, the breaking of sexual mores and stereotypes, the total rejection of parents' values, were the norm. If you weren't involved politically or in grassroots work, you were nothing. The poverty in India that we so easily turn our faces away from today, burnt guilt in our bourgeois minds that could only be calmed by activism.

More than anything else, there was passion. A motivating belief that you can and must change the world as it exists. It is, perhaps, difficult to imagine the excitement of that life which made every moment a challenge, every decision, even not wearing a bra, a political statement; and the bra business had nothing to do with feminism. It was about living in total freedom without pre-decided, illogical social restraints. In comparison to today's life, where the only excitement is where the next party is and how to squeeze on to Page 3, it was LIFE in capital letters. In other words, if you missed that time, you really missed the party of your life.

As Abbie Hoffman, leader of the Yippie Party said,

> We are here to make a better world. No amount of rationalization or blaming can pre-empt the moment of choice each of us brings to our situation here on this planet. The lesson of the 60s is that people who cared enough to do right could change history. We didn't end racism but we ended legal segregation. We ended the idea that you could send half-a-million soldiers around the world to fight a war that people do not support. We ended the idea that women are second-class citizens. We made the environment an issue that couldn't be avoided. The big battles that we won cannot be reversed. We were young, self-righteous, reckless, hypocritical, brave, silly, headstrong and scared half to death. And we were right.

Everyone fought these battles in their own little worlds, in their personal lives, in their own way. In India, people like Bunker and Aruna Roy gave up the option of making money and went to work in the village of Tilonia. They are still there and their work speaks for itself. Aruna Roy has continued her activism today, fighting for the Freedom for Information Bill as a constitutional right. Brinda Karat, now the first woman in the Communist Party's Politbureau and Subhashini Ali, a member of the Communist Party, were inspired to start their political involvement at that time and their commitment has not slacked over the years. Ela Bhatt set an example working with women in crafts, followed by Laila Tyabji and both continue to do so.

The idea that we could actually change what we had unwillingly inherited enveloped us. The Beatles sang: 'We all want to change the world' in *The Revolution*. The amusing aspect is that we all believed it.

In that atmosphere, for Jaya Jaitly, it was conceivably the right and best thing to do. Many brilliant and attractive women got politically involved and became life partners of their 'comrades'. You married your activism and your mate was an activist. What might seem an unusual lifestyle now, Jaya was only following the norm then.

Jaya, with all her usual enthusiasm, worked on the development of crafts while she lived with her husband in Kashmir. She worked as the design and marketing consultant for Gujarat handicrafts and handloom. Jaya has written and produced several books on crafts and craftspersons. She was responsible for the revival of pottery in Nilambur, Kerala, where women had turned to prostitution to support their families. Jaya organized them into a cooperative with their own selling outlets. In 1985 Jaya founded Dastkari Haat Samiti, an organization of crafts people. Jaya was instrumental in the creation of Dilli Haat (1994), which showcases art and crafts from all over India. It is a magnet for young people and tourists as a place in which to hang out, eat, and indulge in inexpensive shopping. Her involvement with Dilli Haat continues, with periodic exhibitions of crafts from all over Asia.

Jaya's political involvement became serious when she got involved in organizing relief camps during the anti-Sikh riots after Indira Gandhi's assassination. She joined the Janata Party, then the Janata Dal (party) and was appointed National Secretary in 1991. After four years, Jaya joined the Samata Party, following her political mentor George Fernandes. In 1998, Fernandes was appointed defence minister in the newly elected NDA government. In January 2000, Jaya was elected president of the Samata Party.

When you enter 3, Krishna Menon Marg, it evokes the period of the late 1960s. The place is maintained and run like a regular *jholawala's* home. It was common during the hippie/activism period to wake up in the morning and discover various bodies asleep on your living room floor. Although not quite that extreme, it is quite normal to see various people from different states in India and other nationalities roam the house as if their own. Jaya's lawyers are treated as part of this great, socialist family. The place is as undecorated as any *jholawala's*. Paintings are obvious gifts from admirers and not chosen by collectors or lovers of art. The place is untidy. An old, dust-covered television set looks barely used. There are piles and piles of papers and books all over. The three, rather charming, dogs have the run of the place and the choice positions on the sofas. There is dog hair everywhere. At the Commission in Vigyan Bhavan, while talking to Jaya's lawyer, I pointed out to him that I could tell where he had been: he had dog hair all over his trousers. Amidst it all, Jaya with her gentle voice, even when she's angry, and her incandescent smile, presides over the casual disarray. No matter how upset she is, she rather unconsciously never loses her allure. Always dressed in beautiful, simple sarees and fashionably unmatched blouses, she is not above wearing pretty, pink-flowered, lacy bras under the *jholawaia* uniform, as I noticed while pinning the microphone on her. Her hair colour is defiantly unusual. Black on top, white at the edges. Jaya's looks, manner, and magnetism completely belie her 65 years. Okay, I forgot, this is the new 65. Jaya has the most important ingredient of allure in a woman: her disengagement with her appearance. Okay, so Frenchwomen have the elusive *je ne sais quoi*, even though they *sais* rather well. This is such a mysterious constituent that American *Elle* magazine flew a reporter to Paris to crack the French *je ne sais quoi* code. (Literally it means 'I don't know what.')

Jaya seems to embody this subterranean sensuality. And, some Indian women have moved it a bit further. Their look can only be described as message dressing and the sexuality is incidental, which makes it even more enticing. The way they appear is a statement of their beliefs. They want the purpose in their lives out there. They are not following fashions. They choose instead how they want to be perceived. Kindly view me as a political activist, a media tycoon, an intellectual. There is no *koshish*. They do not face insecurity that is only soothed by 'phoren' designers and the expensive chiffon-chikan saree uniform. Their obvious rejection of days at the beauty parlour and cool intelligence is Jaya's manner of life. Her breezy detachment with her looks, her intensity in what she believes, her independent personal choices, her confidence in her own aristocracy, her inexorable loyalty to her children and George, are all part of her chosen nonchalant grace.

Jaya was generous with her time with me. It is an awkward relationship, between a journalist and the interviewed. So often, a subject will happily cooperate, speak at will, divulge confidences, and then feel cheated when it appears in print, sometimes even on visual tapes. We both tried to clear the deck as honestly as possible. Clearly, what was in it for Jaya was that her story was correctly told, and that is what I wanted to do. Jaya asked me whether I had a bias, and was I taking sides? I had no preconceived notion of the direction this book would take. That could only come after all the interviews had been conducted and research completed. There was no guarantee that I would view all the issues in the way Jaya saw them. Or, in the way the Tehelka journalists viewed them. Were the interviews with Jaya going to be what is initially a mutually agreed exploitative encounter between us that would end in unpleasantness? The facts of the story were already on an interpretative keel. Would I be able to control my tendency towards the Stockholm syndrome: a basic partiality for every subject interviewed, even someone like Bangaru Laxman for whom I felt nothing but pity? It was difficult, for me as a journalist not to enjoy my entire canvas because such a wealth of exhilarating material is dangerously seductive.

Jaya is obsessed with Tehelka. She doesn't need any encouragement to talk. She has all the facts which roll out of her at break the tape speed. She forgets nothing. She remembers verbatim every word Tehelka journalists uttered in their cross-examinations before the Commission, which she attended every single day. She was rather bitterly not working for the Samata Party ever since she resigned as president on 15 March 2001, in the wake of the Tehelka revelations. She felt let down by the party, which did little to stand by her and support her struggle to revalidate herself. Jaya was in it alone and she was in battle gear. She said she fought by gaining new skills, such as learning how to use a computer, which was a procrastinated New Year resolution. Jaya said, 'I feel quite strengthened by the fight because it has helped me overcome the initial misery of having to explain to the world that I am not corrupt, because that is the core of the accusation.' Jaya needed to go through the Operation West End CDs and type out her defence often late into the night when there was no one else around. I asked, 'Where, at home?' Jaya answered, 'Yeah, here'.

Here Jaya slipped up on an issue that really interests nobody, but she has vociferously claimed that her place of residence is a flat in Sujan Singh Park, repeatedly asserting that she does not live in 3, Krishna Menon Marg. She comes in the morning with her dog and returns with her dog after her day's work. 'Where, at home?' Jaya could have said, 'No, not at home; over here, where I work.' Her natural instinct was to call 3, Krishna Menon Marg home. Not a big issue; nobody really cares where Jaya lives, but, there it is. Jaya said,

I feel that I have overcome that initial strong feeling of insult and humiliation that I felt at being accused of something which was so completely contrary to the very basis of my beliefs. Because whether it's my family or my background or my political work and my closest political colleagues, integrity has been

245

fundamental to our lives. To the extent you don't even have to go around saying, look I'm honest. Because we all come from that kind of society where you don't even think of saying such a thing: you just are. And the other thing is a question of patriotism; not letting one's country down. The phrase that was, the kind of sub-title of Operation West End, was, "The Suitcase People Who Compromise the Nation's Defence." So the nation's defence being so fundamental, that what they were trying to say is that I'm habitually carting around suitcases or meeting people with suitcases and taking money, to sell my country's interests down the drain. I was, in fact, being accused of being a traitor also. It made me very, very angry, which made me get into this fight so wholeheartedly. The second was that it was really insulting. Just a day or two before I had to do my deposition, I was utterly sad at having to stand in the dock and have to say to anybody that I do not indulge in anything which could be called corruption. So it was that agony that I'm referring to.

Despite Jaya's obsession with clearing her name, she did get her book, *Vishvakarma's Children* published, which she said she did as an instrument of self-empowerment, yet it was still the corruption accusations that motivated her. She said, 'I was so determined that I must show the world that this is my real concern. I don't care what they say. I have to bring this book out to show that my real care is for the crafts people's lives.'

On 13 March 2001, Jaya did not react instantly when she received a call from Zee TV that she was being shown in the Operation West End tapes. She did call George Fernandes's secretary who described what he was seeing on TV. Puzzled about what she was hearing, she rushed to George's South Block office. She said she was completely aghast at what she saw. Jaya said she did not remember the visit or the incident. According to her:

They talked about a General Murgai speaking to me. I had never met a General Murgai in my life. As I again mentioned in my deposition, they never introduced [him]. I had no idea who that man was sitting and talking. But since our lives are full of talking to so many people, from all over the country, who you don't ever know who they are. And since this kind of office and our politics is so open, other than the fact that the government now requires guards to be there and all that. Nobody gets checked and nobody gets asked anything. If you come in, you come in. Everybody's meant to deal with people as they think best. And even if a crook comes in, if you are not a crook, you don't have a problem about meeting a crook. He may turn out to be a crook, but the fact is as long as you know your conscience is going to function properly, nobody has any lack of self-confidence that you have to screen everybody. When they said Murgai was talking to me, I said how could it possibly be? I haven't met any Murgai. Army officers never come. In fact it never was clear that day that it was a retired fellow. Then they said, West End. I said but I have never even given an appointment. I don't give appointments to companies. So without an appointment, how am I sitting there and talking to these fellows? I don't understand. Something is funny. So that was around 5.15 p.m. I told George Sahab, I said "please for God's sake, tell the Powers-That-Be, that call these people in, question them, they might have compromised God knows what national security, where they've gone, who they've spoken to. Have they come across some security secrets in some installations that nobody should get into?"

A suggestion from Jaya to call in and question journalists is simply not ethical under the circumstances.

> I think the government should check on that, and secondly, why don't you ask some top most CBI officer to seize all these tapes that they have and take them abroad immediately and have them checked. I'm still fighting for the same thing to be done.

Jaya could not fathom why the tapes were not taken into custody immediately. She pointed out that George Fernandes was looking at it from a different point of view. He was worried that security had been breached in his ministry and whether the defence of the country had been compromised. Jaya complained that George did not say what she had told him to say in the cabinet meeting that was called. She said,

> Everybody was stunned – at the government level. Everybody has this automatic, old-fashioned view, that what you see is the truth. So they thought, well, that's how it is. And George Sahab was thousand per cent clear in his mind that no such thing had happened in my case; that I would not do these things. But I believe it took a while to inquire from Bangaru as to what happened and did he take money and was it for the party.

Both George and Jaya read the transcripts of Operation West End through that night. They had no idea it was an edited version and they had no inkling that Tehelka actually had 105 unedited tapes. Jaya said, 'The more I read, the more garbled it was. The more it seemed to be a complete fiddle of a whole lot of garbled conversations, cut and put together. I started picking holes in it and I have that copy with my notings even now.' A friend called her the following morning and told her that he could clearly see dissolves in the tapes. One would imagine it to be too obvious a fact to consider that the tapes had been edited to be a great discovery. To Jaya it was the proof of the fiddle. Jaya said,

> **Jaitly:** It took a while to make everybody understand that. I was always a step ahead of everybody else, because I knew that something was so wrong; that I kept asking everybody about the technology part. But it was such a political battle. Everybody else was concentrating on the political part of it. Parliament

not being allowed to function. George Sahab not being allowed to speak. He had got the details overnight about all those deals and what actually took place. There was no question of him overruling Kalam as Jain is supposed to have been saying.

Madhu: The question here is that they conducted a sting operation and had 105 hours of tape. They had to edit it down for viewing. Lawyers in the Commission have constantly mixed up editing with doctoring. Are you saying they should not have edited it as it was a sting and it should not have been treated as a news package, where you do cutaways [footage taken later to supplement a news story] of the house later, which maybe showed the events in a different light? They did have to edit it down.

Jaitly: Agreed. But if I had said I agree with you when we discussed this, this would be for a seminar on journalism ethics. But at that point of time, as a political person, being hit in the manner that I was, if I had started talking like this, people wouldn't have listened to me for a second. So, one: I knew that the tapes were tampered with: doctoring and tampering, there are all different meanings to these words, but the tapes are not the true reflection of events. Secondly, I have said that what they're making out, which they have themselves concisely put on their website, was that we are all corrupt people who sell our country down the drain as a matter of routine. It happens right under George Fernandes's nose, right in his house, so there is this illicit relationship also which they *chalao* [run].

Jaya declared that George was more concerned about the demoralization of the jawans, and that he offered to resign at the cabinet meeting. Rumours filtered out that George had been asked to resign but had refused, saying he had done nothing wrong. Jaya said,

Jaitly: My reaction was completely the opposite of his. I said, "Please for God's sake, nobody should resign, because there is some major fraud in this. I believe this is a political fight and I think everybody should get together and fight back. This is not something where everybody resigns." Four days later, George Sahab, myself, everybody resigned. That was because the party was under so much attack, then PM finally decided to accept George Sahab's resignation. Then as a party we took a decision that if George Sahab is resigning, then all of us resign. Including then, if you remember, the four ministers also resigned. Me, George Sahab, Nitish, Digvijay and Srinivas Prasad. And then after much confabulation and two weeks later, they went back into the ministry. George Sahab persuaded them.

Madhu: Why did you not simply say that you accepted money for the Samata Party and leave it at that? Why the frenzied defence?

Jaya: Yes, if they say, we want to give something for the party, yes, but what was their accusation? The accusation was that I knowingly met these people as arms dealers. In their website, I come in a Rogues Gallery saying all these things. One: I never knew they were arms dealers. They weren't even arms dealers. Two: I never gave an appointment. Three: all their things, their proximity with all these things were all lies. Now, I took the position of fight back, not in self-defence. My fight back has been to point out that if these people claim to have done an investigative job and claim to be journalists, then they are frauds. Unless people are exposed as being frauds and every single one of their mistakes – in quotes – is not pointed out and they are not exposed before the public all over the world, the way they have gone around all over the world about us. Tomorrow we can have somebody destabilizing the system much worse than they have done. It wasn't a small thing that they achieved. They knocked the defence minister out of his *kursi* [chair] for seven months. They've still given enough handle to the Congress to say why is he back at all. When my resignation issue came, I said, do you think by my resigning, everything is going to stop? It'll be me today, George Fernandes tomorrow and the PM the third day. In a way, George Fernandes's resignation being accepted was like stopping the flood from reaching Vajpayee's door. I seriously believe they thought the whole government would go.

True. The Tehelka team was certain the government would, indeed, fall.

In Jaya's cross-examination before the Commission of Inquiry, she admitted that she did tell Mathew Samuel that if there was some hanky-panky, if there was any unfair practice or complaint that she thought was genuine and 'the government is paying off somebody' she would then forward their application to the ministry. The acceptance by Jaya of an established corrupt system in the defence ministry while George Fernandes was the minister was revealing. When asked about it, Jaya said,

George Fernandes is a minister who is way above all these things. The corruption could be at the level of some official down below. If you ask George Fernandes today, he won't say his ministry is corruption free. He is fighting a constant battle trying to make it so. The trouble is that I, and he also believes, that because he has tried so hard to make it so, that is one of the reasons he has been targeted.

Kavin Gulati, counsel for Tehelka, dealt with the issue of how the residence of the defence minister was used to meet Samata Party donors:

Gulati: The office of the Samata Party which is at Vital Bhai Patel House. In the first place, why was that not being used by you as the official place where you would conduct party work and why in an office room in Mr George's house?
Jaitly: I use the Samata Party office to conduct party work. This, in no way, can be described as party work. It is a common facility work in Krishna Menon

Marg that people use from all across the country, our trade unions and other colleagues, to conduct various types of work that they may be doing, which is not party work. I work for handicrafts, somebody else is doing something for the trade union. There is no designated place that anybody sits [in] and does any specific work. Party work is done at the party office.

Gulati: Have party presidents prior to you, and now some other person who is the party president, are they also using the same room at Mr Fernandes's residence for similar purposes?

Jaitly: The president prior to me – certainly – yes, because that was Mr George Fernandes. The subsequent party president very often comes to Krishna Menon Marg to conduct meetings with other colleagues and he would certainly use this room.

Many lawyers would have torn Jaya to shreds on her use of George Fernandes's home. "How many hours a day do you spend in George Fernandes's home?" "Where do you spend the night?" "Why is your dog in George Fernandes' home?" "What is the connection between the defence minister's personal home and the Samata Party, when the party has its own office space?" Unsavoury stuff, yes, but that's what lawyers do, right?

Jaya seemed to be completely oblivious of the gossip about her relationship with George. That can be expected because nobody would dare gossip to her or repeat any gossip to her. Indeed, their relationship was so taken for granted that there really wasn't much to gossip about. The truth is that no members of the Samata Party came to her defence, and that was a telling enough statement. Her fury and rage about being spoken of in such a leery, cheap manner triggered her into the best personal defence mode she could muster.

Neither the Tehelka journalists nor their lawyers were interested in Jaya's personal relationship with George. It was only when she filed a criminal defamation complaint that an application was moved by Tarun Tejpal where she was asked how she felt defamed by the use of the word 'companion'. She was also asked why she assumed that being a companion of a person like Fernandes, who according to her, had a sterling reputation was at all defamatory. Yet this was a subject that did upset Jaya.

Madhu: I don't think they ever wrote anything about your relationship with George.

Jaitly: "Companion" is something they keep saying. Why is it that I'm not a political colleague? Why, when it's a woman, you call it a companion every time? They showed on the very first day, over and over and over, R.K. Jain saying, "*Haan, haan*, yes, there are two defence ministers in this country; she's not really his wife, but like a second wife …," and that sort of cheap, crude talk.

Madhu: In India, journalists don't usually go into politicians' personal lives. They don't seem to be interested in exploring your personal life.

Jaitly: They aren't? Then why did these people put this out in this manner?

Madhu: If you are George Fernandes's companion, nobody is getting moralistic about it. The prime minister has a foster family living in his house and it is respected.

Jaitly: Yes, I know.

Madhu: Mayawati's relationship with Kanshi Ram is totally acceptable. Nobody writes about it or says it is wrong. There are numerous examples.

Jaitly: I don't care. I know, but here why did they do it? If it had been in isolation, fine. Madhu Kishwar has an answer for that: she says Jaya Jaitly's always led a very, rather, kind of an unusual private life, but of course nobody needs to talk about it. But when it's a question of interfering with the country's interests and taking bribes, then yes, everybody has a right to discuss it. That's what Madhu Kishwar has said in her interview with Tejpal for Tehelka, on their website. I've got all this material here with me. I was horrified with her. She's been my friend. If anybody has an unusual lifestyle, it's her. [Laughs.] But I never talk about anybody's lifestyle or personal life.

Madhu: But Jaya, why would you be defensive about your relationship with George, when nobody is getting moralistic about it?

Jaitly: I'm not, no, for one: because it's not true. Two: I don't, because here you use it only to establish the fact that George Fernandes is the one who's corrupt. "George Fernandes incriminated beyond redemption" is what this fellow keeps saying.

Madhu: So are you saying that you do not have a personal relationship with George?

Jaitly: I have a personal relationship, which is not at all a romantic one. Let me put it that way between you and me. [Laughs.] If it's recorded, it's recorded, fine. But if anybody knows George Fernandes and his commitment to his work, he couldn't even have his own family life, where is he going to have any extracurricular family life? If you again know the person closely and you know his establishment, in the sense, his trade union, which means establishments all over the country, there are people who will on a phone call give their life for him. People who have so much faith in him, because he is a very straight, honest, fearless being.

Madhu: How would your describe your relationship with him?

Jaitly: I look at him as a, as a, what shall I say? A senior; at closest one could say [he] is like a family member if you like, but it's not even like a family member. Anybody can bully him and say, your kurta is crushed, please change it. There are friends of ours who get his kurtas made and stitched and send it. I don't get his clothes made. I look after this establishment because it's a public establishment. Unfortunately, it's always dumped on the woman to give tea to everybody. [Laughs.] But otherwise…

Madhu: Jaya, let me be honest …

Jaitly: *Haan* [Yes].

Madhu: I find it really difficult to believe that you don't have a relationship with him.

Jaitly: No, it's a very close relationship, but it's nothing …

Madhu: You're an attractive woman, he's a good-looking man. You have had a long association with him. How is it possible not to be attracted to each other?

Jaitly: It's an attraction, you can say, of mutual respect. Of mutual respect, of perhaps intellect; I would like to think intellect, but I still look to him for compliments or admiration in my work. Never, I don't think he even notices what I look like or what I wear or anything.

Madhu: [Laughs.]

Jaitly: No, really, seriously. Maybe it's funny, but he is an odd man.

Madhu: That is very difficult to see. I'm looking at it from a man's point of view, looking at you and you are working around him all the time and then expect a man not to react. After all, he is a man and you are an attractive woman.

Jaitly: But he's a highly, I don't know how, what he would react at all but I do know that he's a highly motivated and self-disciplined person. If at the age of 72 he can sleep at two in the morning, get up at four, wash his clothes, and catch a flight for Siachen at five, when everybody else is exhausted and doesn't want to get out of bed, something about him motivates him which is beyond [what] any of us can figure out.

Madhu: Do you love him?

Jaitly: Certainly, the way I would say I love him but I can find you 20 men right now who'll say the same. He's that kind of a person. Either you hate him or you love him. Men have no awkwardness about saying they love George Fernandes because he is like that. People who have a little bit of cynicism, or a little bit of distance, or a little bit of a different kind of a world, who don't know him, will find it hard to believe all these things. But he really is a completely different kind of a person. He has to be. To be a person where no caste, no religion, no minority, religion only now is some value, earlier it didn't, but no money, no nothing, thrown out of his household and other than Lohia and his ideology and his hard work. How many people in India can get to be where he is now?

Madhu: But you are separated from your husband?

Jaitly: I'm not with my husband for a reason that, I think, because of my total involvement with politics, with public work. I think every man doesn't like to be overtaken by a woman or think that he's being overtaken or that she doesn't have time for him or his life. But I can't share a bureaucratic life, other than going out in the evening for tea and coffee. But I'm a very instinctive, activist, kind of a person. I can't sit back and comment on things. I have to go out and do something about it. I've got more and more bothered by being a part of a society that would talk about oh, how bad everything is, and not do anything. And I, because of George Sahab, I've got the opportunity, for the first time ever, to watch election campaigning. This was in the 1980 election in Muzzafarpur. I said, "Let me go and see how it is." So I went and joined up with the whole team over there and we'd go to each house and tell the women how to fold the ballot paper, where to stamp it and so on. Simple little things like that, just to get a feel, because we were close to a person. Tony (Jaya's husband then) was completely bowled over by George Sahab. He just couldn't stop talking about what a wonderful man he was. So George Fernandes came into our household like a wonderful person. Not physically but Tony would work till three and four in the morning. They'd work together and then they'd again [at] 6 o'clock get up and go and fly off somewhere. His pace of work is tremendous. Fearlessness and integrity: these were things we've always valued and these are what we found in him. But after the government fell and George Sahab wasn't in the government any more, he was shunned a lot by the socialist colleagues who felt he had let them down with that, 1977 speech about, you know, you speak for the government and then you quit the government the next day. There was a big story behind which involved Madhu Limaya. But that's a different thing. However, they felt that for the first time ever they had all come to power, socialists, like Madhu Dandavate, and they felt that George had let them down. So nobody went anywhere near him. I being the kind of person I am, warm, friendly, informal, I said, "Oh gosh, I don't care that he's a minister or he's not a minister; it didn't bother me either way". So if he was sick or with a toothache, there'd be nobody there to look after him. He was isolated completely.

Madhu: Was this in Delhi or Kashmir?

Jaitly: In Delhi. I stayed back because my children were at school. Tony had to keep coming and going from Kashmir. So I'd say [to George], *oh hoh* come here [and] I'll get you medicine or *chalo* [let's go] let's take the children out for ice cream. His little kid was with him also, so, you know, everybody was kind of ...

Madhu: He's been married before?

Jaitly: He's still married.

Madhu: Oh?

Jaitly: *Haan*, to Leila Kabir. She, long before, I think, he became a minister, she was, this is completely off the record, ...

Madhu: So then because Tony was in Kashmir and you were in Delhi, you spent time with them?

Jaitly: I would also be there. Once when she felt very low she called me and I spent a lot of time with her. I used to take her shopping. I used to do her vegetable shopping for her. I just felt, we are people who are families who should care for each other because we've been through a lot together. I'm like that. I don't care about how it looks. Somebody has to be looked after, I'll look after them and I can't be formal with people. I'll either joke or I'll just keep quiet completely. My mother was also like that. We come from a matriarchal family in Kerala where women don't feel oppressed or cowed down in any way. We just believe in ourselves and we just do what we have to do. I do it because I am doing it. I don't think of myself as a woman. I've sat in big trade union meetings, halls, with two thousand men and at the end I realize, oh god, I'm really the only woman here. But I'm not conscious of it. This is the way we are brought up. It's sort of a pre-feminism feminism maybe. [Laughs.]

Madhu: There are a lot of stereotypes we get trapped in.

Jaitly: Yeah. So it's the same way. Maybe it's odd that I'm sitting here and doing all this work. No other woman would sit in a man's house and do this, but I don't see it that way. I see all of us are people, working for a cause. So I'm here. I accept that our society is also very critical and very peculiar, and maybe all societies are, and therefore to a certain extent, I'll answer.

Madhu: But society is also accepting.

Jaitly: They may be accepting, I don't know. It really never strikes me even, do people accept or not accept. I have never wasted any moment thinking about these things. But when they use this constantly, to say that I am a companion of George Fernandes and that's how I'm sitting here. That's why Laloo or all these people in Parliament keep attacking George Sahab on the fact that I'm sitting here. There are hundred and one men sitting here also. If somebody has to give George Sahab money for his election, any of those men could collect it. It would be in the defence minister's house. It's for the party, because he's a party person; what does that mean then? You make it look bad because it's me. So I'm not going to get cowed down by that and that's why I say I'll fight it out. I'll say all right, relationship okay, if there was one. I'm not going to hide it. But if there isn't one, I'm explaining at length to you because you're asking one-to-one and you're curious, or whatever, but that's how it is.

Madhu: The issue that you accepted the money in the defence minister's house has been brought up repeatedly. So in that sense, your relationship then does become relevant.

Jaitly: Because they make it look like a residence. The implication always is that I'm living here.

Madhu: If you are here all the time, then most would presume that there is a relationship. I guess nobody is checking what time you leave.

Jaitly: Yeah, so many people think I live here. But I don't. I make it a point, [laughs]. People ask, "Oh, these are your dogs?" Then I have to go into a whole rigmarole: no, actually these two dogs are not mine. All three dogs are there, but this one goes home with me in the evening and comes back in the morning. I feel that I hope I'm giving a little message to them that I don't live here, if that's what you think.

Madhu: Have you found that your relationship with George Fernandes has changed because of Tehelka?

Jaitly: No. Not a bit. As I say again, there isn't a relationship. There is only whatever is solidly binding, is one: a common belief, again, integrity. And two: courage to fight out things. There will be controversy. There will be adversaries if you don't work within a system. If you try to buck the system, if you try to change things, like changing corruption, there are so many vested interests; you've got to have the courage to face it and fight it out. This is a major lesson I've learnt from him. I feel, I hope, I'd like to believe somewhere; and he doesn't say anything, he doesn't say, well done. If I make him read an article I've written and he'll read it, and I'll say, "Say, what do you think?" and he'll say, "Very good," and I'll say, "Ah, see, I was waiting for you to say very good". [Laughs.]

But he doesn't confide like normal people do. He'll never share his thoughts. He will, with twenty people in the room he'll give his political view about things, but if he's worried or upset about something, he won't open his mouth. So I'll babble from my side, this shouldn't happen, or that should happen and he'll just listen very quietly. So in all this, I keep telling him what I'm doing or what's going on. Once in a while he'll make a little comment, that yes, I've been the only one who's really fought it out. But otherwise, he expects me to do all this. I believe that if he thought I was doing something wrong, he'd say don't do it. But he's actually so liberated that he doesn't even tell you if you're doing something wrong. He wants people to do things for themselves. I think personally I would presume that he's quite proud of the fact that I've dug my heels in and dug my teeth into the whole thing. Because, like you say, why have I fought it out? But in the political class, there are grassroot BJP people whom I don't know, from all over the country. I hear people saying, there'll be some common dharna, and they'll be with other parties and our party people and they'll all mention that *dekho Jayaji ek hi hai jinho neh inkeh samneh himmat karkeh lada* [look, Jayaji is the only one who faced them with courage and fought]. This is how I'm viewed in political circles. I don't care either way. I did it because I felt I had to do it that way. George Sahab didn't say get up and fight. He did what he had to do, left me to do what I wanted to do.

Madhu: In his cross-examination before the Commission, George's stand was very different from yours. He basically told them, this is my position, you do what you like. Whereas, you went into very detailed explanations and defence of your actions.

Jaitly: That was because I was asked to, because I'd taken up that fight right from the beginning. And as you could perhaps see, it was most visible on my tape. But, otherwise, I don't know. I just felt that these allegations really hurt. So when something hurts, you want to argue it out. You have to explain that look, for instance, why should people question why I'm here? People question why is this house used? Now I can argue at length on that. Why should it not be? These are public houses, public money, it's for public work. If we had a big fat family like Laloo's and everyone sat here in all the rooms, was that better?

I don't believe so. I believe that's also a part of the socialist thinking. Lohia always says to have twenty children with your legitimate wife, it might just be worse than having one child with an illegitimate thing. If you care for that woman and you give her respect and you produce only one child, isn't it better than disrespecting your wife and having so many children? So politically, that's how we think. Ideologically that's how we think. So for him this house is not for his personal comfort. It's always been there for Tibetan, Burmese, this that, thousand and one people who want to use this address for any *andolan* [movement] can do so. I believe Indian politics of the freedom movement variety accepts that. It's only the new variety of modern thing, that you must have a fancy house and have it all wood-panelled and have lots of ...

Madhu: Potpourri?

Jaitly: [Laughs.] *Haan* [Yes]. For that, they find it funny it's like this.

⌐

During her cross-examination, Jaya was asked 322 questions, Mathew Samuel 5044, Aniruddha Bahal 5016, Tarun Tejpal 2149. The Union of India lawyers did not question Jaya at all. Bangaru Laxman was asked 186 questions, George Fernandes 150. Doesn't that just say it all?

It was impossible to ignore facts as I dug them up. Facts that would not wear well with Jaya. When I began investigating how the sex tapes story by Anjali Mody appeared in *The Indian Express* (22 August 2001), it was personally confirmed to me that one of Jaya Jaitly's lawyers, who had been a college mate of Anjali Mody's husband, planted the story. Jaya told me she knew nothing about it:

> Vaguely, I heard, that some tapes had been given to the army, right in the beginning, which had been put a lid on. That's all I had heard. But then suddenly we see this transcript coming out in the newspaper with all this foul stuff and in fact, I believe, I was asked in that Sab TV programme whether I had leaked it. I didn't even know about it, let alone leak it. I wouldn't have leaked it. I would have had a big press conference and said, "Look what they've done."

Tough to believe that the lawyers who were with her all the time would have failed to inform her about the sex tapes and their subsequent action. When I questioned Shekhar Gupta, editor-in-chief of The Indian Express Group, he told me, as any hardcore journalist would, 'A story is a story at that point. It doesn't matter where it comes from.' Agreed, no problem. But, it does give you an indication of the kind of information war that was being fought on all fronts.

Then there are discrepancies in the Gopal Pacherwal account. In his deposition before the Commission, Pacherwal said he could not recall whether he was there or not. A man in a kurta pyjama, who intriguingly does look like Gopal Pacherwal, is addressed repeatedly as 'Gopalji' in the Operation West End tapes. Jaya said he was not there. She insisted she would not speak to him in English. She said she was addressing Samuel when she said that the money should be sent to Srinivas Prasad. Jaya said the tapes were patched together from some other day. Then Tehelka made the horrifying error by initially identifying the person in the room as Srinivas Prasad, who had a clear alibi of his party work activities in other towns on those dates. In an interview, Arun Jaitley said,

> The next day [after the Tehelka exposé] I got through to Jaya Jaitly and George Fernandes. Jaya came and saw the tapes and was hysterical. I called Srinivas Prasad to check with him if he had been in the room with Jaya on that day. Fortunately, there was a record of his whereabouts on that day. He was in his constituency on December 28. There was a party conference in Bangalore on January 9 and 10, which he had gone to organize. Then he got some ailment and was in Mysore and then Bangalore. He only came to Delhi on February 23. So there were records of his tour programme. Srinivas Prasad then addressed a press conference along with Venkaiah Naidu and told the press about his whereabouts on those dates.

Tehelka then said, 'Our transcripts were wrong. It was actually Gopal Pacherwal.' In Arun Jaitley's Rashomon, he said,

> There are two conclusions one can come to. One: Jaya said, "Send it to Srinivas Prasad" so it is clear it was meant for the party. Second: if somebody offers a donation through Gopal Pacherwal to be sent to Srinivas Prasad, you have a party president collecting money only for the party. Technically, Jaya did nothing wrong.

In Tehelka's Rashomon: yes, but what was she doing collecting money from a supposed arms dealer in the defence minister's house and promising to help them with a defence contract?

In Jaya's Rashomon: the house is used as the Samata Party office and no company by the name of West End was mentioned. She offered to help if they had been treated unfairly, as one would help any of the people who come to her for help on many different issues.

Later, when Tehelka corrected the identification of the man in Jaya's room as Gopal Pacherwal, Jaya totally denied it. Then who was the individual in the kurta in the tapes? It had to have been somebody in the Samata Party. Why did he not come forward, tell the truth, and clear the air? Jaya's answer to this turned out to be just so politically incorrect, 'So many men in kurta pyjamas come and go. They all look alike.' When you see people in your scenery as all looking alike, they don't exist as individuals. When told it was difficult to believe that with all her resources she could not trace who the mystery man was, Jaya got terribly upset. Jaya raved:

> Who on earth do I ask to come forward and admit he was there? I do not sit in splendid isolation. People come and go. It was so long ago, how would

one remember? How would he remember and then come forward? It is unfortunate that wretched face is not shown properly.

What about the possibility that the man sitting next to her took the money and kept it, which precluded him coming forward. Jaya was adamant: 'If I said, "Send it to Srinivas Prasad" it was to Mathew Samuel. There is no question of any of our people swiping the money.'

Then there were Jaya's repeated applications to the Commission of Inquiry demanding a forensic examination of the Operation West End tapes. This was rejected three times by Justice Venkataswami. This issue created the maximum confusion in the Commission. Tehelka never denied editing the tapes. Yes, the editing was slanted to prove the corruption network, but there is a long stretch between inventing people and creating their actions on the tapes, specially the army officers. As far as Mathew Samuel was concerned, he said, 'Then another one, this Jaya Jaitly trying to send this tape to forensic exam. She knew everything that is the truth. In my mind, I got my day. I don't have any problem.'

On 28 May 2003, the first order Justice Phukan passed after replacing Justice Venkataswami was to send 16 Tehelka tapes to the UK for forensic examination. One of Jaya's lawyers said rather smugly: 'If the tapes are found to be tampered with, then the entire case against Bangaru Laxman, Jaya Jaitly and others will fall flat on its face.' Yes, fine, but what happens if the forensic examination finds that the tapes have not been tampered with? He looked puzzled for a second, as if the thought had never occurred to him, and then said in a quiet tone, 'Then there will be a problem'. More important, are you seeking to win a case on a technicality or is the Commission of Inquiry there to unearth the truth? There is a great qualitative difference between lawyers winning a case in a regular court of law and the purpose of the Commission of Inquiry. In the Commission, truth is the issue, not who wins. What would matter to journalists and editors is whether a law of precedence is being created; that it is possible to create enough legal confusion to completely destroy any truthful journalistic investigation on legal technicalities. Why, for example, did the Army Court of Inquiry not entertain such fanciful proposals? The army officers deposing at the Commission were openly hopeful that if the forensic examination results proved that the tapes were doctored, they could use the evidence in the Army Court of Inquiry. If you read the transcripts of the Army Court of Inquiry, it was conducted in a manner that brooked no nonsense from the officers and mocked their excuses. When the tapes were first exposed, none of the officers claimed they were doctored. This happened only when Milin Kapoor (freelance film-maker) raised the issue with Jaya and then Jaya herself, on careful scrutiny of the tapes, felt that the words 'two lakhs *doh* [two]' and 'West End' were subsequently inserted. Knowing Samuel, it was also highly likely that in his nervousness he forgot to say 'two lakhs' when he handed the packet over and said it when he was about to leave, when he remembered. The increase in audio volume of those words would be because he turned his face downwards to get the mike in his tie to record them. It is possible, but, yes, it is also possible that he altogether forgot to say 'two lakhs', and then it could be said that he handed over nothing more than a packet of *mithai*. It is conceivable that those words could have been inserted later when Tehelka realized Samuel had forgotten. Obviously, however, if the tape was doctored, it would have been placed when he was handing over the packet. Besides, there are some facts that even Jaya cannot dispute, which are: Samuel was in the room with Jaya. That was not doctored. He did offer her a packet. That was not doctored. There was money in it or Jaya would not have gone into the long explanation she did on how the Samata Party was going to use the money. So, it was money. That was not doctored. The amount of money could have been questioned. The fact that Jaya did see Samuel without knowing who he was and take 'some' money from him, albeit not directly, but even taking her word as she says, she asked for it to be sent to Srinivas Prasad. Whether she said it to Gopal Pacherwal as Samuel claims or to Samuel himself as Jaya claims, remains a question, but immaterial. Money was accepted for the use of the Samata Party from unknown persons.

Jaya's behaviour in public fora has been puzzling. In a question-answer session at the annual India Today Conclave (2001), she asked Al Gore (former US Vice President), what should be done to root out corruption in public life. The question raised loud titters from the audience. It was an unnecessary question that drew embarrassing attention to her. In NDTV's 'The Big Fight' she was put in an awkward position when she raised questions about the press's integrity and Shekhar Gupta (*The Indian Express*) responded with, 'How can a politician who has been taped taking money from a supposed arms dealer raise these questions? Why should the press not report it?' I believe her behaviour can be explained if you understand how Jaya views herself. She knows she is scrupulously honest; is functioning as she has always functioned. Although obsessed with Tehelka, she still has the passion for social activism ingrained in her and she has harnessed all of that zeal in her battle with Tehelka. Her email activities in relation to the lawyers, which Jaya termed her 'sting operation', smacked of revenge.

Of all those caught in the Operation West End sting, Jaya was the only one who worked on discrediting the Tehelka journalists. She said,

> **Jaitly:** Not only did the government not fall but they got this pest, Jaya Jaitly, who is pursuing them relentlessly, to show that what they did was a fraud. I can't sit back and say that I'm holier-than-thou. Why should I answer and I've done it perfectly. But that doesn't put them in the dock. Politically my battle is to fight against people who do wrong against our government or our country. I think they've done wrong. They've done it right across the world. *The New York Times*, the first time ever had India on its front page, on something nasty like this. The whole world was made to believe that the defence establishment, including from the prime minister downwards, is corrupt. Of course, there is corruption in every establishment. But if you are going to say that these people exposed, from the prime minister to George Fernandes to his inner coterie, then you cannot have that happen. Somebody has to fight back. Since I found most people incapable, for lack of understanding or lack of interest, I just took this up as a cause that it was my political battle.
>
> **Madhu:** Your aggressive defence, debunking the tapes and all that makes you appear far more involved and guilty than you probably are.

Jaitly: I don't know if it makes me look guilty. I don't care about that.

Madhu: If you say that this is what I said and that's that. Nobody can question it and there it ends, but the fact that you have been aggressively working to show that the tapes are doctored only raises more questions about what you did.

Jaitly: I still say even today that my attempt to get the tapes examined is not in my defence. If the tapes come back saying they weren't doctored, I don't think it shakes my defence at all. So I'm not concerned, but I don't want Tehelka to get away. If I kept quiet, the army officers were like stunned rabbits. They're scared, because their whole lives have crashed. They only have one kind of a life. Bangaru Laxman is a political person, he looks at himself as Rajya Sabha or not, or Dalit or not. For him, politics is everything. They don't have much other dimension other than their position in society and their position in the party. But somebody like me, I feel that I'm not that kind of a politician that I can just shrug off an accusation and not bother about the way these people have made that accusation. If political people [had] made this accusation about me I wouldn't mind. I know how to fight that back and I wouldn't bother. There are a thousand things I don't bother about. But the meticulous way in which they have claimed that what they've done is correct and the way that they have gone on every public platform all around the world, talking about how disgusting the system is in India. How they broke us all down and how they've exposed this "venal underbelly". The words that they used, I just can't stomach from people claiming to be investigative journalists. They can say we are your enemies, therefore we say, fine, we are your political opponents and we say, fine. But you can't sit on the high horse they are sitting on, claiming credibility from that high horse; then I have to demolish their credibility. Because as I've been arguing even otherwise, videotapes are a very important thing. It's a systemic change that I also want. I want that from now on, any videotape, whether it's a Mayawati one or an Osama or a Saddam or anything, we should have a system. We don't even have a system in this country. We don't have the state of the art facilities to forensically examine videotapes. Our forensic laboratories are only up to voice recognition. For Rs 10 lakhs or maybe all together in a combination it comes to Rs 42 lakhs, you can set up a basic facility in India and train people to do this. With tapes being used, more and more, for all kinds of things, including traffic violations, we need this facility in India.

Madhu: The implication here is that Jaya Jaitly is seeking forensic examination to prove that the tapes have been doctored, it is because she's denying she has taken money.

Jaitly: No, no. See, where is it doctored that I have said? Two lakh and West End. Right? My point at that is that, for one: no money was ever mentioned. I had no discussion about money. Two: nobody ever mentioned any company's name. So I had no awareness that I was meeting, had given an interview to or appointment to any West End company. It was to answer only those two questions that I'm saying they had some mala fide intention, in wanting to show that I had already pre-arranged and that I already routinely take money. That I very well know that it's Rs 2 lakhs that I've swallowed. To show that, they have put these two things in. So then it becomes important. What are they trying to say about me and do about me? It's not just that I am clean. It's that they are rotten.

How much of Jaya's behaviour stemmed from revenge and teaching Tehelka a lesson? In February 2003, University of Arkansas psychologists Julia Steel and David Schroeder presented results of their research [Study titled: *The Effects of Counterfactual Thinking and Outcome Closeness on Post-Decisional Reactions in Social Dilemmas*] on 'revenge' and cautioned that one should beware of the one who seeks revenge because these people want to do more than just settle the score. 'When someone has "done you wrong", there's both an emotional and behavioural reaction,' said Schroeder. 'People feel compelled to restore justice, and that's what to human nature, serving its own dark but necessary purpose.'

'I think people use retribution to teach others about appropriate behaviour,' said Steel. 'Maybe it's not our best quality as human beings, but it isn't done purely out of cruelty or malice. It has its own function within society.' History and literature are replete with many examples of revenge going awry and destroying the person as he seeks to annihilate the perpetrator. The revenger's tragedy.

At a press conference on 26 November 2002, Jaya Jaitly announced her own purported sting operation which she had carried out on the lawyers for both Tehelka and the Commission. Jaya said it all began when she filed a writ petition in the High Court asking the court to direct the Commission to send the tapes for forensic examination and that she should be allowed to depose after the Tehelka journalists (which was ultimately decided against her). She thought it would be unfair if she deposed first and then Tehelka journalists got away with all their allegations. In the High Court, in August, Jaya said she noticed that the Commission's counsel and the Tehelka lawyers came in together, would sit together, talk to each other, and carry each other's books. In fact, the Tehelka lawyers and Commission lawyers were sitting together because both were on the RESPONDENT side and were required to sit on the left of the court room facing the judge as per the norms of the High Court. According to Jaya, 'If you're on the Commission's side, then you can't be every day interacting with the lawyers of the people whom you're inquiring into.' When it was pointed out that there was no rule in the Bar Council of India ethics barring this, Jaya insisted, 'You're not even supposed to talk to each other and meet. They didn't even have the courtesy to look our way or greet us or anything.' She also noticed that the lawyers were constantly whispering to each other and Prashant Bhushan (Tehelka's lawyer) would often assist the Commission lawyers on facts. Jaya said she got suspicious of their behaviour and asked her lawyer to ask them for their telephone numbers and addresses. Now this is odd since all the lawyers' addresses were on record in the pleadings and were public knowledge.

Apart from that, all the lawyers met outside the Commission for lunch and tea, and talked to each other irrespective of whom they were representing. Quite a few of them had worked together and even during the Commission and had non-conflicting assignments together. According to Sidharth Luthra, Siddharth Aggarwal had worked with him from July 1998 to June 2000. Aggarwal had joined a corporate law firm for a year and then joined Gopal Subramaniam in 2001. Luthra said, 'My addresses were recorded in the High Court, Supreme Court and Tis Hazari directories. My sister had been her lawyer for some years and we (my sister and I) shared a chamber in the High Court. So what was there to investigate on my addresses?'

According to Jaya, she then sent someone on her staff to that address, pretending to look for a job. In Jaya's Rashomon, he asked for Luthra Associates and was told that this was only the branch office and the main office was in Defence Colony. According to the lawyers' Rashomon, no such thing happened. Aggarwal did not have an office at home, though his doctor parents had a small clinic (his parents are specialists in paediatrics and gynaecology). Sidharth Luthra had no branch offices except a chamber in Tis Hazari and in the High Court and an office at his residence. Incidentally the same office from where his late father had defended George Fernandes 25 years earlier. Jaya said then she got one of the 'colleagues' to phone Aggarwal's number. He spoke to Dr Vijay Aggarwal, father of Siddharth Aggarwal, pretending he was from a law firm in Dubai. Jaya's 'colleague' told Dr Aggarwal that his clients wanted to set up a hospice in Haryana. While talking to him about the possibility of the project, he also asked Dr Aggarwal for legal advice and whether Siddharth Aggarwal and Sidharth Luthra worked together. Dr Aggarwal replied that they were not partners but they had worked together in the past. Dr Aggarwal then gave him Siddharth Aggarwal's email address for further questions. Jaya then followed through by sending an email to Siddharth Aggarwal and asked for a firm profile. In response to the mail, the firm's profile was sent as an attachment. In that profile, Sidharth Luthra was listed as one of the two partners of the firm, while Siddharth Aggarwal only as an associate along with a dozen other lawyers. According to the lawyers, there was no reference of Siddharth Aggarwal's residence as a branch office. Yet for Jaya, this was enough to assume that there was collusion between the Commission counsel and Tehelka lawyers. Jaya said,

> I showed it to some important people in the government that somewhere they were being advised wrongly. Somewhere we are getting the short end of the stick. It's not fair or legally functioning correctly [the Commission of Inquiry]. Everybody sat still and looked the other way and looked back at me and that was it.

Jaya's reaction began when she read a report in *The Times of India* that the government itself had sabotaged the position of Judge Venkataswami, the judge presiding over the Tehelka Commission, because George Fernandes and other government people would be indicted. Jaya insisted she knew that this report was incorrect and untrue. She believed that the Commission lawyers had leaked these stories. So, Jaya retaliated: 'They were leaking wrong information to the public. I thought the only way to stop it, was to blow these lawyers up. That is when I summoned the press and gave all this proof of the email.' The manner in which lawyers for the Commission had aggressively interrogated Jaya, obviously doubting her statements, could not have played a small part in Jaya's need to expose them. Jaya said that she suspected 'something funny was going on behind the scenes'. She was highly suspicious of the Commission lawyers because, as she saw it, ministry officials were interrogated aggressively on 14 defence deals and errors in tape transcription were not corrected. The Commission lawyers did not interrogate Tarun Tejpal extensively, and that certainly rankled Jaya. Since Tejpal had taken the stand that it was Aniruddha's project, he was not aware of the details. Jaya was confused why the Commission lawyers were not sensitive to her and the defence ministry's defence. Perhaps the theory that the government had decided to let Jaya and George hang while protecting their own has some credence.

Well, Jaya could congratulate herself on her sting operation, as she called it, but it did not create a drop of anxiety amongst the lawyers she targeted. The Commission's counsel, Gopal Subramaniam, calmly confirmed that Siddharth Aggarwal had been his chamber junior for the past year and there was no question of his working for some other firm or lawyer. Does Jaya really believe that lawyers get emotionally involved and identify with the client's cause? Lawyers accept the brief given to them. Often, lawyers who are close to each other find themselves adversaries in some cases and working as a team in others. Tehelka's lawyer Sidharth Luthra pointed out, 'In the public domain lawyers regularly fight cases against each other and at other times work with each other. I had been on cases with some of the counsel who were appearing for noticees in the Commission even in the last one year while the Tehelka Commission proceedings were going on. Ms Jaitly's allegations are incorrect.' The reason why nobody in government took any action was because they did not really see it as an issue. More than anything else, it showed how the Tehelka issue consumed Jaya's inner being in a way we typically think of as revenge. The need for revenge seems to be intrinsically linked

In May 2004, the BJP government lost the elections and a Congress Party led alliance, UPA (United Progressive Alliance), was sworn into power. Equations quickly changed in the Commission of Inquiry as well as how the new government would view the Tehelka question. H.R. Bhardwaj, the law minister of the UPA government, announced on 4 October 2004 that the Commission of Inquiry on Tehelka would not be given an extension and the CBI would now investigate the Tehelka case. Bhardwaj also brought up the issue of a 'private person' functioning in the defence minister's home. Jaya was outraged and called a press conference on 6 October 2004. She demanded an apology from the law minister. Jaya ranted,

> If I don't demand an apology, what else do I do? Acknowledge and accept it? He has raised questions about my character. He neither knows the facts nor the law. He doesn't have the decency on how to address a woman who has been the president of a party in a coalition government. So to call such a person a "private person", so then who is public and who is private? What

about the private person in her party who lived in Indira Gandhi's house for 15 years and did all kinds of things. She was the director of Maruti, running an insurance business. So you put her in India's electoral rolls so she becomes an Indian citizen? That's all okay but here, I am doing social work with craftsmen. Every member of Parliament's house is used by many people for all kinds of work. In Ram Vilas Paswan's house a magazine *Naya Chakra* is being produced. What all goes on? When Sonia Gandhi was in the Opposition her house was used for all kinds of work. Members of Parliament's houses are public houses for everybody to use. That is what they are meant for: to do social work. I come here in the morning, do my work and leave in the evening. And he calls that living here? Such words coming from the law minister are not acceptable.

An irate Jaya walked into the house after the press conference and rather prima donna-ishly said, 'Let's have some tea. Nobody is going to give us any? For all my pains I am not even getting a cup of tea.' Now we were back to the same issue: where did Jaya Jaitly live? While sipping her tea, Jaya said,

One of the reasons for him saying that we are giving it to the CBI is because a private person staying in the defence minister's house is conducting defence deals. I don't say don't look into defence deals. I am saying that don't term me as a private person staying here. He ought to know that. He can't be such a, you know, pig, that you don't care what women are all about. You can just call them anything and do anything just for your own political thing. If you call Sonia Gandhi a foreigner, it's the biggest abuse on earth. But you can say I am a private person. What does that mean? Just tell me. Perhaps he was being subtle otherwise it would have been some cheap word. But when a person is a president of a party, you don't call them a private person. Either he is ignorant or he was purposely denigrating and defaming me. Everybody knows that I don't stay here. I work here like everybody else works her. Just like people go and work in Sonia Gandhi's house and people work in every member of Parliament's house. They aren't all termed as staying there.

I cautioned Jaya that she was over-reacting to an issue that would only draw greater attention to it. Jaya said, 'I don't care what the media says. I just wanted to tick him [the law minister] off. The media is irrelevant to me. After all that they have said and done about all these things, if they are not willing to correct themselves I am not going to change.'

I told her she could have reporters staking her out every night to see where she actually lived. I was wrong. How did the media handle this press conference? All the television channels, though present at the packed press conference, chose to ignore it in their news bulletins. Only *The Hindustan Times* carried a three-inch, two-column report on Page 15. Basically, the media showed its disinterest about where Jaya Jaitly actually spent her nights.

When the Commission of Inquiry closed down, the question remained on how Jaya would handle the issue. She said she expected the government to continue to use their party spokesmen to present their point of view and mislead people but said she had not lost her voice. She would handle it and fight when necessary. Otherwise, she would continue her work with crafts. Where did she see herself a year from now? With an easy laugh, she said,

> Never thought. Here, it's never a dull moment, in the kind of life that I've somehow got into, so I never know what's happening next week and there's no use planning it. I will say 20 times, if you like, that I am quite happy. I have nothing else to do now. I don't have to run to the Commission every day.

From 13 March 2001, everything changed in Jaya's life. From the national president of the Samata Party, she became a professional, full-time defendant. Jaya was put on Joseph Campbell's hero's journey that she would never have wanted. She was flung into an orbit of the unknown, with all its uncertainties and turbulence. Jaya was no different from Samuel, Aniruddha, and Tarun. She was also, along with the others, no different from Joseph K. in Kafka's *The Trial*. Her interior life was usurped even more violently than that of the rest, because she felt she had been trapped, misled, and would find no peace within herself until she won a 'not guilty' verdict blasted to the world.

I will risk a generalization: how many people do we come across who feel misunderstood by the world? The opinion we have of ourselves usually varies hugely from that of other people. There is nothing more discomfiting than when a person feels that he is not being seen in the way he feels he really is. Most people view themselves as kinder, much more generous, and easy-going than what other people experience of them. Once labelled by other people, it is often impossible to change other people's perceptions no matter how much a person changes or is transformed. Someone may indulge in the most cruel, ruthless action but with a 'good' reputation, people's response will be that of incredulity: 'He is not capable of doing such a thing.' Personality characteristics are not carved in stone. John Huston, playing Noah Cross in Roman Polanski's film *Chinatown* delivered the most oft-repeated quote: 'You see, Mr Gitts, most people never have to face the fact. At the right time and the right place, they're capable of … anything!' This acknowledges that all men/women have the potential to commit the most evil act. So, before judging the Tehelka team as opportunistic and sleazy or Jaya as one of the 'suitcase people', one has to block off one's preconceived notions of their character. Operation West End has to be seen in isolation. Is it possible that Jaya's own self image is so contradictory to what she saw herself doing on the tapes that she could not accept what happened? In comparison to what others said and did in Operation West End, Jaya looked like an angel. She spoke about the best price and quality being the deciding factor, taking into account the nation's interest. This was not a performance since she did not know she was being taped. Why not just acknowledge that she accepted money for the party and walk away? Why the obsessive, passionate defence? It is because it is not enough to be honest; one must ensure that one is perceived to be so.

Until the nut of the self-image fits snugly into the bolt of the public image, there can be no peace of mind.

There is also the question: When we think we know ourselves, are we deluding ourselves? How on earth can you ever know that even when you genuinely perform a good deed, especially when you are alone, are you doing it to feed your own perspective of being a good person? Is it even possible to separate the purely altruistic, when every selfless act makes you feel happy?

The only way Jaya could heal the wound in her life and soul was to fight to the end. What could be more bruising than a perpetual mindfulness that she was now viewed by the world through the prism of the Operation West End tapes: a continuing negative meditation. Everywhere she went, she could feel on her skin how they saw her. The only one thing that remained constant was the way Jaya viewed herself.

15 Who's Afraid of Shaggy (Woolf)?

But she caught me on the counter (It wasn't me)
She saw me bangin' on the sofa (It wasn't me)
I even had her in the shower (It wasn't me)
She even caught me on camera (It wasn't me)
She saw the marks on my shoulder (It wasn't me)
Hear the screams getting louder (It wasn't me)

– *Shaggy's song:* It Wasn't Me

Gopal Pacherwal, president of the Samata Party, Rajasthan, generally unknown and innocuous, proved to be the cornerstone of one of the most disputed points in the Commission. Tehelka blundered by first identifying the person present in Jaya Jaitly's room as Srinivas Prasad. When it transpired that Prasad had a documented alibi of having been in other towns during that period, Tehelka made the correction and announced the person was Gopal Pacherwal. On tape, Samuel is heard asking him where he is from and 'Gopal' says he is based in Rajasthan. So, it fits. If not, then why doesn't the real Gopal come forward? There has to be some Gopal from the Samata Party who floats around 3 Krishna Menon Marg. Why does the Samata Party not produce the Gopal who could stand as a witness and say Jaya did not take the money?

The Commission lawyers did not cross-examine Gopal Pacherwal, nor did Union of India lawyers. The only person to cross-examine him was Sidharth Luthra, Tehelka's counsel. Pacherwal's answers show how deeply caste differences are entrenched in the psyche, where every incident is viewed through the prism of caste-discrimination:

> **Luthra:** Why did you file your Statement under 5(2)(b)?
> **Pacherwal:** I filed an affidavit when I heard from the transmission things which are disparaging to me and which hurt my reputation. I belong to that class of persons who are even lower [than] the Dalits, i.e. the sweeper community, and when I found in that telecast matters which really were of disrespectful nature in relation to Mr George Fernandes who has helped my class with the upliftment programme, I thought that was my duty to place before the

honourable Commission my impression of what I found regarding this most disrespectful and disparaging telecast by whosoever did it. I belong to Maiter class and I am being persecuted by Manovadi people.

⌒

For urbane Sidharth Luthra, this was a new-fangled point. My guess is that if this were a question on *Kaun Baneyga Crorepati*, 'Which is the higher caste: Maiter or Manovadi?', Luthra would have had to ask for the help-line. A bemused Luthra ignored all the caste connotations and carried on. For high caste city people, it is a bit of, Hey, what's the problem? We are all equal. Not true in rural India. In 2008 a little Dalit girl was burnt for passing a Thakur house.

Luthra: Now please tell me in respect to para 14 of the 8B Affidavit:
"I state that since it is admitted that call girls have been used by Tehelka. com in making of Tehelka tapes and that army officers have been filmed in such activities with call girls, there can be no credible basis for any inquiry in connection with the allegations levelled through the said tapes. The blackmailing of persons through the threat of possible public disclosure of such tapes becomes a distinct possibility and given the conduct of Tehelka. com in doctoring the tapes, the honourable Commission may be pleased to dismiss the allegations levelled through the tapes in question. In this connection, I draw the attention of the honourable Commission to the fact that as on today the Tehelka.com has not handed over the entire footage of their original tapes to this honourable Commission."
Since you had not seen the unedited tapes, on what basis did you derive the knowledge of contents of this paragraph?
Pacherwal: I based the content of para 14 on the basis of newspaper publicity which was given where all the facts which I had objected to were written. Being a political person, I felt it was my duty in this time of crisis when our armed forces are stationed along the border defending the country that they should not be demoralized in the manner in which it was represented, that army officers were more keen in making merry with characters like call girls. Even the home minister's reputation was not spared in that publicity. I felt that those so-called call girls might be belonging to the lower caste and in an indirect manner, it was an attack on the chastity of the women who belong to that category and that caste and they should be punished.

⌒

Why did Pacherwal believe that the prostitutes might be from a lower caste? A sad statement that exposes more about us than Pacherwal thinks. Luthra was suspicious about Pacherwal's point in his affidavit, in which Pacherwal pointed out that the Tehelka tapes showed they were taped separately, one in daylight and one at night. It was a point made repeatedly by Jaya Jaitly's lawyers and Jaya herself. Luthra tried to prove that he had been coached by Jaya's lawyers. Pacherwal stated that he got that point from newspaper reports in *Rashtriya Sahara*. Fine, but was he there or not?

Luthra: On 28 December 2000, when Mr Surender Sureka met you, he said *"Jairamji ki Gopalji"*. Is it correct?

Pacherwal: You can put this question to Mr Surender Sureka. I do not remember.

Luthra: When Mr Surender Sureka met you on 28 December 2000, you responded to his greetings and sat down with him and had a conversation?

Pacherwal: Where did we sit?

Luthra: On 28 December, you met Mr Surender Sureka at 3, Krishna Menon Marg?

Pacherwal: Whenever I come to Delhi, I visit 3, Krishna Menon Marg. There, I meet many people. Many of them have [a] nodding acquaintance with me.

Luthra: On 28 December 2000, when you met Mr Surendra Sureka, Mr Mathew Samuel and General Murgai at 3, Krishna Menon Marg, your conversation and meeting were recorded and you have been shown in Tape no. 73.

Pacherwal: It is quite possible as I frequently visit 3, Krishna Menon Marg. That on 28 December, I might have been there and [was] caught in any of the pictures but I do not know anybody by the name of Samuel Mathew or General Murgai. If casually anybody had taken that shot, it can be possible. I may have greeted them. I do not know.

Luthra: On 28 December 2000, at 3, Krishna Menon Marg, you were present when the packet of Rs 2 lakh was prepared by Mathew Samuel under the instructions of Mr Surendra Sureka?

Pacherwal: It is not correct.

Luthra: On 28 December 2000, you were present at 3, Krishna Menon Marg when in response to Madam Jaya Jaitly's statement, *"ab khatra hai tab bolna ke 'aoji, khulla hai aao ji …'* [when there is danger, say 'come in, it is open, come in', you said, *'haan, usse kafi* [yes, that is sufficient]*."* This conversation was in relation to the articles in the press regarding the defence minister's house being an open house, and you had this discussion with Ms Jaya Jaitly on 28 December 2000.

Pacherwal: There is no question of any newspaper reports that it is an open house. Everybody knows that it is an open house.

Luthra: On 28 December 2000, when Mr Surendra Sureka talked about beginning some industry, you said, *"subhey maine bataya* [in the morning I told you]*"* in response to what Mr Sureka said.

Pacherwal: I have got nothing to do with industries and I do not know anything about industries. I am not a businessman. I do not recollect.

Luthra: On 28 December, you were sitting on that day in that room, and while you were sitting, Mathew Samuel handed over a packet containing Rs 2 lakh, which was taken in your possession?

Pacherwal: I did not accompany these people to Mrs Jaya Jaitly's room. I did not receive any packet of money. I do not know any one of them. This is not a correct story. I deny it. No packet was given to me or handed over to me or in my presence.

Luthra: On 28 December 2000, when the packet was offered, Mrs Jaya Jaitly said, "*Gopalji, ise rakh leejiye* [Gopalji, keep this]" and you accepted the amount of Rs 2 lakhs.

Pacherwal: I was not in that meeting and this is not correct. If Mrs Jaya Jaitly has said this, ask her. I was not there in that meeting. There might be some other Gopal. I am not that Gopal. If this sentence has been uttered, I am not that Gopal. Jayaji is elder to me. She would not say, "Gopalji". She addresses me as "Gopal" and not "Gopalji". I am in age younger to her. Same is with George. He also never addresses me as "Gopalji". He addresses me as "Gopal". We respect age in our party.

Luthra: What is your age?

Pacherwal: I am 53 years complete.

Yes, boss, but your answers and story are very incomplete, *yaar*. Who was this Gopalji, then? Incidentally, Jaya in her deposition stated that Gopal Pacherwal was senior to her and she would never order him to take money like that. The only-in-India-moment here is, Gopal's testimony rests on the respectful term '*ji*' which he says she would never call his name with! How does one crack this? In the tapes, everybody addresses the man in the kurta as Gopalji, he looks like Gopalji, he walks like Gopalji, talks like Gopalji, so he really was Shaggy.

Gopal Pacherwal, along with Surendra Sureka and Jaya Jaitly, was charged with corruption by the CBI on 6 December 2004.

16 The Minister's Last Sigh

Mujhe kharidne wala koi paida nahin hua hain. Main sari zindagi bhrastachar ke khilaf lada hoon [*there is no one born who can buy me. I have fought corruption all my life*].
– *George Fernandes in the Lok Sabha on 18 August 2003*

George Fernandes's life has always been a juxtaposition of contradictions. He studied to become a priest, but unsubstantiated gossip points to his personal life being not too Catholic. In 1974, as president of the All India Railwaymen's Federation, George led a railway strike with 1.5 million workers participating. Fifteen years later, ironically, he became minister for railways (1989-90). The strike was one of the events that triggered Indira Gandhi's imposition of the Emergency in June 1975. George then went underground to fight against Emergency rule. He was arrested in June 1976 on charges of attempting to overthrow the government, and the case became famous as the Baroda Dynamite Conspiracy. He stood for election from jail and won his second term in the Lok Sabha. Later, when he was minister for industries from 1977 and 1979, he was responsible for throwing Coca Cola and IBM out of India. He is an avowed socialist, but he was at that time in a coalition government, allied to a party that aggressively believed in capitalism. Fernandes was defence minister in 2001 and part of a government that ironically heralded foreign investment and welcomed multinationals like Coca Cola and IBM. Like any good peacenik, a photograph of devastated Hiroshima hung in his office. He has campaigned against nuclear weapons all his life, yet he was India's defence minister when India tested nuclear bombs in Phokran. If all that isn't enough, Fernandes has written three books: *What Ails the Socialists; Railway Strike of 1974*; and *George Fernandes Speaks*.

When asked about her relationship with George, Jaya Jaitly said, 'I love him but lots of people love him'. A senior minister in the BJP government told me, 'Everybody loves George', and this is true. He is an extremely likable man. Even Shankar Sharma laughed when he spoke of George: 'He has got a point, *yaar*. He has all my sympathies. If somebody did that to your girlfriend, trapped her, of course it will make you angry.' George's unflinching simple way of living, without any pomp and protocol endears him to people. It is true that anyone can walk into his house. He washes his own clothes every morning, which for some reason, I find disturbing. Shouldn't every minute of his life be focused on India's defence? It could, of course, be his form of meditation. Fernandes's visits to jawans in border areas, and particularly to Siachen, have endeared him to the rank and file. He eschews any motorcade, likes to ride in any army truck and eat with the jawans. George has the distinction of having the highest record of any defence minister for the number of visits he has logged to Siachen. Visiting that ice-bound border is no trip to Goa. It is a physically gruelling and debilitating place.

Now, despite a stellar reputation for integrity, he was now under a cloud of corruption of the worst kind. Tehelka said that their investigation led them right up to the defence minister. In truth, their investigation led them to his address, not him. Fernandes never met them and was not in any way involved in the corruption found on the tapes. The question is, do you find him responsible if money is taken for his political party in his house, from unknown donors? Even R.K. Jain, treasurer of the Samata Party, who initially gossiped about him in the Operation West End tapes, ended up saying: 'George won't take money. He won't take money.' There were stories of quite a bit of dissent in the Commission on whether to issue a notice to George Fernandes at all, as some felt there was no basis to do so.

On 13 March 2001, George Fernandes had roster duty in the Lok Sabha and sat on the front bench. He noticed that Congress party member and chief whip in the Lok Sabha, Priya Ranjan Dasmunsi, got up and left the hall. A few minutes later, Das Munshi ran back, waving a file folder, shouting: *'Ho gaya, ho gaya, sarkar khatam ho gaya, chala gaya* [it's happened, it's happened, the government is finished, it is gone]'. George said, 'It didn't make any sense to me but I kept looking at what he was carrying in his hands. That also did not make any sense. In the meanwhile, I get a small slip from the official gallery, and that is from my private secretary: 'Please come to the office, something serious has happened.' George was informed that a defence scandal was being broadcast on television. When he reached his South Block office, Operation West End was being broadcast on TV, he said, 'The whole thing as it was being shown made me feel that there is an attack on my ministry. And an attack on my ministry is an attack on me also.'

Ministers sent messages to Fernandes, from a normally scheduled Cabinet meeting at 7.00 p.m., to show up but he didn't want to go until he had figured out what the exposé was about. He sent a message back that he was busy 'with something on TV' and it would take some time. When Fernandes arrived at the meeting, the Cabinet wanted to hear his explanation of what was being broadcast. Fernandes said he told Prime Minister Vajpayee that he would resign immediately because he wanted to step outside his ministry 'to fight it out'. According to Fernandes, 'As if everyone had earlier decided to make a statement to me, collectively everyone said, no way, you cannot resign. We are all in it together. We will fight it out.' But I continued to tell Atalji, "No, this is a very big matter and that I have to stand outside and fight it out".' Vajpayee did not accept the resignation at that meeting.

Why did Fernandes offer to resign when he was not personally caught in the sting operation?

Fernandes recalled,

Fernandes: Everyone, my colleagues, told me that I should not resign. Colleagues in the government told me there is no reason for you to resign. My party president was Jaya Jaitly at the time. She told me: why should you resign? But by now there was an orchestration by the other side; that is, by the Congress, the Marxists, and such others allied to them. It started with the government should resign. I was not prepared that this government should go and I decided that I shall resign and fight it out. Because I knew that there was nothing in it and all that I needed to do was present the facts and that was all.

Madhu: Did you resign because you felt that if you didn't the government would fall?

Fernandes: The government was under attack from all of them. The fellow who came running in, *subh khatam ho gaya, government chala gaya, koi nahi bacha sakta* [everything is over, the government has gone, no one can save it].

Madhu: You thought that to save the government your resignation was necessary?

Fernandes: Absolutely.

Madhu: And in retrospect you feel that it was a mistake to resign because it undermined your ability to fight back?

Fernandes: It undermined the fight back, hurt a lot of people who should not have been hurt, one of them being Jaya Jaitly. She was the president of the party. There was pressure on her that she should also resign. And I do feel that.

Madhu: Why did the Samata Party not support Jaya in this fight? There were no demonstrations or support.

Fernandes: There was no support for her and, by and large, everyone tried to keep their hands off this.

Madhu: Why? After all it was your party and she was one of its prominent members.

Fernandes: Yes, I feel that there are people who do not like women in politics. Jaya's capabilities, her competence, her understanding of political minds, all these were not to the liking of people. I cannot think of any other reason why everyone should have turned their backs.

Madhu: You have been the president of the Samata Party until you were appointed defence minister. One would think that the party would do whatever you told them. Did you not tell them to organize demonstrations of support?

Fernandes: In that sense some of them spoke in Parliament. Outside Parliament there were people who stood up, but it was not adequate. Also, the closest of my colleagues believed that I must have made money. Congressmen and

Marxists and such other characters who are accustomed to making money and therefore must be thinking that everyone must be making money. I can understand such people. But people who were very close to me, in the socialist movement for years together who had worked with me, worked under me, when they thought I had made money ….

Madhu: So you felt betrayed?

Fernandes: Betrayed is not the word. I can never forget this.

Madhu: Devastated?

Fernandes: That's the word; that my own colleagues should talk such rubbish.

Madhu: In the Samata Party?

Fernandes: In the Samata Party and in the socialist movement. The entire socialist movement. Shows how fragile relationships are. How people crowd around you when they think you are powerful and when someone makes a charge against you that is totally beyond all imagination, they go by that. They take the word of the enemy as the right word and they attack you or they run away from you.

Madhu: So you would say that this incident has actually been a watershed in your personal life as well. It has changed you?

Fernandes: It has, it has.

Madhu: In what way?

Fernandes: In the sense that I have always been a frontline fighter, and for the last three years am being written about as a tainted person. Right across the world this word has gone. Your capability to do what you wish to do and what you need to do has been affected to a very great extent.

Madhu: Do you find that you trust people less?

Fernandes: Unfortunately I place a lot of trust in my colleagues, my friends, people whom I might have just got acquainted with. I take people at their face value. That's why I have suffered quite often. I go all out to solve their problems and then I have to take the blows, which I have done and continue to do. I cannot change myself.

Madhu: Having been disillusioned, why have you not changed?

Fernandes: I cannot change my character or my thinking process. I trust people because I believe that trust begets trust. But we are running through experiences when that trust is betrayed. But next time around with that betrayal, you may let go. Another person comes with another problem and you repose trust in that person and carry on doing what you should be doing for that person, you may again run into that same situation. And I have run into such situations. The most important point is I felt so betrayed by my own colleagues, my socialist colleagues, the way they went about making statements. The way they went about treating me as someone who has betrayed them. The betrayal was on their part.

Madhu: You are upset that they believed it but when one reads or watches R.K. Jain's statements in Operation West End, the descriptions are so vivid. The reason why they believed it was because of the way R.K. Jain described his meetings with you and the Russians. It would be difficult to imagine that he could invent so much information on procurement. He has this Russian guy's conversations with you in minute detail.

Fernandes: That man was never allowed to be with me anywhere even for a minute. He was the treasurer of the Party, and that's about all. In the defence ministry there are a whole lot of people. People have access to someone inside. What about this very Tehelka; people who had nothing to do with the Ministry of Defence went deep into it, did they not?

Madhu: Isn't it the treasurer's job to accept money for the party?

Fernandes: Treasurer's job is to accept money for the party, naturally, but it is not the only job. The treasurer's essential job is to keep accounts. And if someone is coming and giving, to collect it and keep it and keep accounts. That's the treasurer's job in the constitution of the party. But the treasurer's job does not permit anyone to go on interfering with the work he is not expected to do. That is not the job given to him.

Madhu: Would you say that it is acceptable for the president of the Samata Party to accept money for the party in your house?

Fernandes: Yes, it is legal. It is absolutely legal. For that matter, any person in the political party. When I go on tours, at the end of the day, at the end of a meeting, or where I have gone to attend a function, at the end of the function when anyone says "I have this cheque, this money for your party," I collect it. As minister of defence I never went asking for money at any given time. I kept my distance.

Madhu: Do you think that Jaya might have been wiser to check Operation West End's antecedents before accepting the money?

Fernandes: Jaya also has this sense of wanting to help people and that's it. Most of her life has been related to being with people who are in distress. Her work among the artisans, the craftsmen or her work during the time [when] the Sikhs were subjected to a pogrom right here in the city of New Delhi. She spent God knows how many months with them, looking after them and thereafter, when she found that nobody is now willing to pursue that case. I don't know how much of her time and resources she has devoted. So that is her personality. And you see how they tricked her and despite their tricking her what did she say? What did she do? She didn't touch the money; that's there on tape. She didn't say, I will settle your problem, don't worry. She didn't say that. Every word she uttered, I must have said or written those words to thousands of people in my life.

Madhu: But Jaya said that if any injustice was being done she would speak to George Sahab. I'll send the word down.

Fernandes: I don't think she said that I'll speak to George Sahab. I don't think so. She must have said that I'll tell his staff to speak to him. If my memory is right. It's part of the record. If it's there, it's fair enough. I don't think speaking to me is an offence.

Madhu: The issue that has been raised is that Jaya is interfering in matters in the defence ministry.

Fernandes: Let them provide an iota of evidence that she has interfered in the matters of defence. They are a bunch of liars. A bunch of perverted people.

Madhu: There is a big difference in Jaya's case in the Operation West End tapes and the army officers who were seen taking money, giving documents and fooling around with prostitutes. Why are you clubbing the defence of the army officers with Jaya's case, when they are clearly guilty?

Fernandes: The army goes by its own law, the Army Act. The night of the so-called exposé, I spent the whole night in my office. All the names that had appeared, I had them summoned. Whether they were in uniform or they were in civil clothes. I had them summoned. One of them gave in writing a long statement that so and so came to me and made such and such a proposal and I told him that this cannot be done, this item has been closed. Nevertheless he offered me a lakh of rupees and I have taken that lakh of rupees. One of them gave me in writing in these words. They went to people's houses and offered them women, prostitutes. And nobody seemed to be bothered about that. The fact that here are a bunch of people who claim to cleanse the world and they are muck. They are just muck. Boozers, looters, liars. This is the human material that Tehelka is.

Madhu: The Army Court of Inquiry started off aggressively; within three days they had ordered an inquiry but the defence ministry has been slow in implementing the court martial proceedings. Defence expert, Jasjit Singh, said that the guilty officers should be severely punished so that honest officers are not demoralized. Also, that officers who are in sensitive positions get the message that this kind of thing will not be tolerated.

Fernandes: I endorse that statement. In this case, the army has its own procedures. There are people who misuse those procedures by finding several ways to circumvent them and in the process delay things. Then there could be someone, at some level, people who would like to save someone, and therefore at the prosecution someone may go on playing for time.

Madhu: There have been reports that officers from the same regiment are trying the accused officers and deals are being made for leniency and bending the law.

Fernandes: What I am saying is that there could be different reasons for each of these delays.

Madhu: But while you were defence minister did you not tell them to move quickly?

Fernandes: From day one I have been pursuing, but then this is entirely the preserve of the army. They are covered by the Army Act and I cannot interfere with the way they are operating so far as going by the rules.

Madhu: But there were people in the defence ministry, for example people like P. Sasi, L.M. Mehta who were not covered by the army. They were directly under the defence ministry.

Fernandes: Yes, but I think in their cases the case went on fairly fast, as far as I can remember.

Madhu: They were not covered by the Army Court and the Commission as you know is still in process. So nothing really has happened to them in the ministry.

Fernandes: The Commission's report would have come a couple of years ago but Tehelka was scared about the fallout of this on the fellows who funded them. They created a situation where Justice Venkataswami chose to go. The whole process began again. It's taken double the time. It's not that the defence ministry got any roadblocks in any kind of action.

Madhu: There may not have been roadblocks but the people who were in the defence ministry were not really punished or prosecuted at all.

Fernandes: They all figured in the Commission of Inquiry.

Madhu: Do you feel that the Commission of Inquiry will take care of it?

Fernandes: Yes.

Though Fernandes had a reputation for honesty, he was minister of arguably the most corrupt ministry in India. Billions of dollars are at stake. Did Fernandes institute any changes in the system? He said he ensured that no middleman came near him. Cynics would point out that no middleman would be fool enough to go near George when he allegedly had other people accepting money on his behalf. Any changes in the procurement process? He replied,

Fernandes: Procurement procedures had been inherited by me from our predecessors. From the look of it and from the way things were moving I felt that by and large it was a foolproof procedure but after the Tehelka experience we did bring about a revision, and today those procedures are in place. So we did learn from it.

Madhu: Could you give examples of some of those procedures that would prevent a middleman from playing a role?

Fernandes: Now there is another aspect to it. We have now, on the recommendation of the CVC, decided that we should register those who are agents for defence. Companies, whether they are domestic companies or foreign companies, have to be registered. And in the registration process they are told how much commission they can take, how much they cannot take.

Madhu: Rather than banning them and letting them function underground, you accepted them and made it official. So whatever commission they are paid is all above board.

Fernandes: Yes, that's right; so we have done that.

Madhu: So people like Suresh Nanda can register their company and get official commissions?

Fernandes: That's right.

Madhu: What you are saying is that they don't have to bribe people?

Fernandes: All these things depend on how people want to behave and want to find their way in the world, because there will always be criminals. There will always be fellows who will do one-upism on you and say that torpedo this thing and find your way out. So one can never say the last word on these matters, and particularly defence is one area, from what I have read in my lifetime. I have been associated and I know how these things move in the defence ministry, and no matter how many stratagems you try, there could be someone who will circumvent these things.

Madhu: What about something more draconian? Did you think of something more dramatic, where officers would feel that they are being watched every second? Where if deals were being made, they would be caught? This is a rather pleasant thing you have done, enabling middlemen to register themselves, but did you think of any action that was tougher; that would keep army officers in line?

Fernandes: Let's face it, in the army there's the jawan. He is not involved in any of these deals. He is the man who gives his life at the end of the day. Then you have the middle-level officers, many of them under the aegis of some officer or the other. Their jobs are such that they have no initiatives where they can go out and do some mischief. Then you have the higher level. Now, that there is corruption is beyond dispute. You never believe that it's all a very clean sheet before you. There are black spots. I do feel that any kind of continuing exercise where the officer feels that he is not being trusted is counter-productive. In defence, in my experience that I have gathered in the six years, I personally feel that putting the man under that kind of pressure would bring his morale down. He will think I am not being trusted. Here is a man who at the end of the day may not be living. I have gone through these experiences where I have gone to the mountain-top, spent time with the troops, had a meal or tea with them, addressed them, made them feel happy and I have just come down and that evening they had to bring his body. So to put a man always on trial and that also a person who has started as a first lieutenant, had climbed up the ladder, had gone through innumerable experiences of fighting. You have generals who are walking with a stick; some of the finest generals [are] walking like that because they have been wounded in their younger days as captains or lieutenants and majors. Then to suddenly keep a constant watch on them, I personally would not recommend it to anybody. Because morale is very important. This will apply to any walk of life, but more so to defence because they are staking their lives.

Madhu: When the Bofors scandal was exposed, many important decisions were held up regarding procurement of equipment. Nobody wanted to take the responsibility. The T-90 deal was held up for six years. Do you think that the army will suffer for the fear of exposure of corruption and that it will deter everyone from taking decisions?

Fernandes: The new minister has also spoken about files not moving, decisions not taken. In the aftermath of Tehelka that was the case. Nobody wanted to take decisions. I take a decision and tomorrow I am accused, why did you take this particular decision? Once you are treated as someone who is now to be examined, then there is no ending. This is something in defence I would never do. All that Jaya said was that if you have a problem you can tell me and I will convey it and for three years now her life is in ruins.

Sidharth Luthra, counsel for Tehelka, was going through his own personal dichotomies when he grilled the defence minister of the nation, George Fernandes. But that did not stop him from what he set out to do:

Luthra: You have no personal knowledge that the tapes are tampered, rigged or doctored.

Fernandes: I have personal knowledge, because I saw the tapes the day they were released. I could not find anything on television as to what exactly the tapes were trying to convey, one saw it all dark, then there were a few heads, there were no legs, some movement here and there, somebody speaking. But what struck me was what was coming on the screen. One of the things that was said was that, finally all the tracks led them to the defence minister's residence and what they now have with them proves that the defence minister is beyond redemption.

The Cabinet was scheduled to meet at 7.00 p.m. that evening in the Cabinet Room, in South Block. Fernandes's colleagues started contacting him to find out what was going on. He got a message that Prime Minister Vajpayee wanted to know what his explanation was.

Fernandes: When I read what I had in this document, I found that the whole thing was an attack on me at one level, trying to involve a whole lot of other people, colleagues of mine, people in the army, people in the ministry. And things were written as commentary or whatever that some of us were absolutely rotten and I could not believe, I could not believe myself. I have to believe myself, but I could not believe that I had become that, what these people were trying to present me as. So, how can I accept that this was something that was genuine? I had to accept the whole thing was a sham.

Luthra: You have said that the tapes are doctored. Whether doctored or not, let us see the transcript for a minute. Mr R.K. Jain says, "George won't take money. He won't take money." Are you trying to say that this is doctored as well, Mr Fernandes?

Fernandes: No. There he is speaking the truth. I think what happened was that those who were editing the tapes decided that it was irrelevant.

Luthra: Let us turn to the next page where Mr Jain talks about Mr Sinha. Then he says, "George doesn't take money". This is also doctored, Mr Fernandes?

Fernandes: No. I said here he is telling the truth.

Luthra: Come a little below that. Mr Jain made a statement, "it is not easy to give money to George". Is this also doctored?

Fernandes: He must have said that. I am not challenging whatever has happened here. I am only challenging the veracity of certain things: No. 1, and the truth behind it. Is there truth behind it? This document says that the prime minister was involved in this whole deal, that he sent money to me. Is that the truth? It says a lot of things about a lot of people. Is it the truth? That is the point. I am challenging the truth of this document.

Luthra: Do you have anything to say about the tapes to suggest that Mr Jain did not make these statements?

Fernandes: I am not saying that whatever is put in his name, I have never said that he did not say that. I am challenging the truth of it. What he has said, he has said.

Sidharth Luthra took a logical, legal position and questioned him on that platform. If Fernandes is saying that the tapes are doctored, then all the positive statements made in his support would also be doctored. Luthra said, you cannot claim selective doctoring.

In the middle of this interrogation, Fernandes interrupted the proceedings with an 'only-in-India-moment'. Fernandes looked at the judge and then looked at Luthra and said in a slightly choked voice, 'Do you know who this young man is? His father (K.K. Luthra, senior advocate) stood by me during the Emergency when few people dared to. And he stood by me even after the Emergency.'

Luthra's sensibilities were already raw on this. His father was a close friend of the socialists, especially George Fernandes. When George married Leila Kabir, the bride and groom invited only a handful of guests each at the India International Centre in New Delhi. K.K. Luthra was invited, along with his wife and three children, which included Sidharth. One night during the Emergency, CBI officers arrived at the Luthra home. The family presumed Luthra was being detained under the draconian MISA Act. But no, it was George Fernandes who had been arrested and had asked for K.K. Luthra's presence. The night before Sidharth was slated to cross-examine Fernandes, he went to his mother for guidance and spoke to her about his discomfort. Was he being disloyal to his father's memory? His mother told him, 'Go do your duty fearlessly. Maintain your dignity and his. But do not shirk from the task at hand and do your best.' Sidharth said he had a restless night. 'When I walked down the path to the entrance door of the annexe, the media had taken over the entrance, I went and sat on my seat. I felt it would be the most important day of my career. Mr Fernandes walked in and the hall went silent. Mr Fali Nariman had specially come that day to represent him. It was going to be puny David, me, versus Goliath, Mr Fernandes. It was only when Mr Fernandes stood up to take his place as a witness that our eyes met for the first time that day. All night long, my sixth sense told me that he would say something personal and feared I would get unnerved so I kept addressing him as Mr Fernandes.' Half way through the cross-examination, Fernandes did exactly what Luthra had feared. He spoke about his relationship with Sidharth's father.

Sidharth recalled, 'After the proceeding was over, I immediately walked to the door of the hall with our team when Mr Nariman called me back and said Mr Fernandes wanted to meet me. Then, Mr Fernandes embraced me, asked about my mother and sisters and told me he remembered my father as a great man. It is a day I will never forget all my life.'

Sidharth is in turn gracious in acknowledging the generosity of his colleague in the Tehelka legal team, Kavin Gulati,

> To Kavin's credit, he insisted I do it although it was his brief and it was the most prestigious part of the Commission. Kavin is a unique friend and magnanimous in ways I cannot describe. That night I sat and prepared with my associate Pramod Dubey till late at night but was still restless. We had amazing guidance given by my mentor the late P.R. Vakil (senior advocate) who had come for the cross examination but by then Tehelka had no funds to even pay Mr Vakil's travel expenses. We had no choice but to go ahead without him. The issue in front of me was not the questions to be asked of him but where to go with the questions and how to tackle one of the most impressive personalities of my childhood; someone who I had grown up around. He and other socialists were regular visitors to our house. We also felt that the judge would be monitoring us closely and any, even slightly, offensive question about Jaya Jaitly would be shot down. So one had to tread very carefully, as the impact of being cut down publicly by the judge or a damaging answer by Mr Fernandes to our case would overshadow any benefit we had made till then. Mr Fernandes was in that sense, the star of the show.

So Luthra, treading carefully but doggedly, put Jaya Jaitly and George Fernandes's relationship under a microscope:

Luthra: How long do you know Ms Jaya Jaitly?
Fernandes: I know her for 25 years or more.
Luthra: You knew her before she joined the Samata Party.
Fernandes: Yes. She was one of the founders of the Samata Party.
Luthra: Do you know anything about her political background?
Fernandes: She is one of the finest political activists today in the country.

Frigid Jones-Shones: Hmmmm. I need a man who talks about me like that. *[Editor: You're giving a handle to critics by bringing in frivolous trivia.]*

Well, it takes all kinds. Even, Bridget Jones. Camille Paglia writes in her essay about 'intellectual' Susan Sontag:

> Sontag's calculated veering away from popular culture is my gravest charge against her. When in a 1988 profile *Time* magazine, she denied she had ever been that interested in pop and boasted that she did not even own a television set. I was appalled and disgusted. Not having a TV is tantamount to saying, "I know nothing of the time or country in which I live".

Being 'sombre' about everything, to my mind, is plain pretentious and insecure. Just how seriously should one take oneself? It is the difference between dancing spontaneously to Nusrat Fateh Ali Khan because his music hits your soul as opposed to sitting gravely listening, stone-faced, posing as an ever so serious connoisseur of music.

> **Luthra**: She was working with you in respect of any political or social work?
> **Fernandes**: Yes. She has been the assistant general secretary of the Hind Mazdoor Kisan Panchayat, which had a membership of a million and a half. She is perhaps the best-known authority on crafts, handicrafts and so on. Her role in human rights movement is second to none. She organizes Haats for the artisans and craft persons. She goes and works in all natural calamities and man-made calamities like when the Sikhs were massacred here in this city. She did more work for them than any other single person I know. She was there in Gujarat after the earthquake, spent time in Kutch and found out what had happened to all those Kutchi, the very poor, the very deprived artisans and craftsmen, worked among them, stayed among them. She is a person of great distinction. She is an author, going beyond that. She is a person of great distinction.

Frigid Jones-Shones has turned green, put two socks so far into her ears she is having trouble breathing.

> **Luthra**: And she is one of the most trusted workers of your party, isn't it?
> **Fernandes**: Yes, she is and we are very proud of her.

Jones-Shones has fainted from Inadequacy Trauma. Where did she find this man?

> **Luthra**: Are you aware that Ms Jaitly in her 5(2)(a) affidavit has stated: "all I can try to ensure [is] that everyone gets a fair opportunity to compete". Just read the whole paragraph.
> **Fernandes**: [Reads] "Subsequently the visitors made some complaint about

being unable to have their product tested and being denied a fair opportunity of competition in the Ministry of Defence. I made it very clear that I did not know about such things, but I would believe that anything will only be accepted on its merit and that merit has two components, price and quality. I also conveyed that we could not and do not take up matters on behalf of anyone to anyone else's detriment. All I can try to ensure is that everyone gets a fair opportunity to compete. I also made it clear that fair competition is in the interest of the nation. Completely shutting one's eyes to an available product is to act against the national interest, because that very product might turn out better than others, and others may be benefiting because of some injustice and unfairness. A plain reading of the relevant extracts from Tehelka's own transcripts under the title Operation West End reveals the following." This is what anyone should say; any public person should say this.

Luthra: Read it a little further.

Fernandes: [Reads] "When General Murgai speaks about short-listing, I responded in general terms about the procedures that are presumably followed on such matters in the ministry."

Luthra: It says further: "In the context of any unfair practice taking place, we, that is the party, would step in by forwarding the complaint to the concerned minister for examination, as is the normal practice followed and described earlier in this affidavit."

Further, she says in the next page, "Our endeavour in this regard is not limited to any particular ministry and is a practice followed by the functionaries of all political parties …"

Fernandes: Yes, yes, I do it. Even as minister, I do it, when people come from my constituency, they have a problem, they are small businessmen, they are not getting their bank money. I write to the finance minister and say that injustice is being done to this person. I do it on a daily basis, in government or outside the government; in fact, more outside government than inside government.

Jones-Shones, now coming out of her faint, is confused. Does this mean that in India, the only way you can get money out of the bank is to personally meet the defence minister? Forget Elizabeth Hurley and her stud Nayyar. Maybe Englishmen are not so bad, after all?

Luthra: Definitely, Mr Fernandes, but we are not talking about people from your constituency. We are talking about a foreign vendor who wanted to supply defence equipment.

Fernandes: It was not a foreign person; it was an Indian person, I am sure.

Jones-Shones: And what's so bad about foreign? I heard Indians loved everything foreign?

Luthra: But representing a foreign company, West End International.

Fernandes: Yes, that may be. But then he came to say that injustice is being done. We have a better product. Injustice is being done. All that she says is that we will see that injustice is not done. That is all.

Jones-Shones: See, in Salma Hayek's film *Frida*, Frida Kahlo tells Diego Rivera, she doesn't care if he is unfaithful, she only wants him to be loyal. George, this fab man George, is being loyal, and I'll bet my last cigarette he is faithful too.

> **Luthra**: In what capacity was the president of your party wanting to write to the defence minister to entertain somebody's request for a fair trial, a fair deal?
>
> **Fernandes**: I do not think she has written to me on this, nor has she …
>
> **Luthra**: In what capacity was she talking about speaking to you for getting them a fair deal?
>
> **Fernandes**: I do not think she has said that she will speak to me. Has she?

Jones-Shones: Oh George, don't flap out now!

> **Luthra**: Yes, she has.

Jones-Shones: This Sid fellow is beginning to get on my nerves. Doesn't he see what a great relationship they have? There are plenty of fish in the sea, do I know that? But not this kind of fish.

> **Fernandes**: Well, if she has said that, there is nothing wrong about it. After all, what is wrong in speaking that here is some injustice being done; will you please look at it? And it is my job to look at it and see that injustice is not being done.

Jones-Shones: Give it up for George. He's there for her. Isn't that what that Vietnamese monk Thich Nhat Hanh tells us to say: 'Beloved, I am here for you'?

Sidharth Luthra changed his focus to R.K. Jain, former treasurer of the Samata Party, who had so babble rattled gossip it would put a lunching lady to shame.

> **Luthra**: According to you, you were defamed by R.K. Jain. Did you send him any notice, take any steps against him or prosecute him?
>
> **Fernandes**: He apologized publicly, advertised in the newspapers saying that he regrets all that he has said.
>
> **Luthra**: But you never took any action to prosecute him, did you, Mr Fernandes?
>
> **Fernandes**: Well, I felt that ultimately a person, who was a member of my party, who was a colleague, who was an office bearer, if he has been trapped into making such statements and getting into such situations, I would like to …
>
> **Luthra**: How are you assuming he was trapped?

Fernandes: Because it is so obvious from these files/this record. It is so obvious. The man has a desire to have a hospital built up in the memory of his mother and someone decides that we will get you all the money and we'll put a hospital. We'll give you 90 per cent money, all kinds of things. The man has been subjected to the kind of conmanship by people who should be running schools for conmen.

Luthra: What you are saying is what Mr Jain said was justified, but not what the Tehelka representative said?

Fernandes: What I am saying is that people have been waylaid in a manner of speaking: army officers have been made to say and do things which they would never ever do in their lives. There is so much that has been done, that is against just about everything that is decent.

৯

Tehelka really had no proof against the defence minister himself, so George Fernandes was not in a bad position in Operation West End Jones-Shones: Check out what this cheeky chap Sid ended with, and to the defence minister of the world's largest democracy: even I know that. I heard it on Kumars At 42 on TV.

Luthra: I put it to you that you have concealed facts from this Commission.
Fernandes: I deny it.

৯

Fine, this was the standard concluding sentence from the lawyers in almost all the cross-examinations, and equally the denial, was true to format.

Dayan Krishnan, one of the lawyers for the Commission, was no less firm with George Fernandes. Krishnan pointed out dialogue where the Samata Party treasurer, R.K. Jain, admits how he collects 3 per cent commission for his party. George insisted that Jain never collected money for the party.

Krishnan then focused on Jaya Jaitly's dialogue in the Operation West End tapes where Jaya said, '… if they are refusing to test it, that … then we can step into the picture'.

Krishnan: Now, Mr Fernandes, my question to you is this. A high functionary of your party, operating from the office inside of your house, portrays that she has access to you and the decision making in your ministry. Is that correct?
Fernandes: I do not think that is what it conveys. It only conveys her commitment to seeing that if there is injustice anywhere, she would like to fight against it. She would like to help any person who is facing injustice in any form, in any place. That is all it conveys. Not a day passes when I do not receive at least half a dozen from the Members of Parliament on these lines, that so and so thing is not being done. There is injustice here. This morning I received two of them. I get them on a daily basis. That is what I am. That is the kind of culture I want my political party to have.

Bridget: This woman seems to have gotten this unbelievable guy into a lot of trouble. What he needs is a woman who doesn't understand and is not interested in politics. Say, someone like me. If he knew me, he would really understand how my ignorance would bring him bliss.

↬

Fernandes has not been able to shake off his socialist bent of mind, and over the years repeatedly attacked Rajiv Gandhi and now Sonia Gandhi on the Bofors gun scandal. Since the Tehelka exposé, he often targeted the Hindujas and pointed out that they had supplied the money for Operation West End. How did he come to that conclusion?

Fernandes: When I became minister of defence, at the very first press conference I had to hold in the defence ministry, I made some statements that no middlemen would be allowed in the radius of ten or twenty kilometres of my office. Second, I'll see that there is the maximum transparency in defence purchases. I was aware that there are known identified defence related businessmen in our country and the Hindujas head the list of that. My preventing these fellows from coming anywhere, the transparency that I brought in defence procurement will have hurt a lot of people and the most hurt were the Hindujas. So I came to a conclusion that some of these people are involved with those who could not get their commissions and who could not get to approach me. I had been going through snipes from various people. I assumed that this would be the father of the whole exercise. And I think that was proved right. This understanding was proved right.

Madhu: In what way was it proved right?

Fernandes: In the way that the three fellows that were the so-called Tehelka, their relationships with this company and its proprietors or partners.

Madhu: With the Hindujas or First Global?

Fernandes: With the Hindujas became obvious. It became public that of the three, one went to London and went straight to the Hindujas.

Madhu: But Tarun Tejpal went after the exposé to sell content, and he did not meet them. He sent Charulata Joshi.

Fernandes: Yes, that's what I am saying. I was vindicated thereafter. I didn't say that I had, but suspicion went straight on him.

Madhu: If Tarun Tejpal had made a deal with the Hindujas to put in money in Tehelka so he could do this sting that benefited the Hindujas, he wouldn't be stupid enough to publicly go to the Hindujas' office when he already had dealings with the Hindujas.

Fernandes: Well, sometimes the cleverest of crooks also make mistakes.

Madhu: Did you get this information from RAW or IB?

Fernandes: I did not personally ask the IB or the RAW. In the normal course, the RAW is not concerned with domestic intelligence. The IB is concerned with domestic intelligence and the IB would have had some information. But I never sought any help or assistance from them or any kind of investigation from them because once this whole thing began and I came out of the government and the Commission of Inquiry was appointed; thereafter there was no purpose.

Madhu: Even out of government, on a personal level, it wouldn't have been so difficult for you or anyone in government to obtain the phone records of Tehelka talking to Hindujas prior to the exposé. That by itself would have in some sense incriminated them. But there were no such records.

Fernandes: Well, you have a point there. I know that could have been done, but for me it's now all kind of looking at what all could have been done but was not done. I do feel that the resignation was the biggest mistake. One should have slugged it out and shown these fellows their place.

One of George's errors was to have combined his defence of Jaya with that of the army officers and even R.K. Jain. He could have defended Jaya's actions as what he believed was right. Instead, to have clubbed it in with the army officers and Jain, when each case is different, made all the statements of defence appear to be without basis. It became loyalty for the sake of loyalty, not for what he believed was right. He could not have possibly believed that all the army officers caught taking money, selling documents from his ministry, cavorting with call girls, were innocent and just trapped. Why was George viewing it in this manner? This was his Rashomon. There is no way he could see Jaya doing anything that was not honourable. In fairness to Jaya, Sidharth Luthra excluded all the sentences where she clearly stated that the quality and price had to be right in the interest of the nation. She repeatedly said that decisions were taken in accordance with what was best for the country. That very sentence, however, exposes and begs the question: How is she in a position to know that? Luthra's and Krishnan's point was, how much influence did she wield if she could sit in the defence minister's house, meet strangers, accept party donations, and promise to help them for any injustice they might suffer. George chose to see all that as an extension of her social work activities, where her goal is to alleviate suffering.

Another mistake: when the Army Court of Inquiry was doing well in coming down hard on the COT (Caught On Tape) army officers, why was George defending them in the Commission? By speaking up strongly against the army officers COT, he could have actually raised army morale. He would have shown the jawans who are risking their lives on the border that he would not let their reputation get tarnished by bad apples. By defending them, it can be construed that he is saying: 'The army is corrupt. There is nothing I can do about it. Stop talking about it or it will demoralize the army.' Wrong. It is in not talking about it and in not calling their behaviour irreprehensible and indefensible, that he is demoralizing honest officers. His approach would make an army officer in procurement feel a fool for not making money on the side. Would George have defended the army officers had Jaya not figured in the Operation West End tapes? Would his reaction have been one of feeling betrayed and unforgiving? Would he have nurtured as much anger towards Tehelka at all? Because he felt that Jaya had been trapped, was he unnecessarily extending his sympathy to the officers? After the initial shock, one must presume George must have examined the army officers' behaviour separately. Should not his reaction also have been separate? Why was George not furious with the officers for letting him and the nation down? Where was his anger? As Malcolm X said: 'Usually when people are sad, they don't do anything. They just cry over their condition. But when they get angry, they bring about change.'

What happened to the fiery George who railed against the corrupt system and led a railway strike in 1974? Why has George not felt the misalignment in his life? Shouldn't he be feeling just a little bit splintered? Don't the dichotomies of his life today grate against all the principles that he so publicly stood for? George has enough people saying that he is an honest man. Why then has he not attempted to kill the corruption in equipment procurement in the army?

Enough people have also said it is near impossible to root out corruption in arms procurement. There are too many powerful people involved with huge stakes in the game and they would not allow it. But, if George could take on Indira Gandhi, he could take on the multinationals of the world who often function like mafia; why did he not focus on the disease festering in his ministry? George's own history is that of a man who has always been introspective, motivated by ideals, looking to change a corrupt system. Why is George so far from what he used to be? On numerous issues. How does he reconcile his position of always speaking against nuclear proliferation and then proudly announcing on 5 October 2003, that nuclear missiles were now ready for deployment by the Indian Army? When writer Amitav Ghosh questioned George on how he could be sincere in being comfortable with India's nuclear tests [Interview in *Outlook* magazine, 11 May 2002], George said:

> I went through a deep anguish – an atom bomb was morally unacceptable. I had campaigned against it in Britian. But, I said that if today the five nations which have nuclear weapons we should have, then I should say that we keep all our options open … by all options, I mean every option. I did not say that we make the bomb but that was implied.

Ghosh did not let it go at that and grilled him further:

> **Ghosh**: You claim to be an admirer of people like Mahatma Gandhi, the Dalai Lama, Suu Kyi and others. So how do you then reconcile yourself to these nuclear tests? How do you live with your job as defence minister?
>
> **Fernandes**: I believe that in the scheme of things which exist in this world and with nation states having to survive and protect themselves, those who are in positions where they decide the best use must have first and foremost in their minds the need to protect the nations which don't. And if their perceptions take them to a point where they have to compromise with their conscience on the issue of survival of their people, then I would say along with Mahatma Gandhi – that I shall risk violence a thousand times, rather than risk the emasculation of an entire race. The anguish was there but taking the decision on the bomb was not that difficult in terms of reconciling one's beliefs on

matters of this nature, then taking a conscious decision that if India must make a bomb it is for her own security. Once I had reached a position on the CTBT and the nuclear option, there wasn't a need for me to have a problem for introspection.

Ghosh's choice of words in his question was particular. 'How do you live with your job ...' He was asking: how do you live with yourself? India has seen numerous politicians who have high ideals, but who do change when in power. Why? Becoming a politician in India means, sooner or later, compromising your principles. We have seen that happen repeatedly. The seduction of power, the necessity of going along with the government of which one is part, having access to all the information that triggers the same decisions from any political party in power, the fear of losing a powerful position, all contribute to rationalization of compromise with one's ideals. It is difficult to fathom the dichotomy of a man who once was so against nuclear weapons now saying they are important for our security and he doesn't like superpowers dictating to us. There are many examples of politicians who have lived their lives according to their principles, and at the last count of surviving in power, have acted totally contrary to character.

Why could he not have set up a special commission in the army to create and institutionalize systems that would make army corruption at least difficult, if not impossible? The Army Court of Inquiry looked into Operation West End and took strong action against the accused officers. However, the army appears to have stopped short of looking at the loopholes existing in the system that allow easy graft. There has been no change in these established procedures since the Tehelka exposé. Both Jaya and George acknowledged that there is corruption. Why then has nothing been done about it? Why are we piddling around about a handful of officers who were caught, when the real arms dealers manipulate products based on profit motives and continue to endanger India's security? When questioned about this in the interview given after the NDA government was voted out of power, George spoke about how he had initiated a system of Complaint Boxes in his ministry, adding that he had these placed in every defence establishment in the city. He said he carried the key with himself and every Friday these boxes were opened. Anyone who had a complaint about anything, including corruption, could simply slip in a note. Fernandes said that they had received some complaints and the defence ministry did take action or the matter was sent to the CBI. Complaint Boxes? Quaint. Defence ministers around the world perhaps carry the so-called black box with nuclear deterrent buttons (or hopefully some high-tech defence auto-destruct command tools) but George is proud to carry this key. Are we in boarding school, putting complaints about the cafeteria food in a Complaint Box? Charming, yes, but it doesn't take a village to understand that Ghauri and Shaheen are not pretty Pakistani girls.

If George felt, appropriately, as betrayed and angry as the jawans were with these corrupt officers, then perhaps some corrective action would have emerged. It is now apparent how far George is from the old (actually young) George. *George, George na raha.* The manner in which he handled the Tehelka issue was to ignore it unless he was forced to deal with it.

The old George would have shaken up his ministry and the army. When he spoke of what Tehelka had done to Jaya, his voice choked and his eyes filled. His mind digressed more to the entrapment and sullied reputation than the betrayal by army officers and officials in his ministry. In this imperfect world, as we do have to have a defence minister, give us a macho macho man. This is the Indian Army not the YMCA. Hey, who makes up this stuff: 'We get the government we deserve?' You know who? Joseph de Maistre, in 1811, wrote that in reference to the unsettled state of affairs in Europe after the French Revolution. The only government that Maistre approved of was that of the Pope, who he believed was absolute. According to Maistre, the foundation of social order was the executioner. So clearly, Maistre's famous saying must be simply dismissed as only applicable to the post-French Revolution era. How about: We get the government we deserve to remind us we deserve better?

It was apparent that George felt more grief than anger. More suffering than anger. More hurt than anger. Whatever anger George felt was directed towards the 'boozers, looters, liars' of Tehelka. Three adjectives that would have been better applied to the army officers who boozed, looted, and lied on camera. More than anything else, George Fernandes comes across as a good man with his heart in the place where it idealistically should be. But when you are defence minister, the place in your heart should be reserved, above all other engrossments, only for your nation. Please do not tell me we got him because we deserved him. In India, you can only survive if you doggedly believe that this is *Not As Good As It Gets*.

17 Tropic of Cancerous Corruption

No drug, not even alcohol, causes the fundamental ills of society. If we're looking for the source of our troubles, we shouldn't test people for drugs, we should test them for stupidity, ignorance, greed and love of power.

– P.J. O'Rourke, Journalist, Writer and Humourist

For the Tehelka journalists, Major General P.S.K. Choudary was a substantial catch. It wasn't easy getting to him. Choudary was no retired army officer fishing around for jobs. He was in service and was additional director-general (weapons and equipment) attached to the Quarter Master General's Branch, Army Headquarters. He played a pivotal key in arms procurement. He would meet about three or four arms vendors every single working day. It can be presumed that Choudary thought that Mathew Samuel was just another. His excuse for accepting Rs 1 lakh was a bit of a lengthy stretch: to help care for the stray animals his wife brings home. The gold chain? We'll just have to resist bad jokes begging to be told.

Major General Murgai invited Major General P.S.K. Choudary to a five-star hotel to meet West End's representative, but aware he was under surveillance, he showed reluctance. Murgai followed up with a dinner invitation to his home, which Choudary accepted.

Choudary questioned Samuel instantly. Had West End ever done any defence work? Samuel said, no. What's in the deal? Samuel came up with Mathewisms, 'Sir, that specification and magnification, that I will give you … that I will give you'. Choudary told Samuel it was a 'no-go' case. He said, 'No point going through with it. I believe in total honesty that if somebody asks me for advice, I tell him, "Do this and then do this." Because there is no way you are going to get it.' Choudary explained to Samuel that the army had already bought one-third of its requirement for hand-held imagers from two different sources. He said these required maintenance, spare parts, and he could not increase his product range. Choudary elaborated, 'The logistics problems are going to be there. After all, this gadget is going to be with us for the next 15 years. Right? The maintenance support for next 15 years is going to be very heavy, when you have four-five items of same product.' He informed Samuel that they had already bought '400 odd systems against a requirement of about 1,200'.

Choudary suggested that Samuel should mention products that West End could supply and he would say 'yes' or 'no'. Samuel then threw up the tank navigation system. Choudary said 'yes' the army needed it but the PSUs (public sector undertakings) – HAL (Hindustan Aeronautics Ltd) and BEL (Bharat Electronics Ltd) – were supposed to supply them. Although the trials were supposed to have been conducted two years earlier, Choudary mentioned that US sanctions had delayed matters.

Just before Choudary left Murgai's home, he accepted a gold chain. After Choudary's departure, Murgai allegedly accepted Rs 25,000 from Samuel for arranging the meeting. In their post-meeting discussion, Murgai told Samuel that he gave Choudary a choice. Murgai reported, 'I said, "*Yaar*, if you want to take it, take it, it's open. Otherwise, let's close the chapter." He said, "Okay, I have taken it."' Samuel, obviously excited with these developments, said, 'What I've given that small gift. I want to know what his response. Otherwise, bloody he will refuse it. That is confirmed. He will take the money. He will accept it. He will give the order also.'

At their next meeting at Choudary's home, Choudary explained to Samuel that it was impossible for West End to enter the fray at this point. He said the army had already bought 200 hand-held thermal imagers from the Israelis and 200 from the French. Choudary clarified, 'But we had already taken a limited technology. That means, up to component level. In all electronics, if you have the component level technology, you can buy the same components in the world market and fabricate the damn thing.' They could buy more of the same type of product but they could not opt for a different range of it. Choudary said that he had already negated the product offered by Sagem (which was recommended by the defence secretary) so it would be impossible for him to now explain why he was bringing in a new company. Choudary did not give up, though. He asked Samuel, 'Have you got something else where I can advise you?'

In December 2001, the CAG (Comptroller and Auditor General of India) report highlighted irregularities in the purchase of hand-held thermal imagers. It is revealing that Choudary told Samuel, 'I know that this particular Gen 3 technology, Sagem is far superior in the world … I have said "No" to Sagem. In fact Sagem had approached the defence secretary. The defence secretary was keen that we try to evaluate'. But the army refused. The reason is now clear.

Choudary suggested to Samuel that after evaluating West End's brochure, if the product fit the bill, he would advise him to go to ECIL (Electronics Corporation of India Ltd). As the product had to be integrated into a tank, it would come through ECIL as a collaboration product of theirs. Choudary broke down how the sellers got their orders, 'You look after the minister; I get my stuff. Something comes to the army. You look after the minister or whomever you want.'

Choudary illuminated how the system worked:

Initial job is mine. To put everybody who's approached or who has … whom I know is capable, I put him in the play. Then we ask them for technical proposals. Full specifications, what are the capabilities of your system, and then see is it matching with ours. What we need. Out of ten, five will be weeded out when we take the evaluation. Without even seeing the equipment, based on data that is provided. Balance five people, after technical evaluation, are asked, "Bring your stuff for trials immediately on no-cost basis." Then you carry your trial and evaluation. In the trials, out of five, three may get weeded out; only two may come out winners.

Samuel asked, 'In shortlist?' Choudary nodded and went on, 'Till that is my job. After that, between the two, who gets it is the ministry's job. That's on commission.' Choudary could be seen in the Operation West End tapes rubbing his index finger and thumb, indicating that money was involved at the 'commission' stage. Choudary later said he did not say 'commission' but 'commercial'.

Samuel: In the bureaucrat, what ... what they will play the role? See, because major role will play the user, that's you ... your side.
Choudary: That is my side. That's what I said.
Samuel: Now ... not ... now, not in the bureaucratic or politicians' side?
[Choudary shook his head.]
Samuel: Awkay.
[Samuel slapped his thigh in excitement.]
Choudary: Thereafter, it's entirely with the ministry to call for the commercial ...
Samuel: And who will decide the PNC and everything?
Choudary: I am a member of that too. To advise ... but it is generally chaired by the joint secretary of the ministry.
Samuel: Awkay sir, it's right information. Now I got the right information.
Choudary: No one individual can assure you.
Samuel: Yeah. I can give a ... small gift for you?
Choudary [smiled]: You already gave me a ...
Samuel: No, sir. This is my ... I am not saying that anything ... *haan*?

Samuel opened his briefcase and took out a wad of currency notes and handed the money to Choudary.

Samuel: Sir, one lakh.
Choudary [expressed surprise but accepted the money anyway]: Money?
[Choudary put the money in the right pocket of his trousers.]
Choudary: This is not ...
Samuel: No, this is ... my ... my ... happiness.
Choudary: But, please remember. There is no one individual [who] can help you in this.
Samuel: Yes, sir.

Choudary: We can only put in … put in our bit.
Samuel: Awkay.

On 20 March 2001, Major General P.S.K. Choudary was the first witness called at the Army Court of Inquiry. Choudary, who was so natty and smart at the Tehelka Commission of Inquiry, presented quite a different persona at the Army Court of Inquiry (ACI). First he informed the ACI that he 'did not know the nature of the allegations for which I have been called to depose before the court. I do not know the terms of reference of the inquiry. I would, therefore, submit that I may be provided a copy of the convening order.' The court coolly informed Choudary that there was no provision in the army rules to give him a copy of the convening order. The purpose for which the Court of Inquiry had been convened was, however, read out to him.

Choudary then proceeded to read out a lengthy statement outlining his areas of work and the methods prescribed by the army for procurement of weapons and equipment. The Ministry of Defence laid down the procedures in 1992, ostensibly in an effort to eradicate corruption. Or, some people speculate that it was to spread the decision-making process to such a wide stretch that enough officials got an opportunity to make money to keep everyone quiet and happy. I counted approximately 37 steps in a variety of departments and committees [see Note, pg 308]. If you work out that each step takes one week, which is hopelessly optimistic, in reality it could take up to a month or two, but let's stick to a week, the procedures for acquisition would take over three years. By which time, either the requirements have changed or the item itself is obsolete. It is not unusual to read that any particular military equipment has taken over 15 years to acquire. It is common knowledge that our neighbouring countries go shopping and buy their military equipment like they are in a grocery store.

Choudary submitted to the ACI, 'I would like to submit that as per procedures where a vendor is offering better equipment or due to various constraints, we need to go to additional vendors, Army Headquarters and the Ministry of Defence do not entertain additional proposals from other vendors for an equipment already selected and fielded into service.' With this statement, Choudary attempted to cover himself for anticipated questioning by the ACI as to why he recommended the West End brochure to Infantry School, Mhow.

Okay, so Choudary knew what he was supposed to do. Very well. He then informed the ACI that before he could make any statement relating to the allegations he would like to examine the complete transcript of the allegations made by Tehelka. But, Choudary was a shrinking man. We have all been in that place, whether in childhood or as an adult, when caught doing something one should not have. The need to escape is an animal instinct. Choudary was fluttering in a panic to save his life.

The ACI handed over a copy of the transcript of Operation West End, downloaded from the Tehelka website, and gave him two hours to read it and then complete his statement.

Choudary returned and dug out that old bogey, the conspiracy theory. 'The allegations levelled against me by Tehelka appear to be part of a larger conspiracy. The reasons and details of which can be established only by the government. Though the team had met other ministries and ministers, yet they choose to target only the defence ministry.' (Choudary clubbed his own predicament with the supposed victimization of the defence ministry. A rather obvious psychological ploy to manipulate the court.)

'Even in the defence ministry, though the agents/middlemen had indicated their involvement in certain acquisitions, bigger deals such as MiG, Sukhoi, Barak Missiles yet their total energy were devoted towards targeting the army personnel.' Choudary went on to explain that, as this was the edited transcript and had been selectively edited by Tehelka; he would not be able to give a full response until he saw the unedited version. He did point out:

> Firstly, Colonel Anil Sehgal is alleged to have suggested HHTI as a product. This is a product he very well knows is not handled by Ordnance Directorate, but by the WE Directorate as per charter of duties. I fail to understand as to why he should suggest such a thing [that is] not dealt [with] by him. Similarly, Brigadier Iqbal Singh, Major General Ahluwalia, Major General Murgai indicate that for this product the Tehelka team had to lobby with me. Even Narender Singh of [the] Ministry of Defence is alleged to have said that the item is dealt by me. In view of the above facts, I have become a victim of circumstances.

Swift and smart Choudary may well be, but he did himself no service by making this statement. The questions from the ACI were the antithesis of what happened in the Tehelka Commission of Inquiry. The court did not allow games of semantics and subterfuge. There were no pyrotechnic antics of creating confusion.

At the Army Court of Inquiry, Choudary was questioned about his dinner meeting with Mathew Samuel at Major General Murgai's house, which he acknowledged. Choudary admitted to his discussion with Samuel about procurement of HHTI but said that he informed Samuel that the trial evaluation was already over. The army court then reminded him of his sensitive position as ADG WE and asked why he did not think it appropriate to check the company before entering into any discussion with a civilian. Choudary's answers were priceless:

> **Choudary**: After I met this individual, I was not behaving naturally or behaving in normal self. It appears that I may have been mesmerized or hypnotized.
> **ACI**: In hindsight, don't you feel that this was an unbecoming conduct on your part?
> **Choudary**: Yes.
> **ACI**: Did you accept a gold chain from that individual on that day?
> **Choudary**: Yes, I did accept [it] in that unnatural behaviour.

Choudary informed the ACI, 'I explained to him that I cannot do anything. Yet he thrust Rs 1 lakh to me.' The gold chain too was presumably thrust on him.

Choudary was questioned by the ACI on how much property he owned. He informed them that most of it was owned by his wife and daughters, which is what was explicit in the Operation West End tapes. (It is normal practice that homes are put in the wife's name when it is paid for in unaccounted income.) The ownership of the properties is, however, convoluted. On the first day of his questioning, Choudary told the ACI that he did not know the details of the cost of the Vasant Vihar flat, which had been purchased by his daughter by raising loans all by herself as she was a working woman. On the second day, Choudary said that the flat was purchased by mortgaging property held in his name in Lajpat Nagar. Choudary and his children had given a power of attorney to his wife to manage the flat in his absence.

Now get this: it transpired that Deepak Chabbra, the alleged wheeler-dealer middleman, who also starred in the Operation West End tapes, was the original owner of the plot bought by Choudary at Vasant Vihar. The Choudarys paid Rs 27 lakh for the flat. The ACI pointed out to Choudary that a flat of 1350 sq ft at market value in Vasant Vihar normally costs over a crore. There was no denying that Choudary and his entire family were involved in collecting real estate of a value that stretched the imagination and credibility considering his army income. Choudary had also failed to take the required permission from the authorities, according to Army Regulations (1987), to mortgage his flat in Lajpat Nagar as well as to buy the flat in Vasant Vihar.

In the Commission of Inquiry, Choudary dragged out the proceedings all he could, nit-picking over sentences in the transcriptions, nuances in the voiceovers, and discrepancies in the Operation West End tapes. According to Choudary, he 'had negated the proposal of Tehelka on file and I did not permit its further progress for evaluation. Based on my directions, the file was closed.' Not quite. The eighteenth witness in the Army Court of Inquiry, Colonel A.P. Singh, would reveal more elaborate details which did not match Choudary's Rashomon. Additionally, according to Aniruddha Bahal and Mathew Samuel, they had been told the evaluation letter was ready for them to pick up, but their cover blew before they could.

Mathew Samuel stated in his affidavit in the ACI that Deepak Chabbra had informed him that Major General Choudary's wife had bought a house in Chabbra brothers' building in Vasant Vihar worth about Rs 1.86 crore. Samuel said he had been told that Mrs Choudary handled all their finances.

There is no end to convoluted arguments attempted to cloud the issue. The facts remain: Choudary was one of the most important players caught on tape. He was still in active service in the Indian Army. He was in charge of procurement and intimately aware of every aspect and nuance of the system. He did accept Rs 1 lakh and a gold chain from the West End operatives. Also, why was he giving out information about defence equipment to men whose antecedents he had not bothered to check? Choudary could contort all he liked, but these facts were on tape, he had admitted to them, and nothing he said could make him look all right. There are two ways of handling the fall out of committing a crime. You can look the facts straight in the eye, admit to them, take the due punishment, and walk out with as much dignity as possible. Alternatively, you can do what almost all of them did. You can shout, 'doctored', you can snivel, find minor errors and quibble, circumvolute deformed stories, and end up behaving like men suffering from anorchism with no sense of honour or dignity. These are, after all, men who put their country's defence at risk all in a day's work.

Major General Choudary, in his own defence, told the ACI:

> At the meeting with Mathew Samuel and Major General Murgai, the recording of this meeting, according to the original transcripts exists only for about nine minutes after my arrival, and thereafter the audio had failed. Thus the edited version that has been broadcast over the TV network has been fabricated totally by Tehelka. They must be made answerable for such a fabrication and telling the court under oath that the edited version had not been doctored.

Yes, but did they doctor the tape of the money and gold chain that was accepted?

On 6 May 2002, Major General P.S.K. Choudary was asked by Tehelka's lawyer, Sidharth Luthra, whether he had declared the Rs 1 lakh he had received from West End in his income tax return.

> **Choudary**: That is not my money. I have not declared it. I thought that at some point of time I would be asked to return it.
> **Luthra**: Have you offered to return it or return it to Tehelka?
> **Choudary**: I would like to return it.
> **Luthra**: You received the amount of Rs 1 lakh in the meeting on 24 December 2000. Sixteen months have expired and no efforts have been made to return it.
> **Choudary**: It is not a question of efforts being made. I was contemplating in my mind at that point of time, what I should do. Whether I should bring it to the notice of the authorities, make a police complaint. While I was still contemplating all these actions, the Tehelka story was published. After that, when it came in the public domain and the story was published, thereafter I was waiting for the various instructions from the army authorities on what to do with this money.

Choudary's answer about declaring the gold chain was the same: that it was not his so he did not see the necessity of declaring it. He was holding someone else's property for safe keeping?

Luthra then asked him why he had not checked the company's antecedents. Choudary told him, 'Hundreds of brochures which are coming if I sit down to check; as it is I was leaving my office at 8.00 p.m. at night. I would be sitting 24 hours in my office only making these checks.' Luthra highlighted that military attachés posted all over the world are meant for this purpose.

Dayan Krishnan, counsel for the Commission, drew attention to the sentence uttered by Choudary in the tapes: 'If there is a chance, we will include you, now that I have your thing but this point of time at least for one year, I cannot.'

Krishnan: I put it to you, General, that your processing on the file of the equipment, which purportedly was manufactured by West End, was in pursuance of this statement made to them.

Choudary: It is not true. [And pointed out all the sentences in the transcript where he discouraged the West End operatives.] Now all these indicate that I have negated him repeatedly, repeatedly, repeatedly.

Krishnan: Yet, General Choudary, you say, "based on the above, keep your mind open for taking the decision at a later date".

Choudary: Because it is a product which is, as per the analysis, it is a superior product based on a superior technology. I said, keep your mind open for the future. That's all.

Krishnan: If I understand you right, what you are trying to convey here is that as a single individual you could have done nothing to help them because of the chain of procurement. Am I correct?

Choudary: It is not a single individual including the defence minister, he cannot say that your product will be accepted. Anybody, because the procedures are such that there are a large number of agencies involved so there is no one individual who can help a particular vendor.

Krishnan pointed to the West End transcript and read.

Choudary: "The initial job is mine to put everybody who has [to be] approached or whom I know is capable, I put him there." [He continued,] "We can only put in, put in our bit."

Krishnan: I put it to you that what you were portraying was that you could do whatever you were allowed to do within your power to assist Tehelka in their endeavour.

Choudary: My Lord, [could he be praying?] it is not true. My actions on file indicate that it is not true. Again it is a casual conversation. One line from a casual conversation cannot be quoted. You have to take the overall context and I have read through the entire transcript of [the] tape where this figures and the overall gist is, it is not acceptable.

Interviewing the army officers, who appeared reduced and pitiable, was not an exhilarating experience. Most of them were impenitent. Major General P.S.K. Choudary agreed to an interview because he felt he had nothing left to lose and wanted his side of the story told. Choudary said,

Everybody believed Tehelka. I am speaking to you now because from my heart, whatever you may do, I know nothing can happen to me. I am at a stage where a criminal case has been started. A court martial is a criminal case, where I am going to come out scot-free. For the benefit of rest of the people, you must know the truth.

Choudary was furious with Tehelka. He objected that they had decided on a particular agenda and did not project both sides of the story. When asked what could be the other side of the story when an army officer is on tape accepting money, Choudary replied that it was on tape that he had told them about twenty times that he could not help them, but they edited it out of the broadcast version. He told them that the transfer technology had already been bought. Choudary narrated how he did not want the equipment they desperately needed for Kashmir to be stalled by bringing in a new company. Why then did he accept the money? And why did he officially forward the West End brochure and write that they should be considered in the future? Choudary explained that if West End offered better technology there was a reason to bear them in mind, if only for the future. He pointed out that Tehelka had stated that the Army Vigilance Commission was investigating a case against him. He said this was not true. Tehelka announced in the tapes that they had managed to sell equipment to the army. Choudary said they had not reached anywhere near that stage. Finally, he said that Tehelka declared that in the third week of January L.M. Mehta had sent him a letter and he had then issued a trial evaluation letter to them. This he said was also not true. Choudary argued that if he had gone to Murgai's house in January and learnt that the West End representatives were actually journalists, then why would he have written on the brochure in February that West End should be considered? Choudary said Tehelka had lied and told me to check the dates mentioned in the Army Court of Inquiry, presuming I would have no access to them. On checking the transcripts of the Army Court, I found Choudary's notings were not in February but in January.

Choudary was convinced that the kind of money Tehelka had spent would only be done if there were large financial stakes involved or the motive was to bring down the BJP government. Choudary said, 'Nobody would spend that kind of money purely for satisfying journalistic instinct'. It is difficult for a man who is only exposed to action motivated by financial gain to comprehend journalists who not only spend money but also often risk their lives for nothing more than just getting the story.

For a man who was in a security sensitive position, why did Choudary agree to meet Mathew Samuel in the first place? Choudary said that the army needed the tank navigation system that Samuel offered, and he was on the lookout for someone who could provide it. He mentioned that Tehelka had tried to get to him through twenty different people, all of whom pretended to know him to make money out of Samuel. Choudary recalled that both General Dhillon and General Ahluwalia had told Samuel they had no access to Choudary but Samuel lied to everybody to con them. Choudary said that when Major General Murgai came to him, he followed army decorum and treated him as a retired senior officer and colleague, so accepted his invitation to meet a friend who wanted his advice. Choudary refused to meet them in a hotel, which showed he knew he had to protect himself. Noticeably, when Murgai was in the army he was directly involved in quality assurance in the procurement process.

Choudary was incensed with Murgai:

The way Murgai himself, greedy for money and he is advising this chap. He as a retired gentleman and army officer, and he may be a general but he is trying

to trap me. Murgai is one suspicious character. I don't treat him as an officer of the army. For example, Sayal took the entire blame on himself. Whether it was Ahluwalia or whether it was Iqbal. He said, because of me, these people got involved. There are certain things I cannot tell you. How he has taken the blame because it will be incorrect on my part, hitting my friends. He tried to cover up for their mistakes. On the other hand, Murgai, to save his skin he is telling lies to say I wanted to meet this chap. He said, I never told him that I wanted to take up a job. In the court martial, the court asked did you have an inclination for taking up a job. He said, "yes". It proves my point.

Choudary said that in the unedited tapes, Samuel and Murgai plotted on what snacks and drinks to offer. Choudary recounted:

Choudary: So Murgai is telling Samuel, that I served him a large drink whereas for ourselves we are serving small drinks. When a drink is mixed with water comes to you, you don't know whether it is small or large. Now that is the character of Murgai.

Madhu: So were you drunk?

Choudary: I don't say I got drunk. I was still in my senses. After giving this so-called gift of chain to me, which I didn't see what it is in a packet. He said, now we can finalize this. I said, no. As a person who is supposed to look after the interest of the army, it will be incorrect on my part to do anything which is against the army. All along I have said, your case is a no-go case. Yet, I have been ultimately called corrupt. Now tell me, is it correct for a journalist to keep on offering inducements one after the other just to twist me? I was offered a house by Samuel. I was offered a job after retirement. I was offered a US visa. They keep on offering inducement after inducement. I said, no, I don't. I just ignored all this. But if somebody puts something in your hand, what do you do?

Madhu: You say "no thank you" and return it to him.

Choudary: Whatever. Whether it's my daughters' earnings, my wife's earning or my earning, we said 10 per cent of it goes for animal welfare. That's how we look after so many animals. My wife wanted to live in a place like a farmhouse because she wants to look after the animals. We had seven in my earlier house. Now, seven have become ten. And plus we have added three cows.

Robin Choudary Hood riding down the glen. Robin Hood with his band of men. Feared by the bad? Loved by the good? Oh, poor Robin Hood.

Why did Choudary not refuse the money? He justified his actions:

I was telling him I could not help him. I told him repeatedly, there is no way your case is getting through. Despite that he wants to give you something. I said, *kya farak padta hai* [what difference does it make]? My wife looks after a lot of injured animals. Right now in my house I have ten dogs and three cows. One's leg is broken, one is blind. We have been looking after these animals for a number of years. My wife has been picking up dogs from the roadside. People have been giving her donations. So I said, okay, we will use it for that purpose. I just took it. Basically I am a rich man. I mean I am the only child of my parents. I got married into a rich family. My wife is herself quite a rich person. We don't need this kind of money. I have never got involved in this. That's why I said even after he gave me that money, I will not help you. It is there in the transcript. I am not going to budge from my stand. I cannot help you. Despite that, you give something, okay, I will use it for some purpose. That was the basic attitude I had.

Choudary despaired at how the media had treated him. He said, 'What was hurting my mind is that somebody is saying people had taken money and screwed the country and bought some third-rate stuff. That hurt me. No third-rate equipment can enter this system, because our procedures are such.' Choudary agreed to an interview with Star TV and Zee TV and told them they could say whatever they wanted about the acceptance of money but to ensure that the part about third-rate equipment was also broadcast. Choudary said in anguish that they cut that part out.

Choudary's anger and pain was not that he did the wrong thing. He elaborated, 'They wanted to sensationalize the story and they want to make scapegoats of people like us. Their basic aim was the politicians at the highest level. We were some of those scapegoats who got caught.'

Choudary was the only army officer who admitted his guilt on the night of 13 March 2001, when he was called to Army Headquarters. He was suspended instantly and now he said, 'I do regret it [telling the truth]. Everybody tried to tell me, any number of people who said you have done yourself harm. In fact it is also recorded in a meeting on the file. The Vice Chief wrote: "Choudary is trying to crucify himself".' But, on the basis of a technicality, he saw the advantage. Choudary said the time limitation for the court martial ended on 14 March 2004. The court-martial proceedings actually began on 28 May 2004. Choudary believed that the army had no legal right to proceed against him. Choudary stated that although seven army officers (one lieutenant general and six major generals) agreed that Choudary's case was time barred, the Conforming Authority, Lieutenant General J.J. Singh (Western Command) overruled the verdict of the army court. Choudary said, 'It was the judge advocate general of the army who advised Lieutenant General J.J. Singh to go ahead and court-martial me'.

Did Choudary consider the option of keeping quiet and not admitting his guilt? He said, 'No. If I had I wouldn't have been suspended. My being suspended, I have lost Rs 22 lakh. Twenty- five per cent of my pay was cut for two-and-a-half years. The others who did not say anything, they got away scot-free.'

When asked about the corruption culture in the army, Choudary retorted, 'In which department in India is there no corruption? Just tell me. Everywhere there is. You don't get involved. You close your eyes. Because if you try to do something, you will be picked up and thrown like a stone somewhere.' He gave the example of the mine-protected vehicle that was purchased by the army from South Africa. When the army tried to buy more from the same vendor, the defence ministry pushed through a new vendor even though the army objected. Although this was sorely needed for soldiers who were being killed by mines in Kashmir, the trial evaluations for the new equipment delayed the supply for two or three years. Choudary said the army raised objections but was forced to carry out the trials for the new vendor because he presumed that somebody had got to the top in the defence ministry. He said, 'It becomes clear, but you can do nothing about it. If you have seen the budget every year, the armed forces surrender a lot of money because you are unable to procure.'

Choudary recalled that he was directly involved in getting the Krasnopol (guided artillery projectile) during the Kargil war. Choudary said that it was actually between 1992 and 1994 that the army had decided that the Krasnopol was a worthy product. The file was just going back and forth because there was no middleman to push the case. The army saw the Kargil war as an opportunity to push through acquisitions that had long been pending. According to Choudary the army knew that the Krasnopol proved to be accurate only in the desert and was not effective in the mountainous regions. Reports from other sources stated and published in the press that Krasnopol munitions were able to hit only 25 to 30 per cent of targets in the Kargil sector during field trials. When the Russians were asked to make modifications for Kashmir, they said they did not have mountain ranges at that height to try it out. It was eventually tested in Kashmir and the army reported that it had 60 per cent accuracy. Despite that, the army was anxious enough to get the Krasnopol through for other areas, so it was purchased under the pretext that it was for the Kargil war. In August 1999, the Comptroller and Auditor General (CAG) accused the Ministry of Defence of purchasing 1000 Krasnopol Terminally Guided Munitions at a cost of $31 million without validating their usefulness. The CAG noted that 'it appears that Operation Vijay [Kargil war] was an excuse for pushing through procurement that otherwise may not have qualified.'

Choudary spoke of the time when the army was in the process of upgrading 103mm guns that had been bought in 1965 or 1966. These guns should have been junked but India could not afford to do that. Some trials were conducted and an Israeli company was considered capable of delivering. The tender was issued and price negotiations were in the process of finalization when an arms dealer brought in a Czechoslovakian company. Choudary said it was just fortunate that the Czechoslovakian company failed to produce their equipment in time for the trials. Choudary did say that although pressure might come from the defence ministry, from anybody from the defence minister downwards to the junior-most clerk, it was near impossible to pass off any substandard equipment to the army. There were too many checkpoints.

He did mention that the middlemen do pay for information on the position of particular files, what kind of notes or objections have been made about their equipment, and of course, the quotation of bids. Middlemen also pay to delay or speed up a file. There might be two dealers, one fighting to delay a file while another tries to speed up that same file. Meanwhile, those who are in the coveted positions of manning the desks where the file sits, make money from both dealers. Ironically, Choudary pointed out to alleged arms dealer Mohinder Singh Sahni's admissions in the Operation West End tapes, on how he got himself deals. Choudary confirmed his methodology. Choudary stated that somebody higher up pushes a particular company, but said that the army usually resisted a new supplier because of the delay factor.

Choudary described how the arms dealers do not come into play until after the equipment and companies have been shortlisted. According to Choudary, first an RFP (Request for Proposal) is sent out to all the vendors who are likely to offer the equipment. They send their tenders in two sealed covers. One is the technical bid and the other is called the commercial bid. The technical bid is sent to the army for paper evaluation. This provides the technical details and characteristics of the supplier's equipment. The user in the field, the EME (electrical and mechanical), the quality assurance, the Ministry of Defence with the DRDO are all involved in checking the technicalities. According to Choudary, when there are over twenty agencies involved, it is impossible to bribe so many people. The arms dealers wait until the item is shortlisted. Not true; that is when the big money starts to roll in. Operation West End amply demonstrated that you can bribe right from the lowest section officer to the senior army officers, bureaucrats and politicians.

The shortlisting is done on the basis of technical evaluations, for which over five people have to put their signatures. The file then goes to the finance ministry for approval, who sends it to the defence ministry. Based on the technical evaluation report, those who have been short-listed, are asked to bring their equipment for trials.

In Choudary's assessment, middlemen are required because the failure of the DRDO makes India dependent on imports from abroad. All suppliers do not have the capacity to establish an office in India. He said he was certain that no single person could assure that a particular product was bought, because the trial evaluation was the deciding factor. Choudary had utter contempt for DRDO, who he said had given the army nothing but rubbish. He gave the example of the Arjun tank that took them twenty years to create and was forced down the army's throat. Choudary narrated that in a conference with Defence Minister George Fernandes and the then Scientific Adviser Abdul Kalam (director of DRDO) insisted that the army accept the tank. Choudary said,

> When the army brass objected, Kalam said, "Stop, I don't participate." And walked out of the conference. The aircraft DRDO produced took so long that all the equipment was outdated. For the tank, DRDO imported everything they put in it, including the power pack, from Germany. The power pack alone cost as much as the T-90 tank. DRDO was supposed to deliver radio sets that never materialized so they were finally imported from Israel. While other countries are using infrared camouflage nets that absorb detecting rays, DRDO is struggling with fabric.

The worst that Choudary said was that the DRDO produced disastrous ammunition for the T-72 and T-90 tanks. There were reports of barrel bursting and several soldiers died. The DRDO tried to copy the 105 gun of World War II vintage and failed in that too. They were able to copy the technology but not the methodology, and the barrel was unable to withstand the pressure.

Choudary explained,

> That is why hundreds of brochures by suppliers are sent to Army Headquarters. They are just seen and sent out to subordinates to examine. Like I did. That doesn't mean that just my sending the brochure you give and get a trial evaluation order. It's all bunkum. But the public who is listening to the story does not know all this. Even within the army people do not know what are the procedures followed unless you are in that job itself. So it's lies after lies told by them. Swallowed by the people. In the media, they all take care of each other because no media is going to contradict another media organization.

In the Army Court of Inquiry, Choudary had declared that his daughter bought the Vasant Vihar flat from loans she raised independently. The following day Choudary's story changed. Choudary said he had raised the loans himself and given the power of attorney to his wife to manage the property. When I questioned him, he said, 'No, no. I purchased a small flat in Lajpat Nagar in 1995. Four years before I came in this job [procurement]. That flat was in my two daughters' names. I was in the field. So all three of us gave my wife the power of attorney to rent it out.' What about the Vasant Vihar flat? Choudary replied, 'That is in my daughter's name.' When somebody says that a property is in someone's 'name' does it not immediately connote that it is only in name while it is actually owned by someone else? When it was pointed out to him that it could hardly be a coincidence that alleged arms dealer Deepak Chabbra's family owned the flat, Choudary claimed, 'No madam, we didn't know about it. It's my wife who selected that place. My mother had sold my land at that point of time, therefore we had to put the money somewhere.' Choudary had filed depositions that his income was way beyond his salary because he was an only son and had inherited a lot of property.

Choudary said he was convinced that the tapes had been doctored. He believed that Tehelka had changed the word 'commercial' to 'commission'. He did not think much of the forensic report that declared the tapes had not been doctored, saying that the tapes had only been examined visually and not electronically. Choudary strongly believed that the expert had not done his job. Besides, he said, 'I suspect he has been bought off by the Hindujas. The people behind the whole thing were the Hindujas, because the BJP began to pursue the Bofors case. Once this took a serious turn, that's when they got worried.' Choudary was certain that the money came from Mauritius, and said it had not been established from where Shankar Sharma had got the money. He said,

> Believe me, just for satisfying journalistic instinct, you don't throw away four crores. If you are spending four crores, you expect to make ten crores out of it.

Nobody throws good money just like that. The motive was to bring the BJP government down; because if the government did not fall as expected then Tehelka does not make any money except for selling the tape to Zee TV. Fifty lakhs, for what? That is all the money they got back. All this points out that Tehelka themselves have not been honest. They had a motive and they had to sensationalize.

Choudary railed against Tehelka:

Everything done by Tehelka is against all rules and regulations of this country. There is no way you can keep on offering inducements to a person to somehow catch them. Even the police are not permitted to do that. Is this the journalistic norm? Because everybody has a price. Even the prime minister of this country can be bought if the price is right. So you cannot keep offering things for the heck of it. This is not done. If this thing happened in the US, Tehelka would be in the dock. But [the] unfortunate thing is, our systems are such. Everybody is scared of the media.

In the USA? I think not. The equivalent of the defence minister, the secretary of state for defence would be investigated in senate hearings, his colleague who accepted money would be interrogated, and if found guilty would definitely be spending quality time with some butch ladies in San Quinton prison. American army officers have faced court martial for less. When your daughter has been raped, you complain about the punishment for rape not being tough enough. However, if your son has raped someone, you complain that the punishment is excessively severe. If you belong to the rich pack (I will not use 'élite' because the dictionary defines the word as: 'the best of everything in a class'), you actually sympathize with the son of a wealthy man who ran over and killed seven poverty-stricken people with his BMW. But if a poor truck driver runs over half a rich kid, the rich pack want the driver strung up to snivel and die. That is the perspective of right and wrong as seen through the lens of who you see yourself as. Looking through self-coloured glasses. Narcissistic morality. Can we transcend our own sense of class/self and look beyond ourselves? Choudary at no point showed any regret for doing something wrong. He was upset that he was the one who got caught, and his major regret was the cut in his salary.

Choudary said bitterly,

There must be some kind of laws formed even for the so-called journalists. Anybody in the public domain doesn't have the right to privacy. But to what extent that privacy can be exploited, that is what one has to look into. You cannot con an individual to do something wrong. We have been conned to do something, which you would not have done normally. Unfortunately, about thirty minutes of tape transcript is not available of my first meeting. If that is also taken into account, I must have told him in the first meeting itself about twenty times: "sorry, your thing is a no-go case". Is that person entitled to keep on exploiting that man somehow, turn him, turn him, turn him, keep offering something or the other to change his attitude? Purely for your own benefit of your motive? Is that correct? Nobody wants to listen to me because Tehelka's lies totally projected a wrong kind of a story to the whole world. When nothing has happened, they have claimed that I have sold that equipment. If it was that simple by paying a couple of lakhs here and there, if somebody could get a contract, then why would we be struggling for 20 years to get our equipment through?

True, a couple of lakhs don't cut contracts. A lakh only gets the brochure recommended for future consideration. Multi-crores win the actual contracts.

Choudary said he got taken in by Samuel because the journalist had met 50-odd people before he got to him and so knew all the details of requirements, 'That is how I got taken in'. That easy?

Choudary believed that the BJP government made the correct move in placing in the directive to the Commission of Inquiry that the motives of the journalists should be investigated. He mentioned that the newly elected Congress alliance (UPA) removed the order to investigate the journalists. Choudary railed,

Money has come through Mauritius. They know it. Unless that money is being thrown free to you with a further motive, who would do it? The moment they learned that the Commission is not satisfied with the report given by the forensic expert, the Commission is dissolved. Never happened in the history of this country. No commission has been dissolved. Because they were worried that this forensic expert has been bought off. After all, what is a million pounds to Hindujas? If a million pounds is offered to that foreign, forensic company they would do anything.

This, I'm afraid is illogical and again looking through self-tinted lenses.

In the court martial Choudary faced three charges. One was accepting money and the gold chain, which fell under the Prevention of Corruption Act. Choudary confidently said:

Choudary: They are unable to prove it. Simple reason, there has to be a motive. There has to be a demand that I asked for money in exchange for a favour to be done. Whereas it is quite clear from the transcripts and also the evidence by Samuel that I did not ask for anything. I did not agree to help in any manner. There was no motive so they cannot level a corruption charge.
Madhu: What about not reporting the meeting to authorities?
Choudary: Not reporting the meeting is the only thing, which is there. For which they can't hang me. There are a number of people whom they already

ignored, for example, Ahluwalia, Satnam Singh, B.B. Sharma. All of them had not reported. So they were dealt with administratively by giving some displeasure or something like that. They can't decide to do something more severe to me.

Madhu: How is your family coping with the fall out?

Choudary: I won't say they have had any repercussions. When this thing came out into the open, my daughter was working for a firm. Her boss said, "Everybody has skeletons. Nothing to worry." That's the attitude of that gentleman to my daughter. She had no problems. Despite the stigma, my younger daughter got married in October. What everybody knows, as far as corruption prevailing in this country, in every department something is going on. I go to renew my driving license: for that I have to shell out money here and there because we are not willing to drive twenty kilometres and take twenty trips every time. So, okay, I gave Rs 200 to some clerk and got my license. It's become part of our system. Everybody knows it is there. People who know me intimately, they know I am not a bad chap. If somebody gives me two crores, pass my case, I did not do it. Somebody offering me a house, I did not fall for it. It is just that at that moment, you don't think if somebody is giving you something when you have said, "I cannot help you". Despite that he just puts something in your hand, that is because he wants to film you and show you as a guilty person.

So did he actually regret anything? Choudary did, and by now you won't be surprised at what. He said,

I do. After all my life is gone topsy-turvy for the last four years. First it was the Commission. Now, I am in the court martial. I am only facing inquiry after Inquiry. They took one year to record the summary of evidence. Then the general court martial started. So I am just spending money on lawyers for more and more reasons. It's just fortunate that both my daughters were earning and I could support myself. Otherwise, it is very difficult financially. Besides the financials, a person who is known for his honesty suddenly became a persona non grata in the face of everybody else. Few friends have ignored me. Only now that they know that there is nothing really serious, people talk to me.

What did Choudary see for himself in the future? Rather dejectedly he said, 'God helps those whose remorse is that he has been punished wrongly. There is no way anybody can prove corruption charges against me.' The dictionary defines 'remorse' as: 'Moral anguish arising from repentance for past misdeeds.' Choudary showed no evidence of that.

On 2 March 2005, Major General P.S.K. Choudary was sentenced to one-year rigourous imprisonment and dismissed from service. Director general artillery, Lieutenant General C.

S. Chhinna led the seven-member general court martial that found Choudary guilty on the basis of the Teheika videotapes. The GCM found him guilty of accepting illegal gratification and committing professional impropriety. Choudary was stripped of his rank and all retirement benefits.

NOTE

. According to Major General P.S.K. Choudary: The military acquisitions procedure starts with the Service Futuristics Requirements (SFR) worked out by the Service Headquarters. The army requirements are prepared by the Perspective Planning Directorate, Army Headquarters. The DRDO is required to carry out studies in terms of indigenous capability. The Service HQ then formulates the General Policy Staff Policy Statement (GPSPS), and this is then prepared by the User Directorate. It is then analysed by various agencies and finally approved in the General Staff Equipment Policies Committee (GSEPC), which is chaired by the deputy chief of army staff (DCOAS). Based on GSEPC approval, the concerned Line DTE formulates the draft General Staff Qualitative Requirement (GSQR) for each item of equipment. The draft is then sent to the DRDO and DGQA for their comments. The draft GSQR is fielded for approval in a GSEPC meeting, which discusses at length the issues approved and adopts the GSQR. The minutes of the meeting is ultimately approved by the Ministry of Defence. In the event of a Buy decision, the line directorate submits a statement of case justifying the need, quantity, and time-frame along with a draft Request for Proposal (RFP) to WE Directorate for examination and onward submission to the government. The RFP, which is like a tender document, is issued by the Ministry of Defence to selected vendors after the list has been vetted by the User Directorate, WE Directorate, and Ministry of Defence. The response to RFP comes from vendors in the form of Technical and Commercial Offer separately in sealed covers. The technical proposal is opened in the presence of the vendors by the constituted Price Negotiation Committee (PNC). Those that meet the parameters are recommended for trial evaluation and the .

balance rejected. The proceedings of the technical evaluation committee is then sent to the ministry for approval. Then, on approval, vendors whose equipment has been short-listed for trials are informed by the Ministry of Defence to bring their equipment for trials by a specified date. The WE Directorate further interacts with the concerned vendors to coordinate this aspect with the vendors, particularly in terms of what should be brought, customs exemption certificate, where the equipment should be consigned, and what would be the duration of the trials. After intimating the vendors to bring the equipment for trials, the concerned section of WE Directorate prepares the directive for conduct of trials in consultation with the user directorate. The trials directive is sent out to all concerned by WE Directorate. Choudary drew attention to the fact that it is not given to vendors but only to the agencies under the Ministry of Defence who are involved in the conduct of the trial evaluation. This is the only document issued by WE Directorate with the approval of ADGWE for evaluation of equipment. On completion of the trials, the trial report is circulated to all concerned for their comments and recommendations, and an overall performance evaluation is conducted by WE Dte which is called GS Evaluation. This indicates acceptance or otherwise of the equipment evaluated for introduction into service, and after approved by DCOAS (P&S) it is sent to the Ministry of Defence for approval. After the commercial offers are opened in respect of selected vendors, negotiations are carried out with the vendor by the PNC. In the event of better products based on improved technology become available during the process for procurement of particular equipment after evaluation and approval, a fresh GSQR is prepared or the existing one modified. A new RFP is then sent out to all vendors and the same procedures restart. Under such circumstance, physical trial evaluation is carried out only with regard to equipment that had not been previously evaluated.

18 The Scarless Letter

Absence of evidence is not evidence of absence.

– Dr Carl Sagan, (1934-1996), Astronomer, Scientist, and Writer

Mathew Samuel and Aniruddha Bahal were looking for access into the defence ministry because it was clear that Major General P.S.K. Choudary could not do much unless there was some push from the bureaucracy. Major General Murgai took Samuel to meet L.M. Mehta, additional secretary in the defence ministry on 24 December 2000. Murgai introduced Samuel:

> **Major General Murgai:** Sir, there is one UK-based company, West End International. It's a multinational spread over various countries. Their basic range is … they are making electronics products and electronic testimonials. Rest, they have got these night vision devices. And now, they are spreading their tentacles, trying to come over to various countries, including India. They have made a beginning. So, in due course of time, they want to … he is representing them.

Samuel handed over his visiting card and said,

> **Samuel:** Sir, it is written the liaisoning, but I am not liaisoning. But, I am the chief representative of this company. I am the staff of, I am a employee of this company.

When Mehta asked Samuel about what product range he had to offer, Samuel blustered, 'Sir, we have a tank navigation system. And that is smart ammunition and some very typical type of bombs. So, a lot of products. We are supplying NATO countries also.'

Mehta was obviously not impressed. Who would be? He advised Samuel to change his designation on his visiting card to director or something close. Murgai and Samuel sensed Mehta's cynicism. Murgai said, 'Actually, he is not a technical … ' Samuel added, 'Sir, I don't know any technical things'.

At this point, the West End transcripts stated that Mehta accepted a gold chain, but when Samuel offered the gift, the audio went like this:

Mehta: No, no, no, no, *nahin, nahin.*
Major General Murgai: Sir, this is nothing.
Mehta: What shall I do with this?
Major General Murgai: Sir, there is nothing sir.

According to Tehelka, at this point, Murgai placed the gift box under the table.

Mehta: Please, no.

According to Tehelka, Mehta picked up the box and kept it. According to Mehta, he picked up the box and returned it.

Major General Murgai: Should we leave? Sir, this is …
Mehta: Please keep this back.

Camera shifts to give the full view of the living room.

Samuel: No, no, please.
Mehta: No, no, it is okay.
Samuel: Nothhhhing, surrr.
Mehta: *Nahin, nahin*, this is not good.

Mehta had joined the defence ministry in August 1987 as joint secretary and chief administrative officer. He went abroad for a master's degree and on his return joined the Department of Defence Production. He remained in charge of ordnance factories till 1992, when he was posted to Haryana. He was back in the Ministry of Defence as joint secretary in 1997, dealing with army procurement. In 1999, he took over as director general of the Employees' State Insurance Corporation in the Ministry of Labour. He returned to the Ministry of Defence as additional secretary in October 2000. Mehta said that there had been no vacancy in the Ministry of Defence until 2000, when he got his appointment. Was he waiting for the vacancy? Clearly it was a preferred posting. In his job as joint secretary and additional secretary in ordnance he dealt with army procurement.

In the transcripts of the tapes, Mehta had marginal interaction with Mathew Samuel. He listened more than spoke. Many of his reactions were: 'Hmmmm', 'achcha', 'okay', 'I see'. He did not appear to be angling for a bribe. His advice to Samuel to change his designation,

Mehta said, was a polite way of telling him that he lacked competence. He was also aware that according to the rules, only paid employees or authorized representatives could liaise for companies in arms sales. Mehta was part of the tiny group in Operation West End who was not just literate, but educated. He pointed out Samuel's spelling mistake of 'Liaison' on his visiting card, and when Mehta was offered a 'packet' by Samuel, he refused it. Tehelka insisted he accepted it.

L.M. Mehta got acclimatized to Major General Murgai when they met at meetings of the price negotiating committee when Murgai was working in the Directorate of Quality Assurance. What gave Murgai the comfort level to bring Mathew Samuel to Mehta with a plan to bribe him? They popped up at Mehta's house without any appointment on 24 December 2000, possibly aware that he would be home on a Sunday morning. When Sidharth Luthra questioned him at the Commission on 24 April 2002, he was adamant about returning the 'packet':

> **Luthra**: Do you recall or would you like to see the edited tapes that when Major General Murgai left your house, his hands were empty?
> **Mehta**: Let us see. Let us see whose hands were empty.
> **Luthra**: Now, Mr Mehta, there is a bag, a yellowish bag, light-coloured bag, containing something, which is being placed on the table. Can you tell me what this bag contains?
> **Mehta**: Actually, this was not there in the transcript. This by way of voice over, which has since been deleted under orders of the Commission. This is a person who was not there. This is the interpolation. When this bag was being kept, I was not in the room even. Let us see it again. It is important from my point of view. It has to be seen that it was not L.M. Mehta who moved out of the frame; the focus of the camera shifted with mala fide intentions to prevent the return from being videographed.

Luthra played the tape.

> **Mehta**: When this person is coming out, even here I was not there. I am not in the room. It has been interpolated. At this particular moment, my Lord, I was not there in the room. It may kindly be noted of and apparently, either, there is some sequence tampering or interpolation.
> **Luthra**: The person shown in this shot is your employee Sanjay and the person to the right, whose silhouette you can see, is Major General Murgai, when they were being made to sit in your living room.
> **Mehta**: I cannot make out. Just if you could backtrack this shot for a while and show it in motion. Somebody is trying to project empty hands to give a particular meaning.

Luthra played the tape again.

Mehta: I am not in the room. I am not on the sofa. Now, I am there, sitting with Major General Murgai. So, that means there is something wrong somewhere.

Luthra: Whose sleeve is in the bag?

Mehta: White sleeve is mine.

Luthra: Putting the hand in the bag?

Mehta: To pull it out and give it back. Match it with the dialogue.

Luthra: Mr Mehta, what you are telling me is that at this point of time, the white sleeve entering the bag is yours, is it not?

Mehta: Yes, and before that the rustling sound of pulling it out should also be seen in conjunction with that.

Luthra: Who handed over the packet of the gold chain to you?

Mehta: There is no such mention in the transcript. There is no such allegation. Just show it to me from where you are reading in the revised transcript.

Justice Venkataswami had ruled that the voiceovers in the transcript were not to be included in the questioning. The only place where the gold chain is mentioned is in the voiceover. Neither Mathew Samuel nor Murgai say anything related to handing over the gold chain so there is no audible proof to transcribe. Justice Venkataswami asked Luthra how he could determine that there was a gold chain when it wasn't visible. Luthra said, he would then call it a packet. He then took Mehta through the tape, frame by frame.

Luthra: Now whose hand was it in the yellow packet?

Justice Venkataswami: He has already said it.

Mehta: There is a rustling sound. The camera is not in my hand. They wanted to create a story.

Luthra: Who was putting the packet under the table in this shot?

Mehta: This is Major General Murgai.

Luthra: Who has picked up the packet and begun opening the box?

Mehta: It is me, who picked up the box. Since they were leaving, I wanted to return it to them immediately, lest they should run away from home and it would be difficult to return it them. But I did not try to open it.

Luthra: Mr Mehta, you picked up the packet?

Mehta: Yes. Then I said, "Please keep it back. *Yeh rakhiye aap*". It is so clear. Why did not they even catch this scene? The camera was not with me. *Baaki theek hai* [rest is okay]" means once you have taken out this thing, the cake or pastries is all right. This is what I meant to say when I said, "*Baaki theek hai*". This clinches the issue.

Luthra then asked Mehta why he had demanded Rs 2 lakh from Tehelka. Mehta went ballistic, 'Who says so? Where is the allegation?' Mehta pointed out there was no video footage of any such demand, to which Justice Venkataswami coolly educated him that he could not put a counter question to the lawyer. Mehta stated exasperatedly,

There is no video footage. There is no document. There is no statement even of a third person saying so. Allegation was raised by way of Roll Over Text, voiceover, and it did not have any video backup, but I can reply to your question also. I never demanded. There was no question of my demanding and nobody, in fact, even broached the issue with me.

However, Luthra was relentless and said, Mr Mehta, you received a sum of Rs 50,000 in your office as advance through Major General Murgai …

Mehta: It is utterly false. Major General Murgai did not come to my office. There was no question of receiving any money. Even he has denied it so categorically in his own affidavit and in his cross-examination, which was conducted by you, Mr Luthra.

Luthra: Mr Mehta, I put it to you that you issued the evaluation letter to Major General Choudary in the second week of January 2001 and since you and Major General Choudary had access to that letter, it was destroyed after the exposé.

Mehta: It is a very wild figment of imagination. It is not only wild but it is very malicious. How could I? There was not even a stage set for the procurement; even the first step towards procurement had not been reached. So, where was the question of any trial evaluation letter being issued by any one of us, much less me, who was not even connected with the joint secretary in charge of Ordnance, who was not placed under me? Anybody who is familiar with the defence procurement procedure, would bear me out; there was no occasion for issuance of any letter. In any case, the allegation in the Roll Over Text about me was confined to sending a letter to Major General Choudary, based on which he would have issued a trial evaluation letter. Both the things are wrong. But my defence is confined to the first part of the allegation. I never issued any communication to General Choudary, written or oral or otherwise.

Luthra: In fact, the gift that is shown on the shot in Operation West End was offered to you, you took it in your hand; and you accepted it and retained it.

Mehta: No. It is utterly wrong, and if you carry the tape forward I can prove my innocence still further.

Luthra: You have deposed falsely and you are concealing material facts from this Commission.

Mehta: Absolutely wrong.

Was there a possibility that Choudary, Murgai, and Mehta realized the Operation West End operatives' incognizance of procurement procedures and believed they could milk them with a letter that looked official but had no substance? All the defending individuals pointed out that this was not the way evaluation trials were carried out, nor were letters for evaluation trials issued in this manner. But Mathew Samuel and Aniruddha Bahal did not know that.

They were told they would get the letter. Could it be that the defendants were now using the bluff they created, which was not according to procedure, as a defence? Since it was not according to procedure, it could not have happened. But what about the niggling thorn of the letter issued to the Infantry? A copy of that would have been enough for Operation West End to believe that they were getting somewhere and more money would have changed hands.

Major General Murgai's lawyer, Mohit Mathur, then sought to prove that Major General Murgai did indeed leave the gold chain packet with Mehta, since he shook hands with him before they left and Murgai's hands were empty. Mehta pointed out that the packet could be with either Murgai or Samuel. Mehta also denied that he had had a telephone conversation with Major General Murgai agreeing to the meeting. Mathur, in accordance with established procedure, accused Mehta of deposing falsely.

Dr Khetarpal, the lawyer representing Major General P.S.K. Choudary, demanded that Mehta outline army procurement procedures. Khetarpal hammered the point that Major General Choudary could not have issued the trial evaluation letter without Mehta first writing a letter from the defence ministry.

Mehta: I was not officially connected with the matter. The allegation against me was confined to writing a letter to General Choudary, based on which, allegedly, he would have issued some trial evaluation letter. So, my knowledge and my defence is confined to saying that I did not send any communication to Major General Choudary at all in this matter.
Khetarpal: Whether you were empowered to issue any such letter?
Mehta: Actually, as I have submitted earlier before the Honourable Commission, I was not even connected with the matter. The Ordnance Wing of the ministry worked under a different additional secretary. It, in any case, would not have come to me. General Choudary could not have issued the trial evaluation letter on his own. It would have to be issued by the ministry. That much I can clarify.
Khetarpal: Is it true that some vendors, whose product was not short-listed after technical evaluation or rejected during the price negotiation, approach the press or various dignitaries and make all sorts of allegations so as to delay the finalization of the contract?
Mehta: People do adopt such tactics. It is not very uncommon.

It was Tehelka's principal objective to bring to the surface the mechanics of muck in arms procurement. It does not all happen without the cooperation of those in charge of these operations. All those Caught on Tape were in some way connected. If vendors understood that implementing their tactics would not be successful, they would not waste their time and money on it. If the matter was not in Mehta's domain, as he claimed, why did he meet Mathew Samuel and ask him details about the equipment? Yet, he was not impressed with Samuel and did ask to meet his boss in order to evaluate the company's credentials.

Although Prime Minister Manmohan Singh's government handed over the Tehelka case to the CBI on 4 October 2004, and the CBI has since charge-sheeted seven individuals related to the Operation West End tapes, I have been unable to find any report about L.M. Mehta.

COLONEL A.P. SINGH

Mathew Samuel continued with his meetings to bring the operation to a close. In their last meeting, Murgai told Samuel that Surendra Sureka was trying to get in touch with Samuel to get more money. Murgai said that Sureka had told him that he had already allegedly paid Jaya Jaitly Rs 3 lakh and now demanded Rs 10 lakh. Sureka wanted the payment in cash in advance and said he could then get the evaluation letter issued in 24 hours. Samuel requested Murgai to tell L.M. Mehta to write the letter from the defence ministry and he would pay the money. Murgai agreed to do that.

The Tehelka journalists believed they would be handed the letter they critically needed to clinch the sting. R.K. Jain, remember him? The Samata Party treasurer whose misanthropic eloquence about Jaya Jaitly and the numerous arms deals he had swung that made him so conspicuous. Jain got suspicious of Samuel and traced his cellular phone number to the Tehelka office. Not a difficult thing for him to do. A little grease to one of the cell phone company guys was easy enough. Jain sent his nephew to the Tehelka office, and he discovered it was a news organization and Mathew Samuel was a journalist. Before Samuel and Aniruddha Bahal could pick up the hot letter, the alarm bells rang all the phones of those who had been stung. The blood ran backwards in the network. The evaluation letter was essential to successfully complete the sting. The moment of holding the evaluation order letter in their hands, that frozen moment, was everything that the Tehelka journalists had worked for. That missing should-have-been moment becomes a lifetime of regret for a journalist.

When Aniruddha and Samuel went to Murgai's house to pick up the 'letter', they discovered to their dismay that Major General P.S.K. Choudary and Sureka's cars were parked outside. For three days they tried to get to Murgai and found the same cars parked outside. They then realized their game was up.

Tehelka operatives may not have had the letter in their hands, but they were vindicated by the eighteenth witness in the Army Court of Inquiry on 19 April 2001: Colonel A.P. Singh. Singh was Director WE-4 at Army Headquarters and dealt with the trial and procurement of infantry weapons and equipment. According to his testimony,

> An unsolicited offer was received from M/s West End, UK in October 2000 by AGDWE. The literature was forwarded to users, i.e. Infantry Directorate for study in comparison with in-service HHTIs. The Infantry Directorate carried out an in-depth analysis in consultation with Infantry School, Mhow and in January 2001 recommended trial evaluation on "No cost. No commitment" basis. The recommendations of Infantry Directorate were, however, analysed by WE Directorate and it was decided that trial evaluation at this stage was not

warranted as M/s BEL was still in the process of establishing production line based on TOT acquired, we had already procured two varieties of HHTI and the case for procurement of additional 208 HHTIs was in a very advanced stage with the government. M/s West End has subsequently turned out to be a fictitious company.

Bahal and Samuel never got to hold that letter in their hands, but there is no doubt that Major General P.S.K. Choudary did forward their brochure to Infantry Directorate for evaluation. Choudary had begun what was a normal process for him, until the next step, which would mean bigger bucks.

No, West End did not sell their fictitious product. But they proved how army officers routinely accept money and forward brochures for consideration. For each step, money is handed out. They did contaminate the first step inside the procurement process in the army. Yet, the virus continues. The proof? Take a real hard look at the reputed arms dealers.

BRIBES PAID DURING THE COURSE OF OPERATION WEST END
(According to Tehelka)

Colonel Anil Sehgal   20,000.00
     Date: 5 Sept. 2000
     Place: Arjun Vihar

Colonel Anil Sehgal   20,000.00
     Date: 21 Sept. 2000

P. Sasi (Sashi)   2,000.00
     Date: 6 Sept. 2000
     Place: India Gate

P. Sasi   20,000.00
     Date: 25 Sept. 2000
     Place: Hotel Orchid

P. Sasi   10,000.00
     Date: 1 Nov. 2000
     Place: His house

P. Sasi   20,000.00
     Date: 18 Nov. 2000
     Place: His house

Lt Colonel Sayal (Retd)   10,000.00
    Date: 6 Oct. 2000
    Place: Hotel Orchid

Lt Colonel Sayal (Retd)   5,000.00
    Date:18 Oct. 2000
    Place: DSOI

Lt Colonel Sayal (Retd)   15,000.00
    Date: 20 Oct. 2000

Lt Colonel Sayal (Retd)   10,000.00
    Date: 1 Nov. 2000

Lt Colonel Sayal (Retd)   10,000.00
    Date: 2 Nov. 2000

Lt Colonel Sayal (Retd)   20,000.00
    Date: 5 Nov. 2000
    Place: Park Hotel

Lt Colonel Sayal (Retd)   10,000.00
    Date: 7 Nov. 2000
    Place: Connaught Place

Suresh Kodikunnil   7,000.00
    Date: 10 Oct. 2000
    Place: His house

Maj. Gen. S.P. Murgai (Retd)   20,000.00
    Date: 19 Oct. 2000
    Place: His house

Maj. Gen. S.P. Murgai (Retd)   25,000.00
    Date: 24 Dec. 2000
    Place: His house

Maj. Gen. S.P. Murgai (Retd)   25,000.00
    Date: 25 Dec. 2000
    Place: His house

Maj. Gen. S.P. Murgai (Retd)   20,000.00
    Date: 29 Dec. 2000
    Place: His house

Maj. Gen. S.P. Murgai (Retd)   50,000.00
    Date: 8 Jan. 2001
    (for L.M. Mehta)
    Place: Murgai's house

Raghupati   16,000.00
    Date: 4 Nov. 2000

Narender Singh   10,000.00
    Date: 4 Nov. 2000
    Place: B-21, DIZ, CP

Brig. Iqbal Singh   50,000.00
    Date: 5 Nov. 2000
    Place: 1015, Park Hotel

H.C. Pant   20,000.00
    Date: 22 Nov. 2000
    Place: Lodhi Road

H.C. Pant   20,000.00
    Date: 25 Nov. 2000
    Place: C-6, Qutab Institutional Area

Mr H.C. Pant   10,000.00
    Date: 28 Nov. 2000
    Place: Inside the car

Mr H.C. Pant   **10,000.00**
    Date: 18 Dec. 2000

Mr L.M. Mehta   Gold Chain
    Date: 24 Dec. 2000
    Place: Chanakya Puri

Maj. Gen. P.S.K. Choudary   1,00,000.00
    Date: 24 Dec. 2000
    Place: His house

Maj. Gen. P.S.K. Choudary   Gold Chain
    Date: 16 Dec. 2000
    Place: Murgai's house

Mr Surendra Singh Sulekha (Sureka)   1,00,000.00
    Date: 28 Dec. 2000
    Place: Murgai's House

Ms Jaya Jaitly   2,00,000.00
    Date: 28 Dec. 2000
    Place: George Fernandes's residence

Mr R.K. Jain   50,000.00
    Date: 3 Jan. 2001
    Place: Akashdeep Bldg.

Bangaru Laxman   1,00,000.00
    Date: 5 Jan. 2001
    Place: At his residence

Raju Venkatesh   10,000.00
    Date: 23 Dec. 2000
    Place: Bangaru's residence

TOTAL : 10,08,000.00

19 Enforcement Inferno

Hume tedhi oonglee sey ghee nikalna ata hai [we know how to use a crooked finger to extract the butter].

– Indian Proverb

Shankar Sharma and Devina Mehra made a pilot's error when they invested in Tehelka. One small step of an investment led to a giant leap into a downward spiral of police raids, interrogations, endless litigation, courts, and yes, even jail. This was no moonwalk. Shankar Sharma's and Devina Mehra's lives turned on them. All their branch offices closed down, their properties were attached, their home and offices were raided 26 times, their computer hard disks and servers were seized. They were banned from trading on the stock exchange, which was their livelihood, their bank accounts were frozen. They were physically detained three times, Shankar went to jail for nine weeks without bail under a law that had been repealed a year and a half earlier by Parliament, and within the year, they received over 300 summons for personal appearances from various departments and agencies of the government. The Income Tax Department, the Enforcement Directorate (ED), the Excise Department, the Department of Company Affairs, and the Reserve Bank of India all investigated Shankar and Devina. The Income Tax Department raided them 15 times. Twenty-two were cases filed against them under the Companies Act, plus one FERA case and five FERA civil proceedings. Shankar's passport was confiscated and it took him a year to retrieve it. Devina got a stay order against her passport being impounded, which required yet more appearances in court.

Who then are Shankar Sharma and Devina Mehra? Not exactly household names, even after the Tehelka exposé. Shankar and Devina both come from what would be termed 'humble backgrounds' in Hinglish. They graduated from institutes of management and incorporated First Global Stockbroking Pvt. Ltd in 1994. They are both directors of the company. Shankar looks at trading research and Devina into fundamental research. In the course of seven years First Global became one of the largest securities companies in India. They work sitting next to each other and say they experience separation anxiety if they are not with each other all the time. They bounce ideas off each other, and when Shankar was in jail, being out of touch was the most difficult aspect. Both say they can guess what the other will say and function in complete tandem. Before the Tehelka chapter, they had 18 branches and employed over 300 people. They have offices in London and New York that trade internationally. The First Global Group is the first Indian company admitted to membership of the London Stock Exchange. It was rated among the three top brokerage houses in India by *Asia Money* magazine. In January 2001, the Securities and Exchange Board of India granted First Global the status of a deemed Foreign Institutional Investor. This enabled First Global to raise money from overseas. The trading turnover of the First Global Group in the year 1999-2000 was Rs 7,432 crore. Devina Mehra and Shankar Sharma were individually among the top taxpayers in India. During their 10 years of doing business, they had never been hauled up for any tax or legal infringement. Their success story crashed when First Global was forced to close down in April 2001.

Shankar Sharma and Devina Mehra are a couple that in many ways exemplify the new, emerging India, but now, if anything, their story also exemplifies what is wrong with India. Their Rashomon of what happened to them after Tehelka, exposes the hidden membrane of perdition that simmers under the sanitized, orderly veneer of an investigation. There's no inherited money here. No special contacts or godfather politicians. Their families are solidly middle-class who believed that education was the best they could give them. Devina won eight gold medals during her college education and broke a 60-year record for the highest aggregate marks in her undergraduate course at Lucknow University. During her two years at the Indian Institute of Management in Ahmedabad, Devina was a gold medallist and had scholarships for both years. Shankar received an MBA from the Asian Institute of Management in Manila, where he made it to the Dean's list. Devina worked with Citibank after she graduated, but her interests lay more in research. She said the biggest kick she got in life was learning new things in her field. She had got admission in 1990 to the University of California, Los Angeles, for a PhD but realized there was not much she could do with a PhD in finance. When the markets in India opened up to foreign investments in 1993, research into industries and companies became relevant to the stock market. That is when Devina joined Shankar's business.

Sharma: The business really took off when she joined. That was the turning point. Because I was struggling and Devina coming on board was the big, big, change. It was a before and after story.

Madhu: So you had the larger vision and Devina had the skills or was it vice versa?

Mehra: No, we have skills that are, in many ways, complementary. For example, on the marketing or getting business side, those would be his strengths, whereas my strengths will lie more in analysis and research.

Madhu: So you married her for her skills?

Sharma: Partly. She's smarter than I am. It's always smart strategy to marry a smarter person. I don't know why men have this problem.
Mehra: A lot of people in Citibank had warned him that why are you thinking of getting married to her?
Madhu: She's too smart for you?
Sharma: Yeah. But then, that's okay, *yaar*. You should know how to handle smart people. That's part of the whole management thing.
Mehra: But yes, when I joined, then the vision would have been his because it was a business that he had started.

Despite the fortune they made, the two have lived a low-key, simple life with no garish cars or opulent homes and offices, and have stayed away from the vacuous party scene. Shankar switched from cigars to bidis in jail and continued smoking them for a while. Devina is a surprise. She has a shock of thick, wavy unruly air, no make-up apart from lipstick occasionally, and clothes that show a complete oblivion of style. She tends towards plumpness but is on a diet and is working it off. She is not beautiful in a conventional sense, but after you've spent time with her and listened to her, you understand why Shankar, unashamedly, unequivocally adores her. They work together, live together, built their company together, were virtually destroyed together, and are now fighting for their survival together. Often they answer together, using the same words and just as often complete each other's sentences. Yet, both are very different from each other. Shankar is tall, good looking in the boy-next-door mode, and at first glance they seem an odd couple. Shankar's language is more impulsive and macho, peppered with '*yaar*', 'fucking', and 'boss'. Devina has yet to use any such words in my presence. She is more aware of who she is talking to, the consequences her words will have, particularly in print. Perhaps because Shankar so uninhibitedly praises her worth, she has an inner confidence that precludes the need to prove herself. She is unquestionably strong, yet is not above breaking down and crying. Her pain when she recalls the time Shankar spent cold winter nights in Delhi's freezing jails is obvious. But that does not stop her from laughing uncontrollably when recalling that his sisters broke down after visiting Shankar in jail, crying: 'he doesn't even know how to fold his clothes.'

Devina and Shankar both come across as financial and business intellectuals. Testimony to this is to be found in their many articles published internationally. Even more so it lies in their perspective of the cauldron of problems created by the Tehelka connection. The clearest example, of course, is Devina's Kafkaesque statement in one of their long conversations with me:

Now you realize that anybody out there is only there because nobody wants you inside. Any time somebody wants you inside [jail], you can be inside.

It is so much easier to identify and write about overtly totalitarian regimes. In India, as is our culture, cruelty is rarely practised openly. It is insidious, carefully orchestrated so as to appear that whatever is happening is a matter of course and the law is being impeccably observed.

Much like the stereotypical venom filled mother-in-law or sister-in-law, who spends her days in prayer and social work, while being covertly mean and evil when not observed by men. When the Secret Auto Destruct System (SADS) is activated, no instructions are given in writing. Often, not even over the phone. Just come and see me. The drift of the destruct is given face to face with no witnesses. It is far worse than in any openly totalitarian regime.

～

When Shankar first spoke to Tarun Tejpal on the morning of 13 March 2001, his only concern was that Tarun was going to blow his financing away and thereby forestall his forthcoming exit plans out of Tehelka. Although he believed at that time that Tarun could have waited until Subhash Chandra invested in Tehelka, in hindsight, knowing what the government was capable of, Tarun had no choice. Shankar said,

> When you've done a sting operation, probably your cover getting blown by these goons would mean that you would end up behind bars for spying, some shit like that. Imagine, if this had not become public and these guys had caught hold of Mathew Samuel or somebody, they would have just thrown him away, called him an ISI spy or some Mujahideen guy smuggling.

On the morning of 13 March, Shankar called his office and asked his staff to switch off the terminals and stop all trade until after the tapes were shown. At that point, Shankar and Devina had no thought whatsoever that the echo of the exposé would destroy their work and personal lives. On 14 March 2001, *The Economic Times,* strangely enough, ran a story with the headline, 'First Global's Broking Licence in Danger', a story that had no apparent evidence or basis. At this point SEBI had not started its investigation.

> **Madhu**: When was the first time that you felt the repercussions of investing in Tehelka?
> **Sharma**: That happened when the planted stories started coming in *The Economic Times* in Delhi. From March 15 onwards, weird tales started coming out. The reporters were Sanjeev Sharma and P.R. Ramesh. That sort of told us that something is brewing. Then Jana Krishnamurti [the new BJP president, who succeeded Bangaru Laxman when the latter resigned] comes out and says it's a conspiracy. Somebody else comes out with that it's a Congress conspiracy.
> **Mehra**: BJP takes out a morcha in Bangalore saying we have to find out who is behind Tehelka.
> **Sharma**: Questions were being raised that what is the source of the financing of Tehelka? We started getting more than a little scared. We held a press conference on March 16, 2001, in Mumbai. We gave all the records of our transactions. We said, go and chew over this, guys. And even if it's me saying so, in our 10 years in business we built a sterling reputation.

The Mumbai press knew Shankar and Devina well from previous business-related interviews, none of them even remotely political. But, the press reports emanating from the conference also said that First Global was looking for an exit from the Tehelka investment. On the same night they flew to New York for their NASDAQ accreditation interviews. Although they believed the press conference went off reasonably well, they were somewhat apprehensive as they had never had bad press. In the waiting lounge at the airport, Devina went to chat with an old classmate from IIM, J.R. Verma, a board member of SEBI. When Devina returned, she told Shankar in hushed tones that Verma had been extremely guarded while talking to her and she found that strange. On the flight they talked about possible harassment they could expect and were quite calm about it. Shankar said, 'We thought the worst the government can do is income tax raid *ho sakta hai, woh sab ho sakta ha* [income tax raid is possible, all that is possible], but if they don't find anything, what are they going to do? Every business house in India lives with this thing that sooner or later these guys will land up. It's not the end of the world by any stretch of the imagination.'

Shankar and Devina planned to stay in the United States till the first week of April, but a call from their Mumbai office jettisoned their schedule. Income tax officer A.A. Shankar spoke from First Global's office phone and abruptly told them that the Income Tax Department had sealed the Sharma/Mehra home. A.A. Shankar curtly asked them to return immediately and open the apartment, as they had the keys.

Shankar and Devina caught the next flight out and were received by a friend at 4.00 a.m. They went straight to their apartment in Colaba, but had to check into a hotel close by.

Sharma: I remember it was a very, very weird feeling. You're outside your home. You're not allowed to sleep in your own home. It made me very angry. I can't enter my own home, *yaar*.

Mehra: The irony of it was that in the previous year we had paid over Rs 20 crore in tax. Then what's the point, if you do not even buy immunity from this kind of stuff after paying so much tax?

They called up the Income Tax Department the following morning and about a dozen officers arrived at noon to open their home. The officers then began to pull the place apart, going through their clothes, examining underwear, reading letters, rifling through cupboards. Shankar and Devina were shocked when they turned on *Star News* and watched a story that reported they had been arrested at the airport. Devina said, 'Of course it was planted. All kinds of wild stuff was getting printed and shown. We were thinking, suppose somebody in the family sees it, they will panic.' Shankar added, 'It's also about your repute, *yaar*. Getting arrested, getting raided is not something … You get used to all this shit later when nothing fazes you any more. But then, it was like a big thing.' They called their families to tell them they were at home. Shankar then called Raj Roy at Star News and demanded, What the hell are you running? I am sitting at home.' Roy told Shankar that this report must have come from Delhi and it was corrected in the 9 o'clock bulletin.

The income tax raid continued until midnight. Shankar and Devina refused to feed them.

Sharma: They ordered food. You get angrier and angrier. You feel violated. Very, very violated. Somebody comes into your home like this and goes through all your stuff.

Mehra: Of course, on an individual level, they were all saying this is all because of Tehelka.

Sharma: They were saying, *hum kya karey, Dilli sey orders hain. Humey karna pad raha hai. It's nothing personal lekin humey karna hai. Mainey kaha, theek hai, sala, karne do* [what can we do, we've got orders from Delhi. We are forced to do it. It's nothing personal but we have to do it. I said, okay, bastards, let them do it].

Mehra: Very soon they knew there was nothing to be found at home. Our office guys were laughing, what will they find in the raid? They know precisely how much jewellery she will have. [They both laughed easily.] Obviously, there was nothing. There are mostly books at home, nothing else.

Sharma: The only thing we are proud of is our library; that's about it.

Mehra: By the time they got to the second bedroom, they lost interest. There was nothing there. They left everything open that they had gone through. There was a pile of papers left in the middle of the drawing room, which didn't get cleared up till months later. They had done no homework before raiding us. If you read the income tax manuals you are supposed to do a lot of work and make sure you are going to find some unaccounted income before you raid anybody. They didn't even know how many offices we had. They'd just been told to go and raid. They didn't know we had a locker. Our lockers had not been sealed. They asked us, "Do you have a locker?" We said, "Yes, here's the key". Then they went and sealed it. They opened that after two days. By then they had finished everywhere else and they had not even found Rs 5,000 that was not in our books. Not one piece of jewellery, not one piece of property, not one share that was not on our books. So by that time they were panicking. There were no seizures at all.

Sharma: So what are we going to tell the guys in Delhi? *Itna raid kiya aur kuch nahin mila*? [we raided so much and found nothing]? Then they opened the locker ...

Mehra: ... which had not been operated for two-and-a-half years.

Sharma: We showed them that the last time we had opened this thing in 1999 or something. The only thing there was a few papers and our home papers.

Mehra: A little bit of wedding jewellery, all of which was in the records. The only piece of jewellery which I had got made, Rs 1.5 lakh, not any great money also ...

Sharma: ... that too fully accounted for and disclosed in our personal balance sheet.

Mehra: Every invoice, everything. Then the guy called up his boss and said, *Kuch nahin mila yahan, kya karey* [haven't found anything here, what should we do]?

Sharma: He called up on his mobile. I heard him. He said, *Sahib, yahan kuch nahin mila* [Sir, we found nothing]. The guy on the other end said, *Kya jewellery-wellery nahin mila? Sahib, woh toh accounted for hai* [didn't you find any jewellery? Sir, it is all accounted for]. The valuer came and he evaluated it at Rs 1.5 lakh. Then I immediately called up the office, asked them to bring the invoices, showing the proof of the cheque payment and everything, as well as the personal balance sheet, saying, look this is where it was disclosed. She has paid Rs 3 crore in taxes individually. She's entitled to a *daed lakh rupya ka piece* [she's entitled to a Rs 1.5 lakh piece]. Even if I don't produce an invoice, you have to give me the benefit of the doubt. You can't say, *television ka invoice nahin hai toh main television le ke jaoonga* [you can't say, you don't have an invoice for the television so I am going to take your television away]. This is ridiculous, *yaar*. They had to shoot and say, *humne jewellery seize kar li* [they had to shoot and say we have seized jewellery].

Mehra: They took the jewellery. In income tax law, there is a ruling that 500 grams of jewellery is allowed. Their way of interpreting it is that even if there is one diamond in it, therefore you can take it away.

Sharma: *Toh leh gayeh* [so they took it]. It's completely illegal.

First Global had six offices in Mumbai. The income tax team confiscated 300 personal computers from their Vizag and Salem offices. Devina said,

> These guys were not very sensible, not very educated, so they don't know actually how to cripple a business. They can only do what a *thelewala* [street seller] will do. Take away visible stuff, but they don't realize that you have backups and you can put a lot of the stuff back together.

Despite writing letters to every official from the finance minister down, Devina has yet to get her jewellery back. That same evening, 27 March 2001, they received a call from an employee that an official from SEBI's Delhi office, Salil Gupta, was flexing his muscles in the First Global office. Why somebody should be sent from Delhi when the SEBI head office was in Mumbai was a mystery. While their home was being raided, Gupta interrogated Shankar and Devina. The first thing he asked for were papers related to Buffalo Networks and Tehelka. Although SEBI has no regulatory control or power to enquire into unlisted companies such as Buffalo Networks, it continued to ask for information and documents related to Tehelka. Most of these requests were not made in writing but the compliances to those requests by First Global were put in writing. Gupta made copies of all the documents related to Tehelka and Buffalo Networks.

Shankar and Devina were interrogated for 9 days for up to 12 hours at a time. The income tax officer told them unofficially that the raids were in connection with the Tehelka issue and not to uncover any undeclared income. He said that a case relating to Tehelka had to be built up. He also said that the finance ministry was 'looking for a Taj Mahal in Delhi, while it is actually in Agra'. SEBI officers assured them that they had nothing to worry about as they were net buyers on the day and so could not be connected to the stock market crash of 2 March 2001, the ostensible purpose of the investigation.

> **Sharma**: We were still pretty wet behind the ears then. So we said, *de doh, kya farak padtha hai, yaar* [so we said, give it, what difference does it make, buddy]. Little did we know that all the papers we would give them then would keep getting filed in Delhi six months later in the Venkataswami Commission, whatever that means. Gupta sat and read the Buffalo Networks file, made a photocopy of it and left.

Following that, a series of summons, about 230, were sent to them to appear at the Income Tax Department office to answer questions. On some days, they were summoned to appear at 11.00 a.m. at three different places.

> **Sharma**: They pick out one piece of paper in which you've written, whatever, "Madhu Trehan 10". So they'll say these are all cash payments to Madhu Trehan. So I'd say, wait a second, here is the cheque payment. Anything written on a piece of paper is all cash payments to Mr X. Even if you're making your *hisaab* [calculations], these are the cheques you've got, these are the cheques you've got to pay, they won't cross-check with the books whether these payments were cheque payments or not. In a nutshell, none of these agencies came to find out the truth. Their mandate was to invent. Don't discover. Those were the innocent days, when we thought we could reason with them and explain to them, say, look guys there's nothing here. This realization started dawning on us gradually. *Ismey koi logic nahin hai, ismay koi explanation nahin hai* [there is no logic or explanation in this]. That was the point [when] we decided we are going to stop talking to these bastards.

Their life became cocooned in a dense smog of fear. For three nights a white Maruti van was parked outside their home, observing every move. Shankar and Devina laughed as they said that the first thing they did was to go out and buy books on 'Search and Seizure'. They studied enough to be aware of an Indian citizen's rights.

> **Sharma**: None of these bastards will tell you your rights. They all say, no, *aap ke paas koi rights nahin hai* [they all say, you have no rights at all]. *Sara power government key paas hai. Sari power Income Tax key pas mey hai. Hum kuch bhi kar saktey hain* [the government has all the power. The Income Tax Department has all the power. We can do whatever we want]. Average guy has no idea, what they can do, what they can't do.
> **Mehra**: They tell you, you can't make a phone call. Actually, if you read the law, they can't stop you from making a phone call. You can call your lawyer. You can

call your chartered accountant. It says that it is the responsibility of the officer to make sure you have calmed down enough that you are in a proper frame of mind, before you give your statement. What they actually do is try to threaten and intimidate you.

Sharma: Pure and simple terror tactics.

During the income tax raid at their office, they confined a twenty-five-year-old staff member in a room for 24 hours without food and water and continually threatened him. Neeraj Khanna, who worked as a consultant for First Global, was interrogated through the night, not allowed to sleep, while various officers took turns snoozing and interrogating him. Khanna was threatened that his licence would be cancelled if he did not sign a statement against Shankar Sharma and Devina Mehra. They kept other staff there for 36 hours at a stretch.

Sharma: Anybody will break, *yaar*. And they'll say, *yeh likho, yeh paper jo mila hai, usko bol doh sara unaccounted cash hai. Nahin karogey toh abhi hum police koh bulateh hain* [and they'll say, write this, this paper that has been found, say that all this cash is unaccounted for or we will call the police]. People don't know whether the police have anything to do with a raid or not. Who knows? If you do a poll in this room, most people will say, *arrest toh nahin ho saktey raid mey, yaar. Nahin ho saktey, pur kisko maloom hai yeh baat* [most people would say they cannot arrest you in a raid. Can't be arrested, but who knows this]. They have the licence to do these things. It's just *goonda raj, yaar* [it the rule of the goons, buddy].

Mehra: We documented it right then. We wrote to the whole hierarchy, saying these are the specific threats.

When Shankar and Devina started quoting sections from the Search and Seizure Act, the officers got even more upset with them. The first questions they asked were all related to Tehelka. When Shankar informed them that the statute says that a citizen has only to answer questions relating to assessment of income, the officers were furious. They threatened to file criminal prosecution against them under Section 179 of the Indian Penal Code. Shankar still refused to answer questions that did not fall within the purview of the income tax laws.

From 3 April 2001, right up to 17 April 2001, Shankar and Devina were questioned, principally about Tehelka. The only correspondence that was seized related to Tehelka. No questions were asked about any other First Global investments, while in the context of their entire business, Tehelka was probably their smallest investment.

Harassment began from the Reserve Bank of India (RBI), an institution one would tend to believe is above such pettiness. RBI asked on 9 April 2001 for the Annual Performance Report (APR) of First Global's subsidiary in London, which was not due until 31 July 2001. The RBI threatened to refer the matter to the ED if the APR was not filed. The APR was filed in time.

On 17 April Shankar received a call from an income tax officer saying he should appear before them the following morning. When Shankar protested that he had organized meetings, the officer insisted that he show up. When they arrived in Deputy Director R. Laxman's office at 11.00 a.m. next morning, there was a man sitting with a note pad and pen in the room. Laxman told Shankar they were going to start recording his statement. Shankar asked him how could he start recording a statement if he hadn't given him a summons? Laxman said they didn't need a summons, to which Shankar replied that he had read the law and knew it was essential. This argument continued for an hour and a half and at 12.30 p.m., Laxman served Shankar a perfunctory summons. Shankar then demanded to know who was the man sitting in the corner and asked that he identify himself. The man did not move and did not say a word. Laxman said he did not have to identify anybody in the room, while Shankar insisted that he would not record his statement in front of someone he did not know. In an amazing coincidence, in the 17th sentence of *The Trial* by Franz Kafka, the 'hero', Joseph K. utters virtually the same sentence in uncannily similar circumstances. Joseph K., in *The Trial*, says, 'I will neither stay here or be talked to by you unless you tell me who you are'.

> **Sharma**: I said, fine, we'll sit here all day long and waste time but you are not getting anything out of me. He would not disclose the identity of that person. Finally, that guy had to leave. I think he was from the IB or something. He looked like a weird, weird, spook.
>
> **Madhu**: What did he look like?
>
> **Sharma**: Completely impassive. Blank look absolutely. In his 40s, tall, about six feet two, fairish. He was wearing a striped shirt and he had a moustache.
>
> **Mehra**: He had a squint or something.
>
> **Madhu**: Did he say anything?
>
> **Sharma**: Nothing!
>
> **Mehra**: Even when this argument was going on, he said nothing. That was the strange part.
>
> **Sharma**: Look, I'm talking to you. You're the income tax guy, this man is sitting there. I am sitting here and I am saying, this guy has to leave or I'm not going to give my statement.
>
> **Mehra**: Who is this guy? It's like he's made of stone.
>
> **Sharma**: You'd imagine this guy would react or something. Like, *nahin, sahib, main toh yahin ka hun* [no, sir, I am from this department]. Nothing. He just kept looking at me.

After the unidentified man left, Laxman began to record the statement.

> **Mehra**: What used to happen in our normal statement also was, we'd record one page, this guy would go out, go to his boss, proudly fax the page to his boss, who would then call back and say, these are the questions you must ask. So it was actually, each page was going all the way to Delhi and back.

Sharma: So this thing continued. I think I recorded a couple of pages of statement that day. Finally at 2 o'clock in the afternoon, I said, Mr Laxman I really have to leave. He said, "No, no, you must complete this thing." I said, Your statement is going to carry on till 10 at night. You haven't even given me valid summons. You please serve me valid summons, I will make sure I come within 24 hours notice. But, today I have to go. He kept insisting. I said finally, enough is enough. I really have to leave. And, I closed my statement saying, I am leaving now and 2.05 p.m. I signed it and left.

Mehra: Before that what happened was, it was lunchtime. They said, have lunch. We said, lunch *toh hum log layey hain* [we have brought lunch with us], but we can't stay beyond a certain time. I opened the lunch box and I said, *chammuch nahin hain* [there is no spoon]. He said, *merey lunch box mey sey chammuch leylo* [take the spoon from my lunch box]. I brought an apple also. We gave him the apple. The last thing we did was, I went to the pantry, cleaned the spoon and gave it back to him.

Sharma: Then he wrote after that, Shankar Sharma left abruptly without answering questions. So that's what happened that day.

Mehra: We started making it into bit of a picnic, in terms of reversing their mental thing. In the beginning their tactic was, you would get upset, you have a business to run, sitting in the income tax office for 12 hours a day, you say anything just to get out of this. We said, no, we've kept five years aside to keep coming here during the day.

Sharma: Ha! Ha! Ha! *Sahib, aap thak jaogey. Hum nahin thukney valey* [sir, you will get tired. We are not going to get tired]. It's a mental game. If you show you're scared, they're going to run all over you, *yaar*.

Mehra: Then we'd generally take along food and I laugh pretty loudly. Then [the] income tax chap would say, *ap chup kariyey. Lageyga bahar picnic ho rahi hai* [the income tax guy would say, Keep quiet. It will appear to people outside that a picnic is going on]. Ha! Ha! Ha!

Sharma: I said, picnic *hee toh hai. Apney par kuch hai nahin* [I said, it is a picnic. You don't have anything on us]. You have to cook up something. I'm not going to help you do that, *yaar*.

At 9.30 p.m. on 18 April Shankar got a call from the office that there was a fax without a letterhead but it appeared to be from SEBI. They left their dinner and rushed to the office. Shankar said the fax looked weird, it had no letterhead, no signature, and looked incomplete. They thought it could be a hoax. It was an order to First Global offices to stop their business pending an investigation, under Section 11B of the SEBI Act. No board has to consider and approve this decision. A single man has the licence to stop a listed company's business. It was SEBI Chairman D.R. Mehta who took the decision under Section 11B of the SEBI Act that enables the SEBI chairman to debar a broker pending an investigation. This Act is supposed to be used in an emergency situation, so the SEBI chairman stretched the Act to its extreme.

Shankar and Devina then dashed to SEBI's office where a guard told them that all the officers had just left. Shankar got the home phone number of an officer they had met earlier. Shankar said, 'He was really nice. He asked, *Order mil gayah aap ko* [have you received the order]?" I asked him, "Why has this been done?" He answered, "If there was a reason, I would tell you." We asked to meet him. He said, "I feel so ashamed, I can't meet you. It is the worse thing I have done in my career. As it is an interim order, it cannot be challenged and it is impossible to get immediate relief to run your business." Shankar and Devina began to discuss the inevitability of firing 300 employees and shutting down their branches. Devina said, 'If somebody is not performing and you tell him to go, it is not a big deal. But to tell people who are doing well and who you really like, for no fault of yours or theirs, you have to tell them to go. It is very tough. That was a really hard part.'

Coincidentally, all this happened when First Global was going through the process of getting their NASDAQ membership. The NASDAQ team from the US was visiting India and they questioned First Global about their own regulator shutting them down. The NASDAQ team examined all the First Global papers with a fine toothcomb and concluded that Shankar and Devina were being railroaded for no reason based on their trading. They did mention that if NASDAQ had done this kind of thing in the US, they would have been sued and taken to the cleaners.

Shankar and Devina were in a panic that morning, frantically talking to lawyers, figuring out what they should do next. At 3.00 p.m., three police sub-inspectors in civilian clothes arrived in Shankar's cabin. They asked whether he had fought with someone in the Income Tax Department the day before. When Shankar answered in the negative, they insisted that that is what they had heard. The cops then told Shankar that an income tax officer had filed a FIR (First Information Report) against him and asked Shankar to accompany them to the Tardeo police station to record his statement. Shankar agreed to go with them as he felt the whole thing was so far-fetched that there shouldn't be any problems. In the car, one of the cops sitting with Shankar informed him that he was being arrested and charged with threatening to kill an income tax officer. Shankar couldn't believe what he was hearing. Devina, who had met lawyers for the first time in her professional life that morning, had no idea which criminal lawyer to call. The 'could-only-happen-in-India' part of the story is: the cops did not come in their own car. The car they were being driven to the police station belonged to Shankar's friend Jai. Near Kala Ghoda, a man on a motorcycle was run over by a water-tank truck. Jai decided to give chase and stopped the car in front of the truck and forced the driver out. The driver started running and the cops jumped out to chase him. What were Shankar and Devina doing when all this was happening? Sitting in the car and waiting for the cops to return. The cops then called officers in the Colaba police station. Constables then arrived and arrested the driver.

Shankar was taken to Tardeo police station and Devina called up (a name suggested by friends) Girish Kulkarni, a criminal lawyer, begging him to do something. The cops in the car had already told Shankar and Devina that the income tax commissioner had called the police commissioner and said that Shankar Sharma must be arrested that day under any circumstance. Shankar said that the cops were really good with him and assured them that there was no reason for him not to get night bail. They told Devina, he would have dinner with her at home that night. The police took him to the magistrate's house to apply for night bail. The police did not oppose it but the magistrate rejected it and insisted that Shankar would have to remain in jail.

> **Sharma:** I think he was under a lot of pressure. Definitely. Because if the guy arresting you doesn't oppose, why should he reject it? Hundred per cent he was told.
> **Madhu:** What did the cops say to you when you came out?
> **Sharma:** They were very sorry. They were also shocked.

Shankar said that the cops were kind to him. They let Devina stay, as well as some staff from the office. They sent for food, which has to be tasted in front of the cops by the person who brings it. They took Shankar for a medical check and finger-printing.

> **Sharma:** We came back to the police station around ten. We sat around, had dinner; these guys were very, very nice. They kept saying, sorry. These guys had to leave around 12. Then I went to the lock-up for a while. The lock-up is not in that police station. It's somewhere else. I think it's at Nana Chowk. It was my first sight of a lock-up but I'm sure it's not the last.
> **Madhu:** What did you feel when you walked in?
> **Sharma:** Scared. Bizarre. Depressing. They took me behind, up the stairs, into the lock-up area. Straggly bunch of guys there. Junkies, pimps, I don't know. Three or four of them. The light was very dim. I didn't go to the loo. The floor was stone, all broken. Three walls and the bars and mesh on one side. There was a window very high. You couldn't look out. In all jails the ceilings are very, very high. The walls were dirty; quite pathetic. There was no fan. Then they just lock you in. I sat down on the floor.
> **Madhu:** What were your first thoughts?
> **Sharma:** I was just saying to myself, where does this thing end? Or where is this thing leading to? How did this happen? It must be some bad dream. It can't be happening. Then I came out in about an hour's time. They basically locked me in, as having been there, and then they took me out and took me back to the police station.
> **Madhu:** On what basis?
> **Sharma:** Just being nice. *Raat bhar yehan nahin rehengey* [you don't have to spend the whole night here]. They had to show entry *ho gayee thi*. They were being nice because they knew it was a complete frame-up. If the cops are doing it themselves it's another matter, but if somebody else is getting them to do something, they ...
> **Mehra:** They knew they were doing a frame-up of a good respectable guy. Maybe if it was a slum dweller they would have been different. That's a fact of life.

Sharma: Maybe I was lucky, pure and simple. I don't know if other people would be that lucky in a cop station.

Shankar was then brought back to the Tardeo police station where he spent the night sleeping on a bench in one of the officers' cabins. He woke up at around 6.30 a.m. and wandered out into the courtyard. He said: 'There I see a whole battery of cameras and the entire fucking press and I said, shit! Spare me, *yaar*. They were all arrayed outside. They were not allowed to come in.'

The DCP then called Shankar in and with great hospitality gave him a (inexpensive) cigar. They served him tea and bread pakoras. Meanwhile, Devina was running around in search of a criminal lawyer. Shankar had no access to the FIR against him and was unaware of what the charges against him were. Devina connected with H. Ponda, who said he would appear for Shankar in the Sessions Court the following day. When Devina arrived there, H. Ponda told her that he would not be appearing but his mother would stand in for him. His reassurance that she was an experienced lawyer in her mid-70s did little for Devina when she saw the tiny, stout Freny Ponda. Devina briefed Freny.

Mehra: Then I sat with her in the canteen and told her stuff. After 15 minutes, I was saying something about Shankar and she says, "Who is Shankar?" I said, Oh! God! Ha! Ha! Ha!

Shankar's case was coming up in fifteen minutes and Devina had no choice but to go with Freny.

Mehra: The magistrate came. We watched a few other cases, pickpockets, this, that. Then Shankar's case was called and we suddenly found the whole courtroom, all the people sitting on the benches, came forward and you realized they were all journalists who were waiting for this case. Mrs Ponda turns to me and says, "I thought all these girls had been picked up for soliciting! Ha! Ha!"
Madhu: And they were journalists. Lovely!
Sharma: It was hilarious! I really cracked up, because I got freed as she was saying this. It was the high point of this entire episode. Ha! Ha!
Mehra: But when she argued, she argued very well.
Sharma: We had no idea. She was very, very good.
Mehra: Suddenly you find there is utter confusion. The magistrate asks for the bail application. We find nobody has a bail application because Girish Kulkarni's firm thought that Mrs Ponda's firm is doing it. Ponda's thought Girish was doing it. The other people had not even brought the night bail papers and you're just panicking there. Shankar was later on telling me you were looking very upset in the courtroom. I said you don't know what was going on.
Sharma: I was blissfully unaware. I was sitting with the pimps and the

334

prostitutes and generally enjoying life, not knowing I don't even have a bail application to be filed with the magistrate.

Mehra: Fortunately in Mumbai they are not so formal about bail applications as in Delhi. So somebody just scribbled something and that was good enough. Then the magistrate said, "I will give the order at three". There was press all around, so the cops took him by the back door into the jeep.

Sharma: Straight to the police station.

Mehra: I was really scared that there would be phone calls to this magistrate between eleven and three. God knows what will happen. At 3 o'clock we came back and he gave the order. They give it in Marathi so we didn't quite follow what he said. In fact Shankar thought he had remanded him for another …

Sharma: Yah, yah! At twelve it adjourned and he said something like *teen* or three or something. I said, shit, he's given me three months. Ha! Ha! Huh!

Mehra: We didn't even know that you cannot be remanded for more than 14 days at a time.

Sharma: We had no idea, *yaar*. I said, shit, *teen maheeney key liyey gaiyey, yaar.* Then I asked the cop what's this, he said, *nahin, nahin, sahib, theen bajey bulaya hai vapus. Aap ko aaj bail mileyga.* The cops are saying, *Sharma sahib, main bol rahan, 100 per cent aap ki bail mil jayeygee.* I said, *Chodo yaar, tum aisay boltey rehtey ho, raat bhi bola tha, raat kya hua? Chalo bidi peethey hain,* whatever happens, we will see. [I said, shit, I'm in for three months. Then I asked the cop what's this, he said, no, no, sir, he has called you back at 3.00 p.m. You will get bail today. The cops are saying, Sharma Sahib, I am telling you, you will get bail today one hundred per cent. I said, forget it, buddy, you keep saying that, you said it at night and what happened? Let's go smoke a bidi and see what happens]. At 3 o'clock again these guys herded me into the police jeep and all these bloody television guys. To get a shot, they would kill you. Mad guys. Finally we came to the courtroom, this guy read out bail is set at Rs 4,000 or something. It's like passing an exam or something.

Madhu: That's a very reasonable amount, considering your turnover. Did they know?

Sharma: No, he had no idea, otherwise it would have been like four lakh rupees or something. But he gave a very good bail order. It was like an acquittal.

Mehra: They said no such thing happened. We don't know from where the police came to the conclusion that such threats were given, because the threats are not even there in the FIR. Because the income tax officer actually filed a report in the income tax that …

Sharma: Instigated by the other guy.

Mehra: It is to break you. You stop the business then you arrest the person the same day. Now we laugh about it but at that point it was unimaginable.

Sharma: And you say, this is not happening in India. I really can't believe, through this process, all these incidents, *yaar, yeh Hindustan meh ho raha hai. Yeh toh Malaysia mey hota hai* [this is happening in India? This only happens in Malaysia].

The presiding magistrate granted Shankar bail, stating in the order that there was no case for arrest and that it had been an abuse of power by the police and the Income Tax Department.

Getting out of the courtroom was another project. Shankar had been told that he should wear a black jacket (like a lawyer) to fool the press and they had decoy cars at all the entrances.

Madhu: Did the press catch you?
Sharma: Yeeeaah! These guys will catch you dead or alive. When I got into the car, an office colleague was driving, he took off at a hundred kilometres an hour and almost knocked down a guy. I said, *ismey toh undar mat kara doh muhjey aaj* [I said, don't get me thrown back in again today]. I've just come out. In his eagerness *key chalo nikal jayen, nikal jayen* [let's go, let's go]. Guys were bloody hanging on to the tailgate and all that, these Aaj Tak, or whoever the hell it was, *yaar*.

The funny part was that none of Shankar's friends believed that he had not threatened the income tax officer. Known for his quick temper, they all believed that Shankar must have lost it and cussed out the guy. Shankar said, 'If I had to go in, I should have gone in after saying it'.

In June, Devina got a letter from the Passport Office stating that her passport was being impounded. Shankar said it was like a punch in the gut. They had to leave in seven days, so on two working days Devina worked on her petition and filed it herself. She asked for a stay order against the passport authorities. The judge had obviously read the petition before he heard the case. Before any lawyer could start arguing, the judge looked at the ED and passport office counsel and said that this case was clearly mala fide. As soon as he said that the two lawyers backtracked. They said we have no objection. We will withdraw the notice. They didn't want a negative order from him. Shankar's passport was also impounded when he was arrested in 2002, and was forced to appeal twice. He finally got it back in July 2003.

On 25 September 2001, Shankar and Devina were at Chennai airport to catch a flight to London. After checking in, they proceeded to the immigration counter. The immigration officer looked at Shankar's passport and stopped them. He took them into the immigration office and called someone, speaking in Tamil or Telugu. He returned and asked, 'Are you the same Shankar Sharma who has invested into Tehelka?' They asked what that had to do with immigration clearance. He informed them they would have to wait until he received instructions from the Ministry of Finance in Delhi. The officer made them wait for hours and refused to explain anything to them. Finally, he had their luggage off-loaded. There were 15 officers staring at them, whispering in a language neither of them understood and pointing at their luggage. The last international flight had left and the airport was virtually empty as they sat there for four hours. With their passports impounded, not allowed to make phone calls, waiting for instructions from the capital, Shankar and Devina said it was like being in a foreign country. They were also apprehensive of drugs or anything else being planted in their suitcases. Chennai was an alien city to them. Aside from the five staff members in their Chennai office, they knew no one. They had gone to Chennai only to meet their staff. Shankar said they were both so scared that had they had been 15 years older, they would have suffered heart attacks.

Ironically, on the same night, Tarun Tejpal was being felicitated in Mumbai by the Media Brief Awards for the best media story of the year. Shankar said with a bitter laugh, 'It was a gala night in Mumbai and in another part of the country, something else was happening.'

The immigration officer then demanded that Shankar and Devina hand over their cell phones to him. When they pointed out that he had no authority to sequester them, he said he would sit there and not allow them to make any calls. When Devina went to the ladies toilet, this officer rushed into the toilet and banged on the cubicle door, shouting that she was not permitted to go in with her handbag.

When Sharma said that they could not wait forever, the officer said they were not going anywhere until he received instructions from the Ministry of Finance. Sharma retorted that he had a valid passport, a valid visa, and an airline ticket so he should be travelling. The officer was impervious. At 3.30 a.m. the senior officer arrived and informed Devina and Shankar that a look out circular had been issued against Shankar Sharma to prevent him leaving. Such a circular is usually issued to all airports and exit points out of the country to prevent fugitives from absconding from the law. Shankar informed him that he was living in his home in Mumbai leading a normal life, so what was the necessity and high drama to look for him in airports? When Shankar asked the officer to show him the circular, the man refused. At 5.00 a.m. two income tax officers arrived. They took out their notepads and told them that they were going to question them. When Shankar asked them under what section of the law they were proceeding, they replied that they were from the Income Tax Department and could ask any questions. The income tax officers began their questions by asking them their names. Shankar told them: 'If you have to ask my name and then you search me, then there is a disconnect somewhere. You had better know my name before you search me.' When Shankar quoted from the Income Tax Act and demanded to know why he had to answer their questions, they gave up and said they would wait for their boss to arrive. Their boss showed up shortly with a search warrant that said they had information that Shankar and Devina had valuables in their luggage. Shankar asked how they had discovered this when nobody knew they were in Chennai and wondered how they had come to such a conclusion. The officers then searched the baggage, opening out every single garment, turning the bags upside down and even looked under the lining. They found nothing. They searched his laptop computer and again found nothing. At 11.00 a.m. they signed the *panchnama* and finally decided to let them go. As they were forced to spend the night in Chennai, in front of the officers Shankar called up the hotel nearest to the airport, which happens to be Trident.

They got to the hotel after being awake for over 30 hours. They brushed their teeth, showered, and prepared to sleep, planning to catch the evening flight to Mumbai.

Mehra: And then this phone rings.

Sharma: Devina picked up the phone.

Mehra: *Haan*, so, may I speak to Shankar Sharma?

Sharma: In Chennai nobody knows that we had just checked into Trident Hotel. That's like 10 minutes. Not even our own guys know this.

Mehra: He said some Pradeep Saxena. I said, who? I had never got the name. So I said, who are you? I am an old friend of his. Sounded very shady. I said, old friend meaning what? How do you know him? No, I know him from college. I said, which college? So it went nowhere. He wanted the room number, because the hotel would not give out the room number. So then finally I put down the phone. After five minutes these 12 people land up at the door saying that we have a search warrant to search the hotel room.

Sharma: Same people plus some more people. I told this guy that you son of a bitch, you searched me at the airport. I made this bloody booking in front of you and I come here and I am supposed to suddenly sprout valuables in a hotel room I have never ever stayed in before in my whole life. It was …

Mehra: Bizarre.

The officers searched the hotel room and their luggage all over again. This time they had brought a computer expert who examined Shankar's laptop. Shankar asked them why, since the same laptop had been examined by income tax officers in Mumbai, then again at the airport, it was necessary to repeat the exercise? Shankar said he had little in his laptop since he isn't really into it. The expert announced there was nothing in the laptop.

Sharma: I had said there was absolutely nothing in it. He was shocked because in their image I am like James Bond. [Laughing] I am carrying my suitcase, my cigarette lighter. Keeping a laptop and nothing is there in the bloody laptop. They said that is not possible. I said that is how it is.

Mehra: There were only four to five word documents which were all letters to lawyers or drafts of petitions, which under the law actually they are not supposed to see. Your communications with lawyers is privileged information. But who is to listen?

The IT raiding team got a call from Delhi and the computer expert then said there was some code lock on the laptop. As they had to crack the code, they announced they were confiscating the laptop. Shankar immediately obtained faxes from his Mumbai office that showed the laptop to be a disclosed asset, a copy of the invoice, and a copy of the cheque. The fax showed the entry in the office accounts with tax paid money so there was no legal reason to seize the laptop. They said they had been instructed by Delhi to seize it, so they did. The laptop was worth Rs 1 lakh but Shankar said it would cost him Rs 2 lakh in legal fees to fight to recover it, so he has written it off.

When they arrived in Mumbai on 26 September 2001, they found an order waiting for them that accused them of unaccounted income of Rs 149.35 crore, the tax liability for which was Rs 89 crore. Shankar and Devina pointed out that the allegation was baseless and no demand had been made or notice given in that context. However, the order did impose a requirement to obtain a clearance to travel. The reason was that, according to the order, Shankar had not filed block returns, although that assessment procedure did not come into effect till 12 October 2001. The order also accused Shankar and Devina of attempting to leave Chennai on 25 September 2001 without clearance, although the order to obtain clearance was only issued on 26 September 2001.

On 25 September 2001, the RBI issued a showcause notice for revoking permission for the US subsidiary even though the APR had been filed in time. Approvals for the NASDAQ listing had been delayed due to the SEBI actions against First Global and were finally given on 26 June 2001, after the regulators recognized the absurdity of SEBI's charges. First Global was threatened with the revocation by the RBI without being given an opportunity to start business.

In September 2001, the excise authorities began a detailed audit of First Global's transactions to assess service tax liability. In the seven years First Global had done business, there had never been any problem with service tax issues and no audit was ever undertaken. The audit for five years was completed and the excise authorities made a demand of Rs 1 lakh for the five years audited. Although Shankar and Devina felt it was untenable, they paid it rather than contest. Considering all the cases in which they were already neck deep in, they could ill afford yet another.

Although Shankar's lawyers responded to the summons issued by the ED, another official from the same office issued yet another summons demanding Shankar's passport and numerous documents relating to all transactions, agreements, correspondence, financial statements of First Global, Mauritius. Shankar's lawyers repeatedly requested disclosure of the alleged offence being investigated and its basis, but received no response. First Global, Mauritius had filed its balance sheet two months (January 2001) prior to the Tehelka exposé.

When Shankar showed up at the Income Tax Court in Mumbai on 28 September 2001, as directed by the summons, the officer said that he had never summoned him and had no knowledge of the summons.

On 3 October 2001, the ED, without any ongoing case or charge, issued a summons to Shankar to appear with his passport on 9 October 2001. There was clear collusion between the Income Tax Department and the ED to prevent Shankar from travelling.

Early in the morning of 7 October 2001, a sleepy and severely under-dressed Shankar opened the door to the police who escorted him to the office of the Economic Offences Wing (EOW) of the police on what evidently appeared to be trumped up charges. The police refused to let him dress decently, until Devina pleaded that he be allowed to do so. On his arrival at the EOW office, the investigating officer informed Shankar that he was under arrest. Shankar then spent the whole of that day sitting at the EOW doing nothing. They neither arrested him nor let him go. When Shankar's lawyer asked for the CR number so he could approach the night magistrate for bail, the officer said he would only affect the arrest after 10.00 p.m., so Shankar could not apply for bail that night. However, the officer did allow Shankar to go home at 9.30 p.m., after extracting a written assurance that he would present himself again at 10.30 a.m. the next day.

This detention was based on a complaint of a disgruntled former employee whose services had been terminated over a year earlier, in August 2000. Although the employee had signed a letter declaring that full and final settlement had been made to him, when he was unable to find a job for some months, he filed a complaint with the EOW.

On 8 October 2001, Shankar and Devina received a showcause notice alleging that First Global had carried out short sales after this was banned. It accused First Global of having entered proprietary sales and avoided payment of margin money. They were also accused of not complying with summons listed, even though clarifications had been sought by their lawyers and no response given. By not responding to First Global's lawyers, they gave themselves the opportunity of filing non-compliance accusations.

The ED then issued a summons under FEMA (Foreign Exchange Management Act) on 15 October 2001, to appear with their passports. Although Shankar's lawyers asked the officials about the alleged contravention under FEMA, another summons was served on 23 October 2001 for the same information as the earlier one of 15 October. Shankar's lawyers pointed out that the ED could not proceed with the investigation under both FERA and FEMA to seek the same information.

At the time of his arrest, Shankar was the first person ever to have been arrested for an alleged violation of Section 19(1)(b) of FERA, a 1973 law, since its repeal in June 2000. An article 'So Is FERA Dead?' in *Business India* (June 10-23, 2002), said:

> What is clear is that the ED cannot propose any cases to be initiated. That it has been doing so with impunity right up to and beyond May 31, 2002, is indeed a rear guard action by the enforcement agency to retain some of its turf even after the law (FERA) has called for its termination. Large numbers of people "settled" so that no notices were issued.

A position in the ED is a lucrative one. The benefit of businessmen 'settling' matters is profitable and generally preferred to spending money on lawyers and months in courts. All the evidence used against Shankar Sharma and Devina Mehra was based on documents routinely disclosed by them to the Reserve Bank of India.

Shankar also complained to the Commission that the authorities had been illegally tapping their phones, which was a breach of their fundamental rights. The Intelligence Branch office collected names from the phone taps and contacted First Global's Chennai branch manager, Rajiv Purohit and Shankar's travel agent Mr Bhasin.

On 22 October 2001, the income tax authorities issued an order of provisional attachment for the NSE and BSE cards of First Global, even though the assessment had not begun and no demands had been issued.

On 29 October 2001, Satjit Singh Dhillon, First Global's chief executive officer, was taken in for interrogation by the ED. Dhillon said he was taunted, mocked, and threatened from 11.30 a.m. to 9.00 p.m. Dhillon informed the officers that his knowledge was limited to matters to which FERA did not apply. That notwithstanding, he was interrogated and intimidated into responding to matters that all related to Tehelka and Buffalo Networks, none of which related to FERA. The addresses of Dhillon's parents, uncles, and aunts were taken with a view to harassing them in the future. His lawyer was not allowed in. The ED also raided Dhillon's residence when only his teenage children were in the house. The children were told that their parents had been arrested and they would be arrested too if they did not allow the officers in. The children managed to call their mother, who was also harassed and intimidated. The raiding party reminded her of people who had died in the ED's custody.

On 5 November 2001, Shankar and Devina received an order dated 22 October 2001, attaching their residential properties in Mumbai and Delhi.

On 24 November 2001, First Global's auditor's office was also searched. He was taken to and detained in the ED offices until 9.00 p.m. and then released without being asked a single question.

The raid continued on 26 November 2001, when the ED took away all hard disks and the computer servers, which effectively brought all work and business transactions to a complete halt. Attempts were made to browbeat junior employees into making incriminating statements but they left without any statements having been recorded.

After repeated threats of cancellation of membership, the Bombay Stock Exchange finally cancelled First Global's membership in January 2002. First Global asked how it could be included in the initial investigation, as it had been a net buyer during the time under investigation – when the markets were allegedly manipulated by a bear cartel – but were not given any response. The Bombay Stock Exchange (BSE) suspended the registration on the grounds that money had not been deposited; according to Shankar, the BSE already held money from First Global. Regardless, BSE initiated disciplinary proceedings against First Global on the same grounds. Shankar said, 'How can we be punished twice for the same offence? We have stated that there are adequate funds lying with the BSE and have permitted the BSE to appropriate these funds. The BSE refuses to do so but insists on independent payment.'

Besides that, to add to the list, the Department of Company Affairs (DCA) and its agency the Registrar of Companies (ROC) issued dozens of summons, conducted inspections into all the companies associated with First Global, and filed 10 criminal complaints in Tees Hazari Courts in Delhi. These included technical violations, such as sign board not being displayed, which happened for a few days while the office was being shifted; late filing of the Annual Report (by a few days); some item in the balance sheet not being shown in a manner required by the Act. All these 10 cases were filed at a time when the law ministry had stated that DCA would not be filing prosecution for technical violations and only cases of fraud would be prosecuted. Obviously, an exception was made in First Global's case.

After the Chennai airport incident, the ED got into the act. They sent summons asking for information under FEMA, which does not provide for any powers of arrest. Then the summons, asking the same questions, mysteriously changed to FERA (Foreign Exchange Regulation Act, 1973). They obviously wanted to use an Act that had the power to arrest. Shankar reminded them in a letter that FERA was no longer applicable and they should summon him under the current FEMA Act. Shankar and Devina were in Delhi and the summons continued to chase them in Mumbai as well as Delhi.

On 17 December 2001, which happened to be a holiday for Eid, Enforcement Directorate (ED) officers arrived at their Delhi home at 6.00 a.m. A sleepy Shankar opened the door to them. The officers then told him they needed to take him in for interrogation. They took him to their Lok Nayak Bhavan office. Shankar's lawyer, Rani Jethmalani, waited outside since the ED did not allow any lawyers to be present. They proceeded to ask strange questions: 'What is the stock market?''How does it work?' Shankar was kept inside the whole day. The law says that within 24 hours of an arrest, the person has to be produced before a magistrate. In order to prolong the harassment, the ploy is to detain the person without arresting him, and then issue the arrest warrant much later.

The officers had tried to send Devina home at 8.00 p.m., who was waiting outside the ED office, saying that because of her, the female police officer had to stay and she had children at home. Devina was adamant and was not interested in anybody else's sob story. They told Devina that they were not allowed to arrest anyone after sunset, so she could go home. Shankar's arrest warrant was issued at 12.40 a.m. An arrest memo was handed over that said there was prima facie violation of Section 19 of FERA. This section does not require evidence that gives reasons for suspicion of wrongdoing. The ED officers then decided to hold Shankar for two days, without producing him in court. At that point, Devina lost her cool:

> I really screamed at the whole bunch of them. I said your whole hierarchy is here and not one of you has the guts to say, I will not do a wrong thing. Not one of you has the guts to say I will not put my signature on something I don't believe in. I told them, you talk about being God-fearing and this is what you do.

The officers looked sheepish and shifted their eyes away.

> **Sharma**: They are so rotten. The bureaucracy is the enemy of this country. It's not the politician. Remove the bureaucrats, keep the same politicians, we'll still progress. Politicians do not have any power. He derives his power from the bureaucrats.
> **Madhu**: You are saying that the bureaucracy just buckles?
> **Sharma and Mehra**: Oh yes. Big time.

Shankar was then sent to the Tughlak Road police station lock-up for the night. The Tughlak Road lock-up is outdoors with just bars. The temperature recorded in New Delhi that night, on 17 December 2001, was 10°C and the wind speed 9mph. He was not given any blanket or quilt, nor allowed any food between the time he was arrested and produced in court. The police said that Shankar was in the custody of the Enforcement Directorate and he would not be allowed food unless permission was granted by the ED. No ED official could be found. Shankar was taken to Patiala House at 3.00 p.m. Meanwhile, Devina gave some television interviews, emphasizing that he had not been allowed anything to eat. Devina got in touch with lawyer Kapil Sibal and asked him for suggestions. Sibal told her it didn't matter which lawyer she chose, Shankar would be remanded anyway.

Three lawyers, Rani Jethmalani, Sidharth Luthra, and Anil Sharma, appeared for Shankar. Additional chief magistrate heard the bail application and promptly announced he would hear the case on 25 December which was of course a holiday. Most senior lawyers are out of the country for the Christmas vacation. The SADS ensured that not much could be done to release Shankar for at least 15 days. Rani Jethmalani tried to argue that it should at least be heard on 24 December, but the additional chief metropolitan magistrate would hear nothing of it. Shankar was not arrested for murder or any other heinous crime. The crime had yet to be established. There was no logical reason for him not to get bail. But, as SADS does its work, you see good men functioning in a cloak of fear and helpless obedience.

The case was heard by another magistrate, metropolitan magistrate Surinder S. Rathi on 25 December 2001. The ED accused Sharma for alleged violations of provisions of the Foreign Exchange Regulation Act (FERA) when First Global allegedly transferred Himachal Futuristics Communications Limited (HFCL) shares to Foreign Institutional Investors (FII). ED stated in court that they had examined the balance sheets of five associate companies of First Global for the period ending 31 March 2000, and found that transactions of sale, purchase and profits of HFCL shares were not recorded by these companies. The ED accused Sharma of issuing fabricated bills to the five companies and conducting transactions without the permission of the Reserve Bank of India.

According to Sharma, HFCL transactions deal with unlisted shares and it is for the FII purchasers to approach the Reserve Bank of India, not individuals. According to ED, First Global sold 5,92,000 equity shares of HFCL to FIIs at an average rate of Rs 1,060 a share against a market price of Rs 2,100 to Rs 2,250 a share. Then, ED said, Sharma siphoned off the rate difference on each share from the FII's subaccounts. According to Sharma's lawyer Sidharth Luthra, the Exchange Control Manual permits the purchase of sales by FIIs. The ED has ignored that this transaction related to an open bidding of preferential allotment of unlisted HFCL shares between 17 February and 24 February, when the prices were approximately Rs1,400 for listed shares. If the contract notes were signed on 3 March 2001, it should not be held that the transactions were tainted, according to Luthra.

Well, Rathi rejected Sharma's bail plea and extended his remand for another seven days. Additional solicitor general K.K. Sud said, 'It is wild imagination to say that Sharma is being targeted because of the Tehelka exposé. We started our investigations on 4 March 2001 while the Tehelka exposé took place on March 13. Shankar Sharma has been uncooperative from day one of the investigation. He has always adopted a threatening posture against the authorities. He did not provide the ED with the required information, hence his arrest became necessary.'

The ED lawyers said they wanted to take Shankar to Mumbai so they could open up his home in his presence. While Shankar was in custody, Devina went underground because friends warned her that she too would be arrested. Shankar's sister Rita took food for him. One evening when Rita arrived at Lok Nayak Bhavan, the guard informed her that Shankar had already been taken to Mumbai. She saw his clothes lying around and cried uncontrollably, just unable to leave. Rita said it was the worst night of her life. The following morning she caught the first flight to Mumbai.

Shankar said there was no question of taking his clothes. They just picked him up, bundled him into a car, and took him to the airport. He arrived in Mumbai at 11.00 p.m. and was taken to the lock-up in Azad Maidan Police Station. When Rita arrived at the police station with food for Shankar, they said he would not be allowed home food because the order permitting him home food was a Delhi order and it had no validity in Mumbai.

〜

Sharma: It again comes down to a simple thing. You might be under instructions, but that doesn't mean you act in a manner that is inhuman. *Theek hai* [okay], you can say it is a question of my job. But you can still do it in a manner which is decent.

Mehra: There was no reason to tell Rita the wrong time. Tell her we are taking him in the morning and then take him at 7 o'clock in the evening.

Sharma: Nobody is going to compensate you extra for being bad. He's going to say, go and arrest him. Okay, you said to arrest him, I arrested him. That's a report he's going to file. But it's not the circumstances that are dictated by the ministers or by the political masters. Those are their own innovations by the bureaucracy, not by the politicians.

On 27 December, while Shankar was in the lock-up and Devina was in hiding, the ED officers opened and raided their Mumbai home again. A couple of staff members from the First Global office were there. No lawyer was permitted.

There is no bed or mattress in the lock-up. Shankar spread a few newspapers on the floor to sleep on. On 31 December, the ED brought him back to Delhi and Rita tried to see Shankar that evening. They kept her waiting for three hours and then finally told her that no meeting would be allowed that day.

Although Shankar had landed in Delhi at 5.00 p.m., they decided to transfer him at 10.30 p.m. to the Tughlak Road outdoor lock-up. Temperature recorded in New Delhi that night was 8°C and the wind speed 8mph. Devina got word that Shankar was being moved to the freezing lock-up, so she called up her brother and asked him to take some warm clothes for him. He took what he could rustle up. When Devina went to see him the next morning, it was so cold that the fog had a visibility of only two feet. That was the first time Devina saw Shankar since his arrest. He had high temperature and was feeling ill. Shankar was then produced before a magistrate and since the 14 days of remand were over, he was sent off to Tihar Jail.

Shankar was in the general barracks for the first four nights. It is one large hall, meant to accommodate about 50 people. There were about 300 prisoners there with only one toilet. Finding space on the floor to sleep was a challenge. Yet Shankar was surprised at the affection and care he received from other inmates. They would console him when he missed Devina and assured him that there was no way they would not be reunited. They had no idea how many years he could be incarcerated.

> **Sharma:** I realized, so many of the people are just good human beings. In a place like jail, they are not supposed to be nice. You just turn around, "Biscuit *kha lijiyeh, ya chai pee lijiyeh, ya toothbrush, ye plate …* and say *yeh achha admi hai, voh sala badmash admi hai* [have a biscuit, drink some tea, here's a toothbrush, a plate, tell you who is a good man, who is a goon]." You haven't asked for anything. Then, you can see the public beatings and lashings, *sab kuch hota hai wahan par* [everything happens there]. But otherwise, if you are educated, that is a big thing in jail. *Ki sahib, dekho mere koh nahin padna atha, toh aap pad keh batao* [sir, I don't know how to read, please read this for me] – letters, petitions to magistrates, all kinds of things.
> **Mehra:** You can advise people *na*, like Shankar was saying, *ki* somebody told him *ki* he got beaten up, so he said, next time you are in court, you show it to the magistrate, that this is what's happening. People don't know even that you can do that.

For the first four days in jail, Shankar was in shock and depressed. He had never seen anything like it. He had kept his spirits up for the first fourteen days of his custody but actually being thrown into a regular jail for criminals shook him. After a couple of days, he came out of it and began to find it interesting. There was a time when prisoners were differentiated by their class. There used to be a separate section for taxpayers called A-Class prisoners. Now, Shankar was with pimps, rapists, drug addicts, murderers, and terrorists. After a couple of days he began to figure out the system in jail. For a couple of hundred rupees he could take a hot bath in the deputy superintendent's bathroom. To increase meeting time with a lawyer or a relative, Shankar would pay off the guard, otherwise the man in charge would look at his watch and shuttle Shankar away. The guard had to be paid if a legal document was handed over.

Devina was in a dilemma about whether she should go to jail to meet Shankar. Various lawyers had advised her not to do so because she could be arrested. On the first day, Devina's brother and Rita went to see him. When they returned they told Devina that Shankar really wanted to see her. The meeting hall is divided by netting two feet apart. There are plastic glass sheets covering the netting. The visitor and inmate are supposed to communicate using telephones lying next to each chair, behind the plastic sheets. But often the phones don't work. Soon Devina realized that the glass sheet is only up to waist level. Below the waist, there is nothing. When the phones are dead, everybody squats on the floor beneath the tables and shout across to each other. When they met, the first time since his arrest, they both broke down. Shankar told her that she had to get him out of there somehow. Devina was traumatized.

Devina was told that the court that had heard them for 60 days had no jurisdiction over the case and therefore could not grant bail. They stated that Shankar had to be produced in a Mumbai court. Shankar's lawyers argued for transit bail. Again, the additional solicitor general, argued against Shankar's bail. Bail was denied and he was not released but taken in custody to Bombay (Mumbai). Sidharth Luthra, who was arguing for Shankar's bail said, 'This was a shocking game they played on the sixty-first day, when they filed a complaint in Mumbai while Shankar was still in jail in Delhi. That day Shankar broke down for the first time in court.'

Luthra recalled sadly, 'Their story is tragic but shockingly true. I was part of what happened in Delhi and trying to get him bail. I witnessed them breaking down. We were afraid Devina would be arrested. I remember Devina having lunch at my place and then we smuggled her out of there through a back alley.'

Shankar recalled that the court dates were quite traumatic. It took the whole day. Prisoners are stuffed into over-crowded buses and the court lock-ups have no water and the toilets are stomach-churning filthy. Prisoners sit on stone slabs all day until their case is called. They are brought back to jail at around 7.30 p.m., by which time Shankar said, 'You actually look forward to returning to jail. Your jail cell is your home.'

Travelling in the police buses was dangerous. Even if a riot broke out in the bus, it would not stop until it reached the jail. Stabbings are not rare. Shankar figured out a safer way to come to court. He got himself shifted to the high security zone and would travel in a less crowded bus with accused terrorists. There he met all the notorious names he had till then only read about in the newspapers.

Devina was with her lawyer when she heard that Shankar had been taken to the lock-up in Vikaspuri. As the jail does not open before sunrise, prisoners are taken to the Vikaspuri lock-up for the night to catch early morning trains. Devina dashed to Vikaspuri but they only allowed her to meet Shankar for five minutes. She was shattered. Shankar was then transported to Mumbai by train, in keeping with the jail budget for travel. He was handcuffed through the night, while the police constables slept. In Mumbai, Shankar was taken to Arthur Road Jail, which he said made Tihar Jail look like the Emirates Palace. He shared a tiny cell with five other prisoners, who were in for smuggling. The food was meagre and disgusting. Prisoners were given a bowl of daal for breakfast and various versions of the same thing for other meals. No outside food was allowed. Whereas in Tihar, visitors could hand over food and clothes, none of that was allowed in Arthur Road. There was an eight feet long room to meet visitors. Netting and plastic glass separated the visitors from the inmates, and there were no phones, so everyone screamed at each other. Visitors were allowed only five minutes, and this could be accomplished only after some bribing.

On the 68th day of his incarceration, Shankar was produced in the Bombay sessions court. The prosecution continued to play for time. The magistrate said he would hear the case in a couple of weeks. The prosecution messed around by asking for more time to file a response to the bail application. The magistrate gave them two days but was not available on that day. When the matter was finally heard, Shankar's lawyer, Mahesh Jethmalani, argued that nobody could be held in jail unless he was charged with murder. Despite that, the magistrate reserved the order for the next day. Jethmalani and his team were shocked when the magistrate denied bail. Jethmalani told Devina that it was unlikely that Shankar would get bail in any court below the Supreme Court.

Devina waited for four hours outside Arthur Road Jail to tell Shankar that his bail had been rejected, but was not allowed to meet him. He read about it in the newspapers the following morning. Devina finally got to meet Shankar and they decided to prepare an application for the sessions court to try again. The prosecution took an extra day because they said the lawyers in Mumbai would not argue. The additional solicitor general of India, K.K. Sud, flew to Mumbai to present the prosecution's point of view. He told a shocked court that if Shankar were allowed out he would kill all the witnesses. Who were the witnesses? The ED officers. Mahesh Jethmalani, representing Shankar, said, 'If the government officials are that scared of my client, they should resign. And, in any case, if he wants to get anybody killed, jail is a better place than being outside.' When Shankar was granted bail, their lawyers feared that the ED would get a stay order from the Supreme Court.

Was Shankar a free man at 5.30 p.m. after bail was granted to him? Not quite. Getting out of jail again is yet another challenge. There are persons who have got bail but are still in there after a month. The jailer goes to the prisoner and says, 'Not today, tomorrow'. Everyone has to be paid off. Devina waited outside from 7.00 p.m. until 10.00 p.m., when he was finally allowed to go home.

Mahesh Jethmalani's perspective of the events:

Madhu: The first time when Shankar's bail was rejected, what happened?
Jethmalani: I think it was K.K. Sud [additional solicitor general] who came down. K.K. Sud defended the government and I think he had mixed instructions. The [L.K.] Advani group was telling him that listen: enough is enough. Let this man go, because K.K. Sud was Advani's man. So he actually came to court and not with a great deal of conviction in his case or hostility either. He was very friendly, "*Mahesh, mil jana chahiye aaj* [you should get (bail) today]." Which is why we were shocked.
Madhu: He actually said that to you?
Jethmalani: Yeah. Yeah. In fact he told me, "There's nothing". K.K. Sud actually empathized with Shankar Sharma, if I remember right. In between he may have got counter-instructions, because when the case started he became a little bellicose. It appeared to me, but this is pure educated guessing, that he was trying to keep two competing sets of instructions happy. I had a little information that a particular group had told him, in the then BJP government, to go easy. And the other group had said no, no, no, you've got to continue to teach this guy a lesson. But in the end it was in the magistrate's hands.
Madhu: And the magistrate …?
Jethmalani: The magistrate looks at the posture of the prosecution. The real civil liberties preservation in the judiciary comes from the higher courts. Even today you'll find even the magistrates in the Sessions Courts are very pro-prosecution. Most of them come from the ranks of public prosecutors.

Madhu: So then what happened? He rejected the bail on the basis that Shankar might run away? Tamper with evidence?

Jethmalani: No, no, he didn't reject, he just said you come back after a week. So I was going to the higher court. Then, most of the lawyers who practice in that court, said, "Mahesh, come back a second time to him. He just rejected for a week, don't go to a higher court." So we took a second chance and it worked. I had some hope in the magistrate, Tavare, because he was a liberal. The guy actually gave him bail. He's quite a liberal-minded magistrate.

Madhu: So who do you think was the person who coordinated the Secret Auto Destruct System? There was an additional solicitor general flying into Mumbai to argue against Shankar Sharma's bail application.

Jethmalani: I have a feeling it was a concerted policy. I feel that the entire victimization of Tehelka and all that completely unpardonable vindictiveness was of the law officers appointed by the government. You know who they are. My friend Honku – Upamanyu Hazarika. They were all in it. There is no question about it. I had conversations with Honku at that time. Upamanyu was defending Jaya Jaitly before the Commission. I asked Upamanyu what has happened in Tehelka? Shankar Sharma in jail for 73 days? At one stage Upamanyu actually told me, if this is the kind of rubbish you do with the sort of false allegations – of course he was defending – then you have to face the might of the government.

Madhu: He said that?

Jethmalani: Yeah. And Upamanyu was put up for George and Jaya by Arun Jaitley. They were all part of it. This was very well thought through. There was a whole kind of very nefarious political management going on. This was a team.

Madhu: But you know Arun Jaitley and you know Soli Sorabjee. Both of them have a background and history of fighting for the freedom of the press. How is that possible?

Jethmalani: How does a completely human rights oriented liberal, liberal in inverted commas, a man like Arun Jaitley or even Soli Sorabjee, justify something like Gujarat? It's the same thing. I think years of being out of power and then finally seeing their government in power, and then actually believing their own hype that this was never going to end. India was shining and the BJP would shine forever. That made them a little pompous. Then, the trouble is once you're there, you realize how powerful you are, and how completely emasculated all the other organs that are in theory supposed to be checking you, are. The press, make no mistake about it is the biggest let down in this country, from the Emergency till today. It is just the three s's: sex, sensationalism and sound bites. Nothing else. The press has become so glib in this country. They take handouts. Some journalists just really want to curry favour with people in power and take their say. Protect them from any criticism.

But, this is speculation and there is no proof. In fairness to Arun Jaitley, he was entitled to a rebuttal to all of Mahesh Jethmalani's accusations:

Madhu: Other lawyers have said that you were involved in the harassment of Tehelka and their investors. For example, why would the solicitor general and additional solicitor general be representing the government in arguing against bail for Shankar Sharma, or the case to give him permission to travel? These are too minor to justify the solicitor general and additional solicitor general flying to Mumbai to appear for the government. There are accusations that there was collusion between the law ministry and the lawyers for Jaya Jaitly, such as Upamanyu Hazarika.

Jaitley: As far as Mukul Rohatgi [additional solicitor general] is concerned, he has only appeared predominantly in the cases that were in the Bombay High Court, which had nothing to do with Tehelka. It had more to do with some finance company …

Madhu: First Global.

Jaitley: Yes, First Global. Therefore as a law officer he had to ably argue his case before the Bombay High Court as per the instructions of his department. Upamanyu Hazarika being bracketed with these two, I think, is highly improper because Upamanyu Hazarika was part of Jaya Jaitly's team. As far as I'm concerned, the law ministry did not directly, indirectly or even informally deal with this whole issue, because it was either the defence ministry that was concerned with the defence transactions and it was the Department of Personnel dealing with the Commission of Inquiry. As far as the Commission was concerned, it was either Sorabjee [attorney general] on a few occasions or it was substantially the late Kirit Rawal who was appearing.

Madhu: But why would the additonal solicitor general, Mukul Rohatgi, and additional solicitor general, K.K. Sud, go to Mumbai to argue what is a small, routine matter of a finance company?

Jaitley: No, the matter has some kind of legal importance, commercial importance or even a political importance. Because an allegation is being made that we are being victimized and the government says, "No, we have some element of material against you". The fact that important lawyers appear against you, every party is entitled to its best lawyers. If you can engage Shanti Bhushan and Ram Jethmalani to fight for you, it is unfair to say please give us a piddling little lawyer to oppose. The government is also entitled to the best of legal advice.

Madhu: Why was the government interested in First Global in the first place? Only because they had financed Tehelka?

Jaitley: I don't want to get into that issue because it is a matter that I have not dealt with. The finance ministry was dealing with it. But if there was some independent material against First Global, then certainly any government would be entitled to look at it.

Madhu: But doesn't the extraordinary interest shown by the government in First Global affairs appear odd to you?

Jaitley: I don't think there is any inequality in the violation of law. This is no argument to say that hundreds have violated the law, why are you picking on me?

Madhu: You have the additional solicitor general and solicitor general flying to Mumbai to fight such a case. It is extraordinary, isn't it?

Jaitley: We have law officers flying all over the country to appear in cases. We now have an additional solicitor general in each of the four major metros in the country who look after the local cases of that region.

Madhu: So if they were not called then the ASG in Mumbai would have taken care of it?

Jaitley: I can answer that question. There are hundreds of people who owe taxes to the government. Sonia Gandhi hasn't written for all. She wrote it for First Global. So obviously there is more about First Global than meets the eye.

Madhu: The Department of Company Affairs was under the law ministry when you were law minister.

Jaitley: I do not recollect a single paper from the Department of Company Affairs having come to me for the purposes of any Company Law complaints. You will have to verify the date when these complaints were filed, because the Department of Company Affairs was with me till about June 2002, whereof I went out of the government. When I came back on January 29, 2003, the Department of Company Affairs was no longer with me. It was with the finance ministry. So you will have to verify the dates when these complaints have been filed. In any case, I do not recollect any of the Tehelka complaints coming to me. This is either dealt with at the ROC [Registrar of Companies] level and I don't recollect a single file of this having come to me.

Madhu: Related to Soli Sorabjee, who was the attorney general at that time …

Jaitley: Soli and I have on one or two occasions informally discussed this. That is part of a casual conversation. But I've never been present as a part of his official briefings on the Tehelka Commission. The officers of the concerned ministries, the defence ministry, must have been going.

Madhu: But the particular issue where Soli Sorabjee argued for the tapes to be sent for forensic examination. Did you discuss that with Soli?

Jaitley: I don't recollect having discussed this at all. Things have been discussed. As attorney general and law minister, we used to meet frequently, and even informally, several times and discuss what was pending. But what brief he should accept or what stand he should take in the proceedings, was something that was entirely between him and the officials of that ministry.

Madhu: You have always been known as a champion of the freedom of the press. Did it ever become a conflict for you personally: the freedom of the press versus the preservation of the political party to which you belong?

Jaitley: Um, yes and no. When these disclosures were made, even though I was not directly connected with it and neither was the law ministry, except it is the job of the law ministry to provide lawyers to contest the cases. But as a part of my own personal and political interest, I went through the manuscript in its entirety. In order to satisfy myself as to what I thought the facts were. Now so far as a media organization catches some kind of sleaze on camera and exposes it, I think it is welcome. I would not be a privy to harassing it for that particular reason. I felt that in a number of cases, some of the exposés that they brought out probably would serve the public good. I also felt in some cases, they had a definite political agenda. Their subsequent association, the patronage Mrs Sonia Gandhi has given to them and their funding companies, the manner in which they caved in on the Rahul Gandhi interview, the manner in which Mrs Sonia Gandhi has helped them with their funding companies to do away with outstanding tax demands.

In September 2005, Tehelka published an interview with Rahul Gandhi to which the Congress party took strong objection. The Congress stated that Rahul believed he was having a 'casual' conversation with a reporter in Amethi. Tehelka initially dismissed that by reiterating that 'there was nothing casual about it and it was a formal interview'. A few days later, Tehelka strangely backtracked and issued a statement that it was a clear misunderstanding and any errors were inadvertent and regretted.

Jaitley: Subsequent facts have shown that they did have some kind of a political agenda. And now, that has been repaid back. Specifically, at that time, I felt on two issues they were guilty of gross misrepresentation. And the two issues related to two people who I always perceived to be very honest. The first is George Fernandes. I am mentioning this for the first time. I must disclose that even though I was not directly involved with it, my name was being thrown up by them, saying I was also a part of a group of people who was harassing them. Now to the best of my memory, my ministry had done nothing. I was not officially involved in this except to the extent that I had a political interest in the image of my government and my party. So I did communicate with Tarun Tejpal on this issue. I therefore invited him to my house and we had dinner together in my house. This was about a month or a few weeks after the exposé. There was just the two of us. I assured him that I had no personal agenda against them. I wouldn't be speaking to him if that were so. The first was in the context of George Fernandes. As I perceived, George was an honest man. Always has been, lives a very austere life, he has good values, he has a 40-50 year career behind him. The impression that was being given that George was a dishonest defence minister and somebody in his house was fixing deals. This was a direct reflection on George. Parliament got paralysed because of that. Finally George had to resign and after some time he was re-inducted. Now, having hurt an honest politician particularly when there was nothing on the tapes against George. I recollect having told Tarun Tejpal at that time … They had made a short script of what Gupta had said, what Jain had said, Jaya's conversation with those other chaps was, that when Jain was trying to pull for defence ministry deals, a stage came when those people wanted to know if Jain could directly speak to George about it. And Jain threw up his hands and said: no question of it. George is an extremely honest man. He would be furious even if he heard about it. This was deliberately concealed. So even the so-called middlemen or the dishonest characters were not even willing to allow George to hear a whisper of this because George was an independent honest man. Now if on day one, this had not been dishonestly edited out, the whole country would have known the entire exposures. These are the people who are the black sheep and this was the man being perceived to be honest. At least George would not have been harassed. Therefore, in the absence of any evidence against George and the tape containing a statement that George is a very honest man, editing that out was an act of dishonesty. I don't think Tarun had much to say on this because this editing was part of the political agenda that the tapes had. There may be other exposure agendas that the tape had, which they were legitimately entitled to. I also thought that from the conversation in entirety that the tapes showed with Jaya Jaitly, she did not come out to be, to me, as a person of questionable integrity. Now when people come to politicians and office bearers of political parties and want to give donations, there is a discipline you follow. Please go and deposit it in the party office. If they want to give it to you, we normally say, no. We'll send somebody with you. You deposit it in the party office. You will get your relevant confirmation from it. Broadly, Jaya being a little garrulous in her conversation, speaking about textiles, speaking about IT, being over talkative and then saying there is a party conference in Bangalore, probably being organized by this gentleman Srinivas Prasad. He needs money so it should be sent to him. Now there is a doubt in that area as to whether the money was received there or it was to be sent to Srinivas Prasad, because her conversation is: "Send it to Srinivas Prasad". When you say, "Send it to Srinivas Prasad" you mean, send it for the party conference. This [the Tehelka tape] clearly shows that somebody gave her a token Rs 1-2 lakh, and she instructs either the donor or associate, that this money should be sent to Srinivas Prasad. In that context, she is the party president and for the party conference, some donor has come, so she says give it to the man organizing the conference. Now to project her as some kind of a wheeler-dealer when she clearly says I don't interfere in these deals … So I had mentioned both these cases when Tarun Tejpal had met me. To the best of my memory, I don't think he had much of an arguable case to make on George. On Jaya, there were some areas of disagreement.

Madhu: Both you and Soli Sorabjee are known to have very liberal views about the press, but the image that comes through on this issue is very different. Soli appeared very often in the Commission. In fact if anyone was to count how many times Soli was in the Commission and argued for Jaya's position, it would be very unusual.

Jaitley: I feel strongly that George had been completely wronged in this and that Jaya had been substantially wronged. My impression from my informal discussions with Soli has been that he probably shared the same perception. I don't think there was any further brief that he was keen on.

⌒

Clearly, Arun Jaitley and Soli Sorabjee loved and admired George Fernandes, and enjoyed a good personal equation with him. Jaitley and Sorabjee believed Fernandes had been trapped in an unfair noose. The fact that their defence minister had to resign and Parliament could not function appeared to them a gross miscarriage of justice. The slanted editing in removing all reference to George Fernandes's honesty did no service to Tehelka's credibility. In my assessment, poor journalistic judgement, rather than any dark political conspiracy. A common habit amongst us journalists: often the angle of the story becomes so powerful, it subconsciously turns into a motive.

The letter that Shankar Sharma had written to Sonia Gandhi, was the same letter that Sharma had written to the prime minister and numerous other ministers in the BJP-led coalition government. The difference was that Sonia Gandhi had forwarded the letter to P. Chidambaram, now finance minister, with the following covering letter:

Dear Shri Chidambaram,

I am enclosing a copy of a letter written to me by directors of First Global regarding alleged harassment by some agencies under Finance Ministry. I have been informed that this matter has already been discussed in a high-level meeting and certain corrective measures have been agreed to. I would like you to look into these issues on priority in order to ensure that no unfair and unjust treatment is meted out to the petitioners.

With good wishes,

Yours sincerely,
Sonia Gandhi

⌒

Sonia Gandhi's letter is perceived as proof by the BJP that the Congress had a hand in the Tehelka exposé. I don't think so. The letter is dated 25 September 2004. Two years later, Shankar and Devina still could not travel freely abroad, so earning their livelihood from their companies based abroad had virtually come to a halt. The Congress was in power in early September 2004, when the Income Tax Department attached all their businesses and all their deposits in the BSE. The ED had not returned their legitimate funds, seized during the raids. They had not even returned their computers. Shankar said,

> The ground level remains the same, even though the government has changed. They have to unwind the wrong and for that they have to admit they were wrong. They find it impossible to do that. To revoke their own acts is a problem for them.

The time limit for the assessment order is two years from the search. Although Shankar and Devina received the assessment order on 25 September 2003, that stated: No undisclosed income, no undisclosed assets found, nothing incriminating found. Until the month of November 2005, over a year later, Shankar Sharma and Devina Mehra were still fighting numerous income tax cases.

Many lawyers working in the Commission whispered about how the Commission was allowed to function the way it did because of internal fighting in the administration between the pro-George Fernandes group and the anti-George Fernandes group in government. Obviously, the Commission and Tehelka had become pawns in a larger chess game played out by much bigger players.

This also graphically illustrates how the SADS works. The highest authority can attempt to fix a problem, but it is the lowest bureaucrat down the line who implements it. It is in his discretion how to deal with it. There are many ways and explanations to counter and delay implementation of an order. But, most important of all, he has to admit that his department was wrong in the first place. How does he place that on record without repercussions? He is stuck with it and undoing a wrong placed on record is next to impossible.

Going back to September 2003, Shankar and Devina filed for permission to travel to New York for their delayed interviews with NASDAQ. Beni Chatterjee, the lawyer representing the Income Tax Department, asked for three weeks. When it was argued in court in September 2003, Chatterjee got up and said,

> My Lord, they were trying to flee the country in September 2001. When we searched them they did not have a single dollar with them. That means they have siphoned off all the money abroad. They were leaving with nothing in their bags. Who in this country will leave without even $1,000?

Shankar asked his counsel to show the *panchanama* of 2001, which recorded that they had declared $1,000.

The two-judge bench gave Chatterjee 10 days to file his reply because they said the matter was urgent and there would be no more adjournments. Chatterjee said that Mukul Rohatgi, the additional solicitor general had to come from Delhi and asked for another adjournment. The judges told Chatterjee to get another lawyer but there would be no further delays. The day before the matter was to come up, Chatterjee arrived in court and said there was a personal request from Mukul Rohatgi to postpone the matter for another week as he was unable to come. Chatterjee said, 'Pleeeeeease your Lordships, might give another one week's extension. He is making a personal request to the bench.' The judges told Chatterjee that they had made it absolutely clear there would be no extensions and no adjournments. Chatterjee continued to plead for postponement for four more days. The judges were adamant that the matter would be heard the following day, as it was an urgent matter involving fundamental rights. Chatterjee rose up and said, 'Lordship why are they assuming that this court is going to grant them permission? They have made their booking of tickets as if they are going to get the permission to travel.' The senior judge retorted, 'How are you assuming they are not going to be given permission to travel, when you, Mr Chatterjee, have no basis of assuming that they will not get this permission? So you finish your argument, then this bench will decide.' The bench asked whether the Income Tax Department had recorded any reasons as to why permission should be denied. Under the law they are supposed to state reasons. Chatterjee said, 'No, no your lordship, but there might have been. I will get back to you tomorrow.' The judges told him, 'If you have any reasons you just show it to us now. If you don't have reasons, you tell us you don't.' Chatterjee replied that he might have. The judges responded by stating they would give the order at 4.00 p.m. the next day. When Shankar's lawyer, Jehangir Mistry, tried to refute some of Chatterjee's arguments, the judges asked him whether he wanted to use up the time they needed to give the order in time for his clients to travel. The following day, the judges delivered a 40-page, carefully reasoned order that tore the Income Tax Department to bits. They stated that it was a complete travesty of justice. They also said there had been a total non-application of mind and it was a perfunctory way of dealing with a citizen's fundamental rights. It was so well argued that it made it impossible for it to be appealed before the Supreme Court. Shankar said, 'We were really floored. The judiciary really went out of its way to protect our rights.' Shankar and Devina caught a flight to New York the next evening, in time for their NASDAQ exam.

⌐

The Commission of Inquiry on Tehelka was a separate book in the chapter of Shankar and Devina's lives. In August 2001, Devinder Gupta, under-secretary in the Department of Revenue, Ministry of Finance, filed an affidavit accusing Shankar and Devina of instigating Tehelka through First Global in order to make a fortune on the stock market. It was intriguing that Gupta stated that the affidavit could not be filed earlier as the relevant facts were being collected. He specifically mentioned that various agencies of the government – the Director of Investigation, Income Tax and SEBI – collected information during raids on their offices and home. According to Gupta, First Global started building a bear position just before the exposé, presuming the markets would fall. However, anybody could look at the transaction figures of that period and conclude that First Global was actually not a bear but a bull. The figures were clearly manipulated. Gupta stated, 'BSE Sensex fell by 227 points on 13 March 2001 and by 604 points in the next 30 days.' From which date did the market fall by 227 points? Then he takes the next 30 days but does not disclose the direct effect of the exposé on the day and how the market recovered following it.

Date	BSE Sensex	(Percentage change from [Closing] previous day)
8 March	4056.94	0.25%
9 March	3881.96	-4.31%

12 March	3767.89	-2.94%
13 March	3540.65	-6.03%
14 March	3725.03	+5.21%
15 March	3819.86	+2.55%
16 March	3745.74	-1.94%
17 & 18 March	BSE closed for weekend	
19 March	3722.49	-0.62%
20 March	3672.40	-1.35%
21 March	3791.07	+3.23%
22 March	3713.97	-2.03%
23 March	3635.28	-2.12%
24 & 25 March	BSE closed for weekend	
26 March	3636.32	+0.03%
27 March	3694.82	+1.61%
28 March	3788.21	+2.53%

Gupta accused Shankar, in collusion with Nirmal Bang, of hammering down share prices from January 2001 till the Tehelka exposé. But according to the figures in the days leading up to the exposé on 13 March 2001, First Global was a net purchaser to the extent of about Rs 37 crore. This behavioural pattern is not exactly indicative of someone who is anticipating a fall in the market. Even in the month preceding the Tehelka exposé, First Global had been a net buyer to the extent of Rs 41 crore of stock.

What Gupta failed to bring to the Commission's notice was that the BSE Sensex was falling prior to the exposé and had already fallen from a high of 4,446 to 3,767 on 12 March, the day before the exposé. In reality it started rising a day after the exposé. Two days after the exposé, the BSE Sensex was actually higher than it had been on the day preceding the exposé. Even on 28 March, a fortnight after the exposé, the Sensex was nearly 250 points higher than it had been on 1 March. As seen from the figures, the fall actually took place on or after 30 March 2001, on Ketan Parekh's arrest in connection with the Madhapura Bank scam. It was SEBI's and the government's position that the market was artificially high, manipulated by Ketan Parekh and his associates.

It is also odd that Gupta presumed that the market would react adversely to an exposé of corruption and the prospect of a clean up of corruption. Was the investing public then in favour of corruption?

Shankar and Devina got embroiled in court cases in the Mumbai High Court, trying to get the ban on their trading lifted. SEBI, meanwhile, continued to issue summons to them. They received over 45 summons/notices from SEBI. Thirty-seven notices were issued to them under section 11(3) of the SEBI Act and a further nine were issued by the inquiry officer under diverse regulations. Initially, Shankar and Devina were asked to disclose details that had nothing to do with the crash of 2 March 2001. When they protested, they were informed that open-ended inquiries had been launched. When they asked for disclosure of the authority for initiating such inquiries, they were told there was no requirement for them to be informed. What could be more Kafkaesque? It became obvious that SEBI was conducting secret investigations about the funding of Buffalo Networks and the trading on and after 13 March 2001.

SEBI had granted First Global three new licences between April 2000 and January 2001. The scenario completely changed after the Tehelka exposé. SEBI debarred First Global from conducting any business, using a section under the SEBI Act (Section 11B), normally only brought in for emergencies to stabilize markets. First Global was a net buyer but selective data was attached to prove its position. SEBI deliberately used data from five minutes of a specific trading session to present First Global as a seller. What First Global was doing for the remaining six hours of trading session was completely excluded. SEBI provided 'evidence' that First Global sold Rs 6 lakh shares of Satyam at Rs 300 on an average, when the Stock Exchange records show they actually bought the stock.

From mid-February to mid-March 2001, SEBI stated that First Global had 'a consistent pattern of selling.' The figures, however, show that First Global had a pattern of buying for 11 trading days and selling for the rest of the trading days.

SEBI went on to accuse First Global of 'exceeding exposure limits'. This is apparently technically impossible as trading is controlled by a centralized computer system that does not allow such a transaction to be honoured.

When First Global challenged SEBI's order blocking their trading in the Bombay High Court, the judge directed SEBI to convert the executive order into a showcause notice, giving First Global an opportunity to defend itself. In early May, when First Global submitted their side of the story and SEBI reaffirmed their ban order, First Global turned to the SAT (Securities Appellate Tribunal). An interim order was issued that said, 'First Global has, no doubt, made a very good prima facie case in its favour'.

After three long months of hearings and not allowing First Global to conduct any business, SEBI was unable to produce any evidence to prove guilt. Despite that, on 18 September, SAT ruled it would not comment on the merits of the case and SEBI should get another 10 weeks to investigate First Global. But SAT did add that if SEBI had completed the inquiry within 10 weeks, First Global's business must be permitted to resume. After 10 weeks, guess what? SEBI went back to the Tribunal and got another extension.

Finally, on 3 December 2004, SAT set aside SEBI's order. It was intriguing that the tribunal pointed out that the SEBI chairman had persistently refused First Global's requests for an oral hearing along with their written submissions. SAT stated that SEBI's order had violated SEBI's own laws and regulations and was against the Fundamental Rights guaranteed by the Constitution, laws, and procedures. The tribunal also noticed that SEBI over-stretched its arm when it engaged a solicitor to send a lawyer's notice to Shankar Sharma, rather than dealing with it in accordance with the law. The order stated categorically: 'This we find a little unusual in view of the fact that the enquiry was pending before SEBI. A regulator does not send lawyers' notices when the matter is pending in enquiry.'

What does this amount to? Ten months of investigations to analyse three days of trading. First Global could not function until the investigation was over. Shoma Choudhury, of Tehelka, pointed out, 'It is interesting to note that the Securities Appellate Tribunal comes under the Ministry of Law and Justice and the Ministry of Finance pays its bills.'

Back to Devinder Gupta – he then came up with a mind-boggling claim:

> Going by the actual state of affairs, it would appear that the amount shown to have been received by way of share premium actually represented and reflected compensation/renumeration/professional receipts paid by First Global Stock Broking to Buffalo Networks for producing the Tehelka tapes [Operation West End]. Since the money was paid for producing these tapes, it was but natural that these tapes could have been conceived, designed and produced in a manner which could sub-serve and advance the interest of First Global Stock Broking. Therefore, it is necessary to find out and identify as to what were the actual motives and interests of First Global in arranging the production of Operation West End tapes.

Such magniloquence only exposed the government's fear-psychosis. Justice Venkataswami responded to this affidavit by pointing out that there was no proof of conspiracy by First Global to bring the markets down. He gave them until 8 October 2001, to substantiate this.

In an affidavit filed by the union government lawyers in the Commission of Inquiry, it was stated that Shankar Sharma and Devina Mehra were involved in a conspiracy to bring down the government. They wrote that the two NRIs on the board of First Global Mauritius were the Hinduja brothers or fronts for them. This is factually incorrect. The two are residents of Mauritius. If they are fronts for the Hindujas, no shred of evidence has been brought forward to substantiate it. According to the government, the Hindujas hatched this conspiracy because they could no longer buy the silence and inaction they wanted in the Bofors case. That was the reason Tehelka targeted the defence ministry and army personnel. They alleged that Shankar Sharma and Devina Mehra created this company in collusion with the Hindujas as part of a master plan to destroy the defence minister, George Fernandes, bring down the government, and reduce the Bofors case to cobwebs. Then, the affidavit stated that Shankar and Devina spun an elaborate conspiracy with Tarun Tejpal to play the markets and make a killing with inside information. There is no evidence or proof provided by this affidavit.

On 10 October 2001, Devinder Gupta filed an affidavit in the Commission that admitted, 'Although the investigations have progressed substantially, some further investigations do remain.' It is important to notice here that First Global was not being investigated because of any known violation of law, despite a determined search for it. They had found nothing substantial enough to include in the affidavit. This notwithstanding, Gupta did have the unfathomable confidence to proclaim:

> I, however, submit that the facts unearthed up till now themselves definitely show that "Operation West End" was not a bona fide journalistic endeavour. It appears to be clearly a venture – principally if not entirely – of Shri Shankar Sharma, the evidence shows has indulged in various undesirable activities as

a stockbroker in transgression of the Regulations. Thus the facts already unearthed bear out the statements made in the earlier affidavit filed before the Commission.

Gupta failed to muster any facts whatsoever. 'It appears to be,' maybe, but on what basis does it appear to be?

Gupta, confidently went on to state,

> For the sake of convenience, I would set out the facts under broad headings of the inferences which may legitimately be drawn from the material gathered so far by the Income Tax Department and the SEBI. I submit that these inferences, considered cumulatively, lead to a conclusion that Operation West End was not a journalistic endeavour. The department of revenue has collated the respective investigations.

Can you draw inferences leading to conclusions with no proof whatsoever? The proof Gupta offered are entries made in Devina Mehra's personal diary where the word 'Tehelka' appeared along with those of other media companies in December 1999. The domain name was registered on 23 December 1999. This, according to Gupta, proved that they had plotted the conspiracy when they invested. The domain name was actually registered by Aniruddha Bahal, along with other fanciful domain names, when he was fantasizing about various projects, hoping to use them if he could make his dreams come true.

Gupta stated,

> Shri Tarun Tejpal's suggestion that he established the portal is not borne out by the facts. Shri Tarun Tejpal was engaged as a journalist working with *Outlook* magazine. It was in February 2000 he resigned and joined UD & MD as a Director without any shareholding whatever.

Gupta's further evidence:

> The funding of the portal Tehelka.com has always been almost exclusively by Shri Shankar Sharma and his First Global group of entities. A sum of Rs 2.45 crore was placed at the disposal of UD & MD by First Global – Shri Shankar Sharma during the period April to July 2000 as unsecured loan for funding expenditure incurred by UD & MD. This is consistent with the fact that the said company including the portal Tehelka.com was owned and controlled by Shankar Sharma and First Global.

Gupta then got carried away in the thick of his conspiracy theory:

> The equipment bought in 2000 by Tehelka was eventually used for Operation West End.

All this information was acquired through raids in First Global offices and was in their account books. Gupta admitted as much when he said,

> The seized material also shows that he continued to exercise control over the activities of Buffalo Networks. Records in possession of the Income Tax Department show that First Global – Shri Shankar Sharma continued further funding of Buffalo Networks through July 2000. Besides, certain documents seized by the department from First Global indicate various expenses and outgoings of Buffalo Networks were incurred out of unaccounted cash available with First Global. Thus the entire expenditure by UD & MD and, thereafter, by Buffalo Networks came from funds provided by First Global. Seized records also show that the accounts of Buffalo Network were consolidated with those of UD & MD. This is clear circumstantial evidence of the fact that First Global – Shri Sharma considered the portal Tehelka.com and its activities as its own.

Beyond investing in the portal, which Sharma did, and following the expenses, what other proof is there of Sharma editorially controlling Tehelka?

Going through First Global's account books, there are cash expenditures of gifts and commissions given to various people. Even though Tehelka's own expenditures are written in by name, the rest of the cash flow to other people is officially 'presumed' to be for Tehelka to finance Operation West End. With almost every paragraph prefaced with 'presumably'. Gupta then concluded,

> In sum, it is submitted that facts unearthed so far lead fairly to an inference that Tehelka.com and Buffalo Networks were the companies of Shankar Sharma. Shri Tarun Tejpal's affidavit is based on the misleading suggestion that Buffalo Networks was the promoter of Tehelka.com, whereas the truth is that the portal was registered in December 1999 and was established/set up at least seven months before Buffalo Networks was incorporated. The explanation of Shri Tarun Tejpal on affidavit that Shri Sharma was a mere venture capitalist appears to be untrue – which fact itself is suggestive of the fact that the Operation was not a journalistic endeavour.

After he admitted using presumptions as a foundation for his affidavit, Gupta ended with an 'inference' with what 'appears to be untrue' and concluded that it is 'suggestive of the fact' that it was not a purely journalistic exercise. The fact that Shankar Sharma was a venture capitalist discredits him sufficiently to assert that there was a motive in the investment.

Devinder Gupta filed yet another affidavit in the Commission that accused Shankar, Devina, and Tarun Tejpal of a conspiracy to launch Operation West End only to make money in what was not a journalistic enterprise at all. Gupta said, Shankar Sharma and Devina Mehra took over a shell company in February 2000, UD & MD Agencies Private Limited.

Gupta charged in the Commission of Inquiry that Shankar Sharma, who was allotted 2500 shares on 30 June 2000 at a face value of Rs 10, transferred his entire shareholding in favour of Tarun Tejpal without charging any premium. However, on the same date, 6117 shares of Buffalo Networks were allotted to First Global at a premium of Rs 5711 per share. Again on the same date, 2753 shares were also allotted to First Global Broking (Mauritius) Pvt. Ltd, a subsidiary of First Global Broking Pvt. Ltd. No premium was charged from this company either. In all, 5050 shares were allotted on 1 December 2000, at a face value of Rs 10 to other shareholders, whereas 6117 shares were allotted to First Global at a premium of Rs 5117 per share. According to Gupta, the amount of Rs 3,49,38,830 shown to have been paid as premium for acquiring 6117 shares of Buffalo Networks Pvt. Ltd did not appear to be in the nature of share premium for different reasons, all of which he deemed suspicious. According to Gupta, Shankar Sharma and Tarun Tejpal did this to give the impression that First Global controlled only 10 per cent of Buffalo Networks. Gupta stated that in reality 98 per cent of the finances came from First Global.

Shankar Sharma and Devina Mehra, as directors of First Global Stockbroking Pvt. Ltd, did invest in 14.5 per cent shares in Buffalo Networks that owned Tehelka. On 1 December 2000, shares were distributed. First Global took a 10 per cent stake in Buffalo Networks at a valuation of 35 crore, that is $8 million. In dot-com ventures, before the bubble burst, the investment banker was paid a fee. At that time, typically, investment bankers would make a deal, put in their own capital or others' capital, and get paid in stock. As the investment banker, First Global would be paid that fee. Out of Rs 3.5 crore, the company issued stock at par as fee payment. Therefore, for a start-up company, it didn't involve payment of cash and it conserved the entire capital. If an investor has raised cash and he is getting stock at par, he would do it. Why would he take cash and exit if he believed it was a good investment? The investor then received between 2 to 5 per cent for capital raised. When First Global invested 10 per cent, it received 14 per cent; the additional 5 per cent got diluted by half per cent so the eventual share was 14.5 per cent.

Shankar explained why that particular transaction on that day:

> By mistake, Tarun allotted the 5 per cent, those at par shares to us individually. We told him, that is a mistake. It has to go to the company, because the investments don't come from us personally. All our investments are made through our company and not in our personal capacity. Tarun said, "Now it is done, what do we do then?" There were two options. The options to rectify the shareholding the way it should be are very simple. Either the company, that is Buffalo Networks, buys back those 5 per cent shares issued to me and reissues it to the company, First Global, at the same price. He can buy the shares on the same day, and reissue it to the entity it should be issued to. The first option involved a lot of time. Again, you have to apply to the FIA, and five other places. It can take anywhere between three months to six months. It is a more cumbersome process. The second option is the identical thing can be achieved by our selling the stock. The stock that was mistakenly allotted to us personally,

that stock is sold to another stock holder, which is let's say the promoter, Tarun, so now we are back to 10 per cent. Then a fresh equity issue of 10 per cent is made to the right entity. Which is what we decided upon; that it is a far quicker solution to realign the shareholding as for what it should be. This is why on that day, the share was sold to Tarun and the company issued it. It was worth 5000 for 10 per cent and at par for 5 per cent. It was a mistake that Tarun had made. There are forms that show how this was rectified. It's as simple as that. Tehelka was a portal that Buffalo Networks owns.

According to B.B. Nanavati, additional director of income tax (investigation), when Shankar Sharma and Devina Mehra took over UD & MD Agencies, they owned the entire share capital of UD & MD Agencies amounting to Rs 32,000 on 31 March 2000. In February, Tarun Tejpal, Aniruddha Bahal, and Kunwar Jit (Minty) Tejpal were inducted as Directors of UD & MD Agencies. According to Nanavati, Tarun Tejpal 'had no proprietary interest in the company – it belonged to Shankar Sharma and Devina Mehra'. The entries for purchase of initial equipment, which were ultimately used in Operation West End, are reflected in the accounts of UD & MD, and these relate back to the period prior to 31 March 2000 and April 2000. Nanavati questioned how a company in which Tarun had no shares at that time made these purchases. These expenses were transferred to Buffalo Networks of which Tarun did hold shares. Nanavati, in his affidavit described the manner in which Shankar and Tarun conducted their business but it is completely confusing in what is the illegality they are guilty of?

Was there any possible political and/or financial conspiracy between Tarun Tejpal and First Global? The government floated many tips to suggest that conclusion.

Madhu: A minister in the BJP government told me that he had researchers check and compare the dates of the deal you made with Tarun for investing into Buffalo Networks with the dates of what Operation West End had got on tape that same day. They discovered that it was the same week that Operation West End had got R.K. Jain, the first week of December 2000.
Sharma: Unbelievable. Really? What is R.K. Jain's testimony, I don't understand? It is all just fucking shooting his mouth off.
Madhu: So the scenario they made was: Tarun Tejpal called up Shankar Sharma, told Shankar, this is going to be something big. We've got R.K. Jain, so this is the time to put in money. Shankar Sharma, with the knowledge that they now had R.K. Jain on tape, then invested into Buffalo Networks that is Tehelka.
Sharma: I don't believe it! *Kehan sey kehan pahunch gayee* [from where to where have we reached]? The money goes in tranches, because they can't use Rs 3 crore right away.

In reality, Shankar sent his first investment cheque of Rs 27 lakh to Tehelka in March 2000. Would Shankar Sharma, a savvy stockbroker, risk his entire career and life, aware that the money would be used to sting a government? Shankar's interest and business is to make money. He is not an idealistic journalist who champions any socially correct cause.

Madhu: Did they tell you that they would be doing sting operations?

Sharma: No. Even in the cricket match-fixing story, we got to know at the absolute end.

Madhu: Did they tell you they would be doing investigative stories?

Sharma: Yes, they said they would be doing investigative stories. Like *The Indian Express* will only do investigative stuff, but they will also cover a Sonia Gandhi rally, or Vajpayee rally, apart from doing a petrol pump scam exposé. They will do anything that comes within the ambit of media. But tomorrow if they want to dabble in cement, then the shareholders will stand up and say that is not within the ambit of what you can do and what you can't. The stupidest thing which I can't figure out is that somebody will want to play the stock market and destabilize the country and put it all in my name? Credit me with some intelligence, for Christ's sake. Then sit around and wait for the cops to land up and bloody ransack me?

Madhu: If you wanted to do what they claimed you did, how would you go about it? If you were playing the market and wanted to destabilize the government, how would you have done it?

Sharma: It's not possible. It's as simple as that. It can't be done. If you have to bring down the government and make money, Tehelka is not the answer. You pay 50 MPs to defect and when they defect and then give it to the President, and that kind of shit shat you have to do … You can't go on the bizarre theory like fund a sting operation, know fully that R.K. Jain will come on board and Jaya Jaitly will also be very, very conducive to the whole thing.

Madhu: What about politicians playing the stock market when they get information, as has been rumoured?

Sharma: Very different, I'll tell you why. Because they will play the stock after having decided in the cabinet meeting that this is the decision to be taken, which will be announced to their leader. They get a two-day window to play. This is not a two-day window. This is a year and a half. You have no idea where it is going to go. If he is talking of December and then March, believe me, December and March are ages. It is like two eras. Markets don't get driven by one BJP scandal. Markets are driven by a multitude of factors in which politics plays a very, very small part.

Madhu: What was your motivation for investing in this company when they first came to you? Did you see it as a company that you could list later?

Sharma: The plans that any normal investor will have when he is investing in a company that is unlisted. There are two exit options. The first question every investor asks when making an investment is, what are the exit options? So your exit options are two. One, you can sell it to another company, which is what we actually did. The deal fell through, which is another matter. That was with Zee Telefilms or TV. We shook hands on February 12, that we are selling our 14.5 per cent and Subhash Chandra (Zee TV) said we want you to keep 4.5 per cent. Out of which they would put money into the company and buy us for the 10 per cent that we had. So, we would retain 4.5 per cent and retain a seat on the board if we so desired and whenever the company makes a listing then we would make the rest of the exit. And SEBI despite, all the pressure on them, never made charges that we traded with the inside information of Tehelka. It's not there.

Madhu: Sucheta Dalal of *The Indian Express* has questioned why, if you were the only investor, you took only 14.5 per cent?

Sharma: Huh! And she's a financial journalist. That's like saying why is the fucking coke black? Because the valuation is Rs 30 crore. To get to Rs 30 crore, you want to buy over 10 per cent, you have to invest Rs 3.5 crore. That's it. If we had put in Rs 25 crore, we were about 80 per cent of the company.

Madhu: But could you have asked for a larger percentage?

Sharma: But ultimately it's a game of negotiation. So when you say that look these are comparable companies out there. When you say okay, it makes sense. That's fine. It's a reasonable transaction and a reasonable offer.

Madhu: Sucheta Dalal wrote in *The Indian Express* that: "All of us know that the financial or businesses especially dot-coms does always call the shots despite the minority stake".

Sharma: Yeah, of course I call the shots.

Madhu: Which means you called the shots on Operation West End?

Sharma: No, no, no, no, no. "Call the shots" is a particular context in shareholding. In shareholding, you say you do not get into areas that are off limits as a media company. If tomorrow you start to do cement: sorry, not on. If you start to invest the capital that we have put in, into the stock market: not on. In Apollo Hospital somebody holds a 20 per cent stake or a 10 per cent stake, he will make sure that the promoters tomorrow do not start to think about starting an automobile dealership.

Madhu: But in the context of Operation West End, Sucheta Dalal says you must have been calling the shots.

Sharma: There is no calling the shots on a particular thing. I have no idea what Operation West End is. I have no idea what stories they are doing. The only thing that I am concerned about is that the money is not pissed away on things not within the ambit of a media company.

Madhu: You were not concerned with what they were doing with the money in the company?

Sharma: Yes, I am concerned. If tomorrow they started playing the stock market, I would be very concerned. As long as they stick to media, which is the mandate for the company. So they can do a newspaper, they can do a television programme, they can do a portal.

Madhu: Sucheta wrote: "In fact, Shankar's claim that had they known about the sting job, they would have stopped it, is a dead giveaway ... it proves he had that power.'"

Sharma: Yeah, have you stopped beating your wife?

Madhu: Sucheta says you had the power to stop it, implying that you didn't because you planned to make money in the markets.

Sharma: What is the power? The power is only to tell promoters that guys, you are not doing this. But tomorrow, if they say fuck you, I am doing it, then there is nothing a minority stockholder can do.

Madhu: Sucheta also wrote that First Global was surreptitiously buying HFCL stock through other shady companies.

Sharma: What is surreptitious about it? It's a listed company. We have investment companies through which we make investments. What is shady about it? It is fully disclosed. Every single day it is reported to the stock exchange and to SEBI.

Madhu: Sucheta wrote: "The RBI inspection report documented how First Global obtained clean credit from Global Trust Bank (GTB) to surreptitiously buy HFCL stock through investment companies such as Panchal Components and Appliances, First Global Stock Broking, Vitra Trade & Agencies, Top Gear Leasing & Finance, Vruddhi Confinvest India, UD & MD Agencies, Naulakha Financial Services and Mohan Fiscal Services. It listed 46 instances where a total of Rs 354 crore was released to these investment companies based on oral sanctions."

Sharma: Oral sanctions, that's fine. That's not my problem. That's the bank's problem. Go and ask them. My job as a borrower is to take money and return the money on the due date with interest. Till date, can she say that we have even one rupee outstanding with any bank? Ask her that. And none of the money is used to buy HFCL shares by the way. It is used for working capital purposes. Banks give brokers working capital advances. It's a settled method of doing transactions in the stock market. They will give it to the top fifty brokers.

Madhu: Sucheta wrote: "GTB also subscribed to non-convertible debentures of Rs 15 crore each issued by the investment outfits. First Global also got a hefty overdraft of Rs 44.5 crore from GTB to buy HFCL equity. Instead of placing the shares directly with foreign institutions, First Global's investment outfits first bought the stock at 1050 a share and resold it to the foreign institutions at a premium of Rs 10 to Rs 25."

Sharma: Nonsense. You make a brokerage of one percentage. Standard. No, no, but what is the answer for that? Holding private profits you make a 1 per cent commission on every single transaction. That you do as a brokerage house. That's a legitimate earning.

Madhu: Did you at any point refuse to answer questions to the Joint Parliamentary Committee, as reported by Sucheta Dalal?

Sharma: Yes.

Madhu: On what basis?

Sharma: When Kirit Somaya was taking off on the life and times of Shankar Sharma, I said, "Look, the Joint Parliamentary Committee is circumscribed by x-terms of reference. I will not go beyond the terms of reference. I will say this to his face and I said it then." It's on record.

Madhu: Sucheta wrote: "To me, the first sign of their rhetoric not matching their actions was the private placement of Himachal Futuristic Communications (HFCL), a controversial company run by Vinay Maloo and Mahendra Nahata. As sole coordinators, Devina and Shankar raised Rs 7.35 billion ($161 million) through private placement of 10 per cent of Himachal's equity at Rs 1,050 a share."

Sharma: I don't understand. Thousands of crores of private placements are done. That is the nature of the beast. It's all nudge and wink, so what is controversial? One hundred and twenty-five major financial institutions from all across the world participated in that issue and that included SBI Mutual Fund, included LIC, included UTI and included a hundred other major FIIs. What is controversial about it?

Madhu: Sucheta wrote: "Documents seized by the directorate of income tax during the course of search at First Global indicate that cash aggregating to Rs 96.6 lakh has been received on different dates during the period January to March 2001 by First Global. Nirmal Bang and Shankar Sharma were business associates hammering down the share prices during that period."

Sharma: Nirmal Bang has been exonerated by the same Tribunal.

Madhu: Were you dealing with Nirmal Bang?

Sharma: Yeah, absolutely. Fully disclosed. Nothing against the law.

Madhu: And you got this money?

Sharma: No, no, no. We got nothing. We make payments on account of dealings. This is not cash. These are all cheque payments.

Madhu: To Nirmal Bang?

Sharma: To his company, not Nirmal Bang. Nirmal Bang Equities, or whatever it is called.

SEBI accused First Global of routing proprietary trades through an unregistered sub-broker, Palombe Securities. Sucheta Dalal reported it.

Madhu: There is this affidavit where First Global's relationship with Nirmal Bang, which is under investigation, was irregular as per law.

Mehra: What was irregular about that relationship?

Madhu: They mentioned an unregistered sub-broker Palombe Securities.

Mehra: In fact, our counsel stood up in Bombay High Court and said, "You show me one transaction with Palombe and I walk out of this courtroom, on that one thing alone." There was silence.

Sharma: Nirmal Bang is a broker; is a member of the Bombay Stock Exchange.

Madhu: They state that First Global itself being a broker, dealt in very large volumes through Palombe Securities, Rs 600 crore last year.

Sharma: Let them show one contract of FGSB dealing with Palombe, for that matter Nirmal Bang.

Madhu: "There were unaccounted financial transactions between the Bang group and First Global: already evidence has emerged of unaccounted cash transactions amounting to 96 lakh."

Sharma: Where? Show me.

Mehra: Show me what is the evidence? You can keep writing anything you want.

Madhu: "And this perusal of accounts shows that the balance sheets stand in debit for the most part of the year 2000-2001."

Mehra: What is the crime?

Sharma: And this predates Tehelka by a whole year, by the way. The Venkataswami Commission was not constituted to go into the life and times of Shankar Sharma and give him a character certificate.

Mehra: And as far as the SEBI charges are concerned, the JPC has gone into them and has exonerated us. The statement made is that SEBI has shown no evidence.

Madhu: Did you make money during the post-exposé time?

Sharma: I always make money. We stopped trading on March 13th morning. So if I have to make money in Tehelka, it can be only post-Tehelka right? Because market is not going to fall before Tehelka. Right? Let Kirit Rawal disprove this thing and I'll bloody quit this business.

One can presume that the late Kirit Rawal would have disputed Shankar's statement.

Madhu: Sucheta has questioned the sudden jump in your profits and tax payments.

Sharma: That is the nature of the beast. You have to grow. That's what I go to the office for every single day. I don't go to shrink. Everybody has increased. Every single brokerage firm in India has gone from zero to hundred. We are hardly the exception.

Madhu: In your records, have your profits increased since the Tehelka exposé?

Sharma: I lost Rs 100 crore. It's on record. Because if I lose my business in March 2001 and from three years I am down a hundred crores straight away. It's not rocket science. It's very, very simple.

Madhu: Sucheta has written that if the Chennai office had closed down; what were you doing there in the first place? She said you were trying to flee the country.

Sharma: Even if you are running a *paan ki dukan* [paan shop], you tell your people why you are laying them off. I can't send them a fax that from tomorrow stop coming to work. I have an organization of human beings, not of robots. This is the fucking limit. It's my regional office. I am closing it down. I have to inform my people. They are young kids. I have to sit with them, hold their hands and talk to them about their future. Everything is an allegation. Why did I have cornflakes for breakfast instead of parathas? I had everything at stake and more so the fact that this is September 2001. Six months after the exposé. After the raids have happened and after the arrests have happened. If I had to flee I could have fled any time between March and September. Why should I wait for six months? I am not a dodo who will figure only six months later that, hey, the government is very, very vindictive.

Madhu: How much was your business worth at the time when you were accused of running away from India?

Sharma: Anywhere Rs 50-100 crore. Besides, I would have left everything behind: my repute, my honour, my family.

Sucheta Dalal, columnist for *The Indian Express*, has written critically of Shankar Sharma:

> It is not only Income Tax officials that he threatens, but journalists. He holds press conferences and issues belligerent press releases to amplify SEBI's minor mistakes while keeping mum of many other substantive issues. Anybody who dares to disagree with his position is immediately treated to abuse. Though many of SEBI's findings have little to do with Sharma's financing of Tehelka. com, his constant refrain is that he is "victimized by SEBI which is acting on behalf of a totalitarian regime".

There have been nasty e-mails exchanged between Sucheta Dalal and Shankar Sharma. It only got worse when Shankar sued Sucheta and *The Indian Express* for defamation in January 2005. When you are fighting hundreds of cases against you, one filed by you is a mere drop in the ocean, for Shankar.

⤻

B.B. Nanavati's, (additional director of income tax) affidavit described the business done by First Global with Tehelka, and for each business move and every business decision, he proposed an ulterior motive. If Shankar had invested money in Tehelka, it was because they had agreed to an exposé that would shake the government and, therefore, crash the markets. If Shankar responded to Tarun in an email that stated he was not interested in the day to day running of Tehelka, only in returns for his investment, that again was interpreted as Shankar making a *show* of distancing himself. None of their accounts, balance sheets, cheques, investments, in fact, any of their actions, were taken at face value.

Nanavati's affidavit took an email from a friend in London to Shankar Sharma, congratulating him on Operation West End, as evidence that 'the friends and associates of Shankar Sharma were also aware of the fact that this entire operation of Tehelka.com was one of Shankar Sharma'. In fact, every move, every doodle in a diary, every email, every decision, every communication, back or forth, Nanavati interpreted as a conspiracy. An email from Mahim Mehra (Aniruddha's cousin) who wanted to sell his shares to Shankar Sharma, was used by Nanavati as evidence: 'The entire contents of this email clearly show that the entire operation was that of Shankar Sharma.'

Shankar has said that First Global's investment in Tehelka was merely as an angel investor with no managerial control. In fact, some of the email messages intercepted between Shankar and Tarun were about Tehelka complaining that First Global was not taking enough interest in the company. Shankar's view was that once he has invested, as he did in any number of companies, he was only interested in the bottom line. It was not his business to run the portal. Shankar began to scout around for a round of funding in August 2000, with a view to pull out. Given the dot-com climate in 2000, it was not unusual for First Global to have invested Rs 3.50 crore in a website like Tehelka.

Tarun Tejpal, after reading Nanavati's allegations, decided to file his own rebuttal in the Commission. Tejpal clarified that the valuation of the shares had been made at Rs 35 crore, not by Shankar Sharma but by Ashok Wadhwa of Ambit, who they had approached for funding the project in February 2000. For handling the process to raise funds, Wadhwa had sought 5 per cent equity in the new company to be formed at par value. These discussions had taken place in the presence of Suhel Seth of Equus Advertising. Tejpal pointed out that Shankar Sharma was not even in the picture when the Tehelka project was first conceived or first valued. Sharma came on the scene later while the talks with Ambit had yet to be finalized. Tarun explained that as no company had been incorporated for this project and its incorporation would take some time, it was decided to take a shell company to start immediate operations. UD & MD was picked up by Sharma and the Tehelka team began hiring reporters and began creating the website. By the time it had been set up and was online in June 2000, a new company Buffalo Networks had been incorporated in Delhi to take over the website. Tejpal addressed Nanavati's scepticism as to why the website was transferred from UD & MD to Buffalo Networks without any charges or premium, on the grounds that this was the original arrangement. The transitory use of UD & MD to set up Tehelka was simply to expedite matters and to get down to work immediately. Tarun said, 'There was no question of Shankar Sharma trying to appropriate a not-agreed-upon share of the company because in ventures like this the world over, the entire value of the company vests in its promoters and their ideas'. Tarun tried to explain the logic of the dot-com era investments:

That is what the venture capitalist invests in: the people. And by extension their ideas, their energy, their hard work, their beliefs and commitment, and their ability to create value out of nothing. Without the core people the company has no value. In fact, as companies grow, investors, around the world tie in their key people with labyrinthine contracts because they know the company has no future without the people who dreamt it up and with their energy created it.

The director of income tax creatively argued that the premium charged by Buffalo Networks from First Global for the allotment of 6117 was highly exaggerated and could not represent the premium on the shares and, should therefore be treated as a business receipt in the hands of Buffalo Networks which is taxable. He also pronounced,

> Since the money was paid for producing these tapes, it was nothing but natural that these tapes could have been conceived, designed and produced in a manner which could sub-serve and advance the commercial interest of First Global Stock Broking.

Tarun demanded to know,

> How and on what basis does this income tax officer come to the conclusion that this money [share premium] was paid for producing these tapes? If he had bothered to look at the accounts of Tehelka.com/Buffalo Networks (which presumably he must have seen), he would have known that the total amount spent by Tehelka on Operation West End was not even 5 per cent of the share premium money given by First Global.

On 10 and 11 September, A.A. Shankar appeared as a witness before the Commission of Inquiry. Observers in the Vigyan Bhavan room were treated to Ram Jethmalani's award-winning performance. Jethmalani hammered at A.A. Shankar until the government officer admitted he had no knowledge of Devinder Gupta's [under secretary, finance ministry] affidavit and had only put his signature on it as a 'witness'. Despite constant objections from Kirit Rawal (government counsel), Jethmalani pounded A.A. Shankar, asserting that the financial motive that had been planted on Tehelka was a motivated smear campaign that was wholly untrue. Jethmalani warned A.A. Shankar that he could be tried for perjury. A visibly shaken A.A. Shankar had obviously not anticipated that he was the *bakra* [sacrificial lamb] in the income tax department who had been sent to the Commission. It was reliably learnt that after Jethmalani's demolition missile, the income tax officials declared they would no longer be party to these shenanigans. From then on, Tehelka lawyers kept pushing for the 'financials' to be argued but Justice Venkataswami said he would hear the financials at the end of all the other depositions. In Kirit Rawal's Rashomon, he disagreed with all of it in his interview with me and said, 'A.A. Shankar did not capitulate and withstood the cross-examination'.

‿

According to Aniruddha Bahal:

> The government went after us on this stupid stock market thing. They knew there was nothing. Privately all these government lawyers would say, there's nothing, and they would come up to us, "Sorry, sorry *yaar, kya* instructions *hai yaar, kya karey? Yeh sab toh chalta hai* [we are doing it under instructions. That's how it goes]." *Arey! Kya* [hey, what]? And these were the worst guys. Even in the

government witnesses, whom they were producing, there was some of them, young ones saying, "Sorry, sir, we're just being told to do it." *Arey!* What is this, *yaar*? They were the worst people, who would come up and commiserate with you, "*Yaar* it is not me, they're putting it." And they were the guys who have fucked us the most. Be honest about it. Why are you coming out and commiserating with us?

Then Shankar filed the affidavit, in which he said that Kirit Rawal's sister, Dharmishtha Rawal, was in SEBI. And the JPC report indicts her for SEBI transactions with the Calcutta Stock Exchange or something, big time. And Shankar put that in passing, that how can Rawal ignore this? And your own sister, in SEBI, from where possibly all this whole concocted theory was being created, because SEBI they were *chabi banoing* [churning up] SEBI. There was a conflict of interest. You are trying to protect your sister by passing on the blame to somebody else. This was pointed out by our lawyer and Venkataswami expunged that.

Madhu: Why was it expunged?

Bahal: Harish Salve made a huge issue out of it: "How can these people write anything against us?" Here we are giving a statement of facts. It is a conflict of interest. It is like a government lawyer coming and prosecuting you for a certain crime that he thinks you have done. And somebody in his own family – mother, father, brother, whoever – is also, indirectly involved with that organization, against whom we are said to have committed some intransigence. So either you take yourself off the case. Then suddenly they are not so interested in discussing the financial part. They got scared after Ram Jethmalani cross-examined the income tax officer. I've never seen a cross-examination like that. He simply trashed him. That man was close to tears. Then suddenly they realized, at that point of time, that this thing can't go on, because we have seven witnesses to come and we'll get trashed on this. Then they started creating all these delay tactics. First Harish Salve got up and said, "I need more time because my wife is sick". They sought an adjournment and after that another adjournment, and then they suddenly, when we moved an application that this thing should finish before closing arguments, should stand, otherwise you're just closing this chapter. Then suddenly the stand was taken that maybe they need more time for investigation. They already had taken eighteen months; how much more investigation do you want? And Venkataswami was supposed to rule on this.

Madhu: When he resigned.

Bahal: Yeah, when this whole episode happened. The whole position was that he would rule on this and I don't know which way he would have gone. But we pushed him into that; either you rule on this, because they got all their chances. He indicated that he will start with the closing arguments, which just means the application for discussion of financials is forgotten.

An atmosphere of shady dealings was created around First Global through all the affidavits. That isn't tough. When they are after you, every 'i' you forgot to dot can become a mountain in a teacup. So how did Shankar explain all the innuendoes?

Madhu: Shankar, in the affidavits filed by the government agencies, they have mentioned that there was some wrong doing in the structure of First Global in Mauritius and the transfer of money and shares. Please explain your position on that to me.

Sharma: This is in India. We have three subsidiaries, one in the US, one in the UK, one in Mauritius; three companies. Tehelka's an Indian company; our investment into Tehelka is from our Indian company. There was an investment of $620 with RBI permission from First Global, Mauritius to buy a 5 per cent stake, which is our company. That $500 was remitted but through our EEFC account. Three and a half crore, from our First Global Stockbroking Private Limited.

Mehra: Out of tax payments.

Sharma: For a three and a half crore investment, why is the whole bloody bureaucracy, the government jumping up and down?

Mehra: In fact, that was another *tamasha* [drama] in between, when Shankar was in jail, around January. *The Times of India* did a lead story saying that money came from overseas to Tehelka. That same evening, I wasn't even aware of it but Shanti Bhushan and Ram Jethmalani held a press conference saying that, "We want to tell the world that First Global has not committed any offence". I went and met someone at *The Times of India* and I said, "What kind of nonsense is this?" You either get my version or you simply check the facts. Look at how much money is come into Tehelka from overseas.

Sharma: $620, for Christ's sake, with RBI permission.

Mehra: And you're saying $620 is some major foreign funding.

Sharma: And even if it is foreign funding, how on earth is that a bloody crime, *yaar*? It's just completely going off on weird tangents. Make a conclusion on 14 March or 15 March than spend two years trying to find each and everything to make it fit. Aniruddha Bahal's cousin is a guy called Mahim Mehra, who owned 6 per cent of Tehelka. He's an NRI based in Singapore. He bought the stock from Aniruddha to just participate in the dot-com boom. In the government's affidavit, he is mentioned as being Devina Mehra's brother. This is after your RAW and IB's great investigative skills. Mr Mahim Mehra, brother of Devina Mehra. *Kahan se bhai* [from where to where brother]? Just because two Mehras are there, *toh matlub* Mehra - *Mehra bhai-bhai* [so it means Mehra -Mehra so brothers]. It is so asinine.

Mehra: And Kirit Rawal and Soli Sorabjee and Harish Salve are looking through these affidavits. This is part of the great affidavit filed by the Union of India, which ends by saying that there were also emails seized which show that

Shankar Sharma has a strange relationship with Devina's brother, Mahim Mehra, who has also invested in Tehelka. Mahim Mehra is a cousin of Aniruddha Bahal. He has nothing to do with me at all.

Madhu: They said in the affidavits that you had differences with him? Did you?

Sharma: I never met the guy. With my brother-in-law, yes, that's a separate issue altogether.

Mehra: [Laughs.]

Sharma: I remember the first affidavit that came in. I said we're not going to open it in office, let's go home and *arram se bethkeh padhegeh* [read it comfortably] … Then when we went, opened and started reading it, and Devina, the problem *kya hai hi ki* [what happened is] once she starts to laugh, she can't control herself. She has this weird problem *ke yeh saans nahin le pati* [she can't breathe]. She fell off the bed. I remember this so distinctly, I said, "*Baba, baba, saans lo saans lo* [baby, baby take a breath, take a breath]."

Mehra: They really did not apply their minds at all. Every time we file a writ, the Union of India's response is, "Kindly don't go into it". They want to investigate further, create another legal proceeding, whether anything exists or doesn't exist.

Sharma: So what do they go and say in court? No, no, your Honour, we are still investigating. For the life of me I can't understand that they know the truth, let them just simply summarily withdraw this whole bloody bullshit about these affidavits – there is nothing in it.

Mehra: In fact, Harish Salve, he was solicitor general, stood up while the cross-examination was going on. The witness, the income tax guy, all his statements had collapsed on the stand. Harish Salve stood up and said, "Regardless of what my witness says, I will make the case for the Union of India". He could not support any of the affidavits. Ram Jethmalani said, "You know what the procedure is, how can you make a comment like that? Your witness has to stand by his affidavit and defend it. If he can't defend it, how can you?"

Sharma: Just leave us alone and let us do our work. From their perspective, sending me to jail has a limited shelf life. Once you see it, then there's nothing to it. You can go in again, come out again; it really has no incremental value. Then why carry on with this whole bloody bullshit? It's Tehelka you're after then you're after the wrong guy in this case, boss. We are not Tehelka. Please make no mistake about it.

Mehra: In fact, in the cross-examination, we went down this stupid affidavit of theirs, and Ram Jethmalani asked them that you are saying that these are cash amounts given by First Global, so if I prove to you that these are cheque amounts, and these are receipts that First Global received, and not given out by First Global, would you agree that this document has been fabricated? This guy says, "Yes". Then Ram went, started going line by line, like this 20 lakh gifts, it's a receipt item, it's a cheque item, it's there in my income tax returns and so on. Every item he started going through. The fact is that this is a fabricated document. Ultimately that guy was just sweating there. So it's like saying, somewhere, there'll be a figure of ten written. They will say that this is 10 lakhs given to Tehelka, on no basis whatsoever.

↩

What did the Enforcement Directorate accuse Shankar and Devina of? ED charged that First Global sold HFCL (Himachal Futuristic) shares to FIIs, neglecting to obtain the required approval from the Reserve Bank of India. ED also charged that First Global sold those shares in an underhand deal at a lower than market price and took the difference abroad in dollars. Shankar demanded to know, 'What is the evidence for these charges?' Under Section 81 of the Company Act, SEBI has guidelines for a minimum price and price bids can be invited. In this case, the Government of India is then accusing Indian financial institutions and FIIs of money laundering. Shankar pointed out, that in the government's attempt to fix Tehelka, they have actually exposed how desperate they were to divert attention from the real issue. There are repercussions to these accusations that can have serious long-term effects. Putnam and Amvescorp-Invesco, two of the funds accused of money laundering with First Global, happen to be among the top five funds worldwide. The Reserve Bank of India, SEBI and the ED were aware of this transaction for 22 months, but an investigation into it was initiated only after the Tehelka exposé.

The Reserve Bank of India's Exchange Control manual states that the RBI grants general permission to authorized FIIs to purchase shares from Indian companies without any additional approvals from the RBI, so if we accept the ED's contention, what happens? Billions of dollars of transactions on the Indian market would be in violation of the rules.

In any case, FEMA replaced FERA in June 2000, which would preclude any arrests, as all the violations would be punishable only with monetary fines. Yes, there is a sunset clause in FEMA that allows investigations initiated before the repeal to be completed under FERA. The accusing finger again points to the government, because the investigation into First Global had not begun till October 2001, 16 months after FERA was repealed. When Shankar was arrested in December 2001, no case reference was made and they had no proof of any misdemeanour.

The Enforcement Directorate stated in its remand application after Shankar's arrest, 'We have conclusive evidence that the accused siphoned off Rs 56 crore in the HFCL deal'. But, the ED did not file a charge sheet against the Rs 56 crore accusation even though the last date for filing charges under FERA slipped by. The charge was simply dropped. Shankar charged that the ED officials committed perjury under oath and the government should call them into account for it.

Shankar and Devina have been incensed with the injustice of it all, forgetting perhaps that living in a labyrinthine maze, India is on an average, just plain normal:

Sharma: What's relevant here is there is no allegation of our having made any money in Tehelka.

Mehra: While in the Commission they are trying to make it seem that there is some nexus with Tehelka. None of the actual charges made by the agencies relate to Tehelka.

Sharma: They pertain to alleged undisclosed income a year back, so nothing to do with Tehelka at all. I don't know what the hell they are there in the Commission for.

Mehra: SEBI has made no allegation of any insider-trading relating to Tehelka. It's just in the Commission there is this overall aura that there is something negative related to Tehelka, when no agency has individually made any charge on that.

Madhu: But Kirit Rawal said that you made money by using other companies and trading in their name.

Sharma: We went to open court and challenged these bastards that you come out and show me who else I have traded through. Just all nudge and wink. So bring it down to fucking facts. You are the Government of India, right? You should be able to find out something. And if you can't find out, then fucking stop talking about it, boss. Till date, Madhu, neither SEBI, nor Income Tax, or any other agency, has made any allegation that we traded with any information about Tehelka. A thing as hair-brained as some tapes will come out and market will fall. It's only a Government of India can even think that.

Madhu: What about the allegations they have made about your company in Mauritius?

Sharma: It's our company in Mauritius, that's fine. So is that a crime? Bansi Lal's daughter-in-law has a company in Mauritius. Yashwant Sinha's daughter-in-law has a company in Mauritius. It's not a crime. I've taken RBI permission to do that. That company does not do any business in India at all. I've lived in the country long enough to understand that. So don't even venture into the territories of this country. What else am I supposed to take, permission from God? I've remitted $5000 from my EEFC account, taken RBI permission from their automatic approval group in December. What else am I supposed to do? This is four months before Tehelka happens.

Mehra: If I wanted to do something shady, why would I officially take over a company? It makes no sense.

Sharma: I apply to RBI on paper and then give those papers to the guys who search, *haanji saab dekho mere paas yeh hai* [yes, sir, this is what I have]. Initially we were so naïve. See these doors, these are all the searches. These are all the wax seals that they put. They've all been sealed at various points for various searches. We gave them everything. Then you find that whatever you give them is twisted around. We realized this is a different ball game. When I paid those taxes, in year 2000 there was no Tehelka. i don't need a Tehelka to make money. Why are they hanging on to a theory which has outlived its usefulness? We have no interest in the fucking tapes and never bloody watched their tapes on Zee TV. I've never watched those scurrilous tapes. I have no investigative journalism aspirations. I'm an investor. I have invested; if that's a crime, then punish me for it, but don't get into Tehelka's crimes and put it onto my head for Christ's sake. If they've used prostitutes, then there is a proceeding under IPC [Indian Penal Code], and then you please proceed against them. I can't do any useful work. Till today, even as you were probably walking up the stairs, what we were sitting and doing? We were sitting and making a writ for income tax. Is that the job of any sensible person in this country?

Mehra: And the Union of India lawyers don't want to defend it in court or in the Commission. There they are nothing. There Ram Jethmalani is screaming, that all your officers are committing perjury and lying under oath. They don't have a reply to that.

Sharma: Natural justice *kya hai* [what is natural justice], because they have not given us anything. The income tax proceedings, nothing has been given to us. It seems you have evaded Rs 100 crore. It seems you have evaded Rs 90 crore.

Mehra: Which transaction, what are you talking about? In any proceeding, if anything is to be held against me, I have to know the charge.

Sharma: What evidence you are relying upon? Give me a copy of that evidence?

Mehra: I can't be asked to defend myself in a vacuum. So that's what our writ is about. We have half a mind to go and argue it ourselves. It is in Kirit Rawal's interest to divert attention from that stock market crash, because his sister was totally involved in that.

Sharma: Dharmishtha Rawal, his sister, is a nominee, SEBI nominee on the Board of the Calcutta Stock Exchange. The cover-up in this goes a lot beyond just Tehelka. The good thing is that what the JPC found and frankly, again that is an amazing thing. I can't figure out how, a bunch of parliamentarians, typically you won't expect them to understand the nuances of something as complex as the stock market. But, there I am floored by even their capacity to ferret out information. Because they had withheld a lot of information which was damaging. In the JPC reports it is very clear which corporate house was the reason why the crash happened. Very, very, very clear. The entire planting of stories in this initial part, that Shankar Sharma behind the stock market crash, all that happened through *The Economic Times*, Delhi. The JPC report is fairly clear in that the withdrawal of funds by a corporate house in the period of February-March period was the reason that caused the crash. Yes, there is no crime in that. But if you are looking for a reason, then that was the reason.

Madhu: When I interviewed Kirit Rawal he was furious with Tehelka for bringing his sister in. He said he would never forgive them for dragging his sister's name in.

Rawal also trashed all of Shankar Sharma's allegations against his sister.

Sharma: He should have revealed his conflict of interest to the Commission. You are saying that I am part of the bear cartel. Whilst in reality that problem has actually been presided over by your sister. No, as a lawyer you reveal that I have got this conflict. They all hushed it up. The thing about the government's whole strategy is that, since numbers are beyond comprehension of everybody – so you just put a lot of numbers in it. And numbers in our business are by necessity large. It's always thousands of crores. That's like saying that you raid Naresh Trehan, and you find that he operated upon three thousand patients.

Madhu: Tell me, how much were you worth before Tehelka?

Sharma: Officially, just Rs 70-80, maybe Rs 100 crore; something like that.

Mehra: We'll have to just check out the numbers.

Sharma: Considering the tax payment, that is a known fact, *na*.

Madhu: And then after Tehelka?

Sharma: After, we haven't even sat and calculated.

Mehra: Yeah. It'll be far, far, far lower.

Sharma: It's too depressing so I don't even go down that path at all.

Mehra: Yeah, actually if you start thinking about the monetary loss, you wouldn't sleep at night. Then there's no point.

The time limit for the assessment order is two years from the search. On 25 September 2003, they received the assessment order that stated: No undisclosed income, no undisclosed assets found, nothing incriminating found.

The Joint Parliamentary Committee report stated that unusual volatility on the Bombay Stock Exchange had been much more noticeable in the year (2000) prior to the one being investigated (2001), but no official thought it warranted an investigation by SEBI. The JPC had a majority of the ruling party's members (NDA) and was headed by Prakash Mani Tripathi, a BJP member of Parliament.

The report read: 'Large falls had occurred at least ten times in the previous year', and further, 'The single day fall has been more on at least 125 days.' The JPC pointed out, 'The market has fallen the day after the presentation of the budget on most occasions in the decade of the 90s. The biggest fall – of 520 points – was recorded the day after the budget was presented in 2000.' The JPC clarified, 'Although the SEBI investigation into the volatility of the market in February and March began on 2 March, the market really collapsed several days later, between 7 and 13 March, by over 150 points compared to the closing index on 2 March, in the wake of the payments crisis on the Calcutta Stock Exchange.' The JPC made it a point to mention that the market, in fact, did not fall in the two days following the Tehelka exposé. Figures show it rose by 350 points in the two trading sessions on 14 and 15 March. Rather than evidence pointing to a conspiracy by First Global to make a killing on a downward crashing market, the Tehelka exposé actually rocketed a depressed market to 350 points. The JPC report concluded that the downward trend turned into a crash on 29 March when the Ketan Parekh-Madhavpura Bank of India mess was splashed all over by the media. The following fortnight the market lost 400 points and on 12 April, the closing index was almost 800 points below the close on 2 March. The JPC report concluded, 'Thus, much of the stock market crash of March-April 2001 post-dated the budget by several days and had, in fact, no relationship with the budget.'

෴

The Times of India, in an editorial on 21 December 2002, wrote: 'Interestingly, the JPC has also cleared First Global, a major investor in Tehelka.com, of charges of "deliberate bear hammering" to discredit the government. Will those responsible for the witch-hunt against First Global's promoters be held accountable? Don't hold your breath.' When a government agency goes after someone, if that person is proven innocent, it matters little to the government. The purpose was to harass, and since that has been achieved, conviction is really not necessary. Are then those who man the agencies answerable for their actions? No, they simply move on to the next victim.

Shankar and Devina still maintained they respected the Indian judiciary. They pointed out that in Russia, an arrest leads to incarceration for two months without any hope of relief. At least, in India, a ten-page order is written and reasons for the rejection of bail have to be recorded. Shankar and Devina believed that the Constitution of India has inbuilt protection of human rights, and even the most perverse judge cannot go against it. Shankar mentioned that Goolam Vahanvati, then advocate general of Maharashtra, had met them on a Mumbai street and with tears in his eyes, apologized to them. Yeah, right! I was frankly sceptical. Tough to believe that a government appointed officer would do that. Subsequently, I interviewed Vahanvati in his chambers in the Supreme Court.

As in everything in India, the opposite parallel always runs concurrently. For all the unscrupulous, *sabh chalta hai* [anything goes] lawyers working the system for their own benefit, there are others who are conscientious to the law and the Constitution. Goolam Vahanvati, was witness to the government churning out the SADS (Secret Auto Destruct System) on Shankar and Devina.

Vahanvati happened to be advocate general of Maharashtra in 2001 when the market crashed after the budget was announced. SEBI believed that Anand Rathi, president of the BSE (Bombay Stock Exchange) had actually spoken to people in the record room on the day the market was fluctuating. SEBI believed that Rathi had sought to obtain price-sensitive information so D.R. Mehta, chairman of SEBI, suspended him on 8 March 2001. This was the first time this power had been exercised by SEBI. The Bombay High Court heard this case from March through April. While this matter was being heard, similar orders were passed in the Shankar Sharma and Devina Mehra's case. Vahanvati, as advocate general, was involved in justifying the legal principle of SEBI's power to suspend Rathi.

Later, Shankar Sharma and Devina Mehra (First Global) filed a comprehensive petition in the Bombay High Court to which they had made all the agencies parties: the Income Tax Department, Union of India, Enforcement Directorate, SEBI. They said that there was a concerted action on the part of government against them, starting from the time they were stopped at Chennai airport. When that case came up for hearing, Vahanvati was not available because he was appearing for the Maharashtra State Electricity Board against the Enron-sponsored Dhabol. First Global's petition was dismissed. In February-March 2004 (when the

BJP-led NDA alliance was still in power), SEBI tried to revive the cases against Shankar Sharma and Devina Mehra, after dropping them earlier. Vahanvati spoke about that case when he was called upon by SEBI to represent them:

Vahanvati: Hmmm. I was briefed. I wouldn't like to really say this. I am saying this off the record …

Madhu: Then don't say anything off the record. Say what you can place on record.

Vahanvati: Okay, let's say for some time I wasn't appearing for SEBI in between.

Madhu: Did you refuse to appear?

Vahanvati: When this case came I thought it was a continuation of the earlier proceedings. I appeared on the first occasion because obviously I wanted to understand how SEBI was justifying its action and I couldn't. In the meantime, I made a statement in the court that no action will be taken on the notices. Then I read the papers. My conscience didn't allow me to continue. So I just said I am not available.

Madhu: Did you think at any time, when you obviously found that they were being railroaded and the facts that were being presented, were wrong?

Vahanvati: No, on the legal principle I thought what they were doing was all wrong.

Madhu: Did you at any point at that time think that it would be good to say that what you are doing is wrong?

Vahanvati: No, I can't as a lawyer. I can't do that. As a lawyer I can't do that. The only option I have, Madhu, is to return the brief. As a professional you have no right to sit in judgement over a client. The only option you have is to say I will not appear. You cannot, I know some professionals are doing this, issuing statements or giving interviews to TV, in respect of matters in which they have appeared. I think it is grossly unprofessional. Just see the predicament you are placed in here. You are privy to what opinions they have got. You are privy to what facts they've got. The only thing is that you have to quietly walk away. This is what I did.

What happened was, I just made an excuse. I said I am not available and I returned the papers. You must understand that I was holding an office as advocate general of Maharashtra. It is a responsible position. I don't want to do anything which will appear to be political thing. I am a non-political person. If I had started making statements and there was a different government over here, it would have looked very bad. So I did what I thought was the only correct thing to do. And incidentally I was walking home and (voice breaks with emotion) – and I feel very strongly about what's happened to these people. Really, it tears me apart. [speaking in a choked voice] I think, it's … the entire government goes after some people. I met them [Shankar Sharma and

Devina Mehra] on the street. They said, "Are you okay?" I said, "No. I returned the papers. That's all I could do." [Trying to control emotion and tears.]

Madhu: Basically you saw on the inside how they were organizing the destruction of First Global?

Vahanvati: Yes. I saw it. Please give me a moment to pull myself together. [Turns his face away and tries to control his emotions for a few minutes.] It was clear to me and I was afraid it wasn't put across the way it should have been. I consider this to be the grossest abuse of powers on entire … how the power of the state was used. You feel so helpless. You can't do anything. [Tears in his eyes; very upset.]

Madhu: That must have been very discouraging for somebody in your position.

Vahanvati: I couldn't, I couldn't agree, I couldn't. What else could I do? The only thing, having appeared in the case once, the only honourable thing for me to do was to say, "No I won't appear again". I met them then and I told them that I am not appearing, because I couldn't bring myself around to agree to a situation where in law, I am just putting it in law. I didn't think that I had the power to reopen the cases. So I just quietly said, "No, I am sorry". I am saying this even though I know the matter will be sub judice today or whatever it is. I am not appearing.

Madhu: What do you think needs to be changed in the system to prevent this kind of a thing?

Vahanvati: When the system breaks down then the people who are in charge let it. That's the problem in our country. We have so many systemic failures.

Madhu: Invisible orders are given where there is no proof.

Vahanvati: There are so many other cases one finds. Footprints. It's a question of footprints, Madhu. There are never any footprints in a file. I've seen that in various cases.

Madhu: In your memory, has anyone been harassed in the way Shankar Sharma and Devina Mehra were?

Vahanvati: I hope not. Frankly, my problem is that I know nothing about the stock market. I hardly have any shares today. But I have tremendous sympathy for Shankar and Devina. I feel that it was an amazing situation where P.C. Chidambaram used to come. He argued brilliantly for them. Ram Jethmalani has done a wonderful job and Ram at least went out of his way to make statements. I admire him for that.

Madhu: Now that you are the solicitor general, what do you see your job as in the Tehelka Commission? Earlier, the attorney general and solicitor general took an extraordinary interest in the Commission.

Vahanvati: I won't. I will not take it up. I will not participate in the Tehelka Commission in any way. Again as a professional I have very strong views in the matter. As I have already explained … I will not get involved in the Tehelka Commission anyway.

Madhu: You will not go there?

Vahanvati: No, I will not go there, unless I have instructions to the contrary. I will not go to justify anything of this kind. I don't have to. I am not a political person.

Madhu: But do you think it is correct? Do you think the solicitor general should be involved in such proceedings, according to the constitution?

Vahanvati: The solicitor general position is not a constitutional post. Each individual has to make what he wants at the office. I would like to set my own standards. I have no right to sit in judgement over anybody, whatever constraints they had. I wouldn't really like to know. I don't even know what games they played. I am not interested in knowing.

Madhu: The previous ones played a very active role.

Vahanvati: Yes, I am not interested in knowing. Whether it's the Gujarat case or whether it's all the cases which I am inheriting now. I am taking my own view, regardless of what happened before. I think it is not proper and wrong on my part to try and say this was wrong, that was wrong. Because then I am trying to promote myself saying what these people have done, which I don't think I will ever do. But Tehelka I will never touch. I will not go to that Commission.

Madhu: Do you think anything at all can be done in the future to prevent this kind of harassment?

Vahanvati: We can put systems in place where this sort of thing shouldn't happen.

Madhu: What kind of systems can be put in place?

Vahanvati: I will tell you. It's very simple. As advocate general of Maharashtra I had a very interesting case. My first opinion, that I had to give, was whether a bureaucrat is bound when wrong orders are issued by the minister. This is on some land matter. I am talking about 1999-2000. Okay, a minister passes an order which the bureaucrat thinks is illegal. Question is: Is he bound by that order of the minister? Does he have to comply with it regardless? My advice was that you are bound because we are living in a parliamentary democracy and if they are responsible to Parliament out of the legislature and therefore if they pass a wrong order you have to comply with it. But, you have to do three things. You have to first put your dissent on the file. You have to bring it to his attention that what you are doing is wrong. Then, if he still insists on passing that order, you have to comply with it. It is the bureaucracy which is really responsible for standing up to ministers and saying, sorry what you are saying is wrong. Now what happens if a minister is giving an oral order? Or what I call, a lack of footprints. It is for the bureaucracy to say, sorry write it down. If you don't put it down, I am afraid I am not going to comply with this.

Madhu: But in reality what happens is that if somebody doesn't comply they are transferred to the boonies.

Vahanvati: You are transferred. That's what the prime minister said today that I will stop all this. You stop it.

Madhu: But it is insidious. It is very difficult to implement.

Vahanvati: No, if you give them a fixed tenure appointment in a particular department then they have the courage to say, that sorry, I will not do it. We have had some wonderful secretaries in Maharashtra who refused to bow down. [Laughs]. For instance, a particular person called a particular person and he was in the midst of a meeting and said give a tender to a particular person and he said, "Thank you very much. I will place it on record that you have called me and asked me to give the tender to so and so, who happened to be related to him." He said, "No, no, no, I am not asking you to." He said, "Thank you very much and I am not going to give it to him." You have bureaucrats like that. But you have to encourage bureaucrats to be independent. At the same time they shouldn't become too independent. Then they will not comply with any orders at all. But you have to have this system. Somebody has to have the courage to pass an order.

Madhu: So you would call this a systemic failure?

Vahanvati: It is a systemic failure. Our system is not wrong. You should have a system in which a bureaucrat stands up and says, "No, I think this is wrong". Unfortunately, what seems to have happened over here is the bureaucracy is screwed up. Don't you think? Because somebody thought somebody is going to be there forever. This is not the only case this happened.

Madhu: It's not so much of standing up. I think it has just been the precedence of obsequiousness and survival.

Vahanvati: *Kya farak padta hai* [what difference does it make]? So that doesn't matter. Standing up for what you think is correct is really not worth it. That's what they feel. You have to encourage them to do this.

⌣

Shankar, in a particularly Indian way, believed it was Divine Intervention that saved them. As Shankar said: Because, you know, when the state is after you, who can save you?

Madhu: Against their divine right, your divine intervention?

Sharma: Precisely. There was something beyond our own skills, our own abilities. It can take you up to a point, but there's something a lot beyond that. Look boss, they have thrown their best bunch at you, okay. They've done everything that they could possibly do. And you're going around in Mumbai. If this is not divine intervention, I don't know what is. *Aur kya* [what else], how do you rationally explain it? You can't.

Mehra: Our organization didn't fall apart.

Sharma: Yeah, everybody stayed.

Mehra: I'm pretty sure it was a big effort on their part.

Sharma: This raiding ED party told our staff member that our aim is that, like

9/11. We will strike in the middle then the whole thing will collapse from the top. They saw that even after all this, because this was midway through the whole thing, that our overseas businesses are running and we're still doing research. They said, we will see how they manage to run. So what they did in those raids was; they took away all our hardware. Then they tried to intimidate these people into leaving. So they said then the organization has to collapse.

Both Shankar and Devina feel it would have been difficult for them to survive if it hadn't been for the support they got from their families and friends. They said everyone was always on standby, and they even received the support of people they did not know. Shankar reiterated, 'That has been really the win factor, frankly. *Accheh log zyada milheh* [met more good people], in this whole process, which is, to my mind, the biggest learning gain out of this whole thing.' Devina added, 'Ram, Tony, Rani (all Jethmalani), all these people – it's not as if we were childhood friends of theirs or anything. We came to know them only now and really they went out of their way.'

After long hours and days of interviews with Devina Mehra and Shankar Sharma, did I believe they were guilty? Were all the accusations made against them a possibility? Of course, there is always a possibility. Did they create an elaborate camouflage network with shell companies and front men where the Hindujas' names were never actually used? Yes, it is possible. When you implement a conspiracy, you don't leave a trail behind for people to catch you. But would they, as professional, financial players risk everything for a relatively small pay-off by the Hindujas? Again, it is possible. The brightest people have been known to be stupid at some point in their lives. Anything is possible. George W. Bush got into Yale University! But niggling little question: Why has the government, with all its ability to use RAW and IB, not been able to unearth a single iota of proof?

In an interview, Mahesh Jethmalani gave his opinion of Shankar Sharma:

Madhu: What do you think of Shankar Sharma and Devina?
Jethmalani: He's not a saint. But I think that as far as statutory compliance goes in this country, he's better than most. The trouble with Shankar is that he is a little outspoken. He has very strong opinions and he advocates them quite vehemently. So he makes enemies. But I think he's honest.

What happens to a man and woman, yet to be proven guilty, when the state so invades their lives on a shock and destroy mission, that the man wholly loses his interior life completely? The only monologue he can have with himself, is about how he will survive the attack on his life, which only he experiences and the outside world cannot see. There is no space in his interior to think of anything else. The term, 'quality of life' becomes an unattainable luxury. You just want your ordinary life back. The idea of seeing a movie after work or having dinner with friends becomes a luxury you cannot afford. The only introspection you have is how to plan your escape from the mental jail into which the authorities have perpetrated on you. A direct outcome of this is an atmosphere of constant paranoia. Shankar received a call from an office employee who accesses their email, asking if he should delete an email that had just arrived from Aniruddha Bahal. When Shankar asked what it was about, the employee read, 'Okay, bye'. Shankar had informed Aniruddha that they were visiting Delhi on a particular date. Aniruddha was only confirming it.

Shankar said, 'There is a shift that is permanent. We can never really be comfortable in this environment. Most of us live under the normal assumption that life will be predictable. If you don't break any laws, you are safe. But, now you live with: anything can happen.' In character, Shankar added, 'On the other side, I feel if life has given you this, it also gave you the tools to fight it, which is how we could actually survive'.

If a psychological survey was undertaken of the people of India, how many of them would say that they were trapped by external circumstance, not of their doing but which had been forced upon them? If you gave this state of mind the colour grey around each person who feels like that, my guess is the country would appear black. Very black.

Now we can certainly address the phrase, First Globalian. What does it mean? It means you have made the mistake of aligning with someone who took on the powerful. It means you will be destroyed. It means you will not be able to identify your enemy, for it will have no name. It means that various departments of the government will cohesively work in breaking your spirit and harassing you. The normal freedom to function is overtaken by being forced to continually smack a blanket over little fires that keep erupting from nowhere. The degree of transparency demanded of your personal life is overwhelming. There is a selectivity from whom such transparency is demanded. No politician would survive for a day if his books were examined as relentlessly as First Global's have been. And, this could happen to anyone. Politicians do it to one another as soon as they oust others from power. But for the grace of the Powers That Be, you and I go free. Given the wrong time, given the wrong place, given the wrong circumstance, any one of us could be In. Stay on the right side or spend the rest of your life dodging bullets. As Shankar says, the average Indian, the ordinary rickshaw-puller faces this fear every day of his life. It is as easy as spitting for a factory owner with the right connections to have an employee jailed. The average Indian knows he lives in a First Globalian world and spends his life walking on a high wire. The paradox of this world is that the same people who are instrumental in implementing the machinery of the SADS, are also caught in this world, since they too are watching their backs. The officers who carried out the orders to harass Shankar and Devina had little choice. Obviously, they were looking out for their jobs and promotions and did not relish the prospect of being packed off to a 'punishment posting', a term that is really only used in India. Nothing personal. It is just survival, not even business. The family tree of the SADS also climbs upward. Even the politician/bureaucrat who ordered the magistrate to put Shankar on a terror trip, is watching his *naukri* [employment]. He has to deliver the message to his boss that he is a master spin-doctor for the party. If he fails to make the SADS a success, his own future is in jeopardy.

There were discussions at the Commission that those who had suffered in Indira Gandhi's Emergency were using the same systems effectively against Shankar Sharma and

Devina Mehra. Statements recorded by SEBI, income tax, FERA, and Enforcement Directorate officers are admissible in evidence. The methods used to extort these statements would generally be considered unconstitutional, but Indian courts have treated financial crimes with seriousness and made it near impossible to retract such involuntary statements.

The Indian government follows standard procedure, no matter which political party is in power, when a journalist writes damaging material. The politicians never go after the journalist. The government is acutely aware that if a journalist is harassed, the press rallies around him; he becomes a martyr. They know that no political party can afford to alienate the press. What then do they routinely do? They go after the owners or to revert to the somewhat archaic term, 'proprietors' of the media organization. Human rights activists are on the watch for any violation of the rights of journalists, but is anyone watching out for the rights of the owners? The journalists, quite frankly, don't give a damn and stories about a businessman being harassed hardly make hot copy.

The lower courts often became inimical tools in maintaining Shankar's and Devina's no-exit labyrinth, the one place in a democracy from which you would hope to get justice. Devina and Shankar's story is not fiction, and that is why it is so petrifying. It is happening now. It is happening to millions of others. It can happen to you and me.

~

For Devina, there was also hurt that fractured her love for India. She said, 'The two worst things in this was letting go people [who worked for them] and secondly was the fact that your own country was doing this to you. Al Qaida comes and bombs you, at least they are the enemy. This was your own country doing it to you. That was the hardest.'

Despite Devina and Shankar's resilient fighting spirit and their ability to laugh in the face of the worst circumstances, there was a natural resentment towards Tarun Tejpal for the repercussions of Tehelka's sting. Shankar never verbalized it to Tarun. Shankar said, 'Tarun knows. I don't have to say it. And there's no point in you saying something that the guy is feeling bad about. There's no point in rubbing it in.' Devina added, 'There's nothing you can do about it.' Shankar was clear that fighting amongst themselves would have undermined the platform they were fighting on and they had to stay united. As a couple, they could have also got into the blame game, but Devina refrained from reminding Shankar that all of them were, after all, his college friends. Shankar, who is closer to Tarun's brother Minty, did tell Minty, 'I said, *kehan phassa diya tum logon ne* [I said, where have you people got me stuck]? This is not my life and what am I doing here? Not once. Several times, over the past one and a half years.'

Yet Shankar's frustration and anger with Tarun, though never expressed, is palpable. He spoke about his feelings on 13 March 2001:

Sharma: I was so mad at Tarun that morning. Boss, if you're funded and you're through and you're cruising, then you can take a little bit of a risk. You have to think like a businessperson. You can't think like an idealistic journalist. Those are two different things. If you have an artist in a garret mind set, *phir voh karo, jhola lutkao aur phir karo* [hang a shoulder bag and do it]. But if you've got to run a business, what you are professing to run, then there's a huge difference. It's not as if you're going to feel any less about corruption or anything. You're just delaying it a little bit. By all means, do it. Nobody's denied you that right. You're a journalist, do it. Timing *dekho, yaar* [watch the timing, buddy].

Mehra: It was the wrong stage of their evolution to have done something like this. It's not the same thing as *India Today* doing it.

Sharma: I don't think Aniruddha understands even today.

Mehra: And then, you are putting a whole lot of people in danger. You are taking a decision for yourself, that's a different thing, but there are other people involved.

Sharma: You can become a celebrity journalist, but at what cost, ultimately? If that's what you want to become, then your strategy is a very different strategy. There's no business angle to that, whatsoever. You can be a loose cannon journalist in another set up and the management will give you just that much leeway to do those things. But if you are the businessperson, you have to think differently. Irreverence, going off on a limb, all those are nice things if you can carry it off, boss. Then it becomes a part of your persona. Business has too much at stake. People don't realize, especially people in the media. Everybody tells me, every business associate, every friend, every time we sit down for a drink, *Yaar, Shankar, tu itna bewaqooof tha, mujhey nahin patha tha. Mainey kaha, kyon? Yaar, tum paisey daikar kyon nahin nikal saktey they* [hey, Shankar, I didn't know you were such an idiot. I ask, why? Why didn't you just pay them off and get free]? I try to tell them, *yaar agar mai gyarah saal pehley aaya tha, char paanch paisey leykar Mumbai mai,* and I've built a business this size, *kuch toh dimagh hoga merey mey. Kuch toh dimagh hoga* [I try to tell them, if I came to Mumbai 11 years ago with very little money, I've built a business this size, I must have a little intelligence]. Bribing an income tax officer, are you trying to tell me I have never heard of it? That it doesn't happen? Boss, in my case, let me be absolutely honest with you, there was no option. If I'd tried to, I would have gone behind bars all over again. They had come with a mission. They want you to give money so they can trap you. So they can say, look, look, "Tehelka Investor Caught Trying to Bribe Income Tax Officials". *Voh kal keh paper mey aajayeyga* [it would be in tomorrow's papers].

Mehra: Anyway, you don't want to pay off if you have done nothing wrong.

Sharma: *Sawaal hi nahin* [the question doesn't arise]. I have nothing but contempt for these guys. Every time we are in court I have a good slanging match with these bastards.

Mehra: They can't believe it because they are used to doing anything to business people and business people still *haath jodd kay khadday ho jathey hain* [stand up before them with hands folded]. From day one, we showed them no respect, the way they are used to.

Sharma: The whole tragedy of Tehelka is for what good, for what purpose, what did it achieve? Something leads to something, actively beneficial to society. Even if there's a price to be paid for it, *paanch pachees log marey. Ismey kya hua, yaar* [if five or twenty people were destroyed. What happened here]? Complete exercise in futility.

Madhu: Was it, perhaps, because Tarun believed that by doing great investigative stories, Tehelka would become a magnet for investors? Perhaps misreading that business people would not touch it?

Sharma: Not just business people. Even if you get purely a financial investor looking to invest, you still have to get ad revenues. Not the investment angle, I'm talking about the bread and butter angle. Just running it as a business. You need ad revenues. You can't sell it on your two rupees *mey toh kuch nahin milney vala* [you won't get anything]. *Kaun dehga* [who will give it]? No government will touch you. Obviously. No state department will advertise with you. It will go to *The Times of India*. There are ways to get to the businessmen. You have to think through these things in a very systematic manner.

Madhu: When I met Tarun on 13 March at the screening of the West End Operation tapes, he said to me, "The government is going to fall".

Sharma: But you can't run a business on that premise. And even if it is so, what if it falls? What do you think investors are going to flock to you because the government has fallen? Businessmen play it both ways. They are in bed with everybody. Regional parties, opposition parties and always the ruling party. *Kiskey paas jaogey tum* [who will you go to]?

Mehra: That's what happened with Subhash Chandra.

Madhu: Subhash Chandra chickened out?

Sharma: No, Subhash Chandra did not chicken out. He came back with a lower figure of the valuation. That's all.

Madhu: How much lower?

Sharma: Not a whole lot lower. We were discussing Rs 40-45 crore effectively, right?

Mehra: 45-50 I think.

Sharma: He came back with Rs 26-30 crore. First they came with 20, then with that meeting with Devnag Anand, he came with 30. Tarun didn't take it. Again, you have to alter strategy as you go along. I trade for a living; rather I speculate for a living. That's my life, okay? Sometimes you're in a bad trade then you take any price that comes your way, boss. Then you don't sit and wonder.

Madhu: When Subhash Chandra came with the Rs 30 crore valuation, did you advise Tarun to take it?

Sharma: It was in a meeting. Tarun himself turned it down. I was there in the meeting.

Madhu: Didn't you have a say in it?

Sharma: Tarun was, at that time, very confident that NRIs are going to give money. I would have told him, if he knew NRIs the way I know NRIs, you will get jack shit out of them. So Subhash Chandra didn't back out, to put the record straight. I don't think the number Subhash Chandra came up with was in anyway an absurd number, because the market had crashed, dot-coms had gone out of favour.

There was a transformation from the ready for battle cloaked with the gear of optimism of their early interviews, to the later ones, where it was beginning to get to them. Yes, really get to them.

⌐

The ED had conducted raids on First Global employees, associates, lawyers, and auditors. Old parents, wives, and children were threatened and some associates manhandled. Shankar's travel agent was so terrorized that he terminated all dealings with them. First Global's overseas clients stopped doing business with First Global worldwide, as they feared government reprisals.

Two years later when Shankar actually found time to clean up his papers he found his bail rejection orders from the Delhi High Court, which was opposed by Harish Salve. Shankar said,

That order boggles your mind because it uses facts which were never urged by either side. It uses my statement to SEBI in which I said, "Tarun called me up on March 13th morning and told me this and I told Tarun that this is what will jeopardize your funding and I think you should just get your financing and then do whatever you want." How come the judge quotes this statement in the order? From where did he get it? In the SEBI matters, we went to the Tribunal. The Tribunal rejected our stay application and refused interim relief. The Tribunal wrote that we do not think that SEBI has any cause to be angry with the applicants because the Tehelka tapes have been viewed and there is no mention of SEBI on the Tehelka tapes. So why should SEBI be antagonistic towards them. All these were in camera dictations given in private.

The government's behaviour has been largely suspicious. Why were no raids conducted on all the people found accepting money on the Tehelka tapes, even though N. Vittal, commissioner of the Central Vigilance Committee, asked for it? Why were no charges filed by the government against all those caught on the Tehelka tapes? Should SEBI not be functioning as an independent adjudicator rather than a slave at the whims of the government? The Joint Parliamentary Committee, after investigating all the accusations, announced, 'SEBI has not so far provided conclusive evidence to substantiate its conclusions'.

It must be asked: Did the government's damage-control team ever discuss what the *right* thing to do was? Was it ever discussed by the ministers in power, that if corruption has been exposed, they should not become party to the cover up? Was there, at least, a redeeming dilemma of values? Is everything discussed on the basis of immediate expediency for the survival of a political party and is a vision for the country a naïve, impossible utopian dream in the formulation of damage control measures?

The SADS has been instutionalized and will be used by subsequent governments as a blueprint, just as precedence is used in the application of law. What do we have here? Obsequious bureaucrats with a reputation of being instruments of terror taking orders from self-serving politicians versus First Global, with a reputation of business success, huge tax payments, employment-generation, and intellectual strength? First Global received virtually no support from the media and no celebrity made it a fashionable cause to fight for. It simply did not touch the general public.

Shankar's lawyer, Mahesh Jethmalani, spoke about the on going cases against Shankar and Devina:

Madhu: But Shankar Sharma's cases are winding down now, aren't they?

Jethmalani: Nothing is ending. They're all there. They have to be argued out and then wound down. When the new regime comes, it is not as if all the old victims of the previous regime get automatic redressal of their grievances. The new system also takes some time.

Madhu: In the Commission it happened instantly.

Jethmalani: Because the Commission has wound up. Not before that.

Madhu: It was so funny to see Khanna, Iqbal Singh's lawyer get up and complain about how everything had changed because the government of India lawyers were not allowing them to badger witnesses.

Jethmalani: No, that happens overnight. Even these enforcement guys came to me and they said, please make sure that you tell, sir, we only did our duty.

Madhu: The ED guys. They went to Shankar also.

Jethmalani: Yeah. They went to him as well. They came to me and said, please tell sir, we were only doing our duty and make sure we don't get victimized. Complete rats. Doing a quick volte-face. But that's the bureaucracy and that's the entire revenue department. They are all just the master's voice.

During Shankar Sharma's last interview, conducted when he was in Delhi to argue his own case (one of the 22 filed against him under the Companies Act), he spoke about how he had had just about enough of it all. He was in Delhi for a case where their office signboard had been taken down while it was being repainted and they were charged for not having a sign outside their office. The magistrate threw out the case and castigated the prosecuting counsel for wasting the court's time. The FERA cases are still pending, and Sharma said, 'The worst thing is the courts will not do a wrong thing. But they won't do the right thing either. They will just keep pushing it away.' There are still some income tax cases pending. Sharma ostensibly got permission to travel but was stopped at the airport. 'It's like Hydra, multiple heads. If one guy will tell me it is okay to travel, he will also alert the guy at the airport to tell him to stop me,' he said.

Devina took the whole experience in a doggedly determined stride. She said that their goal was to break your spirit, and both Shankar and Devina resolved that they would not allow that to happen. A senior income tax officer had suggested to them that they would face huge mental problems living through this. Shankar and Devina informed him that they experienced no mental stress. They told him, 'Our parents gave us a great education, we built our business ourselves and we can rebuild it all over again.' He disappointedly responded that he had heard from colleagues that they would be tough to break because they were self-made successful professionals.

It wasn't as though they did not have their disheartening moments. The fact that they had just expanded their offices, a few weeks earlier had completed the interiors, and now had to let all those young people go, shattered Devina's feelings for India. Devina said she had always held patriotism close to her heart. Before Tehelka, they often found themselves in furious arguments with Indians settled abroad and they pointed to their own success as an example; that it was possible to make it without political godfathers and connections. In Shankar's opinion, Indians, despite individual success stories, as a people cannot make it work because there is something intrinsically wrong. He said that although India has English-speaking manpower, accounting systems, and everything else going for it, we still can't seen to make it happen. The same Indians go overseas and do well. Shankar said he believed he now had the answer. 'Free enterprise that has to build bridges with the bureaucracy or government ministries, just can't work. This model cannot work,' he said.

Sharma: Until you have a rule of law you can't make a successful model out of anything. Either you have a dictatorial regime the way China is, so at least you understand the rules. So this halfway thing is there, where you believe that law will protect you and then you realize there is no enforceability of your rights as an individual or as a business person or as whatever you are.

Madhu: Have you lost faith in India now?

Sharma: I have. I make no bones about it.

Madhu: And you Devina?

Mehra: Definitely. This system does not work. Specially the bureaucracy.

Sharma: *Aur agar iss thereh sey business karna hai, humney nahin karna hai* [and if this is the way business is to be done, we don't want to do it]. If I have to cow done in front of a bunch of corrupt ministers or bureaucrats, *nahin karna, yaar* [I don't want to do it buddy]. That's a waste of my energy.

Madhu: Are you planning to move abroad?

Sharma: Eventually, I don't see any other way out. That is a decision we have taken. It's been like a near death experience. I can't stay in a country, boss, *yeh* [this] regime change can't determine whether I like a country or don't like a country. It's not comfortable, *yaar*. That small guy can screw with your life like this, *yaar*. I want rule of law. I am very clear. I do not see us doing the model that is time-honoured in India. And everybody has to do it, whether it is a Narayan Murthy, or a Wipro, no matter what they say. Not one of these guys,

I've known them for years, Narayan Murthy, Nandan Nilekani, would they ever come out and say something in support of us? No, they are too damn scared.

Mehra: We've got a lot of support through all of this. That's been the good part of all this that so many people have gone out of their way to help, but not a single business person. Not even in private. No one has even called.

Sharma: *Itna darthey ho, yaar? Kis cheez sey darthey ho* [you are so scared? What are you afraid of]? Are we Pakistan? Are we China? But maybe deep down there is this fear that somebody can ruin your life and there's nothing you can do about it. We are educated. We know our rights. We can fight a legal battle. *Hum agar iss haal mey hain* [if we are in this condition], why even talk about 99 per cent of this country, who are anyway leading lives of quiet desperation. Here, despite having means, somebody can just take it away.

Mehra: And all these senior lawyers will tell you the same thing, that you can't depend on the judiciary. Justice may not come at all, and if it comes it is so late … what is justice? If somebody robs you, after three years, *tumarah saamaan vapiss aajayagey* [you'll get your stuff back]. That's it.

Sharma: *Humarey mey Devina ki jewellery mil jaayeygi*, because that's our rightful thing. *Kab mileygi? Doh saal key baad mileygi. Voh meyra hai, voh meyra huck hai* [we will get Devina's jewellery back because that's our rightful thing. When will we get it? After two years. That is mine, that is my right]. What are you going to do this bastard who unlawfully took our legally acquired possessions away? He's not accountable for what he did. He gets away with it.

Madhu: You may not realize it but from the time I started interviewing you till now, how you have changed. Earlier you said, *"Kya kar lengeh? Main kabhi nahi yahan seh jaunga. Inko mar keh jaunga* [what can they do? I will never leave. I will destroy them and go]."

Sharma: *Nahi, nahi, nahi. Vo karkeh bhi jaunga. Aisa bhi nahi hai ki* [no, no, I will do that and go]. I am not going to let these bastards live in peace. I will live in peace. That's the difference. I am not going to forgive and forget.

Madhu: How will you fix these guys? The guys who ordered these ED and income tax raids are out of power now.

Sharma: Correct. I can't fix the politicians.

Madhu: Can you fix their jokers?

Sharma: I can fix the jokers through departmental proceedings. Absolutely. *Unkeh saath bahut asaan hai* [it's real easy with them]. That's why I am very relaxed about it.

Madhu: They committed perjury.

Sharma: Perjury and going beyond the Act. The Income Tax Act doesn't allow you to file conspiracy theory affidavits in Commissions of Inquiry. It is not your job. You can't become a tool to the political vendetta. *Tumko aapna kaam karo* [you do your job]. If George Fernandes has a *panga* [grudge] with me, let him do what he can do.

Shankar spoke about how this whole experience had made them re-evaluate their priorities. He said, 'You can say everything can be so fleeting. Why then shut out something just for the sake of some work? Whatever you do in your work, somebody can bloody come and do something tomorrow. So may as well have this end of it also figured out. And by God's grace, we will have the baby in December.'

Devina gave birth to a baby girl, Precia, on 7 December 2004. At least one part of the story should have a happy Bollywood-shtyle ending. 'The baby,' Shankar said, 'was a big, big, big gift out of this whole thing.'

Shankar Sharma and Devina Mehra only invested in Tehelka Rs 3.5 crore for a 14.5 per stake. At that time small change for them. Babes in the Wood who made one Pilot Error. Now they are in a state of Amazing Grace trying to piece their lives together again. And it is not sweet.

The story could have some value, if you feel their story could be, but for the Grace of those in Power, your own.

20 Why the Caged Reporter doesn't Sing

Tom Joad [Henry Fonda]: If there was a law, they was workin' with maybe we could take it, but it ain't the law. They're workin' away our spirits, tryin' to make us cringe and crawl, takin' away our decency.

- *John Ford's film*, Grapes of Wrath *(1940)*

Kumar Badal was an unlikely candidate to play the hero in the cause of journalism. Badal spent six months and two weeks in jail, sent there by the SADS (Secret Auto Destruct System). He did not become a hero. Not because what and how he suffered was not heroic, but because he was an inhabitant of Insectpur. Too insignificant to be noticed. Unlike Tarun Tejpal, he was not a sought-after speaker throughout India. Tarun Tejpal was a hero because of his class, his education, and how he presented himself to the media. It was an obvious outcome of his background. Badal did not belong to the right class, did not have fluency of speech nor the ability to present his cause to the press. He could not even envision how he could use his persecution (and prosecution) to his advantage, as Tarun had quite naturally done. This is significant in India. It is easy for 'high profile' people to wage heroic battles. Rarely will they feel the constant uncertainty of an interminable time in jail. Even if they do go to jail, it will only be for a symbolic day or two. For Insectpurites, it can be the end of a regular life. Except for their own family, nobody knows or notices when an Insectpurite is thrown into jail.

Tarun Tejpal could not have guessed that Badal would be a target of the SADS. There was not much Tejpal could do once Badal became embroiled in the SADS and his story quickly became Kafkaesque. The strangest part was Badal's inner life: he was a hero in his own eyes. He felt good about himself.

Badal was an easy victim of the SADS. He is a symbol of how India's democracy is so distant from being universally accessible. You think and believe you are living in a democracy, until you become inconvenient for someone who has power. Suddenly, you find yourself in ex-Soviet Gulag. So how and why did Kumar Badal get arrested?

According to Kumar Badal: The police arrested two poachers in Biharigarh and reportedly did not register the arrests in their records. The modus is that you arrest people, don't record it, and negotiate for money to let them go. The police followed the routine, took money, and let the two men go. However, the press got wind of it and reported that two poachers were in jail. To cover up, the police then arrested two other men at random, Meherban and Imam, who were actually innocent. The police found Kumar Badal's cell phone number on one of the arrested men. When the police saw 'Tehelka' on the card, they gained their own brownie points when they called authorities in Delhi to tell them they had a golden opportunity to use. Kumar Badal was traced to the Tehelka office. Suddenly, stories 'appeared' that Tehelka had paid for poachers to kill protected wildlife to film it.

Kumar Badal said he had on occasion gone to Dehradun to pick up medicines from a famous Ayurvedic doctor since his wife was having problems with her pregnancy. He said, like most reporters, he would talk to people sitting around him in the bus. He said, 'I may have given my number or card to someone I met on the bus'.

On 3 July 2002, Badal went to the CBI office and was taken into custody at the CBI office, New Delhi. Overnight Badal was rushed to Saharanpur. Sidharth Luthra assigned one of his juniors, young Haryanvi lawyer, Satya Narayan Vashisht, on Badal's case. Vashisht, chased the CBI cars through the night in desperate pursuit to Saharanpur. Once there, Vashisht convinced the magistrate to hold Kumar in jail for a day. When Vashisht pointed to injury marks on Badal's abdomen, which he had sustained during the CBI interrogation, the CBI stated they had no idea how he got them. The judge then reassured Badal that one of his lawyers could stay with him for 24 hours.

According to Badal's lawyers, 'On 4 July 2002, the police deposited him in Saharanpur jail and he mentally bounced back. Though the following day he was handed back to the CBI for three days, the one day in jail had toughened him up'. On 8 July he was sent back to Saharanpur jail and remained confined there for 11 days. On 17 July 2002, Badal was transferred to Dasna Jail, Ghaziabad, and was incarcerated till 4.30 p.m. on 15 January 2003.

Badal was accused of paying poachers to kill three leopards in the Shivalik hills of Uttar Pradesh. Apparently, Badal was in the middle of doing a story on poachers. District Forest Officer Paramjit Singh had apparently told the CBI that Badal had approached him to do a story on poaching. However, no such evidence was ever produced. On two subsequent occasions, Singh said that although Badal had come to him to do a story on poaching, there was no criminal activity involved.

A lawyer closely involved in the case had his Rashomon to this story. According to him, "My take on this is different. I think the CBI or IB etc. had Kumar under surveillance, that is, phones were tapped, as was the case with most, if not all, Tehelka staff. This was a bonus the CBI ended up with. Kumar thought this wildlife poachng sting/story was his path to fame. He was oblivious that he was shadowed or his phones were tapped. They (those who were tapping phones) then tied up with the UP police and/or the wildlife department. The CBI then took over the case and arrested Kumar."

Tehelka lawyer Sidharth Luthra said, 'Vashisht was a discovery of legal talent. Since my whole office was caught up in Tehelka's defence in the Commission, I talked Vashisht into following up on Badal's arrest. He tenaciously spent night and day pursuing the CBI and made sure he was with them every inch of the way. Wherever they went, he followed or even reached before them. Vashisht ensured that no harm came to Badal. No confession could be extracted by the interrogators. His television bites were earthy but cutting edge. He taught Badal how to fight back and not buckle under pressure.' Badal said that every 14 days his hearing would come up and he would appear in court. When the beating issue arose, the media got activated. Badal said, 'When I came to court, people would come to look at me, as if I was some animal from the zoo or some joker'. There was a huge crowd, including the media, when he left the court. They shouted slogans against the CBI and the government. When Badal was being herded into the police van, somebody from the press pulled his shirt up to expose the marks of his injuries. That was broadcast on all the television channels. It was only when the beating issue arose, the media got energized.

How then did Kumar Badal end up in jail for over six months? He said he learnt about the true nature of justice in the lower courts. His bail was rejected three times, for no reason other than the charges being of a serious nature. His case then reached the Sessions Court. R.K. Anand volunteered to do the matter pro bono. It took four visits to Ghaziabad and lengthy arguments but again his bail was refused. When the Allahabad High Court heard Badal's case, he was hopeful. The judge reprimanded the CBI for jailing journalists while poachers roamed free. The judge gave a date after a week for his decision. After a week, the judge deferred his decision. When the decision came two weeks later, the same judge who had ticked off the CBI, rejected his bail plea yet again.

Aniruddha and Tarun were working behind the scenes to help Badal. They approached Kapil Sibal, eminent lawyer and member of the Congress Party, who took up the case and argued it in the Supreme Court. A special leave petition was filed but the courts' winter vacation postponed the hearing again. When it came up on 13 January 2003, before a two-judge bench, Raju Ramachandran, additional solicitor general appeared for the CBI and said bail should not be granted as they required a further two months to complete the investigation. The judges told him that if the CBI wanted to they could complete the investigation in 24 hours or they could take 24 years to complete it. They asked: He has already been in jail for six-and-a-half months, what else do you want from him? They demanded to know how Badal could hamper their investigation? On 15 January 2003, Kumar Badal was released. He was a changed man.

Kumar Badal is again part of the Actualized Man group. Born in Muzaffarpur, his family moved to Bombay when he was three. His Bihari father was a partner, along with 14 others, in a pharmaceutical business. After being ousted from his position as managing director, he started a pharmaceutical business of his own. Badal's father was married to a woman from Bihar and had six children from her when he began an affair with a Bengali woman. After Kumar's grandfather died, his father married the Bengali lady who then gave birth to three children, one of whom was Kumar. His mother died when he was six years old. He said, 'I was treated like a prince when she was around'. His early schooling was in a missionary school called Notre Dame. He recalled a delightful childhood with his doting mother coming to school every day to feed him his favourite food. They moved to Bombay, and Badal attended Cardinal Gracious High School. He got admission because of all the scholastic medals he had received in Notre Dame School.

The night before Badal's first day of school in Bombay, he went to sleep excited about his new school bag and books. The next morning when he answered the doorbell to let in the garbage remover, he heard his father shouting, trying to wake his mother. He told Badal to rub her feet while he called the doctor. His mother died of a heart attack. Badal recalled that all the neighbours who she had planned to invite for his birthday a few days later, were now in his house, mourning.

His father's first wife then arrived to take care of the children and Badal's misery began. His stepmother played the stereotypical role of being nasty and mean to him. Badal said, 'I was like a friend with my mother. I don't know why I became a target for abuse from my stepmother.' Badal refrained from complaining to his father because he was afraid of fights between them. He lost interest in his studies and began bunking school to go to movies. After receiving complaints from his school his father transferred him to Holy Cross School. As he was now short of money, he earned some by giving tuitions to younger children in his building and sorting bangles in a bangle factory. When his father realized the situation, he sent Badal back to his hometown, Jamalpur, where he was blissfully happy with his loving grandmother. But in the tenth class, he was again brought back to Bombay.

Badal then went to a Parsi college where he studied electronics. After graduation he joined a friend in Jamalpur, who had started a shirt-manufacturing factory. He went to Calcutta for a foreign trade management course and then arrived in Delhi. He had fallen in love and his girlfriend found a job as a journalist in Sahara. Badal got a job with a small ad agency in Daryaganj but hated it. He found himself fascinated by the journalistic work his girlfriend was doing. He heard that *Outlook* was looking for people and accosted the editor, Vinod Mehta, outside his office. Badal showed him a story he had written and he liked it. Tarun directed him to Aniruddha who hired him for Tehelka.

Why was Kumar Badal harassed if he had nothing to do with Operation West End? Badal knew nothing about Operation West End while it was being conducted. However, a few days after the exposé, Tarun and Aniruddha sent Kumar Badal to Rajasthan to locate Gopal Pacherwal, president of Samata Party in Rajasthan, when they needed to identify who was disputedly in the room with Jaya Jaitly on the tapes. It was Badal who found him. It was that act that made his name a target.

Badal was transformed during the time he spent in jail. He said, 'Because I had the feeling that we are on the right side, that kind of heroic feeling. I was considering it as a sort of freedom struggle. Even our freedom fighters had to go through this.' His wife, as a journalist, was supportive and knew that Badal had not done what he had been accused of. I asked him: 'Were you carrying cameras when you were doing the poaching story?' He replied, 'When in the first place I am not going, where is the question of cameras.'

Badal said that he saw men in jail who had been in there for thirteen months for stealing a couple of garments, another was in jail for over a year for picking up two vegetables that had fallen off a bicycle. Although journalists in Saharanpur marched in protest against Badal's arrest, the national media did not take up his cause. He said a few journalists came to interview him but he was puzzled by the lack of any strong protest from the major dailies. Aniruddha Bahal was a regular visitor, barring lawyers.

In jail, Badal turned to the Bhagawat Gita. He said,

> The Gita asks you to do things without expecting any result, *nishkam karma* [selfless action without reward] and to have *samabhava* [the equality of all religions leading to one God], treat everyone alike. So I put it into practice. I gained my strength. I didn't like the way they were treating the prisoners, hanging them upside down and beating them. The prisoners didn't know they had any rights. So I confronted the officers. The prisoners came to know someone was standing up for them. Then they would come to me with their problems. They wanted to play cricket, so I started a cricket team in the Ghaziabad jail.

Apparently, Vashisht in his *jugad*, got through to Vikas Yadav's *pairokars* (Yadav is in jail for the murder of Nitish Katara and was sentenced by a trial court to a life sentence on 30 May 2008) to take Kumar under his wing. Yadav, son of D.P. Yadav (a don-politician who had nine murder charges against him and has been a minister in Mulayam Singh's government) made sure that Badal was comfortable, safe and protected. Badal enjoyed Yadav's largesse but ironically while still in jail, he wrote an exposé of his jail term, naming Yadav as one of the major powers that controlled Dasna jail. Weird! Yadav was reportedly confused and furious that the same man whom he had taken care of and helped to survive in jail, wrote an article about Yadav's 'extraordinary' privileges in jail which were then endangered because of the article! One would expect Yadav to have then 'sorted out' Kumar, but in true Don style he was angry yet amused, and continued to help Badal.

Sidharth Luthra recalled, 'Soon after Badal's arrest when Aniruddha and I were visiting him, the jailor at the gate asked us who we were there for. So I said we had come for the Tehelka journalist. The response was, "*Haan, abhi toh hamare paas ek hi andar pahuncha hai* (yes, right now only one has reached here)*",* anticipating more to follow'.

Badal believed that his study of the Gita and following it through with action, saved his sanity. He believed that his experience was beneficial because he came out of prison a better person. His greatest challenge now was to maintain the *nishkam karma* and *samabhava* that he began in jail. Badal articulated how he saw his jail term as an opportunity to follow a spiritual path. He said that with the Gita guiding him, he felt light and free. He did not wish to harp on all the injustice meted out to him with his friends and decided he did not want to go berserk enjoying things he had been deprived of in jail. He said, 'I decided to be very cool about it and not try to get sympathy from people'. When he left jail, Badal told the CBI officer that he had done him great service by keeping him in jail. The officer looked at Badal, clearly puzzled.

21 Oops, Sorry, Sorry, Sorry

Ben Bradlee [Jason Robards]: All non-denials denials. They doubt our ancestry, but they don't deny the story is inaccurate.

– Alan Pakula's film, All the President's Men *(1976)*

Freelance television producer Milin (Bobby) Kapoor, handed me a thick file titled, 'BOBBY BIBLE'. In this, Milin painstakingly scrutinized the Tehelka transcripts and compared them to the Tehelka tapes. He found hundreds of mistakes and discrepancies. Milin also marked all the cuts in the footage. The cuts do not mean tampering, as was often misinterpreted in the Commission by lawyers. Cuts in the footage can mean that the camera was switched on and off, without a dissolve being inserted in the editing as is often done, to make the viewing smooth. A cut can also be seen if footage is removed and it jumps to the next part of the footage, without the benefit of a dissolve. The first question: Why did he do this? Why would a television producer who is an ordinary citizen, go to the trouble of pouring over the transcripts and go through this utterly tedious exercise? Aniruddha Bahal and Tarun Tejpal had ready answers. They pointed out that Kapoor has been commissioned to make films for the army through DRDO and wanted to ensure he gets more. There is no doubt that he is in Jaya Jaitly's camp and his work focused on points she found damaging. Second question: Is there anything morally wrong with helping out someone from whom you hope to get work? The answer depends less on your own moral code and more on, whose side you are on. If you lean towards Tehelka, then Milin is tainted with motive. If you favour Jaya, Milin only did what anyone would do to help a person to whom he is grateful for the past and wants to ensure that he has reason to be grateful in the future. (The technical mistakes have been noted by Milin Kapoor. The journalistic mistakes are discussed by the writer.)

Milin started on Page 1, 'Reference Cast – In order of Appearance'. Twenty-seven characters are listed, out of which Milin found four of those mentioned are not present in the edited tapes. Although Milin found seven with wrong names and designations, I found three incorrect names and five incorrect designations. He has stated that the title of National Trustee of the RSS given to R.K. Gupta does not exist. Milin has questioned the title of 'defence middlemen' given to seven men. These men could be loudmouth gossips making all kinds of wild claims and there was no actual proof of their work as middlemen. But, after listening to them, it is indeed difficult to believe that they were not in some form involved in defence deals. It seems to me these names were included by Milin to make the mistakes list longer.

Aniruddha scripted a rather misleading lead voiceover/editorial:

> We at Tehelka.com managed to sell the Lepage 90, the A LION and the Kreuger 3000 to the Indian defence establishment – ostensibly fourth generation hand-held thermal cameras and, needless to add, non-existent.
> This is the story of how we did it.

Fact: This was journalistically incorrect. Tehelka did not actually sell any of this fictitious equipment. They did meet all the officers in the tapes who did promise them a letter for trials of evaluation of the equipment. Before they could pick up the letter, Samuel's cover was blown.

Voiceover 2:

> Soon enough comes a demand to be entertained in a five-star hotel. Brigadier Sehgal comes there with a Lieutenant Colonel B.B. Sharma, who is an army officer posted in the Air Force procurement section. Here, they are entertained and disclose how to proceed.

Fact: Brigadier Sehgal is actually Colonel Sehgal. No demand is made on camera. More likely, Samuel offered the entertainment, as he did the money, in order to lure the officers into the sting. Even if no demand was made, why did the officers go to the hotel at all?

Voiceover 3:

> After enjoying the hospitality of West End International at a five-star hotel, Brigadier Sehgal demands Rs 2 lakh to give further documents relating to the procurement of hand-held thermal cameras and other equipment that West End might be interested in supplying to the Indian Army. He accepts Rs 20,000 and a little while later another Rs 20,000. He also advises on how to proceed in the matter of bidding for the hand-held thermal cameras.

Fact: There is no demand on camera for Rs 2 lakh. But, it is quite clear that Sehgal is ready and willing to accept money. He is just unhappy that Samuel is giving him only Rs 20,000.

Voiceover 5:

> As a matter of fact, Sasi himself was setting up different channels for us that would take us right up to Defence Minister George Fernandes and the then minister of state for defence, Harin Pathak…

Fact: Well, the truth is, they never got to Defence Minister George Fernandes. Yes, they got into his house. Samuel offered money to Jaya Jaitly for party funds and she explained how the party would use it. She was not seen handling the money herself.

Voiceover 7:

> Brigadier Iqbal Singh then spells out the commission that has to be given to General Dhillon.

Fact: This cannot be found in the tapes or the transcripts.

Voiceover 8:

> Here Brigadier Iqbal Singh takes his little gift from West End.

Fact: On tape, Brigadier Iqbal Singh is seen refusing the money and handing it over to Colonel Sayal, who said he would deliver it to Singh later. In the Commission, Sayal said he pocketed the money himself.

Voiceover 10:

> Our next meeting with General Ahluwalia takes place 10 days later. Here he accepts a token bribe of Rs 50,000 which is never delivered to him.

Fact: Major General Ahluwalia did not take any money on camera. It is unclear that Ahluwalia acknowledged that he would accept it in the future. Ahluwalia seemed uncomfortable taking the money.

Voiceover 11:

> Sayal goes near Ahluwalia and tries to hand him Rs 50,000, which he accepts later.

Fact: Read the transcript that follows directly after.

Voiceover 11:

> **Ahluwalia:** This is, this is … Sayal please, don't be stupid.
> **Sayal:** Okay, later. Then …
> **Ahluwalia:** Okay.

Fact: There is a possibility that Sayal took the money and did not give it to Ahluwalia or he covered for Ahluwalia who was still in the army.

Voiceover 29:

> Within the RSS, Gupta's known as a "super trustee". His proximity with both Prime Minister Vajpayee and L.K. Advani is lore. Both have been tenants at his properties. He has also established the RSS headquarters in Jhandewalan, Delhi in 1967.

Fact: Milin Kapoor wrote on the transcript: 'No such thing I'm told.' I found it impossible to verify the 'super trustee' status as everyone in the BJP distanced themselves from R.K. Gupta. In the tapes, H.C. Pant does state, 'He's the trustee All India …' Gupta boasts about his power over the BJP: 'I can also slap them on the face if they don't do the work.'

Voiceover 46:

> Elsewhere, the brew is simmering. After hearing a lot of talk about R.K. Jain, the treasurer of the Samata Party, being the briefcase man of George Fernandes we at West End decided that a direct approach was called for. The series of meetings with R.K. Jain proved to be a goldmine of information about past and present defence deals. It incriminates beyond redemption Defence Minister George Fernandes and the Samata Party. Jain was conned by emphasizing the size of West End as a group, the contributions it would make to the Samata Party fund and to Jain's own coffers. An introduction to Jain.

Fact: There is no proof of the involvement of George Fernandes in defence deals in the Tehelka tapes. Aniruddha stated that he would naturally believe a man who happens to be the treasurer of the party. Giving Fernandes the benefit of the doubt that Jain seemed to be on a boast trip the question still arises, how would he know all the details about the defence deals so intimately if he were not involved in them? Jain gave details of trips to Russia and discussions with various officials. Tough to invent. Jain told Samuel that he became treasurer of the Samata Party when Fernandes needed money (Rs 2.5 lakh) and he got it for him in two days. Could be boasting.

Although the Tehelka transcripts read: 'Though I am not allowed to fly without the permission of Jayaji' – in the tapes, 'Jayaji' does sound more like 'George.'

Voiceover 50:

> There is another Suresh Nanda deal in which he gave an advance of Rs 1 crore to R.K. Jain for the Samata Party. This time for getting an air-to-air and surface-to-surface missile system through the Indian Navy. In fact, the Israeli missile system called Barak was objected to by Abdul Kalam, scientific adviser to the Indian government, as he was in favour of the indigenous varieties – Trishul and Prithvi variants. But Abdul Kalam was overruled by George Fernandes. And this is why Fernandes did it.

Fact: The manner in which Jain described the Barak deal sounds highly credible. But, Tehelka could have played it journalistically safe by writing a voiceover with the onus on Jain and his claims. By creating the hype and presenting it as a story stemming from Tehelka, it slanted the angle. Why was Abdul Kalam never called by the Commission to check if he had recommended indigenous missiles and nixed Barak? Why was George Fernandes not questioned on the reasons for ignoring Kalam's advice? Tehelka made a mistake in not getting interviews with Kalam or Fernandes on this issue. They could have done just this without blowing their story. It would have brought credibility to their story which could now be dismissed as cheap boasts by a greedy man.

Voiceover 51:

> In an explosive revelation, R.K. Jain continues to spell out the incredible corruption and compromise of the Indian defence at the highest level. He explains how the actual monetary transaction takes place in a defence deal, and how much money he has made for Samata Party – so far Rs 50 crore, for himself a rather substantial sum of Rs 10 crore. In the beginning, he speculates about whether the prime minister forwarded some of the Sukhoi fighter aircraft money to George Fernandes.

Fact: Jain gave minute details of the deals and money exchanged. We have to weigh Fernandes's reputation of being honest against Jain's revelations. Even if one does not want to believe Jain, the question arises, how can Jain, the treasurer of Fernandes' party, know such detailed information with credible sounding conversations, unless he was involved and it was true. Or Jain is the best scriptwriter in the world. The mistake Tehelka made was in not sending out reporters to confirm if the bald facts about the deals were true or not. When did the deal take place? Did the dates match? Then the story would not rely on only Jain's version.

On page 98 of the Tehelka transcript, Satya Murthy, Bangaru Laxman's private secretary is talking to Tehelka:

> "**Satya Murthy**: Because after P.V. Narasimha Rao, he is the only South Indian who is involved in this.

Tehelka: Yeah!

Satya Murthy: And this kind of deals in India only South Indians can do. Nobody else can do.

Tehelka: That is true! True fact.

Satya Murthy: We do in a systematic way and we are the trusted people. Maybe our charges may be one or two per cent higher than …

Tehelka: Yeah! Yeah!

Satya Murthy: But we don't cheat people.

Tehelka: No, no. You know, if we can go through one or two per cent, that is not a problem. I am telling frankly. But our work should have the best.

Satya Murthy: First we'll shortlist it. And this, if you give him the dollars today … so that your, your credibility will increase.

Tehelka: Okay, today I will give the dollars.

Satya Murthy: Okay. Security money.

Tehelka: $31,500 I will give you."

[In the sub-titles on the tape, the number written is $21,500.]

On page 105 of the Tehelka transcript, there are words that are the focus of a consequential dispute between Jaya Jaitly and Tehelka. Jaya Jaitly stands accused of entertaining defence dealers with unknown antecedents in the defence minister's house. Mathew Samuel insists that he had been introduced as a businessman who was interested in supplying defence equipment. Jaya is adamant that Samuel was introduced to her as someone who was dealing in electronics. An excerpt from the significant transcript:

Surendra Sulekha (Misidentified by Tehelka. Actual name Sureka): Madam, he is Mr Samuel.

Tehelka: West End …

Sulekha: He's dealing in electronics and …

Jaya Jaitly: Hmmmm.

Sulekha: Now they'll be starting something with the defence. He's brought something for the party.

[Jaya laughs.]

According to Milin Kapoor, Sulekha (Sureka) does not say 'with the defence' but says 'for this'. However, 'Now they'll be starting something for this,' does not make a sentence that conveys any meaning or sense at all. Given all the multitude solecisms committed by many of the heroes on the tapes, that doesn't amount to much. But there is no explaining away or substituting words in the conversation Jaya had with Major General Murgai in the same meeting, who spelt it out succinctly:

Major General Murgai: This company is making quality products …
[Jaya Jaitly nods]

Major General Murgai: And now they are going in a big way for commercial selling. And also make a mark in defence.

Jaya Jaitly: Hmmm.

Major General Murgai: That is what they're doing. And they are making these night-vision binoculars, cameras …

Jaya Jaitly: Naturally, probably as far as I know because I don't know much about these things, but you all have to … whenever some new entry into … entrant into the field, they have to test the things.

Page 116 of the Tehelka transcript has a prickly contention over four words, which had Jaya Jaitly in enough of a twist to repeatedly ask for forsenic examination of the Tehelka tapes, until she got her way.

Jaya Jaitly: And also, you know what it is. I have no … I will not have any direct this thing. I would only request sahib's office that somebody is not being considered even. So please send a word down that if anybody is fairly offering a good quality thing at a good price, they should also be considered.

Tehelka: Okay.

Jaya Jaitly: Now … when that happens, we don't want anybody to feel that anybody has any extra interest.

Major General Murgai: That's true.

Jaya Jaitly: Because we don't have any extra interest in anybody. We have extra interest in the good quality and good price.

Surendra Sureka: That's right.

Jaya Jaitly: In the interest of the nation. So that we'll ensure that they don't neglect you.

Tehelka: Okay.

Jaya Jaitly: After that, it's up to you and your product.

Tehelka: That's all. That's all we're expecting … that's all.

Major General Murgai: So let's go?

Tehelka: That's two lakhs. Two lakhs.

Jaya Jaitly insisted that, 'That's two lakhs. Two lakhs' was inserted later and is adamant that the tapes were doctored. Milin Kapoor provided his proof of the doctoring in the Commission. [See Chapter 22 on Doctoring of Tapes] It is with Milin Kapoor's 'proof' that Jaya Jaitly repeatedly petitioned the Commission to send the tapes for forensic examination.

On Page 134 of the Tehelka transcripts, a crucial sentence was omitted:

Major General P.S.K. Choudary: Thereafter, it's entirely with the ministry to call for the commercial bids.

Tehelka: And who will decide the PNC and everything?

Major General Choudary: I am a member of that too. To advise … but it is always generally chaired by the joint secretary of the ministry.

Tehelka: Okay, sir, it's right information. Now I got the right information.

Major General Choudary: No one individual can assure you.

Tehelka: Yeah.

The transcript left out:

Maj. Gen. Choudary: You already gave me a gold chain.

Tehelka: No, sir. This is my gift. I am not saying that anything … *haan?*

Voiceover 75:

Surendra Singh makes a demand of Rs 10 lakh to get the evaluation letter issued from Choudary little knowing about our own lobbying with him. General Murgai explains to West End about Surendra Singh's new demand.

Fact: To be journalistically correct, Tehelka should have said that Murgai made a demand of Rs 10 lakh for Surendra. Given the packets of money swishing around, it should have been left for the viewer to decide whether Surendra had actually made the demand through Murgai or Murgai was making a demand on Surendra's name hoping for a cut.

Concluding Roll Over Text:

Additional Secretary L.M. Mehta issued a letter to Major General Choudary in the second week of January. He asked for Rs 2 lakh in cash. He was paid Rs 50,000 by Major General Murgai as advance in his office and the rest was promised upon the receipt of the letter. Of course, we just planned to collect the letter and run.

You see we couldn't go any further. We couldn't produce hand-held thermal cameras and submit them for trials.

Major General Choudary issued a trial evaluation order in the third week of January. It was a 26-page order. Major General Murgai collected it for us. Mehta's dilemma was that he couldn't organize an evaluation letter just for West End and had to include 3-4 more companies. He did that.

Fact: Tehelka was told that a letter was issued. They did not have the letter in their hands. There is a possibility that Tehelka was being misled by Mehta, Choudary and Murgai. L.M. Mehta was not in charge of procurement for the army, so a letter from him was doubtful. But, the fact remains, Tehelka had gained access to people such as Major General P.S.K. Choudary, additional director general (WE), and L.M. Mehta, who was additional defence secretary, although he was in charge of procurement for the air force only.

Aniruddha Bahal spoke about how the transcription errors were manipulated by the noticees caught on tape.

Bahal: There was this big confusion in the judge's mind about transcription errors. And these noticees made a big thing about it: *yeh dekho* (look at this) transcription. They were not only pulling out half a dozen mistakes in the four-and-a-half hours, out of which only one was a gross mistake. The others were, it doesn't make any difference. One was a really stupid mistake you know, *pata nahin kaiseh ho gaya voh* [don't know how that happened].

Madhu: Which one was that?

Bahal: That was about Sehgal, where something about ten lakhs. He didn't say ten lakhs, he said something else, undertake something. That was really, really stupid, but apart from that, the others were just normal mistakes which happens every day. Every day a channel is doing sub-titling, it's going all over the place. Our stupidity was that we went through so much time and effort, we should have put a disclaimer in the beginning of the movie, saying that the tapes are only the prima facie thing. The sub-titles are just an aid to the listening process. We're just doing it to help you. Which movie documentary release have you been to, where they are giving you a transcript? Just imagine it, we went through all that effort, *ki sab log aah rehain hai* [all these people are coming]. Even till two hours before the press conference we were correcting the transcripts, that otherwise it becomes too difficult, *ki transcript toh hai mathlub* [if there is a transcript then it has meaning]. We give them the transcript and in the four-and-a-half hours of public domain, there must be, like, half a dozen mistakes. They made such a big thing and then they started pulling mistakes out of the unedited tapes, which didn't go in the public. *Arey bhai hamneh toh dala hi nahin hai, usme mistakes toh hongey hi, kaunsa ham baith key usko theek keh rehain hain* [hey, we didn't put it in, so there will be mistakes in that, where are we saying that it is all accurate]? They were for me to write the script, for my purposes. *Jab hamneh chey ghantey sadey char ghantey jab bana, toh usko hamney cross-check kiya. Hum toh yeh baki nabbey ghantey thodi cross-check bethengey, purpose kya hai cross-check karney ka? Yeh hum aap ke liyey thodey kar rehey hai. Voh toh apney purpose kay liya kar rehay. Usmey toh bahut saarey errors hongey. Public domain mein toh sadey char ghante ki hai na* [when we reduced it from six hours to four-and-a-half, then we cross-checked. We are not going to cross-check the rest of the 90 hours. What would be purpose of cross-checking that? We are doing this for the public. We did ours for our own purpose. There will be lots of errors in that. Only four-and-a-half hours went into the public domain]. They started pulling out errors from there, look at this, here it is, it is doctored, it is doctored. First of all there was a big confusion in the Commission what is doctored? Transcribing errors started becoming doctoring. *Yeh dekh, yeh dekh,* mistake, *bahut doctor kiya hai unhoneh* [look at this mistake, they have doctored a lot]. All of the lawyers realize this, but this is the point, what else is their defence? So they started coming out with all this, this is not transcribed. Then, which is what I kept saying on the stand. There was a big confusion in Venkataswami's mind also, in the beginning he couldn't understand. The whole editing process, it just didn't sink in him.

Besides all the minor word glitches, there are scores of pages in the transcript which are missing in the tapes. Probably some last minute editing to shorten and tighten the length. Ram Vilas Paswan who is included in the transcript for a touch of comedy in an otherwise tragic story, is finally eliminated in the tapes. Dr Ketan Shukla, former private secretary to minister of state for defence, Raju Venkatesh, personal secretary to Bangaru Laxman and Santosh Gangwar, minister of state for Petroleum and Natural Gas, are all mentioned in the Cast in the transcript but are all missing in the tapes that were shown. Additionally, there are pages that are in duplicate. Evidence that there was no fine toothcomb checking before it was released to the press, as one would expect in an exposé like this where they should have expected to be deluged with dung blasts. It is intriguing that no journalist found the mistakes.

When Milin Kapoor pointed out all the mistakes in the transcripts to Aniruddha Bahal, there was a shrug of the shoulders and a laugh, 'I am surprised that there weren't more mistakes.' To my mind this does not display a cavalier carelessness. What Aniruddha is saying is, given the circumstances under which they were working, they had to run with what they had. Journalists pride themselves on their ingrained scepticism, living by the credo: 'If your mother says she loves you, check it out.' Yeah, but what if her boyfriend has a gun to your head and you do not have the time to check it out? You run.

22 Spin the Dog: Doctoring?

Conrad Brean [Robert De Niro]: What's the thing people remember about the Gulf War? A bomb falling down a chimney. Let me tell you something. I was in the building where we filmed that with a 10-inch model made out of Legos.
Stanley Motss [Dustin Hoffman]: Is that true?
Conrad Brean: Who the hell's to say?

– Barry Levinson's film, Wag the Dog *(1997)*

Milin Kapoor is the fifteen-minutes of fame hero of the Tehelka saga. I interviewed Milin and his wife at their home in Gurgaon. Their television production company, Nishan Communications, was established nine years ago. Their company has made films for the government, Indian Airlines, the Army's DRDO, NTP, BHEL, and some fashion shows. They are young, obviously trying to make it in the diabolically competitive world of television programme production. Milin Kapoor has no warm, comforting presence of inherited wealth. As was venomously excavated by the Tehelka lawyer during Milin's deposition in the Commission, he had no formal education beyond his high school 12th class. Like many in the television production business, he learnt on the job. As with millions of the middle-class, Milin and his wife are the victims and beneficiaries of the economy's liberalization. Yes, there are more opportunities but it comes packaged with barbaric competition. Editing machines, tapes, papers, all covered in dust, confuses their home into a messy workplace. There is a pertinacious undertow of bitterness emanating from the grinding wrangling for elusive success. It isn't easy. The question is: Would Milin Kapoor's name ever have appeared in the newspapers during his lifetime had he not raised the bogey that the Tehelka tapes were doctored? Thirty-eight-year-old, Milin stated in his affidavit, that he had made films from the age of nineteen and specialized in the digital format for the past six years. But, as Tehelka's lawyer Sidharth Luthra, gouged out, Milin had no degree in physics or engineering. Milin said he had taped the Zee TV broadcast of Operation West End, as a 'concerned citizen'. There are thousands of filmmakers in India, so why did Milin Kapoor choose to do what he did? Not only that, he put in long hours, meticulously examining the tapes and manuscripts in microscopic detail, marking the mistakes in the transcription and logging every point in the tapes where he thought they had been tampered with. Was it his not so magnificent obsession? He generously shared the transcript with his markings with me.

Milin filed his affidavit in the Commission on 8 May 2001. Two months had passed since the Operation West End tapes had been broadcast on television. The obvious question it raises is: If the tapes were doctored, why did Bangaru Laxman, Jaya Jaitly, the army officers, bureaucrats, and all the others not bring up this issue right from the first day on? All of them spoke up, seethed and ranted, but not one of them ever mentioned that the tapes had been doctored. That's exactly what they said after Milin Kapoor raised the Doctoring Demon (DD).

It took Milin two months to file his affidavit. For good reason. He put in a lot of work. He examined every frame to figure out any discrepancies. In Milin's statement, he said: 'Even though it was stated at the beginning of the broadcast that only expletives had been deleted and there was no editing, on noticing a couple of places where dissolves, i.e. indication of editing, were clearly visible, I proceeded to record the broadcast in order to examine the contents in my studio'. This is entirely misleading. At no point has anybody on the Tehelka team ever said there was no editing. This gave the lawyers a manoeuvring handle to take the Commission through an interminable labyrinth. This stratagem was then used to point out 'doctoring' areas on the tape where there had been legitimate editing. The same mendacious demagoguery was drummed repetitively and it morphed into the Commission's theorem, the Doctoring Demon (DD). Every edited point became a 'doctored' point. There were 105 tapes. They had to be edited for broadcast. How could 105 tapes be shown on commercial television? Not unless Bertolt Brecht owned Zee TV and demanded connoisseur discipline from viewers, laughable in this attention challenged 'give-em-what-they-want' age.

Milin's affidavit hijacked the Commission into a tailspin of doubts and stretched the time for months, then years. After Milin starred in the DD, all the lawyers were galvanized into this new issue. Rather than addressing the real issue of politicians, army officers, and bureaucrats taking money from Tehelka operatives, Tehelka's lawyers were forced into having to prove that the tapes had not been tampered with. On the other hand, all the lawyers of those caught on the tapes, rejoiced that a red herring had fallen into their laps and they were going to milk it. The army officers' lame excuses, that they had been hypnotized or drugged by the Tehelka operatives were not necessary when Milin served them this wonderful diversionary tactic.

Milin said in his affidavit: 'I have the experience, capability and academic interest to apply my mind and time to such matters. The reason for my curiosity was that in television journalism this kind of unannounced and unspecified editing is considered unethical'. There was some realization that he had to explain his extraordinary interest that led him to spend two months, assiduously putting it all together.

Is it unethical to edit? Obviously, editing is done in all news stories. If it was maliciously done, that was for the lawyers to point out. Malicious editing is not doctoring or tampering. How do you, announce, an edit? The whole idea was so far-fetched that it was surprising that such an affidavit was even put together by lawyers and accepted in the Commission. It also laid bare how uninformed the lawyers and the Commission were about television production to even entertain such an affidavit. It was a conspicuously sycophantic and self-serving position. Obviously, Milin Kapoor gave Jaya Jaitly and her lawyers what they wanted to hear and they took off from there.

Why did Milin do it? He answered facetiously: 'Because I am stupid.' He went on to explain seriously:

> Because I thought that I was genuinely putting forward a very important point of view, being in this business. I've made three hundred of these films. And I know the ins and outs of how this can be done. So from that perspective, from that point of view, when this big ad came in the paper, can you help the Commission in any way? I said, hey yeah, I'm doing my job, yeah. I'm giving back something. And I wrote this whole thing.

Milin, clearly on a high with himself, continued:

> But the problem is that one of the things that surprised me right at the beginning of this whole situation, was that I was the only guy who came forward to do this. I mean, nobody else in this country came forward to help or to forensically examine anything.

Perhaps there was a good reason why nobody else jumped forward for fifteen minutes of glory. It came to light in the Commission that no one in India really had the technology to forensically examine videotapes.

Milin stated in his affidavit that he digitized certain portions of the tapes in professional non-linear editing systems and discovered, according to him:

> Definite editing of the video material in the middle of conversations which were not indicated on the manuscript by notings, as professionally and ethically required if any part of the dialogue is cut.
>
> A crucial word such as "defence" was not said in the audio but has been transcribed as such in the manuscript and sub-titles.
>
> Anomalies in the soundtrack which definitely indicates tampering with the audiotrack, such as original soundtrack.

In addition, Milin added that he had a detailed explanation in images, graphics, and text. If the journalists' motivations were examined microscopically, it would only be fair then to analyse Milin's motivations, and this does not in any way imply he must be blamed. I do believe, he must be understood, because this is an illustration of Indian zeitgeist. Were his motivations completely altruistic? To be purely altruistic, Milin should stand to gain nothing by putting in so much hard work into proving that the tapes had been doctored. He was making films for the defence ministry's DRDO, and this was a question that was obviously raised by Tehelka's lawyers. The lawyers had anatomized Tehelka's motivation for Operation West End. As the Tehelka lawyer Sidharth Luthra pointed out, Milin stood to gain by getting access to Jaya Jaitly and consequently, to the defence ministry. Would Jaya Jaitly or George Fernandes have even known Milin Kapoor's name before he came up with the DD?

Milin justified his extraordinary interest in the Tehelka tapes by explaining in his affidavit that he was the son of Lieutenant Colonel Kapoor (Retd) and it was his defence background that led to his concern about the defence deals. On 24 September 2001, Valmiki Mehta, senior counsel for the Commission was frankly comfortable in his suspicion of Milin's extraordinary choice of the specific portions he claimed were doctored. They just happened to be the two areas that bothered Jaya Jaitly the most. Milin justified his focus:

> My wife and me sat down, we both decided to concentrate on the Jaya Jaitly sequence. It was the most talked about portion of the Tehelka tapes during that time. A defence minister had to resign which made it a very big thing and we decided to take up that particular point because we were limited in what we could do ourselves.

Are we to believe that out of the 105 tapes, Tehelka chose to doctor only the two instances that make Jaya Jaitly uncomfortable? Sidharth Luthra asked Milin:

> **Luthra:** Now specifically answer the question, if there are ten simultaneous sounds in an uncontrolled environment, is it possible to remove one while not affecting the others? Let us say, there are eight of our colleagues speaking, there is an air-conditioner, there is a dog barking, there is a sound. Can you delete the sound, the dog barking without affecting the other sounds simultaneously, other sounds remaining, can one sound be deleted?
> **Kapoor:** No, not possible.

That is the defining point. Television experts brought in by Bangaru Laxman and Jaya Jaitly's lawyers befuddled the Commission by switching dialogues and placed them as emanating from someone else's lips. The excitement amongst the lawyers in the Commission was like children watching a magic show. 'You can make anybody say anything! You can switch words around! You can do anything!' Not quite. Two crucial facts were ignored. Firstly, it was done in a controlled environment. Secondly, it was easy to detect that the lips moved differently from the words. The magic show exhibition tapes were not forensically examined. If Tehelka editors wanted to add words, they would have to create the same ambient sound, that is, the hum of the air-conditioner or fan, the distance between the microphone and the person speaking would have to be the same, it would have to be in a room of the same size with equivalent height of ceiling. They would have had to have the time to place it in special editing machines and then replace each sound, along with the ambient sound. The website internetmarketingmagician.com explains what it means to 'render':

When a video is created it consists of many separate elements: the video and sound-track, still shots, sound effects, background music and special effects, such as a green screen.

Rendering means reducing all this information down to a single stream of code that can be burnt onto a DVD or put on an Internet server and streamed to visitor's computers on demand. The striking aspect of rendering is the sheer amount of time it takes! As a round guide – depending on the amount of additional material involved – rendering takes three times as long as the actual playing time. So a twenty-minute video will take about an hour to render.

It is easy to do it in a commercial feature film where anything can be done because you control the lighting, set, and ambient sound. In journalistic tapes, where you are recording in whatever existing conditions are presented to you, it is near impossible to recreate the exact ambient sound in a recording studio that existed in the room or locale in the original tapes without being easily detected.

Milin had submitted to the Commission, along with his affidavit, what he called a sonogram. He also put this on a website with a coloured graph of the sound pitches in the 'doctored' sections of the Operation West End tape. The website explained that the tape was doctored because the pitch of 'two lakhs' was higher and the intensity of those words shown in a different colour was disproportionate compared to the other voices. It must have appeared impressive to the layperson: high-tech coloured graphs shooting up and down. In reality, all it showed was that at some point of time Mathew Samuel spoke louder or his face came closer to the mike in his tie.

Milin had examined a VHS copy he had made of Zee TV's broadcast, which was at least three or four generations away from the original tapes. There was no way Milin could have been so certain. In Milin's techno-babble: 'A sonogram shows you time on the horizontal axis, frequency on the vertical, and the colour of any dot in the image shows how strong the particular frequency was at that instant of time.'

This is odd. A 'sonogram' is a term used for the visual image produced by reflected sound waves in diagnostic ultrasound examination. Basically, it is a coloured graph of sound waves.

Milin pointed out that the green points in the diagram show the pitch rising suddenly when Samuel uttered the words, 'two lakhs'. So the snap conclusion he came to was that those words were recorded in another room. How? Just because it is louder? Had he pointed out that the ambient sound had changed, that would have meant something. What the 'sonogram' did show was that the 'pitch' of the voices rose and fell. That is all. A pitch can vary even when the same person speaking, depending on how he modulates his voice; implying not much beyond that.

At the Commission, Tehelka's lawyer questioned Milin Kapoor about this:

Sidharth Luthra: Can you tell me if there is a failure of the mike or a change in the camera or the change in the lens or if there is a sharp spike in the current, would it not produce a wave form view which would be similar to what your sonogram of a cut was?

Kapoor: In a lot of cases you will find that an error on a sonogram or on a wave form is very similar to, for example, a dog barking or a sudden closure of a door or of clapping of a hand, also creates a similar spike; a change in frequencies entirely, a change in the whole amplification of the sound. These things do happen. As I said yesterday, it is not just one thing we are looking at the sonogram. We are looking at a sonogram and saying this sonogram is it. We are saying the sonogram does not take sides; it tells you what is there in the frequency range. The wave does not take any side. It tells you what is there on the amplitude or the volume of the sound, the waves. It takes a little experience in this business to differentiate between a natural occurrence like a door closing or a funny occurrence like something being cut in the middle. It is a combination of these events that leads you to the conclusion that this part of the audio should be checked, this part of the audio is okay. It is the natural sound, which sounds to me very clearly like a door closing, like a dog barking, somebody speaking over a door. No problem there; doesn't look like a cut. So these are things you look at and you hear for when you are doing a normal recording. It is a combination, Sir.

Good lord, assure me that I am sane.

A sonogram or spectogram is part of a software package called the signal analysis tool, which is easily downloadable from the Internet. Milin Kapoor's techno-*bhashan* beclouded everyone in the Commission.

Luthra asked Milin:

Luthra: Can you tell me what, in technical terms, AFM is?

Kapoor: This is a radio term. I think in my terms it would refer to Amplitude Frequency Modulation.

Luthra: Actually, I am referring to Audio Frequency Modulation.

Kapoor: Sir, there are a lot of generic terms used within the engineering aspects of any audio or television studio. There are some terms which are engineering based on both audio and video environments. It is, as I said earlier to the Commission, that I am a filmmaker who has a lot of experience working within these mediums. My strength is having done so many audio and video productions. It is very easy for me to pick up on variations or a slight problem on tape and analyse them up to a level. So, I should not be expected to go and become an audio engineer suddenly or a video engineer suddenly. I am basically a filmmaker. I just want to make this clear, Sir.

What we must accept here, then, is that we have a filmmaker with some experience of the profession, who has an opinion. It is not exactly based on any valid scientific equipment or data. Measuring pitch frequencies is a long distance from forensic analysis of tapes. His opinion may be valid, if you so choose, but it is not based on infallible machines.

In his interview, Milin Kapoor made an important journalistic point. He said that in a sting operation, you should not apply the same rules of editing as you would on any other film. If you are presenting the Truth, then, it should be undiluted. That is tough if you have 105 tapes. The best Tehelka could have done was to keep it as objective as possible, with minimum editorializing and no malicious editing.

Milin said, 'Be honest. You can't really notice it unless you are looking for it'. He pointed out that the dissolves in the tapes were so rapid and close together, as to be barely noticeable. He suggested that if obvious fade-in and fade-out effects had been used it would have been obvious to viewers that some time had elapsed between frames. Milin said he realized it wasn't possible to do it in entirety but if the camera was not moving for an hour, if there was a long dissolve between the start and the point that was cut, it was acceptable. On the other hand, if the discussion went on for two hours and you present two or three bits of five minutes each to a viewer it is made to appear as if the conversation lasted fifteen minutes. Milin insisted that it would have been ethical to inform viewers that the conversation actually lasted three hours and was edited down. He believed it would have added to Tehelka's credibility.

What was Milin's definition of doctoring a tape? He said, 'Replacement of any audio part or slowing down of any audio or visual part'. That could only be done, he said, if it is transferred to a computer system and then transferred back to a tape.

How else then could Tehelka have edited the tapes? It had to be transferred to a computer. Milin stated that every camera had a signature that is imprinted on the tape and there is no way that can be falsified. But, Milin had neither examined the camera or the original footage to ascertain whether it was a different signature.

Milin said he also noticed there were 'sound drops'. This could have been, he said, because something was erased from that point, or that a visual was added and it was longer than the sound, so there would be a blank sound for that duration. True, but it is just as easy for an editor to close the gap. Milin added, 'Let's not jump to conclusions that something bad has been done. I'm not saying that. I am saying, let's check it'.

In a discussion that displayed my doubts about Tehelka's technical capacity to successfully 'doctor' tapes and my scepticism about Milin's sonogram theory, Milin said:

Kapoor: M'am, I've shown this; I normally don't take just my opinion. I normally show this around to people. I've shown those two segments to about six or seven engineers and two of them very, very senior in the business.
Madhu: Who are they?
Kapoor: I can't tell. They don't want to be involved. I almost got into trouble with them because *The Times of India* printed it.

Milin admitted that the only way to really check whether the tapes had been doctored was to examine the original tapes. He said, 'I cannot do this on a copy. But ultimately, if you want something in a court of law, it has to be the original tapes.'

⌒

To be absolutely certain regarding the tampering issue, I grilled Aniruddha Bahal. In answer to a question about the sound drops, Aniruddha explained that they had some problems with the mike hidden in the briefcase. They found that when the briefcase was placed on the ground, the sound would just go off. When they picked it up, it would start again. Anyone who has worked in television will reassure you that these maddening things do happen. It proved to be some 'soldering problem' that took a while to identify. On certain occasions, they took two cameras to be on the safe side, to ensure that if one malfunctioned, the other would pick it up. Aniruddha also mentioned it was socially odd to walk into an office and immediately place the briefcase on someone's desk.

Madhu: Let's go to Jaya's tape, where she has said it was doctored and that the "two lakhs" was inserted later. Was "two lakhs" said earlier and edited in at that point or was it said exactly as it played? Milin Kapoor showed the Commission that where the audio goes higher it shows up in green and indicates where the audio was subsequently inserted from another audio.
Bahal: Not possible.
Madhu: So, explain it. How is Milin Kapoor showing that it was inserted later?
Bahal: This point never came up initially, when reporters went to Jaya and asked her these questions in which she's saying political parties do that. This point came up when they got a chance to read the transcript which we have distributed, then they construct a defence. I think just one person out of thirty-six noticees questioned that they were not the original tapes, before Jaya raised the issue. What I would consider doctoring is when you're putting things which have not been said by those people. Doctoring would be when you're putting in images which obviously did not happen. In Jaya's tape I have not broken it up, as far as I can remember. There are some dissolves between conversations.
Madhu: Or would you transfer part of the audio to another point of the visual? Meaning, alter an audio track.
Bahal: No, no, that hasn't happened.
Madhu: Or lift a section of audio from one point and insert it elsewhere?
Bahal: On another visual?
Madhu: Yes.
Bahal: Obviously that would be doctoring. Nobody does that. I'm talking about say a portion of video that has both audio and visual. So what you are saying is, remove that particular stretch of audio from that visual and slap it on another visual? No, no.
Madhu: You didn't do that?
Bahal: No, no, no, no; what largely these people mean by doctoring, or what

they're pretending to say, is that the transcribing errors, which they've made a big thing out of, which are nothing actually. I was cross-examined extensively on this and I stand by whatever I've said in the Commission, which is all true. All the dissolves had been marked in my original script when I first wrote the script.

The original script was over six hours. Tarun Tejpal wanted it cut down to three but Aniruddha insisted that it be allowed to run for four-and-a-half hours. At that point, when they were racing against time, they started cutting on the monitor. Aniruddha said,

> **Bahal:** The editor didn't take care to take out printouts at every stage of the cut, so that the dissolves would be there. In the transcripts that we gave in the press viewing, the dissolves were, maybe, 70 per cent of the dissolves were marked. It was very clear that it's a cut here and then it goes to the other thing, but the transcripts were an aid to the whole process.
>
> **Madhu:** What about the chronology of events?
>
> **Bahal:** I think largely the four-and-a-half hour story was a very linear story.
>
> **Madhu:** Nothing was sequentially altered or jumbled around?
>
> **Bahal:** No, no, no, no, that, I'm not sure. It may have been done on a few occasions, but it didn't go date-wise. It went as a narrative. It went from one link to the other actually. It went from one person to the other person who connected. It was a very linear story.

Why did Tarun and Aniruddha resist the demand that the tapes be forensically examined? Aniruddha explained that they were confident that when they first handed in the tapes they would be examined. One of the Commission officers told Aniruddha that they had examined the tapes and they had come to their own conclusions. Aniruddha said, 'We knew that was the first thing they would do. You don't ever give tapes which you say are genuine and your whole career depends on it.' In the original affidavits none of those Caught On Tape (COT) questioned the veracity of the tapes. It was only after Milin Kapoor's testimony that all the noticees added the DD to their affidavits and depositions. Tehelka learnt only two days before Milin Kapoor was supposed to appear in the Commission about his position on doctoring. Aniruddha said that they did not know of any expert but contacted Umashankar, reputed to be the best audio expert in India. Umashankar asked them which format they had used. They had no idea. When Umashankar checked the tapes and cameras, he informed them that they had used Hi8 AFM and it was impossible to doctor anything in that format. He explained to them that the audio and video are on a single track. According to Aniruddha, after Milin Kapoor made a fool of himself on the stand with his innocence of the most basic information about Hi8 AFM, Umashankar gave his deposition that included brochures with all the technical specifications.

Aniruddha said,

The only way they could attack the tapes was by this fantastic theory. Imagine what it suggests: that 105 tapes are not original. What does it mean, practically, for someone to pull something like that? It's four-and-a-half hours which you are doing in bits and pieces. Vijay Raman, our editor, was breaking it up because one computer does not have the capacity. The rendering takes forever. After ten or fifteen minutes of rendering, the computer would crash and then you have to do it all over again. The four-and-a-half hours of tape took more than fifteen days just to render. It would take your bloody NASA to do something like that.

Aniruddha said that they were accused of doctoring inconsequential portions when the real issue was that Choudary, Laxman, and Sayal all admitted to taking money. He said that Jaya was quibbling about areas where she is directly compromised: the money and entertaining arms dealers in the defence minister's house. Aniruddha said that none of them stated that it was not their image on the tapes. He said that Umashankar (audio expert who appeared at the Commission) had pointed out that Milin Kapoor was making a fool of everyone because there was no way in which he could analyse the audio tracks with the ancient software he possessed. 'They should have had the tapes forensically examined in the beginning, before they sent notices to anybody and then started the proceedings,' Aniruddha said. 'They should have given the report on the tapes to all those people, so then they could not take the plea that this is not my face. In their own affidavits they admitted everything first,' he added.

Sidharth Luthra focused on the Catch-22 of it all: 'The means adopted by the Tehelka team may have not be acceptable or palatable but by admitting and seeking prosecution of the Tehelka team for inducements of sex and money, etc. those caught on the West End tapes accept what happened. How then can there be a denial of the entire content of the tapes? Or allegations that when the tapes were recorded the incidents were not real or whatever so we must prosecute the Tehelka journalists for inducements AND falsifying some tapes but not others! Obviously it was not logical.'

Aniruddha said they could not take a public position that the tapes should be examined because they were not certain what the process would be. He did believe that the demand for tests would have been valid had it been made earlier. Bahal said,

Now a big doubt has been created and they just kind of manoeuvre public space on that basis. Then send it to an agency which they can control. In a sense, they are trying to derail the entire thing. So why should we give them the pleasure to do all this and participate in it willingly?

In an interview with Mathew Samuel, I tracked down how the tapes were handled. He said he always gave the tapes to Aniruddha and nobody else. Aniruddha would record the numbers in a log register and then deposit them in a locker.

Madhu: The one that is lying with the Commission is a copy or an original?
Samuel: This is the camera original. *Pukka*!!!
Madhu: There's no fiddle in this?
Samuel: *Kuch nahin* [none at all]. I'm very much known this matter. Camera originals. I know vaat was in the tape there. Vaatever tape I did, I know vaat is there. I don't think there is any possibility of doctoring.

Kajal Basu, features editor in Tehelka, said that Minty Tejpal was the only one who knew anything about editing. Aniruddha and Tarun had only a print background and knew nothing of the editing process. He said that Vijay Raman did the bulk of editing and there was constant tension between Minty and Raman. Towards the end, Raman actually pulled out. Was Minty taking editorial decisions on his own? Basu said,

> No, he doesn't have the wherewithal for that. I know it sounds condescending but he doesn't have the intellect for that. He was terribly in awe of Tarun who is like a father figure to him. Minty worships the ground he walks on. I do know that Tarun wouldn't allow any infusions or external interventions.

There was a glaring absence at the Commission of someone who could have clarified the doctoring issue in a flash: the person in charge of the editing of the tapes, Vijay Raman. The Commissioner never thought of sending a notice to him. The lawyers of those COT must have been afraid to, in case a few damaging truths emerged. Vijay Raman, a man in his late thirties, came across as someone who had thought through the value of Operation West End in the context of a larger horizon and was disappointed. He had an objective perspective that journalists usually lack, as we all tend to fall in love with every word of our stories. He reiterated a point that was nagging about the doctoring. How could Aniruddha Bahal and Mathew Samuel, not conversant with the technicalities of editing, have found the sophisticated equipment and a skilled editor to deliver them doctored tapes in such a short period of time? Vijay Raman explained the details and complexities of editing 105 videotapes.

The editing began around the second week of February 2001. The tapes were given to Raman in D8 (Digital 8) format. He transferred them to mini-DV and then to a computer. All the editing was done on that, using three computers. They worked on Macintosh computers, Mac G3 and G4. Raman said Aniruddha handed him the tapes, gave him a script and told him to pull in a team from the Tehelka office and put the story together. There were A, B, C, D teams who transcribed 105 tapes and handed it all to Aniruddha.

What instructions did Raman receive from Aniruddha? Raman laughed and said,

> Aniruddha briefed me the way only he can brief: *Behanchod, yeh story karni hai* [sisterfucker, this story has to be done]. So *behanchod* [sisterfucker], *maderchod* [motherfucker], nobody should know. And you pull six people together and say the same thing – *behanchod* and *maderchod*, nobody should know I think,

amongst all of us, like *andhon mein kana raja* [a one-eyed person is king amongst the blind], probably I was the most competent to put it together. Aniruddha and Tarun are not computer savvy.

Raman said there was nothing creative about the job: just follow the script, do mechanical work, and get the film out. At some point, Raman realized that their computers did not have the capacity for the six-hour script Aniruddha had written and asked him to chop it down, which he did.

Raman mentioned that Aniruddha was very particular about the tapes. He would ensure they were transferred and take them right back. Raman said, 'Aniruddha was very smart in what he did. Everybody knew a part of the process. Nobody knew the whole. I am sure Aniruddha knew.'

Raman lived for 14 days in the editing room, sleeping there and only leaving to bathe and rush back. They covered the windows with black paper. Raman said, 'I don't know if that makes it more dramatic or less. Somehow, people in Tehelka knew that these secret little things were happening. Things get into the consciousness and everybody gets an idea. By January, I knew something like this was on, without knowing exactly what.' There were six people rotating on three computers and two small computers to add the subtitles. They finished the job just two days before the date of the exposé. While the Operation West End tape was rolling in Imperial Hotel, the last part was still receiving finishing touches.

Raman said, 'It was also a question of when they would get to us. We knew our phones were tapped and they could come any time. People were on our track and it was like any time the place could be blown up or something could happen. There was an urgency to release the story.'

Were there any correspondents standing behind them, directing them about what to do? Raman answered, 'No, correspondents. There was poor Samuel who would come and ask, 'Ah! [groan] *Taiyyar ho gaya* [is it ready]? *Nahin* [No]? Ah! [groan] If you have met Samuel you know what he is capable of. He was really surprised that the film was not ready in about two hours.'

Was he asked to take Mulayam Singh's name out? Raman said he had not seen that footage and only followed the script that Aniruddha gave him.

Madhu: Did you at any point add on any new words that were recorded in the studio? Did you add on anything afterwards, other than voiceovers?
Raman: I can say this, Madhu, there was nothing. If I had thought, I am a person of conscience and if I had thought there was any hanky-panky with it, I wouldn't have been a part of this at all. I am talking about my own sense of what was right. One thought, maybe naively, who would have thought it was against the BJP?

Raman would have wanted to get eminent people on camera, would have liked idealistic people to debate what they saw, accepted the visible corruption and discussed what could be done to eliminate it. He said, 'It became a free for all. Truth, but without any boundaries for people to debate on'. Raman raised the question: 'I don't know if we as journalists should limit ourselves to exposing a story or should one create a political platform? Is that jumping the line and are you entering politics? Is there such a division at all? I don't know.'

In pursuit of creating a positive impact with the Operation West End story, Raman called up N. Vittal (commissioner, Central Vigilance Commission) on the morning of 13 March 2001. He did not know him but Raman said, 'He looked like a good man'. Vittal missed the press conference but picked up the tape in the evening. Vittal then lauded Tehelka and said, 'There are middlemen in defence deals. Tehelka was right in pointing out corruption. Corruption in defence and politics is regular in the system. Nobody is answering that.' Vittal contemptuously spoke of critics of Tehelka, 'Fools are looking at the finger and not where it is pointing to.' Coincidentally, Vittal had written a book *Fighting Corruption and Restructuring Government* in 2000.

What did Raman think of Milin Kapoor's accusations that the tapes had been doctored? Raman replied,

Raman: Nothing was put in later, if what is being alleged that some recording happened later with poor Samuel. Nothing like that happened. It seems vulgar to me to even respond to these kinds of accusations. This didn't happen, Madhu. Between journalists, it was just a straight story.

Madhu: Were words taken and another part of the conversation put in there?

Raman: No, no. If they mean anything has been fixed in order to say something that has not been said, I can say, even though it is like two years now, I can say that with my life that hasn't been done. Remember it is a three-hour film which we showed on Zee. I am talking about the tape which went on air. Not talking about the original tapes. I got a set of tapes which I, to my life, believe are completely original. I don't see why they shouldn't be and why they should be fixed. What is this huge controversy? Where will these guys fix them? These idiots [referring to Tarun Tejpal, Aniruddha Bahal, and Mathew Samuel] who know nothing about technology, yes, in technical terms they know nothing. Where would they go and fix them? Fix them and against who, against a Jaya Jaitly? Who is Jaya Jaitly, in the larger scheme of things? Okay, a Vajpayee or Advani understandable. But a Jaya Jaitly of Samata Party?

Madhu: Could it have been taken from another part of the conversation and inserted there?

Raman: No, no, no. I would have to go into this footage and see what has been done, which I don't know if I am capable of now. It is only possible if you were there right then. What could have happened is typically what we do in any editing. There were long segments with Jaitly or a Bangaru with a long empty span. You are like, *esko saale ko nikalo* [take out this bastard]. Shorten it. That's what you are doing while editing. What else are you doing? So initially I used to go into a tizzy when they said this has been edited, cuts and dissolves. Obviously, there are cuts and dissolves.

Whatever we have reduced X number of hours into four hours, we are showing you something. It is edited and there are portions which are not there. Whether Jaya took the money from the footage that I got. She did, much as I respected her then. I even do now if only she had not made such a hue and cry. I thought when I saw the footage, one was sad. She spoke eloquently and articulately. Who was the other person in the room? If you take it or your secretary takes it, what's the big deal? She made it clear it was for the party. One would have expected her to say this is how Indian elections run, the party needed the money and how does a party like the Samata Party survive if it doesn't take money? If she had said that then we would have all said, wow, here is a woman who stood up for what is so.

When informed of Milin Kapoor's accusation that the sound drops were a sign of doctoring, Raman said,

The DV is an excellent format at one level. But is not designed, at least so far, to handle tons and tons of footage. Shooting in a drunken stupor, as it ended up. It is designed for little subtle things where you make [a] one-minute advertising film. There might have been a slip or two. I am not saying this is a squeaking, perfect film. I can say this much: nothing has been fixed. If sound has dropped in a couple of places, sorry, we were afraid that we would be bombed any day. We used to talk amongst ourselves. One of these days they are just going to plant a bomb out here and all of us are going to go for a six. That's what we were working under.

About Bangaru Laxman's allegation that the audio is not in sync with the visuals and the audio is being slowed down to fit a visual from somewhere else, Raman responded:

Raman: We were not under any instructions to not slow it down. If there was a whining fan somewhere, we put Bangaru, which was at least of some interest. If we had to stretch it, we stretched it. But this is from the tapes that were shown on air. The original footage would have it.
Madhu: When two cameras are used, say one in the briefcase and one in the tie, you have images of the same scene, which one is the original?
Raman: I think this kind of thing happened in Jaya's case. I think maybe also in Bangaru's. We used to call tapes, toffees, or toffee number. Now if there was a problem like suppose we had some footage it seemed more unclear than usual, we would tell Aniruddha that *yeh theek nahi aah raha* [this is not coming properly] and somebody might remember *uska toh aur ek tape bhi hai* [it was from that and there is another tape of it]. So then he would give us that tape.

We would copy it and fix it. That's all that happened. That might explain a lot of things.

Madhu: In the Commission, one of the lawyers showed two tapes. He said these are identical but in one tape, one glass is missing here, a bottle of Bisleri has come there. So it was doctored.

Raman: Suddenly the angle is changing with Samuel sitting here. Yes, two cameras were used in Jaya's story. I am not sure if two cameras were used in the Bangaru story.

Hi8 tapes have the audio and visuals embedded together and, therefore, it is impossible to fiddle with the original tapes. Raman said, 'What stops us if one had to fix it?' But, he maintained it was not done. He was terribly disheartened about the demand for forensic examination of the tapes. 'What does it take now to do anything except for a Gandhi,' Raman said, 'I felt if Gandhi had done the story he would have followed it up by walking in satyagraha with the tapes.'

Raman said the public might perceive Tarun and Aniruddha's refusal to allow the forensic examination as having something to hide. 'What they are saying is that so much has happened and now there will be another drama of forensics,' Raman explained. He said he had no problems in sending the tapes for examination, but was disappointed that in the ultimate analysis that the story did not achieve anything more.

He was disgusted that the 'sex tapes' had been used to discredit Tehelka journalists. He said,

For example none of us ever saw the prostitute tapes. I never had the need or the desire to see those tapes. A big deal was made out of that. Nobody is defending it. I am not saying it was the best thing to do but in the context of the story and what was happening: it happened. This happens in India when people ask for favours and this is one of the favours they ask for.

Tarun and Aniruddha were just a bunch of very young guys just going and doing a story. They were dealing with something like the BJP. Personally, I would have loved it if they could have also fixed some Congress people. It doesn't look like a story against the BJP then, which it wasn't intended to be. If the Congress was in power and Tehelka was there, it would have been the same thing; just the characters would have changed. I don't know if that would have helped them, in any case. It would have become very big. Everybody would have gotten after them and killed them.

Raman said that he used to play with Jaya's son as a child,

Raman: *Merreh ko chot lag gayee ek bar* [I got injured once] and Jaya washed it. I haven't forgotten. Jaya was among the people one thought had possibilities. What is her story? Why is she so on and on about it?

Madhu: I told her you could have said it was money for the party and then just left it. She said it is the principle of the thing. She said, how can journalists come in and misrepresent themselves? She said she has taken it up for the issue, not for herself.

Raman: I am sure it hits people who see themselves as honest. I suppose if somebody filmed Vijay Raman buying a tape in Pallika Bazaar and pulled it out like I was smuggling. Yes, probably one would, in the goodness of things, also. Maybe somebody just needs to give her a hug and say, "Come on, get over it".

⌒

Jaya Jaitly is not one to get over things with just a hug. Along with other 8B notices, Jaya had made repeated applications to gain access to the original tapes.

Jaya Jaitly was scorching with anger at the Commission for setting stringent rules on how the tapes would be watched.

Jaya: They go there, in the heat of summer, all these boys sat all summer watching those unedited tapes. How can you watch tapes, which nobody let's you stop, pause, listen again? You can't. If you go out to have a glass of water or go and have a pee, you miss, you miss – too bad. If you find that you know it's saying inaudible in your transcript, but you can hear what's being said. You say *zara sunao* [play it again] – No. Can't touch it, watch it, watch it, *jao* [go].

Don't blame her. Does sound unfair. But, there is the other Rasohmon here. In the process of Pause, Rewind, Play, it isn't too difficult to press Record, which would immediately Erase any portion anyone saw fit.

Jaya said she sent her 'experts' (the ubiquitous Milin Kapoor?) and asked them to listen carefully to 'the same peculiar "CD West End" and "funny two lakhs". They told her it sounded exactly the same as the edited tapes. That should have hit the note that it was not doctored. Instead, Jaya's interpretation was that the original tapes were doctored! Jaya's lawyers used the unedited original recordings in the Commission to prove that the same difference in pitch proved there had been a fiddle. Jaya bristled:

Somebody has to explain this. It's all that Jaya Jaitly is talking rubbish, but then somebody has to accept the fact that there's something strange. And, on the basis of your claiming that it's all there, you are condemning me to having pre-arranged deals with arms dealers. But you make me into a traitor, a corrupt person, who is knowingly doing all these things, in league with the defence minister, under his nose, in an illicit relationship … what more could anybody pile on my head? And you really expect me to sit back and say, "Oh, well, too bad, doesn't matter?"

Yes, it is a lot on her head and Jaya is not one to sit back at all.

After the tapes were sent for forensic examination, I asked Jaya what would happen if the forensic experts declared that the tapes had not been doctored? She said she was not asking for the tapes to be examined to defend herself but in the interests of journalism and in the interests of the country. Jaya said that this would establish a precedent that in any inquiry all tapes should first go for a forensic examination. She did add,

> Even if they're not doctored, supposing he'd even said that two lakhs there or he'd said that West End there, I still haven't said or done anything wrong. I am disproving by this: that they never mentioned and I never heard the company name. They are trying to say I knew from beforehand, that I was meeting arms dealers and that I accepted the money. And that they, in fact, put in the transcript, when they say two lakhs, thank you very much, Jaya nods. You don't see me nodding at all. It's not in the picture. All this is being pushed on later. So I'm trying to show their mala fide intentions.

Jaya insisted it was not her personal problem but that as a political person, 'apart from fighting for my own reputation, I have to fight for something which is in the interests of the country. Therefore I have to fight to expose people who do wrong and also the next time, if some such things happen, they won't be this blind acceptance of any sort of tape.'

What do you call a decision-making procedure that chooses selective facts and ignores those that are inconsistent with the urge to produce a desired result? The process includes the entirely unconscious area of how you perceive your problem, how you use the information given to you, and how your judgement gets affected by your own unconscious need to fix the concluding result to your own satisfaction. The most brilliant people's unconscious strings can pull them into areas that are self-serving and just erroneous. Milin Kapoor had served up the DD to Jaya on a platter. In Jaya's Selective Perception, she saw Milin Kapoor's confection as apodictic. That is fine, but what Jaya neglected here was the real possibility and probability factor of the result of the forensic examiner's report not agreeing with Milin Kapoor. I brought up the point that the examiner could declare the tapes not doctored, what then? Jaya responded: 'If the tapes come back saying they weren't doctored, I don't think it shakes my defence at all.' Why did Justice Venkataswami turn down Jaya's requests for forensic examination three times? Jaya said, 'This is a big misconception. It wasn't turned down three times. He has always deferred it. He said there was no prima facie case made out at this juncture.' Jaya pointed out the 'juncture' was the point when her lawyers were supposed to prove their case without access to the original tapes.

According to Aniruddha, the only reason why Justice Venkataswami kept the issue of sending the tapes open by adding 'at this juncture' was because if he gave a final ruling, they could contest it in court. Aniruddha believed it was a smart legal thing to do because then when Jaya went to the High Court, her plea was shot down on the grounds that the issue had not yet been decided.

'This,' Jaya said, 'is the most ridiculous legal or technical situation, which I don't know how any judge could have possibly accepted.' They were forced to use flawed multi-generation copies of the tapes to point out the problems in them. Jaya stated, 'Venkataswami is advised by Gopal Subramaniam – who gives a lengthy submission to the judge, saying why they need not be examined. The curious part is Gopal Subramaniam is in Madras when the presentation is being done. So how a lawyer who didn't even see what was going on, give a submission?' Jaya said the submission was based on taking Tehelka's word and discrediting Milin Kapoor. Jaya believed that her lawyers had in fact discredited Tehelka's 'experts': Pradip Krishen, ostensibly because he happened to be married to Arundhati Roy (Indialnk, a publishing company in which Tarun Tejpal was a partner, published Arundhati's bestseller *The God of Small Things* in India) and Umashankar (also according to Jaya), because he admitted that he did not have the technology to ascertain the veracity of the tapes. Jaya bristled, 'Despite all this, if a senior lawyer advises a judge that there is no need to examine the tapes now, I find it very questionable'.

Jaya seethed at the unfairness of having to defend herself before the Tehelka journalists were to depose in the Commission, without access to the original tapes. For this, Jaya petitioned the High Court that she should be allowed to depose after Tehelka. The High Court took six months to turn down the request and said: let the Commission do its job. They were not going to interfere.

Gopal Subramaniam went by the Evidence Act which states that if a person admitted it was their picture and voice it was acceptable evidence. Then there was only the question of the tampering of the tapes to be dealt with. When enough technical knowledge had been shared that it was impossible to tamper with the originals, Subramaniam advised that there was no need to check the tapes. But Jaya fumed:

The custody of the tapes remained with Tehelka for six weeks, during which time everybody had already come out with their accusations of where exactly, what had gone wrong. They had ample time to sort out the Srinivas glitch, to do anything else they wanted to. I was told by Bobby [Milin Kapoor] who knows about these things, that they probably, the very first day, when we all met, he said I have a feeling they have been filmed on mini-DV. And they have transferred all this to Hi8 and this whole big yarn that Hi8 has been used. You don't need much to transfer from Hi8 to a computer.

Bobby knows about these things? Then Bobby should also know the t-i-m-e it would take just to transfer 105 tapes before an edit. Jaya said, 'Later on they admitted they transferred it on a computer'. How else could it have been edited? There was no 'later on' admission. Was it possible to transfer all the mini-DVs and different tapes and then again transfer all of it to Hi8 and bring out a final tape? Yes, of course. But that defeats the logic of how computers function and the pressures under which the journalists were working made it implausible that they would undertake such a time-consuming useless exercise. What was the need to tamper? They had got all the footage they required without going through the cumbersome technical burdens of doctoring it. Should Jaya have trusted Milin so blindly? What about Milin, who was obviously feeding Jaya's need for information that would rest her case? Did Milin think of the repercussions if his allegations turned out to be wrong?

Jaya said that Justice Phukan, who replaced Justice Venkataswami, did not want to deal with the custody issue because if the report said that the tapes were doctored, it would also resolve the custody problem. Jaya said, 'So he'll decide to throw out all or keep some or do whatever he wants to do'.

Madhu: Why is your fight to get the tapes examined so personal?

Jaya: I don't want Tehelka to get away, if I kept quiet. The army officers were like stunned rabbits. They're scared because their whole lives have crashed. Bangaru Laxman is a political person. They don't have much other dimension other than their position in society and their position in the party. But somebody like me, I feel that I'm not that kind of a politician that I can shrug off an accusation and not bother about the way these people have made that accusation. But the meticulous way in which they have claimed, that what they have done is most correct and the way they have gone at every public platform all around the world, talking about how disgusting the system is in India. How they broke us all down and how they've exposed the "venal underbelly". The words that they used. I just can't stomach from people claiming to be investigative journalists. You can't sit on your high horse claiming credibility. Then I have to demolish their credibility.

Why did Milin Kapoor give an affidavit in the Commission that stated he was convinced that the tapes had been doctored, when he had not analysed the original tapes?

Chris Mills did the same thing. Jaya Jaitly said she turned to Christopher Martin Frederick Mills, director of Network Forensics (United Kingdom), on a recommendation of the then British High Commissioner. Mills's company is part of the Control Risks Group, incorporating audio, video, computer evidence and investigation, fingerprint and questioned document services. In his affidavit he stated that he was the senior audio/video consultant and provided audio and video enhancement and authentication analysis services to prosecution and defence teams as well as commercial organizations. He had experience as an electronic engineer in the navy, which involved sonar and electronic surveillance. Mills worked with the Metropolitan Police Audio Forensic Laboratory for eight years. His work included analysis and authentication of recordings, utilizing analogue and digital enhancement equipment and examination techniques. He had an impressively long list of cases where he had been called on to examine audio and video recordings, such as the FBI recordings of the Davidian Compound siege in Waco, Texas and the Bloody Sunday incident in Derry, Northern Ireland, in 1972, analysing recordings produced by journalists. He also enumerated all his professional degrees. How did Jaya Jaitly pay for this remarkably high power and expensive-sounding expert? This is a marvellous aspect of *jholawalas* and leftists. They profess a simple life, but when money is required for something, there is always a capitalist friend to pick up the tab. Jaya said her friend R.V. Pandit paid for him. Fine, that done, but what did Mills actually have to say?

Mills said that he received an M.PEG1-Compact Disc of 17 minutes from Jaya Jaitly, which were sections of the programme broadcast. She also sent documents, transcripts, and orders given by the Commission. He was given three months to complete the job. Mills stated at the outset:

> That based on my experience with the various forms of electronic equipments (audio and video), I would offer the opinion that where events on copy tapes indicate a degree of uncertainty in their continuity, or that events indicate that something untoward has happened, in the interests of all parties, it would seem a sensible approach to allow independent forensic examination of the "original recordings".

Mills said that since the tapes were disputed it would be inappropriate to rely on them as representative of the whole truth as the content and context of copy material is open to manipulation during the process of 'reorganizing' the original material.

Significantly, Mills added,

> I understand that the original material was recorded in Hi8-AFM format. This format creates tapes where the audio and video signals are intertwined in such a way as to make any alteration of the original recordings technical(ly) unfeasible. Attempts to tamper with this type of original recording would be eminently detectable by qualified examiners.

Now this directly refuted Milin Kapoor. Jaya Jaitly had paid for an expert witness who was not doing her cause any good, but rather convolutedly he quite cleverly, also put in what Jaya Jaitly wanted said. Mills wrote:

> This however does not prevent any copy material from being manipulated before final presentation. It is technically possible to record separately, in a digital system, the video and audio from a Hi8-AFM recording. The individual components can then be edited before being reassembled as a product for onward transmission.

So, tell us something new. Tehelka had never denied editing the material.

Mills then attempted to make Jaya feel she had not entirely wasted that money. He pointed out there were 'at least three instances where the audio information is interrupted whilst the video information appears continuous'. Mills concluded that,

> ... where without examination of the "original" recordings, the finished transmitted programmed may well be misleading and prejudicial to those who appear in it. Only by examining the original material will it be possible to determine if the transmitted copy material does indeed represent or

misrepresent the true version of events. Until the "original" recordings are examined who can say what the truth of the matter is.

If Mills, with all his high-tech equipment as well as professional degrees and years of experience in the field, cannot determine the truth until he examines the original recordings, how did Milin Kapoor insist that the tapes were doctored? With neon coloured sonogram graphs, no less? Yet, Jaya Jaitly and her lawyers ignored all these comments and focused on the three instances Mills found suspect. But, Mills was in no way conclusive.

Kavin Gulati, Tehelka's lawyer questioned Chris Mills on 3 January 2002:

Gulati: As of today, therefore, you cannot conclusively say, one way or the other, as to whether these interruptions have deliberately been caused or they are as a result of such errors as you point out in paragraph 15?

Mills: When you undertake copying, editing and you haven't looked at original material, which is the whole point. How can we know what caused these interruptions?

Gulati: Supposing Mr Mills, the Commission is having in its possession, as we say the originals, and if we are able to say for example show you the first generation tapes, and those breaks as you point out do not occur in those first generation copies, would you reconsider your opinion which you have given in paragraphs 10, 11 and 15?

Mills: I would be reluctant to examine any copied material in terms of its authentication.

Gulati: You may be reluctant to examine the copied material. But you have given an expert opinion on the basis of copied material. Isn't it?

Mills: Yes, because that is what has been made available to me.

In answer to Gulati's question, Mills said he worked five days to analyse the material. Methinks Jaya may have gotten ripped off here. Jaya had sent her own CD/DVD copied from the broadcast version, so it was already many generations removed from the original. If nothing could be conclusive unless the originals were seen, why did Mills not refuse to carry out the analysis?

In answer to Gopal Subramanium, the senior counsel for the Commission, Mills answered:

The difficulty that you have is that you are working on material that is so far removed from the original material. All you can say is that there is an inaccuracy or an indication that something has happened at this point. Now without backtracking and referring to original material, as far as an expert goes or as far as I am concerned …

Mills also confirmed to Subramanium that it was technically unfeasible to make an alteration in the Hi8 AFM original recording without it being detectable.

Jaya and her lawyers spun Chris Mills's testimony as corroborating everything she had said in the first place. Jaya wanted sufficient doubt created for the original tapes be examined, and Mills certainly helped her in that. Speaking over the telephone to Chris Mills in London, followed by a subsequent email to him, I received no response to my question about why he did not refuse to examine tapes that were not original when the result could not be conclusive.

Jaya was not happy about how the Commission treated Chris Mills. Jaya said:

> A man like that, they used him for only twenty minutes. I would have thought the judge could have even called him privately and educated himself on this whole procedure. Because of his high level of qualifications, they couldn't demolish his credibility. Tehelka, the government and Commission lawyers asked him questions. Very interestingly, everybody got up and wanted to ask: "No, sorry. You didn't stand up quickly enough. Your chance is gone."

Jaya believed it was all pre-planned because, she said, in the entire two-and-a-half years it was the only occasion when people were not allowed to ask questions when they rose. She recalled that the Tehelka lawyers objected when government lawyers asked Mills questions. Gopal Subramaniam asked three or four brief questions. Jaya said, 'Then he said, thank you, bye, bye bye and he was stunned that nobody had anything else to ask him'. Jaya had gone to England herself to speak to Chris Mills, spent Rs 5 lakh to fly Mills to India, so the lukewarm response his testimony received was harshly disappointing to her. That was the point when, Jaya said, she got suspicious that the Commission's counsels were acting in Tehelka's interests and not in public interest. This is a serious charge.

> **Madhu:** Are you saying that Justice Venkataswami was biased against you?
> **Jaya:** I believe that there was collusion between Tehelka and Commissioner's counsels. I'm afraid Justice Venkataswami, for the first few months, didn't apply his mind. He relied on his counsels, in all good faith.

Jaya went on to say, 'When Bobby [Milin Kapoor] showed this interactive thing, I think it went over everybody's head'.

Let's get this straight here. What Milin showed was definitely not 'interactive'. He lifted sound from one tape and placed it in another person's lips on another tape. The technique is the simplest form of editing. It did not go over anybody's head.

> **Jaya:** But by the time I came along, one; I did it in a layman's language because I am a layperson, and secondly, by then so much time had passed, so many questions had come up, that the judge actually listened. Maybe a woman is more interesting to listen to, or a curiosity or something, so he listened. Earlier when the judge was really not clued in enough, he was letting things go by, in the way that he was being advised. According to my senior lawyer, he feels the

turning point came at my deposition. Perhaps, I got a little more attention, because I was a woman and it was a change of voice or a change of person there, so everyone listened more carefully. Probably the kind of person Venkataswami is, he would be interested to know what a woman had to say. They also, I think, had the impression that I wouldn't have a clue about all this tampering and how to describe it. But I had gone into it in so much detail that I was speaking like an expert myself. And the fact that I was capable of doing that and the way I explained it to him, because I had by then understood what kind of a person he was and I felt you had to say it to him very carefully, like you're almost explaining it to a child.

What can one say, except, 'Oh ho!' in dismay?

↩

On 26 September 2001, Tehelka retaliated with their own sound expert, Umashankar. A capricious maverick, Umashankar was ambivalent about Tehelka and not interested in taking sides. Fifty-six years old, he looks like a prototypal mad scientist. Uncombed hair, slapdash clothes, gives whimsical directions to his six-floor walk-up so you are lost for an hour. I walk up six floors and see him waving madly from the sixth floor of the building opposite. He has an obvious, trenchant intelligence. In 1967 he joined *The Indian Express* in Chennai, having talked his way into the job with no qualifications. 'Nobody in the Tehelka Commission asked me about this, so they don't know I was actually a journalist,' he chuckled. He edited a weekly arts page and wrote a science column, until 1976.

During the Emergency, he played the unenviable role of Internal Censor for *The Indian Express*. The position the newspaper had taken in a court case against the government was that they were not publishing anything that required to be censored. During the three months when the case was being fought, Umashankar ensured that the newspaper appeared that way. He said it was a challenge, but a depressing one. After the court ruled in favour of *The Express*, he quit the job.

Umashankar then took his 'Joseph Campbell's heroic step'. He shed his historical limitations and took a leap. He had some friends in Delhi so he decided to pursue his hobby of audio engineering. He became friends with Pradip Krishen, who was a history professor at that time. Umashankar: 'We were gambling friends. You don't have to say that, but if you want to, you can say. I have no objection.' Krishen received an offer to make a series of films on science and roped in Umashankar who was writing a science column for a newspaper. He knew nothing about films. Umashankar discovered that more than writing scripts, he enjoyed building amplifiers and found himself doing the sound for the programmes.

Umashankar became a sound engineer for films, documentaries, news programmes, and chat shows, and has about 25 years of experience in the field. Since 1982, Umashankar has worked as a consultant to a project in Gurgaon, advising them on how to preserve archives of traditional music. Umashankar works at the American Institute of Indian Studies, rather more specifically, the Archives and Research Centre for Ethno-Musicology. In his research into the acoustics of a third century theatre in Bhubaneshwar, he has used extensive analytical techniques for sound. When asked about the spectrogram shown by Milin and that it shows interpolations, he said he couldn't understand what Milin was showing other than spikes in sound that occur in any conversation.

> **Madhu:** Milin Kapoor has said that the green wave shows that it is coming from somewhere else.
>
> **Umashankar:** It doesn't show anything of the sort. All you have to do is listen to this. [Umashankar played the sound with the visual graph.] He thinks these are bands of sound, looking very different because of inter-positioning. There's no real reason to think that it shows anything of that sort. Any noise, what that particular spectrum analyser does. This is the sound that is on the tape. [Umashankar played the tape again] This is one way of representing it. Frankly, this is one way of representing sound. *Haan?* What you're seeing visually is a representation of sound.
>
> **Madhu:** Are you saying that Milin Kapoor represented sound peaks as interpolation?
>
> **Umashankar:** The thing is, I am not in competition to Milin Kapoor, who is an ass. I have some reputation as Umashankar. I don't want one-to-one with him.

When asked by Tehelka, Umashankar examined the cameras they had used for the recordings as well as a copy of the original tapes. In his deposition at the Commission, Umashankar refuted Milin Kapoor:

> One of the peculiarities of the 8mm format has been, specially in the Hi8 format, is that video and audio are recorded together on the same layer of tape, one under the other and it is not possible to record one without the other. And that is an incontrovertible thing.

Umashankar then handed over to the Commission some technical literature supporting what he had said.

Umashankar went on to explain that when you are looking for any tampering, it would be easily detectable because the background noise is not reproducible. If a word is cut, the background sound breaks, and that is more noticeable than listening to the words. When questioned by Rani Jethmalani (Tehelka's lawyer), about his opinion on Milin Kapoor's deposition, Umashankar explained in detail that the material Milin Kapoor was examining was over five or six generations removed from the original tapes. He said if he were given material such as that to analyse, he would refuse. Tehelka had informed him that they had already handed over the originals to the Commission, so they gave him the closest copy they had. On examining it he said, 'I can say very confidently the drop out is not there.' Umashankar confirmed that after examining the Hi8 tapes no words had been edited out.

Rani Jethmalani questioned Umashankar about the portion that Milin Kapoor had demonstrated where 'CD West End' is said during the meeting with Jaya Jaitly. According to

Kapoor, it was odd and peculiar. He had alleged that there was some kind of manipulation of the tape.

Umashankar went into a lengthy explanation about the techniques he used to check the tapes, which involved removing the background sound and slowing down the words. He also removed the words and retained the background sound to check for uniformity or interruptions. Umashankar demonstrated this on the tapes for the Commission.

> **Jethmalani**: What could be the words that were being uttered where Mr Kapoor suggests that "CD West End"?
>
> **Umashankar**: I thought it was a fairly standard way of saying "have you explained" but said "you explained" with an interrogative two-word sentence, which is quite common usage in India.

Umashankar clarified that if a word or two were added, unless it was done with high-quality equipment and controlled surroundings that replicated the room exactly where the original recording was done, with the same distance of mike to ceiling etc., it would be near impossible to match words recorded later that would naturally carry their own ambient sound in the fresh recording. In removing all the words and only listening to the background sound, he could confirm that here were no later additions and no tampering.

Jethmalani then asked Umashankar about the disputed words, 'two lakhs', which had really put Jaya Jaitly in a twist. Of course, Milin Kapoor had volunteered to twist with her. Since the pitch of these words was different and higher, did it mean they had been inserted later? Umashankar demonstrated to the Commission when he removed the words that there was no audio break in the transmission and no audio drop out at all, as alleged by Kapoor. Umashankar explained that because the mike was placed on Samuel's body, the pitch of his voice would only naturally record louder than the rest of the group.

Umashankar did explain at length that the reason why he did not use a sonogram, which he preferred to call a spectrogram, was because he did not consider it a sufficiently suitable tool for detecting something like a dropout. He said it was much more useful if you want to compare two microphones or two recordings to match more accurately while editing. He preferred to use a waveform and believed that the dropout Kapoor found was probably because the material had been transferred so many times. Umashankar suggested that another copy be made to see if the same break occurs at the same point.

Jethmalani then questioned Umashankar about the words, 'I know him' allegedly uttered by Bangaru Laxman. Umashankar played the tape repeatedly but said he did not have the voice recognition equipment required to be certain. He did say:

> If you saw the picture, the gentleman in question is eating *paan*, he spits at least in frame twice and I do not know if the mouthful of *paan* juice, the speech tends to be somewhat difficult to follow. I am not 100 per cent sure, but what

> I am quite sure from looking at the noise, the background pattern is that this is not something that has been put in later.

Rani Jethmalani then produced Major General P.S.K. Choudary's affidavit in which he alleged that the tapes had been tampered with or doctored, and says 'that is on commercial basis' has been converted, doctored as 'commission'. Jethmalani sought Umashankar's opinion on this. Umashankar confirmed that after slowing down the audio he believed the word was indeed 'commission'. He again demonstrated to the Commission how he checked for tampering, by removing words and playing the background noise where he found no breaks at all. Umashankar stated comfortably, 'I am reasonably certain there has been no tampering at this part.'

↩

Nilay Dutta, Jaya Jaitly's lawyer, then thrust out his tentacles. Thirty questions which meandered around hypothetical technicalities designed to bamboozle Umashankar and the Commission, succeeded only in prickling Umashankar's disposition. Umashankar had no interest in being at the Commission and found it a profound waste of his personal time. When Dutta asked his thirtieth question, a rather innocuous one, 'When you were asked by Tehelka to see the footage, how many shots did you see?' Umashankar lost it and went off on a wild tirade in frustrated exasperation:

> I was not planning to be a witness. I was planning to advise them and they did not know what expert evidence was going to be presented in opposition. They said, look, this is the kind of complaints that have been made. I was willing to talk about it because I have my reputation to defend.

Blah Blah Blah he went on and on. Who can blame him? He concluded with:

> So the five segments that were mentioned in that charge I looked at only those which I transferred to a laptop. I was reasonably convinced that what they are saying is justified; and that is when I decided I will come and stand up to what I am saying.

To Umashankar's tirade, a bemused Dutta responded, 'This process reminds me of P.C.Sorkar [India's renowned magician],' to which Umashankar countered with 'Yes. I was very worried about.'

↩

It was Umashankar's startlingly independent, eccentric persona, and its unpredictable quality that made him a wonderful advocate for Tehelka's credibility. He made it quite clear he was no admirer of the Tehelka journalists. Indeed, he believed they were stupid to have gone to the Commission to try to defend themselves. Umashankar said they should have done what other journalists have done. Publish the story and leave the Commission and lawyers to go figure. Umashankar told me,

I gave evidence because Milin Kapoor is a joker. Otherwise I wouldn't have, because I'm not interested in it. And, in fact, I told whatever is the name of the guy who is the boss of Tehelka, I am bad at names, the Commission is not inquiring into Tehelka. It is inquiring into arms deals. Why are you defending it?

Dutta asked Umashankar 214 questions, attempting to demolish his credibility, twisting him with hypothetical technical scenarios but Umashankar, besides his irritation that he was in the Commission at all, was unshakeable.

On 29 September 2001, K. Madhavan, the lawyer representing R.K. Jain, took pot shots at Umashankar, pointing out he had no technical degrees or technical knowledge. Umashankar couldn't have cared less. Narender Singh's lawyer, H.R. Khan Suhel, then joined in the Umashankar gang bang.

On 3 January 2002, Bangaru Laxman produced his own 'technical expert', Kartic Godavarthy. A producer, director, and editor of films, Godavarthy runs Studio 7 (Hyderabad) which has digital and analogue editing machines. His educational qualifications include a postgraduate degree in anthropology. Godavarthy said that anthropology and film-making are 'two sides of the same coin'. Right. So are obstetrics and architecture. Godavarthy said, 'I have gained knowledge and how to appeal to the human mind, human heart in anthropology and I tried to use this knowledge in making films when I direct them or when I script them or when I actually edit them. I don't really consider both of them to be very separate.'

The less said. Now you know the level the Commission had hit. Godavarthy then proceeded to show 20 points on the tape which he believed had been doctored. These included jump cuts, lips out of sync with actions, lack of audio continuity, dissolves in the middle of conversations, missing audio, etc. He pointed to Bangaru Laxman's lips moving with no words coming from them. As far as I recall, isn't that how *paan* is chewed? Godavarthy pointed out to the court any amount of manipulations could be done on the tapes. Justice Venkataswami asked a crucial question:

Venkataswami: From the copy you have done all these manipulations, but even the camera original Hi8, can you tamper with it?
Godavarthy: Once I transfer the footage on …
Venkataswami: Transfer is all right, but before transfer?
Godavarthy: Once I transfer and do my manipulation, I can put it back on a Hi8 AFM tape and I can always claim it as a camera original. I just want you to watch this bit of manipulation.

Godavarthy then proceeded to show an edited tape that took the voice from one interview and transferred it so as to emanate from someone else's lips. Yes, but it was transferred and edited, a fact that was continually misrepresented. Godavarthy gave 21 demonstrations based on a VHS copy of the edited broadcast tape. He pointed out sudden jerks, visuals stop in jerks but audio continuous, no sync between audio and video, the sound of a cough coming five seconds after the visual cough, video slowed down to fill up audio gaps, and specifically, exactly the point that Bangaru Laxman was uncomfortable about (much like the Milin Kapoor and Jaya Jaitly's ratio), Godavarthy found there must have been tampering. On the tape Laxman says, 'I know him but'. Godavarthy said, 'But there seems to be some kind of residue in the audio which cannot be explained in the video. It apparently is a residue of some of bit of the sound that has been taken away.' Godavarthy showed a demo of Laxman moving his lips without any sound. Did we forget the ubiquitous *paan*? Again and again, Godavarthy was seeing it on a copy of an edited VHS. All this meant nothing at all in terms of tampering with the originals. These points and demonstrations should not have been allowed or recorded in the Commission.

R.P. Sharma, counsel for Colonel Anil Sehgal, asked Godavarthy:

Sharma: Yesterday you had shown us the instances of tampering, doctoring, editing and what not; these are the technical terms in the tape of Bangaru Laxman, Colonel Sehgal and Brigadier Iqbal Singh. Now, as an expert kindly opine whether the authenticity and genuineness of the entire tape in question gets shattered, clouded once these instances of tampering, doctoring are detected in it.

Godavarthy: Yes, the entire tape's authenticity will be questionable and yes, it will be shattered.

Mr R.P. Sharma sat down satisfied.

Brigadier Iqbal Singh's impetuous lawyer, C.M. Khanna, asked Godavarthy that if there were instances of no sound audible from Laxman's lips, was it possible that the same problem existed in other parts of the tape? Godavarthy most readily agreed.

With such goings on, perhaps the only point left to be debated, was to Commission a Measure for Measure play or No Ado About Much? Lawyers representing Colonel Anil Sehgal, Lieutenant Colonel V.P. Sayal, Major General S.P. Murgai, R.K. Jain, Jaya Jaitly, and P. Sasi all had a charming rendezvous with Godavarthy, where he served up delicious scenarios of how tapes can be manipulated. All the lawyers repeatedly asked the same questions about points on the tape that were edited and therefore, presumed manipulated. None of these could of course have been done on any Hi8 tape, but it was a successful circus of postulation.

Sidharth Luthra, the lawyer for Tehelka, the lone fox among wolves, then proceeded to pound, pummel and finally annihilate Godavarthy. He got Godavarthy to admit he had no knowledge of editing guidelines issued by the Press Council of India. Actually the Press Council does not even deal with the electronic media. Luthra asked, 'Have you ever shot a film in your life?' Godavarthy declared he had a shot a corporate film for a resort club in Hyderabad called Cosy Retreat. Of course, this is begging for bad jokes. Luthra then got Godavarthy to admit that he had not seen the original West End tapes, that he was not an audio engineer, that he had not done any audio analysis, that he did not get Bangaru Laxman's voice print, could not define 'wave form', 'pattern', 'carrier wave', 'modulation', or 'demodulation'. Godavarthy did his best to salvage his glory from the day before when he was such a hero showing his 'doctored' tapes. But he was the easiest piece of cake Luthra ever devoured. After generally battering Godavarthy down, Luthra closed in for the kill of a puny adversary. He asked Godavarthy that if Chris Mills had taken five days to examine 17 minutes, how did Godavarthy manage it in only four-and-a-half hours? Godavarthy said the whole process took him about three or four days.

Luthra established that Godavarthy came to the conclusion that the tapes had been doctored without seeing the originals, without seeing transcripts of the original tapes nor transcripts of the edited tapes. Under these circumstances, Luthra questioned how Godavarthy could conclude that the edits were 'unethical'? Godavarthy justified it, saying, 'One, that if it was ethical edit, how can we justify a non-sync between the audio. And the video, if you are really talking about ethical edit, then how can we justify the various discrepancies that I have highlighted?' Try looking at the originals. Luthra had an easy time making poor Godavarthy look rather worse than an amateur.

Luthra then moved on to a decisive point which had not been sufficiently stressed: the technical impossibility of doctoring 105 tapes.

> **Luthra**: In an uncompressed or non-compressed situation if I was wanting to put one second of film on a camera original, can you give me a guess as to approximately how much hard disc space would I use?
> **Godavarthy**: Uncompressed? What is the resolution we are talking about?
> **Luthra**: 720 by 576.
> **Godavarthy**: 72 GB approximately one hour, one hour twenty minutes – that is what my system takes.
> **Luthra**: If I were to do a computation that means for hundred hours of tape you are talking about 7200 GB, is that correct?
> **Godavarthy**: Yes. If the math is right, I am not sure.
> **Luthra**: A normal computer not the state-of–the art equipment you have, about a year ago, March-January this year, the standard space in a computer would be 10 to 20 GB of hard disc space?
> **Godavarthy**: I wouldn't be able to comment on this because if you have access for higher hard disc, you can always get that.

Godavarthy caught on to where Luthra was leading him.

> **Luthra**: I am asking you a specific question, if I were to pick up a machine, official that would be 10 to 20 GB of hard disc space one year ago?
> **Godavarthy**: If you pick up a video workstation. I wouldn't know when how much GB of hard disc have been introduced in the market.
> **Luthra**: If I were to say that a year ago 10 to 20 GB hard disc space what is available that means by computation 7200 GB of hard disc space will be available in 360 computers.

Godavarthy: 7200 GB, but you want to edit the entire 100 hours in one single go.
Luthra: Exactly.

Tehelka would have required 360 computers and that many editors to edit and doctor the tapes. Even if they rented 10 or 20 computers, the time required to log, script, record voiceovers, and then perform delicate doctoring would stretch to virtually a year. Luthra asked Godavarthy how much time it would take to edit 100 hours of tape. Luthra asked him six questions, the same one in different ways, trying to elicit an answer. Godavarthy hedged his way through. Finally Godavarthy confessed, 'I have taken one whole day to edit 38 seconds of the video footage. It took the whole day to render it, but depending on the nature of the data the time is defined'.

It took an entire day to render 38 seconds. Now figure 105 tapes that have to be edited down to four-and-a-half hours. Even if certain areas were picked by Tehelka to doctor on the original tapes, logging those points, rendering them on a computer, playing with audio and editing it again on the original, then making a new 'original' that matched at every point is inconceivable. It makes doctoring an extreme possibility. More logically, why would Tehelka feel the need to doctor the tapes? They had on tape Bangaru Laxman taking money. He never denied it. They had on tape Jaya Jaitly's lengthy explanation on how the money would be used. As far as the Tehelka journalists were concerned, they had proof of corruption. Why would they feel the need to spend aeons of time and money to add a word or two here and there?

Luthra asked Godavarthy if he was correct in assuming that he had no experience in forensics. Godavarthy replied, 'No sir, I don't'. What Bangaru Laxman's lawyer had done was to bring a man who owned an editing studio, who showed editing tricks on tapes and lawyers in the Commission, unfamiliar with editing, reacted with enthralled awe: 'See, anything is possible. They doctored the tapes'. It was strange that Justice Venkataswami, who could be quite firm in stopping irrelevant questions sometimes allowed these dramas to be played out on copies of edited broadcast tape as the template. All questions on doctoring should have been restricted to the original tapes.

Gopal Subramanium, counsel for the Commission, asked Godavarthy, in a suspicious tenor, about his attendance of the Commission on two days when he had signed the visitors' book once as G.S. Kartic and the second time as Kartic C. Godavarthy. He also asked Godavarthy about the address he had written in the visitors' book, 3 Kushak Road, which happened to be Bangaru Laxman's address.

Well, if Jaya Jaitly can spend Rs 5 lakh to obtain a report from Chris Mills and fly him from London to Delhi, surely Godavarthy flown in from Hyderabad by Bangaru Laxman is not something to get your gown in a twist about. Crucially however, it revealed the Commission counsel's perspective of the witness. Subramanium was unimpressed by Godavarthy's act.

Anand Patwardhan was Tehelka's next witness on doctoring. Patwardhan has made some groundbreaking films, and his work has inspired respect. His educational qualifications, which were brought out in his deposition are really redundant, since his films have far surpassed the weight of his college degrees. For the record, he has a BA degree from Bombay University, a BA from Brandeis University (USA), and a master's degree in Communications from McGill University in Canada. In his testimony, Patwardhan saw no possibility of doctoring and said there was regular editing in the four-and-a-half hour version.

Hariharan, lawyer for P. Sasi, asked him 201 questions. Again the questions revolved around creating confusion between the edited tapes and the originals. An example:

> **Hariharan:** The second aspect that I wanted to put to you is that did you think that a layperson, by just simply viewing, would be in a position to say whether the edits, the cuts, the dissolves have been ethical or unethical or they have been at the right portions or whether there has been tampering?
> **Patwardhan:** I think the word tampering in regard to editing is a redundancy because editing means tampering. Editing means that you have changed the original. If you say that it is an edited tape, it is obvious that it is an edited version and not the original version.
> **Hariharan:** Then you said that if it is an edited tape, it is a tampered tape.

O, let me out of here. The vacuity of Hariharan's questioning that followed showed nothing more than the goal to delay, distract and destroy the Commission. Hariharan asked around 15 questions about who asked Patwardhan to look at the West End tapes, on what date, at what time, under what conditions, whether he lived near Hindu College and the digits of his phone number. You would think all this was leading somewhere. Think again. Is there someone in some corner of the world logging every second of how he spends his day, just in case he has to account for it in court one day? And then to show his sleuthing acumen he shouted that Patwardhan could not have seen the Operation West End broadcast because the cable supplier in the area that he lived in Mumbai (INCABLE) did not broadcast the one from Zee TV. Hariharan then announced that Patwardhan was lying to the Commission. Lying about what? That he sneakily watched the Operation West End tapes on a different day than when they were broadcast?

Hariharan asked Patwardhan to explain why he had written in his report that if a word here or there did not make a difference if it was changed in the tapes. Patwardhan stated that if visually you could see money being handed over it made little difference if Bangaru Laxman said 'I do know' or 'I don't know'.

Patwardhan had made a point in his affidavit that he had noticed that the audio and visuals were out of sync in the Zee TV broadcast. It is not an unusual phenomenon in television broadcasts and can occur with the most superior equipment. Then Hariharan gave Patwardhan a platform to display what he thought of him, the lawyer:

> **Hariharan:** Who told you that it was done on Adobe Premier software?
> **Patwardhan:** I do not remember who told me. But I have a distinct impression that it was done on Adobe Premiere software. I might have heard it from

Tehelka people themselves or I think I have read it here. I am not sure. It is one of the two.

Hariharan: Whosoever has told, you believed it?

Patwardhan: Yes, I believed it.

Hariharan: If I tell you that it was not done on Adobe Premier software, will you believe it?

Patwardhan: Not as readily.

Hariharan: You will not believe me. What is the reason? But you will believe others. Do you want me to change my language?

Patwardhan: No, I am just saying that my belief system depends on my overall evaluation of the people. So, I cannot have the same yardstick or belief.

You asked for it, Hariharan, you got it.

Patwardhan didn't get all those degrees for nothing. The rest of the questions consist of Hariharan doubting Patwardhan's credibility, technical knowledge, and juxtaposing Godavarthy's deposition against his. If the lawyer's aim was to create reasonable doubt about the authenticity of the tapes, the only point that was successfully established was that the various lawyers of those Caught on Tape were taking the Commission on a long diversionary ride.

The lawyers representing Lieutenant Colonel V.P. Sayal, Narender Singh, Bangaru Laxman, Jaya Jaitly, all frolicked through the same shenanigans. Patwardhan was asked a total of 690 questions.

Tehelka then produced their third witness in relation to doctoring: Pradip Krishen, who has 30 documentary films to his credit as well as three feature films. His first film *Massey Sahib* won two international awards. His other two films, *In Which Annie Gives it Those Ones* and *Electric Moon* both won national awards. Krishen has lectured at AFTERS (Australian Film, Television Radio School in Sydney). A history graduate from Delhi University, and the recipient of another arts degree from Oxford University, Krishen taught history at Delhi University for five years before making films. He viewed around 15 tapes of the camera originals when the Commission was showing them.

Krishen, in his low key, unpretentious manner, junked Milin Kapoor's contentions, explaining that in looking at the original tapes all the points raised by Kapoor were clarified by what you observe. Krishen said that dissolves in editing are a simple, transition device. They are not in any way indicative of tampering. Krishen said that the sudden sounds that Kapoor treats as proof of tampering are normal in any uncontrolled shoot, such as doors banging and teacups being put down. He did say that it was fortunate that Tehelka happened to use Hi8 with AFM sound, where it is not possible to add or remove any piece of sound without adding and removing the corresponding picture. He stated categorically that Milin Kapoor was misinformed when he said it was possible.

Krishen reiterated Umashankar's view that the audio blank spots on the VHS tapes that were reviewed by Milin Kapoor would have occurred because of dropouts caused in making of copies. What about the examples of tampering, where Milin Kapoor demonstrates how you could take out words and put different ones in? Krishen pointed out that if there was any lesson to be learnt from Milin Kapoor's demonstration of 'doctoring', it was that it was so easy to catch that kind of tampering. There was a clear discontinuity in the background sound, despite the advantages Kapoor had over Tehelka with superior equipment, directional mikes, a DV camera and an environment completely under his control. This was exactly what Umashankar had demonstrated by removing the words in the audio and only listening to the background.

Nilay Dutta, Jaya Jaitly's lawyer, zeroed in on Krishen about 'leading the cross-examination' of Milin Kapoor the day before. Aggressively, Dutta demanded, 'Do you think it behoves on an expert's independence to help?' Krishen was not in the least defensive, 'In the same way that you have claimed that you know this is outside the area of what you are familiar with, they expressed the same sentiment.' Krishen, in fact, went even further and said, 'In fact, I was rather surprised that Mr Milin Kapoor, who initially said that he was an objective film-maker who was presenting certain testimony, later turned out to be Jaya Jaitly's witness. I mean, that struck me as being rather odd and certainly shook me when I was sitting there and listening to him.'

In his effort to discredit Krishen's deposition, Dutta then got personal:

Dutta: Are you married?
Krishen: Yes.
Dutta: Can I have the name of your wife?
Krishen: Arundhati Roy.
Dutta: Arundhati Roy published a novel called, rather wrote a novel called *God of Small Things*. Who is the publisher?
Krishen: The publisher of which edition? There are 43 editions. Well, shall I start with the Norwegian edition, the publisher is someone called …
Dutta: Was this novel at any point of time published by IndiaInk?
Krishen: IndiaInk, that's correct.
Dutta: Who is one of the co-founder of this IndiaInk?
Krishen: Mr Sanjeev Saith and Mr Tarun Tejpal.
Dutta: And this Tarun Tejpal is in Tehelka.
Krishen: Yes.
Dutta: Your wife Mrs Arundhati Roy had to file an affidavit in reply to the honourable Supreme Court regarding Tehelka tapes. She brought in the matter relating to Tehelka tapes in her affidavit in reply to the Supreme Court. Are you aware of it?
Krishen: Yes, I am.
Dutta: Can you tell the Commission the contents of that portion regarding Tehelka tapes?
Krishen: Arundhati Roy made the point in her reply to the Supreme Court that if the Supreme Court – the Chief Justice had said that they could not spare a sitting judge to look in the affairs of the Tehelka tapes – how come that they

could spare a sitting judge to look into a case that was as frivolous as the case brought against Mrs Medha Patkar, Arundhati Roy and Mr Prashant Bhushan together. That was the substance of what she said. I don't see the connection but …

Dutta: Shall I say that you are not a very independent witness and your opinion here is faulted by bias, in favour of Tehelka?

Krishen: I deny that completely.

Krishen was then questioned by the babble rouser C.M. Khanna, counsel for Brigadier Iqbal Singh. The Commission was treated to hilarious, phoney, techno gobbledegook. Sample this:

Khanna: This merging which you has said so that it does not pinch the eye, so the merging which takes place a transition when it is made smooth is in terms of one parameter, both the parameters and I said parameters light and sound I am concentrating on that. In case of light and sound it is the both. If it is both, if both the parameters are corrected, I am using the word "corrected" for the purpose of – you have used the words "toning down", "merging" because from cut to a dissolve when the transition is taking place, so that effect of one place to the other has got to be merged in fashion some sort of compromise, some sort of a treatment to both the parameters has got perforce technically to be given both to the light parameters as well as to the sound parameters.

Krishen: I fail to understand your statement that is made. You said some sort of treatment has to be given to the parameters?

Khanna: Treatment in the laymen's terms, technologically how you produce the effect of this, that is what is called treatment. Some sort of what treatments will come subsequently. Some sort of treatment has got to be given for the purpose of creating a dissolve which deals with both elements, the sound as well as the light.

Krishen: I am really not sure what you mean, but shall we proceed beyond that because …

Khanna: You are a technical man. You may not have technical qualification but you have got sufficient experience.

Krishen: Your question is not sufficiently precise. You said some sort of "treatment" is given. I don't know what you mean.

Khanna: In creating a dissolve and the merging has to take place on the one side it is very bright thing other side it is very dull. From bright to dull when you are the two frames are being made to other. Naturally that particular effect which is brightness here you may be sitting here in Kashmir and tomorrow you are in Kanyakumari and when you are, that particular dancer may be carrying out her performance in the one frame up to a particular frame, and in the same type of environment it may be created another frame and the two are merged, when they are merged together naturally both the light and the sound parameters have got to be adjusted so that you do not feel the transition. The transition remains smooth. This is what you have said, smooth case of a dissolve. That is what I am saying the treatment now, is it clear. The treatment in both the parameter …

Krishen: I am sorry, it is not clear at all what you are saying.

I would like some of whatever Khanna is smoking. Krishen's behaviour is completely inappropriate. He is steadfastly polite. More appropriate behaviour would have been if he fell down roaring with laughter.

If it wasn't costing the country so much, Khanna should get an award for his futile ingenuity. Get this:

Khanna: Can I request you and tell me that what type of these glasses you are wearing?

Krishen: What is the power of it?

Khanna: Yes.

Krishen: The power is −2.5.

Khanna: Only −2.5? [Sounds disappointed.] Something more also? Is it bifocal?

Krishen: No, it is not bifocal.

Khanna: Yes, yes, because you have been, I asked your capacity to judge. Because the question is, you said that you have been viewing the tapes and you have been able to identify, I do not know whether you can possibly or …. Mr Dutta is sitting there. Can you give a description of his right hand which is there now from where you are standing?

Krishen: His right hand is clutching a black pen between his index finger and his middle finger.

Khanna: It may be noted please. Your Lordship, it is between the little finger and …

Krishen: I didn't say "little" finger. I said middle finger and index finger. His chin is resting on, probably his thumb which is hidden behind his hand …

Khanna: I will now request that we have talked regarding the dissolve, the words interpolation and there you have said certain things that things from one place to the other like the example what Milin Kapoor gave us regarding the Bush and Osama. It can be interchanged, certain portion can be cut. By this interpolation, does within the definition of tampering, the addition also comes?

Krishen: I'm not sure I understand your question.

Bang your head three times and it makes sense. Or does it? Checking on the power of his glasses? Could Khanna have seen *My Cousin Vinny* (1992; film starring Joe Pesci and Marisa

Tomei) or is he following the Bollywood justice system? Khanna was giving his client his money's worth. Now this:

Khanna: Basically the light is composed of as we have learned seven colours and those are the colours of the rainbow. Is this theory still good?

Krishen: If you like. It is more complicated than that. Let's assume for a moment that you are correct.

Khanna: I am asking is this theory in keeping in view you being an expert in this, this is a question with the subject of the science of light, I have asked you this question whether this theory is still good?

Krishen: Well, light is composed of wavelengths …

Khanna: I said the basic elements like colours such as VIBGYOR what we say, the seven colours of the rainbow, this theory is still good or is there any other elements more than those seven elements?

Krishen: Are there any more primary colours other than those colours; no, there are not, if that is the question.

Khanna: If I suggest to you that all the innovations which are taking place with the advancement of technology, they are based on the Vibgyor resolution by digital stimulation and collative techniques, do you have got any comment on this? Can you say this is correct or wrong?

Krishen: Can you repeat the question?

Khanna: In the field relating with this type of technology where the analysis of light is the subject matter. There is this Vibgyor resolution by digital simulation and collative techniques, is the basic science which is in use. These are the basic techniques which are used.

Krishen: I am not sure. I am not a physicist. I am not aware of this. I have no opinion on the matter. I am not a physicist, but I am aware also that through digital techniques you can do a lot of simulation which certainly bypasses the kind of fundamental physics you are talking about.

Khanna: The theory of these techniques, if it is put across to you with its mathematical interpretations, when if you put across these mathematical interpretation.

Krishen: I would not understand. If you gave me a theory with mathematical interpretations I would not understand it.

Khanna: The basic terms, the mathematical terms, the integration and differentiation, not only that I have heard but just from the working knowledge, do you understand these two terms?

Krishen: Do I understand what differentiation and integration are? Well, only from school days maths, not beyond that.

Khanna: School days, when you say that is up to class?

Krishen: Class 11, in my days …

Khanna: Why I have asked this question is, I will put for you because these are the basic qualifications which are required to understand technological development and a scientific basis to come to the conclusion whether there is a possibility in science of these development or it is not. I will explain this position to you. I hand over a Rolls Royce car to you. You may be a good driver. You may be able to maintain the car very well. I am suggesting to you that you do not have the technical qualification to comment upon the technicalities which are involved in the present issue about the possibility. It is only your experience but technically you are not qualified.

Krishen: I am not an audio-engineer. I don't have any engineering background. Yes, it's only based on my experience. I accept that.

Khanna is Puff the Magic Dragon flying with Lucy in the Sky with Diamonds. Khanna's method of investigation, dialectical obfuscation, was the leitmotif of the Commission of Inquiry. Pradip Krishen was asked 292 questions of a similar nature. More repetitive questions, the biggest disadvantage to anyone attending the Commission every single day. The lawyers were not and did not know what had been asked previously.

On 12 October 2001, Justice Venkataswami turned down Jaya Jaitly's plea that the tapes be sent for forensic examination. He said in his order, 'No prima-facie case about doctoring has been made out at all. It is inappropriate at this juncture to refer the unedited tapes in the custody of the Commission to a panel of experts.' On 14 January 2002, Justice Venkataswami again rejected Jaya Jaitly's plea to send the tapes for forensic examination. His order read, 'It finds no reason to send the tapes for examination as there was no case made out so far.' Again he found no prima facie evidence to support Jaya Jaitly's plea. Venkataswami did add that after the examination of all noticees, 'If a case is made out for examination, the Commission will consider it.'

On 29 April 2003, when the newly-appointed Justice Phukan chose to listen to arguments on Jaya Jaitly's plea to send the tapes for forensic examination, C.M. Khanna, the lawyer for Brigadier Iqbal Singh began the arguments, making a case for the necessity to ask Tehelka to submit their cameras and the editing machines on which they had worked. Khanna pointed out that Tehelka was using the cameras for all kinds of things, such as, filming wildlife poaching. The cameras could be confiscated or destroyed. He asked the Commission to ask Tehelka to submit the cameras.

Jaya Jaitly's lawyer interrupted, 'If the cameras have been destroyed, does it mean the veracity of the tapes cannot be determined? The tapes should be sent for examination even without the cameras.' He wanted to ensure that the forensic examination of the tapes was not derailed if the cameras were not available. Khanna then detailed the discrepancies he saw in the tapes. He pointed out that Aniruddha Bahal had admitted in his deposition that copies had been made of the tapes, even though he said the originals were with the Commission. According to Khanna, Mathew Samuel is seen in two different coloured shirts in the tape that is supposed to be one continuous tape. Then he went into some contortionist argument about Samuel's shadow falling in a different direction than earlier. It sounded like feverish detective work but what on earth did it prove? Khanna said that Tarun Tejpal had admitted that Anand Patwardhan had made a film using the Tehelka tapes. Therefore, in Khanna's view, there was no way of figuring out who had the originals.

Sunil Kumar, Bangaru Laxman's lawyer, stated that the onus of proving the genuineness of the tapes lay on Tehelka. Kumar said they had only received copies of the edited tapes which had no evidential value. He had brought in an expert to prove, on the basis of the VHS tapes he had, that they had been doctored. He said that as Tehelka had not provided the make of the camera and had not produced any member of the editing team, there was no evidence to prove that these were the original tapes. Kumar pointed out, 'In view of the evidence recorded, the tapes stand totally discredited'.

Hariharan, P. Sasi's lawyer argued that it was clear that copies of the tapes did exist. He said, there was no telling whether or not it was the originals that were with the Commission. If it turned out that the tapes were copies, he argued, they could not be used as evidence. Hariharan showed examples in the tapes that, according to him, were discrepancies. He said the same girl was in Tape 1 and Tape 4, though there were supposed to be two different girls. Hariharan pointed out that two tapes had been submitted that were identical. If they were originals then how could there be two tapes of the same event? He also said that when two cameras were working on one event, only one tape had been submitted. That could only mean some tapes had been withheld from the Commission. When Mathew Samuel was questioned about a break in the tape, he answered, 'I do not know'. Hariharan shouted, 'Their saying, "I do not know" is fatal to them. They are the makers of the film. They cannot say, "I don't know"'. The break in the tape could be for any number of reasons. The camera could have been switched on and off. There could have been a technical problem. There could have been a sound drop while editing. But this was an invidious interpretation to an answer.

Then the attorney general, Soli Sorabjee took the floor and set forth his argument: All doubts about the tampering with the tapes should be put to rest by sending them for forensic examination. Jaya's knight in shining armour played his role well. Sorabjee is naturally chivalrous. His court craft, reputation, logic, wit, all combined to lend his argument weight. Justice Phukan was a good listener.

Soli Sorabjee had participated in the Tehelka Commission innumerable times. As attorney general, was he making this plea to ensure justice was done? Were the Union of India lawyers not representative enough? What was the necessity for the attorney general of India to argue in favour of a plea put in by Jaya Jaitly?

Sorabjee read Venkataswami's order rejecting Jaya Jaitly's plea rather selectively. He stressed, 'so far' and further stressed, 'the Commission will consider it'. He simply eliminated, 'It finds no reason to send the tapes for examination as there was no case made out' and reiterated 'so far'. Sorabjee, in his wisdom, pointed out that the Commissioner had kept an open mind on this subject. The fact that Venkataswami had not changed his mind despite three pleas from Jaya Jaitly was not touched upon. Sorabjee stated, 'It must be proven without reasonable doubt that the tapes have not been tampered with.'

Jaya Jaitly whispered to me, 'This is the first time the government is standing up and saying what I have been saying. Even in the High Court they didn't say it.' Jaya continued,

'The option is the judge can reject it and not even send it to forensic experts. We could have had it thrown out in the earlier arguments on custody, but the mood was not right. I wanted hundred per cent proof that they were doctored. Nobody would have listened if I had said, "don't look at them".'

Sorabjee continued, 'The possibility of tampering is there. Today the gaps are there. The doubts are there. My learned friend, Hariharan has so vividly shown. I haven't seen a James Bond film for a long time, but this was better than that.' He just made it sexy for the lawyers, and this evoked titters in the sleepy room.

Sorabjee insisted,

> Every possibility of tampering or of erasing part of the tape must be proven before they can be admissible as evidence. Has there or has there not been tampering on the tape? It boils down to the conscience of the Commission. Does it require a probe to say there has been no tampering? Should a paper dogma of infallibility be followed? The Commission should not deprive itself of getting down to the bottom of this.

The attorney general's movement in sitting down was neutral.

A simple question: should it boil down to only the Commission's conscience or should somebody else's conscience also be considered? During Indira Gandhi's Emergency in 1975, those who opposed it, not only went to jail but suffered severe harassment. As for the collaborators, there were people who made the choice of clinging to jobs that could only be maintained if they supported Indira Gandhi. When the Janata Party took over from Indira Gandhi in 1977, collaborators heads were not shaved, as was the done in World War II to anyone consorting with the enemy. Had there been, there would have been thousands of bald heads which would have included some in the media, judiciary, senior bureaucrats, and a president of India. Indian history is replete with examples where choices made by key people who decided to collaborate with power, even though it was against moral conscience. This happened even during India's struggle for freedom from the British. In the fight for independence, in the battle for freedom of speech during the Emergency, the battlelines were drawn clearly in black and white. In smaller instances, when the individual is not particularly aware of public scrutiny and their judgement, a dangerous insouciance, deliquesces the conscience. It is easy to be brave when you are a soldier amongst legionnaires, but true valour is when you stand alone. Many will never forget, that on 5 June 1989, in Tiananmen Square, Beijing, an unfaltering man stood alone in front of seventeen or more tanks, unwilling to step out of their path. As the tanks attempted to go around him, he would step in towards them again and again. After blocking the tanks for nearly 30 minutes, he climbed up on to one of them and spoke to the driver. No one has ever identified him for certain. He disappeared. That kind of valour is indelible. The Tehelka episode introduced a new set of collaborators who worked with the government in power to destroy journalists and their investors. These collaborators must know in their hearts that they are tonsured.

One of the lawyers for the Commission, Sudarshan Mishra, then stood up and said that it was not a question of whether there were sufficient grounds for forensic examination. It should be done if there was reasonable doubt about the originality of the tapes and their having been doctored. Another lawyer for the Commission, Kotoki, declared that as Tehelka had withdrawn from the Commission, it was even more vital to take into account Tehelka's view. He drew the Commission's attention to the fact that the Tehelka team had stated under oath that these were camera originals. Kotoki said, 'They would not lie'. He went on to say that Tarun Tejpal had stated repeatedly that he was not involved in the editing process. Anniruddha Bahal had said in his deposition that the sanctity of the tapes was maintained and copies were made under his supervision. Kotoki reiterated that Tehelka had said the question of the custody of the tapes was never brought up. He reminded Justice Phukan that the question before the Commission was whether the tapes with the Commission were originals or copies. Jaya Jaitly's expert witness on doctoring, Chris Mills, had stated that tampering is impossible on original tapes because the audio and visuals are intertwined. They could be transferred to digital format where anything can be manipulated.

Justice Phukan then asked Kotoki, 'Except for Umashankar [Tehelka's expert witness on doctoring of tapes] they are all saying that they can be tampered with. What is Chris Mills saying?'

Kotoki answered, 'Mills says it cannot be done unless it is transferred. The question before your Lordship is, that the opinion should be sought under the Evidence Act to determine whether they are original tapes. Your Lordship is not bound to accept their opinion.'

On 9 May 2003 Justice Phukan, in his first decision as chairman, dramatically reversed Justice Venkataswami's rulings and, in a detailed 31-page order, ordered a forensic examination of the tapes. This was Phukan's answer to Jaya Jaitly's new application to send the tapes for forensic examination overruling Justice Venkataswami's earlier decisions. Phukan wrote in his order: 'These doubts have to be removed and the truth has to be found. The examination of the original is essential in order to come to a conclusion as to the veracity of the tapes.' He said he believed that, 'In any case, no prejudice will be caused to Tehelka if the tapes are sent for forensic examination'. Phukan said in his order: 'It has definitely come out that once an Hi8 tape with AFM soundtrack is put to a computer, editing, tampering, doctoring etc. can be done.' Tehelka had never claimed that editing was not done for the four-and-a-half hour broadcast. Phukan stated in his order:

> These instances have prima facie created serious doubts in the mind of the Commission that the tapes submitted by Tehelka might be tampered and/or not the camera originals. This view is not only based upon the evidence on record but also based on watching the tapes and the demonstration of the videotapes.

Phukan pointed out that law must be in a state of progress and adapt itself to change and should not remain behind the times. The commissioner was quoting almost directly from Sorabjee's plea. He maintained that the tapes were primary evidence and a foundation of the present inquiry. Sixteen tapes were sent for forensic examination, excluding the so-called 'scurrilous tapes'.

Justice Phukan asked the noticees where the tapes should be sent for forensic examination. A curious enquiry that could be likened to asking a murderer to suggest a judge under whom he would like to be tried. In India, that choice can mean whether you live or die. Jaya Jaitly and other noticees' lawyers were at a loss. Justice Phukan then asked them to find out and return on 19 May with the names and addresses of forensic laboratories.

On 27 May 2003, Kirit Rawal (the late), counsel for the Union of India, said in the Commission hearings that they had some names of laboratories that could conduct the forensic examinations. He clarified, 'We are only suggesting names but it is entirely up to the Commission because tomorrow I don't want it said that we influenced the conclusion.' Rawal reassured the Commission, 'As far as expenses, there is no problem. The government will provide it.' Yes, but why is the government so willing to pay for it? As taxpayers, do the people of India want their money spent on this exercise?

Nilay Dutta, representing Jaya Jaitly, wondered how it could be ensured that the packets were not opened by the customs authorities at airports. It was his view that the sealed packets should only be opened by experts.

Kirit Rawal was quick to assure him that the tapes could go in the diplomatic pouch. At this point, Brigadier Iqbal Singh's lawyer, C.M. Khanna jumped up and said, 'Without knowing the cameras, how can we ascertain they are the camera originals?' Justice Phukan informed Khanna that he had decided that if the forensic experts asked for the cameras, they would be sent. When Khanna continued to push his argument that the tapes should not be sent without the cameras, Justice Phukan, visibly amused, told him, 'You are opposing your own affidavit.' Rawal interjected and said, 'Let the tapes go. If required we can issue warrants for the cameras.'

Then the scene turned into a satirical comedy. Justice Phukan asked all the noticees or their lawyers to come to the centre of the room and witness the tapes being placed in sealed boxes. Small steel boxes that are normally used by government employees to carry lunch were brought in. They all gathered around the tapes and boxes. There was an air of great satisfaction as they witnessed the tapes being placed in the lunch boxes. How they ascertained which tapes were being put in is anybody's guess. Documents containing the depositions of various noticees, with markings of the disputed portions of the tapes were also included. The Commission also put in Aniruddha Bahal's affidavit with details of the equipment used in the recordings. Jaya Jaitly's expert witness, Milin Kapoor's deposition, including a spectrogram made by him formed part of the package. The Commission enclosed a sealed envelope with the keys of the box and a sample of the seal of the Commission. Justice Phukan stated that the identity of the expert would not be disclosed to any party and would be maintained in a confidential file.

That afternoon, Jaya Jaitly and her lawyers stepped out of the Commission room laughing and congratulating one another. Jaya invited all of them to 3, Krishna Menon Marg to celebrate with cake.

The army officers looked a little more optimistic than usual. If the tapes were declared to have been doctored, there was hope for them.

On 19 September 2003, excited COT and LOCOT, along with reporters, jostled with each other in the Commission room. There was anticipatory excitement that the forensic reports had arrived and Justice Phukan would declare that the tapes had been doctored. It turned out to be a bore of a limp squib when it was announced that the forensic laboratory could not say for certain whether the tapes had been doctored or not. They were doubtful about certain areas of the tape. The forensic examiners said they needed to look at the original cameras to be certain. Tehelka, faced with the confiscation of their cameras and lacking any faith in the direction the Commission was going, found themselves back in the Commission. Prashant Bhushan argued vociferously that if their cameras were going to be confiscated, they wanted to ensure that the signature numbers of the cameras were recorded in their presence in the Commission. Tehelka was also interested in the possibility of having the forensic experts flown in so they could observe them examining the tapes in their presence in the Commission. Two weeks later, Tehelka returned to the Commission with their cameras, where the numbers were recorded.

The tapes were sent when the BJP coalition was in power. By the time the report came in, the government had changed. Now it was the Congress-led coalition. On 31 May 2004, Kapil Sibal, minister of state for science and technology, pre-empted the Commission of Inquiry by announcing that the tapes that had been sent for forensic examination had been declared genuine. On 21 June 2004, the forensic expert, Mathew J. Cass, Bureau of Forensic Science Ltd, appointed by the Commission to examine the Tehelka tapes, handed in his report and declared that the tapes were originals and had not been tampered with. The Bureau of Forensic Science also included a letter that declared to the Commission that Tehelka.com had contacted them by email requesting an interview with Cass. The letter stated that the Indian correspondent of *The Guardian* seeking interviews had also contacted Cass, but he had refused all interviews. The Bureau also pointed out that, 'However, from what they [Tehelka and *The Guardian* reporters] said it would appear that a minister has pre-empted Mr Cass's evidence to the Commission and we have found reference to this on at least one website.'

Mathew Cass is associate director for the Department of Electronic Evidence and senior video audio and imaging expert at the Bureau of Forensic Science. Cass has a BSc degree in Photographic and Electronic Imaging and Science, and an MSc degree in Medical Illustration. He has worked on hundreds of cases involving processing, enhancement, and presentation of evidential video and other imagery. The Bureau of Forensic Science charges £150 an hour or £1000 a day. Cass was sent 15 Hi8 tapes and one Mini DV tape for examination. He also received five CDs, which were exhibits from Jaya Jaitly's lawyers and three volumes of supplementary paperwork. The applications were from Colonel Anil Sehgal, Brigadier Iqbal Singh, Major General P.S.K. Choudary, R.K. Gupta, and Jaya Jaitly. Cass chose to view the tapes in short periods of time, no longer than 20 minutes each, with frequent breaks to ensure high levels of concentration. The tapes were seen on a monitor with an under scan facility, so that he could observe the entire picture area, even that obscured by the normal 10 per cent masking. This allowed him to observe the head-switching points on playback of the analogue tapes to check whether there was any evidence of previously recorded points. He examined the structure of the signal coming from the tapes to ascertain whether there had been any sign of re-recording using an H-V delay monitor, waveform monitor, and vector scope. He examined the points on the tapes when the recording ended to ascertain whether there was any discrepancy between the ends of the recording on any of the tracks on the tape. The general characteristics of the material recorded on to the videotapes, such as noise in the picture, geometry of the optics used, edits, type of material being recorded, and type of audiotrack used on the system were checked.

Cass also took a look at the edited programme to assess the standard of sophistication involved in the production. He evaluated the level of technical expertise that would be required to produce a 'false original' tape that could pass all the tests he applied to the tapes given to him as originals. Cass appraised the Tehelka cameras in the briefcase, handbag, tie, and satchel.

In Cass's written opinion: 'There is nothing to indicate that the tapes supplied to me by the Justice S.N. Phukan Commission of Inquiry are not the "camera originals" made at the time of the incidents depicted. There is significant evidence to support the contention that they are the 'camera originals'.

About the edited tape, Cass said,

> If edits have occurred, it is no surprise that they are missed by the lay viewer, because the sign of a good editor is that their work goes unnoticed by the viewers. However, if the viewer is looking for edits and has experience of editing then a straightforward edit can be identified. There is also a language of editing, in which certain type of edit is used to convey an impression to the audience. Modern audiences know this language as they are exposed to it every day while watching films and television. Therefore, they accept these conventions subconsciously without realizing why. If these conventions are contravened then this will usually disturb the viewer.

Cass had found discrepancies in both the transcripts of the tapes, which did not surprise anyone.

With reference to a point at which Milin Kapoor and Kartic C. Godavarthy had identified tampering, Cass said the edit only removed a 'bang' sound in the background and no words had been removed. A question had been raised by Brigadier Iqbal Singh's lawyer that the sequences of the meeting were wrong. Cass's response was that the tapes appear to be recorded in chronological order. The money does appear to have been handed over at the end of the meeting and the mention of '50,000 bucks' is at the beginning. He stated that 'the implication that the chronology of the meeting has been changed is inaccurate in my opinion'.

In answer to the question about non-synchronized audio and video, Cass said,

> I have mentioned above that there is evidence of poor proofing of the final master and my opinion is that just because the audio and video are "out of

sync" does not imply that the material contained in the sequence is suspect. It does match to the original even though it is "out of sync". There are a number of ways that one can "un-sync" audio and video in Premiere without any great difficulty and on a four-and-a-half hour video this would be very easy to miss.

Major General P.S.K. Choudary's lawyer had asked a question about the word 'commission', as he had sought to believe it was 'commercial'. Cass disagreed and said that the word, was indeed 'commission'.

On Jaya Jaitly's tape there were two cameras used. One in the tie and one in the briefcase. Her lawyers asked Cass to explain the difference between the two recordings. Cass said, 'This is explained by the fact that Tape 73 has been recorded in Standard Play mode while Tape 74, like all other tapes, has been recorded in Long Play mode, which will reduce the quality of the recording.' Why then is the image from the tie camera better?

The subject matter is different in both. In the room on Tape 73 there is a light source, which means the AGC in the system will not try and compensate for the low light levels. This will result in a less noisy picture. Finally, Tehelka did not state it was of a much lower quality, just that it was "defiantly inferior", which is true.

They also asked, 'Do the two tapes run concurrently. Is there a break in the recording of Tape 73?' Cass replied,

The tapes do run concurrently until 00:20:37 on Tape 73, when a break of approximately 22 and a half seconds occurs. The tapes then run in sync with noises recorded on both. This is most likely because the system was paused then re-started. It is my understanding that the wearer could control the system.

How did Cass explain the switching off and on during the recording? In this, he reiterated Mathew Samuel's position that he was switching it off to conserve battery. Jaya said it was done deliberately but Mathew Samuel countered, 'If people are just doing social chit chat, I switch off. Nothing deliberayte. How I know vaat she going to say?' Cass stated,

The only break during the meeting is the one already stated, and as stated, the wearer could control the system. One reason for this could be an attempt to conserve tape time, as this is the only tape recorded in Standard Play mode, thus reducing the available time for recording. There is no break in recording at this point.

On the crucial words 'CD West End' and 'Two lakhs, doh', which Milin Kapoor had insisted were insertions, Jaya's lawyers wanted to know why there were differences in tone and audio level during the utterance of specific words. Cass pointed out,

This is down to the speakers being in close proximity to the microphone and the AGC [Automatic Gain Control] on the audio system being set for quieter speech. There is also the possibility that the microphone has moved. I cannot hear any musical beats on the original tapes or my copy of the edited tapes.

On the same tape, the lawyers asked about the words 'speed *meh lelo*' said by Samuel in a panic after his meeting with Jaya. Cass answered,

Yes, at 00:38:04:00. There is another break in Tape 73 at approximately 00:37:29:00. The conversation is therefore truncated, which is most likely due to a pause in recording, then a restart.

Cass concluded his report with,

There have been no "high end" special effects applied to the edited material and material itself does not lend itself to this type of work. If special effects are to be used in a programme, the material is specially shot. This would require a lot of time and patience to achieve a believable result.

In a mega-spin doctoring exercise, Jaya turned Cass's forensic report around in a statement given through her counsel:

In view of the various specific opinions of the expert, it would be naïve to conclude the allegations regarding tampering and malicious editing of the tapes have in any way, been disproved. In fact, the expert has simply referred the matter back to the Commission for final decision on the issue of malicious editing, which he says he is not competent to render an opinion on.

Jaya's lawyers also said that 'several allegations raised against the veracity of the tapes were prima facie substantiated by the opinions contained in the report', adding,

The findings rendered on various specific queries have greatly strengthened the case of Jaya Jaitly. Certain specific queries do not appear to have, however, been adequately dealt with in the report and we intend to explore these areas in course of the examination of Mathew James Cass, the expert on June 23.

So? On 23 June 2004, Mathew James Cass appeared before the Commission. Cass had handed in the report, he stood by it but was unwilling to take a position on 'malicious editing', which he believed was not his job in any case. Yes, the Commission could declare that there was malicious editing but there is a huge gulf between tampering with the tapes and malicious editing.

On 23 June 2004, S.K. Misra, senior counsel for the Commission, got Cass to clarify what he meant:

Misra: The very first point in your report: "There has been editing of the material contained in the original tapes." What is your reference with regard to original tapes and the released tapes of four-and-a-half hours? Could you please clarify this?

Cass: For me the material contained means material taken from the original tapes onto an editing suite and if that has been edited. I do not mean that the original Hi8 tapes have been edited, and I apologize if that has caused confusion.

C.M. Khanna, lawyer for Brigadier Iqbal Singh and Nilay Dutta for Jaya Jaitly interrogated Cass and attempted to re-establish that the tapes had been tampered with. Dr K.N. Khetarpal, lawyer for Major General P.S.K. Choudary and R.P. Sharma for Colonel Anil Sehgal joined in the attempt to try to discredit Cass's report. The Union of India lawyers repeatedly objected to the badgering of the witness. In truth, Khanna was caught unawares at the sudden change of stance in the Union of India lawyers, as they had been replaced by the new UPA government, which he pointed it out to the judge, 'See, what is happening here. How things have changed. I don't know what is going on.'

According to Sidharth Luthra, 'The defence for the COT was focused to prove the journalists to be liars. This was of no help to them as that alone would not affect the veracity of the contents of the tapes. The Tehelka teams testimony was not shaken and those COT admitted their actions during their cross examinations.'

The question remained: Why was Jaya so obsessed with the 'doctoring' of the tapes? Was it enough for her to create a doubt so her lawyers could use it? Okay, let's give her the benefit of the doubt and accept she did not hear 'West End'. But that turns out to be immaterial. Jaya accepted money in the defence minister's home. If she was absolutely straight, why did she not do what the honest bureaucrat Doodani did, which is, throw them out of the office and scream that such hanky panky does not take place here. One would imagine that she would be incensed that someone could come into the defence minister's home and presumptuously offer her a packet of money. She could have told them that yes, such practices do take place, but not with her. She could have told them that there was a proper route for a party donation. She did nothing of the kind. Instead, she elaborated on how the party would use the money.

Jaya Jaitly fumed throughout this hearing, muttering in frustration, while Milin Kapoor, the architect of Jaya's belief that the tapes had been doctored, gave up picking his nose and dozed off. It was more than disappointing for her because Jaya genuinely believed that the tapes had been doctored. She had fought and fought hard for the tapes to be forensically examined because she had faith that it would expose Tehelka. It was her 'cause'. How was it that she never thought of the alternative? What if? What if the tapes proved to be genuine with no hint of tampering? It had all turned on her. How would she look back at this period in her life? Would her grandchildren be taught that this was the one story they should never ask Jaya to relate? Tehelka was an eyelash on her hand which, no matter how hard she huffed and puffed, would not blow away and make her wish come true. But, she had the politician's congenital talent for self-preservation. The Tehelka episode would stick to her reputation like her third name: Jaya Jaitly Tehelka. She had not come into politics for this. Her motives were at best altruistic, at worst, romantic. Her reputation would now always remain in perpetual cognitive dissonance. Even so, Jaya was not dispirited: There was a much loved man who carried the bitterness against Tehelka for her.

23 The Omission of Inquiry

Judge Dan Haywood [Spencer Tracy]: But this trial has shown that under the stress of a national crisis, men – even able and extraordinary men – can delude themselves into the commission of crimes and atrocities so vast and heinous as to stagger the imagination. How easily that can happen. There are those in our country today, too, who speak of the protection of the country. Of survival. The answer to that is: survival as what? A country isn't a rock. And it isn't an extension of one's self. It's what it stands for, when standing for something is the most difficult. Before the people of the world – let it now be noted in our decision here that this is what we stand for: justice, truth ... and the value of a single human being.

– Stanley Kramer's film, Judgment at Nuremberg *(1961)*

On 16 March 2001, the law ministry issued an ameliorative notice that the Union cabinet had approved the setting up of a Commission to probe Tehelka allegations. The government, presciently satirical, fixed a period of four months to complete the inquiry.

Justice Venkataswami, a retired judge of the Supreme Court and predictably patrician, was appointed by the government to preside over the Commission of Inquiry into Tehelka. Although Justice Venkataswami was appointed on 25 March 2001, the first hearing took place on 31 May 2001 and sat six times in the first two weeks of July. The Commission had issued notices to forty-five persons, including defence secretary Yogendra Narain, Union home secretary Kamal Pandey, Intelligence Bureau (IB) Director Shyamal Dutta, as well as Tehelka reporters Aniruddha Bahal, Mathew Samuel, and Tehelka's chief executive and editor Tarun Tejpal. The hearings began in an atmosphere of excitement and yet much apprehension. Of course, anything new when it begins contains a strain of naiveté in hope. Yes, the subterranean subversives were already beginning to grind into position. Those caught on tapes were naturally in a state of fear but ready to do battle. The journalists were wary about how the government in power would allow an investigation into their own people. Few were cynical enough to realize what a u-turn the inquiry would eventually take.

The Commission hearings were held in the Annexe behind Vigyan Bhavan, New Delhi. It was open to the media and the public. Basically, anybody could walk in after getting a pass made at the reception. Mr Sharma, in charge of issuing the entry passes, helpful to the press, became friends of the regulars and would take the time to engage in pleasantries. Security women, with a distinct resemblance to Gabbar Singh examined the contents of your bag and asked what each thing was used for, with a touching curiosity about any make-up lingering in your bag. The Annexe is a large room with semi-circular seating. There are desks in front of each seat with a microphone attached, which is switched on from a control panel set behind the judge in a glass cabin. The judge sat behind his own large desk and microphone at a raised level facing the desks. Just below him, at a right angle, the Commission's secretaries and recorders sat at desks burdened with relevant reference books and documents. If you were facing the judge, the Press was seated on the left of the semi-circle. In the centre sat all those COT with their lawyers. On the right, there was usually a contingent of army officers COT sitting in a carapace of guilt. The first rows were reserved for the attorney general, the solicitor general, the Union of India lawyers and the Commission lawyers. The back wall is lined with seats for visitors and random observers. When any individual was being interrogated, he stood behind a lectern to the left of the judge. The décor of the Annexe had the customary debility of design of government interiors. To be dull is thought to represent a virtue and so it perseveres to be. As the Commission proceeded with its work, the stillness of the room was not your imagination. The Commission was running in the same place. The veneer of activity kept all those involved buried in supplying documents and talking to their lawyers. Most of them ensured that there was the longest distance between any two points. There was an utter malevolent vacuum of impatience.

Justice Venkataswami, sixty-seven years old when appointed, is a man of stereotypical sobriety, bespectacled and most often wore grey and beige suits; a habit veered towards by most judges to distinguish themselves from the black and white of the lawyers. No matter how boring the depositions proved to be, Venkataswami continued to pay attention, never fell asleep, and remained focused. Often, he would reprimand lawyers for sliding on to the wrong track, and correct them if they misinterpreted an answer to their advantage.

The format of the Commission is confounding to a layperson. Lawyers ask random questions, not because they expect an answer but only to put on record a bizarre suggestion that would be included in the report. The question could be a world away from the scope of the investigation.

The atmosphere in the Commission was six feet under with affidavits, documents, and twisted legalese. Walking in at any time, you would hear ranting vituperation from one of the lawyers, who were intent on twisting and turning the Commission into any direction other than from those COT. And, they were succeeding. Simply by distracting arguments, making them as convoluted as possible, hanging on to tangential technicalities, they succeeded in prolonging the duration of the Commission. There was no hurry and there was no detail small enough to ignore. The more protracted the proceedings were the more lucrative for all concerned. So, hey, what's the rush? The Tehelka team did shoulder a concern for urgency. Some of their lawyers were working without a fee and therefore wanted to get on with their working lives that had choked to an unexpected halt. Tehelka had also run out of money. The Commission sailed quietly along on a slow sludge of paperwork and a turgidity of words. The liturgical passions of the lawyers did little to lift the hypnotic pallor. It could be any bureaucratic office in government. But, there was no one you could bribe to speed up your work, as is the case in other government offices. Noticees, culprits, victims, perpetrators, all arrived and sat through, stone-faced, with no end in sight. For those seeking results, the Soviet-like drone of the Commission going nowhere was suffocating. For those who were not looking forward to the consequences of their actions, it was perfect.

The Commissions of Inquiry Bill was passed in both the houses of Parliament in 1952 and became the Commissions of Inquiry Act, 1952, after it was assented by the President of India. It has been amended in the years 1971, 1986, 1986 again, 1988 and 1990. The Act states that the Central government shall appoint a Commission of Inquiry for the purpose of making an inquiry into any definite matter of public importance with a time specified in the notification. The government shall place the report in Parliament and in the public domain if it chooses to.

If you read the Commission of Inquiry Act, 1952, it appears to be an Act written with the clear purpose of helping a government in power to bury a problem it doesn't want to deal with or expose. It seems impossible to pin down who drafted the Act and what the motivation was. Although the Act [Section 3 (4)] the report before Parliament, there is nothing in the Act that says that the report has to be made public. The report is only to be considered as recommendations for action. The government has no legal binding to follow any of the recommendations.

It is true that the government is required to table the Commission's report, together with an Action Taken report (ATR) before the Parliament. However, the question is that if it does not, what will happen? The Opposition may make a noise in Parliament and that may compel the government to act. Alternatively, a writ could be filed in court asking for a direction that the government table the report and its ATR before Parliament. (Whether the court can issue such a writ is still unclear and the Supreme Court is considering this issue in Haldea's case as to whether if a court issues such a direction it will be a breach of privilege of the House.) But these are theoretically effective mechanisms to ensure that the report is tabled in Parliament.

The reason is that Commissions of Inquiry often work as means to bury a problem that the government does not want to deal with is that: the Commission of Inquiry is appointed by the government. It appoints people it wants and the report it makes favours what the government wants it to say. Moreover, the Commission is told to take its own time to decide the issue (and the lawyers unwittingly help this process!) and while the Commission is deciding the issue, the Opposition or anyone else cannot make a noise about the issue – the answer is simply that the Commission is inquiring into it! Even the press remains silent and everyone is waiting for the report of this 'impartial' Commission. By the time the report is submitted, it is a dead and forgotten issue. Or the report doesn't say what the Opposition or the other people want to hear.

What this really means is that the Commission is sent out to play *kabadi-kabadi* with a problem, have a really good game, write up a report, and there is no pressure on the government to take any action on it or even make the report public. The only power the Commission has, is to enquire and submit a report with recommendations. The Commission has no power of adjudication and cannot pass any decree that has to be enforced. A senior lawyer at the Commission commented that although Commissions of Inquiry rarely produce any results, they provide a great training ground for lawyers to showcase their talent and make their reputations. Oh ho! There has to be a better way where the important issues are not buried and citizens pay for it all.

Ironically, the NDA government even bettered the existing ambiguity and impotence of the Commission of Inquiry Act when it notified the Commission of Inquiry into Tehelka on 24 March 2001. The terms of reference of the Commission are unique, inasmuch as it introduces for the first time the need to inquire into the conduct of journalists who exposed the corruption:

(a) To inquire whether the transactions relating to Defence and other procurements referred to in the said videotapes and transcripts have been carried out in terms of the prescribed procedures and the imperatives of national security;

(b) To inquire whether in any of the aforesaid procurement transactions, illicit gains have been made by persons in public office, individuals, and any other organization as alleged, and if so, to what extent;

(c) To suggest actions that may be taken in respect of persons who may be found responsible by the Commission for their acts of commission and/or omission in respect of the transactions referred to in sub-clause (a) above;

(d) To inquire into all aspects relating to the making and publication of these allegations and any other matter which arises from or is connected with or incidental to any act, omission or transaction referred to in sub-clauses (a) and (b) above.

A.G. Noorani, constitutional expert and lawyer, wrote in *The Hindustan Times*, 31 March 2001:

Never in the half century of the Commission of Inquiry Act, 1952, was the body ever asked to probe into the credentials of those who had made the charges. The focus was on the message, never the messenger.

He clarified,

The widely worded remit – d (of the Venkataswami Commission, dealing with Tehelka) includes everything except the kitchen sink. It is not only invidious to single out the press for discriminatory treatment, it is also unconstitutional to do so.

If this move is allowed to pass muster, the press will be effectively muzzled.

Well, it did pass muster, and the press did not react. It was treated as 'Tehelka's problem' which did not affect the Indian press as a whole. The direction to investigate the Tehelka's motivation and methods gave an impetus to all the lawyers (LOCOT) of those caught on the tapes (COT) taking money and involved in sexual acts, to grill Tehelka on issues that had little to do with what was seen on the tapes. Get this equation. There are 26 persons shown on Operation West End tapes. All the lawyers of those caught on the tapes questioned Mathew Samuel, Aniruddha Bahal, and Tarun Tejpal. Even those who were not in the tapes but whose names were mentioned had lawyers questioning the Tehelka team. One Tehelka lawyer at a time questioned all the 26. Just think of the ratio. The appointed judge is listening to over 26 lawyers grilling Tehelka for hours, days, months. Sometimes the COT had several lawyers taking turns. The attorney general, the solicitor general, and their juniors did not question any of the COT. The Union of India lawyers also glossed over the COT but did extensively interrogate the Tehelka team. The journalists logged in the longest hours at the Commission.

Sidharth Luthra (Tehelka's lawyer) pointed out that the Commission's proceedings were marred by continuous disputes on the procedure to be followed. He said,

> **The Tehelka legal team faced combined hostility from the government lawyers and the lawyers of the noticees. After evidence began, it soon became apparent to us that a strategy had been evolved by the other noticees, where demands were made that after we had cross-examined a witness/noticee, the other noticees' lawyers would cross-examine the witness. This was a strategy to try and destroy the effect of any incriminating statements that the Tehelka legal team brought out during the cross-examination. The technicality behind this is that whereas examination-in-chief is limited in scope, in cross-examination leading questions can be put, that is, questions that contain the answers. This enabled a numbers of noticees to try and cover up the damaging admissions obtained during cross-examination by Tehelka or the Commission lawyers. Initially the judge did not appreciate our concern, however later the collusive strategy adopted became apparent even to the judge who then made appropriate modifications.**

In the interest of the Indian public, forget about the content, where is the focus supposed to be? Was the nation waiting to find out about the motives and methods of Tehelka or did they want to know what was going to be done about the army officers who sold documents, gave advice and information, as well as placed themselves in a highly compromising position with sex workers? Since the 'public' was not shouting in the Commission about their right to know what was going to be done about the politicians who took money, why would it be considered? This is the trap in which Tehelka found itself. The Commission had ruled that the videotapes were genuine but under Term D, it allowed all the lawyers to explore 'all aspects relating to the making and publication of the allegations'. The result was that every sentence in over 105 tapes was scrutinized and had to be defended. Tehelka had around 14 lawyers to defend itself. Initially, as many as seven Tehelka journalists had been assigned to deal with their defence in the Commission. According to Tarun, Tehelka spent 30,000 man-hours on Commission-related work.

The Commission dawdled on for 20 months under Justice Venkataswami, when on 22 November 2002, the Opposition parties staged the most bizarre turn of events. Priya Ranjan

Dasmunsi, (Congress chief whip) raised a question in the Lok Sabha, demanding to know how Justice Venkataswami could head two commissions both appointed by the government. Congress party members had discovered that Justice Venkataswami had also been appointed as chairman of the Committee on Advanced Rulings on Customs and Excise in the finance ministry in May 2002.

The then Finance Minister Jaswant Singh attempted a response in the Lok Sabha. He said, Justice Venkataswami was appointed as chairman of Advance Ruling Commission for CBEC in May 2002. When the finance minister had asked the chief justice of India to nominate a retired Supreme Court judge to the Commission in September 2001, Justice Venkataswami's name was suggested. The ACC (Appointment Committee of the Cabinet) approved the appointment in April 2002 and the appointment orders were issued in May 2002. Priya Ranjan Dasmunsi demanded to know how Venkataswami could have been appointed in May 2002, when he was already heading the Tehelka Commission which began in March 2001. Jaswant Singh, not quite prepared for the barrage the Opposition parties were flinging at him, answered as best as he could. But the screaming and chaos barely gave him a chance. The House was adjourned to give Jaswant Singh time to get more information.

On the same day, Kapil Sibal (Congress Party) raised the same question in the Rajya Sabha, where Najma Heptullah (deputy chairperson) presided. Sibal said, 'This, Madam, is a matter of great concern, because it indicates how authorities are compromised'. Balbir Punj (BJP) yelled, 'I object to the word "compromised". What does he mean "compromised?"' While Sibal continued to raise the issue of two appointments held by a single retired judge, the rest of the House created utter pandemonium. A normal day's work in the life of a member of Parliament. The leader of the Opposition, Dr Manmohan Singh said,

> Our system of government rests on a combination of checks and balance, and appropriate respect being shown to constitutional norms, proprieties and considerations of morality applicable to high offices of our Republic. Madam, it has shocked us that a person who was appointed to head a Commission of Inquiry is simultaneously being appointed to another office, in the Ministry of Finance … [members of Parliament screamed and created utter chaos.] He is looking into the conduct of a particular ministry, a particular minister, and matters relating to certain defence deals of the government. For the government to offer an appointment to the same person, is violative, in my view, of all norms applicable to appointment to such high offices. Therefore, as a mark of protest, we are going to walk out from the House.

Venkataswami had accepted the second job in May 2002 so why had the Congress Party woken up only seven months later? The Commission was bleeding Tehelka. They were left with no staff and no finances. Did Tehelka gamble that the Commission would be shut down and they could get on with their lives? Contrarily, the Opposition parties provided the BJP an opportunity to replace a judge who had not given any favourable decisions to those in the government caught on tape. The chief justice had taken five months to recommend a name for the post of chairman of the Authority for Advance Ruling (Customs & Excise). Could the chief justice and the finance ministry not have anticipated the potentially dangerous situation? Is it not the responsibility of the attorney general and the solicitor general to inform the government that there could be a problem?

On 23 November 2002, Justice Venkataswami announced to a packed press conference held in the Annexe, that he had sent a letter to Prime Minister A.B. Vajpayee that he was resigning from both his posts. Looking visibly upset but controlled, he said that he had pointed out in the letter that the government job was offered to him on the recommendation of the chief justice of India last year and that he had never sought the post. Justice Venkataswami said, 'Of course, I was deeply hurt by all the allegations'. He said he had done nothing unethical by accepting the AARCE offer.

> No, I do not see anything wrong in accepting the second offer. As has been made clear, this was not the first time a judge heading one commission was assigned another task.

He added,

> I did not accept the post straightaway. I took time to consult my wife. She said if the Chief Justice of India was recommending my name, I should honour his word. That is how I came to accept the second job. So far as hearings and proceedings are concerned, no one has complained about the proceedings.

Justice Venkataswami read from a prepared paper:

> I held 181 sittings and examined 75 witnesses and noticees under Section 2B. 720 interim orders have been passed. I had almost prepared the rough draft of the findings. The first draft of the defence transactions has been prepared. Only the final touches are to be given. The time was set for financial arguments. Only three or four witnesses had to be examined. With one more extension, I could have completed the job in time, but this controversy arose.

He concluded with more than a little regret and anguish, 'Do you think that a sitting judge, a retired judge, can be influenced by the government?' There was no dearth of journalists ready to orate to that.

One cheeky journalist earnestly demanded to know in what capacity he was holding a press conference at the same venue as the Commission hearings since he had already resigned and had the government provided him this facility? Venkataswami was beyond caring.

Attorney general Soli Sorabjee met Justice Venkataswami on 24 November (2002) hoping to convince him to continue, but Justice Venkataswami reiterated that he would not take his job back.

Tarun Tejpal complimented Justice Venkataswami for resigning and not buckling under government pressure to give a favourable report. Aniruddha Bahal said that the government had never wanted the truth to emerge and was saddened by the resignation. It doesn't take long to wise up. Tehelka too had mastered the art of spin doctoring.

The BJP adopted a blustering stand, with Arun Jaitley stating that, 'The blame for this lies entirely with the Congress, which made irresponsible allegations against Justice Venkataswami. This is not the first time that a judge heading a particular panel has been assigned another job.'

The Congress Party did not know whether to laugh or cry. They ended up saying that the resignation was a vindication of their stand. Which stand? How? What was achieved, except more delays?

The joker in the pack who started all the trouble, Priya Ranjan Dasmunsi, in justification of raising the issue in Parliament in the first place, said, 'The way the government tried to cover up the whole thing put him in a trap,' blaming the BJP squarely for the fiasco. Who then was responsible for the conspiracy? It was Kapil Sibal who was in touch with Tehelka. There was a feeling that Justice Venkataswami was not looking quite as favourably at Tehelka as he had at the beginning of the game. In this case, was Jaya Jaitly correct in the direction she pointed her finger. It was the easiest thing to create a ruckus in Parliament. On speculation, I believe Tehelka just wanted it all to end, but what they didn't have was the foresight to realize that this time around the government would ensure that they had a judge who would, in their reckoning, be favourable to them. Better the devil you know than the devil you don't. From the frying pan to the fire. Don't cut your nose to spite your face. But here it was: a stitch in time put the ball in their own court.

Six long weeks later, on 6 January 2003, Justice S.N. Phukan, another retired Supreme Court judge, was appointed to take over the Commission of Inquiry into Tehelka. Ironically, he continued to hold the post of chairman of the Assam Human Rights Commission (AHRC). When questioned by the press on this oddity, Justice Phukan replied that he was able to handle both the assignments. Did Phukan then have capabilities that Venkataswami lacked? Not surprisingly, the Congress Party did not raise the same issue this time. Phukan started bravely, saying, 'It does not matter if anybody is holding high political post in the country. If I find during my investigations that those top political and powerful people are involved then I will recommend necessary action.' He also said, somewhat painfully out of context, that being an Assamese it was a great honour for him to be appointed to the post, and that he would ensure that Assam's 'good name outside was upheld'. However, Justice Phukan did not come without his own controversies. In 1998, in a letter to the then president of India, K.R. Narayanan, Phukan had threatened to resign in protest when three judges junior to him were slated to supersede him to the Supreme Court. In a forty-year long career he had served as chief justice of Orissa and Himachal Pradesh. The manner in which he undertook the probe into the Tehelka tapes would test his integrity and comprehension of the serious precedent it set.

Justice Venkataswami often showed impatience with repetitive questions from lawyers and did seem protective of the Tehelka team. Three times he pointedly turned down Jaya Jaitly's requests for a forensic examination of the tapes.

Soon after Justice Phukan's appointment on 28 February 2003, after long discussions with their lawyers, Tehelka decided to withdraw from any participation in the Commission of Inquiry. (Many people have wondered what they were doing there in the first place. There was a discomforting naiveté to this. Journalists have said, they did a story, they should have said the usual, 'I stand by my story' and left it at that.)

In Tehelka's letter of withdrawal to the Commission, they listed all the reasons for their exit. The obvious points were the evaporation of funds, no staff, continual harassment from the government, no action taken against the guilty group in the tapes, spending between two weeks to a month each on the stand, and the inability to work and support themselves and their families. Tehelka added: 'The message from the establishment has been continually clear: those who exposed the corruption have to be targeted; those found guilty of corruption have to be protected.' Tarun Tejpal said that 114 people had been working for Tehelka, now not a single paid person was left. Tarun, with outrage in his voice, said, Tehelka had given the Commission 100 hours of tapes, transcripts of the tapes, every possible relevant document, had cooperated in every possible way, 'now we cannot possibly participate because of financial and moral reasons'. In Tarun's perception, the government had taken a completely partisan view. (So what's new?) Tarun, even charged up, seemed emotionally drained and exhausted.

At a press conference in the small room in the Press Club, New Delhi, Tarun said:

I have a sinking feeling about what is happening. The question of doctoring of the tapes should have arisen if any of the actors on the tapes had disputed any material accusation against them. The first point is, Jaya Jaitly had entertained arms dealers at the residence of the defence minister. Secondly, she admitted to accepting the money for party funds. And thirdly, Jaya Jaitly agreed to intercede in case they were treated unfairly and not shortlisted. Jaya Jaitly challenged the Venkataswami Commission in the High Court and her case was dismissed in the High Court. She has admitted all this in her affidavit. Now an absurd basis is being used for sending the tapes for forensic examination.

It appears the Commission has become a charade. We have done everything we could do to the best of our ability. Now other arms of society have to kick in to see this through. We showed 15 deals being made on camera. What happened to Venkataswami's report which he said was ready? Why is it not out?

When asked, 'Why now? After all the hours that were spent and when you are most required to defend Tehelka's integrity, why withdraw?' Tarun responded, 'We just don't have the people or finances to do anything. We do not have an office. There are no paid people working for Tehelka. The Commission is going to do what it's going to do. Anything we say is not going to make any difference.'

Tehelka's lawyers, who had joined the crusade following their own ideals or the excitement of getting valuable experience and media exposure, were also worn out. For how long can lawyers give hours of their time without compensation?

The government just wore them down. The one individual who had continued to be loyal to Tehelka was Arun Nair. A *chust* [energetic] young man, whose faith in Tehelka gave him a wired energy, Nair exuded sparks of earnest sincerity and had taken it upon himself to do the running around required for the Commission. Tarun relied on him to deal with all the logistics. Would you believe, that a few days before Tehelka decided to withdraw from the Commission, Arun Nair died in a freak accident, ramming his motorcycle into a stationary bus at about ten in the morning? What was Tarun doing for luck? It would seem that not only did the proverbial hit the fan, it seemed to rain exclusively on Tehelka. Geetan, Tarun's wife said, it was the first time that she saw Tarun break down. I would guess, that day Tarun crossed the border to the other side. Like Franz Kafka's hero in his brilliant book, *Metamorphosis*, who wakes up to find he has turned into an insect. Tarun entered the land of Insectpur, where the majority of Indians live. Insectpur is your place in society and your state of mind that has only known the hopelessness that stems from events that are never within your control. You can at any moment be stepped on and squashed, at any given time.

Kafka's metaphor borders on cliché in India. Government and their network of departments have perfected the art of reducing human beings to insects. Tarun had said to me, 'Everything in this country is to make you less than who you are.' The élite are born with the privilege of believing that if they work hard, they do the right things, they can achieve anything. That attitude is to be more envied than the money and status with which they are born. It cannot be acquired. If, from the moment you are born, life teaches you that whatever you do, you cannot change your life in any way, helplessness becomes a constant companion of the Insectmind. You cannot have any real ambitions, because you will never break out of what you have been born. So easily have people mocked and marvelled at Indians for resignedly believing in kismatfate rather than fighting for our right to change circumstance. In reality it is not really our belief in kismatfate but living in the surround of Insectpur. As we proceed to grow from childhood to youth, experiencing the frustrations of a life where the wrong caste, the wrong schools, the wrong accent, the wrong manners, devoid of networks and contacts, thwarting any hope at every step, it is logical when to fail at everything you attempt. It is because other people take decisions you cannot control, that you finally succumb to residence in Insectpur. The only dreams you can permit yourself to have, are watching Bollywood fantasies. You have the subconscious licence to dream of going on a picnic with Katrina Kaif, because it will never happen so there's no harm in revelling in imagination. Everyone around you is aware that you are indulging in mere fantasy without any real hope of it ever becoming reality, and so it is merely amusing. An Insectpurite would be mocked if he claimed an ambition is to work for NDTV or become a business tycoon and buy politicians at will. He would appear to other Insectpurites as an idiot with no conception of the 'real' world. To dare to hope to realize real ambitions, appears self-delusionary and foolhardy. Even privileged people in India, who experience great personal tragedy, cross into Insectpur. When for the first time, it sinks in, there are some events that occur in life over which they have no control. Tarun had belonged to the Winners Side of the Border; those functioning with the confidence to actually nurture ambition with a chance of it being realized. With some advantage of an army background and education, Tarun had worked himself out of there. He could have been mediocre but he pushed his way up to cross the border. It is the class of people who are used to getting things done. The possibility of possessing the characteristics of experiencing joy in one's work, efficiency and achieving success, can only exist if there has been some ancestral, historical precedent, and experience of it.

But the vast majority of children grow up in India surrounded by those who can never accomplish what they aspire to, no matter what they do. If all a child has ever seen is that in every attempt to better one's life, it is met with kicks meted out by the more powerful, how does s/he break out of the Insectpur mindset? The miniscule number who do, are extraordinary people. Abdul Kalam, Dhirubhai Ambani, and Kalpana Chawla crossed the boundary. But few, too few. Clearly Abdul Kalam also retains the aura, and delight, and astonishment of *main kehaan se kehaan pahunch gayey* [imagine from where I came and where I am now]. His insistence on including children at his swearing in ceremony as president was because he wanted to show them that it is possible to have a dream and achieve it. Education cannot be just learning maths. It also has to generate in young minds a belief in the possiblity of achievable goals.

From a man who once felt the power of bringing down a government, Tarun now faced the same helplessness of a man in Insectpur, unable to control the manner in which the Commission functioned. The government was treating Tehelka as if they were guilty criminals conspiring to bring down the government for personal financial gain. He could not control the government lawyers' obfuscating questions. He could not control Tehelka's lawyers return to their paying legal cases. He could not control people leaving Tehelka for jobs that actually paid a salary. He could not control the reality that they had no more money. He could not control Arun Nair's death. He had lost control of making things happen in the way he wanted. He had crossed the border and was in the same state as a man with the wrong caste, wrong school, wrong accent, wrong manners, no contacts. Kismatfate had hit him between the eyes. Arun Nair's death, the evaporation of funds, and sheer mental and emotional fatigue caused the bell to toll.

But, even withdrawing from the Commission was not as simple as just walking out. On 28 February 2003, when Tehelka lawyer, Prashant Bhushan, attempted to submit their letter of withdrawal from the Commission, Soli Sorabjee, the attorney general, objected to the language in their letter. Well, it was easy to see why. The letter:

The highest law officers in the land – the solicitor general and attorney general of India – for instance, have personally spent days targeting Tehelka in the Commission. Some of them even spent days personally cross-examining the Tehelka journalists while not cross-examining a single person found taking bribes on the Tehelka tapes.

Was it then the 'language' or the content? The attorney general demanded that the submission should be in the form of an affidavit and the letter should not be admitted in the court records as they were handing it in. Bhushan then asked for permission to allow Tarun Tejpal to make an oral statement. Sorabjee, in a raging pique, objected and insisted that Tejpal should not be allowed to speak. An acrimonious exchange between the attorney general and the Tehelka lawyer woke up all the catnappers. Bhushan pointed out that Tehelka had a right to put their views before the Commission. Sorabjee shouted that Tehelka had maligned the officers of the court and should not be allowed to speak. The attorney general prevailed of course and Tehelka had its last day in the Commission with the most pernicious denotation. This attorney general, the same man who had appeared pro bono for cases fighting for freedom of the press during Indira Gandhi's Emergency, did not allow Tehelka to speak. This was narcisstic legalese.

Later, Tarun said,

When Justice Venkataswami has stated he had completed the investigation on the defence deals, then the first thing Justice Phukan should have done is completed that report. He should have said whether those transactions were above board or not. But the first order he passes is to do what Jaya Jaitly wants him to do and that is send the tapes for forensic examination.

Despite this official withdrawal, Tehelka found itself forced to deal with the Commission. Five months after Justice Phukan gave his order for the forensic examination, the technical experts who were examining the tapes asked for Tehelka's cameras. On 19 September 2003, Justice Phukan ordered Tehelka to hand in their cameras to the Commission to send to the forensic experts. Prashant Bhushan, while arguing against it, also happened to make a remark about the delay of the report of the Commission when the report on the 15 defence deals was ready. This stirred up Justice Phukan quite a bit and he demanded that the Tehelka lawyers file an answer as to their source of this information. The lawyers and public had no access to the proceedings related to the defence deals. They were held in camera citing reasons of national security.

Two weeks later, Prashant Bhushan returned to the Commission and brought along newspaper reports of Justice Venkataswami's statements about the completion of the report on the 15 defence deals.

On 4 February 2004, there was high drama when all the television news channels ran stories that Justice Phukan had given a 'clean chit' to George Fernandes. Justice Phukan called a press conference on that day at 2.30 p.m. in the same room in Vigyan Bhavan, where the Commission hearings were held. He stated that he had gone to the prime minister that morning to hand in Part 1 of his report. Obviously, to his disappointment he found no media there. So he took the unusual step, as judges are not supposed to speak to the press, to call for a press conference. Why is the report of the Commission going to be in three parts? In answer to my question, Justice Phukan said, 'One of the Tehelka lawyers accused me of delaying the report, so I decided to do it in three parts'. So now we have a judge who responds to accusations of any kind with a report that is not quite ready and then calls for a press conference because nobody noticed.

At no point during the press conference did Justice Phukan say, 'I have given a clean chit to George Fernandes'. Why then did the television channels run this report? 'They can run what they like. They are independent,' said Justice Phukan dryly. Right. They may be independent but could he not confirm or deny it? 'No comment,' he said repeatedly to the same question asked in many different ways by highly frustrated journalists, who were incensed at being called for a press conference and getting no information to write about. What were the issues from which George Fernandes had to be exonerated?

1. Defence Minister, George Fernandes's home was used to entertain dubious arms dealers, without their antecedents being checked.
2. Was Fernandes allowing Jaya Jaitly to interfere or offer suggestions in the procurement of arms?
3. The veracity of the numerous statements made by, and stories concerning arms deals recounted by the treasurer of the Samata Party, R.K. Jain, about Jaitly and Fernandes.

According to the transcript of Justice Phukan's press conference, he is clearly non-committal about George Fernandes. He repeatedly said that Fernandes's reputation was not examined in this part of the report.

How then did the television channels begin running the 'clean chit for George Fernandes' campaign even before the press conference? It doesn't take a genius to figure out that the spin-doctors, now increasingly media savvy, clearly planted the story from the prime minister's office. The report was handed in at 10.30 a.m. to the PMO and soon after that the TV channels began running the 'clean chit' story. It is the government's prerogative on whether or not they make the Commission's report public. Justice Phukan did tell the press that his report dealt with 15 defence deals discussed in the tapes and George Fernandes's name did not figure in those deals. That, however, did not give a 'clean chit' to the fact that the defence minister's house was used to accept money from dubious dealers for the Samata Party.

After the Commission hands in the report, it is left entirely to the government to decide what to do with it. The spin-doctors faced four clear options. The first option: they could fling it in the shredder. Second option: they could dump it in the garbage. Third option: they could hold a funeral service over an already crowded Commissions of Inquiry file cabinet and bury it there, with the stipulation that there would be no *chautha* [memorial service]. The fourth option: they could table it in Parliament, at which point it would be made public. Well, we know it wasn't tabled in Parliament at that time and it wasn't made public. Should one therefore presume that one of the first three options was exercised? A terribly simple question: If Part 1 of the Phukan report gave George Fernandes a 'clean chit', why did the government not make it public? Why did Justice Phukan hold a press conference when he was not in a position to elaborate on the contents of the report? Why did the government not hold a press conference and exhume the details of the 'clean chit'?

Television journalists who attended the press conference and witnessed Justice Phukan declining to confirm he had given George Fernandes a 'clean chit', still filed reports in the evening that did not contradict the earlier 'clean chit' reports. The disinformation initiated by the spin-doctors in the morning continued to be repeated after the press conference and also in the nightly news reports.

Justice Phukan stated that he had made his report on the basis of top secret documents on arms deals. He had not yet heard any depositions from people mentioned in these deals. Justice Phukan said he would now issue notices based on his findings. Why did he not hear these noticees first and then file the complete report?

The *Asian Age's* headline screamed, 'Phukan Report Clears Fernandes'. The story reads, 'The Justice Phukan Commission, inquiring into news portal Tehelka's defence exposé, has cleared Defence Minister George Fernandes of "impropriety" in any of the defence equipment purchases it probed.'

The Hindustan Times shouted: 'George Not Guilty: Tehelka Panel Phukan Commission finds no impropriety in 15 defence deals'.

The *Pioneer's* headline: 'George Cleared'. The story leads with: 'The Justice Phukan Commission, probing the Tehelka's "revelations" has exonerated Defence Minister George Fernandes of charges of impropriety.'

Even *The Indian Express* ran the headline: 'Tehelka Judge says George did no Wrong, Opp Cries Unfair'. The report said: 'Though there is no connection between the tapes and the report presented today, his response to a question that there was no impropriety on the part of Fernandes set off smiles and celebration in the NDA and protesting voices in the opposition.'

The Hindu was the only newspaper that carried a slightly more accurate headline and report: 'No Impropriety in Defence Deals by Fernandes: Panel'. The report stated: 'He said that "no impropriety has been committed by the Defence Minister in these transactions," in which the procurement procedures were dealt with'. The story continues: 'Asked whether Mr Fernandes had been exonerated of the charges in the report, he said, "No comments. I have submitted my report to the government and I personally feel that the recommendations should be accepted"'. Justice Phukan made no effort to correct the erroneous reports the following day or any day after that until it showered on him in May 2005. When his impartiality and integrity was at stake, he corrected the impression that he had given George Fernandes a 'clean chit'.

The media was used by the spin-doctors. Either they were not aware of it and chose to run the story so as not to be left behind in the race of reportage or they willingly ran a planted story to curry favour with the PMO. The *bhed chaal* [sheep following sheep] trend of the media exposes the reality that there are many reporters running around who are unwilling to stand up and say: 'This is not the story. The real story is ....'. Twenty years ago, if anyone asked an uncomfortable question at a press conference, fellow journalists would get terribly upset. I was once reprimanded by another journalist for 'spoiling the mood' at the press conference when I asked a question that raised an issue the government wanted buried. A press conference used to be a 'suck up' conference. That has completely changed. One now sees a wonderful irreverence of authority and power at press conferences. There is no shortage of aggressive journalists who are totally unafraid to ask all kinds of irritating questions. In fact, the more audacious the question, often playing to the gallery, the more *bhau* [admiration] he receives from fellow journalists. But where is the courage when it means breaking ranks from fellow journalists, by not accepting a 'plant' or a handout and giving the real story behind the plant? If we expect politicians to accept and deal with our criticisms, why are we unwilling to brook any criticism from fellow journalists? Why was there no editor at the desk at the television stations, who after seeing Justice Phukan's press conference footage, questioned the earlier story? Why was there no attribution for the 'clean chit' story? 'Clean chit' according to whom? One didn't have to look too far. There was only one department in the government which had the report that morning. This was a serious breach in Indian journalism that exposes the ease with which stories are planted.

In this epidemic of *bhed chaal*, journalists missed the big story. Only six weeks earlier, in the last week of December 2004, Justice Phukan, accompanied by his wife and eight other lawyers of the Commission, including the counsel for the Commission, enjoyed the hospitality of the defence ministry. The junket took them to Shirdi, Pune, Ahmednagar, and Mumbai. The Supreme Court was on its winter vacation and the official reason for the trip was to familiarize themselves with the weapons systems they were inquiring into. Official approval from the Ministry of Defence had been given as required for civilians to use defence aircraft. They were entertained with dinners and lunches at army and naval headquarters. Justice Phukan did view some presentations on weapons but one was cancelled to enable him to make the pilgrimage to Shirdi. In Mumbai, the entourage stayed at the Western Naval Command officers' mess. They used a chopper to fly from Ahmednagar to Mumbai. *Outlook* magazine broke this story in its 9 May 2005 edition. It was Aniruddha Bahal, still sleuthing around, who had tipped them off. Various judges interviewed by *Outlook* voiced their disapproval of acceptance of such junkets, especially from an organization whose members are the target of a probe. Imagine the consequences if just one of the reporters had stepped out of the crowd in Justice Phukan's press conference on 4 February 2004, and asked a question about the junket he had enjoyed just around a month earlier.

On 4 May 2005, Pranab Mukherjee, the defence minister in the UPA government, raised the issue in Parliament. He reiterated the facts on the Phukan junket and added that they had also visited the Ajanta and Ellora caves. Well, no weapon presentations there. Mukherjee said that the Commission of Inquiry's secretary wrote to the defence ministry on 19 December 2003, saying that Justice Phukan had directed that equipment bought in transactions being investigated be inspected in Pune, Ahmednagar, Bangalore, and Mumbai. Quite creative on Justice Phukan's part. How did looking at the equipment affect the murky deals that were made to obtain them? He would have learnt more had he had sat in on just one price negotiating committee meeting.

On 22 December 2003, George Fernandes, then defence minister, approved the use of an Indian Air Force plane for Justice Phukan and his entourage. The aircraft that was used is supposedly strictly reserved for the use only of the president, the vice president and the prime minister. Justice Phukan said he had no idea that he was flying an aircraft meant only for VIPs. He had thought the government was providing the aircraft as he had got in touch with them. What then was his wife doing with him on a weapons inspection trip? Justice

Phukan said that when he had gone to Chennai for a briefing with Justice Venkataswami, his wife had been allowed by the government to accompany him. Oh, well, ignorance of a law and breaking it never got anyone off in court. It was only on 4 May 2005 that Justice Phukan said, 'I had never used the word "clean chit". It was the media that coined this word on its own.' Not true. It was made up by the spin-doctors. Justice Phukan went on, 'I had said that I did not find any measure of irregularities in the defence deals in question.' True, but why did it take him over a year to correct what the newspapers had erroneously reported? And did George Fernandes really believe that such a trip would remain a secret? George Fernandes was furious all over again and said that he had not committed any impropriety in sanctioning the aircraft for the Commission's use. Fernandes said that when the Commission asked to inspect the arms and equipment that was being investigated for improprieties, the service headquarters were told to prepare a programme and send it to the defence ministry. The Air Headquarters then wrote to the joint secretary in the defence ministry requesting approval to provide an aircraft. Fernandes pointed out, 'Had I refused permission for the use of the service aircraft, I would have been liable to be accused of obstructing the work of the Commission whose mandate was to probe acts of corruption concerning the defence ministry.' True, true. George Fernandes also accused the Congress Party of planting the junket story in the media.

On 7 May 2005, George Fernandes threatened to sue in the Supreme Court if the UPA government did not table the Phukan Report in Parliament in three days. 'If they don't table the report, I have no option but to go to court. I am ready for a legal battle.' He said, 'They are legally bound to table that report. When a Commission finishes its report, legally it is supposed to be tabled in Parliament.' Yes, but how many Commissions of Inquiry reports are never tabled, no questions asked?

This is truly odd. Justice Phukan had actually handed in the first part of the report to the NDA government, of which George Fernandes was defence minister. They did not table that report. At that time, not a word was uttered by Fernandes or anyone from the NDA government that the report should be tabled. Now they insisted that the present UPA government table a report that they themselves had failed to do when they received it on 4 February 2004. Fifteen months later they decided to agitate for it to be tabled. Fine. Accordingly, on 13 May 2005, the UPA government tabled the report in Parliament and immediately trashed it as 'incomplete' and 'bereft of reasoning'. Although the report investigated 15 defence deals, found procedural lapses (read corruption) in 13 of them, there was no nexus established between the army, bureaucrats, middlemen, and politicians. Figure this. On 4 February 2004, Justice Phukan did not deny that he gave George Fernandes a clean chit. On 5 May 2005, after *Outlook's* report surfaced about the junket to view weapons, Justice Phukan denied he gave George Fernandes a clean chit. On 10 April 2005, the intrepid *Indian Express* got hold of a copy of the Phukan report and published a summary. Then we discover that Justice Phukan's report stated that George Fernandes did not commit any irregularities in any of these deals.

On 13 May 2005, George Fernandes, at his residence talking to the press, read from a copy of the report:

The Commission, after examining the records of each past transactions and the evidences, both oral and documentary, has recorded specific findings in each of the reports relating to 15 past transactions that no illegality or irregularity has been committed by George Fernandes.

George further hit back and said it was the Opposition that was completely bereft of reasoning. It would be interesting to know how the judge justified repeatedly trimming his sails to the direction from where the wind blew.

On 7 February 2008, George Fernandes wrote to the Central Public Information Officers of the home ministry to supply him a complete copy of the report under the Right to Information Act, 2005. This request was forwarded to the Ministry of Defence who, on 14 March 2008, declined Fernandes's demand. In the letter of refusal, the Ministry of Defence wrote that since the report had already been tabled in Parliament and the cases were now all with the CBI, there was no basis to give him the report. Then in the wildest enactment of Catch-22, the Appellate Authority rejected Fernandes's appeal without a hearing on the grounds that the volumes containing the Commission's detailed recommendations on the 15 past defence deals had not been tabled in Parliament and supply of this information would constitute breach of privilege of Parliament.

On 20 May 2008, George Fernandes wrote a letter to the speaker of the Lok Sabha, 'bringing to your notice, the blatant fraud played by the government on Parliament and the nation. The contents of the present letter will indeed shock you and I have no hesitation in my mind that it will compel you to take suitable action against the government after calling for an explanation from the prime minister.' George pointed out that, 'When this document as tabled, reached me I was shocked to find that the document tabled was not the report of the Commission in its entirety but was only the prologue, conclusions and interim recommendations running into 57 pages which were only a part of the complete report.' He stated that Part-I of the report consisted of 700 pages and more. Fernandes's letter ended with, 'It is obviously part of a dirty political ploy to relegate the work of a former Supreme Court judge to the dustbin, hide it from Parliament and the country, portray the judge did no work or very little work and place ministry files and the Commission's papers in the hands of a police agency like the CBI so that a cloud hangs over the political opponents.' Fernandes urged the Speaker to 'take strict and appropriate action in the matter, with the urgency the issue deserves.' So is any political party or poltician better than the other? The one who is in power will rattle the skeletons in the other's closet.

UPA defence minister Pranab Mukherjee responded in a note to the Parliament by pointing out that the Commission had failed to investigate the serious charges of procurement transactions, illicit gains made by people in public office, so, 'Even the conclusions arrived at by Justice Phukan are bereft of reasoning.' Mukherjee then said that his government found it impossible to accept the report's findings so the CBI had been entrusted with further investigations into the corruption.

Subsequently, Fernandes attempted to raise the issue again with press releases and letters to members of Parliament, but nothing happened.

The Commission of Inquiry on Tehelka only followed the tradition of commissions of inquiry. Nothing of any consequence happened as a result of the report.

One must also examine the psychological make-up that reiterates journalists' basic collective cynicism that the Commission of Inquiry on Tehelka is the government's whitewash circus. If George Fernandes has been given a 'clean chit' then it only goes to show that this government's intentions are exposed. The Tehelka team would agree with this. This is exactly what Tarun Tejpal and Aniruddha Bahal had been saying from the outset. They could now point out that they have been vindicated because the Commission is biased. Journalists are not a congenitally cynical breed. The attitude has developed through the evolution of events. They have seen umpteen commissions appointed, seen them go through the deposition-*leela* of witnesses with lawyers singing their ghazals. In the state of Karnataka alone, in the course of 23 years, 15 commissions of inquiry have been appointed, eleven reports accepted, and action taken only in two instances. In the education ministry, 80 commissions on literacy have been appointed since 1947. Our literacy rate screams for itself. The Liberhan Commission was appointed soon after the destruction of the Babri Masjid on 6 December 1992. Over the past 16 years, the Commission has held 325 hearings, examined 99 witnesses, and has been given multiple extensions by governments. It actually concluded recording of evidence on 22 January 2003. On 2 May 2005, we were told that the report was about to be submitted. The Liberhan Commission was given its forty-fifth extension on 1 May 2008. The Commission has already cost the nation Rs 717.66 lakh. There is more to it than meets the eye. The report could swing a political party's fortunes in a particular direction if the timing is wrong. The Jain Commission, appointed on 23 August 1991 to inquire into Rajiv Gandhi's assassination, submitted its final report on 7 March 1998. The Nanavati Commission appointed on 8 May 2000, to re-inquire into the 1984 anti-Sikh riots received its sixth extension in October 2004. It was the third commission to be appointed to inquire into the anti-Sikh riots. Ten committees had already been appointed for the same purpose. Twenty-one years after the massacres took place, Justice G.T. Nanavati finally submitted his report on 9 February 2005. A minimum of 15 to 20 commissions are appointed every year. The highest number recorded was in 1966 when Indira Gandhi became prime minister for the first time, when she appointed 72 commissions. She had to ensure that all those who had called her a *gungi gudiya* [dumb doll] were kept occupied with worthless activities. In 1977, 49 commissions were created. This was the post-Emergency era when the Janata Dal came into power. Again, they had to keep Indira Gandhi and her family too preoccupied to meddle.

What were the purportedly learned authors thinking when they sat down and wrote the Commission of Inquiry Act of 1952? It is commonly believed that the Indian constitution is based on the British constitution. As we all know however, the British constitution is not codified in the form of a written document. British law is based on the laws and customs of Parliament, case law, and constitutional experts who have written on the subject. With what alleged wisdom then did our legal experts come up with the Commission of Inquiry Act?

The Constitution of India came into force on 26 January 1950. Although it follows the British parliamentary system, the American Bill of Rights were used as the basis for the

Indian Constitution. As British law was based on precedents, the authors of the Indian Constitution looked to British precedents. But, should one look at a colonizer's methods of suppression of uncomfortable truths as a format for a newly independent nation? The British had repeatedly appointed commissions in India to look into natural and unnatural disasters, as well as other issues. The Famine Commission was appointed by the British viceroy, Lord Edward Lytton, in 1897, after millions died of starvation. Lytton's purpose in appointing the Commission was to ensure that 'high prices, by stimulating imports and limiting consumption, were the natural saviours of the situation'. Lytton also ordered that 'there is to be no interference of any kind on the part of the government with the object of reducing the price of food', and denounced 'humanitarian hysterics'. He labelled those who wanted to save Indian lives as victims of 'cheap sentiment'. The British government passed The Government of India Act of 1919, in which, under Section 84, a statutory commission was to be appointed at the end of ten years to determine the next stage in the realization of self-rule in India. In 1927, the British government then appointed Sir John Simon to head the Simon Commission to recommend the future constitution of India. Every Indian child knows that those who were part of the independence movement boycotted the Simon Commission. It took from the year 1919 to 1947 for India to gain independence from British rule. The British were able to stall the independence movement for 28 years through the Commission raj.

In 1920, the Hunter Commission recommended suspension for Sir Michael O'Dyer, Governor of Punjab, who was held responsible for the Jallianwala Bagh massacre of 13 April 1919. It proved even then to be the diversionary instrument commissions were and are, since the British Parliament cleared his name and praised O'Dyer. So, didn't our venerable constitutionalists get the message? The British used the commissions on a colonized population to maintain a humanitarian veneer, if and when required. Why would we need such a ploy? Why, indeed, should we allow such a ploy? Clearly, the time has come to remove the toothless Commission of Inquiry Act completely and replace it with one that metes out real rather than pseudo-justice. A more accurate term would be in Hinglish – drama*baji* justice.

It is no surprise then that the general public is cynical about commissions. When a journalist goes into a press conference being held by a judge appointed by the government to look into its own wrongdoings, the journalist cannot have expectations other than that the government will exonerate itself from all accusations and give itself a 'clean chit'.

The public's perception has become so palpable, that the then chief justice of India, R.C. Lahoti, on 31 December 2004, expressed his dismay with the shortcomings in the Commission of Inquiry Act. Lahoti, part of a generation that is now not as reverent of things past or British, said he had reservations about the effectiveness of Commissions of Inquiry. He told a correspondent of *The Hindu*, 'Personally, I feel that no judge should accept the responsibility of heading commissions unless it is guaranteed that their recommendations and findings will be implemented'. Lahoti pointed to the Justice B.N. Srikrishna Commission of Inquiry on the Mumbai riots, where none of the recommendations were considered by the BJP government. He went so far as to say that the appointment of commissions of inquiry was a diplomatic way of diverting the attention of the people and called it a waste of time.

Mahesh Jethmalani spoke about what he saw as the correct direction for commissions of inquiry:

Madhu: How should the Commission of Inquiry Act be improved or amended?

Jethmalani: The first thing I would do is time limit a commission. I would say no adjournments before the commission. Anybody, any lawyer who wants to appear can't say I'm busy in other courts. This commission has to publish a report within six months; no further extensions. They always keep a loophole saying "and it may be extended from time to time". This should never be done. This commission will complete its report within six months because time is of the essence of this entire activity.

Madhu: Well, the Army Court of Inquiry completed its work in three months.

Jethmalani: Exactly, and they court-martialled all of them. So there you are. If you want to have speed, you can have speed. But these commissions are only used as stumbling blocks. It's only to buy the government time, nothing else. If they wanted this Commission to reach a verdict, it would have seen them through the next election.

Madhu: What about clause (d), in the terms of reference for the Commission of Inquiry on Tehelka. The Commission was asked "to inquire into all aspects relating to the making and publication of these allegations." This required the journalists and investors involved to be investigated.

Jethmalani: Actually it's been a howler for them. The press didn't realize what it does for their own future. You're sitting on a branch and cutting it off from beneath their feet. It sounded the deathknell of freedom of speech in this country.

Madhu: But there was very little reaction.

Jethmalani: Crazy. There should have been *dharnas* outside Parliament. There should have been protests all over the country. But it didn't happen. We were all amazed. It was the press's job. You can't get lawyers going to court and taking up these saying clause (d), when the press itself is not vigilant about its own rights.

It is important to be aware of the situation in which judges find themselves when they retire. The miniscule pension, no housing and the urge to continue to make their lives useful, naturally makes them look forward to appointments to commissions or other bodies. Quite a number of Supreme Court judges have large and lucrative practices as arbitrators and giving legal opinions, which are used to lobby the government. Will a government appoint that judge again if he has not given favourable reports about it? It is important that the government reconsider the retirement benefits of judges so that honest judges do not find themselves scrambling even for a home with hardly any money. Why do we, indeed, treat to whom we owe the most so badly?

On 1 October 2004, the Union of India counsel (now appointed by the new UPA government that had come to power) submitted to the Tehelka Commission that any investigation into journalistic ethics in Operation West End was beyond the scope of its inquiry. The counsel said that the question of motive behind the exposé was not relevant and could not form part of the inquiry of the Commission. The Union of India said the Commission should limit itself to probing the bribes paid in defence deals as shown in the Operation West End tapes. Ironically, an affidavit was submitted signed by the joint secretary in the finance ministry, D.P. Sengupta, that stated allegations of violation of taxation laws, SEBI regulations, enforcement and other regulations should be completely beyond the purview of the Commission.

Jaya Jaitly immediately accused the government of trying to save Tehelka and First Global. She charged, 'The truth would never be out if there was no probe into the journalistic ethics of Tehelka and the motive behind the making of the tapes.'

On 4 October 2004, in the afternoon I received a call from Jaya Jaitly: 'So you have a juicy ending for your book,' she said, with a bitter edge to her voice. The law minister in the UPA government, H.R. Bhardwaj, had just announced at a press conference that his government had decided not to grant a further extension to the Commission on Tehelka on the last day of the three-month extended term of the presiding judge, Justice Phukan. The Commission was initially set up for four months and subsequently obtained numerous extensions. Bhardwaj stated that the government had asked the CBI to probe the 'various personalities' who figure in the Operation West End tapes. The CBI would begin a preliminary inquiry, study the Tehelka tapes to examine whether leaders such as George Fernandes and Jaya Jaitly could be booked under the Prevention of Corruption Act.

Bhardwaj had a point when he said that although George Fernandes may have claimed that he was given a clean chit in the defence deals, in the interim report filed by Justice Phukan there was no clean chit. This would mean that defence deals struck during the NDA government's tenure would be investigated. Bhardwaj said that the previous government had deliberately misdirected the inquiry to shield George Fernandes. He stated, 'The only thing the Commission has done so far is to send the tapes for forensic tests abroad and the report in this regard had said the tapes were genuine.' The law minister believed there was no reason to probe the motives of the journalists, 'who had done a great service by exposing the widespread corruption in defence deals'.

All the players were confused. The same government had granted an extension to this Commission in July. The Commission was in the process of completing the second and final part of its investigation. The final arguments were about to be heard.

George Fernandes said, 'If the law minister has taken the decision not to extend the term of the Tehelka Commission and instead refer the case to the CBI, it is *bakwas* [rubbish] for it tantamounts to showing distrust in Justice Phukan.' Jaya Jaitly, in a fury, said, 'The motive is obvious. They did not want the Commission to unearth the truth. It is a dirty, political witch-hunt to divert national attention from the tainted ministers issue.'

The people in power and the Opposition always seem to be in a state of ecstatic amateurism playing in a sandbox, indulging in childish revenge.

Anyone could have seen it coming. The UPA government had replaced all eight counsels representing the government in the Commission. These counsels had repeatedly sought adjournments in order to give themselves time to read the inquiry papers. Justice Phukan, rather shaken, pointed out that it was these counsels who had delayed the proceedings. He said that he had made substantial progress and was poised to submit his second and final report when the government decided to scrap the Commission. Justice Phukan said he would have handed in his final report in two months. In an interview to rediff.com, Phukan said,

> I had no clue. I read about it in the papers like any other person. Even as we were talking, my secretary came back from the law ministry and told me that the government will be sending a formal letter to the Commission intimating its decision to wind up the Inquiry panel, either later in the evening or tomorrow [8 October 2004].

He pointed out that it took over a year to check whether the tapes were authentic, and he had no control over that. He said that over 500 top secret files were part of the proceedings. In between, the Commission's counsel resigned (change of government) and the new one wanted time to go through the files. Phukan ruefully said,

> Yet, I completed the hearings within six months of the first argument and then took another two months to submit the interim report, which consisted of 700 pages and included several recommendations. The matter would have been disposed off in another six months.

That then was the snail's pace he had set himself.

At the last hearing, Justice Phukan had said, 'I am feeling uncomfortable. I don't know how to proceed', just before adjourning for the day. He was acutely aware that although it was the last working day for the Commission, the government's silence on the matter of his extension was a nagging buzz in his ear. Often, when one is at odds with a decision but cannot fight it, the anger is then directed at the *way* it was done, and so it was with Justice Phukan. The government did not inform him personally. He learnt of the decision only through media reports on Bhardwaj's press conference. Reacting strongly to the prime minister's remarks that the Tehelka Commission had not produced a single report, Justice Phukan pointed to a long list of the work that was done during his one-and-a-half-year tenure as chairman of the Commission. He said that within a year of his taking over, on 4 February 2004, he had submitted a 700-page report on the fifteen defence deals cited in the Operation West End tapes. (How much of it was actually written by Justice Venkataswami?) Justice Phukan refused to elaborate on his findings, because he said the content was 'extremely sensitive'. He did say that he doubted the report on the fifteen defence deals would ever see the light of day, as it would be difficult for the government to make defence secrets public.

In another twist, the then BJP President Venkaiah Naidu said, 'It seems the Congress leaders fear that the allegations made by them on the Tehelka issue may prove wrong if the Commission continues the probe'. Strange stuff. Then, why hand it over to the CBI? However, Naidu said that the UPA Government was being vindictive by handing over the investigation to the CBI and it was 'politically motivated with an ulterior purpose'.

Prime Minister Manmohan Singh was categorical when he said on 6 October 2004 in Mumbai, 'The Tehelka Commission has not come up with a report after three-and-a-half years. What is the guarantee that it will come out with a report after getting another extension of three months sought by it? We play the game straight and the government is not vindictive.' The BJP General Secretary Arun Jaitley took strong exception to Manmohan Singh's remarks and stung back, 'The prime minister's statements are dangerous. If the reasons furnished by the prime minister have substance, namely non-completion of work, how come the Jain Commission has continued over so many years? Liberhan Commission has continued even after twelve years, despite having prosecuted people.' Jaitley stated that Singh's statements did not behove the office of the prime minister, and his party did not accept the contention that the Phukan Commission had to be wound up because it had refused to produce a report. Jaitley said ruefully that it was the first time a Commission of Inquiry had been wound up before completing its work. Union Information and Broadcasting Minister Jaipal Reddy defended his government's decision, saying, 'We also need to note that the defence personnel who figured in the case have been punished based on the same Tehelka tapes. You can't have two stands, one for defence personnel and another for politicians. Reddy clarified that as the tapes had been certified as genuine, 'appointing an Inquiry Commission is a diversionary ploy, particularly when influential politicians are caught taking money, from immediate criminal action.' Jaya Jaitly, traded accusations and charges with Congress Party spokesman, Anand Sharma, who she alleged had brought an arms dealer to her pleading for help, three years earlier. Jaya stated that there is a difference in the Army Act and the law applicable to civilians. Again, that raises the question – why was Jaya Jaitly meeting arms dealers at all and that too, through a Congress Party politician?

There was speculation that the reason why the UPA government had scrapped the Commission was to ensure that the first part of the report already submitted by Justice Phukan would never be exposed. This report dealt with fifteen defence deals, which had of course taken place under previous Congress governments.

Did she believe that the CBI would do a fair job? Jaya elaborated,

See, governments are always slow at paper work for one thing. Secondly, they probably also want to test the waters. Other than one paper or two, even *The Hindustan Times* has said, there is no need for this. Don't misuse Commissions. This will be seen as political vendetta. Specially, the Hindi *Dainik Jagaran* has come out quite strongly, very strongly. And once you start going on hounding people, people are not going to appreciate it. Nobody liked Indira Gandhi being hounded. Although she hounded the whole country during the Emergency but once they got after her with Commissions and what a big, fat drama. They made a mockery of that also. So, she came back and everybody was willing to wash away her genuine sins. Here, when everybody knows that George Sahab was a very popular defence minister, if there are deals, then they have enquired. At least say that you are not satisfied with these reports. But to just say that there is no interim report given, the term was already over and it wasn't going in the right direction because the motives of journalists were being enquired.

The Commission had come to an end and now this appeared to be a new beginning. Was Jaya now tired? Can a politician be honest and say what any normal person would say: 'Enough is enough'? Jaya answered with full political grandstanding:

When there is wrong-doing, having to fight it can never make me fed up. Because once you get into public life to make things better around you, then there is no end of it. If it had not been this, some other battle would have cropped up, in some other sphere. But, as much as I keep fighting, I do so much of constructive work, that I think that I keep a balance. I don't feel fed up. I just feel utterly disgusted with the kind of behaviour that government has shown because it has shown no respect for any norms or any sort of judicial processes. What's really happening is that by each one flinging mud at the other in any way that they can and using institutions to do it, they are making Indians look like criminals across the board all over the world. Everybody seems to have forgotten the politics of debate, of dialogue, of discussion or basic decency. CBI is to catch crooks who misuse the system, in ways where there is proper evidence, there is complete autonomy. The trouble is when you are in the Opposition you ask for CBI inquiries. When you are in government or when you accuse those who are in government of misusing so the CBI gets a big question mark on it. Now Commissions of Inquiry get a big question mark on it. Are we really cleansing the system or are we dirtying ourselves? These are issues which you can't say *ki* [that] now I am tired, I am going to sit back. If you are willy-nilly thrown into the thick of it, then you are going to deal with it.

Whew! Many would suggest a hug with an attempt to lighten up!

How did Tarun Tejpal react to the scrapping of the Commission? No, they were not exuberantly celebrating. He was indifferent. Tejpal said, 'We have not participated in the proceedings before the Commission as it was not interested in finding the truth. Only time will tell whether the CBI probe will be just and fair.' Aniruddha Bahal just guffawed his trademark hyena laugh. He was watching the *leela* [drama] of life.

On 6 December 2004, G. Mohanty, spokesman of the CBI, announced that the organization had formally filed criminal cases against Bangaru Laxman and Jaya Jaitly under various provisions of the Prevention of Corruption Act as well as Section 120-B of the Indian Penal Code for criminal conspiracy. It was reported that there was a dilemma within the CBI on what to charge Jaya Jaitly with. She was eventually charged of taking a bribe in order to influence the defence minister. Besides, the CBI was keen that the government should file a complaint, which it did in the last week of November 2004. The CBI registered cases under the Prevention of Corruption Act against ten persons in the Operation West End tapes. Among the ten were Major General S.P. Murgai (Retd), Gopal Pacherwal (president of the Samata Party in Rajasthan), S.K. Sureka (businessman from Kanpur), P. Sasi (assistant, Ordnance Services), H.C. Pant (then deputy director in the Ministry of Defence), Narender Singh (then assistant financial adviser in the Ministry of Defence), Uma Maheshwari Raju alias Raju Venkatesh (personal assistant to Bangaru Laxman), Satya Murthy (personal secretary to Bangaru Laxman). Reportedly, the group of ministers who have been meeting to work out a plan of action on Tehelka were Union Home Minister Shivraj Patil, Defence Minister Pranab Mukherjee, Law Minister H.R. Bhardwaj, and Science and Technology Minister, Kapil Sibal, (also a senior lawyer).

Last I heard, Jaya had been summoned and questioned by the CBI. Later, the CBI took the unedited tapes to Umashanker, the audio expert, and asked him to verify Jaya's words on the tape: 'Gopalji, *yeh rakh leejiyeh* [Gopalji, please keep this].'

Tejpal was cautious when he said, 'For the first three-and-a-half years the NDA government hounded us. We don't know how the CBI investigation will go. We have to see how the CBI does the job.' Bangaru Laxman said, 'When we had waited for nearly four years for the Tehelka Commission's report, why couldn't they have just allowed them to complete it? Why did they have to give it to the CBI? Obviously, it is a political game.'

Jaya hardly seemed surprised and was calm when she said,

This is a *sarkari tamasha* [government theatrics]. The CBI will try to do their job. But, in their investigation there has to be a fact. If there is no proven fact then where will they go? This is the Congress Party's political ploy. They have to cover up all their own scams, such as the Bofors scam. I did not accept the money nor did I say that I would help them. So what will they charge me with? I am not going to waste my time on this at all. If they want to play their games, let's see how far they go.

It begs repetition: Jaya Jaitly did verbally acknowledge the money for the Samata Party and Jaya did say she would send word to the ministry if West End was treated unfairly.

It was comedian Groucho Marx who said, 'Who are you going to believe? Me, or your own eyes?'

24 Not so Fine a Balance: Ethics and Journalism

Nelson Chaney [Welsey Addy]: All I know is that this violates every canon of respectable broadcasting.
Frank Hackett [Robert Duvall]: We're not a respectable network. We're a whorehouse network and we have to take whatever we can get.
Nelson Chaney: Well, I don't want any part of it. I don't fancy myself the president of a whorehouse.
Frank Hackett: That's very commendable of you, Nelson. Now sit down. Your indignation is duly noted; you can always resign tomorrow.

– Sidney Lumet's film, Network *(1976)*

In 1964, media critic Marshall McLuhan said, 'The medium is the message'. McLuhan induced us to examine whether we were absorbing the information/entertainment content or simply gazing vacuously at a television set. In the Tehelka sting operation, the medium of the clandestine shoot became the message. You could not think or speak about Operation West End without the undercurrent of the medium used: The Tehelka journalists had used hidden cameras to capture people. As a metaphor in journalism, what did Tehelka do? They crossed an unwritten line. They proved what could be done. They showed no mercy. They trapped their victims, some of whom were only living out what they thought was their work. Some of them were even likeable characters. Some, you felt downright sorry for.

The government instantly fell into its own trap in their determined belief that there had to be a conspiracy hatched by the Opposition or an arms dealer with a vested interest. Their monomaniacal corrupt atavism could not accommodate an altruistic motive. They could not believe that journalists would spend that kind of money or take such risks just to get a story. They set out to unearth a treacherous plot, and when they didn't find one they began spin-doctoring. They had no notion of what a conglomerate a journalist is.

Why does any person become a journalist? Tom Stoppard said, 'I still believe that if your aim is to change the world, journalism is a more immediate short-term weapon'. I would hazard a guess that there are few in India today who would not want to change the world around them. But journalists are often blamed for focusing on stories that many would prefer ignored or covered up.

The most unsurprising response of anyone caught in any scandal is, 'the media is the problem'. In other words, if the scandal is not exposed to the public, it remains small. But, should it? Roger Rosenblatt said, 'The principal reason journalists exist in society is that people have a need to be informed of and comprehend the details of the experience'. That is what our TV channels did in Gujarat. They brought the carnage into our living rooms. Should they have? Pressure exerted by the American public on politicians to bring an end to the Vietnam War came only after they saw their young men dying on their television sets.

If you listen to the politicians, journalists have an agenda to sensationalize events and exacerbate the problem. Many would be surprised that often, when you talk to some of the journalists directly involved, they evince a commitment to do their job fairly, honestly, without any agenda. The question of the capability of any individual being totally objective has long been debated. Can a journalist, who is supposed to report a plane crash and not a plane landing safely, point the camera at what a politician would want him to show? Should the television crews have pointed their cameras at the areas in Gujarat that were peaceful and ignored the violence? Should they have shown both to display 'balance'? That would have been like showing planes landing safely to give balance to a report on a plane crash.

What motivates these messengers of bad news? Journalists tend to be adventurists and danger junkies, imbued with an urge to be where the action is, to expose wrongdoing, injustice, and suffering, to catalyse change, to be an eyewitness to unfolding of historical events. To make money? Not in India. If your response is that many journalists take money from political parties and business houses to make enough, then so does a doctor who performs unnecessary operations. A good doctor's motivation stems from a desire to heal people. A serious journalist's motivation is to get a good story and give it to the people. It can be as simple as that. It can be. But, was it, in the case of Tehelka?

Frank Luther Mott wrote in *American Journalism* (1941), that although Joseph Pulitzer (*St Louis Post-Dispatch*) in 1883 and William Randolph Hearst (*San Francisco Examiner* and *New York Journal*) in 1895 pioneered yellow journalism, there were not only sensational headlines but also, 'ostentatious sympathy for the underdog'. Hearst clearly saw money in siding with the underdog. His avowed purpose, 'To make a great and continuous noise to attract readers; denounce crooked wealth and promise better conditions for the poor, to keep readers. Increase circulation.'

Essentially, that is what Tehelka sought to do. Was it a purely journalistic exercise with no aim of financial benefit? Of course not. Creating a sting operation that would push journalism and raise the value of their website is not a crime or even a misdemeanour. It can be applied to any profession. Tehelka chose investigative journalism because that was their passion, corruption their muse, and then their aggrandized website would be their crown. It turned out to be a crown with more than a few vicious thorns.

At the Commission, lawyers of those Caught on Tape repeatedly raised this issue. They insisted that the only motive Tehelka had was to make money. So? Tehelka never claimed to be a charitable organization.

Was then everything they did journalistically correct? Tarun Tejpal, Aniruddha Bahal, and Mathew Samuel all admitted in their cross-examinations before the Commission of Inquiry that they had never read the Press Council guidelines. Few journalists do until the

Press Council hauls them up; which is at best a small yelp, not even a bark, and certainly has no teeth. But Press Council regulates the print media and the relatively new broadcast journalism is not covered. The Press Council of India was first constituted on 4 July 1966, as an autonomous, statutory, quasi-judicial body, with Justice J.R. Mudholkar, then a judge of the Supreme Court, as chairman. It was abolished during Indira Gandhi's Emergency in 1976 and then re-constituted by the Press Council Act 1978 after Indira Gandhi was voted out of power. That it was abolished when Indira Gandhi scrambled to control the press is self-explanatory. The Press Council exists as much to protect the press as to control it. In assessing the Acts and Regulations in its formation of the Press Council, one cannot but conclude that they are deliberately liberal in favour of the freedom of the press and provide little or no power for any serious action against journalists. Other than upholding a complaint and censuring the publication concerned, the Press Council is not vested with any powers. It cannot even ask a journalist to reveal his sources. But the Press Council does publish Norms for Journalistic Conduct which should be required reading or at least, skimming for every working journalist.

The Cable Television Networks (Regulation) Act, 1995, covers all the usual – obscenity, national security, etc. If the government chose to go after them, they could have. This did not happen not because of any ethics or goodness of heart, but only because they know that every government that goes after the press rarely comes out a winner.

On 21 April 2001, Justice P.B. Sawant, chairman of the Press Council, gave his approval of Tehelka's methods of uncovering corruption. He pointed out that the undercover operation was done in public interest and did not infringe on the right to privacy. He believed that individuals holding public office must maintain a consistency in their public and private lives. 'The right to privacy has a limit. It ceases to be a right the moment it is used for anti-social activity. You cannot make bombs at your home and claim a right to privacy,' Sawant stated. He went so far as to say, 'There is no reason why society should not come forward and reward such organizations, who do excellent service to the nation.' Justice Sawant could have hauled up Tehelka had he been so inclined. Tehelka broke a number of the Press Council's guidelines. In the second paragraph of the Norms of Conduct:

Pre-publication Verification
2) On receipt of a report or article of public interest and benefit containing imputations or comments against a citizen, the editor should check with due care and attention its factual accuracy – apart from other authentic sources with the person or the organization concerned to elicit his/her or its version, comments or reaction and publish the same with due amendments in the report where necessary. In the event of lack or absence of response, a footnote to that effect should be appended to the report.

In the Operation West End tapes, there were enough allegations and stories spun that may have had no basis whatsoever. Getting a reaction from those who were mentioned on tape would admittedly have meant blowing their cover, in some instances. Giving Tehelka the benefit of the fear of sabotage, they could have editorially added in their voiceovers that none of what was being said on camera had been substantiated. It would not have substantially detracted from the weight of the statements made and the public would have been free to come to their own conclusions.

In the sixteenth paragraph of Norms of Conduct:

Right to Privacy
16) The Press shall not tape-record anyone's conversation without that person's knowledge or consent, except where the recording is necessary to protect the journalist in a legal action, or for other compelling good reason.

There is no provision in the Indian Constitution that enumerates and ensures the right to privacy. Surprised? You shouldn't be. Think. The concept of privacy does not exist in Indian culture. Relatives walking in and out of a newly married couple's bedroom is common. Locking a bedroom door invites raised eyebrows. A relative going to chaperone a couple on a honeymoon trip is normal. A parent knocking on a child's room before entering is only practised in Westernized homes. In many homes it is not unusual for the patriarch to open all the letters that arrive, no matter to whom they are addressed. Ask any ordinary Hindi-speaking person the word for privacy in Hindi, and the chances of his being unaware are high because in common parlance it is barely ever used. The concept of privacy is alien to Indian culture: in the Indian mind, why should anyone want to be alone? There must be something wrong with you if you do.

The issue of the right to privacy has been argued endlessly in the courts and judges have resorted to Article 21, 'No person shall be deprived of life or personal liberty except according to procedure established by law' to twist it into including the 'right to privacy.' A 1994 judgement passed by Judge Jeevan Reddy and Judge Suha C. Sen, ruled that writers had a right to publish the life story of the complainant Auto Shankar based on public records, even without his consent or authorization. 'The press has the right to publish life story of a private person subject to their being liable for consequences if they invade his right to privacy.' The judges quoted from precedents of American and British judgements. This meant that the petitioner could only file a case of invasion of privacy after the publication because there was no law to prevent it from being published.

The All-India Newspapers Editors have published a Code of Ethics, but Tehelka violated only one code in that:

4. Journalists should endeavour to ensure that information disseminated is factually accurate. No fact shall be distorted or the essential facts deliberately omitted. No information known to be false shall be published.

Essential facts were omitted. R.K. Jain's statements vouching for George Fernandes's honesty were edited out. Tehelka cut out an encounter they had with an honest bureaucrat in the defence ministry, Mr Doodani. He was furious with Mathew Samuel for offering him money and threatened to call the CBI if he did not leave immediately.

From the unedited West End tapes, Mathew Samuel offered Doodani a packet of money:

Doodani: No, no, no, sorry.
Samuel: Awkay, awkay, I am sorry. Sasi told me.
Doodani: Please never do this. Never. No, absolutely not.
Samuel: I am sorry.
Doodani: I will see Sasi.
Samuel: Sasi told me.
Doodani: No, no. no. I am very much against these things.
Samuel: Sasi told me.
Doodani: No, I told Sasi.
Samuel: I'm sorry. I'm sorry. I'm rrrreally sorry. I'm rrrrreally sorry.
Doodani: I'm never for these things. You've got a … he just told me that you wanted some advice, I said, "Okay. Friendly advice I can give to him." But, your this thing, sorry!
Samuel: Sasi told me.
Doodani: I'll just ring up Sasi.
Samuel: Sasi, I'm calling from Mr Doodani's home. You told me, "Give the money to Mr Doodani." I did, one moment.
Doodani: Hello? Sasi? What is this you are doing? What's this nonsense? No, that day when you spoke to me, I told you very clearly if he wanted friendly advice, okay, welcome. But, then do you think he can bring the money over here and put it before me? Am I that kind of man? No, no, no, no. I don't want to hear.
Samuel: He told me to give.
Doodani: Yes, I am very disturbed.
Samuel: I am rrreally verrrry sorry.

This was a serious breach of fair journalism. Tehelka said they wanted the public to know about the corrupt system. The public was equally entitled to learn that there are honest officers. In this, senior editors in any organization play a crucial role. They ask for the other side of the story, ensure all the facts are double-checked and that no journalists push an agenda. Tarun Tejpal was too busy trying to run the website and Aniruddha Bahal was in charge of the investigative cell. Bahal was also the man running Operation West End. There was no objective eye looking at editing decisions. Journalists habitually fall in love with the angle of the story on which they are focusing and any point raised that moves it away from that angle, is dropped. The integrity of George Fernandes and Doodani moved them away from their exposure of corruption. That was a 'Tipping Point'. It made their report appear biased.

When Tehelka hired sex workers for the army officers they violated the Immoral Traffic (Prevention) Act, 1956, conviction under which could mean imprisonment from seven to ten years. The government, cognizant that it was done in pursuit of a story, did not follow through on this. Tehelka also broke the law in offering bribes to defence personnel and bureaucrats. According to the law,

> Whoever abets the committing of mutiny by an officer, soldier, sailor or airman, in the Army, Navy or Air Force of the Government of India or attempts to seduce any such officer, soldier, sailor or airman from his allegiance or his duty, shall be punished with imprisonment for life, or with imprisonment of either description for a term which may extend to ten years, and shall also be liable to fine.

In many ways Operation West End carried a whiff of a boarding school adventure. Aniruddha and Samuel were going in there with their cameras blazing. What was the atmosphere like in Tehelka? Kajal Basu, a journalist with twenty years of experience, was features editor in Tehelka during the sting operation. He spoke about the best and worst about Tehelka. According to him, he had only heard rumours about a sting operation in progress but Tarun, Aniruddha, and Samuel never spoke to anyone about it.

Basu said that transcribing the tapes was a massive affair. People were locked in a room for weeks. It was messy because the audio quality was so bad, they couldn't understand many words. Basu recalled:

> **Basu:** One part with Samuel, it took about half a day to transcribe. He kept using the word "wax". Now no one could make out what "wax" was? Till it turned out to be "hoax.'"

Basu believed that if Aniruddha had only vet the transcriptions, they would not have had to face all the problems that arose in the Commission. Basu said he kept asking him to, but Aniruddha was busy setting fires elsewhere.

> **Madhu:** Was there any tampering with the tapes or audio-recordings being generated and inserted in different parts of the tape?
> **Basu:** It wasn't possible with the kind of technology we used. It did not permit tampering either by digitizing or whatever. I have known Tarun for a long, long time. There is absolutely no way he would do that. Nor Aniruddha. I don't doubt their characters. They will not do that. Where the doubt comes in is the way they used sex workers. That's where you might find fault with them. There was no time for tampering. While the first part was being shown at Imperial Hotel, Minty was still editing the ending.

Basu said he disagreed with Tarun about how the story was handled. He said, 'The story had enthusiasm, journalistic pulse, a word Tarun used a lot but the story lacked journalistic vigour.' Basu felt that in a story of such magnitude, Tarun got pushed into releasing it before it was ready because the players got to know about it. Basu said,

> **Basu:** You sort of build up a fortress somewhere. You stop the government legally. You get a stay order. There are ways and means to stop the government from acting. In the meanwhile, what you do is you hole up and you finish your work. Even if it takes a week or a couple of weeks, and that could have been done.
>
> **Madhu:** Did Operation West End damage journalism?
>
> **Basu:** No, very brave journalists will not say that. Whether the government is going to come down on your head or not, you don't know. But a lot of journalists did ask at the end of the day, "What did you get out of it?" You got unemployment out of it, which is stupid really because it doesn't really work that way. The government is going to fall, is again overstating the case. It is cowboy journalism, young, enthusiastic, without anchors. And Minty's words, he is so much more brazen than Tarun is again: "Screw them. We will screw them." In Hindi, "We'll screw them". Let's take away Goliath because you will never get a chance like this again. And the mere fact that you have taken away a Goliath is a story by itself. So whether the story turns out to be good or bad can be handled later. But you've taken away a Goliath, that's your story. And what a wonderful story it was.
>
> **Madhu:** Do you think that if they had followed the basic tenets of journalism, which is that if somebody said that Brajesh Mishra controls everything, they went to Brajesh Mishra and said, look, we have got this statement from someone. And they had the denials on tape. Do you think that would have made the story stronger?
>
> **Basu:** They could not have done that. I don't believe that. Had the government got to know one tenth of what they got later, they would have destroyed it. They would have burnt Tehelka to the ground. They would have bombed Tehelka. They would have done something. Just look at their reaction after the story came out. Before the story was out, to kill the story they would have done just about anything. Tehelka wasn't known. Tarun wasn't known. Ani wasn't known. If you burn down Tehelka, who would have gotten to know? There wouldn't have been any difference at all. There is no way. I think they could have taken two or one Supreme Court Justice into confidence. Or several like-minded, into confidence and told them that listen this is what we are doing. Maybe it would have worked. I think it would have made it more responsible.

⌒

But the obvious dangers of sitting on a story like that cannot be sniffed at. And every single person remotely connected felt they were targeted. Sidharth Luthra recalled,

> The pressure was great for all of us. Surveillance was expected, phone tapping a norm. In the last days when Kumar Badal got arrested, there were times when we felt Aniruddha would also be arrested. On a couple of occasions, I drove to Noida at midnight and we walked into a public park to talk, fearing tapping while deciding on strategy in the event he was arrested. I cannot describe to you the atmosphere at that time. I was afraid for my mother and children to go out alone.

In 1981, Arun Shourie, as executive editor of *The Indian Express*, on line to expose corruption, directed a reporter to expose the buying and selling of girls. The reporter, Ashwani Sarin, filed his story after going to Madhya Pradesh and buying a girl called Kamala. Sarin and Shourie broke the law. Shourie, cognizant of correct conduct, wrote to five eminent persons, including two Supreme Court judges that *The Indian Express* planned to violate the law to expose this racket. On the day of publication, Shourie and Sarin filed a writ petition in the Supreme Court seeking an investigation into the trafficking of young girls. But, it must be noted, unlike Tehelka's exposé, this corruption did not directly affect the government in power.

Arun Shourie has always been a crusader, whatever tools he uses. It could be writing articles, books, and yes, even politics. He was the first in India to become an activist-journalist, a path that many subsequently sought to follow. Shourie holds strong views on the method of journalism. He believes that sting operations are a valid form of journalism because 'there is such a stone wall and when deals are struck in shadows, then you really have to have night vision of some kind'. Shourie did have a problem with including the girls, and felt that was going too far. He clarified,

> The line is this: that then the person you're asking a question of, you put him in a situation where you could actually blackmail him subsequently into saying things. I'm not saying that that is what happened. That's the distinction – you may do something to inveigle a person into disclosing the truth, but not put him in a position where you can then later on cause him into saying something. Because then it's your word against his word, he will say, "I was coerced into saying something", and the journalist will say, "No, he wasn't". That was the only distinction.

Shourie believed that Tehelka could have informed a few trustworthy, eminent people that they were carrying out a sting. He pointed out that certain factual errors were made in the tapes, where somebody made a claim that he had made money on a particular missile. Later it was discovered that the government had not bought that item. Tarun told Shourie in a discussion on television, that they had already worked nine months on the story, so there was no time to check. Shourie's view is that they had all those nine months to check. He believed it was important not to simply broadcast allegations without substantiation. Tarun responded, 'Let the public decide'. Shourie said that could take two or three years, and in the meantime great harm is done. He believed that if the allegations prove to be false, then besides destroying lives and reputations, it discredits journalism and weakens an essential instrument for ensuring democracy. When I pointed out that their cover had been blown so they were under pressure, Shourie responded, 'That is one point. But what Tarun was saying, from the way he put it at that time, it was as if it was enough to broadcast the allegations.'

On the state of journalism in today's India, Shourie expressed his shock that editorial space was being sold and the average reader did not grasp that it was not news but a promotion. He added,

> I regard Samir Jain [*The Times of India*] as a good person, but I regard his approach as completely, but completely, destructive of public discourse and of journalism in India. This whole emphasis on lifestyle journalism, this whole business of newspaper as a product like soap, this whole business of deliberately slapping the editors down, sometimes there are response managers, sometimes papers are without editors; this business of having two editorials on the same subject as if it's just a high school debate. All these; now for instance, treating the great aspect of political life of India, the five-yearly elections, as just a comic show going on. This is destructive of journalism and it is fatal to political discourse in India. I really feel *The Times of India* is up for being taken on by somebody who will spend money, fifty crores or hundred crores, in Bombay itself, who will put in that investment and have a credible newspaper. It's necessary in Bombay because that's where the money comes in for advertising. It is this business of suborning the advertising agencies and thereby getting the money.

Meanwhile, *The Times of India* is laughing all the way to expansion, joint ventures, and multi inter-connected products. It was reported in January 2005 that *The Times of India* had struck long-term advertising deals with clients by picking up equity stakes in companies and bartering promoting those brands in all their media. Clearly, journalism is low on the agenda. The proprietor of one of the largest newspaper chains reportedly said that for him his newspaper was the same as selling soap. But, the average readers are not aware that what they are reading is soap. About selling editorial space, Shourie said,

> **Shourie:** That is why it is all the more destructive, and that is why it is the duty of everyone, even by word of mouth, to spread this fact. We are, as you said, going through great transition and globalization does not mean trivialization. After all, *The International Herald Tribune* or *The Washington Post* or *The New York Times* or *The Los Angeles Times* or *The Wall Street Journal*, they're responsible, and there they are the mastheads of globalization. I know that when they come to interview any one of us they check it three times, later on. Then somebody will ring up from Hong Kong, then somebody will ring up

from Washington, is this what you said? What is the background to this? *Par yahaan, joh marzi karte jao* [here you go on doing what ever you please]… I see this in disinvestment, in stock markets, that there are so many of these plants in economic papers for instance, you don't know whether this is a newspaper or it is a part of the horticulture department. Absolutely so many fabrications. And then when I mentioned it to somebody he said *nahin, nahin saab, voh toh stock market mein player hai khud* [no, no, he plays the stock market himself].

Madhu: In your view, how should Tehelka have been dealt with?

Shourie: I think journalists must always deal with things by focusing on the facts. Whatever the motives of the journalists, my responsibility is to answer the facts. That was certainly my plea within government.

Madhu: In the end, do you think Tehelka did the right thing? Besides the girls, did Tehelka serve the cause of good journalism?

Shourie: With those two caveats, yes. Checking allegations and not putting other people in a position where the viewer could presume that the person could be blackmailed into saying things. With these two things, yes, whatever the journalists did, in my view, was correct.

Madhu: The investors Shankar Sharma and Devina Mehra were particularly harassed. The government filed nearly 300 cases against them.

Shourie: Firstly, it is my view that I have often articulated within government, it is the manifest record in India that any government that raises a hand against the press will have the hand singed. And there are other views. Some governments will say that, no, might as well make an example of one and see everybody else will learn. There's a phrase [that] you kill one and frighten a thousand. But my view has been quite contrary, and these people have certainly given me the time for me to articulate this. Second, I think the lesson is, we learnt this in *The Indian Express*, if you are going to stand up to the State, then please don't expect the other fellow to be Snow White. This doesn't mean the State should not, I am not condoning what the State does, but from the journalists' point of view, we notice this. You take up something and there will be an income tax raid on Ramnathji's [the late Ramnath Goenka, owner of *The Indian Express*] house, this inquiry, customs inquiry, excise, something or the other. So you must be absolutely above reproach.

Madhu: But hasn't this been a bad sign for journalism, in the sense that the investors have had to pay heavily for the sting operation?

Shourie: My own view about the State is it should not be doing this. If this was the reason behind the State, in the end, I'm sure it will recoil on the State itself. The second aspect really is, that everything depends upon your persevering in that conduct. What happens is, *The Indian Express* does something. The State comes down on it. When that was happening, everybody was against us. Giri Lal Jain used to write one-and-a-half page articles against me: a Galahad of the Press. When *The Indian Express* edition in Delhi was closed, it was *The Times of India* workers and union which then came and beat our people up when we were trying to go in. That is on video. Now supposing *The Indian Express* at that time had given up and recoiled, or did not have the resources to go on, or Ram Nathji was not that much of a fighter, then there would be no lesson in it at all. But because it persevered, because the owner persevered, therefore that government went and the paper continued. That was the contribution to journalism. In this case what's happened is, for economic reasons, or maybe because others did not take up the issue, both reasons, Tehelka did not then survive. Or that kind of operation was then given up. Therefore, it becomes a warning rather than an example to other journalists. It really depends upon other people taking up that kind of work.

Madhu: Friedrich Nietzsche wrote about the two classes of Man. He said that all of history was a metaphysical struggle between two groups, those who "will to power" and those who are poor and impoverished. It seems that struggle continues to this day. In this case, does Tehelka fall in the category of the weak? You have said, "The proposition that man is not an effective agent for changing the man-made world strengthens the inertia of the oppressed and rationalizes the callousness of the rulers." Tehelka, in their way, saw themselves as agents of change by exposing corruption. Would you question that?

Shourie: Well, yes and no. See, one is that it is not just that there is one group that has the will to power and the rest of the people, no. I think the great contribution of the 1990s has been that now there are more centres of power. The people in politics are not the only powerful people now. The great power that the bureaucracy had is much diluted today. We are now getting what the Americans' strength is, centres of countervailing power. Some is with industries, some with individual industrialists, some with CII, FICCI – in terms of legitimacy, in terms of research – and some with politicians. Very few politicians command power today because of moral authority. The state apparatus itself is able to get one Shankar Sharma, but in general it is not able to wreak revenge, because it's a palsied hand.

Madhu: You've written and spoken very often on the code of conduct for journalists. You have written criticizing the journalism of today, but it doesn't seem to be reaching many journalists. More and more unsubstantiated stuff is being printed. More reporters seem open to plants. There is a serious reluctance to admit mistakes and make corrections. If one TV station reports an erroneous story, all follow without checking the facts. There are no corrections; they just move on to the next story.

Shourie: Right. That's the way things are. In the sense, that I see that even in [the] Department of Telecom or Disinvestment. Absolute fabrications against individual officers come out. I ring up the people, I try to get to them, they just don't even respond. So what to do about it? I think we just have to either ride through this or use every little, feeble occasion to make this point in public, with actual examples. I try to do my little bit in that regard.

Madhu: There is a movement in America amongst senior editors to protect their product; that is their credibility. In India, the proprietors do not view credibility as their product.

Shourie: Therefore, it is very sorry to see that organizations like the Editors Guild, on the one side, and the Press Council, on the other, have just, sort of, faded away. A generational change in owners, a generational change in editors, absolute youngsters coming out of college, suddenly becoming so powerful because of this television journalism, so all that has contributed to this. I don't have any ready solution for that, except for people to talk about it and write about it as much as possible. Even fifteen years ago, ten years ago, a number of columns had started, attempts even at TV portrayals, "This last week in journalism," people were writing about the press. Even that has now been given up. Because everybody feels that he is now a part of the same crowd.

Arun Shourie's position on the ethics of Tehelka is not unusual for an activist-journalist. However, it does make him a maverick as a minister appointed by the party in power that decided to go after the journalists. In this situation, it just so happened that the BJP was in power. It could have been any party and the story would not be much different. Any degree of difference would only be the level of vindictiveness, which definitely could have been worse.

The inevitable, contentious debate began in the press on whether Tehelka was correct in its approach to the story, correct in undertaking sting journalism in the first place, correct in using money, alcohol, and sex workers as lures. Needless to say, there was microanalysis on every issue and there wasn't anyone who didn't have any opinion. Once the initial shock began to wear off, so did the support for Tehelka's actions.

Vir Sanghvi, editorial director (during the Tehelka exposé) of *The Hindustan Times* was one of the few who supported Tehelka through numerous articles. In answer to my question, Sanghvi said,

In principle I don't think you can take a black and white position about sting journalism and say it is a good thing or a bad thing. Having said that, all the usual rules apply. I think traditionally the profession all over the world is uneasy about sting journalism. Nobody is willing to say it's a bad thing but equally there seems to be some kind of consensus that it cannot be your raison d'être. You use it sometimes, as rarely as possible and only when nothing else will work.

In the case of the defence deals it was justified, yes. Because it is talked about that there is corruption in defence deals but nobody can prove it, which is why I have supported them on this. What else could they have done?

When a journalist conducts a sting operation against the government in power, he is obviously putting his organization at risk. Doing sting operations on say, corruption in medical admissions, are relatively low cost, since if they come back it's not going to destroy your organization. I am not so sure when Tarun embarked on Operation West End, he realized that he risked losing Tehelka then. And whether he would still have done it if he knew that then, I don't know. Of course now he would say that. But equally with Tarun, I think that he thought he would get away with it.

The Tehelka journalists believed that when they introduced sex workers they were following the story to its conclusion by showing that the army officers were vulnerable to blackmail. Sanghvi wrote an article expressing his disagreement with that. He clarified,

> Admittedly this was new territory. They were making it up as they went along, but remember, I said that there is no such thing as pimping in the public interest. You have to draw the line. If a guy then said beat so and so up, would you have beaten him up just to keep the story going? So obviously some lines have to be drawn somewhere.

Would Sanghvi accept a story, such as the one about the sex tapes, from a known plant? He would, after verifying such tapes indeed existed, getting Tarun's side of the story and if it was a legitimate story. He would not turn it down just because Jaya Jaitly benefited from it.

When Sanghvi joined *The Hindustan Times*, he changed the policy that you ran a story and if the person complained, there would be an apology the next day. He said,

> I insist that anybody who is involved in a story must get an equal chance to be quoted before the story appears. It doesn't always work for three reasons. One is, often journalists are in a hurry to file stories and say, why should I check with that liar? Two, they also take the line that if you check with the source, your whole story might disappear. They are not willing to take that risk. And three, very often sources believe that if you have this kind of rule, that if you don't respond, the story will go away. So often they won't respond to your calls. I now have a policy, which is that, if the guy doesn't take your calls you have to send him a written questionnaire saying we are doing this. Fax it, e-mail it and keep a record of when the fax is received. So that he can't say later that he didn't get it. And at least in one or two cases, people have called me and said I have just got your fax. It's eight in the evening, I am going out for dinner, can you hold the story over for a day and I have done that.

How does an editor like Sanghvi prevent false reports and plants in a large organization like *The Hindustan Times*? Sanghvi recalled that he had to sack a reporter who concocted a quote from George Fernandes about a letter he wrote to the Speaker of the House. The letter existed but to tart up the story, she added George's fake quote, 'I've had sleepless nights and I can't cope with all this.' Fernandes complained to Sanghvi. After Sanghvi ascertained that she had never met Fernandes and the tape she insisted she had of the quote 'accidentally' broke, he planned to fire her. But the day before this person could be dismissed, she got a television programme on a channel and she continues to be a television anchor doing an interview programme.

How does Sanghvi view the state of journalism today? Sanghvi reflected,

> **Sanghvi:** The first of which were the changes that came about in the 1990s with liberalization where in some sense, our papers moved into the twentieth century, finally. You had for the first time the growth of a consuming middle class. We had a huge demographic shift and the newspapers began trying more and more to appeal to the younger reader. There is that famous, probably apocryphal story about Samir Jain coming to meet a bunch of new people joining *The Times*. He asked, "How many of you come from homes where *The Times of India* is read?" And all of them like *chamchas* put up their hands. And he said, "I don't want you. I don't want your parents to read the newspaper. They are too old for me. I only want younger people." If you see it as a continuum, if you see the growth of these lifestyle supplements, the devaluation of the post of the editor, then the selling of *Delhi Times* and *Bombay Times* is like the logical thing. In the initial days when they started, when you paid for a picture they would have a little thing saying Medianet. Now they don't even bother to say that. So there is no attempt now to distinguish between news and advertising.
>
> **Madhu:** There was a big controversy that erupted over that.
>
> **Sanghvi:** Yes, there was a big uproar. But, they were quite shameless about it. So they don't even bother to say that this is paid for. Now it's only a matter of time when this switches to the main paper. *HT City* is a lifestyle supplement. *Delhi Times* is a Delhi supplement. There will be quite serious stories on roads in Delhi, etc. Even those can be sponsored. They were shameless. In fact, Samir Jain told me that everything else we have done, within a year every other newspaper will do it. Nobody has done it. There still is a basic commitment to truth, to certain standards, in other newspaper organizations.
>
> **Madhu:** Does the Tehelka metaphor now establish that you cannot fight the system?
>
> **Sanghvi:** I don't know. I am beginning to wonder whether you could ever have fought the system. The only examples you have of people trying to fight the system before, were really Ramnath Goenka. In each case, the system retaliated with such massive force. Two things went wrong with Tehelka. One was, not

only was it a little website. All its problems coincided with the end of the dotcom boom.

Madhu: Why did the press not support Tehelka?

Sanghvi: It's not something that reflects well on the press. But my experience with the press is that we don't stand by each other. In the case of many editors and Tarun, it was a very strong competitive element and very strong personal jealousy. Tarun was on television every day. He was being fêted. He was going around the country. They were saying, "Who is this kid? And how is he suddenly become this champion of Indian journalism? He is just a pornographer." Who is this guy? He claims he stands for investigative journalism. What, he thinks he invented it?

Virtually all the editors of the major news organizations mentioned that a pervasive cloud of envy enveloped the journalist community. A caterwauling buzz gushed out in the press about the ethics of sting operations. Looking back, it is astounding that Aniruddha Bahal and Mathew Samuel hurtled into the sting without any discussion, planning, or introspection. In comparison, in 1989, when Long Island's newspaper, *Newsday*, was considering a proposal put up by two reporters that there was racial steering by real estate brokers in Long Island, they took over a year to mull over it. The reporters suggested 200 matched tests, employing ten white and ten black couples. They wanted to blow the belief that blacks can buy homes anywhere in America. The editorial team painstakingly examined the ethics, doubts of authenticity, logistics, deception, and secrecy. Anthony Moro, editor of *Newsday*, seriously considered the proposal but entertained doubts about what he called the 'threshold'. Moro said, 'The question is, should there be a threshold of presumed bad conduct before a newspaper unleashes this sort of thing on unsuspecting people?' His reporters assured him there was. Meanwhile, in November/December 1989, *The Hartford Courant* ran a front-page story describing discrimination after reporters tested fifteen real estate agencies in and around Hartford. Funnily enough, two weeks later, *The Hartford Courant's* reader-representative, Henry McNulty, wrote a dissenting column, pointing out that the reporters had misrepresented themselves and lied. The *Newsday* team continued to labour over the logistics and ethics. In September 1990, *Newsday* ran a series, 'A World Apart: Segregation on Long Island'. It was based on research, personal accounts, and statistics that proved that racial segregation in housing was a reality.

Clandestine news reporting is not new, and there is a long list of them conducted all over the world. The most respectable, conservative press establishments have used clandestine filming to get a story that often ended up in courts. Rarely, however, has it been used only to show people having sex or even proposing sex. One hundred years ago, Nelly Bly exposed the pathetic conditions at New York's Blackwells Island Insane Asylum in an article, 'Ten Days in a Madhouse'. She did it by courageously misrepresenting herself as insane. More recently, the television programme 20/20 (ABC News, US) went undercover to prove that manufacturers had to pay New York stores to have their product placed on shelves. Primetime's programme (also ABC News) is best known for its repeated undercover stories. On 5 November 1992, Primetime showed store employees of the Food Lion supermarket chain take old meat and chicken, relabel it to be sold as fresh. Primetime has shown tele-evangelists performing fake miracles, day-care centre workers slapping babies, doctors involved in fraud and misreading mammograms. They planted a hidden camera in the Malawi president's London hotel room to expose his extravagant shopping while his nation starved. They have gone as far as Peru to broadcast an adoption story concerning Americans who paid for babies who were not permitted to leave. Primetime hid cameras in a filthy veterans' hospital showing devastating footage of a quadriplegic screaming hopelessly for help. Primetime got embroiled in legal battles when they went undercover to reveal the unsanitary conditions in Food Lion supermarkets. In November 1992, Primetime exposed open racism in employment and even in car sales. In 1979, *The Chicago Sun-Times* conducted one of the best-known sting operations in a story about corruption among city inspectors. They nearly won the Pulitzer Prize for it, but notably lost out because the Pulitzer board disapproves of sting operations. In 2003, twenty-six-year-old Jennifer Hersey, an investigative producer with Orlando television station WFTV, nabbed Palm Beach County Assistant State Attorney Ira Karmelin in an Internet sting. Posing as a thirteen-year-old, Hersey engaged Karmelin in sex talk and was recorded masturbating by a webcam. Arrested, and even though subsequently released, Karmelin's life was destroyed by the exposé. There was a serious divide over whether Hersey was correct in her methods. Media ethicist, Jane Kirtley of the University of Minnesota's School of Journalism and former executive director of the Reporters Committee for Freedom of the Press, said she was concerned that Hersey, masquerading as an underage teen had engaged in deception, even though the eventual goal was a worthy one. Kirtley said, journalists are not an arm of law enforcement and must remain independent of it. 'Our role is to report the news, not engage in undercover police work,' she insisted. Surely Kirtley would then have disapproved of Tehelka's methods. However, WFTV's news director, Bob Jordan, said that although he believed that reporters should not misrepresent themselves or use deception, there were a few instances where traditional newsgathering does not work. Jordan believed they had done a public service because when he learnt that people were using webcams to perform lewd acts in front of children, the public, especially parents had to be informed. Jordan had the plan vetted by an attorney before Hersey was told to go ahead. Jordan proclaimed, 'We would do it again. Somebody in an ivory tower may not like it but that's what the ivory tower is for. If we talk about ethics of conduct, let's talk about the ethics of the person who went on the Web.'

Robert Kapler (*The Guide*) went undercover working as a security guard in the nuclear plant on Three Mile Island, to reveal the lax security. During the Gulf War, Jonathan Franklin went undercover in Dover Air Force Base as a mortician to learn the actual casualty figures which he was convinced were being glossed over. He was a freelance journalist but had the support of *The San Francisco Bay Guardian* and *Spin* magazine.

In India's tradition of irony, it was the politicians who swung into the sting mode. On 17 November 2003, *The Indian Express* published transcripts of video footage in which Minister of State for Forest Dilip Singh Judeo in the A.B. Vajpayee's government, was caught accepting money, saying, 'Money isn't God but, God promise, it's no less than God'. The videotape had even greater impact when it was also released to news channels. This was another case of a story with dubious antecedents being accepted and the possibility arises of the press being used by politicians. Arun Jaitley, Union law minister in the BJP government, on 28 November 2003, three days before the Chattisgarh elections, alleged that the sting operation was carried out by Akash Channel in Raipur which was owned by Ajit Jogi's (Congress Party) son, Amit. Jaitley asked the press why the persons who were responsible for the tape had not come forward to claim credit for it if it was a purely journalistic exercise. Jaitley stated, 'I would go so far to say that I have no right to ask them [The Indian Express] who their sources are. We are not questioning them. It is, therefore, not an issue of the party versus the press. It's a political battle between us and our political opponents.' A less sophisticated politician would have gone after The Indian Express.

With BJP being the government in power, it wouldn't have been a problem to ask the CBI to probe the origin of Dilip Singh Judeo tape. In Indian politics there is nothing sweeter than the taste of revenge. On 6 December 2003, Arun Jaitley played a tape of Ajit Jogi, chief minister of Chattisgarh discussing with BJP MLA Virendra Pandey, the strategy to stop the BJP from forming a government in the state. Jaitley showed a stash of currency notes, Rs 45 lakh, which Jogi had allegedly paid. Jogi is heard saying that the Congress would prop up a BJP government led by BJP MLA Baliram Kashyap. Jaitley was unabashed about it being a sting operation and said that two journalists from television channels had witnessed it. The revenge would have come full circle if the BJP had given it to The Indian Express as an exclusive. Tehelka gave birth to an idea and politicians picked it up.

The Indian Express has always been in the forefront in investigative stories. Shekhar Gupta is an editor who is respected for his integrity and perspective. Gupta said that it was impossible to separate sting and investigative journalism, as they require a wide definition. He said he would agree to run a sting like Operation West End but would confine the story to middlemen and brokers. He said, there would be a follow-up on information provided by brokers on weapons system sales, whether or not it actually happened. He added that there were all kinds of people who might sit in the Press Club and gossip about all kinds of big names with great authority without any of it being true. Gupta said he would approve a sting operation under exceptional circumstances provided it did not pry into people's personal lives. Gupta felt it was okay to catch on film, if money is actually being given as a bribe, and if money is being paid to somebody by way of evidence, that so-and-so accepts bribes, then that is legitimate. 'But what I will not do is give someone a lakh of rupees to buy a file. That I will not do.'

Madhu: Would you also bring women in to prove that the officers are vulnerable?

Gupta: I certainly won't, but I will not sit in judgement on whether Tehelka should have done it or not. Except if I read all those transcripts, I do not hear those guys asking for women. In fact, I see on the other hand, Tehelka guys pushing those women on them. In fact, I remember some kind of reluctance, *haaan theek hai* [it's okay]. Now Tehelka can always justify it by saying we had to push the story forward, so we thought pile them with, whatever. But, once you are running a whole sting operation, then you can't say but I will film this and I will not film this. Because suppose you're filming them, and while the guy is having sex with the woman, he may say something, he may tell her something about some deal. I think once you're doing this, you can go the whole nine yards.

Madhu: With hidden cameras you are not always in a position to switch the cameras on and off.

Gupta: Yeah, yeah. But I think, the whole thing became a little childish. I think people were having a lot of fun doing this and that's where they lost their way a little bit.

Madhu: I was told by an extremely reliable source that one of Jaya Jaitly's lawyers, you could say the horse's mouth, planted the story about the sex tapes in your newspaper.

Gupta: I'll be very surprised. You can check with Anjali, she no longer works with us. But even if she did, I have no problem. It doesn't matter where a story comes from, as long as the story is accurate and as long as you've given the other side a right to respond, fairly. I think most journalists get stories, exclusive stories from somebody who's interested. You could apply this even to whistle-blowers. Why do they talk to the media? They talk to the media because through the media they can make a point. But, in this case, I do not think so. I do not think it came from Jaya Jaitly's lawyer. But I do not usually follow the principle of asking the reporters where they got their story from, as long as the story is good. In this case, the story was sound. It was perfectly valid. It was perfectly accurate and more than adequate play was given to what the other side had to say.

Madhu: Why do you think the press has really not supported Tehelka after a point?

Gupta: The press has supported them very, very strongly. They have become household names. They have been on television channels all the time. The newspapers – I don't know of any newspaper that has written an editorial which has not editorially supported them. Beyond that how much can the press do? On the other hand, the media has not supported *The Indian Express* on its exposé of the petrol pumps. The media has not even picked up *The Indian Express's* series on defaulters in the companies banking system. A lakh and ten thousand crores – not a single newspaper has carried even a line in follow-up.

Madhu: What Tarun sees is that he's being harassed and destroyed. Tehelka had to close down for lack of funds. He sees that the government has made that happen.

Gupta: I'm sure there is a degree of harassment, but everybody suffers harassment. We've suffered harassment. Rajiv Gandhi filed nearly a thousand cases against *The Indian Express* during the Bofors story. More than three hundred are still pending. They are still there. Non-compoundable. But in the media, once you decide to do journalism of this kind, you have to carry on. You have to build institutional strength to be able to handle it. When we ran the series on the petrol pumps, we knew the risks involved. These are all powerful people who are well connected, who are networked. Unless they had support in the political system, they would not have been able to get away with stealing a lakh and ten thousand crore. Many of them control a lot of advertising as well. So those are risks.

Madhu: Do you feel sometimes that in journalism in India, one is doing these stories only for one's self, because the impact is minimal and the consequences are not what you expect them to be?

Gupta: Sometimes, but you always make some difference. I'm sure even Tehelka has made some difference. But yes, the media doesn't work together in India. But Tehelka really got a huge amount of support from the media. I have not seen any exposé in the history of Indian media get so much support from the media. But you know, the rest of the media, cannot fight with the government on your behalf.

Madhu: Do you think it was good journalism?

Gupta: It was an interesting story. It was a good story. It's easy to say, but if you're doing a sting, it can be done very differently. It would have made a much, much greater impact. But if you seek a popular view, most people will believe that there was a lot of racketeering and they exposed it.

⌒

Journalism set in motion a disturbing trend on 15 December 2004, when *Mid-Day* (Mumbai) published photographs of actors Kareena Kapoor and her then boyfriend Shahid Kapur French kissing in Rain, a restaurant in Mumbai. Kareena sent a legal notice to *Mid-Day* seeking an unconditional apology but received little support from the Mumbai film industry, with Amitabh Bachchan admonishing that, 'If you allow yourself to be photographed, that is no fault of the media'. Kareena Kapoor claimed that the pictures had been doctored but *Mid-Day* stood its ground and said they had proof that they were genuine.

On 13 March 2005, India TV, a fledgling channel, aired clandestinely shot footage of two otherwise unknown Bihar MLA politicians fornicating with prostitutes. How far does one have to bend one's mind to accept this as legitimate journalism? Indian journalism has always followed the line of never stepping into the personal lives of politicians. Even prime ministers with their paramours were basically left alone. Atal Bihari Vajpayee laid down his rules to a journalist who asked him about his personal life: 'Ask me anything about politics but my personal life is my own.' If some unimportant politicians were doing their thing with prostitutes, how did it in any way affect politics or the public? When Bill Clinton was going through the ringer about his relationship with Monica Lewinsky, there was a general reaction in India: What's the big deal? We were told: 'It is not because of what he did. It is because he lied.' Well, why ask a question that should or need not be asked?

One of India TV's reporters, 'Ruchi', snared B-grade Bollywood villain Shakti Kapoor in a casting couch sting. After chasing the actor for over seven months, begging him to give her an acting role, Ruchi finally got him in a hotel room, gave him whiskey, and offered herself. Kapoor mentioned major Bollywood stars who had made it by sleeping with their directors or producers. He was then ready for action when the cameras were discovered and he proceeded to beat up the cameramen and abuse the girl. When the channel was attacked for using sleaze to raise their viewership, Rajat Sharma, owner of India TV, said, 'For all our sting operations, including the recent ones on Bollywood stars, politicians and sadhus, we have got tremendous public support which is clearly reflected in the recent TAM [Television Audience Measurements] ratings'. Shakti Kapoor went on another channel and apologized to his wife, his family, the actresses he had said had slept around, and everybody else he could think of. It was reported that his family was devastated and his son refused to go out or speak to anyone.

The reaction to the tapes shown on India TV was generally one of distaste. It discredited sting operations and journalism. We were pompously told that city people might be disapproving but the general masses all over India were lapping it up. Well, why not go to Pallika Bazaar and buy porn? The TRP's (Television Rating Points) would really shoot up. Rajat Sharma maintained that his exposés were for larger public interest and there was no breach of privacy. He pointed out that they had also done exposés on hospital waste, synthetic milk, illegal blood transfusions. The Ministry of Information and Broadcasting was not amused. Flexing its muscles under the Cable Television Networks Regulation Act and Programme Code, the ministry sent India TV a notice that the footage of the politicians and prostitutes offended public decency and morality. Sharma responded: 'We did not show anything vulgar or which would hurt the public sentiments. The telecast was done purely in public interest and every precaution was taken to check any vulgarity. There was no audio and we did not even show any parts of the body.' Yes, but was it journalism?

The TAM ratings for that week do show that India TV led with 22.4 per cent against Aaj Tak's 20.2 per cent, NDTV close behind with 18 per cent. However, Sharma denied that the sex stings had been done to boost his channel's ratings. Sounding much like a politician, he said, 'It is a propaganda against us. Our other programmes have been getting good TRPs. A day before the telecast of Kapoor exposé, India TV recorded much higher channel share than its rival channels for its Prime time show, Aap Ki Adalat.' The figures, however, indicate that Aaj Tak and NDTV got ratings very close to India TV without any sleaze on a normal news day of regular journalism. That begs the question: Can TRPs based on sex stings be sustainable if the rest of your programming sucks?

Do the higher ratings mean more advertising for the channel? The competition for the advertising pie is cut throat. The prospect of getting advertising for a sex sting seems remote because it does have to be pre-sold.

For weeks afterwards, 'Ruchi' appeared on India TV justifying her sting operation. Her argument was that the casting couch exists and it was her journalistic duty to warn young girls who were attempting to enter the film industry that they could be victimized. Literary critic Matthew Arnold wrote, 'Freedom is a very good horse to ride; but to ride somewhere.

You seem to think that you have only to get on the back of your horse Freedom, and ride away as hard as you can, to be sure of coming to the right destination.' The word 'Freedom' could well be replaced by 'Journalism'. India TV is riding a wild horse with no destination that includes good journalism. Yet, *The Washington Post* syndicated columnist Colman McCarthy raised an intriguing point when he wrote about clandestine footage, 'It's possible to uncover the truth by being untruthful, but where do television news people secure the right to legitimize their deceits? How about some truth-in-packaging as the program begins: "We lied to get this story"'.

Vinod Mehta, editor-in-chief, *Outlook*, is a strong advocate of solid, old school journalism. Legwork, cross-checking facts, keeping off the record absolutely off the record and being honest in one's approach in getting the story

Mehta elaborated that there is a big difference in catching someone who is doing something wrong and setting someone up to do the wrong. He said that much of journalism is conducted off the record, and if you report anything off the record, you might get that one story but that individual would never speak to the reporter again. Mehta said,

> **Mehta:** If you don't honour those commitments, then we will not be able to do our business. So to that extent, how far this whole sting operation, this whole idea of putting secret cameras, can take the place of conventional journalism, I'm not sure.
>
> **Madhu:** Would you allow it in *Outlook*?
>
> **Mehta:** No, I wouldn't allow it simply because we might do one good story but then we would run ourselves out of business. If somebody is speaking to me off the record and he knows he is speaking to me off the record, then I also have some professional integrity to honour that. But then you can make the case that there are certain things that are happening in this country that never get known and therefore to break the defence scam, you have to use these kinds of sting operations. That is a call that you make at a particular story, but it's the exception. It can't become the norm in the way you work. You might say that this is an extraordinary story and it requires an extraordinary investigative method but you can't tell everybody in the office that we break all the old rules and we set these new rules up.

Mehta felt that Tehelka was a non-starter financially and would have gone bust anyway. 'So it went bust in great style, thanks to this whole harassment and the way the BJP went,' he said. Mehta was categorical about the aftermath: 'Their harassment has been indefensible and unforgivable. They have been broken to the extent Shankar Sharma must be cursing the day he decided to invest in Tehelka.' Mehta believed that two messages have gone out: 'If you are going to start a publishing business, you cannot do it this way. You can't come and trap us and then say that, "Oh in the name of free press, we will not do anything to you". The second is that this is a risky business if you are critical of the government.'

Outlook was subjected to a certain amount of harassment when they ran a story about

Prime Minister Vajpayee's office and the prime minister's foster son-in-law Ranjan Bhattacharya. Vinod said that the Income Tax Department raided the owner of *Outlook*, Raj Raheja and for eight months made life hell for him. *Outlook* Mumbai offices were also raided. Mehta recounted that Raheja was brave and the only thing he wanted to ensure was that the staff in his own office were not harassed. Unfortunately, that is exactly what the income tax terrorists did by calling Raheja's managers and making them wait endlessly outside their offices.

Did Raheja then tell Mehta to stay off critical stories? Mehta answered, 'I don't have self-destructive instincts. Once these raids happened, I put my head under for seven or eight months, because the big thing for me was that this house survives as a publishing house.'

Does Indian journalism forever live under this fear?

Mehta: Absolutely. With any publication which does stories critical of the ruling party and in India today the ruling party has many individual power centres. You may please one power centre but you have alienated another power centre. So you don't know where you are. It's a very risky business so actually you have to make sure that periodically you keep all these power centres happy. At *Outlook* we have to be very careful.

Madhu: So you would not call it a totally free press?

Mehta: No, no, absolutely not. Actually every editor has to spend 50 per cent of his time making sure that nothing like that goes in. How do they get you in the end? I'm not scared of the prime minister of this country. I'm not scared of the home minister of this country. They can put me in prison. What the hell, I'm not worried. So if I'm sacked from my job, I'm not worried. I am in business because of my proprietor. The best way to get me is to get my proprietor. If anything happens to my proprietor, then I sink. So my job [laughs] is to make sure that he doesn't sink.

Madhu: So 50 per cent of your time in *Outlook* goes into being careful and the other 50 per cent is spent in listening to people complaining about stories?

Mehta: Handling those stories, and if I find any time I look into it [laughs].

Mehta elaborated that it was important for an editor to know his staff when hiring people, particularly in the political section of his paper. He said:

The nice thing about Delhi is that it is so well known about every journalist whether he is close to anyone. Actually, what you do sometimes is, if you have someone close to Advani, then you hire somebody close to Vajpayee. So both camps are happy. But there are still quite a few independent journalists and one can find them. But the longer they remain in the field, they get polluted. You have them pure for six or seven years and as they get closer to power centres, as their own ambitions rise, then you lose them. Women are generally, in this respect, better than men in terms of professional integrity. The female correspondents are less easy to corrupt than men. Many women don't have the kind of political ambition that male correspondents have. Rajya Sabha seats, high commissioner, and many of them are not as ideologically driven as males.

Mehta said that over the past five years he has been getting calls from politicians recommending journalists to be hired. Mehta laughed:

My first instinct is that I'm taking everybody but not that son of a bitch. The very fact that he has been recommended by a politician, he's burnt his copybook, as far as I'm concerned.

Increasingly, politicians and political parties have become adept at planting reporters in news organizations, and Mehta said that it was not unusual for him to get a call from a politician about a story that is just in the planning stages, discussed only in a news meeting. The buzz around the journalists was that any positive stories on Tehelka in the Commission were killed by the government news agencies. Although journalists are told repeatedly about 'confidentiality', Mehta said,

Journalists, of course, are big gossips. It's very difficult for them because especially in the Press Club, everybody wants to brag. They may not even mean it. We try very hard to tell them that whatever we discuss in this room, must not go out. Also, I don't discuss too much even in my conferences. We talk about stories and leave it at that. But still, you have to discuss the way you are going to do something.

Mehta believed,

When the history of journalism in India is written, I don't think Tehelka is going to be that great. It will be a small hiccup. I don't think Tehelka is going to determine the way Indian journalists work. What Tehelka has done is that it has planted an idea in the minds of some journalists, that this is also one way to function. But I know of no mainstream editor with whom I have had a long conversation, that this is the way forward. I think most of us still believe it is the old slog. The secret taping actually reflects the insecurity of a news organization or publishing house which doesn't seem to have the time to stay the course. And which wants quick fame, quick returns and they trip up in that.

After all, just think now Tarun is also coming back to conventional journalism after the sting. He is trying to raise money in the conventional way after his great flirtation and great success with this other kind of journalism.

The survival of good journalism has been attacked from many fronts. We have done it to ourselves. Journalists themselves or the proprietors of news organizations have perpetrated most of it. In the hunger for readers or viewers, all norms of old journalism and ethics have been threatened. The very nature of journalism is that it asks a reader or viewer to suspend interpretation, unlike a book of fiction or poetry. He must see it as it is shown. Yet today, we know that suspension of interpretation has disappeared. We are forced to evaluate, interpret, and then come to our own conclusions. Often we read or see a story and the first question one must ask: Who planted that story? That, of course, is the real story. Echoing Marshall McLuhan, we have to constantly look at ourselves looking at a story.

Newstrack, the video newsmagazine (1988-95), repeatedly undertook exposés without clandestine shoots. Although in possession of a camera as small as a lipstick, it was never used and I am sure nobody even knows where it is now. In the early 1990s, bureaucrats and politicians were not as media savvy as today, so it was certainly easier. Nonetheless, the courage demonstrated by Newstrack journalist Alpana Kishore, when she contacted Kashmiri terrorists who took her to film a kidnapped victim while still in their custody, was journalism at its best, and without any hidden cameras. Alpana Kishore was the first to interview Kashmir terrorists in 1989, when the central government continued to deny their existence. Subsequently, the then home minister, Buta Singh, and Chief Minister Farooq Abdullah exhorted Rajiv Gandhi to arrest the producer of Newstrack, i.e. this author right here. Rajiv Gandhi ignored their request. When the Babri Masjid destruction took place, Newstrack teams ran into the violence while others were running for cover. Cameraman Ashok Bhanot bravely ran to hide the tapes inside a temple when journalists were being beaten up and cameras broken. Newstrack showed an inebriated doctor running a clinic, a nonchalant bureaucrat saying it was quite possible for contaminated intravenous glucose to be used in hospitals as well as HIV-infected blood at blood-donor clinics. Yaqub Memon, brother of underworld don, Tiger Memon, was interviewed while he was under arrest in the custody of IB. All this was done without hidden cameras, through contacts and the ruthless pursuit of good stories. Most crucial here, in all of these stories, the viewer could comfortably suspend interpretation. Good journalism can be defined in this: If you can trust what you see and read as the truth, then, and only then is it true journalism.

With the boom of consumerism, the old journalistic approach of doing a story for which there is merit, has been buried. It is the advertisers in the newspapers who, by deciding who their market audience is, command space. That is achieved not by their advertisements alone, but by copy being created that matches the advertisements. The advertisers own the news we read. *The Times of India* was the most creative in launching a city edition of their major cities, called *Delhi Times* or *Mumbai Times*. *The Times of India* was responsible for inventing the Page 3 phenomenon, which became the first page you turned to and was the most talked about. People who attended the parties loved seeing photographs of themselves, and people who were not invited loved to see what they could aspire to or envy. Invariably, the same one hundred or so people were recycled. It became such a potent phenomenon that a Bollywood film called *Page 3* was made that purported to expose the shallow life of Page 3 regulars. Ever ready to make the buck, *The Times of India* then began to sell space to people who wanted their parties covered. The earlier one hundred regulars were then repulsed by Page 3. Reportedly, the practice of selling editorial space then began to encroach into *The Times of India* main edition. There was an uproar in the press and a controversy broke out, with news organizations taking different sides.

Aroon Purie, CEO of the India Today Group and editor-in-chief of *India Today* magazine, has logged in 30 years of experience in print journalism, publishing and relatively recently, television channels. The India Today Group is one of the largest in its stretch across media, including music and education. Purie has the not-so-common combination of sensibility for journalism and a head for business. Purie said that he believed in sting journalism with the caveat that it was in public interest. He felt that Tehelka's Operation West End was a justifiable operation and he would have no objection to such being carried out by *India Today* reporters. But, he added,

> **Purie:** I think that when they start talking about supplying women, that's treading a very thin line between entrapment and investigation. It's okay to have a sting operation where you're out to expose people's public lives and not anything to do with their private lives. I don't think that's of any interest.
>
> **Madhu:** Do you think that Tehelka lost the media's support when *The Indian Express* broke the story about the sex tapes?
>
> **Purie:** I think journalists are basically jealous of them because they did quite a remarkable job in getting, I think for the first time, a real scoop, with the party's BJP's president taking money. That is a huge story. You can go undercover and be able to expose something, which is of public interest. It is valid.

Purie has had his share of controversies and journalistic dichotomies are not new to him.

> **Purie:** In getting the prostitutes involved meant doing things that are illegal and that's where you draw the line. I think, not in this case, but there is always the journalist dilemma, in terms of, say, going and spending time with terrorists. Do you inform the police, do you not inform the police? Is that your job? Is it not your job? I think that's a call you have to take on a case-by-case basis. If you know that somebody's going to declare war on you, do you go and tell the government or do you not? Do you have something beyond your job as a journalist, as a citizen, which you think is a larger duty than everything else? That's a personal call you have to take in every situation.
>
> **Madhu:** Tehelka was criticized for not getting rebuttals and not cross checking with people who were on the tapes.
>
> **Purie:** There were some that were indisputable facts. Like that of Bangaru taking the money. There was no question about that. It was on tape. It happened. He may say whatever he wants afterwards, it doesn't even require a rebuttal. There were conversations, which took place in the defence minister's house, which were, I think, reported verbatim. I think there were certain parts

which were run without checking because they are something which you have established and you're reporting what happened to you. You went to this house, you offered this much and so-and-so was there, you're reporting a conversation. So I don't think there's any checking required on that, because it's your own reporters who have gone and done it. Checking is required when you're accusing somebody of something, which is not on the tape.

In early 2003, Purie came out vociferously against selling editorial space where the reader really doesn't know whether he is getting an article by an objective journalist or a promotional advertisement written by the public relations company of a business house.

Purie: Sadly in India, it's happening in the way that the market leaders have become so soft towards journalism and even towards advertisers. They are giving their space into very intrusive kind of advertising, which in the end actually destroys its readership. So it's actually quite self-defeating. If you allow advertising to become so intrusive into reading that it'll eventually lead to lower readership and in fact, lower viewership of your ads. In a long term it is not the right way to do it. In India, I think there's space for everything. All these publications may be doing very well, and the other one is not doing so well, but there is a space for all of them to survive. It's a market waiting to be taken. Anybody can see that there's a huge amount of money being made by people who are in a monopoly situation. They don't deserve to be in that monopoly situation. They are there because of history and geography and so forth, but not because of journalistic excellence.

Madhu: So far the general reading public is not aware of paid editorials.

Purie: They've hidden it. The fact is that I don't know how they're doing it now, or whether they're doing it, but it's now not apparent. Obviously this outcry made them hide the fact that they were doing it. Earlier it was quite open, they described journalists as "intermediaries" rather than journalists, and the fact that this was society pages in any case, so it really doesn't matter. They're not doing it openly, so they're obviously conscious of the fact that the public will react to this at some stage.

Madhu: There is one publishing house that has established that the owner has utter contempt for journalists.

Purie: I still think it is a noble profession. It is something which you do for the love of it and not because you want money. It gives you a certain degree of satisfaction, that you're doing things for the public interest. Journalists? There are good journalists and bad journalists, the same thing in terms of any other profession. They need greater amount of training and a greater degree of control because the people who are today planting stories have become very smart. That's the big change in India now: sophistication of public relations, of seduction of journalists. It is something which has developed and I don't think that journalists in organizations have developed here enough to counter it. It's like the criminals being ahead of the law. One of the big dangers in the media is the sophistication of people, even the political parties today know how to spin stories. They know how to do sound bites, they now set up stages, they know how to deal with the prime time news, they know which people to put forward, so it's become a very sophisticated game. You have to have an increasingly greater degree of sophistication on the journalistic side to counter this, which has actually yet to develop.

Madhu: Has all the harassment that everyone associated with Tehelka scared journalists and owners of news organizations to tread carefully?

Purie: No, I don't think so. Tehelka's sting had encouraged journalists to look for those kinds of stories. Yes, the government did get after Tehelka. They had some kind of problems about its financing and about Sharma and so forth – and whether it's true or not, I don't know. But they found it a convenient way to get at Tehelka. I think that most journalistic organizations should be able to stand up to the government, in these kinds of issues. I don't think there's been that many cases of government harassing publications, except in the Emergency of *The Indian Express*. But other than that, *The Indian Express* has run a lot of exposés. I don't think the government has gone after them in the way that it's gone after Tehelka.

Madhu: Is Indian journalism divided between those who are in it just to make money and those who still believe that journalism should be practiced with a goal to exposing the truth?

Purie: I believe that good journalism is good business. However, unlike other businesses, there is an element of trust and social responsibility that the information being given is truthful just like a doctor is trusted by the patient to give him the right medicine. The sad part is that trust is being betrayed often now in India.

~

In 2005, the government brought up the possibility of banning all sting operations. Clearly, journalism would be hurt in this. There are stories that would not be possible without stings and there is a need for a continuing exposure of corruption.

It can be said, then, that journalism in India is markedly divided in two cities. Charles Dickens's prefatory sentence in *A Tale of Two Cities* (1859) could well apply to Indian journalism today: 'It was the best of times, it was the worst of times, it was the age of wisdom, it was the age of foolishness, it was the epoch of belief, it was the epoch of incredulity, it was the season of Light, it was the season of Darkness.' India is a country of juxtapositions. While dishonest judges are investigated, the honest judiciary has taken on the role of activism through implementation orders. While senior police officers in Mumbai are arrested for corruption, officers like Kiran Bedi continue to serve as role models for the honest police officer. Why was Kiran Bedi not been appointed commissioner of police in Delhi, which was her due in the normal course of promotions? Simple: because she is not pliable and not open to political interference. While there are lawyers who idealistically gave their time free to Tehelka, others are willing to do anything for a price, even to bribe judges. Why do all obviously guilty criminals go to one particular lawyer who can turn witnesses hostile by paying them off and turn a BMW car into a truck? This juxtaposition exists in every field in India, so it is not surprising that the same co-exists in journalism. While there are journalists like Seema Mustafa, who wrote a scathing editorial in *Asian Age* ('Fourth Mistake', 4 December 2004), about the damage to journalism perpetrated by self-seeking editors and proprietors, there are others who will write anything for as little as social access.

There are journalists in India who continue to be passionate in their pursuit of serious journalism and pay heavily with their lives being damaged. On 30 July 2001, Mool Chand Yadav, a journalist working for the daily *Punjab Kesri* was shot at in Jhansi. He had been investigating organized crime. The story of the murders by terrorists of the owners of *Punjab Kesri* could fill a book. Virtually the whole family has been wiped out and Ashwani Chopra, the only survivor of that generation, travels with Z security, the highest level accorded to any civilian. Despite all the killings and personal tragedies, *Punjab Kesri* continued to publish articles against the Khalistan movement and the terrorists.

On 20 August 2001, Rajesh Bhattaraj, editor of *Aajo Bholi*, was arrested in Gangtok because he criticized the chief minister of Sikkim. On 27 June 2001, Suresh (Sun TV) was arrested when he attempted to verify the quality of grain in a warehouse. On 19 March 2001, the Madhya Pradesh High Court sentenced Rajendra Purohit and Vinay Panshikar, editors of *The Hitvada* and two journalists, to six months imprisonment for contempt of court. The newspaper had criticized the High Court for acquitting suspects in a murder case. Little known freelance journalist Sanjay Arya of Chirapatla village, Betul district in Madhya Pradesh, has been in jail since 21 October 2004 on trumped up charges under the Scheduled Castes and Scheduled Tribes (Prevention of Atrocities) Act. Arya had the temerity to expose government corruption in the public health and educational systems, illegal hunting, tree felling and mining in reserved forests.

In August 2004, Sajid Rashid, editor of the Marathi-language daily, *Mahanagar*, was stabbed outside his office. Rashid had written articles against the Muslim custom of men divorcing their wives simply by uttering the word 'talaq' thrice. On 13 October 2004, Yambem Meghajit Singh, who worked for a television company, North East Vision, was tortured and killed for criticizing separatist groups, local officials and exposing corruption. The struggle for serious journalism continues and it is not short of soldiers who willingly and selflessly put their heads on the line for it.

Even so, the battle is not always between those in power and idealistic journalists. It is also a struggle within the confines of journalism itself. Journalism is, of course, the history of our times. If future generations will judge us on the basis of preserved records of journalism, they will see Frederico Fellini's *Satyricon*, replete with aristocrats decadently feasting in burlesque playhouses. All we will be seen to be doing is being corrupt, dancing, singing, partying, lying, fornicating, committing adultery and murder. This is not exclusive to India. 'Today's journalism is obsessed with the kind of things that tend to preoccupy thirteen-year old boys: sport, sex, crime and narcissism,' wrote Steven Spark in *Atlantic Monthly*. Pick up any newspaper in the world, and you will find it shockingly similar. When Arun Jaitley was law minister, he was travelling with a television star/journalist. He discovered to his amusement that the crowds that he thought were waving to him, were actually focused on the man standing next to him. A clue to the spirit of our times. The power-media star. How ever did the fourth estate get itself in this position where it has become a hated (by all the other estates) necessity of democracy?

What are the principal functions of the press? Gandhiji wrote: 'One of the objects of a newspaper is to understand the popular feeling and give expression to it; another is to arouse in people certain desirable sentiments; and the third is fearlessly to expose popular defects.' The Indian press played a huge role in national awakening during the freedom struggle and was part of the nation-building process. Today, we have become obsessed watchdogs in 'exposing defects', which of course must be done, but we are doing it without a thought for nation building. Here we come to the crucial question: who watches the watchdog? Does the media criticize itself as relentlessly as it does everyone else? Is the media above being influenced by political parties, business houses, and its own owners, the publishers? Possibly the best method of preventing plants is for journalists to include the source of the story whenever possible, along with the report. It makes it a larger story by simply reporting it, which then exposes the motive of the plant.

Today's journalism is not a graceful, light years away from 30 years ago. Over the past decade, it could be likened to the 'Big Bang of Journalism'. It is not just the exposés, but that the exposers have become stars. It could be termed the Vanity Press. There are three varieties within that. There is the *jholawala* press, that reaches out to villages, earthquakes, floods, and gives a voice to people who would never be heard. Not much happens and he moves on to the next story. Then there is the muckraking press that captures politicians with the foot and mouth disease together with the greasy hands disease. What happens thereafter? He is usually hounded out of his job (the reporter, not the politician), becomes a star amongst his peers and the general public, but the politician continues on his greasy path. Thirdly, and most important of all, there is the access press. This journalist moves with the Mighty, begins to believe, he is Mighty. The Mighty, with whom he moves, dislike but humour him for their own safety. He is not above boasting he can install and topple governments, participate in corporate wars, and generally tinker with anyone he chooses. His Mightiness begins to believe that he is a real friend of the Mighty. The truth is that the Mighty wouldn't know him from Bhola Nath had he not the power of the organization that employs him. Access journalism cannot be value-free. Can a journalist who gets an exclusive interview as a reward, be totally unbiased in his questioning? How many interviews have we seen that are obsequious and never ask THE question?

Because of the Big Bang, there are armies of journalists who exhibit an utter ignorance of the ethics of the profession. Newspapers and magazines may have orientation programmes where the ethics of the company are spelt out. But, most often, the code of ethics practised by most news organizations is established by the conduct, decisions, and demands of the owner and publisher first, and then the editor. A proprietor of a business house news organization reportedly justified accepting money for editorial space on the grounds that, 'If my editors and reporters are making money by selling space in the paper, why shouldn't I? So it is better to institutionalize it.' That is, like a senior police officer saying that if my constables are making money, why shouldn't I establish a procedure for it so I can be on the take too? A junior reporter learns quickly which business houses and politicians he must never write a negative story about, those who he must write glowing reports about, which advertisers to be sensitive to, and so the list goes on. In some news organizations, freebie trips and gifts are acceptable, vendetta-motivated planted stories are willingly accepted whether they are true or not, a story is rarely held back to ascertain both sides, any means are utilized to get a story, there is no problem in paying sources for a story, as for privacy, who knows the meaning of the word?

In the race to beat the next guy, unsubstantiated gossip is splashed about, and when the injured party objects, the first sentence in the ostensible apology is, 'I stand by my story', no matter how factually incorrect it may have been. When Priyanka Gandhi wrote a letter to Coomi Kapoor (*The Indian Express*), correcting her on facts, she also mentioned that she did not normally object to every inaccuracy published because that is all she would be doing. What does that say about Indian journalism? We are destroying our own credibility and consequently, the strength of the press.

Despite the brilliant investigative stories of Indian journalism, there are thousands of examples of wild journalism. The most damaging that comes to mind was the reporting on television networks on the Kandahar hijacking incident (24 December 1999). The kind of exposure that was given to the relatives of those on the plane, thereby exerting extraordinary pressure on the government to give in to the hijackers' demands, was mindless. The same terrorist who was released was reportedly later involved in the killing of journalist Daniel Pearl (February 2002) and the bombing of the Indian Parliament (13 December 2001).

Journalism has today become a murky business, bursting with intrigue, blackmail, and fixers. As Dileep Padgaonkar, columnist said, 'So much that passes for investigative journalism, is a leak or a plant given by a bureaucrat, politician or businessman in order to spite someone'. Rarely, in the press, do we turn the spotlight on ourselves. *The Washington Post* columnist, Sydney Schanberg wrote, 'No newspaper is eager to acknowledge its own deficiencies or even those of its peers who might return the favour. Everyone has dirty linen.' We have a history replete with great journalistic exposés by ethical journalists but today the *daal* [lentils] is getting more and more *kaala* [black]. As Elridge Cleaver said, 'If you are not part of the solution, you are part of the problem'. Have we journalists become part of the problem?

Even so, there are journalists who still risk their lives for a story, work in punishing inclement weather, face down terrorists, shrug off threats from politicians, take a 'no' for an interview as only an invitation to ask again, and are unrelenting in their pursuit of a story. There are enough fearless journalists in India who stand up not only to politicians in power but take a stand against their editors and proprietors. A correspondent's worth shot up amongst his peers and funnily enough, with his employers (*The Hindu*), when he took a stand and refused to cover Aishwarya Rai and Abhishek Bachchan's wedding.

In Hermann Hesse's *The Glass Bead Game*, he wrote in 1943 what could be written about Indian journalism today:

We must confess that we cannot provide a definition of those products from which the age takes its name, the feuilletons. They deem to have formed a commonly popular section of the daily newspapers, were produced by the millions, and were a major source of mental pabulum for the reader in want of culture. They reported on, or rather chatted about, a thousand-and-one items of knowledge.

Hesse could be writing about Page 3 today. There are journalists who are examining the *khichdi* [Indian porridge] in which we find ourselves. Sagarika Ghose, in a perspicacious analysis, 'I Think Therefore I am Not' (16 October 2003, *The Indian Express*) pointed to the reasons for the decline of intellectual activity in India. She wrote that there are hardly any academics writing about cricket, emotion, or popular history.

In other ways, the plight of Indian intellectuals is parallel to the predicament of the Soviet intellectuals as described by Russian academic Boris Kagarlitsky. When a new nation "awakens to freedom", it creates its own "state-sponsored intellectuals", whose roots lie in official policy rather than in the pulse of society. Thus India's intellectual community is rooted in the Preamble of the Constitution rather than real social changes. Endless jargon-drenched works that juggle around the words, "civil", "secularism", "society", "politics", "democracy", simply repeat tired official formulae.

The role of intellectuals is crucial today to the evolution of India's modern culture. We need to be examined, analysed, and new concepts put forward which the young can seize as the future. Instead, we are being anaesthetized by academics who are rooted to examining the meaning of a scratch on the stone age rock shelters of Bhimbetaka rather than theories that connect with today. Admittedly, there is value in analysing archaeological sites, but there is a desperate need for academics to relate to contemporary India. Additionally, this needs to be presented in a way that attracts the young, in language to which they can relate. The alarming angle to this is the need to regurgitate formulae successful in the past coupled with a timidity to experiment with anything new.

When Eugene Meyer, father of Katherine Graham, bought *The Washington Post* in 1933, he wrote to a friend, 'My only interest is to make a contribution to better knowledge and better thinking. If I could not feel the ability to rise above my personal interest, I would not have the slightest pleasure in being a publisher'. For those who steer the formidable fortunes of the largest news organization in India, Meyer would be considered an absolute imbecile. Meyer also said, 'In the pursuit of truth, the newspaper shall be prepared to make sacrifices of its material fortunes, if such a course is necessary for the public good'. *The Washington Post* has been challenged numerous times to put this belief into practice for the past three generations.

Any given era invites the end of itself when one formulaic success over-repeated gluts itself to overdose. At this point, the print media is anaesthetizing us with pablum. Television has become the opium of the masses. As far back as 1958, legendary journalist Ed Murrow said in speech in Chicago:

We have currently a built-in allergy to unpleasant or disturbing information. Our mass media reflect this. But unless we get up off our fat surpluses and recognize that television in the main is being used to distract, delude, amuse and insulate us, then television and those who finance it, those who look at it and those who work at it, may see a totally different picture too late.

As much as it is important for doctors to heal, it is for journalism to play the role assigned to the raison d'être of the profession. Murrow added:

This instrument can teach, it can illuminate; yes, and it can even inspire. But it can do so only to the extent that humans are determined to use it to those ends. Otherwise it is merely wires and lights in a box. There is a great and perhaps decisive battle to be fought against ignorance, intolerance and indifference. This weapon of television could be useful. Stonewall Jackson, who knew something about the use of weapons, is reported to have said, "When war comes, you must draw the sword and throw away the scabbard". The trouble with television is that it is rusting in the scabbard during a battle for survival.

There is a remarkable opportunity for purveyors of news to return value to the Credible Word and weight to questioning the new anti-journalistic money-making norms. We should be at the cusp of change to battle against trivia and bring the importance of issues and accountability to all of us. What have you done that is worthwhile? Will you leave anything behind at all that changed something for the larger good?

Cogito ergo sum: I think, therefore I am, wrote Rene Descartes in 1637. What have Indians been thinking? Okay, here's a quickie pop-psychological history. Indians could not be existentialists under 200 years of a colonial power. There was no burden of freedom of choice to haunt the Indian. The age of 'dual identity' was followed by Mahatma Gandhi waking up the crowd. We invited the British to leave, but we couldn't bear to let go all they left behind. With the post-colonial third generation now adults, little British baggage remains. This generation takes their pride in being Indian for granted. It is not to be acquired. It is inborn. This generation is defined as one that has been the most influenced by the media. Yes, we are 150 years away from using chapattis to spread a mutiny, as was the case in 1857. A mutiny could now be a cellphone away. But who is going to mutiny when there is another cellphone to buy? It is the media that is sculpting the national identity. In this decade, 'I am not, until I appear in the media'. This validation of existence and being has become a basic need. Until you are famous, you do not exist. If we could more seriously take who it is that merits the fame, perhaps we would begin to scratch the dawn of a new era.

25 Ubiquitous Presence of Malice

What's the difference between a good lawyer and a bad lawyer?
A bad lawyer can let a case drag out for several years. A good lawyer can make it last even
longer.

Sometimes, there is a clear divide. There were lawyers who ended up working for Tehelka without a fee. Tehelka had promised them a monthly retainer's fee but after two months, their funds dried up. Yet, the lawyers continued to appear for Tehelka. As Sidharth Luthra said, 'We fought the good fight in the spirit that we were up against injustice and wanted truth to prevail'. They did so because they believed it was an important cause: to protect the constitutional right of the press. It was not just a matter of appearing before the Commission for a few minutes. Some of them stopped all their other work, so they earned no income while they spent long hours talking to Tehelka journalists, studying their papers, filing affidavits, besides appearing before the Commission. The point is: There is a choice, and the choice you make shows you exactly what your Being is.

But was the divide so clear? No, because there is a grey area. It is true, lawyers often appear and go in whichever direction they are paid to go. The same lawyers who appeared for an idealistic cause, could very well be appearing for and defending criminals they were prosecuting the week before.

We clearly have a catch-22 here. A lawyer's duty is to protect his client. So in order to do that, any amount of theories, distractions and antics are acceptable in a court of law. But what happens in a Commission of Inquiry? It is there to uncover the Truth. The Commission must go after the facts. If those facts are not favourable to the lawyers' clients, it is their duty to take the Commission as far away from those facts as possible. They are then found to be going against the very nature and reason for the Commission. The lawyers spun a gossamer labyrinth of distortions and led the Commission as far from the truth as possible. The Commission of Inquiry became Rashomon at its best. It was the mother battle of versions.

Whose version was the Truth? Tehelka journalists became the accused and all those on tape appeared to be victims.

What were the lawyers participating in the Commission supposed to do? What was their assigned role? We are constantly reminded by lawyers that every person is entitled to a defence and it is a lawyer's duty to never turn down a case. But, we are never reminded that a lawyer also has a duty to the court and truth. Lawyers have used the reason that everyone is entitled to a defence to justify accepting cases where the guilt is admitted and obvious, but that same reason is forgotten when convenient. When senior lawyer Ram Jethmalani chose to defend Manu Sharma, accused of killing Jessica Lal, his son Mahesh Jethamalani said, 'I, my sister and our entire family have opposed him for defending Manu Sharma. We tried to convince him there is no compelling reason for him to take up this case. This wasn't a case of public importance. But obviously, there are many people who have more influence on him than us.' (*The Hindustan Times*, 19 December 2006)

Lawyers went on strike and held violent demonstrations in 1988 when Kiran Bedi took a principled position to stand by her constable who had handcuffed a lawyer caught stealing. Not one lawyer was willing to defend her. On 19 October 2005, the members of the District Bar Association condemned the murder of Vijay Singh, presiding judge of Chandigarh Labour Court, and there was not one lawyer who was willing to defend the accused. Every citizen is entitled to defence only when a lawyer chooses. The point here is: There is a choice.

In the Commission of Inquiry, the lawyers knew only too well that their clients had been caught on tape engaged in immoral acts, yet continued to clobber into the Commission records that the tapes were doctored although there was no real evidence of this. Not one of the clients had initially claimed that the tapes were doctored. This line of argument was only adopted as a ploy that they all hung on to once the idea occurred to them after reading about similar cases in America. Not one of those on the tapes ever denied that the events as they played out in the tapes had not transpired. Some said they were drunk, drugged, or hypnotized. The lawyers were all well aware that what was on the tapes was nothing but the truth. This was not a court. It was a Commission of Inquiry where the purpose was to get to the truth. Is it too naive to hope that some lawyers may have had a delimma of conscience?

Canadian philosopher and writer, John Raulson Saul wrote in *The Doubter's Companion* (1994), known as the Devil's Dictionary, that citizens have more choice than they are led to believe and the aim of his book is to demonstrate this. He says:

> **People feel they only have two choices, the head and the heart. One is the instrumental, hard-nosed thing, and the other is the marginal, romantic, idealist thing. Well, that is not a choice. The point is to show people they have these qualities they can use. For example, ethics is really very practical, but it isn't good enough to be right. It also has to work; otherwise, it is just good intentions, and then it is romantic. That doesn't mean it's easy and pretty.**

At the Commission of Inquiry the LOCOT strategy was to discredit the journalists by asking questions that bordered on sleaze, attack the veracity of the tapes and allege tampering, claim there was unethical editing and finally give their own version of events highlighting how people were induced into committing acts they would not have otherwise. Sidharth Luthra pointed out, 'To my mind they did not understand the consequences of such a defence since their admission of meetings and explanations of the transactions with Tehelka operatives undermined their attack on the authenticity of the tapes. In a sense, the Commission was a precursor to criminal prosecution and simultaneous to court martial/inquiry proceedings.' According to Sidharth Luthra, 'This should have determined the defence strategy and not just attack on the credibility of Tehelka. Ideally, those on the Operation West End tapes, should have attacked the tapes and denied the incident. But most admitted meeting the Tehelka team. So what business did they have meeting the team or discussing procurement? That to my mind was enough of an admission of impropriety and the cash or sex was the additional evidence for indicting them.'

I asked Sunil Kumar, counsel for Bangaru Laxman, whether he had not tried to prove that the tapes were doctored just to get the evidence dismissed to get his client off, even though his client had never denied taking the money.

Sunil Kumar: No, no, that is not the lawyer's job. We are there to assist the Commission because it is a fact-finding body.

Madhu: Your questions to Tarun Tejpal about sex advice on his website were only to discredit him. How were you assisting the Commission there?

Kumar: No, what is cross-examination? You come forward in your affidavit, to say that we are investigative journalists. So we are cross-examining you and testing your credibility, not that I am trying to put something against you. Are you an investigative journalist and is it a purely investigative journalistic endeavour? A lawyer's job is not to put the person in any wrong dock but it is within the legal parameters. When you put a question regarding the content of the website, it is only to test the correctness of what you have stated earlier.

Madhu: How is that relevant?

Kumar: That is very relevant, because these people have been claiming to be investigative journalists. Their ace man, Mathew Samuel, who is according to Mr Tejpal, one of the best journalists in the world, he was not able to write five lines before the Commission. When I asked him that you being a journalist, can you report on the proceedings before the Commission today, five lines? He could not do that. We say these people were simply out to make money. All that journalistic enthusiasm or motive was just not there.

Madhu: That is not correct at all. When I was running a news-magazine programme, although it was an English programme, I used to hire Hindi-speaking journalists. They could not write the story in English but were far better in getting the stories. They would get the stories, brief me, and I would write them. I think that is how they were using Mathew Samuel.

Kumar: The most important thing is that you must be able to communicate. Whatever stories you're collecting or whatever you're doing, and when you say that you are a journalist and you cannot communicate, that is a contradiction in terms.

Madhu: You should be able to tell the story, and I think Mathew Samuel could do that in his own way.

Kumar: You should be able to tell the story and you can't be a trickster and call yourself a journalist.

Sunil Kumar was far from helping the Commission about the difference between editing and doctoring. Kumar brought in his 'technical expert' to prove that Hi8 tapes can be doctored. How can that be interpreted as helping the Commission to get to the truth?

Kumar: First you come forward to say this can be done. This has been admitted by all the experts produced by Tehelka also. That once you have a tape, you transfer it on a computer, do whatever you want to do and then put it back on the same tape. No one will be able to say which one is which.

Madhu: That is not true. None of the Tehelka experts said it can be altered on Hi8. You can tell an edited tape from an original tape and this is where the lawyers were confusing and misleading the Commission. On Hi8 tapes you cannot separate sound from the visuals.

Kumar: That is also very debatable. Once you have put it on a computer and done whatever you want to do, and transfer it on a separate same Hi8 or whatever tape it be, I come and give it to you, this is the camera original. Then say that, no, no, these are the camera originals, nothing can be done on these Hi8 tapes, then say don't send it for forensic examination. So you have experts coming to say that, no, this can be done. Take for example, the sentence where a clear word has been deleted.

Madhu: The word "don't".

Kumar: Yes, "don't". That day, Mr Shanti Bhushan himself said that yes, Tehelka experts said yes, there is a sound. There is a sound.

Madhu: That does not mean they admit it was doctored. It could be a drop-out.

Kumar: Three different things have been said about it, by their own experts also. And that is why in such a situation Mr Shanti Bhushan said that no, there the benefit of doubt has to go to Mr Bangaru Laxman. I read in a newspaper, which said that Mr Bangaru Laxman had spat on the camera or something. Bangaru Laxman doesn't eat paan ever since his bypass surgery, about four, five years back. Preposterous!

Madhu: He doesn't eat *paan*? He certainly looks as if he's eating paan in the tapes. There is something in the side of his mouth.

Kumar: No, no, he has not eaten paan maybe for four, five years now. Yes, it looks, but he doesn't.

But Laxman never denied accepting the money. Did Sunil Kumar know whether or not the BJP had issued a receipt? He said that was in the BJP records, but no copy of the receipt had been deposited in the Commission. Kumar explained that an individual can accept money for the party but it is the treasurer who issues a receipt. If everything was above board then why did Laxman resign? Kumar replied that that was a political question only the BJP could answer.

When questioned about Laxman's statement about Brajesh Mishra, Kumar pulled out the doctoring demon: 'I've seen the tape also, that it has all been tampered with. And you keep asking me a question about what is on the tapes. First, it is not faithfully reproduced.'

> **Madhu**: In the four-and-a-half hours of edited tapes?
> **Kumar**: As also in the unedited tapes. These so-called unedited tapes, because we have always said the 90-hour tapes which have been submitted to the Commission. These are not the camera originals. This is one issue where the Tehelka people have fought from the very beginning. Saying that no, these tapes should not be sent for any forensic tests. As if after all, if you have made the recording, you're so sure about your tapes. They should have come forward and offered and laid the controversy to rest, right in the very beginning. All this delay of two-and-a-half years would not have happened at all.
> **Madhu**: But what makes you suspect that those are not the camera originals?
> **Kumar**: Oh, there are various instances. If these are the camera originals, then the four and a half hour must contain everything, which is there in the camera originals. But there are things in the four-and-a-half hours which are not there in the 105 tapes. How do you explain this? If something is there in the 105 tapes and it is not there in the four-and-a-half hours. The material has been subjected to a detailed compression of material. The way the tapes have been handled and what all material has come forward in the cross-examination of the three Tehelka people, they leave no matter of doubt, that these tapes have been interfered with. All the three have been contradicting each other. One coming in to say that this is an area about which the number two man coming will explain. Number two coming in the witness box to say this explanation has got to come from number three. And number three actually gets away by saying that I don't know.

Each question that Kumar raised had been answered, but I think he believed himself. It is dangerous when you begin to perceive facts only according to what will exonerate your client.

> **Madhu**: In the four-and-a-half hours version, they have cut out a key sentence. It was in the originals in the 105 tapes, in which Mr Laxman says, "Will you come with cash?" That is not in the four-and-a-half hour transcript.
> **Kumar**: Which transcript are you talking about, because in transcript also there

are various discrepancies? Something which is there in the transcript if you hear it, it is not there in the tape. Then the Government of India's transcripts says something totally different from what the transcript of Tehelka is saying. And when you hear the tapes, you find that nothing is there on the tapes. Someone produces something in one transcript, another transcript someone else produces. And the transcribing done by Tehelka itself is defective definitely. But it seems that deliberately they have put in things, omitted things.

As is obvious in the interview, the same technique is used by picking the errors in the transcripts to distract and twist away from the truth. Kumar said that he did not remember the sentence 'Will you come with cash?' He maintained that Tehelka had not left out anything. Instead, they had juggled the visuals around. Kumar admitted that if he created sufficient reasonable doubt about the veracity of the tapes, 'The law is very certain there. The tapes would be rejected.' As Laxman had not denied taking the money, why was Kumar working to have the tapes rejected? Kumar said triumphantly, 'What is the other material, which is there before the Commission on which any conclusion can be based? That is for the Commission to decide.' When asked if a man came to him and admitted he was guilty of murder or raping a four year old, would he still argue he was innocent, Kumar replied that it was not for him to judge him. Kumar said,

I'll tell you, people, they become childish. They start imagining things. They start dreaming that yes, yes, yes, I remember something had happened. Why is a child's testimony not admitted in a court of law? Because he has an imagination, which adults are not supposed to have. But let me tell you, adults equally imagine and have fantastic ideas about things as children do.

So do lawyers, I imagine. We can then conclude that Kumar could tell the man, you may think you are guilty but you are not. You are just imagining things.

What did Kumar think of Gandhi who refused to lie for clients and refused to defend someone who lied? Kumar replied,

I don't think it is right. If I'm not wrong, there are judgements which say that lawyers have no business to say I will not take up your case. I'm definitely sure. The Calcutta High Court has said that a lawyer cannot turn down a case. There are only certain circumstances under which you can refuse a brief.

It is rare to encounter a lawyer who is not a *phata-phat* virtuoso in rationalizing anything. In Lawrence Kasdan's film *The Big Chill* (1983), there is a superb exchange about rationalization:

Michael [Jeff Goldblum]: I don't know anyone who could get through the day without two or three juicy rationalizations. They're more important than sex.

Sam Weber [Tom Berenger]: Ah, come on. Nothing's more important than sex.
Michael: Oh yeah? Ever gone a week without a rationalization?

Combine a lawyer's rationalizations with our propensity to function without guilt no matter what we do and you have a winner. In the Bhagawat Gita, when Arjuna questions the morality of killing his own kin, Krishna answers: 'Because death is not the end, there will be no guilt on your hands.' Rationalization? It is in our genes. Guilt? If all that unfolds is because of karma, then how are we responsible? Is there a word for 'guilt' in Hindi? This is anti-existential philosophy at its best. As polyphonic as our culture is, so are the rationalizations. They are creative and voluminous. There are any number of reasons not to take up a case when not convenient, even more to take up a case even when convenient.

(The late) Kirit Rawal, the counsel for the Government of India when the BJP was in power, consented to an interview at his home. Rawal said: 'The government has found evidence that people have been used for their own agenda, that is to topple the government.' When I pointed out that no evidence of this has been presented at the Commission, Rawal responded: 'Shankar Sharma definitely knew what Tehelka was doing.' Here again I pointed to the evidence that proved the contrary. Rawal said, 'Tehelka wanted to sensationalize it, thinking it would raise their brand value. They wanted big names.' Well, there is no argument in that. They definitely decided to go after big names or their story would have had no bite. The story was sensational enough without any further need to sensationalize it. Also, it is no crime to attempt to raise your brand value.

Rawal elaborated: 'Bangaru Laxman was not in any defence transaction. He took money for the Party.' Yes, he did, but without a receipt. Whether it actually went to the Party remains an open question. Rawal said, 'If you trace Shankar Sharma's money, there are a number of unanswered questions. Himachal Futuristic Shares were transferred for 1000 and sold for 3300.'

In the Enforcement Directorate's Remand Application for custody of Shankar Sharma before the Additional Chief Metropolitan Magistrate, on 29 January 2002, they stated:

The investigations being carried out by the applicant Enforcement Directorate in India and abroad, are heading towards the conclusive proof that the accused above named Shankar Sharma had illegally received money abroad, the differential amount to the tune of Rs 56 crore approx. (as a conservative estimate) from the said FIIs to whom he had sold the 5,92,950 HFCL shares at rates ranging between Rs 1060 to 1075 per share, i.e. at nearly half the market price which was ranging between Rs 1951 to 2211 per share on the date of the transaction.

Rashomon played it out again. According to Shankar:

The plain truth of the matter is that the ED knew all along that no such siphoning off ever happened. All confirmations by the FIIs for the said transaction records submitted to RBI, as well as in the tax returns filed with income tax authorities. Yet, just in order to secure remand after remand, the ED committed perjury after perjury, and spread disinformation in the media that Shankar Sharma had hawala transactions in siphoning off Rs 56 crore.

Shankar's lawyers filed various documents in the Commission to prove the perjuries committed and the mala fide arrest conducted by the Enforcement Directorate.

Rawal said to me in his interview: 'And that story about Tarun signing the register at Hindujas office and then not going up is impossible to believe.' Rawal ignored my question about why, with all the resources of RAW and IB at their command, the government had brought no proof about the Hindujas involvement with Tehelka.

According to Rawal, 'There were so many procedural lapses. The Commission would have come down really hard on the defence personnel. But Tehelka unnecessarily panicked. If they had just sat tight, not given press conferences about being hounded, Tehelka's credibility would have gone up.' Did I really hear this? This fails all logic. Does that mean that had Tehelka kept mum about the harassment, the government would have assumed they had learnt their lesson and would have gone easy on them?

Rawal was incensed by Tarun and Shankar Sharma's statements about his sister, Dharamishtha Rawal, who was an executive director (legal) in SEBI. Rawal said,

> Dharamishtha is the nominal director of the stock exchange in Kolkata. Tarun behaved like a third rate person by dragging my sister into this. It was totally unprofessional behaviour. For this I will not pardon Tarun. It is hitting below the belt. The allegations are pernicious. I feel sheer disgust. If Tarun had not defended Shankar Sharma and had not gone on and on about how much he was being harassed, Tehelka would have been much better off today.

'If Tarun had not defended Shankar Sharma ... Tehelka would be much better off today', meaning that Tarun, to save himself should have left Shankar high and die.

In an affidavit filed by First Global, Shankar Sharma stated:

> At the height of the payment crisis at the Calcutta Stock Exchange (CSE) during March 2001, SEBI had presided over the sale of a huge amount of DSQ share to UTI by various brokers, in order to bail out the CSE and the defaulting brokers. According to newspaper reports published in May 2001 this purchase was under the supervision of a senior SEBI official who was deputed to the CSE to manage the crisis. Now, according to other newspaper articles about the JPC's draft Report, it is learnt that the said senior SEBI official was its executive director (legal), Ms Dharmishtha Rawal (sister of additional solicitor general, Mr Kirit Rawal) and further, an internal enquiry report of the UTI, conducted subsequent to the S.S. Tarapore Committee's recommendation, has found that this bail out cost the UTI more than Rs 19 crore, as the value of its investment

on account of this transaction had depreciated from Rs 25.13 crore to Rs 6 crore. The Report has further noted "that the primary objective of the purchase of DSQ shares was to help CSE during the payment crisis, which is surely not in conformity with UTI's mandate." It is shameful that senior SEBI officials have misused public (UTI) money to bail out defaulting brokers. The real motives of such a patently illegal and fraudulent act by a public servant can at best be left unsaid. I understand that, in the draft Report, the JPC has recommended strict action to be taken against Ms Rawal in this connection.

Shankar and Devina believed that as there had been this questionable involvement, Kirit Rawal should have recused himself from First Global's case.

In an interview, Mahesh Jethmalani was asked about the role of lawyers in the Commission:

Madhu: But what about the lawyers? The lawyers in the Commission were deliberately subverting the Commission constantly.

Jethmalani: Of course, that was the job. But I've seen this happen. When a new government comes into power, it has its own lure, the spoils of victory and all that. It becomes this whole patronage system. Everybody loves this kind of thing. And it becomes "my Party, my government, right or wrong", then its "Us against Them". You get that kind of a mentality. The problem, there are very few people committed to the law and the judiciary. They're more committed to feathering their own nests, or the government or the Party they belong to.

⌒

As in everything in India, the opposite parallel always runs concurrently. Are we born with no hope in the system? No. Children in India are taught the value of the Indian Constitution, the courts and the protection of their human rights. There is a cross over point in every person's experience when you become the cynical adult. It takes just one incident where you see injustice carried to an extreme. This happens all the time. When journalists began to write about the corruption in the judiciary, lawyers held forth that the press was damaging the institution. Who after all is damaging the institution? The institution is only damaged by those who corrupt it, not by those who report it, quite obviously.

The parallel of the good guys continued with all the lawyers who appeared for Tehelka free of charge. Ram Jethmalani's interrogation of an income tax officer that drove him virtually to tears is now legendary. Ram's daughter, Rani Jethmalani, also represented Tehelka. Others who appeared for Tehelka without charge were the renowned lawyer Shanti Bhushan and his son, Prashant Bhushan. The young but notable Sidharth Luthra, often the most aggressive, led the charge. They obviously believed in the system of justice. Inevitably, some of them found that belief frayed in the course of the Commission's long-drawn out proceedings. Kavin Gulati, a college friend of Aniruddha Bahal, also Tehelka's counsel, was one of those lawyers.

When Tehelka received the first summons from the Commission, Gulati filed a formal application to hand over the original tapes to Justice Venkataswami. Tehelka said, 'We stand by our story. Here are the tapes. You can ascertain whatever you like.' They also gave the Commission a set of VHS tapes.

Gulati said that when the government framed the terms of reference, none of them, neither Tarun, Aniruddha, nor Gulati, realized that the broad terms of reference would shift the focus to an investigation into Tehelka itself. Gulati said,

> You have an investigating agency which is the arm of the government. You have these ministers who are not ready to quit their office handling the show. Files are being sent – what is in those files, who knows? We were not allowed to see those files. We were told they were all security documents related to the security of the country. So, we did not, in fact, know what was happening.

At the start, none of those COT raised any doubts about the authenticity of the tapes, and in their early affidavits they had all substantially accepted their presence and voice on the tapes. This was the first Commission ever held in India that would use videotapes as evidence on such a scale. After the lawyers of those COT studied similar American and British cases, they learnt that the only loophole to slip through towards 'not guilty' was to debunk the tapes. The Commission was derailed for six months on the doctoring issue alone, when the lawyers were using only VHS tapes from the broadcast, which is already a couple of generations down. Why did Tehelka lawyers allow this to happen? Gulati said,

> I was certain that Justice Venkataswami, at least, would do no wrong. Not that I have reason to doubt Justice Phukan, but the way this government has moved, after all he can only do justice with what is available to him. Then there were 30 lawyers on the other side and one lawyer saying, "They are trying to impugn motives on you". In fact, there was this so-called British expert, Chris Mills, you see the first two questions I put to him, you will see what a dishonest man he was. If a person admits to 99.99 per cent of the tape, would you still examine the tape? He said, "Yes." For what?

How did the difference between editing and doctoring get so confused in the Commission? Gulati admitted, 'I have to confess that most of us did not understand what we were saying, neither did they. Most of the lawyers did not know what they were saying'.

Gulati said that they were convinced that as there was no forensic laboratory in India, if the tapes were sent abroad, the government would provide the funds, a person from the government would accompany the tapes, and only the government would know who was examining them, so the result could then be fudged.

> **Madhu:** Switching to a completely different aspect, you know Tarun and you know Aniruddha. Do you see them as having changed as people through the Commission's proceedings?
>
> **Gulati:** Yes and no. Yes, because … [pause] … initially they were very upbeat

521

about being able to see it through. Now, we have come to realize that it is extremely difficult, if not impossible to fight the system. You cannot fix a man who is very high in power in this country at this stage. The kind of confidence which we had at the point when we stepped into this Inquiry is no longer there. You have that feeling that something good may ultimately come out. Something unusual may happen and we may be vindicated ultimately. That's the reason why we've backed out, at least, that's the reason why I decided to move out of this. I told these people that even if you proceed with the matter, I will not be participating because I think it's a waste of time.

Madhu, money apart, my practice suffered because of this. There were about ten to twenty thousand pages which we were dealing with, and every day from 8 in the morning to 12.30 in the night, I was sitting at Tehelka's office. Six to eight months of my life I have given to this case and I think it was an exercise in futility. There's no doubt about that, because what do you get at the end? Nothing at all. Everything's gone waste according to me. We'd reached the end and then this resignation happened. That's when I wilted. There were many occasions where I did receive subtle hints from people and I refused to relent. But when this happened, I myself gave up.

Madhu: Did it change you?

Gulati: Yeah, because it shattered my confidence in the system. It did. I don't want to say it. We faced this case in the High Court and we won. I have no reason to complain. As I said, before, Justice Venkataswami, at least I had a wonderful experience. The judge was absolutely superb. I don't know about the internal pressures which he would have faced. But in the Commission itself, people had become so belligerent and so offensive, it was only that he was a man of God, he kept his cool. I give him full marks there. But when we talk of the judiciary, I talk of the general atmosphere which is there. You look at the trial courts. You look how evidence is being recorded and how witnesses turn hostile in every case. When I talk about the judiciary and my loss of faith in the system, what I mean is not a particular case, but any case which goes to a trial court. All kinds of people frequent the trial court and the manner in which a trial is conducted, is absolutely pathetic. It's only when you start going to the higher courts that you actually get to see some sense of law.

Madhu: So what possibly happened was that Tarun and Aniruddha did not anticipate how they would get attacked from all sides.

Gulati: You're right about that. They were just not aware of what they were getting into when they broke this story.

Madhu: They thought that the government would fall.

Gulati: If they thought that the government would fall, I think that they were being stupid. It's very funny. Tarun, I did not know from Adam. Aniruddha also I think just called me for the moment. He thought he is an old friend. He'll be doing some free service, *theek hai* [that's okay]. Ultimately we'll get him some top guns. That is what I could figure out. But I was also doing it for the sake of experience because I also knew this was a big case. They got me in only thinking that we'll start one or two months down the line, we'll get some big people in. But, somebody can give you a commitment for a day, one hearing, two hearings, not for months because in terms of spending so many months senior lawyers would lose crores and crores.

Madhu: So you think this proves that you really cannot get justice in India? That the truth cannot come out and it can be twisted by the system? The System is bigger than the Truth?

Gulati: I am a pessimist.

Madhu: You became one after this experience?

Gulati: Yes. Though in the court in which I practice, that is the Supreme Court, I still have my optimism because more often than not, it works. A judge may commit a mistake but that does not mean he is doing it for the wrong reasons. We commit mistakes all the time, so do the judges but by and large, the higher judiciary I have great faith. Why is the Commission of Inquiry Act being used? The Supreme Court says this is primarily an Inquiry in order to enable the central government to inform itself properly, so that it can take an appropriate action. The government actually is supposed to play a very, very neutral role.

Madhu: You are speaking of the attorney general or the government lawyers?

Gulati: The government lawyers.

Madhu: Is the attorney general supposed to play a neutral role?

Gulati: Yes. He has to. He has to.

Madhu: But he hasn't.

Gulati: I can't say anything on that because that's for people to judge.

〜

One more with belief in the system bites the dust. The bitter lessons foisted on the surprised victims will never be written up in Indian history. Yes, Gandhi's moral dilemmas, Nehru's identity crisis, Indira Gandhi's Emergency foibles, have all found a warm place in history books. Who will educate the children of India about the Ramayana in reverse played out during our lifetime: the triumph of evil over good? If they are so taught, what will they understand? Don't ever try to buck the system because it will get you in the end.

Why is the Constitution so important and sacrosanct? A drowning man will hang on to a straw to save himself. Simply put, we need it to protect us from the tyranny of power. It is that straw that has saved us repeatedly and is perhaps the only document that is consensually accepted by people from all income levels, all castes, all religions, and even all political parties, including the Communist parties. In the Constitution, the separation of powers between the legislature, the executive, and the judiciary is lucid, but it has not always been unchallenged. There is an inbuilt interconnecting network in the Constitution that separates the three principal organs of state. The executive, that is, the president on the advice of the prime minister and the chief justice, appoints the judges of the Supreme Court. The judges are ensured independence from the executive because they cannot be removed except by impeachment, where a serious breach of conduct has to be proved. If a law is passed in Parliament, the Supreme Court has the power to declare the law invalid if it violates the Constitution. Consequently, over the years, there have been notable confrontations between the legislature and judiciary on this issue. Perhaps more than any other democratic country, India has the most fascinating history of politicians tinkering with the Constitution by passing laws in Parliament to suit their own agendas and in the case of Indira Gandhi, for the protection of her own political power. And in each case, the players get divided quickly into those who will *chamcha* up and those who will stand up for what they see as their principles of a democratic country.

Now it has become a tradition that precedents place the format. But, it was precisely because T.N. Seshan did not look at the conduct of preceding election commissioners that he was able to make the Election Commission's office bite and chew up politicians. He read the rules and actually began implementing them. Before his time the Indian people were barely aware that the Election Commission existed. And, hey, blowing away the cobwebs from 50-year old rules and implementing them makes news in India. Seshan also become notorious for his rude and obnoxious behaviour, which can be ignored as small change for the larger good he did.

So then, are attorney generals supposed to be independent or are they supposed to be at the beck and fall at the government's feet? Men of courage do not look at precedents alone. It is the essence of man that urges him to look at each stage anew: to embrace and battle for the larger vision rather than the next cup of tea. It is the extraordinary men who can see the importance of small and apparently inconsequential events. Besides, we have been so brainwashed by the medium and not the message, that unless the press creates a ruckus about it, how can it be conceived to be an issue at all? The press on its part became disturbingly silent with the sensational stories related to Tehelka, became envious, got bored, moved on. The press can make a thundering issue about Kareena Kapoor kissing her boyfriend, but when the freedom to publish without retribution even such inane piffle was at stake, they were busy looking for their own stories.

The president of India appoints the attorney general, ostensibly, but it really is the political party in power that chooses him. According to the Constitution:

> It shall be the duty of the Attorney-General to give advice to the Government of India upon such legal matters, and to perform such other duties of a legal character, as may from time to time be referred or assigned to him by the President, and to discharge the functions conferred on him by or under this Constitution or any other law for the time being in force. In the performance of his duties the Attorney-General shall have right of audience in all courts in the territory of India.

This is safely vague for it to be interpreted into a hundred Rashomons. But relate it to Tehelka and the Commission of Inquiry. As much as there may be admiration for the man, I am compelled by conscience to ask the question here: What exactly was Soli Sorabjee, the attorney general at that time, doing in the Commission of Inquiry on Tehelka? If he is to 'give advice to the Government of India' does it make the government the attorney general's client? If the government already has lawyers representing it in the Commission, then what exactly is the attorney general's role? He is entitled to speak in any court in the land. Naturally, that expectation entrusts a degree of neutrality to the attorney general, to ensure that, above all, justice is meted out in absolute fairness to all citizens. The Constitution does not state that the attorney general 'represents' the government. It does state clearly that he must 'give advice to the government'. One would expect this to mean that he would advise the government on where it stands on legal issues in any controversy. Does this, however, entail making a case supporting Jaya Jaitly's plea to Justice Phukan? If Jaya Jaitly's own lawyers were capably representing her, why should the attorney general be arguing in favour of her plea being accepted? Here again Rashomon comes in. Renowned lawyer, Fali S. Nariman disagreed. He said, 'The attorney general and solicitor general, when government is involved, are merely spokesman for their clients and one must not confuse the role of the Ombudsman with that of a law officer who appears for and is instructed by his government.' A lawyer for Tehelka said, 'The Union's legal team protected certain individuals and attacked others, which is not their assigned role. Should not a difference be maintained between the government and its supposedly errant leaders/politicians/officers? Did they act as per their higher duty to the court and justice? Or was he only a mouthpiece of the government focused on destroying the messenger to get rid of the message?'

This was an issue that was debated nationally in 1962 when the government proposed to merge the office of the attorney general with that of the law minister. The government withdrew the proposal when the Opposition was so volubly strong. It was pointed out that since the law minister was part of the cabinet, if there wasn't an independent attorney general, the president of India would be denied independent advice when he needed it. [*Constitutional Government in India* By M.V. Pylee p.260] (Cf Ashok Desai, 'Law Minister as Attorney General', *The Economic and Political Weekly*, Annual Number 1963, pp 129-32 and V. Venkatarama Ayyar, 'Attorney General and Law Minister', *The Hindu*, 22 January 1963). According to one perspective, neutrality and commitment to the Constitution are necessary ingredients for an attorney general. In fact, Soli Sorabjee himself, in his interview with me, elucidated quite clearly, 'That was because the British had this idea, with the Government of India Act 1935, they said that the attorney general should be a person who should not be a political personality. He should be a person of independence, who can give objective, sound advice to government.'

Soli Sorabjee, is a man who is generally liked and respected by the public at large. He is known for his love of poetry, literature and jazz. He exudes the air common to many Parsi men: that he was possibly brought up surrounded by crochet lace doilies, fine bone china, antique furniture, charming manners, all spun around him in a delicate cocoon by a frail chiffon and brooch mummy, with beauty parlour hair, flawlessly manicured nails, and whiffs of old-fashioned French perfume. Not the kind of culture that produces bohemians and rebels. Above all, it instils a seasoned respect for things past and the need to repeat them. It would lead one to expect that Sorabjee would respect the Constitution and fundamental rights, including the right to free speech, above all else. Sorabjee's columns in newspapers show him to be analytical, erudite, and au courant in world affairs. When he has chosen to, Sorabjee has been fearless in standing up to differ from the government he has been chosen to advise. How could he have been so tractable that he became party to the exculpation of individuals who were caught on videotapes in questionable activities?

Between 1975 and 1977, Soli Sorabjee, appeared pro bono for many newspapers and periodicals fighting censorship during Indira Gandhi's Emergency. In September 2003, Sorabjee was an invited speaker at the MLRC London Conference and spoke on 'The Constitution, Courts and the Freedom of Expression with Reference to Censorship'. In Mark Stephens' remarks when he introduced Sorabjee he pointedly clarified, ' ... Soli Sorabjee now plays a very important role as attorney general of India, outside of the government. He is independent of the government, not as it says in the biography.' It indicated that Sorabjee sought this clarification.

Sorabjee concluded his own remarks by saying:

> I think, ladies and gentlemen, there can be no hard and fast rule except one: When in doubt, tilt the balance in favour of expression rather than its suppression. And always remember the memorable words of Madison, who said about freedom of the press and I quote, "It is better to leave a few noxious branches to luxuriant growth, than by pruning them away, to injure the vigour of those yielding proper fruits."

In February 2002, Soli Sorabjee argued for the government in the Supreme Court that the particular section of the Industrial Disputes Act, stipulating the government's permission to close an industry, conformed to reasonable restrictions allowed by the Constitution. On 25 July 2003, Sorabjee took a stand in the Supreme Court that differed with the government and in conflict with solicitor general Harish Salve's submission. Sorabjee submitted in the Supreme Court that the rights granted to minorities under Article 30, to establish and administer their educational institutions was absolute and was beyond the purview of the interference of any external agency. Salve had stated, in line with the government position, that the minorities had no absolute rights, as such a right was subject to reasonable restrictions. Ravi Kiran Jain, president of the UP People's Union for Civil Liberties, criticized Soli Sorabjee for appearing in a 'personal capacity' in the minorities' case. He said that if the attorney general differed with the government, he should have resigned. It was Jain's view that Sorabjee had taken advantage of his position as attorney general; that he is permitted to appear in any court of the land, but not in a personal capacity. Many constitutional lawyers disagree. They believe it is not only acceptable but also imperative for an attorney general to present what he interprets as the correct interpretation of law. It is not required that the attorney general agree with the government. He must represent the Constitution and ensure that the government's activities are within its purview. However, Jain's view is understandable. The historical precedent of attorney generals compliant with the government in power had indeed become the common interpretation of the role. It certainly is a political appointment, but the role is lucently consecrated in the Indian Constitution. The attorney general is not supposed to be a political person but must remain above politics, advising the government against any action that is unconstitutional.

At this point the attorney general's role seems to be a freewheeling concept. If Sorabjee agreed with the government's position on any particular issue, he would argue their case. If he didn't, he seemed to be independent enough to either argue against it or refuse to appear. Why then was Sorabjee present in the Commission of Inquiry on Tehelka? On pure speculation, one might assume, Sorabjee was given to understand that there was this minor irritation that was festering in the Commission. Why not just nudge the presiding judge to send the tapes for forensic examination and be done with it? It appears that Sorabjee simply considered the Tehelka Commission a tiny pesky issue. Perhaps he did not view it as a larger moral issue that could culminate in muzzling the press and freedom of speech. His actions in the Tehelka Commission do not measure up to his history of taking positions on similar subjects. There appears to be, prima facie, an element of chivalry on his part, as seems to be his nature, that was misdirected. Jaya Jaitly was being bothered. Sorabjee likes George. Remember, everybody likes George. Just help fix it. The attorney general, particularly this attorney general, should have been above steering the Commission to Jaya Jaitly's advantage and against the freedom of the press. It was reliably learnt by the press that Chris Mills, the forensic expert flown in for his deposition by Jaya, was a dinner guest of the attorney general at his home, along with Jaya Jaitly and her legal team. This is not considered proper at all. Soli Sorabjee, in an interview, clarified what he thought his role in the Commission of Inquiry on Tehelka was as attorney general of India:

Soli Sorabjee: The attorney general, under our Constitution, is not a member of the cabinet. Major distinction from America, Canada, and Australia. He is not expected to be a member of the ruling party. He is not expected to be a member of the House. That was because the British had this idea, with the Government of India Act 1935; they said that the attorney general should be a person who should not be a political personality. He should be a person of independence, who can give objective, sound advice to government. At that time, the attorney general was called the advocate general of India. The role of the attorney general has to be as the first legal officer of the Government of India. In practical terms, I appear in court much more often than my counterparts do in other Commonwealth countries. I give advice when opinions are sent. Apart from that, oral advice is given on difficult opinions, whether it is constitutional or whether this will stand scrutiny, whether it will be in conflict with some legislation. And, I have always believed and I have always said, I see no reason why the attorney general's opinion should not be published. People have a right to know what is the reasoning of the attorney general. I, as attorney general, in some matters I am asked per the court to appear as amicus curiae, then I did not necessarily project the government's point of view. And it happened in the minority case before the eleven-judge bench.

Madhu: So in that sense, you saw in your role as attorney general the freedom to be independent when you saw it differently?

Sorabjee: When I saw that the constitutional provisions did not really totally justify the government's stand. But, of course there would be very few occasions like that. Otherwise, what I would do is, if there is a matter and the government is very insistent upon, quite frankly, for example as it happened with the textbooks case. In that George [Fernandes] was involved. George was one of the petitioners. I would say, I think you had better ask some other officer to do it. My heart is not in the matter, so I won't be able to be convincing. Both sides are briefing me. I am not convinced. So I won't be able to drag home the point with conviction. So tell someone else. I sometimes gave the excuse that I knew one of the petitioners and that I feel embarrassed.

Madhu: Were you comfortable with clause (d) in the terms of reference, which required the motivations of the journalists to be investigated?

Sorabjee: Yes, yes, of course. Of course, very much so. Because they wanted to know what was the motivation? What was the reason? That's the reason that's the clause they wanted to be dropped, very much. That was one of Ram Jethmalani's requests to the prime minister about his not contesting the elections in Lucknow. They dropped the whole thing and particularly this clause. You see, that clause [laughs] the idea was the Commission to go [into] what's behind this? And then the question came up about the funding. The amount that was received by Shankar Sharma and his wife. All this inquiry is going on. Income tax officers were there. So they were very, very, sort of nervous. Yes, were nervous about this Inquiry being drawn into another Commission.

Madhu: But what came out with Shankar Sharma and Devina Mehra was almost six months later. At the time this Commission was constituted, the terms of reference included clause (d), which had never been the case earlier. How would you have known when the terms of reference were framed about any money being received by Shankar Sharma?

Sorabjee: *Haan*, maybe. But, possibly they might have expected or suspected that there must be something else about the funding of it.

Madhu: I will read to you clause (d) included in the terms of reference:

"(d) To inquire into all aspects relating to the making and publication of these allegations and any other matter which arises from or is connected with or incidental to any act, omission or transaction referred to in sub-clauses (a) and (b) above."

Sorabjee: Yeah, so there was a motivation. There were allegations. So we wanted to know is there any political party behind it? Is there some other person behind it? So go into it. That was the terms of reference. But they were wide.

Madhu: Yes, but it was basically giving them permission to investigate the messenger.

Sorabjee: Yeah, yeah.

Madhu: Did you have any information when the terms of reference were being drafted that there was any financial irregularity? Did the government have any information that there was a foreign hand or the Hindujas' hand or was there any evidence of any motivation other than straightforward journalism?

Sorabjee: I don't know. That time, *tho kuch aise nahi tha* [there was nothing like that]. The government definitely had a suspicion, almost a belief in their minds that this is not just a pure journalistic exercise. This is not Mr Tarun Tejpal, sort of very anxious to see accountability in public life and transparency in public life. There was something which more than meets the eye. And this was politically motivated. Their impression, maybe wrong, but they had that feeling. *Hinduja tha ki nahi aur doosra kaun tha* [Hinduja was there or not and who else was there]? Later on it came. The fact of the matter is that we had official information from Mauritius authorities. But the Mauritius banking laws are so strict they would not reveal the accounts.

Madhu: I have seen the documents of the ownership of those companies.

Sorabjee: *Mera kehana yeh hai bank transfer, kisne kiya* [what I am saying is, who did the bank transfer]? They got lots and lots in their accounts.

Madhu: So is it illegal to make a lot of money? They have documents to show they have paid taxes on them.

Sorabjee: But, what is the source? From where did it come?

Madhu: Their sources are their own companies. They are making money in their business. They are paying taxes of sixty crore annually.

Sorabjee: *Nahi*, we are, we are little different. What was the source of the money which came from Mauritius?

Madhu: They are making money in London, on the London Stock Exchange. They are making money in NASDAQ. They are registered there. So they were making money all over the world. They were within their rights to transfer their own money and invest it where they chose.

Sorabjee: Making money all over the world, but the question was where were some other sources? I'll tell you what made us suspicious about this someone, *Hindujas key saath* [with the Hindujas], who is that lady who was in *The Hindu*, that Charulata?

Madhu: Yes, Charu Joshi.

Sorabjee: Right, Charu Joshi. Yeah, Charu Joshi and then ...

Madhu: They were trying to sell content and then Tarun didn't go upstairs but she went and she spoke to them.

Sorabjee: Yeah, yeah, yeah, yeah. Suspicious, suspicion but there it was. But at that time I don't think that at the time of the terms of reference, I don't think this was in their mind. Though, they did that generally.

Madhu: So on what basis did they put it in except to give them a handle to go after them? What did they suspect at that time?

Sorabjee: It was put in because they questioned their motivation. Now let me tell you one thing. They wanted to find out whether the tapes were fudged, whether there was some deliberate interpolation, if anything which was done was faulty. One thing I always ask the people who always hail this fellow as a hero. And Patwant Singh and I had a rather heated conversation. I said, Patwant just tell me one thing. In the thing they relayed to the public, under the media channel, there was one bit which was cut out and it was very important. Where, who is that fellow who was boasting about the deals?

Madhu: R.K. Jain?

Sorabjee: *Haan* R.K. Jain. That bit, "*Nahi, nahi, George Sahab paise nahi lega. Vo tho socialist, socialist sab manta hai. George Sahab paise nahi lenge* [no, no, George will not take money. He is a socialist, he is recognized as that. George will not take money]." That was deleted. Immediately I asked why was it deleted? If you said all the things. If you are fair, this is a very important thing. Some silly excuse like we didn't have time. At that time we are doing it.

Madhu: So you can accuse them of slanted editing, but where is the evidence of a conspiracy in the funding? Did you see the original tapes?

Sorabjee: No, but this particular part, it is omitted. You are suppressing a very important matter of fact. The same R.K. Jain, who was boasting was also saying that George does not take money. But this one showed there was a motivation. This one, as I said, then I doubted bona fide.

Madhu: You could call it immature editing.

Sorabjee: Now that was not bad editing. That was motivated.

Madhu: No, but you can't say it's been tampered with. It's edited.

Sorabjee: No, no, no edited. Tampering *ko chodh doh* [leave tampering out]. But if you edit and under the guise of editing, you delete a portion which shows the other side in a favourable light, I would suspect that person's position.

Madhu: You can call it malicious editing.

Sorabjee: No, it is suppression of facts, because the public was entitled to know. Public would still say, *ki R.K. Jain bolta hai ki George toh socialist, paise nahi lega* [that R.K. Jain said George is a socialist, he doesn't take money]. *Tab bhi* [even then], they still believe he takes money. But if he said that why did they omit it? Why did you ignore that?

Madhu: Did you see the original tapes?

Sorabjee: Original tapes I did. Some parts of it.

Madhu: Did you did you suspect that they were tampered with? Forget the malicious editing.

Sorabjee: Tampered, *nahi* [tampered, no]. *Mereko aise tho laga* from what I saw *ki* [I felt that] they were adjusted in such a way that one scene is shown in one room the other scene is shown in another room. But I am not very technologically savvy about these things. But I did raise a suspicion. I am not a technical man. I said, let the others who are more familiar with it just point out what are the loopholes in the tapes. They themselves admitted many sort of gaps and they explained why the gaps are there. You must have seen there some portions. Jaya must have given you the details. What are the various omissions and what happened and transpositions and other things. But regardless of all this, *meiney tho seedhi baat aisa karta* [I said it straight]. Look, you are supposed to be fair. You are a journalist. If you do not have any other motive or any other thing. You must see both sides of the picture. You presented to the public that thing which is damning. You withheld from the public that thing which is also favourable to the other side. Now if any one does that then I start doubting the motive. *Ki kyun aisa kar diya*? [why did you do that]? Now people are entitled to know. As I said, they can still form an opinion afterwards. This was not fair and objective and impartial.

Madhu: You could say the editing was slanted but to take it to a point where you say that you can put words in people's mouths without it being detected is too far-fetched. This is not a feature film where under controlled circumstances you can do it.

Sorabjee: *Aapneh tape, tapes dekha hai* [have you seen the tapes]?

Madhu: Yes. I knew that they could not have doctored them. It is too difficult to do without it being easily detected.

Sorabjee: And that's what the forensic examiner's report said?

Madhu: It is not possible to do it. They didn't have the machines. They didn't have the time. It's very easy to bamboozle the Commission by showing a few tricks that are possible. But doctoring is an entirely different issue. You can do it in a feature film. You can't do it in an authentic atmosphere.

Sorabjee: *Aacha*, maybe you know.

Madhu: It is impossible. But you argued in the Commission on 29 April in favour of sending the tapes for forensic examination. You cited Malkani's case and other cases as precedents.

Sorabjee: No, no, no. My argument was this. This goes to the root of the matter. Since the other side says, one of the people says that these tapes have been tampered with. Then we must go into that question because if we do not, then differences in the conclusion will arrive. If suppose, that time we didn't know what would be the result of it. But even if it is established they are doctored or tampered with, then naturally the whole other thing will go. So please send them. I definitely argued and I told Jaya and I told George: "If the result goes against you, you must be prepared to accept it." She was absolutely confident.

Madhu: Milin Kapoor had convinced Jaya that the tapes had been tampered with, so she had her own lawyers asking for the tapes to be sent. And the

Union Of India was also pushing for them to be sent. Why would the attorney general go and argue the case for them to be sent?

Sorabjee: I argued the case because I had said that this is their allegation. I don't know whether it's true or not. The other side says *ki* it is not so, it is sure. It's necessary since this goes to the root of the matter and clarifies this issue. What is the idea then doing it much later? I said, send the tapes for examination.

Madhu: But basically you are supposed to be looking into constitutional issues. Why were you as attorney general arguing Jaya's case?

Sorabjee: No, no, not constitutional issues. I am supposed to be looking at how the Commission should function and what is the proper role of the Commission to do. The Commission asked me, what is the stand of the Government of India?

Madhu: But the Government of India lawyers were there.

Sorabjee: I was there. No other. I was not there as attorney general. I was appearing for the Union of India. I was there. Kirit Rawal was there.

Madhu: Kirit Rawal was there for the Union of India. You were there as attorney general.

Sorabjee: I was also for Union of India. I was appearing on behalf of Union of India as I appear in many other matters of High Court and Supreme Court. The notice was not given to me as attorney general. But even if the notice was given to me as attorney general, I still believe that it was the right course to be adopted because then all these wild allegations.

Madhu: Who was briefing you for this? Did you just speak to Jaya or George?

Sorabjee: No, no, Jaya and George only they said they are spurious, spurious, spurious. But we took the decision ourselves with the law officers in the law ministry. What do you think is the correct course? He said, well there are the allegations about the tapes and there are counter-allegations. But [the] best thing would be to have them removed at the earlier stage.

Madhu: But who was actually your instructing advocate?

Sorabjee: Instructing advocate, I don't know who, was from the central agency or from someone from the law ministry. I don't remember his name now.

Madhu: Did you have any direct contact with Jaya?

Sorabjee: *Nahi, nahi* [no, no], on the contrary, I had to avoid speaking to Jaya, just in case. George *ke saath* [with George], I used to talk. I told George informally that "George, you are so confident about it. I hope the result of the tapes is what you expect after Jaya's sort of assertions and allegations." She was absolutely convinced. Now they say *aisa bilkul nahi hai* [now they say it is absolutely not like that]. And I was someone who had said, don't send the tapes to the CBI, because the credibility will be questioned. Send it to some independent foreign agency and let me tell you, I did not know the name of that agency at all. Nor did Kirit Rawal. Nor did he try to ask the judge. *Bilkul* *nahi* [absolutely not]. Because again they decided to keep it under wraps. So I said just as well.

Madhu: But was George talking to you about it regularly?

Sorabjee: No, no regularly, *nahi*.

Madhu: Just when there was an issue to discuss?

Sorabjee: No, not regularly. He was sometimes, he was complaining about Gopal Subramaniam's attitude and I would say "*Yaar*, take it easy, George, come along. Counsels argue this way. Don't read too much into it." You know sometimes he would say, "Look, he's very much biased." Or sometime some judge's observation, because these things happen in court.

Madhu: Were you briefed by anyone to appear in the Commission?

Sorabjee: They brief. The law minister will brief when it's related to Government of India, they brief.

Madhu: Related to this Commission?

Sorabjee: Yes, yes. They briefed me, of course, so they asked for the presence of Soli Sorabjee before the Commission of Inquiry. I didn't go every day. I made it very clear; in fact they were very upset that I should be there every time. I said I only come in the questions of principle, important questions of procedures to be argued. And I did argue in the question of what should be done about those tapes. Venkataswami didn't accept the arguments but he always said, "Not at this stage. Not at this stage." Kirit was appearing more. Because the factual part, I said I won't have the time.

Madhu: I interviewed Goolam Vahanvati. He was advocate general of Maharashtra when the cases were going on against Shankar Sharma and Devina Mehra.

Sorabjee: Yeah, yeah.

Madhu: He appeared once against them and after he realized what was going on, he refused SEBI's brief. This was because he believed that Shankar Sharma and Devina Mehra were being harassed and railroaded.

Sorabjee: Maybe, many people had that impression. Shankar Sharma went to court in Bombay High Court. They made a number of petitions. He went to others with this same allegation. But I don't think the courts accepted that.

Madhu: Are you aware that governmental agencies, the Income Tax Department, and the Enforcement Directorate were carrying out raids on Shankar and Devina Mehra? They were collecting information from their offices and homes and giving it to the Union of India for the Commission.

Sorabjee: For the Commission?

Madhu: Yes.

Sorabjee: What information was being given to the Commission?

Madhu: All the data on their personal computers, all their documents, all their mail, all their accounts of their business, their personal diaries.

Sorabjee: Commission can only be given information in affidavits.

Madhu: Detailed information about all their financial dealings in their business was passed on to the Union of India lawyers.

Sorabjee: They would give to the Government of India. They will give to the counsel appearing for the Government of India. The Commission would never accept any information privately. It would not be proper. Then it would have to be given to the Commission in the form of an affidavit.

Madhu: This was given to Union of India lawyers like Kirit Rawal.

Sorabjee: *Haan*, maybe. Yeah, yeah.

Madhu: All the agencies were looking with the intention of finding something incriminating and supplying information to the Government of India lawyers.

Sorabjee: Yes, yes, perfectly all right. It was very important for the purpose of examining them under clause (d). So I don't see anything wrong in that. If there was information, certainly in order to go into clause (d) that information had to be supplied to the government counsel. And that's the reason some income tax officer was also cross-examined by Ram Jethmalani. And maybe added to the suspicion with Ram coming in and his connection with the Hindujas. That sort of thing, maybe surmise again. Let me tell you, all this saying the government's case has gone completely by default because I told George when we met. I said why don't you just republish their evidence. As to what they have done and some of the admissions, other things. No comments nothing. The media was totally against the government in this matter. They thought he was being hounded. He was being harassed. *Arre bhai* [oh brother], I said publish some of his own statements. Don't make any comments on that. No comments, nothing. The media was totally against the government.

Madhu: You asked them to publish Shankar Sharma's statements?

Sorabjee: No, no, no, no, Tehelka's. What they did, about the methods they employed. What they did in collecting evidence. Those women, prostitutes and there also it says once I have been there and he just went to the shop; this shop turned out to be a shop selling underwear and condoms.

Madhu: Yes, but none of this has anything at all to do with Shankar Sharma and Devina Mehra.

Sorabjee: I don't believe, Madhu, that all these raids were not justified because he had refused to answer so many notices from the income tax authorities. It was very clear sign to avoid the proceedings and income tax authorities.

Madhu: No. I don't know how you got that because that never happened. They did not avoid any proceedings or ignore any notice. They spent, since 2001 all their time fighting cases against them.

Sorabjee: Why?

Madhu: They had over 200 cases filed against them by various agencies in the government. Shankar Sharma and Devina Mehra could not conduct their business. All they did was meet their lawyers, answer notices, and go from court to court. Their offices were closed down. From over 200 employees, the number came down to four.

Sorabjee: Closed down on account of what?

Madhu: Because SEBI took away their licence to trade on the Bombay Stock Exchange.

Sorabjee: No, but they went up against that in court and they lost.

Madhu: They have won it now.

Sorabjee: No, no but …

Madhu: Initially they lost. And they made an appeal, appealing again and again, and now they got it back.

Sorabjee: When? Recently?

Madhu: Recently.

Sorabjee: I didn't know.

Madhu: Two months ago. But for three years they were not allowed to trade on the stock exchange. Their passports were taken away.

Sorabjee: *Haan*, passports so they may not flee.

Madhu: Their passports were taken away on the basis that they were under investigation, not because anything had been found against them.

Sorabjee: But you must, if you really want to write a book, go to the CBI. Go to the people [in the] income tax authority and find out what are those cases.

Madhu: I have personally met income tax officers involved who cannot come on record. They confirmed that they were instructed to go after Shankar and Devina. I have no reason to hold a brief for Shankar or Devina. I came into this story without any preconceived notions. I have carefully examined hundreds of documents of the cases filed against them by these agencies.

Sorabjee: No, but suppose if they filed non-compliance notices.

Madhu: I have documents that show they have filed a case against them for not putting a sign outside their office.

Sorabjee: That's absurd. Really?

Madhu: You have to see. Read the cases. You have to read about the way they have been raided.

Sorabjee: But what about the cases where they refused to reply? They refuse to reply to notices issued by income tax authorities, which is an offence. In the sense, not a serious offence for which you serve notice.

Madhu: It's just not true. You know you can write off a notice and throw it away.

Sorabjee: No, no but just tell me. You just see, what was the notice, alleged violation of that provision and missed the reply to the notice.

Madhu: You might have been told that they did not reply to notices, but that cannot be true. That was all that they were doing.

Sorabjee: I have got an impression because I asked them. I said, "Look, this looks bad. You can't do that. After all, it's a freedom of the press also." They said, "Sir they are not replying to notices." I am also not really concerned with that part of it.

Madhu: [Voice rising.] But, you should have been. I have put their accounts through two separate audits from separate accountants. I told them to look for whatever *hera pheri* they may have done. I don't know how they fudge it in balance sheets. Both of these are two independent accounting firms.

Sorabjee: Correct, correct. Neither would I actually.

Madhu: What they told me was that even if he was part of the bear cartel, he was part of the bear cartel with everybody else; that is a separate issue. That also 'if'. There is nothing else there to indicate that what he did was dishonest. Everything was declared. They were paying their taxes. Even when they conducted the raids, it was Shankar and Devina who informed them that they also had a locker. They didn't even know. They took them to the locker. There was nothing there but one diamond necklace. For a couple who were one of the highest tax-paying individuals in India, all they found was one diamond necklace worth one lakh, which was paid for by cheque and they had the receipt. He was jailed …

Sorabjee: For what? What was the offence he committed?

Madhu: They maintained there were cases against him and he might flee the country. The cases were based on the ground that they wanted to investigate his FERA violations and income tax violations. On the mere presumption that there were violations, they put him in jail.

Sorabjee: No, I want to tell you one thing. Tavleen Singh spoke to me about Shankar Sharma and Devina Mehra. I told K.K. Sud, the additional solicitor general, "Don't oppose bail." I said, "Leave it to the court." He agreed. Then somehow Bombay High Court did not grant bail. I said, "Why, what happened?" I thought we shouldn't oppose bail. Leave it to the court. Just have proper conditions to see that he doesn't flee. And then he says, "No, sir, this, that, rest of it. I didn't know that." I do know there were two High Court judgements which declined his application of bail and some reasons must have been given.

[The following conversation in italics removed by publisher on advice of author's lawyers.]

Madhu: *The reason that was given was that the …*

Sorabjee: *No, no, …*

Madhu:

Sorabjee:

Madhu: Soli, when I interviewed Goolam Vahanvati in the Supreme Court recently, Goolam began crying. He asked me to switch off the tape-recorder. He said, "Let me compose myself." He was extraordinarily upset about what had happened to Shankar Sharma and Devina Mehra.

Sorabjee: Really?

Madhu: Yes. He said, I can't believe this is happening in my country under my nose. He was so upset. He cried. He was really, really upset. Then he composed himself. You read the story of what's happened to them, Shankar and Devina, for an investment into Tehelka which for them was small change. It was the dotcom era. Two crore to them was nothing.

Sorabjee: But then how was it that two courts, two judicial courts, they declined their application on bail for certain reasons?

Madhu: Because …

Again, conversation removed by lawyers.

Sorabjee: *Haan* that's must have. There a debate will open.

Madhu: Bail was refused with no real justification.

Sorabjee: *Haan,* but that means that two views can be taken about it. You can't say that. You can't jump to that conclusion. Everyone says it. He decided in my favour because my case was very strong. Decided against, *yaar ye dekho isska tho pressurize kiya tha. Ussko doosra koi baat kar diya tha* [he was pressurized. Some other thing must have been done].

Madhu: If you read the affidavits filed by the Income Tax Department and Enforcement Directorate, everything begins with the word "presumably".

Sorabjee: *Oh, voh toh hota hai,* "presumably" *hee hota hai na* [oh, that happens …]. That's the first, prima face case *hota hai.* You don't get to see a murder.

Madhu: You have to have some facts on which to base it. If everything is presumed, then base it on at least one proven fact.

Sorabjee: I have an impression, when I asked them, they said, "Sir, these are just numbers of cases. We have served fifteen notices, they don't reply. So we filed fifty cases. In reality it's only one. And number of notices have been sent and they haven't replied."

Madhu: Every time I interviewed them in Delhi they were coming for some case in either Patiala House or the High Court. They were always caught up in cases. It is a story that is so wrong. I was not biased. I did not go into the story with any views. I have had all the affidavits filed by the income tax and Enforcement Directorate examined by lawyers and explained to me. I have had their accounts audited.

Every government, no matter which, that comes to power does the same thing. Whenever there is a report in the press that makes the government uncomfortable, it is historically seen that they do not go after the journalist but they go after the investors. You have always fought for the freedom of the press. During the Emergency you argued cases pro bono because you believed in standing up for the freedom of the press. You said in a speech, "I think, ladies and gentlemen, there can be no hard and fast rule except one, when in doubt tilt the balance in favour of expression rather than it's suppression."

Sorabjee: *Haan*, but that was the context of censorship.

Madhu: Here they were victimizing these investors in every possible way.

Sorabjee: Investors meaning?

Madhu: Shankar Sharma and Devina Mehra.

Sorabjee: Hmmm.

Madhu: They left Tarun Tejpal alone because they knew that if they did anything to Tarun, it would make news. Nobody in India cares about the businessman. The Press Club of India will not go on a *dharna* [protest march] for an investor.

Sorabjee: But Tarun was complaining. Tarun *tho aapse barabar kehate hai. Office ko search kiya tha, vo kiya tha, ye kiya tha* [Tarun had complained that his office was searched, they did this, they did that].

Madhu: They were more careful with Tarun. He was complaining on behalf of Shankar and Devina.

Sorabjee: *Haan, haan.*

Madhu: Nobody was in the least bothered by the fact that Shankar Sharma and Devina Mehra were not only cruelly harassed but their business was destroyed. Two young people from small towns who really made it on their own merit.

Sorabjee: I am glad to hear that. The impression I was given [was] that they are very dubious operators.

Madhu: I got the documents of ownership in the Mauritius company. Kirit Rawal told me that there were shares sold at much lower prices than they should have been. I investigated all that.

Sorabjee: Kirit was really more in charge of that. Because I made it clear that I won't be able to appear in all the hearings of the Commission for this examination and that cross-examination. I appeared [for the] first terms of reference. I appeared mainly to say whether the tapes should be sent for examination.

Madhu: You could have taken a neutral position. You could have looked at what was happening. What repercussions it would have on the freedom of the press. What they were doing to Shankar and Devina. You should have looked into it.

Sorabjee: No, no, no, no, no, not at all. As far as I was concerned, I had to ensure that the Commission was functioning in the way it should.

Madhu: Do you believe that Tehelka and First Global were treated fairly in the Commission?

Sorabjee: I think so. Tehelka withdrew from the Commission. You should read Phukan's order about their application, which almost said we won't get justice from him, expressing no confidence in him. After that, whenever he passed any orders in respect of the tapes, what should be done about them, he yet gave notice to Tehelka. And I said yes, give them notice, if they still don't choose to appear then that's their lookout. So he did that. That's something that is correct and the other thing in the Interim Report, I have the impression that the defence minister, I don't know. I don't really remember that. But, did give a clean chit.

Madhu: But the CAG and the CVC investigated the defence deals and reported misappropriations in that.

Sorabjee: No, but George in that? I don't think so.

Madhu: No, they haven't mentioned George in that.

Sorabjee: George gave evidence for Venkataswami. Now, Venkataswami was a simple, fine man. He just wanted a better stenographer or more assistants. Venkataswami said that George gave good evidence. But George is, you know, George is a good fellow. His evidence was very forthright. I am convinced that George hasn't made a *pai* [penny] out of this personally. There is no question about it. But, very indiscreet to have in his own office.

Madhu: R.K. Jain?

Sorabjee: No, no, apart from that, Jaya had no business as a colleague in the party, to be there. *Ussko* office *mein rakhna kya karna* [why keep her in the office]? Very indiscreet. *Aisay hee controversy ho gaya* [that is how the controversy got created].

Madhu: That is something I have not been able to understand. Everyone in India is very open about relationships.

Sorabjee: Of course, it's an open secret. *Haan.*

Madhu: Jaya still maintains that George is only her mentor.

Sorabjee: Maybe there are some platonic relationships like that. Maybe. Very difficult though, for so many years. But I am very fond of him. Because, he is very clearly honest.

Madhu: Jaya got obsessed with proving her innocence in the Commission.

Sorabjee: May I tell you something? I told George once. George will you please do me a favour? Will you please ask Jaya to shut up and not make any statements about the Commission's rulings. That I used to tell him.

Madhu: But she continued to do so.

Sorabjee: *Bilkul* [absolutely]. Totally, she used to react all the time. Of course, he told me something one morning, "You don't know how difficult it is for me to control her," [laughs] *bola tha* [he said]. He is such a hit. Whenever he used to come home, *seedha ordinary khaana baith keh khaya* [simple, ordinary food, he sat and ate]. No pomp, no airs, nothing. I used to know him from Bombay days. *Isskey saath toh kya kiya* [what they did to him]. They wouldn't let him speak in Parliament. You make accusations against him. Then you let the man defend. Then you will go on saying, *yeh kya baat hai* [what is this]?

Madhu: But the stuff that the Samata Party treasurer R.K. Jain spoke about ...

Sorabjee: He is an absolute lout.

Madhu: But details he came up with are so believable because you wonder how he got this kind of detailed information about the Russians, about the arms dealing companies?

Sorabjee: I know there is no question about it. *Vo tho zarur hoga* [that must be there]. But that's correct. So you do that but also at the same time channels publish his statements, George Sahab *paise nahi leta hai. Vo tho socialist, socialist* [George doesn't take money. He is a socialist]. If Tehelka had included all that, if they had played fair, everything would have played out differently.

Although Sorabjee mentioned that he had told K.K. Sud (additional solicitor general) not to oppose bail, Sidharth Luthra pointed out that the facts do not match with what Sorabjee said. Harish Salve appeared in Delhi High Court and vehemently opposed bail. Luthra said, 'K.K. Sud came to the trial court and he too opposed it to the hilt when Rani Jethmalani and I appeared for Shankar in Delhi. Shankar remained in jail for over 60 days. Once his case was shifted to Mumbai, he got bail in a few days. The most shocking was that he was arrested and kept in a Delhi jail but when 60 days expired, on the sixty-first day they filed a complaint in Mumbai. That was the day that Shankar broke down for the first time in court.' Perhaps the reason was to avoid Mumbai was due to a hostile state government.

Mahesh Jethmalani, lawyer for Shankar Sharma and Devina Mehra, expressed strong views on the role of the attorney general, in an interview:

Madhu: Soli claims, and you could only second-guess it, as I am doing, having just interviewed him, that he was unaware of the extent of what was happening to Shankar Sharma and Devina Mehra.

Jethmalani: What's that famous saying? There are none so blind as will not see. That's complete crap. Soli's too intelligent a man.

Madhu: That's what anyone would think. And when I told him that look, this happened, this happened, this happened, he said no, I told Sud that let the guy go, what are you doing to him?

Jethmalani: Soli was hand-in-glove with Brajesh Mishra. He would do everything that Brajesh wanted. Soli was Brajesh Mishra's puppet, let me tell you that much.

Madhu: So it wasn't Jaya and George who were asking him to appear in the Commission on these doctoring issues? You think it was Brajesh Mishra?

Jethmalani: It may be both. It is typical to say that George and Jaya didn't. But I'm much more inclined to believe that between the grass-root democrat politician that George was, and the completely cynical bureaucrat that Brajesh Mishra is, that the bulk of the pressure came from Brajesh Mishra. George may have, in his old age George may have, for his own survival, shunned a few conventions. Forgotten his hoary past and all that. It's quite possible.

Madhu: But with this Commission, new precedents have been set.

Jethmalani: Nobody will ever go that far. That was the golden age of *The*

Indian Express and it never happened after. Sometimes, I think, *India Today* did it. That's it. They were the only two who were independent. *TheTimes* [of India] and all the others have been so close to the establishment. It's all quick-buck journalism, what do you say? You can sell space.

Madhu: The manner in which the attorney general's role has been spelt out in the Constitution, it is rather vague and subject to a huge range of interpretation. How do you assess Soli Sorabjee's very active role as attorney general in the Commission of Inquiry? The Constitution has left it rather open to interpretation.

Jethmalani: No, no. So much of the effective functioning of these institutions like the attorney general depend not on the letter of the law and what is prescribed for them in the Constitution. It really depends on the strength of the incumbent, the character of the incumbent, and on conventions that have evolved.

Madhu: The convention that has evolved over the years is largely subservient and obsequious to the government.

Jethmalani: Absolutely. This was something which bipartisanship should have taken care of in our Constitution: that no matter which party is in power, these conventions are healthy conventions. If people say "my party right or wrong" and don't put democracy above party, this is going to happen. And that's another failure. We've got the British system, but that works because they have well-established conventions. People don't violate them. Thus far and no further. But here it happens.

It would have also played out differently had the attorney general sought more details on what was being done. In his interview, it comes across that Soli Sorabjee was relying on information provided to him by other counsels for the government who were implementing the SADS. The Rashomon here will be the reader's assessment. Many lawyers have reacted by saying that it is not possible that Sorabjee would not have known what was going on. This comes from the respect he commands in the profession. How could someone so clued in not know about the SADS? In his interview he said he was unaware of the details. Is it possible? If you give him the benefit of the doubt, figure this: a busy attorney general, rushing from court to court, does not examine the details in every case. He is relying on what he is being briefed. Unless he launches his own investigation, it is unlikely he will understand that there is a murky side to the picture. Even senior lawyers appearing in a case are often not conversant with the details. In another conversation years ago, Sorabjee had mentioned how his daughter, Zia Mody, a cracking successful lawyer in Mumbai, had criticized him, saying that you seniors don't even read the cases properly. You get briefed in corridors just before you walk into the courtroom. Shankar Sharma and Devina Mehra never spoke to Sorabjee about what they were going through. It would not have been proper. It was unlikely he would have met them. It is my belief: Soli Sorabjee just missed it. But, grab this fantasy. Sorabjee becomes aware of the SADS. He tells the government, in his assigned capacity as attorney general, that they must bring to an end these trumped-up cases against Shankar Sharma and Devina Mehra. Stop going after Tehelka. Start proceedings against all those caught on tape. Let the law do its duty to the nation. Then we could believe in rock 'n roll again. This was a case in which an extraordinary person, Sorabjee, was placed in a situation to which he reacted by being most ordinary. On the other hand, there were circumstances that transformed ordinary persons, the Tehelka team and their investors, into the extraordinary.

One column of ants struggles to maintain their integrity and faith in the Constitution alive, while the other column works just as industriously to subvert it. It is a living Rashomon. It is much more difficult to remain honest in India than virtually anywhere else in the world. Because not breaking the law, not misusing law, not telling lies, upholding the Constitution means you have to step out of the crowd. Your conscience becomes a lonely place. Your conscience is a private place. In the midst of this, do not forget that in Hindi the word for privacy is hardly ever used.

In the film, *To Kill a Mockingbird* (1962, based on Harper Lee's Pulitzer Prize-winning book), the lawyer, Atticus Finch (Gregory Peck), talks to his eight-year old daughter, Scout (Mary Badham) about defending a black man in a segregated White area:

Atticus Finch: There are some things you're not old enough to understand just yet. There's been some high talk around town to the effect that I shouldn't do much about defending this man.
Scout: If you shouldn't be defending him, then why are you doing it?
Atticus Finch: For a number of reasons. The main one is that if I didn't, I couldn't hold my head up in town.

Scout asks her father whether he thinks he will win the case.

Finch replies:
Simply because we were licked a hundred years before we started is no reason for us not to try to win

26 Conspiracy Curry

Stanley Motss [Dustin Hoffman]: What difference does it make if it's true? If it's a story and it breaks, they're gonna run with it.

– Barry Levinson's film, Wag the Dog *(1997)*

CONSPIRACY 1

During the first week that the Operation West End story broke, alongside streamed a plethora of conspiracy theories. One of the first was that an investigative firm called Gresham & Reed, based in London, had hired Tehelka to undertake an investigation on arms dealers. In March 2001, I checked with Tarun Tejpal on the veracity of the story:

> **Madhu:** Has anyone had any professional dealings, any agreements, or any communication with Verghese of Gresham & Reed, based in London?
>
> **Tejpal:** Aniruddha Bahal had met Verghese when Tehelka was investigating the cricket match-fixing story and accounts of cricket players. So, he knows him. But, Gresham and Reed had nothing to do with the investigation we carried out on corruption in the armed services and the government. We did not have any agreements or professional dealings with them on the investigation related to the corruption on arms deals and the government.
>
> **Madhu:** Has anyone in Tehelka received any payment from Gresham & Reed?
>
> **Tejpal:** No.
>
> **Madhu:** How was it that the address and fax number on the visiting card given to Jaya Jaitly and Bangaru Laxman corresponded to that of Gresham & Reed?
>
> **Tejpal:** We needed a dummy address. So if they asked for George Verghese, they could say he worked there. If they asked for Alvin De Souza they could say he was out of the office. We just used Gresham & Reed as a dummy address.
>
> **Madhu:** Have you had any contact with the estranged wife of an arms dealer?

Tejpal: No.

Madhu: Is it true that Tehelka was hired to investigate Suresh Nanda's arms deals, contacts, and accounts which then developed into a much larger exposé?

Tejpal: This was a straight journalist story. What you are seeing here is a Fascist government at work. All kinds of stories are being planted and spread. Our phones are being tapped. There is a Gypsy parked outside our offices at all times. There is a Gypsy parked outside my house. Everyone who comes to see us, their car numbers are being noted down. No FIR has been registered. All these stories are just bunkum and dishonest.

Madhu: Did you and Charulata Joshi meet the Hindujas in London and did you receive a cheque from them?

Tejpal: A meeting was fixed in London by Charulata two weeks ago which had to do with Tehelka providing content to a website on a monthly basis for a fee. Charu had been working on the deal for some time and felt that my presence would help move things along quicker. The website is owned by the Hindujas. The person to be met was Dheeraj Hinduja. With the current scenario being what it is, I stepped back from the lift and told Charu to go ahead. I paced the street for the 40 minutes she was in there. I envisioned an irresponsible charge like, "Hinduja hand suspected in Operation West End". It was a straight deal for Tehelka to supply content for the Hinduja website.

~

In March 2001, I tracked down Verghese of Gresham & Reed. He happened to be in Dubai and denied any connection with the Tehelka exposé. When he was asked if his company had hired Tehelka to investigate an arms dealer's financial dealings, he said, 'Why would I hire Tehelka to do that?' Because, perhaps India is not your area of operations and you thought Tehelka could do it more easily as they had the experience of exposing the match-fixing scandal? 'Oh! You'd be surprised how much investigative work we do in India. It is definitely our arena,' Verghese replied.

Verghese is involved with eight companies. Gresham & Reed undertakes investigations for banks into companies that have gone bankrupt and insurance companies for fraud. Born in Madras on 18 January 1952, Verghese applied for a five-year multiple entry visa to India at the Indian High Commission in Dubai on 28 March 2001, which he obtained. However, with so many questions being raised about his involvement with Tehelka, it is believed he had second thoughts about travelling to India at that point in time.

Another piece of the jigsaw puzzle was Renu Nanda, the estranged wife of reputed arms dealer, Suresh Nanda, whose name figured in the Tehelka tapes. In the process of negotiating the terms of her divorce, it is believed that she had contacted Gresham & Reed to investigate her husband's accounts and dealings. When I asked the estranged wife to confirm whether she had hired Gresham & Reed, she appeared shocked and said she had done no such thing. But she did go on to say that her husband had already asked her the same question three days earlier and she had said the same thing. Ivana Trump advising her?

CONSPIRACY 2

Sayantan Chakravarty's story

Jaya Jaitly pointed me in the direction of Sayantan Chakravarty, special correspondent for the magazine *India Today*. She said she had given him all the facts, directed him to all the right people (Enforcement Directorate) who gave the interviews but *India Today* never ran the story. Perhaps for a good reason. Jaya told me that she couldn't go on sending reporters to the Enforcement Directorate, who gave the interviews and it embarrassed her that no story appeared. The following facts are according to Chakravarty:

A company called Harrow Enterprises was incorporated in Mauritius in June 1998. There were two NRI's on the board of directors. For a year the company engaged in no activity whatsoever. No work was recorded. In July 1999, the company's name was changed to First Global and Shankar Sharma and Devina Mehra were drafted in as directors. They held two shares, worth $5 or $10. According to the Enforcement Directorate, Shankar Sharma, when being interrogated, refused to divulge to them the names of the other directors on the board. All this is according to the Enforcement Directorate: on 15 November 1999 First Global received $125,000. This amount was remitted by Jamilla Traders, based in Dubai. This was remitted through Nagreb Bank in New York, to First Global, Mauritius, and on to State Bank of India in Mauritius.

Shamshuddin Mohammad, based in Chennai and a partner in Jamilla Traders, was arrested by the Enforcement Directorate for organizing the hawala transaction. He was also interrogated by the Income Tax Department. According to the ED and the Income Tax Department, Mohammad made a detailed disclosure statement in which he admitted to having executed the hawala transaction. He categorically refused to divulge the names of those for whom the hawala transaction was undertaken. Under the FEMA law, any statement made in the presence of officers of the Income Tax Department is valid in a court of law. Mohammad very coolly said, '*Un ney bola, paisa edhar se udhar kar dho, mainey kar diyey. Main kyun poonchoon, kiskey paise* [they told me, pass the money from here to there, I did that. Why should I ask, whose money it is]?'

According to the ED, this money moved to First Global, was further used to purchase shares in Buffalo Networks. $1.1 million was moved from Jamilla Traders to First Global, but there is only proof of the $125,000 amount in bank documents. When questioned by ED officials, Sharma admitted he had received $1 lakh to $1.25 lakh for services he rendered to Harrow Enterprises, but according to the ED, Shankar refused to disclose the source of the funds. Sharma's company in Mauritius had violated FERA rules as he had been making profits from his Mauritian company for years before actually getting around to inform the Reserve Bank of India about it, again, according to the Enforcement Directorate.

In 1999 the company's name was changed to First Global, when Shankar Sharma and Devina Mehra were drafted in as directors. At some point between December 2000 to January 2001, Shankar Sharma asked the RBI for permission to transfer $5,000 to a bank in Mauritius for running this new company. In their investigations the ED found it peculiar that Sharma transferred money for expenses of his company, when he already had $7 lakhs in his bank account in Mauritius. According to Sharma, why should that make any difference, if you are transferring money for business purposes?

As it stands now, the Government of India has issued a Letter Regotary to the Government of Mauritius. This is the formal process a government undertakes to obtain documents from another country. This was employed in Bofors case too. Now it is for the Government of Mauritius to decide if they care to share the information.

Would the story have run in *India Today* without Shankar Sharma's side of the story? I checked all the 'facts' with Shankar. According to Shankar's Rashomon, he confirmed that Harrow Enterprises was incorporated in Mauritius in June 1998. Sharma stated that both he and Devina Mehra held about two shares (something like that, he said) at about a value of about $5 or $10.

Madhu: Is it true that you refused to give the names of the directors when ED questioned you?

Sharma: No, what nonsense. Everything has been explained to them. This company has been known to the Reserve Bank of India from the time we took it over. November 2000, six months before all this Tehelka thing started.

Madhu: According to the ED, First Global received $125,000 remitted by Jamilla Traders.

Sharma: Yes, that is part of the business of the company. What is wrong with that?

Madhu: A certain Shamshuddin Mohammad based in Chennai was arrested by the ED for implementing a hawala transaction?

Sharma: Bullshit, *yaar*. He is a moneychanger. His job is to remit money overseas. A client of ours had sold Penta 4 GDRs. The profit element of the Penta 4 GDRs transaction were remitted to that company. It was in 1998. It was one year before Tehelka. The profit was $125,000. Six months before Tehelka happened we had remitted $5000 from India to take over this company with full disclosures to RBI. There is a full correspondence with RBI.

Madhu: According to the ED, you transferred $5000 even though you already had $7 lakhs in your account, which they find strange.

Sharma: I did remit $5000. I had more than $7 lakhs in the account. I had $1.1 million. The RBI knows all about it. We told the RBI we helped the company make a lot of profit, now we are taking over that company. It was out of my export earnings. $5000 was remitted from my EFG account in India. This was in November of 2000.

Madhu: The implication is that the two other Indians on the board are the Hindujas.

Sharma: No, no, no. They are not the Hindujas. They are business associates of ours. In fact, they are husband and wife. They were taken on the board later. The husband used to work for us in our London office, until very recently. His name was Ashwani Mathur. He is a professional and is an old friend of ours. We have known him since 1994. In fact, he set up our First Global UK Ltd office which is our UK company. We went to RBI and asked how long will the approval process take if I have to set up an overseas subsidiary in UK. Now we are talking about 98-99. They said it will take about 6 to 8 months time. We said we can't wait that long. Then they said, are you going to have somebody working for you there? We said, yeah. So they said, let him float the company, you apply for your approvals here, and when it comes through then you take over that company. It is a very transparent thing. All this has been declared to the RBI much before this Tehelka shit happened.

Madhu: Can you say categorically that the Hindujas had absolutely nothing to do with First Global?

Sharma: I can say, that in the 39 years of my life I have never had anything ever, at all to do with the Hindujas. They are out of their minds. Why will we, barely three months before Tehelka happened, go and take over this company? Otherwise nobody has any knowledge of First Global Mauritius. How would RBI, the ED, and the Government of India and this press, would have ever come to know about this company? I will be the biggest ass in the world to go and declare this to the RBI, give its balance sheet, give its profit-loss account, give its directorships, give everything.

Madhu: It is said you took over this company to do this Tehelka thing with the Hindujas.

Sharma: Then why do we need to take it over? Why do I need to step into the picture, boss? I am a businessman. Why should I put it in black and white with the supreme regulatory authority of the country, the RBI, just barely three months before Tehelka happened? Am I stupid to do that? It is so asinine. Give me credit for some intelligence. Somebody is going to do all this and we declare First Global India, then First Global Mauritius. I am going to announce all the board of directors and everything, three months before Tehelka? And all this shit happens and face consequences for the rest of my life? What Hindujas, what shit? Anyway, what does First Global have to do with Buffalo Networks, in any case?

Point by point, Sayantan Chakravarty's story as given to him by the ED is addressed to Shankar Sharma, who finally sounds harassed and loses it.

Sharma: Bombay High Court granted us permission to go abroad from the 20th to the 28th. Now we get an order that we cannot travel. The whole problem of this is the fucking cost of all the lawyers and cases going on. When we realized they were going to freeze our accounts, we took Rs 30 lakh out of the bank, tax paid money, and kept it in the house for our own use. Then the CBI raids the house and seizes the tax paid Rs 30 lakh. I have already paid Rs 2 lakh in trying to get it back in the courts. In the end I will end up paying 10 lakh just to get it back. Enforcement Directorate can't seize Indian currency. I have written to them a hundred times. No show cause notice has been issued.

Shankar sounded unusually upset. His pitch was high, his outrage at the injustice of it all, his sense of helplessness that reduced him to becoming a puppet in the hands of kismet, the unfairness of it all, finally got to him. I am surprised it took as long as it did: most men would have crumbled earlier.

Sharma: There is no downside for them, *yaar*. Even if we win the case after years in the courts, will anybody be accountable? Will anyone go behind bars? The courts can even rule in favour of us, but what will that get us? Will we get the money and time we spent in the courts back? We can't work any more. All we do is spend time in the courts. Why should I spend Rs 12 lakh to get it back? What do they want? What do they want? Let us get on with our lives, please. The kind of work we are doing gets covered by CNBC, in Europe in Prime Time. Here we are wasting our time for hours in the Enforcement Directorate office and having three cups of tea. Aniruddha and Tarun can get on with their lives. Aniruddha has his book and Tarun is starting a newspaper. They can get on with their lives and we have to pay for their mistakes. They can go everywhere. Boss, the culprits are somewhere else. You are going after the wrong guys. *Acha bhai, jo karna kar lo* [okay brother, do whatever you want]. Strangest things happen. We are propounding great theories in economics and then we are treated like criminals. It took them two-and-a-half years to concoct a story. Before Tehelka happened we were the most respected company in the world, now we are criminals.

In my pursuit of being thorough, I obtained First Global Mauritius's company registration documents. No surprise that Hindujas were not named. If they were involved, nobody would be quite that stupid to actually include their names. Did I believe the Hindujas were involved? No.

↜

I must acknowledge my debt to Sayantan Chakravarty for relating the entire story to me, but there was no choice for me but to get the other side of it too. Clearly the story was a creative plant by the ED. Remember, it was Jaya Jaitly who organized the interviews for Sayantan Chakravarty with officials from the ED, who provided him with all the information they had about Shankar and Devina.

How then is the conspiracy theory being spun out? Okay, connect carefully. The spy cameras, one for the tie and one in a briefcase came from London. Charulata Joshi, Tehelka's representative in London was interfacing with the Hindujas for Tarun. This Tarun admitted in his cross-examination, when he told the Commission about how he had qualms about going up to see the Hindujas in their offices and turned around at the elevators. Charulata went up to see them alone, while Tarun paced the pavement and ate a hot dog. The conspiracy theorists point out that it is public knowledge that Ram Jethmalani is close to the Hindujas and Charu is close to Jethmalani. Charu got married in Ram Jethmalani's house. The two NRI's on the board of directors of First Global Mauritius 'must be' the Hindujas, I was told, or a front for the Hindujas. The conspiracy theorists ask, why the money moved on 15 November 1999 went as a transfer document rather than a foreign investor being directly inducted? It is the prerogative of a businessman to conduct business in whatever way he chooses, for whatever reasons. Why should every move conceal an ulterior political motive?

The Hinduja brothers were most adversely affected by George Fernandes's decision to blank out dealers and middlemen from the purchase of arms and ammunition. According to Sayantan Chakravarty, the Hindujas were not expecting charge sheets against them. It is believed they had lobbied with carrot and carat to ensure it never happened yet the CBI went ahead and filed two successive charge sheets.

Srichand, Gopichand and Prakash Hinduja were charge sheeted on 9 October 2000, a full, ten long years after the CBI registered the case against them. The charge sheet alleged that the Hindujas had received 81 million Swedish kroners ($8 million) as middlemen in the Bofors gun deal. The CBI charged that Bofors had paid the equivalent of Rs 20 crore into Swiss bank accounts that have been found linked to the Hindujas. They accused the Hinduja brothers of bribing politicians and bureaucrats on behalf of Bofors, the Swedish arms manufacturer who was awarded the Rs 1,437-crore arms contract. The conspiracy theorists point out, it makes perfect sense for the Hindujas to have funded First Global and then induced Tehelka to go after George Fernandes. It is impossible to see how free wheeling Samuel, who virtually fell into the sting operation by mistake, was part of this well-planned, perfectly implemented conspiracy. My belief is that Samuel, Aniruddha, and Tarun would have done it regardless of which party was in power.

The real, hard question is: When Tehelka has spoken at such length about how they were acting as crusaders against corruption; when Tarun and Aniruddha have been journalists long enough to know that the Bofors corruption case was the very kind of thing they were trying to expose, why for duck's sake did Tarun send Charulata Joshi up to talk to the Hindujas in the first place? The Hindujas? Wouldn't it have been a much better idea to send Charu up with a tiny camera in her tie? Okay, perhaps not her tie, but wherever?

The principal justification for the kind of sting operation that Tehelka undertook was that it is impossible otherwise to prove the massive corruption in arms deals. That is undeniably true. The real major arms dealers do not leave a trail for the CBI or ED or even Tehelka to pick up. They are mopping up and wiping the muck as soon as it drops. They have cover *jalli* [cover] businesses that are separate, efficiently run, profit-making operations to camouflage the real big money arms deals. Why then go to sell content to those people who have been accused of the same form of corruption and provide a handle for a conspiracy charge?

Conspiracy 3
Jaya Jaitly, at one of her numerous meetings with me, gave me a handwritten letter on her

note-paper, sent by her to senior advocate and member of Parliament, Ram Jethmalani. Jaya complained to me how Jethmalani had let her down and had behaved unethically by first advising her and then accepting a brief to defend Shankar Sharma and Devina Mehra at the Commission. In an interview with Ram Jethmalani's son, Mahesh Jethmalani, I asked about this:

Madhu: Jaya Jaitly gave me a letter she wrote to Ram. She said that he was advising her and then suddenly switched sides.

Jethmalani: Yeah, Ram has never denied that he did touch up a draft.

Madhu: No, but she felt that then he was on her side. So then how did he switch?

Jethmalani: No, no, he had made a very clear condition. He decided because he realized that this was not just a simple defence that was going on. When clause (d) became the main focus of the Commission, he realized what they were up to and they were trying to compromise him. They never wanted Ram to appear for them. They took his advice. And they wanted to compromise him, block him. He put that in his letter to her. Jaya didn't reply to that letter. He wrote her a stinker of a letter, after that.

Madhu: Jaya was obsessed with her defence.

Jethmalani: Well, it's actually very clever. She's a clever lady and she's very convincing. She came to my office with this whole doctored tape thing. She came with that fellow, that forensic expert on tapes.

Madhu: Chris Mills?

Jethmalani: No, no, he was a Parsi chap in those days. Then of course they went to a higher level to try it. She came to my office to convince me that the tapes were doctored. There was nothing to it. She convinced everybody and the government let her have her way. It suited them. A complete red herring.

Madhu: I did tell her there were serious technical obstacles to doctoring a tape like that.

Jethmalani: Well nigh impossible. All the vital institutions were with her. Ultimately the Commissioner allowed her to, because the government knew it would happen. But I must say that everybody put up a very spirited fight, for a long time. It became less and less of an issue, and when the BJP got more and more confident about its possible return to power, after winning those by-elections, then they slipped this in. Just a question of timing. At its peak, they wouldn't dare do this. When public interest died down, then they thought it would be all right now.

Madhu: I asked Upamanyu when she was making these applications and her lawyers seemed to believe the tapes were doctored.

Jethmalani: She was very convincing. The sum and substance is you can't deny that arms dealers for some ridiculous equipment like night vision glasses came to her. She did say, yes, I will take a contribution but give it to Srinivas

Prasad. The sum and substance of that allegation stands unimpeachable. And frankly speaking, what she did is a lot better than most politicians do, that they pocket it, Bangaru was probably …

Madhu: He pocketed it.

Jethmalani: And she made it clear. There was a rider to what she said, silly woman; there was a very clever rider. She said listen, I'm not promising you. This is only to see that you get justice in the matter. Frankly there was nothing illegal and Ram kept telling her that. That was the issue between Ram and her. Ram said, look, so long as you stuck to my defence, but once you started going on this vindictive rampage, then I'm sorry. That wasn't the terms of my engagement. She became a malignant character. She just went on every conspiracy theory. She would spin anything she wanted to in those days. She was so frazzled. The Commission never should have been wound up in public interest. Now, this government would have had a field day and Ram would have had a field day on that revenue under secretary.

Madhu: Yeah, well, he really destroyed him.

Jethmalani: He destroyed him. Not only that, he would have got him to say who had told him to give this false evidence. And I vouchsafe you that implicated that whole clique.

Jaya had handed me the copy of the letter she had written to Ram Jethmalani as proof that he was involved in her defence. It read:

April 28, 2001

Dear Ram,

With some minor changes we have retyped your draft. I shall be very grateful if you have one final look at it and feel free to delete or change anything you feel is not correct.

I shall be at telephone number 66 … or you can leave a message with George if there's anything special.

Thanks for your help and I shall look forward to your return.

Affectionately,
Jaya

The most intriguing part of the jigsaw puzzle is that Jaya wrote *another* letter on a day that will long be remembered by those attending the Commission. The income tax officer representing his department had attempted to defend his department's actions against Shankar Sharma and Devina Mehra. Ram Jethmalani had torn this man to shreds; absolute shreds. He was not left with an iota of evidence or a leg left to stand on. Hearing of this, Jaya was inspired to write a letter to Jethmalani. Had Jethmalani continued in this vein of attack, the government's SADS would be totally exposed. Something had to be done. As any journalist would, I checked out the other side and discovered a very different story. The following letters are self-explanatory.

January 14, 2002

My dear Ram,

I was told that you had appeared before the Justice Venkataswami Commission today on behalf of First Global which, in effect, is the same as appearing for Tehelka.com.

I respect you as a long time friend and a senior in the legal profession. It is because of this that I have spent many hours with you seeking your help and discussing the issues arising out of the Tehelka escapade.

You were kind enough to dictate every word of my affidavit and even signed on the draft that you had approved and settled it on April 29, 2001.

Later on September 10, you advised and dictated applications on behalf of George Sahib and myself requesting the Commission to first frame the specific issues related to his reputation and my conduct before calling us before it to depose. You had also included the clause that the veracity of the tapes should first be established.

Not only that but you told me that according to the transcript I "should be proud of what I have said" and that the transcript of my section of the tapes was enough to exonerate me.

After having given me so much support and legal advice and after having taken the trouble of drafting my affidavit (52-a) before the Commission surely it is unethical of you to defend those who have put money into Tehelka.com's hands to conduct Operation West End in order to besmirch the reputations of both George Sahib and myself?

I request you to please reconsider the step you have chosen to take as anything else would not be proper or ethical.

With warm regards,
Yours sincerely,
Jaya Jaitly

In response Ram Jethmalani wrote to Jaya:

January 15, 2002

Dear Mrs Jaitly,

1. Late last night I received your letter bearing the date January 14, 2002. I am sorry that your letter contains falsehood and half truths. Let me set the record right.

2. Soon after the Tehelka exposure I appeared on television and publicly applauded the producers and the public service that they had rendered. I also publicly declared that the tapes were genuine and when one of the

interviewers asked me whether my legal services would be available to Tarun Tejpal, I declared that I would certainly defend his right to do what he had done.

3. When you and George saw me I pointed out that the tapes on the contrary bring out the character and integrity of George and so far as you are concerned your actions as caught by the tapes can be fully justified as the normal actions of a leader of a political party. When you wanted my legal services I made it very clear that I will do nothing which would put me in conflict with the interests of Tehelka which I am publicly pledged to defend.

4. You recall that I had written to the Prime Minister that there was no reason why George was either allowed or made to resign. I did this as George's friend and as a member of Parliament.

5. Yes I did advise you not to deny anything that the tapes attribute to you. It is true that I helped to draft your affidavit. Since you have got the draft signed by me you should read it again and you will see that it does not contain a word about the veracity of the tapes. I was shocked when I learnt later on that you had changed the affidavit and made an attack on the veracity of the tapes. I now find that you have made it a full-time occupation.

6. You are the best judge of how you should go about before the Commission, but do not for a moment suggest that I had at any time agreed to help you against Tehelka. It is wholly false that I subsequently advised or dictated any application.

7. Having read your letter I regret that I rendered you any help. Fortunately you do not suggest that you had discussed anything about First Global with me. I have not received any information from you which I am likely to use against you. I have more than once told George that I will always defend his interests, I cannot be sure about you though. If George is being criticized it is because of your operations at his official residence, for that alone there are many who do not share my opinion about George's complete integrity.

8. You are nobody to decide that appearing for First Global is the same as appearing for Tehelka.com. First Global's case is that they were not aware of the contents of the production, they did not finance it or in any way abet it much less that the production was intended to depress the stock market for their profit.

9. I consider it my moral and public duty to defend Shankar Sharma and his wife, who have been treated by the government and its agencies in a manner worse than what was done during the Emergency by Mrs Indira Gandhi's government.

10. I have been wondering what has gone wrong with the government of

which I was once a part. I have been trying to find out who is responsible for the atrocities perpetrated on the couple. Your letter fortunately provides some clues. It is the enormity of injustice that has ultimately made me take up the First Global cause.

11. A lecture on ethics from you is laughable.

12. I am not appearing for Tehelka.com not because I cannot nor because I owe it to you but only because I did not feel physically up to it.

13. I will entertain no correspondence from you and you are at liberty to seek your own remedies against me.

Ram Jethmalani

How did Jaya imagine or presume that I would not follow through the letter she handed me?

⌣

Conspiracy 4

It was Jaya Jaitly who first raised the issue of Anil Malviya and then directed me to meet Suresh Kodikunnil, who Jaya told me knew the 'truth' about Malviya.

Jaitly: What did they do to this Anil Malviya? Anil Malviya goes to Kumbh, he dies there, all that thing is another very shady story. If you read Hariharan's questioning and I've had my suspicions from day one about this Anil Malviya.

Madhu: What are your suspicions?

Jaitly: I know in Bombay there is an Anil Malviya household where the husband has died and the wife and children and mother are there. My contention is that Anil Malviya and Rajiv Sharma are two different people. Rajiv Sharma got removed from the scene, either by death or otherwise. Not death, I'm sure there is a Rajiv Sharma who was told, okay, your job is over, now just shut up and disappear. They decided to call him Anil Malviya and say that, well, he's dead.

Madhu: Is there a Rajiv Sharma in Bombay?

Jaitly: Who knows? But why do you check-in in the morning as Rajiv Sharma and sign out in the evening as Anil Malviya? Initially they told the journalists that oh, he was a journalist and he died at Kumbh. So I found out, I rang Rajnath Singh, who was chief minister then. I said, you've all been telling us we conducted the whole Kumbh without a single death. He said yes, nobody died, but I'll ask locally. SP [Superintendent of Police] and everybody was asked, anybody died at Kumbh? No. Then I put it through various journalists back to Tehelka. They said, no, no, he didn't die actually at Kumbh, he died at the railway station. Then I got through to Nitish Kumar, I said can you find out from your railway people, did anyone die at the railway station? No, nobody died at the railway station. Then again found out what's what, no, actually what happened was, he went to the railway station to catch a train, he didn't feel well, he went back home and died there. In Allahabad initially what I found out was that nobody had died. Then they said *haan, haan,* some cousin, some nephew of some former judge or some family like that *haan,* he died. A thirty-two year old man dying? It's very unusual for a thirty-two year old healthy man to die. Was there any post-mortem? Was there a medical certificate? if he had a heart attack it must have been a big thing. They have thanked him in that list. But they have not said 'In Memoriam' or he died during the process or anything. When it was forced on them, they said, oh, he died like this. So okay, you have to get rid of one person, so you call him somebody else who actually died and say it was him. That cuts the trail of who brought the women.

Madhu: Did you send someone at all to Bombay to find any Rajiv Sharma?

Jaitly: No, how can you suggest, find any Rajiv Sharma? In fact the SIT should have done all that. We don't have policemen at our command. I haven't asked the government to do it. The Commission should have done it. They had a whole police team. If they were an impartial Commission, they should have long ago said, find out about this fellow. How did a fellow die? Nobody else has found out. Whatever information I have, I gave to the home ministry. Nothing's being done. But it's very easy, very convenient, if you don't want to find out whether those call girls were part of a conspiracy or they were just brought. You want to avoid showing that you paid for them or not, because if you paid, then it's Immoral Traffic Act. I don't think Rajiv Sharma and Anil Malviya are the same person. You just find a fellow who died because Aniruddha is from Allahabad. He can find anybody who died and say, *haan,* it was him. There is some photograph, which the SIT has, which they showed some people, who've seen it. Hariharan has seen and that Suresh (Rajesh Suresh Kodikunnil) has seen. They say it's not him. Suresh says no, no, he was very fair, like an apple. [Laughs.] His description, typical Malyali, ahpplle.

Madhu: But on some of the tapes, you can see Arun Malviya.

Jaitly: Anil Malviya. Partly. It's a lot of effort, but it needed to have been done. You take those bits of that tape and show it to those hotels and ask did this person ever come and stay? There are ways of finding out, surely, there is enough suspicion.

Madhu: But if there was something fishy it shouldn't be difficult for the government to find him from his image on the tapes? Why haven't they?

Jaitly: Yeah, but to take that picture and go hunting all over the countryside. One, you have to have SIT that is ordered to do it. But what happened? The SIT is also very funny. All the SIT did, there's no reports available now? Where have they gone? If the SIT did any investigation on Anil Malviya/Rajiv Sharma, I don't know if it's there at all.

Madhu: But this doesn't take them off the Immoral Trafficking Act, since Samuel is there in all the tapes.

Jaitly: Yeah, but he's said No, Rajiv did it. That's why Nilay [Datta] very cleverly

555

asked because we weren't supposed to ask who brought the women. Then Nilay asked Aniruddha, who was the deciding person in all these things. Who decides, so sometimes one, sometimes the other. Then who decided on this? Quickly, said Anil Malviya. So he would have paid? Don't know. Finished.

Madhu: But surely with IB and because defence is involved, because George is also mentioned in the tapes, surely somebody from defence intelligence could find out if Anil Malviya really died?

Jaitly: Contrary to what Tehelka keeps shouting, nobody in the government has done any inquiries. They have left it entirely to the Commission. I don't know whether George Fernandes wanted to. I think he was being absolutely correct and proper and saying that whatever the Commission has to find out, let it find out. If he asks the defence intelligence to find out and the defence intelligence comes up with something, which is detrimental to Tehelka, they'll say George Fernandes asked them to say so. What's the point of him getting into that tussle? .

Okay, fine. Then Jaya directed me to Rajan Suresh Kodikunnil, a party member of the Janata Dal (U) who tried desperately to depose before the Commission of Inquiry but his application was rejected. He is a difficult person to interview and comprehend. Kodikunnil is on Tehelka's list of bribe takers for Rs 7000, which he denied. Kodikunnil said he told Samuel, 'I don't have that much relations but there is one Raghupati, secretary in Janata Dal (U), we can ask him to do. So Rajiv Sharma and Samuel came.'

Madhu: You mean Anil Malviya?

Kodikunnil: I don't think there is one Anil Malviya.

Madhu: There is a Rajiv Sharma?

Kodikunnil: Still I am believe like that. That's Rajiv Sharma. I am coming to that point after some times. Rajiv Sharma and this Mathew Samuel they came to my residence. They discuss this business with Samuel. Then I told them, we are not doing this kind of business. We are clear politicians. Then they offered, means they offered more and more things. But I told them I am not a such person.

Madhu: What were they offering you?

Kodikunnil: They offering liquor, this um … this and all. Money. They offered more. Then told them I am not such a person. I don't have that time uh they offered me because I am running some schools in Delhi under Kerala Cultural and Education Society. Rented buildings. We don't have our own buildings. Then my, my tape also I got from Jaya Jaitly. She collected the all things. I asked a permission to submit a affidavit. But I couldn't get the permission. It was also not of that Rs 7000 from my account. Published in newspapers. My name Suresh seven thousand rupees.

Kodikunnil's said that Rajiv Sharma told him on the phone that he had some important information to give him about Samuel but he never showed up. Kodikunnil mentioned that Malviya/Sharma had differences with Samuel and had cautioned him to not trust Samuel. The CBI showed him a photograph of Malviya/Sharma and he said that the picture was 'joined'. He said the upper half of the face was Malviya/Sharma, the rest was not. He pointed out that Malviya/Sharma was not a 'beard person'.

Kodikunnil said, 'Rajiv Sharma death not a common death. He was healthy, handsome man.' He suspected that Rajiv Sharma had been killed and he questioned the fact that according to his phone records, Sharma spoke to him after he was reported dead.

He was convinced that Mathew Samuel was a 'crooker' and 'Tehelka was a big fraud'. Kodikunnil said,

> **Kodikunnil:** Yes I am the gravely I my doubting the death of this fellow because he told me something about the motive of this all. He told me something, something wrong. He told me I will discuss all the things with you. Whenever I come and meet you on January 27 last call. Last one I discuss with him after this is that time.
>
> **Madhu:** Did Rajiv Sharma give you his address in Bombay?
>
> **Kodikunnil:** No. Address is there, na. I got this address from this one Jaya Jaitly. She forwarded the address. They actually, they try to put me in big trouble.

I must admit I too had my suspicions. Not that Tehelka had bumped him off, as one camp, also spread around, but that Anil Malviya had just decided to disappear rather than deal with the Commission of Inquiry. He was no journalist so there was no motivation whatsoever for him to hang around. Also, belling him with the prostitute problem was convenient and let Bahal and Samuel off the hook. Aniruddha Bahal's version of Anil Malviya's death:

> **Madhu:** How did Anil Malviya die?
>
> **Bahal:** That was one of the freakiest things. A heart attack. Went to the train, talked to his wife for a long time after that. Talked to his mother also. He went to Kumbh and he was going with a friend to the station and he complained of pain. I'm telling this second hand, third hand; it's not that I was there. So they returned back to his uncle's place or somebody, where they were staying and complained of chest pains. He lay down and then that's it. Then the doctors came, but it was too late. That's how I understood the sequence of events. I came to know about it a day later. It was a shock. First natural instinct that time, seeing that all this had already happened, this was February, I think, that *kya*, is somebody after us? That's the natural feeling. And then for maybe one or two days, I was unwilling to convince myself that it was really a heart attack. I was in the same thing, shocked out of my wits. Samuel was also shocked out of his wits. Then we made the calls to talk to his wife, his mother, and they explained the whole thing. He had some relatives here in Delhi also.

⌣

Then of course I tracked down Anil Malviya's relatives in Delhi who had no idea I was coming to see them. Many members of the family were there, including teenagers. When I questioned them extensively, Bahal's story did seem to add up. Whether the man who died is the same man in the tapes would require another book.

But, as Sidharth Luthra pointed out, 'The obsession with Anil Malviya/Rajiv Sharma is irrelevant to what those caught in Operation West End. Did anyone put a gun to their heads or force them to meet West End operatives and accept money/sex or whatever?'

Let us do some of our own math here.

1. Jaya Jaitly directed me to Syanthan Chakravarty after she had put him in touch with ED officials. When the attempted plant in *India Today* magazine failed, there was an attempt to plant the story on me.
2. Jaya Jaitly handed me a letter written by her to Ram Jethmalani that supposedly exposed Jethmalani's unethical behaviour. This only exposed another attempt to manipulate and malign those she viewed as her enemies.
3. Jaya Jaitly directed me to Suresh Kodikunnil. He tried to convince me that either Anil Malviya was still alive or he had been killed by the Tehelka team.
4. Jaya Jaitly directed me to Beni Chatterji, the lawyer who was arguing against the Shankar Sharma cases in Mumbai. (Yes, you may well ask, what Jaya Jaitly had to do with the financial affairs of First Global?)
5. Madhu Shekhar was Jaya Jaitly's witness at the Commission of Inquiry and told horrendous stories about Mathew Samuel. Why was a witness who deposed before the Commission that he had been duped by Mathew Samuel presented by Jaya Jaitly?
6. Shekib Arsalan, who related even worse stories about Mathew Samuel, was also Jaya Jaitly's witness.
7. It was confirmed to me by one of Jaya Jaitly's lawyers that the story in *The Indian Express* about the use of sex workers in Operation West End was, indeed, leaked by him. She told me she knew nothing about it.

It does not take much to add it up. Jaya Jaitly said in her interview: 'It's not that I am clean. It is that they are rotten.' A simple question: Why does Jaya have to do this?

Beautiful, intelligent women are used to getting their way. When they don't, it's best to run for cover.

27 The Aftermath: Shattering Heights

Ben Bradlee (Jason Robards): You know the results of the latest Gallup Poll? Half the country never even heard of the word Watergate. Nobody gives a shit. You guys are probably pretty tired, right? Well, you should be. Go on home, get a nice hot bath. Rest up… 15 minutes. Then get your asses back in gear. We're under a lot of pressure, you know, and you put us there. Nothing's riding on this except the, uh, first amendment to the Constitution, freedom of the press, and maybe the future of the country. Not that any of that matters, but if you guys fuck up again, I'm going to get mad. Goodnight.

– Alan Pakula's film All the President's Men *(1976)*

Madhu: So after all this, did you receive *gaalis* and threats?

Samuel: Nobody. They have only contact with my mobile. After Jain's people landed up in our awffiss, Bangaru Laxman calling furiously for my money. R.K. Jain calling continuously for his money. Bloody, I have only hundred rupees in my pocket. Asking two crore, ten lakhs. (Ha! Ha! ha!) That, you know, really verrry intrrusssting part. That time suppose I want to go and buy one packet cigrutt, *paisa bhi nahin hai* [don't have even a paisa]. Rrreally I'm telling you. Bangaru's asking ten lakhs, R.K. Jain asking two crore, Parekh 25,000. So and so asking one lakh I need. Murthy asking two lakh. These people are asking money. I have only thirty-five rupees. Rrreally I am telling you. Touccchh wood. It happened. Uzzzual, daily asking, *doh lakh, theen lakh* [two lakhs, three lakhs]. Bangaru's seketry calling, "Where's my money?" Bangaru continuously calling. He don't know his seketry calling. I will give you my data entry of my mobile. Just you go through, you'll go mad.

Madhu: Samuel, do you ever think of the people who lost their jobs because of the story you did?

Samuel: Of course. Really, I am verrry saaad of that. Verrrry sad of that, they lost their jobs. After that vaat happened. My telephone will go. My mobile will go. Murli is my friend. Lawts of friends calling. The CBI landed up asking hundred of questions. In Kerlla, one of my friend, he is having a teashop, *usko doh din usko huraaahs kar diya* [he was harassed for two days]. Because he's my friend, he's calling me. It's appeared in my mobile his number.

Madhu: What actually happened when you were in Kerala and you said that the home ministry was involved and Aniruddha and Tarun retracted it?

Samuel: Yes, now that story is there. I am working on these stories and I am digging digging. After Kernel Bayry [Lieutenant Colonel Berry] told me, that is recorded, no one has challenged that. This BJP leader guy has one sekitry I don't know name and there is another name, there is a dealing there in the border fencing communication equipment. This sekitry has an account outside. From where he got the money? If I get a chance to go to London, I can get all the dawkoomunts related to this. Maddumm, it is not small, it is 26 crore. Is it possible?

Madhu: I really don't know, unless there is some proof. So this came out in the tape, that money was taken for the border-fencing contract? You said this in Kerala so why did Tarun deny it?

Samuel: I don't know this day itself why Tarun denied it. I ask him. Tarun saying there is not much supporting evidence to establish that those things. Then my question will come: suppose you go through all the tapes. Somewhere they are saying only one way, without supporting every time. Home ministry matter comes up. We are just talking recently, then Aniruddha said, you never told me sorry about ministry matter. I said I will never say sorry about this matter. Why I have to say sorry? He said, "No, no, that is not a good way." I said, "No. Both our voice went to the public. But, I am a disciplined soldier. I am wurrrking with you, I will obey you, vaatever you are saying." But, internally I told him vaat eggzackly happened. But I will not go public. I will not talk second person also this matter. Aniruddha said, there is no proof on this fellow. Only somebody said it. Then I said that is with so many people mentioned in the tapes. No proof, just names mentioned. Then apply same rule. Then why we cut it and put that one. That time he say, "Okay that's up to you but you have to tell me one time sorry." I said, I will not tell you sorry. Very very polite manner. I said, I will not tell you. Becawz I said, vaatever you are doing wrong thing, I am wurrking for you, I will support you, I will say on the outside also. But I will come and tell you personally that I am not supporting this.

Madhu: What you are saying is, why not apply the same rule to everybody else on the tape?

Samuel: Yes. But I am a very disciplined reporter. Suppose I am vurking under you, I will report to you. Lawt of pressure come, like you have to tell like that. But I will not tell anything. I have not even given any interview. Lot of people are trailing me. I say, "No." If this matter will come to the Commission, I will give a hot reply. No one asked this question. No one. They should ask, your editor denied it. But vaat about your opinion? No one asked.

When I questioned Aniruddha about this, his excuse was:

There were two, three things, one was Advani's name doesn't come, home ministry comes, which is the most important thing. Here Bangaru Laxman is naming your Brajesh Mishra. He's taking names. Here, there's no name. Second is, the whole story was about defence procurement. So suddenly we drag in the home ministry. If you notice, the whole script is about defence, defence, defence, defence, all the way down; this is the non-defence thing. So then there has to be some criteria na?

My educated guess is that Tehelka was feeling encircled by the SADS and were wary of opening hostilities on yet another front.

I asked Samuel about his future plans.

Madhu: Tarun has launched a weekend newspaper, Tehelka. Are you going to work for him?

Samuel: No, I won't.

Madhu: Why not?

Samuel: It's enough. It means that, suppose we are doing a story, I know after that, I also suffered, not getting salary properly. And I was mentally low, early morning starting with lawyers, court and everything. Suppose I start wurrking again, again this same court matter will come. I want to away from this lawyers and everything. This kind of wurrk … why I want to do? I am willing to go court and everything but not twunty-four hours dedication with the court and lawyers. And at the end of the day, Tarun become a superrr star. I'm not blaming anything.

Madhu: But Samuel, if you had given interviews and let people take your picture, you would have also become a star.

Samuel: I never need like that, one thing. I never want to be like a celaybrayty, or anything. I have my own limitations. I'm wurrrking. I'm not like a order of the day, anywhere. I'm wurrrking like that. I got many cawls now also to give interviews. But I rrefuse to give interview.

Madhu: Samuel, when you started the story, you had this vision that you would do a historic story, that would bring down the government …

Samuel: No, not at all. Just I started the story, meanwhile this matter happened, which one, that Sehgal matter, so this guy Malviya scared.

Madhu: Did you see it as doing something to push the limits of journalism, or to focus on corruption, for your country, or was it just the story?

Samuel: No, it was not like that, maddumm. Suppose, I remember, we started the story, uh, uh, after the Sehgal's tapes over, fusst tape, then I gone through the … I vaaatch the tapes keenly. There is some mentioning about some deeeeal, what actually happening, then the koooriosity increased. And rrreally excited also. It was the excitement of the story. I never know that the story will build up in a such a way. I never know.

Madhu: Did you not have this ambition to become known as a crack investigative journalist?

Samuel: No, never in my mind, if these internal things will come out, it will be good for the country. So, this stupids should have to punish. Those who are involved. Not like these people, those others also.

Madhu: Were the journalists harassed after the exposé?

Samuel: They do many different things for hurrrahssment. I applied my passport two times. Suppose my passport reached one year back, suddenly I got a news from Kerlla my passport is not reached. So I paid, everything is clear, the passport form and everything. Then from here I gave from Delllhi, again I applied a passport. Fussst passport. Now also, seven-eight months over. That is they are not giving. I went and asked. They never given any reply. Otherwise I can travel lawts of places. This is the thing.

Madhu: Now bearing in mind what actually happened afterwards, would you still do a story like that or do you think it's useless?

Samuel: Maddumm, my question. Verry intrrusssting. I don't know. Hurraaass! Hurraaass! Hurraaass! The question is coming, the gaeurmunt did like that. Of course, gaeurmunt did like that. One time the raid happened and investigation is not coming properly becawz of the gaeurmunt pressure and everything. My this thing is very clear, what I did I never known the story will build up in such a way, will get such a gooduh essposhur also. Now mind is very clearly saying that, why we could not able to, Tehelka could not be able to stand anywhere and Tarun giving lawt of answer, this happened becawz of this happened, that happened becawz of that happened.

Madhu: What does Tarun say?

Samuel: Becawz of gaeurmunt screwed up. Fussst of all, of course one thing I am thinking, vaat we did, these politicians they are roaming around without any ban, then another one this Jaya Jaitly trying to send this tape to forensic exam. She knew everything that is the truth. In my mind, I got my day, I don't have any problem. Reason is I was in south also, many BBC people are calling up to my home about that story. There is not problem for a job for me now. I will go and get it job anywhere. But the rrust of the staff, those who wurrked with Tehelka, they never know vaat this idiot we are doing. They rrreallly suffered. They are not getting job. One time, Tehelka was in such a very good time and finally it's going in such a baaaad shape. They kept some good plant, pot plant and everything, one day the contractor come and taking away all the plant and everything. And those who are financed the vehicle, they're coming and taking all the vehicle back. I saw the coming up and going down. I don't know internal side of what their financial matters anything. I only know they are not giving properly salary, becawz of there is no money. That is a verrrry saaaad position.

Madhu: Do you believe the country benefited from your story?

Samuel: I believe Indian democracy is not that much strong. Of course, we have a good democracy, we are enjoying that also, compared to other countries. But what I esspect, how we will come out, second day the prime minister also given the speech to the nation that's a wake up call. So I also felt it's strungthening the democracy prrawcess. But, finally, vaat happened? Everything turned around. So that is very sad. That is life. I don't know, the rrust of them vaat they are saying. This is my very simpble mind, mentality.

Madhu: Do you believe it is impossible to fight what is called the system?

Samuel: Not like that. Suppose, this not only for the, we can fight, we can fight, but we need a prrroper back up financially to stand.

Mathew Samuel has tried to continue with his stealth journalism but not with any success, which points the finger to Aniruddha Bahal; that it would not have been possible without him. Or, for that matter, without the platform created by Tarun Tejpal for Operation West End.

⌒

When the tapes were made public in March 2001, Tehelka was already in serious financial trouble. Shankar Sharma's 3.5 crore investment had been exhausted and Tehelka was surviving on loans. From September 2000, Shankar refused to give any more money, was looking for an exit, and presentations to second round venture capitalists had begun. In the first fully attended board meeting in November 2000, Shankar informed everyone that Channel Nine, who had valued Tehelka at Rs 50 crore, had now pulled out. Aniruddha laughed, 'Can you imagine the madness of those times? We were all depressed about being evaluated for only Rs 50 crore.' Shankar was confident they could pull in a second round of funding and told them he would give them loans until then. Around January 2001, Shankar was beginning to see the dotcom bubble burst and began to get nervous.

In November 2000, Subhash Chandra of Zee TV had begun talks with Tehelka to revamp his City Channel. This gave Shankar Sharma some hope, otherwise he had thought of pulling the plug. Shankar had stopped sending loans and Tehelka's burn rate was Rs 45 lakh a month. To get out of trouble, Tarun, Aniruddha, and Minty all gave Rs 11 lakh each. They also organized a side deal with Aniruddha's cousin Mahim Mehra and gave him 6 per cent equity. They got around Rs 20 lakh for that and they all put 70 per cent of it into Tehelka to survive.

The deal to revamp City Channel was in process. Subhash Chandra paid Rs 50 lakh to Tehelka to run the Operation West End tapes, and according to Aniruddha, 'was pretty gung-ho at that time'. The Tehelka team was apprehensive about how Chandra would react to the exposé, but decided they could not sit on their story until the money came in. Although Subhash Chandra had initially given an evaluation of Rs 60 crore, a few weeks after the exposé he stopped returning their calls. Aniruddha assumed that Chandra had come under some kind of pressure.

On 5 May 2001, the Special Cell of Delhi police arrested six persons who they claimed were hired by the ISI (Pakistani Intelligence) and were plotting to kill Tarun Tejpal and

Aniruddha Bahal. It is highly possible that the ISI was as surprised to hear this as were Tarun and Aniruddha. Although the police brought six arrested men to Patiala House and stated they had recovered two AK-47 rifles, two Chinese pistols and a bullet-proof jacket, all to kill Tarun Tejpal. I have my doubts about this story. Significantly, the government then gave Tarun and Aniruddha Z security, which meant that they learnt to live with six policemen tailing them wherever they went. Now the government had full licence to watch Tarun and Aniruddha every moment of their lives.

The CBI raided the Tehelka offices on 26 June 2002, on the same day Tarun Tejpal was to begin his deposition in the Commission of Inquiry. On 7 August 2002, the CBI arrested Aniruddha on the day that Mathew Samuel was to start his deposition.

Aniruddha disembarked in the land of Kafka. The sentence of Franz Kafka's book, *The Trial* is illustrative: 'Somebody must have made a false accusation against Joseph K. for he was arrested one morning without having done anything wrong.'

Bahal: There was this case that they wanted to plant on us, the Official Secrets Act case, which is related to a story that we did in October, 2000, which related to some Dutch NGOs funding north-east militants. In that we gave exactly what happened, the minutes of the meeting and so on. The Ministry of Home Affairs never denied that story. Nobody denied that story. Subsequently they filed an FIR after Operation West End, on 18 March, five days after it, because they obviously wanted to get an angle into us. What happened was they had already summoned us two, three times, to interrogate us on this particular issue. We cooperated and everything was over. Then suddenly the CBI officer landed up at my office, maybe on August 6, to interrogate me further on this. I asked him, as all my lawyers have advised me, that anybody coming in you have to ask to officially give a summons. I asked him, what is the notice that you have come under and you have to serve me that notice. We'll cooperate fully, as we have done all the time. But you have to give it to us in writing. For our own record, otherwise tomorrow you can say we never came, which he said he hadn't got. He left the office. The next thing I know, that there's a complaint at the police station, Malviya Nagar that I physically assaulted him and threw him out of the office. There are around fifty guys in office. That time I even had security. There were like ten cops outside. There was Section 506 something, which is obstructing justice. They made out a case and the next thing I know, I come to office the next day and they arrest me. Then, luckily what happened was that I called up Uday [Shankar, who had worked with him in *Down to Earth*], immediately as they were in my cubicle, ten of them trying to arrest me. He put me live on Aaj Tak, which was the best thing that happened. So my entire arrest, I was giving a voice-in live to Aaj Tak. While I was being taken from the Gypsy [car], to the *thana*, and then they took me to the Hauz Khas Police Station. One minute call and then I was live on air. So that happened and for that I'm eternally obliged to Uday and Aaj Tak. [Laughs.]

> Then they took me to court. Somehow the judge gave me bail, Reena Singh Nag. If she hadn't given me bail, I would have gone into judicial custody for two weeks. They asked for two weeks judicial custody. For what? And she gave me bail immediately and they haven't even filed a charge sheet on that. Imagine.

Sidharth Luthra pointed out that when he argued for bail for Aniruddha, the judge asked for surety papers but not one person, including 20 journalists were willing to give even their identity cards or stand surety for him. This, despite the judge pointedly telling Luthra that she would release him if any journalist just showed their identity cards and furnished bail bonds for him. Chander Uday Singh (lawyer for some of Shankar Sharma's cases) had said, 'It is a story that desperately needs to be told – not least because of the abject failure of the Indian press to stand by Tehelka and all the players in the exposés. I've always felt that if the press hadn't been so insecure about Tehelka, they wouldn't have been so supine'.

Other ways were used to get at the journalists. Aniruddha was questioned in the Commission by the late Kirit Rawal about the money he earned from his book *Bunker 13*. What relevance or connection did that have with Operation West End tapes? It was a travesty of fairness to bring random subjects in to create an ambience of shadiness around the journalists. In order to avoid double taxation in the United States and India for his advance royalties, he filled up the form applying to the income tax authorities to certify that he had paid his taxes in India. Obviously, Rawal had been given this information when he began needling Aniruddha about how a novice like him could garner advance royalties of £75,000 from Faber and Faber and a quarter of a million dollars from Farrar, Strauss and Giroux. Rawal then informed Aniruddha that according to information received, these were illicit funds, that had been generated abroad and channelled through these publishing houses in India. Bahal said,

> I really lost my temper then. I said that, "You're demeaning the office of the additional solicitor general by even hinting at such a thing." And then he got shirty and then all these lawyers ganged up together, "How can you say something like this about a lawyer." Unfortunately Sidharth [Luthra] was not sitting there, he had just stepped out of the Commission, so he couldn't participate. I was left alone to face this whole crowd. I said, "You're saying this because you're not only demeaning me, trying to insult me, to calm down." I said, fine, fine. He also knew what was happening. They never brought it up further.

Aniruddha had begun work on *Bunker 13* six years earlier, after investing in a computer at home and taking two months unpaid leave from *Outlook* when his wife was pregnant. When Vinod Mehta threatened to sack him, Aniruddha returned to work with the book unfinished. A chance meeting in February 2002 with V.S. Naipaul's and his own agent, motivated Bahal enough to complete the book. Aniruddha welcomed the money as everything in Tehelka had dried up and many former employees came to him for loans. Aniruddha said in puzzlement,

> Strangely, I meet people on the street and they think we've salted away millions. The general public consciousness is that fame is equated to money. There's a general subconscious and they think that we really creamed and we are in a pretty situation. If they only knew how Tarun has run up debts of about seventy lakh. How to repay those debts? I myself have lent to Tehelka about eleven, thirteen lakh. Even the car that I bought from Tehelka, I paid four-and-a-half lakhs to get that car in my name, out of my book money. If the book hadn't happened I was up shit creek totally, financially; and totally unemployable as you said. We have got a mindset that after you run a place, how can you work for somebody?

When asked whether there was any evidence about the people behind the harassment to which Tehelka journalists and investors were subjected after the exposé, Aniruddha said:

> Not really, there's nothing on paper. You won't get tapes on this. No, there's no way except by the whole ridiculousness of the cases and arrests. But how do you go beyond that? Just look at it. The government affidavits which they filed in the Commission against us, the Commission didn't tell them to file them. Okay? Now there's no process by which somebody's telling them to file them. The government's terms of reference in the Commission was just Term [sub-article] (d), that all aspects will be investigated. And so when this income tax guy was on the stand, it was an interesting cross-examination. Jethmalani kept honing him out. The returns had to be filed by, I think the company returns are filed in October, it is not March. The company closing is different from this March closing, which hadn't yet happened. So Jethmalani was after him. This income tax guy, *vahin uskey muh se nikal gaya ek dum ki, ek dum sey stand peh keh gaya* [it slipped out of his mouth suddenly on the stand], we were under instructions to investigate, investigate, investigate. Then he suddenly started backtracking, *ki, nahin, nahin, nahin, nahin* [no, no, no], it was a normal process. They were claiming these underhand deals, with hawala thing, stock market crash, and all this, they were trying to implicate Shankar in some weird thing. Whereas for that particular year, the time for filing the returns hadn't happened. You can only bring up those transactions, if they are not reflected in that year's return. They formed a report before that. So how do you do that? It was basically fantastic and they knew that they were on very weak ground. This was what the fallacy was and they knew that they were making fools out of themselves on the stand and will make more fools of themselves. I think what had happened was, the government, the witnesses, they went back to Kirit Rawal and this whole gang. This is what we heard, we

don't know if this is true or not: that we're not participating in this anymore. Even the judge got very upset, at the manner in which this guy was giving evidence. Everything he would say, he would get back and it was so prima facie. It was a comedy going on there and they caught on. Obviously they knew and they started catching on and then they suddenly realized that it's not working.

Madhu: Aniruddha, do you have any regrets about this, the way it was done or whatever?

Bahal: No regrets, no. Nothing. People always ask me, "Weren't you afraid" and all that? No, never afraid.

Madhu: No, journalists don't get afraid, but sometimes one looks back and says I could have done it differently.

Bahal: Yeah, with all this hassle that is going on. But anything you can do differently. You learn so much, there are ten, twenty things that I would do differently. But then that luxury is not available to you, when you are doing the story. Nobody knows how it will pan out. Actually there were misgivings even the day we released the story. We didn't know how, whether, *ki media uthayega nahin uthayega* [whether the media will pick up the story or not], that was a real concern. We still had those doubts with us, even the day we were releasing the story. It wasn't that everything panned out the way we wanted. Look, at the end of it – what happened? In a sense, we have been put in the dock: explain yourself.

Madhu: In the Army Court of Inquiry, was it more just than the Commission?

Bahal: Army has their straight rules and I think, they honestly want to get them. I've travelled a lot and met lots of army officers. Even those people whom we're interacting with while the proceedings are going on. There isn't one who hasn't congratulated me on this story. They come up to me and say, boss, you guys really did this thing. There's a lot of feeling in the lower sections, that generals, brigadiers *sab toh choot jateh hai* [all get off scot-free]. So there's a lot of sense in the army that we can't let them go. We have to set an example.

Aniruddha broke away from Tarun pretty soon after the exposé. In one of the CBI raids on the Tehelka office, they had found emails Aniruddha had written Tarun about his resentment and hurt that when he, that is, Aniruddha had done all the work on Operation West End, Tarun had taken all the credit, conducted all the press conferences, given personal press interviews, gone on television programmes, accepted invitations for lectures all over the country. In other words, Tarun successfully used it as a platform for bigger things. Aniruddha was reportedly upset, when he saw that in interviews Tarun kept saying 'I' and not 'we' when speaking about Operation West End, when other people in the organization had done all the work. Aniruddha launched his own company Cobra Post (also a website) and began a series of 40 successful sting operations which he sold to television channels. Following the same format adopted in Operation West End, he succeeded in bribing members of Parliament to ask questions in the House, got doctors to issue fake certificates, hospitalization, and the like. He successfully sold his Tony B. show which is a Borat clone and quite funny. All the while, his mind is continually cooking future projects.

Aniruddha's potboiler mentality has been repeatedly mentioned as his predominant characteristic. Vinod Mehta, editor of *Outlook* magazine, for whom he worked, said Aniruddha was always chasing him to buy hidden cameras. The murky motives attributed to Aniruddha by LOCOT don't really don't stand up. It is clear, Aniruddha is ambitious. Very ambitious. But, ambitious for what? To push the boundaries of conventional journalism. To be more than he was born to be. Or, in his mind, to be what he was really born to be. For all of Aniruddha's journalistic failings, we must value what he set out to do. The fact that he did not execute it faultlessly, does not in any way subtract from the sum of the whole. As Dante wrote: 'In any act the primary intention of him who acts is to reveal his own image.' Nothing could reveal more than Aniruddha's script for Operation West End. Yes, he was motivated by a tendentious approach. He knew there was corruption. He made it his Holy Grail. He wanted to be the hero of his novel where he found it and brought it back. It is the 'coming back' that is the problem in all such adventures.

Is Bahal a hero at all? He undertook a massive adventure: you cannot take that away from him. Yet, the very same section of society that could build public perception of him as a hero, the media, did not do so. Our heroes today are testosterone-inflated men who shake their booties with bleach-haired babes, risking their lives strictly in fiction. For the press, Bahal is a competitor: there is envy. And finally, there is boredom. How many times can you write about the same person and the same subject? It is risky for the market-oriented to fail to remain alert to attention-challenged, easily bored readers.

In Joseph Campbell and Diane Obson's book *The Joseph Campbell Companion: Reflections on the Art of Living* (HarperPerrenial, 1991):

> You do not have a complete adventure unless you do get back. There is a time to go into the woods and a time to come back, and you know which it is. Do you have the courage? It takes a hell of a lot of courage to return after you have been in the woods.

There is also a difference. Bahal's battles were not over when he returned from his adventure. It was on his return that the real war began. Rather than the recipient of a laurel wreath on his return, he faced bullets. Unlike the guerrilla warfare he had been conducting while on Operation West End, he returned to a battlefield that burst into open warfare, where the enemy had identified him to be destroyed.

On 16 June 2005, Bahal was caught up in even more imbroglios. In the court-martial proceedings against Brigadier Iqbal Singh, where Bahal was a witness, Bahal pointed out that additions had been made to his summary of evidence in another handwriting which was not in the evidence he had given. It was confirmed that Bahal's summary of evidence had been tampered with and the accusing finger pointed to the officer taking the evidence:

Brigadier S.S. Gill. Brigadier Iqbal Singh lost it, screamed and yelled, and marched out of the courtroom. He was arrested by the military police that afternoon. On 6 October 2005, an Army Court of Inquiry (ACI) held Brigadier S.S. Gill, blameworthy of procedural lapses while making additions in statements contained in the Summary of Evidence in Brigadier Iqbal Singh's trial by court martial.

On the other hand, the CBI hauled Bahal up for a case the CBI had filed against him under the Official Secrets Act for a story he had done for Tehelka in 2000 about the illegal funding of terrorists in the northeast. Tehelka has become Bahal's own shadow. No matter how hard he tries to shake it off, it sticks to him.

As Bahal would laugh and say: *'Kya yaar, kidhar phas gayeh, boss?* [Translation: What the fuck happened]?'

⌐

Do the many mistakes made by Tehelka, in the transcription of the tapes, their wrong identification of people, their ambivalent and expedient moral code, slanted and sloppy editing, erode their credibility? All the Tehelka deviations have been used to the hilt by the LOCOT. It still doesn't take away from the fact that Tehelka did catch these people on the tapes taking money from a fictitious company without checking on the company or their antecedents. Obviously it can be considered next to impossible to actually catch 'real' arms dealers in operation. In fact, the real ones are the ones they could not get to. Only their names are mentioned by other people on the tapes. The real operators are much too careful in maintaining thick smokescreens. As journalists, Tehelka could hardly interview the arms dealers openly or even successfully reach them. So, Tehelka did the next best thing, which was to create this fictitious company. The people who took the money are not fictitious. The positions they held in the political and defence establishment were not fictitious. Tehelka did prove how easy it is to infect a virus in the system. They did show hard evidence that the system that everybody knows exists and is gossiped about but nobody has been able to prove is, indeed, in full swing. An ex-Army man, now a lawyer defending a client caught on the tapes, told me himself that he had been corrupt and took commissions when he was in the army and didn't think it at all unusual. He said this Tehelka exposé would not stop corruption. Only the price will go higher because the risk is higher now. He also demanded, 'Do you think Tarun Tejpal's father who was in the army did not take money? How did his sons carry on with this lifestyle if he didn't?' The state of amorality is such that it is taken for granted everyone is corrupt and earning an honest living is considered simply impossible.

When Tehelka broke the Operation West End story, Tarun believed the power of journalism would be validated. Tehelka would attract massive funding. They had pulled off the biggest coup in journalistic history. What Tarun underestimated was the government's core organizational spin strength against an easy target. In other words, the question was whose vital organs got caught in the wringer? The Secret Auto Destruct System's (SADS) wheels started turning smoothly. The government's core wringing team, just cranked the machine and squeezed them, utilizing every department, every agency that could search and destroy, then simply moved on to the next crisis that needed spinning and doctoring and forgot about Tehelka. No shock and awe, this. It was Method Screwing. The government appointed a Commission of Inquiry and launched the SADS from all sides. The government transformed Tarun, Aniruddha, and even the concept of Tehelka, into a quick, tiny hiccup in the public's perception of national developments. For editors, Tehelka became an old story, no longer worth covering.

Tehelka's lawyer Kavin Gulati gave his client an opportunity to speak about the harassment:

> **Gulati:** What has been the fall-out of this investigation on Tehelka as a result of this exposé?
>
> **Tejpal:** Today the only casualty of our exposé in corruption is not an individual or political party but Tehelka.com itself. For the last one-and-a-half years, we have been harassed by all kinds of agencies in the government. The angel investors of the company have been destroyed, their business shut down. The man himself has served two and a half months in jail without being given even a proper charge sheet, without really knowing what has happened, his travels have been banned, his properties attached. Thanks to all that, Tehelka.com has not received even a single rupee of investment since we broke the story. Today, of course, it is true that we have not paid salary for five months, there are people who have not received it for eight months and Tehelka is one-fifteenth of the size it was when we broke the story. Every department from the Enforcement Directorate, Income Tax, CBI, we have been harassed by every agency and the kind of harassment has to be seen to be believed.

I asked Tarun about the price Shankar Sharma and Devina Mehra paid for funding Tehelka. Tarun said:

> **Tarun:** Shankar and Devina, that's a really sad story because they had nothing to do with any of it. They were trying to get out of Tehelka from bloody August 2000. Every time we spoke to somebody they wanted to sell their share of the equity. They just wanted to make the money and get out. They were just money people. But I think in some deep level, I think this had been good for them because it's changed them in huge ways also these last two years. They were just a pure and simple money obsessed couple. Today they've become many other things. That life is a big complicated business. That there are moral, spiritual, emotional issues.
>
> **Madhu:** They've been through a horrendous time.
>
> **Tejpal:** Yeah, I know, because it's been a really tough time and it's changed them in very deep ways and I've seen them change really up close.
>
> **Madhu:** Even Kumar Badal is a changed man.
>
> **Tejpal:** Yeah, he just went to Vaishno Devi. It's changed him hugely; his jail book Penguin will probably take, *yaar*, jail stories. They are working on it now. I mean his English is bad and all.

Madhu: All these characters have been through a lot.

Tejpal: Oh, absolutely. No, I have to say you know we were very lucky. Shankar and I laugh about it today because in some sense I think, in some sense both Shankar and I are strong people.

Madhu: His wife, Devina too. The common thread I've found in all the interviews is that the wives are amazingly supportive.

Tejpal: Yeah, you can't get by this otherwise, boss. I am always asked by people, so bizarrely, that did you check with your wife before breaking this story? You put them all into so much trouble, *yaar*. I said you must be out of your mind. Geetan, in any case, is a pillar. She's like Mother Earth. It helps, when people who around you don't have avarice.

The aftermath of course changed Tarun. He said he saw himself differently and believed he was cast in a situation where his cause became the moral burden to push Tehelka into a story with a happy ending. Despite all the harassment, he was energized by the goodwill given to him, especially when he accepted invitations to lecture in small towns. Living with Tehelka teetering on the brink of closure, being an agnostic, Tarun's born again positivism has become his solace and dogmatic religion:

> **Tarun:** One, because I see that it is a moral duty that I need to fulfil, and the second is the business about Tehelka shutting down. The message that goes out, is far greater than Tehelka. The message that goes out then, is that "you can do the right thing and you can be run into the ground and you can be closed down".
>
> Whereas I'm convinced that the message that has to go out is that "you can do the right thing, you may suffer inordinately for it but you'll win in the end". We are a country with too many bad stories, boss.

In spite of Tarun's support system of friends and family, many well-intentioned people, including his partners, who wanted to get on with their lives, advised him to close down Tehelka. Still confident that he could clear his debts Tarun said, 'Here it has been placed in a different zone. Now the thing is to do justice to the zone so, today, it's not about money. It's about just making Tehelka a great, independent, media institution. That's the only obsession.'

Often in his conversations, Tarun relies on his literary life as his spiritual strength:

> I can make the connection today and let my literary sense empower the activist end of my life. It gives me strength. But I am basically a literary animal. I find it very, very difficult to make easy indictments. I find it very, very difficult to deal in black and whites. I am a grey guy. I have a lot of time for people's shortcomings and foibles. I understand the function of literature, which is kind of explication, understanding, insight, elimination, bewilderment. Activism,

even if one practices it at some level, even our own story, at some level you can understand the inherent flaws, the fickleness in everything that you do. But then you understand that there is a leap to be also made into activism, which is important. There are two things: It's not enough to understand, it is also important to do. I think the literary end of me is about trying to understand. So that end of me is a very easy going. But the intensity is because I was really driven both by my personal ambition, which was largely literary. But, there was an ambition of the world, also. I always say when you come from nowhere and you want to go somewhere.

Tarun said that he was driven by activism when he was young, and that became latent during his work with conventional journalism. 'Today I often talk to Geetan about it. She was the first who noticed it. She said, "You're far closer to being the guy you were in your early twenties in the last few years", he said.

Tarun launched his weekend newspaper on 7 February 2004. At a function held at Siri Fort Auditorium, New Delhi, on 30 January 2004. Tejpal was a returning hero, fighting valiantly against injustice and for the freedom of the press. It was a creative launch: quawaals sang a specially composed number about Tehelka, Ram Jethmalani, against the advice of his doctors, flew from Mumbai to give a rousing monologue on the freedom of the press. Unknown at that time, Rabbi Shergill, who would take the music world by storm a year later with his new sound and genre, sang Punjabi songs which he termed, 'not raag, not bhangra but ragda'. Tejpal's speech was an Oscar acceptance speech, and I am not cooking this up: he really did thank his uncle, sister, mom, dad, and wife.

Seated in the audience was Aniruddha Bahal, certainly consumed with a sense of awkward irony that the person who had nothing to do with the sting operation, was now using it as a platform to launch another venture. It had become clear that they could not work together. Bahal owned only 16 per cent of the equity in the company and Tarun owned the majority. Although it was Aniruddha's work in Operation West End that put the brand name Tehelka on the map, that brand was what Tarun was now using and promoting. They had an amicable parting of ways, as amicable as competing siblings can have. One senses they have a fondness for each other that their shared experiences somehow refuse to destroy but yet a recognition that they must also avoid each other.

I interviewed Tarun again after 22 issues of the weekly. He was attempting an unusual and difficult paradigm in that he planned to rely on subscriptions rather than advertisements to cover costs. Obviously, there weren't too many companies willing to stick their neck out to place advertisements, nor was the government going to oblige either. He was full of how successful his weekly was, how he was getting money for it, and how splendid the stories were. Everything about the weekly was so spectacular. Clearly, it was tough going but he was shouldering the struggle with strength. It began as a serious, heavy, paper catering to literary *jholawalas*, and that goes completely against the non-reading, television-watching, Internet obsessed public. It has now evolved a texture more in tune with the times. Quality does not necessarily mean success in India. Often, the lack of it makes it happen. There is an unbridled celebration of mediocrity coupled with a clear rejection of anything that has not proved a consensual tribal success. Look at our 'news' channels. They are not dumbing down. They are crawling and wallowing down there. Breaking news turns out to be – Your horoscope! Sometimes, I find it difficult to meet the eyes of people who run these channels. So Tehelka is in a difficult space when it does not dumb down.

Anyone who invests in the *Tehelka* magazine today, invests in hope, in the idea of democracy and what India was supposed to be. Surely, there must be a few business people who live with courage and not just mere expediency? Am I making a pitch? Yes, I am. I may not agree with a lot of what Tehelka does and publishes, but it deserves to not only survive; it must do well. We owe it to ourselves.

Tarun took the decision to alter the format from a tabloid to a newsmagazine on 12 September 2007, and since then has reported higher sales. On 5 November 2007, Tehelka published and broadcast a sting operation on the Godhra (Gujarat) violence in 2002. They caught on camera functionaries of the VHP-Bajrang Dal testifying to police cover-up and collusion of the public prosecutor in the case. Teeth-gritting accounts of how the killings were carried out including difficult-to-hear details of Congress MP Ehsan Jafri's brutal, slow murder. Most creepy was the fact that these people were 'boasting' of their achievements. Have any of these people been arrested?

The work continues, but the question that must haunt all journalists, including me, is whether our work will actually ever bring about change in this highly cynical, jaded, Machiavellian society?

At this point, intellectually and emotionally, Tarun is happier with the direction his life has taken, even though it is more difficult. He is a driven man, determined to give Tehelka a 'happy ending'. Consequently, Tarun never stops and you can't help but smile. He was a sports star in college, brilliant in debates and quiz competitions, he got a first division in his degree after studying for three days, he was a star reporter in Punjab for *The Telegraph*, he virtually ran *India Today* (how many people have claimed that?), and the Tehelka website was the best the world had ever seen, with its combination of the highbrow and local grit. Tarun's book, *The Alchemy of Desire*, was published in March 2005 and received mixed reviews. In an answer to Lindsay Pereira (rediff.com) who asked him about a remark he had made, 'I don't care about Indian reviews', he said rather bitterly:

> I think between incompetence and malice, almost no decent reviewing takes place in India. Mostly it is the clever, collegiate "quiz competition" kind of notices that pass off for book reviews. Media journeymen – out of work journos, copyeditors in publishing houses, peripheral academics, precious column writers – these are the ones who are handed out books. Most of them lack the skill, the craft, the heart, the understanding of the tradition, to assess serious books.

I spoke to him about a particular review with which I was truly disappointed, because not only was it just a synopsis of the book without a single opinion but it also broke the cardinal rule: the reviewer gave away the ending. Tarun replied with much tension: 'I am not looking at the reviews. I don't care what they write here. Only years from now they will realize how this book has broken new ground in writing. Nobody in the history of India has written like this.' Yes, love, but leave that for others to say. As Ali G would say: wot yous bangin' on about? In the mode for raising funds for the *Tehelka* magazine and the grit required for survival, Tarun has gotten into the same mode as when making presentations. Hype it up. Way up. Okay, but seriously pull it way down for real life. Learn from all the fake modesty flaunted by our ever so filmy film stars. Yes, I liked the book. Tarun's greatest talent is that he is a true craftsman of the word.

Asiaweek listed Tarun as 'one of Asia's 50 most powerful communicators,' and *Business Week* declared him 'among 50 leaders at the forefront of change in Asia.' The December 2006 issue of *The Guardian* listed Tejpal as one of 'India's New Élite – Top 20'. The young people of India must see that a man's struggle is to some measure worthwhile.

In his last interview with me, Tarun said:

It's led me to believe, over the last couple of years, that, everything that's created in the world, is created by an act of will. Someone's act of will. Right from designing an aeroplane, to fucking creating a newspaper, to creating countries. Everything is someone's act of will. So you have to exercise that act of will. You have to have belief. If you feel a belief is grounded in good solid things, then you have to execute that act of will to make it come into being. Everything comes into being because someone believes in it and makes it happen.

Of this he keeps reminding himself. He has to.

In the film *The Hours*, Leonard Woolf asks his wife Virginia Woolf about the ending of the book she is writing:

Leonard Woolf: In your book you said, "Why does somebody have to die?" Why? Why does somebody have to die?
Virginia Woolf: Somebody has to die in order for the rest of us to value life more. It's contrast. The poet dies. The visionary dies.

Tehelka, as Tejpal and Bahal had originally envisioned it, is definitely dead. A new Tehelka is born, yes, but with new players and it is different. It is in the contrast. Will we then value more what we lost?

28 The Unbearable Lightness of Conscience

Howard Beale [Peter Finch]: Television is not the truth. Television is a goddamned amusement park.

— *Sidney Lumet's film* Network *(1976)*

What has Tehelka left us with, besides a metaphor for sting journalism? There is the exterior, of what Tehelka and the SADS did to the texture of journalism. There is the interior of what it did to the psyche of all those involved. And there were those who turned their faces away. Each incident burnt away the possibility of it ever happening in the same way again.

Let's look at where we are. There is no denying that we are in a frenzy of celebrating the great modern invasion, no matter how mediocre or stupid it is. In tandem we are participating in creating a neurotic country while continuing to complain about it. As we struggle to hold on to and rid ourselves of our past, we seek to embrace the modern and are at once repelled by it. The modern is raging around us, generating havoc and confusion, and yet is indiscriminate in its proliferation. It has the making of a schizophrenic India. In much the same way, a woman who runs a successful industry, returns home and then piously proud of her duality, assumes the role of subservient wife. We are continually battling between two worlds every day. The personal moral choices that we are forced to make each day are immediately urgent and ubiquitous. We have to choose whether to be honest or dishonest at innumerable points in time every single day. We have to choose whether to genuflect to the boots of authority and forge ahead; or buck the trend, fight for what we consider the Truth, and suffer for it. So stark is this choice defined in India that it raises the question whether it is possible to stand up for the truth and move ahead. If you don't play along with the system, you become a pariah. Honesty has become a subversive act.

Does India's pseudo neo-modernism include gender equality and a genuine functioning democracy where votes are based on national benefit, governance and educated choices? Modernity is being confused with trappings. Women bleach their hair blond, carry over-priced brand monogrammed rexine handbags with crotch-length skirts and are now modern. In the face of this they have no compunctions about fasting to give birth only to a son, then proudly discriminate in his favour and treat him differently from their daughters. Even the daughters are trained to accept their brother as the special one. How educated or modern is that? Attitudes are not genetic, they are taught. The seed of female infanticide is sown. Parents have become so increasingly intimidated by the onslaught of modernity, that they are afraid to lay down basic rules for their children. As we hover in the twilight of an uncertain identity, what will decide the character of the people we become as a nation? Look at any country's history and development; it is always interlinked with the individual character of the citizens, which then becomes national character. Is it enough to expand globally in technology and industry, if our fundas are not well defined? We have a choice of finding ourselves in the Age of Behenji Turned Mod in Utter Confusion (BTMUC) or reinventing ourselves, where we arrive at a national ambient character that is responsive to a required evolution. An innocuous, brilliant film *Lage Raho Munna Bhai* (2006), helped in taking a tiny step. The move had a catalyzing impact though short-lived. At this point, we are stampeding towards anarchist modernism. A trip to the shopping mall buildings in Gurgaon shouts that this is even reflected in the freakish but much appreciated new architecture. This pseudo neo-modernism has not arrived through a conscious thought process or knowledge. It is wild, unwieldy, and irrational. It is dangerous. The era begs for neo-Gandhians. Which areas of Gandhi's philosophy are relevant, from which we can benefit?

Although the then Prime Minister Vajpayee said immediately after the Tehelka exposé that it was a wake-up call and promised to clean up the dirt, it was clear that the dirt was swept under a Commission. Defence Minister George Fernandes was reinstated after his resignation before the Commission of Inquiry came to any conclusions. Bangaru Laxman, after resigning his position as president of the BJP was appointed president of the Parliamentary Housing Committee. Prime Minister Vajpayee had no problem in sharing a dais with Laxman at a BJP rally in Agra seven months after the exposé. The tainted politician was garlanded amidst resounding, consoling cheers. The BJP government did not file a single charge sheet against any person COT. Subsequently, the UPA government has ordered the CBI to investigate all those COT. The BJP government was gifted a huge opportunity to demonstrate its superiority over previous governments. It could have shown that it would not spare its own if caught in acts of dishonesty. Had they taken cohesive action against those COT rather than Tehelka and its investors, it would have won the public's respect as a party 'with a difference' as it has long claimed to be. But, could the BJP have maintained a stable government had George Fernandes's Samata Party withdrawn its support? It turned out to be depressingly the same. The format of political expediency was repeated. Is this a diatribe against the BJP? It cannot be since all the other parties are no angels.

It is often repeated that Gandhi died at the right time because he had become irrelevant after Independence and was not a leader who could have led the nation forward. As we race or stagger towards the high-tech modern age, replete with shopping malls, multiplex cinemas, a new clued-in Bollywood, jobs in BPOs, we are also caught in the ravages of psychological disorders, stress, epidemics of rape, murder, road rage and the already virtually dismantled joint family, and now indeed even the disruption of just the family. There is a screaming fatuity about how to deal with the BTMUC problems barfing on us. On 12 May 2005, Kanti Singh, union minister of state for human resources, commenting on the spate of rapes in Delhi, pronounced that, 'The clothes of a girl provoke men to indulge in such acts'. On the same day that Singh spoke, a six-year old was raped. Singh was also head of the department of women and child development. A person in an office that is responsible for the well being of women and children is so insentient as to repeat incongruous, archaic clichés? Where did they find this woman?

Social commentators now use television to gauge the temperature of a culture. What do we see? It seems terribly Sangh Parivar and puritanical to say that all one sees are bodies covered with little more than handkerchief-sized pretence for clothes, bodies gyrating to implant images of a range of sexual positions in viewers' minds. But that is exactly what it is. Think of a lonely young man, sitting alone in a room, watching it night after night and not getting any? Where does it take his head? If political propaganda hammered into brains can motivate people towards the most inhumane acts, or conversely sacrifice their lives for a cause, how will the sexual propaganda inspire people? Perception management, the updated term for propaganda, is continually drubbing into men what they could be getting and are not. Censorship would amount to killing the messenger, as Martin Amis pointed out in an article in *The New Yorker* (1993). Actually, he was talking about pornography, so I am stretching it. It only makes the forbidden more exciting. And, it does not stop at sex alone. Television advertisements constantly remind us about what we should possess and don't. We see, more often than not, what is not within our financial reach: cars, television sets, cellphones … all advertised as the completeness of life. If you are an army officer or bureaucrat on a meagre salary, without any ethical agitprop countering the commercial propaganda, the question of a moral crisis or dilemma doesn't arise. You do what everybody else is doing to 'get ahead'. Tehelka revealed it is no longer 'corruption'. It is a normal way of life. In a country study report of India (2003) for National Integrity Systems, Transparency International, Dr R.B. Jain and P.S. Bawa wrote: 'Corruption in India has passed through three different stages (a) gaining legitimacy (b) widespread indulgence, and (c) shameless defence'. When Suresh Nanda and his son Sanjeev were arrested trying to bribe an income tax officer (March 9, 2008), the common refrain was, 'Come on, everybody does it. He just got caught'. Shameless defence. It is also narcissistic morality. It could have been me or my son.

In December 2003, the Bill called The Election and Other Related Laws Act was passed, amending the People's Representation Act, the Companies Act, and the Income Tax Act. Under this, political parties are permitted to accept donations, but the treasurer of the party must submit records of all donations as well as how the money was spent, each financial year to the Election Commission. As has invariably been the case, passing mountains of legislation never changed anything in India. If laws were horses, Dalits would ride. There would be no dowry. There would be no child marriages. The gap between laws and reality is as wide as Mayawati's greedy yawn. It is self-evident that the Bill passed with much fanfare has done little to alter functioning realities. The ambience of *subh chalta hai* [everything and anything goes] and no visible action taken against those who break the law, begets no grain of surprise. Tehelka did not make any new discoveries. They went after what they knew existed but had been impossible to prove.

After Gandhi died, the character of the post-colonial man had little room for compassion, except for the politicians' pseudo-compassion for the poor to harvest votes. The slave became the boss, with all its implications. Hubris-inflated politicians set up paradigms of the poor against the rich, bureaucrats against business, the powerful against the weak. Economic policies were abrasive to one section against the other. Five decades later, when the age of BTMUC engulfed us, compassion was the lowest order in the nation's psyche. In the narcissistic grab to be in on the race, the psyche is damaged. Censoring out all the Kama Sutra *matak* dances on television is not the solution. Banning aspiration advertising will not work. Spreading an alternate perception by widening the scope of an ethical ethos through film, theatre, and television, there could be hope of the development of the concept of the modern Indian being. The power of the film medium became evident when films made soon before a short Indo-Pak détente aided by cricket matches, that caricatured Pakistanis as hideous villains suddenly proved unacceptable to Indian audiences. Did society influence Bollywood to create the suffering image of Meena Kumari or did that character reflect women of the era or did women learn they had to imitate Meena Kumari to be appreciated? Today a woman who suffers is considered an idiot. It works in tandem but if certain characteristics are glorified, people's behaviour responds in resonance. Liberal arts education curricula in schools and colleges could include the massive range of international discourse on sexual mores and civic responsibilities, thereby moulding a conscience that prevents a man from becoming a raging, greedy beast. The men who are today committing rape so nonchalantly are of the same texture as the men who dropped out of well-paying jobs to work selflessly for our Independence over half a century ago. It was the propaganda of a certain way of living planted by the best mindmesser of them all: M.K. Gandhi. We must feel good to be ethical. At this moment, it feels pathetically pious, self righteous and foolish.

In this rapidly flowing river of a consumer driven society, we have also imported America's Individualism in which self-interest is the prime motivating factor and there is a subterranean collective consensus that the benefits will trickle down to the poor. The trickle down is just that – a trickle. This form of individualism has proved to be a malignant growth that is destroying any form of collective responsibility for the underprivileged. This is evident in our not extending even a show of basic courtesy to our neighbours, community, and environment. Every man is focused on himself alone, glorying in the most aggressive, ugly behaviour and exulting in chronic indifference.

Our only hope for the future is India's youth. It depends on the choices they make. Will they get sucked in to just make a buck or can they choose to force the culture to change? Will they insist on and vote in only honest leaders? Will leaders have the guts to make demands of the citizens? A role model is courageous Cuban Yoani Sanchez whose web log has created a worldwide stir about life under communist repression. After the Cuban government blocked access to her blog, Sanchez has been clandestinely uploading from a flash memory card to her website linked to a server in Germany. At an Easter family dinner, she mentioned her sadness for a missing relative, one of 75 journalists jailed by Fidel Castro in 2003. Her young son said to Sanchez, 'So, you are still free because you are a bit cowardly.' Are we just a bit cowardly? Why should courage in India be a limited edition? Is it just too boring for our youth to have the courage to choose what will benefit the future of the nation? I seriously did reflect on how I could make the last chapter a power point presentation. A quickie PPP on how actions that require courage and create change are food for the soul. Is it necessary for our young people to sacrifice, live in poverty and work only for other people's benefit? No, most emphatically, No! It is possible to work to have a good life and still manage it in a manner that you are catalysts for change. There are enough examples of such in every profession, even in business. Look around you. When you are old and the material acquisitions have writ and moved on, you will need to look at your life, what you achieved and what you will leave behind. It is balm to your soul if you have fought and left a legacy of change. Google search 'H.D. Shourie' (1911-2005) and check out how many Acts, Bills and laws were passed because of his public interest litigations that he argued himself, with bemused but highly respectful judges listening to him. Shourie was a bureaucrat who used his retirement by becoming a path-breaking consumer activist. He was also an artist and photographer. Many have repeated he deserved the Bharat Ratna. He was cool. He said, 'I just learned how to say "My Lord" and went with it.'

Is the Tehelka story an example of how you can never beat the system? No, it shows that if you are going to fight the system, you must do it as cleverly as when you strategize for a battle, with enough fall back for the aftermath.

Is it possible to instigate Individual Action for national change? One of the most important concepts Gandhi promulgated was: 'Be the change that you want to see in the world.' Elaborated, this means that if you expect honesty, be honest yourself. Change the word 'honesty' in that sentence to any word that represents what you would expect from other people or your country and you immediately activate your behavioural pattern in a direction that creates the change you seek in others and subsequently your country. Buddhism teaches the concept of Bodhicitta, or the treatment of every person you meet as someone who could have been your mother/father in one of your past lives. This altruistic mind (Bodhicitta) is the first step, not for yourself but for everybody. Wisdom cannot come without compassion. It embodies a universal responsibility for everyone around you. The doctrine of individual independence only exists in modern man-made reality, whereas our subliminal interdependence exists from the moment we are born. A baby may be a separate entity but it could not have taken birth if a male and female had not joined in a physical way. The baby is dependent on the parents for its birth. This continues through your life, in every aspect of it. You cannot eat a single bowl of rice unless hundreds of people are interdependently involved to get it to the dinner table. Does the Western form of individualism where you perceive responsibility only for yourself alone, not lead to alienation and isolation? Even nations that are isolated from the rest of the world, work hard to secure the approval of other countries for their actions. The fact that the ozone layer is being depleted by some is causing disturbances around the world. In a globalized world can we function with just me, myself, and I? It is not breaking news that we are of the same substance and our existence is dependent on the survival of everyone else around us. This spirituality is not of the kind that you can switch off from the material world and live in your own cocoon. This is action spirituality that you work on every moment of your life when dealing with people, and always being conscious of the consequences of any step you take. The end product of what a nation becomes depends entirely on the texture of each individual's behaviour.

Tehelka exposed in every way how far we have strayed from the path of conscience responsibility. Its aftermath displayed how nonchalantly 'life just goes on'. There are no three words more cruel than 'life goes on'. Because sometimes, it just shouldn't. Aniruddha Bahal, Mathew Samuel, Tarun Tejpal, Shankar Sharma, Devina Mehra, Kumar Badal all raged and raged, not gently into Dylan Thomas's 'dying of the light'. The Leela of Tehelka became W.H. Auden's 'Musée des Beaux Arts' where:

> ... for instance: how everything turns away
> Quite leisurely from the disaster; the ploughman may
> Have heard the splash, the forsaken cry,
> But for him it was not an important failure; the sun shone
> As it had to on the white legs disappearing into the green;
> water; and the expensive delicate ship that must have seen
> Something amazing, a boy falling out of the sky,
> had somewhere to get to and sailed calmly on.

How everything turns away quite leisurely from the disaster. So clearly it played out as Auden wrote: 'Where the dogs go on with their doggy lives'. Yes, life went on, as cruel as always.

1984, turbans knocked off, long hair scalped from Sikhs when a big tree fell. We saw, but we turned our faces to the charming new prince. We had somewhere to get to. 2002, little girls raped in Gujarat, while we watched on television and turned our faces away. We had somewhere to get to. 1988 till now, whenever it is, children were blown to bits in Kashmir; we swallowed it with our morning tea. We had somewhere to get to. When Tehelka happened, the messengers were sedulously destroyed; we turned our faces away from ruined lives and a trampled constitution. We had somewhere to get to. Much as we calmly turn our faces away from a common sight, when a Blue Line bus driver, after his bus wheels cut a child in two, runs away to save his own life. If only, yes, if only, that what he *didn't* do, would haunt him.

Index